Classic Edition

Sources

Anthropology

Contemporary Learning Series

2460 Kerper Blvd., Dubuque, IA 52001

Visit us on the Internet
www.mhcls.com

Classic Edition

Sources

Anthropology

Edited by

ELVIO ANGELONI
Pasadena City College

Contemporary Learning Series

2460 Kerper Blvd., Dubuque, IA 52001

Visit us on the Internet
www.mhcls.com

EDITORIAL STAFF

Larry Loeppke, Managing Editor
David Welsh, Developmental Editor
Jade Benedict, Developmental Editor
Joe Offredi, Developmental Editor
Nancy Meissner, Editorial Assistant
Rita Hingtgen, Production Service Assistant

PERMISSIONS STAFF

Lenny J. Behnke, Permissions Coordinator
Lori Church, Permissions Coordinator
Shirley Lanners, Permissions Coordinator

MARKETING STAFF

Julie Keck, Senior Marketing Manager
Mary Klein, Marketing Communications Specialist
Alice Link, Marketing Coordinator

PRODUCTION STAFF

Beth Kundert, Production Manager
Trish Mish, Senior Administrative Assistant
Jane Mohr, Project Manager
Jean Smith, Project Manager
Sandy Wille, Project Manager
Tara McDermott, Design Specialist
Maggie Lytle, Cover Designer

Cataloging in Publication Data
Main entry under title: Sources Anthropology
1. Anthropolgy. I. Angeloni, Elvio, *comp.* II. Title: Sources Anthropology.
ISBN-13: 978–0–07–337969–2   MHID-10: 0–07–337969–7   150

First Edition

Cover image Siede Preis/Getty Images
Printed in the United States of America   1234567890QPDQPD97   Printed on Recycled Paper

ELVIO ANGELONI
Pasadena City College

Elvio Angeloni is a Professor of Anthropology at Pasadena City College in Pasadena, California. He received a B.A. from U.C.L.A. in 1963, an M.A. in Anthropology from U.C.L.A. in 1965 and an M.A. in Communication Arts from Loyola Marymount University in 1976. He has produced several films and has served as an academic adviser for the instructional television series *Faces of Culture*. He is the academic editor of *Annual Editions: Anthropology* and *Annual Editions: Physical Anthropology*, and co-editor of *Annual Editions: Archaeology*. His primary area of interest has been indigenous peoples of the American Southwest.

Preface

*A*nthropology is the study of people—not just some people, all people. As a social science, *cultural* anthropology touches upon such fields as geography, economics, political science, psychology and sociology. As a biological science, *physical* anthropology relates to such areas as biology, anatomy and physiology. Anthropologists even delve into the humanities, such as philosophy and the study of religion. In addition to cultural anthropology and physical anthropology, there are other branches or subfields of anthropology such as archeology (the study of past cultures), linguistics (the study of language), and paleoanthropology (which deals with the fossil evidence for human evolution). In terms of its subject matter, therefore, anthropology can lay claim to being the most diverse discipline in the sciences, ranging from the biological to the cultural, from the individual to the society, from our primordial past to the ongoing present. Anthropology is the process of trying to understand everything that we human beings are, everything we do and everything we produce.

It does not matter that some anthropologists specialize in the study of fossilized bone, while others may be more interested in revivalist religious movements, and still others may focus upon the speech patterns associated with asking for a drink in a downtown bar. All such areas of research are anthropological in the sense that they touch upon such issues as what it means to be human, and how and why we humans have come to differ from each other in all of our wondrous ways, biological and social.

CLASSIC EDITION SOURCES: ANTHROPOLOGY 1ST ED. is a collection of readings in cultural anthropology. It is devoted to the concept of cultural diversity and to the development of the research methods and ideas that have helped us to better understand ourselves. You will find articles that show how the comparing and contrasting of cultures not only leads to a greater appreciation of others, but may also provide insight into our own way of life. One of the greatest lessons that anthropology has to offer is the notion that understanding others is a *necessary means* to understanding ourselves. Some of the articles, therefore, represent a challenge to previous ways of thinking in the field of anthropology itself while others make each of us personally face up to whatever stereotypes we may hold.

A cursory glance at the table of contents will show that many of the authors represented here (either in their own writing or in historical references to them) were and are true pioneers in the field. Over a period of one hundred fifty years, from Edward Tylor to Marvin Harris, they invented and continually re-invent this wonderful science of humanity. Everything about anthropology today, from field methods to theoretical perspectives, would not be the same without the contributions of such notables as Franz Boas, Bronislaw Malinowski, and Margaret Mead.

The articles in this volume are organized into chapters that have to do with major aspects of the anthropological enterprise: anthropology as a science; doing fieldwork; theoretical perspectives; language and culture; social relationships; marriage and family; magic religion and witchcraft; cults and ritual; social change; medical anthropology; and applied anthropology.

While it is true that certain key concepts covered here may also be found in the standard textbook for cultural anthropology, this anthology allows some of the original sources of such ideas to speak for themselves while at the same time enabling the student to explore these topics in greater depth. This anthology, in other words, should serve as a supplement to a cultural anthropology textbook—it should complement it rather than replace it.

The articles themselves have been selected for their readability (without compromising the science), their relevance to understanding the anthropological perspective regarding the human condition, and the degree to which they represent the breadth of cultural anthropology as a whole. Some were written quite recently, while others may go back more than 75 years. In general, I have tried to strike a balance between using the best elements that can be gleaned from original sources, with judicious editing, combined with the more insightful and comprehensive retrospectives written by contemporary anthropologists who, it must be remembered, have the advantage of hindsight.

In any case, what is "classic" about this anthology is not just the writings of well-known anthropologists of the past, whose works have withstood the test of time, but the issues they faced and which we continue to confront as we each strive to understand our place in the broader scheme of things.

A word of caution is in order. As you read some of the articles, particularly the older ones, you may find phrasings that would not be considered appropriate today. For example, references to indigenous peoples as "savage" and "primitive" were commonplace up until the mid-twentieth century. Indeed, the only allusion to Native Americans in our Declaration of Independence was as "merciless savages." Yet, just as we would not want to discount the importance of such a hallowed document as the Declaration in the development of our country, so also we should not discredit the intellectual contributions of the founders of anthropology for having used what we consider today to be abusive language.

Included in this book is a list of Internet resources, with associated links, that pertain to the topics covered. These can be used by the reader as a source of additional information on a particular subject and for further research into related areas. In consideration of how much information is available on the web, I have kept the lists down to a few sites that I have found to be particularly useful.

Each selection is preceded by an introductory headnote which provides some background information about the author, highlights key concepts set forth in the article, and places the essay in its anthropological and historical context.

A word to the instructor: an Instructor's Resource Guide is available to those who use *Classic Edition Sources* in the classroom. This Guide provides a brief synopsis for each selection; guidelines for discussing each selection in class; and testing suggestions (both multiple choice and essay) for each selection. The Guide is available upon request through the publisher.

Elvio Angeloni
Pasadena City College

Contents

Preface   vii

① Anthropology as Science   xx

Selection 1   **FRANZ BOAS,** from "The Aims of Ethnology,"
Race, Language and Culture   **1**

> "The data of ethnology prove that not only our knowledge, but also our emotions are the result
> of the form of our social life and of the history of the people to whom we belong. If we desire to
> understand the development of human culture we must try to free ourselves of these shackles."

Selection 2   **CLYDE KLUCKHOHN,** from "The Meaning of Culture,"
Mirror for Man: The Relation of Anthropology to Modern Life   **4**

> "A good deal of human behavior can be understood, and indeed predicted if we know a people's
> design for living. Many acts are neither accidental nor due to personal peculiarities nor
> caused by supernatural forces nor simply mysterious. Even those of us who pride ourselves on
> our individualism follow—most of the time—a pattern not of our own making."

Selection 3   **RUTH BENEDICT,** from "Anthropology and the Abnormal,"
Journal of General Psychology   **8**

> "It does not matter what kind of 'abnormality' we choose for illustration, those which indicate
> extreme instability, or those which are more in the nature of character traits like sadism or
> delusions of grandeur or of persecution; there are well described cultures in which these
> abnormalities function at ease and with honor, and apparently without danger or difficulty to
> the society."

Selection 4   **ROBERT L. CARNEIRO,** from "Godzilla Meets New Age Anthropology:
Facing the Postmodernist Challenge to a Science of Culture," EUROPÉA   **12**

> "The cornerstone of science has always been the premise that there is a real world out
> there, independent of our individual existences. And it is this world that, as scientists—as
> anthropologists—we should be studying. If anyone still doggedly prefers to contemplate his
> own navel, fine. But let him call his contemplation by a different name than anthropology..."

② Doing Fieldwork   17

Selection 5   **E.E. EVANS-PRITCHARD,** from "Fieldwork and the
Empirical Tradition," Free Press   **18**

> "It is indeed surprising that, with the exception of Morgan's study of the Iroquois, not a
> single anthropologist conducted field studies till the end of the nineteenth century.

It is even more remarkable that it does not seem to have occurred to them that a writer on anthropological topics might at least have a look, if only a glimpse, at one or two specimens of what he spent his life writing about."

Selection 6 **ARTURO ALVAREZ ROLDÁN,** from "Malinowski and the Origins of the Ethnographic Method," *Fieldwork and Footnotes: Studies in the History of European Anthropology* **24**

"I have spent over 8 months in one village in the Trobriand and this proved to me, how even a poor observer like myself can get a certain amount of reliable information, if he puts himself into the proper conditions for observation."

Selection 7 **KATHLEEN GOUGH,** from "Anthropology and Imperialism," *Monthly Review* **30**

"I am asking that we should do these studies in our way, as we would study a cargo cult or kula-ring, without the built-in biases of tainted financing, without the assumption that counter-revolution, and not revolution, is the best answer, and with the ultimate economic and spiritual welfare of our informants, and of the international community, before us rather than the short-run military or industrial profits of the Western nations."

③ *Theoretical Perspectives* 35

Selection 8 **ELMAN R. SERVICE,** from "Evolution, Involution, and Revolution," *Cultural Evolutionism: Theory in Practice* **36**

"We have been long committed to the notion of imminent progress that was associated with the contemporary world view of the 18th century philosophers, and then with the later influence of the organismic analogy. It might be useful to start afresh with a look at the modern world to see what theoretical inspiration can be gained from a more recent perspective, and it may be that a useful theory of evolution thus could be inspired. If it is any good it will apply to the modern world as well as to the 18th and 19th centuries."

Selection 9 **ABRAM KARDINER AND EDWARD PREBLE,** from "Bronislaw Malinowski: The Man of Songs," *They Studied Man* **42**

"Malinowski's creed and advice was, 'never to forget the living, palpitating flesh and blood organism of man which remains somewhere at the heart of every institution.' The history of an institution, its form and distribution, its evolution and diffusion—all these problems are of secondary importance. The important questions are, How does an institution function now? How does it satisfy individual and cultural needs in the given society, and How is it related to other institutions?"

Selection 10 **PAUL BOHANNAN, MARI WOMACK, AND KAREN SAENZ,** from "Paradigms Refound: The Structure of Anthropological Revolutions," *Anthropological Theory in North America* **49**

"Paying homage to one's anthropological ancestors is not enough; one must also supplant the powerful lineage head, either by killing him or her or through 'neolocal residence,' that is, by establishing a new lineage based on a newly generated or newly defined paradigm."

Selection 11 **MICAELA DI LEONARDO,** from "Margaret Mead vs. Tony Soprano," *The Nation* **55**

"In the 1920s, counter to the assertions and interpretations of more recent commentators, Mead's Coming of Age in Samoa was written, and was read, not as a paean to free love

or women's rights or even the romantic lives of 'noble savages,' but rather as a scientific account of certain differing cultural features in a "more simple" society that 'we,' meaning middle-class white Americans, might wish to adopt in order to raise 'our youth' in a less stressful manner."

④ Language and Culture   61

Selection 12   JAMES P. SPRADLEY AND BRENDA J. MANN,
from "How to Ask for a Drink," The Cocktail Waitress   **62**

"Asking for a drink becomes an occasion to act out fantasies that would be unthinkable in the classroom, on the street, and even perhaps when alone with a female. But here, in the protective safety of the bar, a customer can demonstrate to others that he has acquired the masculine attributes so important in our culture."

Selection 13   DEBORAH TANNEN, from "Why Don't You Say What You Mean?,"
The New York Times Magazine   **74**

"I am not inclined to accept that those who give orders directly are really insecure and powerless, any more than I want to accept that judgment of those who give indirect orders. The conclusion to be drawn is that ways of talking should not be taken as obvious evidence of inner psychological states like insecurity or lack of confidence."

Selection 14   EDWARD T. HALL AND MILDRED REED HALL,
from "The Sounds of Silence," Playboy   **79**

"Nonverbal communications signal to members of your own group what kind of person you are, how you feel about others, how you'll fit into and work in a group, whether you're assured or anxious, the degree to which you feel comfortable with the standards of your own culture, as well as deeply significant feelings about the self, including the state of your own psyche."

⑤ Social Relationships   85

Selection 15   MARSHALL SAHLINS, from "The Original Affluent Society,"
Stone Age Economics   **86**

"A good case can be made that hunters and gatherers work less than we do; and, rather than a continuous travail, the food quest is intermittent, leisure abundant, and there is a greater amount of sleep in the daytime per capita per year than in any other condition of society."

Selection 16   LAURENS VAN DER POST AND JANE TAYLOR,
from "Woman the Provider," Testament to the Bushmen   **93**

"Meat may be their favourite food, and the only food to arouse real enthusiasm, but if the Bushmen had had nothing but the meat that the hunters provided, they would have disappeared without a trace thousands of years ago. It is the prosaic unsung work of the women that has kept them alive."

Selection 17   ERNESTINE FRIEDL, from "Society and Sex Roles,"
Human Nature   **100**

"Patriarchies are prevalent, and they appear to be strongest in societies in which men control significant goods that are exchanged with people outside the family. Regardless of who

produces food, the person who gives it to others creates the obligations and alliances that are the center of all political relations."

Marriage and Family   105

Selection 18   KALMAN D. APPLBAUM, from "Marriage with the
Proper Stranger: Arranged Marriage in Metropolitan Japan," Ethnology   **106**

"Clients are buying an imagined community, or 'tradition' as it is now marketed in Japanese popular culture. The candidates are also buying their place in society as well as buying off anxious parents…the pro nakodo capitalize on this wave of cultural nostalgia as well as their clients' uncertainty regarding the appropriate cultural model for one of life's most important rites of passage."

Selection 19   R. JEAN CADIGAN, from "Woman-to-Woman Marriage:
Practices and Benefits in Sub-Saharan Africa," Journal of Comparative Family Studies   **115**

"Despite the fact that woman-to-woman marriage may also be beneficial to men, the institution is not simply given by men to women in order to appease them in the male-dominated system; rather, woman-to-woman marriage has been a way in which women could substantially advance their social status and/or increase their economic standing in their communities."

Selection 20   VEENA TALWAR OLDENBURG, from "Dowry Murder:
The Imperial Origins of a Cultural Crime," Dowry Murder   **121**

"The crime occurs in the kitchen, where the lower- and middle-class housewife spends a lot of time each day. Kerosene stoves are in common use in such homes, and a tin of fuel is always kept in reserve. This can be quickly poured over the intended victim, and a lighted match will do the rest. It is easy to pass off the event as an accident since these stoves are, indeed, prone to explode."

Selection 21   WILLIAM R. GARRETT, from "The Decline of the Western Family:
A Review of the Evidence," The Family in Global Transmission   **130**

"These data indicate that persons who divorce have not given up on marriage; they have simply given up on the particular partner to whom they were married. Or, as Spanier and Thompson have observed: 'Divorce is a response to a failing marriage, not a failing institution. The family system can remain strong while divorce rates remain high.'"

Magic, Religion, and Witchcraft   137

Selection 22   ABRAM KARDINER AND EDWARD PREBLE, from
"Edward Tylor: Mr. Tylor's Science," They Studied Man   **138**

"As modern highways are often laid upon remains of ancient tracks of barbaric roads so, thought Tylor, was modern thought and behavior following the courses of primitive existence. To a university man, steeped in the traditions of academic learning, the commonplaces and trivia of daily life might seem a strange place to look for the origins and development of cultural history. To Tylor, who was denied a university career, it seemed natural to study the living for knowledge of the dead."

Selection 23 **BRONISLAW MALINOWSKI,** from "Essay I,"
Magic, Science and Religion: And Other Essays **146**

"Magic, based on man's confidence that he can dominate nature directly, if only he knows the laws which govern it magically, is in this akin to science. Religion, the confession of human impotence in certain matters, lifts man above the magical level, and later on maintains its independence side by side with science, to which magic has to succumb."

Selection 24 **E.E. EVANS-PRITCHARD,** from "Witchcraft Explains
Unfortunate Events," Reader in Comparative Religion **153**

I found it strange at first to live among Azande and listen to naïve explanations of misfortunes which, to our minds, have apparent causes, but after a while I learned the idiom of their thought and applied notions of witchcraft as spontaneously as themselves in situations where the concept was relevant.

Cults and Ritual   *157*

Selection 25 **PETER M. WORSLEY,** from "Cargo Cults," Scientific American **158**

"However variously embellished with details from native myth and Christian belief, these cults all advance the same central theme: the world is about to end in a terrible cataclysm. Thereafter God, the ancestors or some local culture hero will appear and inaugurate a blissful paradise on earth. Death, old age, illness and evil will be unknown. The riches of the white man will accrue to the Meslanesians."

Selection 26 **RALPH LINTON,** from "Totemism and the A.E.F.,"
American Anthropologist **162**

"A rainbow over the enemy's lines was considered especially auspicious, and after a victory men would often insist that they had seen one in this position even when the weather conditions or direction of advance made it impossible. This belief was held by most of the officers and enlisted men, and anyone who expressed doubts was considered a heretic and overwhelmed with arguments."

Selection 27 **CLIFFORD GEERTZ,** from "Deep Play:
Notes on the Balinese Cockfight," Daedalus **165**

"In the cockfight, man and beast, good and evil, ego and id, the creative power of aroused masculinity and the destructive power of loosened animality fuse in a bloody drama of hatred, cruelty, violence, and death. It is little wonder that when, as is the invariable rule, the owner of the winning cock takes the carcass of the loser—often torn limb from limb by its enraged owner—home to eat, he does so with a mixture of social embarrassment, moral satisfaction, aesthetic disgust, and cannibal joy."

Selection 28 **MARVIN HARRIS,** from "Mother Cow,"
Cows, Pigs, Wars, and Witches: The Riddles of Culture **178**

"To Western experts it looks as if 'the Indian farmer would rather starve to death than eat his cow.' The same kinds of experts like to talk about the 'inscrutable Oriental mind' and think that 'life is not so dear to the Asian masses.' They don't realize that the farmer would rather eat his cow than starve, but that he will starve if he does eat it."

Social Change 185

Selection 29 LAURISTON SHARP, from "Steel Axes for Stone-Age Australians," Steel Axes for Stone-Age Australians **186**

"The most disturbing effects of the steel axe, operating in conjunction with other elements also being introduced from the white man's several sub-cultures, developed in the realm of traditional ideas, sentiments, and values. These were undermined at a rapidly mounting rate, with no new conceptions being defined to replace them."

Selection 30 E. RICHARD SORENSON, from "Growing Up as a Fore Is to Be 'In Touch' and Free," Smithsonian **194**

"This new road, often impassable even with four-wheel-drive vehicles, was perhaps the single most dramatic stroke wrought by the government. It was to the Fore an opening to a new world. As they began to use the road, they started to shed traditions evolved in the protective insularity of their mountain fastness, to adopt in their stead an emerging market culture."

Medical Anthropology 198

Selection 31 ANN McELROY AND PATRICIA K. TOWNSEND, from "The Ecology of Health and Disease," Medical Anthropology in Ecological Perspective **199**

"An important aspect of the training of the young was to pass on knowledge and awareness about the sea ice, the snow, the weather, animal behavior, geography and navigation. Children, learning not from books but from observation and from trial and error participation, became highly sensitive to subtle environmental cues such as shifts in the wind, changing humidity, the color of ice, the restlessness of a caribou herd. This sensitivity was extremely important for survival."

Selection 32 THOMAS ADEOYE LAMBO, from "Psychotherapy in Africa," Human Nature **209**

'The character and effectiveness of medicine for the mind and body always and everywhere depend on the culture in which the medicine is practiced. In the West, healing is often considered a private matter between patient and therapist. In Africa, healing is an integral part of society and religion, a matter in which the whole community is involved."

Selection 33 EDWARD T. HALL, from "Proxemics: The Study of Man's Spatial Relations," Culture, Curers, and Contagion: Readings for Medical Social Science **215**

"Western medicine stresses the isolation of the sick and the minimization of their contact with the healthy. Yet, there are a number of instances, in other cultures, where leaving the patient alone or with only a very few people around him would signify approaching death."

Applied Anthropology 221

Selection 34 MARIANNE ELISABETH LIEN, from "Fame and the Ordinary: 'Authentic' Constructions of Convenience Foods," Advertising Cultures **222**

"Many authors have argued that food provides a particularly suitable medium for representing 'the other,' making ethnic cuisine an excellent paradigm, or metaphor,

for ethnicity itself. However, such representations of the other are also locally constructed, as they tend to be influenced not so much by the 'others' they claim to represent as by cultural configurations of 'otherness' among the consumers they address."

Selection 35 **MONTGOMERY McFATE,** from "Anthropology and Counterinsurgency: The Strange Story of their Curious Relationship," Military Review **229**

"Regardless of whether anthropologists decide to enter the national security arena, cultural information will inevitably be used as the basis of military operations and public policy. And, if anthropologists refuse to contribute, how reliable will that information be? The result of using incomplete "bad" anthropology is, invariably, failed operations and failed policy."

Selection 36 **LEE CRONK,** from "Chapter 7: Gardening Tips," That Complex Whole: Culture and the Evolution of Human Behavior **240**

"College students in particular tend to be relativistic and tolerant to a fault. When I have raised the issue of cultural relativism in my own classes, some students—students with otherwise mainstream political and moral opinions—have earnestly used the idea of 'culture' to exonerate the efforts of the Nazis to exterminate European Jewry. 'It's their culture, so who are we to judge it?' is the reasoning offered, implicitly putting the Holocaust on the same moral level as eating bratwurst."

Acknowledgments   245
Index   248

Internet References

General Internet Sites for Anthropology

http://aaanet.org/resinet.htm
This is the site of the American Anthropological Association. It contains links to just about every anthropological resource imaginable on the Internet.

http://www.trinity.edu/~mkearl/anthro.html
This is an excellent starting point for anthropological resources of every sort, using links.

http://www.indiana.edu/~wanthro/eco.htm
This site is compiled by students in Indiana University's Anthropology Department. It contains links relevant to the various subfields of Anthropology, changes in anthropological perspective over time, and biographies of certain key anthropologists.

http://anthropology.tamu.edu/news.htm
This is an excellent source for the latest news, with weekly updates, in anthropology. It is maintained by the Texas A&M anthropology department. Articles may be retrieved without a fee.

http://www.intute.ac.uk/socialsciences/anthropology/
The goals of Intute: Anthropology, the sponsor of this site, is to match resources to the anthropology curriculum and the needs of researchers. It has links to every type of anthropological interest.

http://www.questia.com
This is an online library of the social sciences with anthropology being a major subject area. For a subscription fee, one can find anthropological texts from books, journals, magazines, newspapers and encyclopedias. It provides a personal "bookshelf," allows one to organize work into separate "projects" and, in many ways, facilitates research.

http://www.usc.edu/dept/elab/urlist/index.html
This UR-List: Web Resources for Visual Anthropology provides searches by cross-indexing 375 anthropological sites according to 22 subject categories.

http://www.mnsu.edu/emuseum/information/biography/
This site contains over 850 biographies of people who have influenced anthropology in some way, including many authors in this book.

http://www.anthrobase.com/default.html
A searchable database of anthropological texts.

http://www.therai.org.uk/
The Royal Anthropological Institute of Great Britain and Ireland (RAI) is the world's longest-established scholarly association dedicated to the furtherance of anthropology (the study of humankind) in its broadest and most inclusive sense

Chapter 1

http://www.wsu.edu:8001/vcwsu/commons/topics/culture/culture-index.html
As one of Washington State University's learning modules, this is a good introduction to the concept of culture as defined and discussed by anthropologists, past and present. It is a work-in-progress that deserves to be monitored.

http://www.anthrobase.com/default.html
This site has a searchable database of anthropological texts, and a dictionary which defines key anthropological terms and identifies anthropologists with their theoretical perspectives and publications.

http://ethnohistory.org/
The American Society for Ethnohistory (ASE) was founded in 1954 to promote the interdisciplinary investigation of the histories of the Native Peoples of the Americas.

Chapter 2

http://www.janeresture.com/trobriand_postcards/index.htm
This site contains images of daily life in the Trobriand Islands. They were taken during the period of 1914-1918, at the time Bronislaw Malinowski was there doing fieldwork.

http://www.socioambiental.org/pib/epienglish/yanomami/yanomami.shtm
This site provides a general description of the Yanomamo along with photographs.

http://69.57.157.207/issues/10.30.00/report.html
Part of an ongoing investigation of the Tierney/Chagnon case by the Dartmouth Review.

http://www.anth.ucsb.edu/images/Aj2it.pdf
This site, which in part consists of an interview with Napoleon Chagnon, presents a discussion of Chagnon's conflicts with the Salesian missionaries of Venezuela, with other anthropologists such as Kenneth Good (author of *Into the Heart*) and with Patrick Tierney (author of *Darkness in El Dorado*, a thoroughgoing criticism of Chagnon's work among the Yanomamo).

Chapter 3

http://www.interculturalstudies.org/main.html
The Institute for Intercultural Studies was established by Margaret Mead and is today directed by her daughter Mary Catherine Bates. With links, it promotes accessibility to Mead's work as well as that of several of her associates, including Franz Boas, Ruth Benedict and Gregory Bateson.

http://www.sciencesitescom.com/CASC/
The Center for Anthropology and Science Communications facilitates improved communications between anthropologists, the public, and science media.

Chapter 4

http://anthro.palomar.edu/language/default.htm
This is a good introduction to the subject of linguistics and includes related websites.

http://www.intute.ac.uk/socialsciences/cgi-bin/browse.pl?id=120052
This site provides links to linguistic associations, journals and links to websites and data bases dedicated to the preservation and study of languages.

http://www.icahdq.org/
This is the site of the International Communication Association, which sponsors conferences and publishes books and journals having to do with cross-cultural communication.

http://www.usal.es/~nonverbal/researchcenters.htm
The site is the gateway for links to all other sites having to do with nonverbal behavior and communication. Site includes links to publications, research centers, experiments, and conferences.

http://members.aol.com/nonverbal2/center.htm#Center%20forNonverbal%20Studies
This is the website of the Center for Nonverbal Studies, dedicated to the development of a deeper understanding of what it means to be human through the study of nonverbal communication.

Chapter 5

http://abbott-infotech.co.za/index-kalahari.html
With maps, photographs and links, this website offers descriptions of the desert, the vegetation, the animals and the people who have lived in the Kalahari

http://anthro.palomar.edu/subsistence/links.htm
This site contains good summaries of subsistence practices, from foraging to intensive agriculture, as well as the effects of the consequent increases in such areas population, warfare and disease. There are also related websites cited.

Chapter 6

http://anthro.palomar.edu/marriage/default.htm
This is a good cross-cultural survey of marriage customs, residence rules and the treatment of homosexuality. Related websites are included.

http://worldweddingtraditions.com/locations/african_traditions.html
Marriage customs are summarized for every region of the world.

http://www.un.org/womenwatch/about/
As part of the United Nations system, Women Watch serves as a conduit for information and resources on the promotion of gender equality and empowerment throughout the world.

http://www.umanitoba.ca/faculties/arts/anthropology/tutor/case_studies/yanomamo/index.html
This site nicely summarizes the kinship and social relations within Yanomamo society.

Chapter 7

http://anthro.palomar.edu/religion/rel_5.htm
This site deals with the various aspects of folk religion and magic, along with related internet links.

http://dir.yahoo.com/Society_and_Culture/Religion_and_Spirituality/Faiths_and_Practices/Shamanism/
This site offers links having to do with shamanic healing.

Chapter 8

http://etext.virginia.edu/users/fennell/highland/harper/religlink.html
Website provides links to a variety of subject areas such as witchcraft accusations and trials, folk religion and magic.

http://www.apologeticsindex.org/site/index-c/
This site offers resources on religious cults, sects, religions and doctrines, including cargo cults.

Chapter 9

http://www.cwis.org/wwwvl/indig-vl.html
The Center for World Indigenous Studies is seeking to create a virtual historical archive relating to the human rights struggles of indigenous peoples. Links are organized geographically.

http://www.cs.org/
Cultural Survival, in addition to publishing its quarterly magazine, provides important links to documents and organizations relating to protecting the human rights of indigenous peoples.

http://www2.etown.edu/vl/humrts.html
This site offers directories, limited area search engines and searchable databases in relation to human rights worldwide.

http://www.inmotionmagazine.com/pacific.html
This site presents articles, opinions and discussions revolving around the indigenous rights movement in the Pacific.

http://www.socioambiental.org/pib/english/whwhhow/wichpe.shtm#t2
The Instituto Socioambiental (ISA) was established in 1994 and has taken as its mission the support of traditional peoples in their struggles for social and environmental rights.

Chapter 10

http://www.medanthro.net/
This is the official website of the Society for Medical Anthropology, a branch of the American Anthropological Association. In keeping with its goal of promoting the study of the anthropological aspects of health, illness and health care, it offers links to relevant medical organizations, academic programs, publications, conferences and other medical anthropology websites.

http://anthro.palomar.edu/medical/links.htm
This site provides an overview of how illness is traditionally perceived and treated in various cultures of the world and provides related Internet sites.

http://sharktown.com/proxemics/intro.html
This website has been set up to disseminate information on psychological aspects of proxemic behavior.

http://ethnopharma.free.fr/
The European Society of Ethnopharmacology represents more than 1500 specialists, including medical doctors, pharmacologists, botanists, anthropologists and historians of medicine and pharmacy whose common interests are medicinal plants, traditional pharmacopoeias and medical anthropology.

Chapter 11

http://www.aaanet.org/apla/index.htm
As a branch of the American Anthropological Association, the Association for Political and Legal Anthropology supports workshops, lectures and publications having to do with issues of contemporary importance in the fields of political and legal anthropology, such as nationalism, colonialism and post-colonial public spheres, multiculturalism, and globalism.

http://www.sfaa.net/
This is the site of the Society for Applied Anthropology, which has as its mission the promotion of interdisciplinary scientific investigation of the relations between human beings and the application of these principles to practical problems. It is affiliated with the American Anthropological Association.

http://www.radcliffe.edu/murray_redirect/index.php
This is the site of the Murray Research Center, which promotes the use of existing social science data to explore human development in the context of social change.

Anthropology as Science

Selection 1

FRANZ BOAS, from "The Aims of Ethnology," *Race, Language and Culture*

Selection 2

CLYDE KLUCKHOHN, from "The Meaning of Culture," *Mirror for Man: The Relation of Anthropology to Modern Life*

Selection 3

RUTH BENEDICT, from "Anthropology and the Abnormal," *Journal of General Psychology*

Selection 4

ROBERT L. CARNEIRO, from "Godzilla Meets New Age Anthropology: Facing the Postmodernist Challenge to a Science of Culture," *EUROPÉA*

The Aims of Ethnology[1]

Franz Boas

In this essay, Franz Boas, who is considered to be the father of modern American fieldwork, sets down several of the basic principles which were to guide his students as they embarked upon their own professional careers as anthropologists.

First, says Boas, look at the crude and derogatory descriptions of other people contained in most travel books destined for public consumption. This *ethnocentrism* (the belief in the superiority of one's own social or cultural group) is the result of the kind of superficial contact that must be avoided at all costs and, so, the way to prevent such shallow thinking is to carry out objective ethnographic fieldwork. Boas was not against making generalizations about other people, but he insisted that all inferences be based upon systematic, thorough-going data collection.

Second, upon closer inspection, Boas finds, people's belief systems, as discerned in their folk tales and mythology, are no less sophisticated than our own. In fact, many of our own myths may have been the result of borrowing or *diffusion* (the anthropological term) from other, more "primitive" groups.

Third, whether similar cultural phenomena found in different areas are the result of borrowing or independent invention, they show that the "human mind develops everywhere according to the same laws." In other words, there is what we call the *psychic unity of mankind*, which is the anthropological equivalent of a declaration of intellectual equality that applies to all people.

Franz Boas was born into a Jewish family in Minden, Germany in 1858. Since his family was more dedicated to social issues than to religion, Boas grew up in a free-thinking family environment. He received his doctorate in physics, but soon gravitated towards anthropology as a result of a trip to Baffinland, where he filed reports on Eskimos for the German newspaper, the *Berliner Tageblatt*.

Franz Boas was to write only a few books, the most important being *The Mind of Primitive Man* and *Race, Language and Culture*. His articles in professional journals, however, number over 600. Beginning in 1899, Boas was to spend most of his career as a professor of Anthropology at Columbia University, during which time he served as mentor to some of the "greats" in anthropology, such as Margaret Mead, Ruth Benedict, Alfred Kroeber, Robert Lowie, and Edwin Sapir (to mention just a few!). If we consider how many students of his students (and so on) there must be in the American anthropological community, we can begin to appreciate how far and wide Boas' influence has spread.

Key Concept: ethnocentrism

Many books of travel give us descriptions drawn in the most abhorrent lines of the people inhabiting foreign countries, describing their mode of life as similar to that of wild beasts, denying that there is any indication of emotional or rational life deserving of our sympathy. In early descriptions of Australians, Bushmen and Fuegians are often described as the lowest forms of mankind, void of all feeling for social obligations, without law and order, without imagination, even without shelter and tools.

If travellers who have seen those people give us descriptions of this type, it is not surprising that others who have never been in contact with primitive people accept their views and we begin to understand the reason for the oft-repeated question: What is the use of studying the life of primitive people?

Even the rudest tribes do not conform to the picture that is drawn by many a superficial traveller. Many examples may be culled from the extensive literature of travel showing the superficiality of the reports given. The well-known traveller Burchell met near the Garib a group of Bushmen and gives us the most wonderful report of their complete lack of reasoning power. He asked the question: What is the difference between a good and an evil action? And since they could not answer to his satisfaction, he declared them to have no power of reasoning and judging. In a similar way the Fuegians were asked about their religious ideas in terms that were necessarily unintelligible to them, and since they could not answer it was said that they cannot grasp any idea that transcends the barest needs of everyday life. Nowadays we know better, and no scientifically prepared traveller would dare to make statements of this kind. We know now that the Bushmen, whom Burchell described as little different from wild beasts, have a well-developed music, a wide range of tales and traditions; they enjoy poetry and are excellent narrators. Their rock paintings show a high degree of skill and a remarkable understanding of perspective. We also know that the Fuegians have a well-developed social organization and that their customs are proof of a deep-seated religious attitude.

The Andamanese are another people that owe their ill repute to the reports of early travellers. Marco Polo, who visited them in 1285, said: "These people are like wild beasts, and I assure you that all the men of this island Angamanain have heads like those of dogs, and teeth and eyes of the same kind; in fact, their faces look like those of bulldogs." An Arabic writer of the ninth century says: "The color of their skin is terrifying; their feet are large, almost a cubit long, and they are absolutely without clothing." Compare this with the description of E. H. Man, to whom we are indebted for a better knowledge of this interesting people. He says: "It has been asserted that the communal marriage system prevails among them, and that marriage is nothing more than taking a female slave, but so far from the contract being regarded as a merely temporary arrangement, to be set aside at the will of either party, no incompatibility of temper or other cause is allowed to dissolve the union, and while bigamy, polygamy, polyandry, and divorce are unknown, conjugal fidelity till death is not the exception, but the rule.... One of the most striking features of their social relations is the marked equality and affection which subsists between husband and wife." Even if this description should be considered as somewhat colored, it shows nevertheless that these people are not "like wild beasts."

Thus a closer study shows that some of the peoples of worst repute are not as crude as superficial reports would make us believe, and we are led to suspect that the cultural conditions among all primitive peoples may be higher than is commonly assumed.

Our knowledge of primitive tribes the world over justifies the statement that there is no people that lacks definite religious ideas and traditions, that has not made inventions, that does not live under the rule of customary laws regulating the relations between the members of the tribe. And there is no people without language.

The task of ethnology is the study of the total range of phenomena of social life. Language, customs, migrations, bodily characteristics are subjects of our studies. Thus its very first and most immediate object is the study of the history of mankind, not that of civilized nations alone, but that of the whole of mankind, from its earliest traces found in the deposits of the ice age, up to modern times.

We must follow the gradual development of the manifestations of culture. The aim we have in view may be illustrated by an example....

The results of philological and historical investigations referring to peoples speaking Indo-European languages demonstrated that the family was the foundation of society and that on this basis the tribe and state developed. From this point of view it seemed strange that among some peoples the father was not the head of the family but that often the mother had rights which in later time belonged to the father. Thus Herodotus tells that among the Lycians the daughters inherited from their parents, not the sons. It is told that in Athens at the time of Cecrops the children took their names from their mothers, and according to Tacitus the mother's brother enjoyed particular respect. The numerous tales of Amazons may also be mentioned. From the standpoint of our culture these customs were unexplainable, but when the customs of primitive people came to be known, the history of the development of the family was more readily understood.[2] (Among many primitive tribes descent is unilateral, the child being counted as a member of either the father's or the mother's line; not a member of both. When the child belongs to the mother's line and position or other rights are held by males, conflicts develop because the child does not inherit these from his father, but from the men of his mother's line, that is to say from his maternal uncle. When the family consisting of parents and children form an economic and social unit, this type of organization leads easily to conflicts between father and sons, and between a man and his wife's brothers. Therefore there is an element of instability in these institutions and they are liable to break down and change to a form in which either the child belongs to the father's line, so that conflicts are avoided, or that it belongs to both lines.)

A conclusion based on investigations of this type should be emphasized. It shows that emotional reactions which we feel as natural are in reality culturally determined. It is not easy for us to understand that the emotional relation between father and son should be different from the one to which we are accustomed, but a knowledge of the life of people with a social organization different from ours brings about situations in which conflicts or mutual obligations arise of a character quite opposed to those we are accustomed to and that run counter to what we consider "natural" emotional reactions to those to whom we are related by blood.

The data of ethnology prove that not only our knowledge, but also our emotions, are the result of the form of our social life and of the history of the people to whom we belong. If we desire to understand the development of human culture, we must try to free ourselves of these shackles. This is possible only to those who are willing to adapt themselves to the strange ways of thinking and feeling of primitive people. If we attempt to interpret the actions of our remote ancestors by our rational and emotional attitudes, we cannot reach truthful results, for their feeling and thinking was different from ours. We must lay aside many points of view that seem to us self-evident, because in early times they were not self-evident. It is impossible to determine *a priori* those parts of our mental life that are common to mankind as a whole and those due to the culture in which we live. A knowledge of the data of ethnology enables us to attain this insight. Therefore it enables us also to view our own civilization objectively.

When it is recognized that similar customs may spring up independently, we are no longer prone to infer from superficial similarities community of origin of peoples. How often have the lost tribes of Israel been rediscovered—in America, Polynesia, and Africa! How often have lost tribes of antiquity been supposed to have migrated by way of the fabulous Atlantis to America! The argument for such extravagant theories is generally the occurrence of some taboo or of an ornament found in widely separated regions.

It is indeed most remarkable that the same cultural phenomena recur in the most remote parts of the world and that the varied complex forms of thought and action which the human mind develops are repeated and so distributed that historical connection is almost unthinkable. The Phaëthon tale is a good example. It is the story of the son of the Sun who drives the heavenly chariot and is cast down by the thunderbolt of Zeus when he scorches the earth. Among the Indians of British Columbia the mink visits his father, the sun, carries the sun in his stead and is cast down by his own father when he scorches the earth. The custom of wearing large ornaments in the lips is found in parts of America, but also in equatorial Africa. Recently Bastian has treated modern spiritism from the same point of view, showing its similarity with the practices of spiritism among primitive people.

The frequent occurrence of similar phenomena in cultural areas that have no historical contact suggests that important results may be derived from their study, for it shows that the human mind develops everywhere according to the same laws.

The discovery of these is the greatest aim of our science. To attain it many methods of inquiry and the assistance of many other sciences will be needed. Up to this time the number of investigations is small, but the foundations have been laid by the labors of men like Tylor, Bastian, Morgan, and Bachofen. As in other new branches of science, there is no lack of hasty theorizing that does not contribute to healthy growth. Far-reaching theories have been built on weak foundations. Here belongs the attempt to explain history as determined by the nature of the country in which the people live. A relation between soil and history cannot be denied, but we are not in a position to explain social and mental behavior on this basis and anthropo-geographical "laws" are valid only as vague, empty generalities. Climate and soil exert an influence upon the body and its functions, but it is not possible to prove that the character of the country finds immediate expression in that of its inhabitants. It is said that the Negro, living in tropical Africa and not troubled by lack of food, is lazy and does not take the trouble to clothe his body. The Eskimo also is said to be made lazy by the long Polar night which dwarfs his imagination. Unfortunately such generalizations are entirely misleading. There are Negro tribes which punish anyone who appears in public improperly clothed; while the tribes of Tierra del Fuego which live in an inhospitable climate are scantily clothed. The Eskimo, during the long winter night, find entertainment in dance, song and story telling.…

I have hastily sketched the scope of our science. I have not been able to do more than to mark the broadest outlines of the aims we have in mind. With a few words I have tried to indicate the methodological means at our disposal.

I hope I may have succeeded in my task: to show that it is not idle curiosity or fondness of adventure that induces the scientist to visit distant people of apparently low grades of culture; that we are conscious of a task well worthy of the most strenuous efforts when we collect the languages, customs, and tales of tribes whose life differs in fundamental aspects from our own.

Notes

1. Lecture given before the Deutscher Gesellig-Wissenschaftlicher Verein von New York, March 8, 1888; New York, Hermann Bartsch, 1889. I have included this paper in the present series because it illustrates my early views regarding ethnological problems.
2. The following passage has been changed, because the current view of a necessary precedence of matrilineal forms of family organization was accepted. This view is not tenable, since it is impossible to derive all forms of family organization from a single source.

SELECTION 2

The Meaning of Culture

Clyde Kluckhohn

So much of the details of our lives—family relationships, economic arrangements, religious activities—are imprinted upon us by our culture, says Kluckhohn (1905–1960), that much of human behavior can be predicted. Is it any wonder that an American-born male growing up in China acquires the mannerisms of his adoptive country? That rattlesnake meat can taste like chicken until you are told what it actually is? That an American Indian product—the tomato—would be seen as poisonous by early American settlers?

Although not identifying the anthropological concept by name in this essay, Clyde Kluckhohn brings home the point of *cultural relativity*, the notion that even our innermost thoughts and feelings are determined not so much by our biological make-up or even the physical environmental in which we live, but rather by how we are brought up.

It is important to remember that, during the formative years of cultural anthropology in the United States, this was not necessarily a commonly accepted view. Just the opposite: it was once widely held that peoples' lifestyles were at least in part a product of their biological nature, a form of *reductionism* in which the explanations for social behavior could be "reduced" to hereditary causes. The most extreme expressions of this form of racism were so widespread that membership in the Ku Klux Klan in the United States grew to several million members by the early 1920s and the Nazi Party rose to power in Germany in 1933.

In writing this essay in 1949 (excerpted from *Mirror for Man: The Relation of Anthropology to Modern Life*), Clyde Kluckhohn was not only promoting the positive benefits of the cultural anthropological perspective, but he was also joining a chorus of anthropologists, led by such pioneers as Franz Boas and Margaret Mead, in condemning biological reductionism.

In fact, many cultural anthropologists would say that there is still too much reductionism in the academic atmosphere (although granted, not of the racist variety), being promoted by "evolutionary biologists" and "evolutionary psychologists."

Clyde Kluckhohn attended Oxford University on a Rhodes scholarship and received his master's degree there in 1932. He received his doctorate in Anthropology at Harvard University in 1936. He is perhaps best remembered for his fieldwork among the Navaho.

Key Concept: culture is a set of learned adaptive techniques

Why do the Chinese dislike milk and milk products? Why would the Japanese die willingly in a Banzai charge that seemed senseless to Americans? Why do some nations trace descent through the father, others through the mother, still others through both parents? Not because different peoples have different instincts, not because they were destined by God or Fate to different habits, not because the weather is different in China and Japan and the United States. Sometimes shrewd common sense has an answer that is close to that of the anthropologist: "because they were brought up that way." By "culture" anthropology means the total life way of a people, the social legacy the individual acquires from his group. Or culture can be regarded as that part of the environment that is the creation of man ....

One of the interesting things about human beings is that they try to understand themselves and their own behavior. While this has been particularly true of Europeans in recent times, there is no group which has not developed a scheme or schemes to explain man's actions. To the insistent human query "why?" the most exciting illumination anthropology has to offer is that of the concept of culture. Its explanatory importance is comparable to categories such as evolution in biology, gravity in physics, disease in medicine. A good deal of human behavior can be understood, and indeed predicted, if we know a people's design for living. Many acts are neither accidental nor due to personal peculiarities nor caused by supernatural forces nor simply mysterious. Even those of us who pride ourselves on our individualism follow most of the time a pattern not of our own making.

We brush our teeth on arising. We put on pants—not a loincloth or a grass skirt. We eat three meals a day—not four or five or two. We sleep in a bed—not in a hammock or on a sheep pelt. I do not have to know the individual and his life history to be able to predict these and countless other regularities, including many in the thinking process, of all Americans who are not incarcerated in jails or hospitals for the insane.

To the American woman a system of plural wives seem "instinctively" abhorrent. She cannot understand how any woman can fail to be jealous and uncomfortable if she must share her husband with other women. She feels it "unnatural" to accept such a situation. On the other hand, a Koryak woman of Siberia, for example, would find it hard to understand how a woman could be so selfish and so undesirous of feminine companionship in the home as to wish to restrict her husband to one mate.

Some years ago I met in New York City a young man who did not speak a word of English and was obviously bewildered by American ways. By "blood" he was as American as you or I, for his parents had gone from Indiana to China as missionaries. Orphaned in infancy, he was reared by a Chinese family in a remote village. All who met him found him more Chinese than American. The facts of his blue eyes and light hair were less impressive than a Chinese style of gait. Chinese arm and hand movements, Chinese facial expression, and Chinese modes of thought. The biological heritage was American, but the cultural training had been Chinese. He returned to China.

Another example of another kind: I once knew a trader's wife in Arizona who took a somewhat devilish interest in producing a cultural reaction. Guests who came her way were often served delicious sandwiches filled with a meat that seemed to be neither chicken nor tuna fish yet was reminiscent of both. To queries she gave no reply until each had eaten his fill. She then explained that what they had eaten was not chicken, not tuna fish, but the rich, white flesh of freshly killed rattlesnakes. The response was instantaneous—vomiting, often violent vomiting. A biological process is caught in a cultural web ....

Culture arises out of human nature, and its forms are restricted both by man's biology and by natural laws. It is equally true that culture channels biological processes—vomiting, weeping, fainting, sneezing, the daily habits of food intake and waste elimination. When a man eats, he is reacting to an internal "drive," namely, hunger contractions consequent upon the lowering of blood sugar, but his precise reaction to these internal stimuli cannot be predicted by physiological knowledge alone. Whether a healthy adult feels hungry twice, three times, or four times a day and the hours at which this feeling recurs is a question of culture. *What* he eats is of course limited by availability, but is also partly regulated by culture. it is a biological fact that some types of berries are poisonous; It is a cultural fact that, a few generations ago, most Americans considered tomatoes to be poisonous

and refused to eat them. Such selective, discriminative use of the environment is characteristically cultural. In a still more general sense, too, the process of eating is channeled by culture. Whether a man eats to live, lives to eat, or merely eats and lives is only in part an individual matter, for there are also cultural trends. Emotions are physiological events. Certain situations will evoke fear in people from any culture. But sensations of pleasure, anger, and lust may be stimulated by cultural cues that would leave unmoved someone who has been reared in a different social tradition.

Except in the case of newborn babies and of individuals born with clearcut structural or functional abnormalities we can observe innate endowments only as modified by cultural training. In a hospital in New Mexico where Zuñi Indian, Navaho Indian, and white American babies are born, it is possible to classify the newly arrived infants as unusually active, average, and quiet. Some babies from each "racial" group will fall into each category, though a higher proportion of the white babies, will fall into the unusually active class. But if a Navaho baby, a Zuñi baby, and a white baby—all classified as unusually active at birth—are again observed at the age of two years, the Zuñi baby will no longer seem given to quick and restless activity—*as compared with the white child*—though he may seem so as compared with the other Zuñis of the same age. The Navaho child is likely to fall in between as contrasted with the Zuñi and the white, though he will probably still seem more active than the average Navaho youngster....

Culture is a *way* of thinking, feeling, believing. It is the group's knowledge stored up (in memories of men; in books and objects) for future use. We study the products of this "mental" activity: the overt behavior, the speech and gestures and activities of people, and the tangible results of these things such as tools, houses, cornfields, and what not....

Since culture is an abstraction, it is important not to confuse culture with society. A "society" refers to a group of people who interact more with each other than they do with other individuals—who cooperate with each other for the attainment of certain ends. You can see and indeed count the individuals who make up a society. A "culture" refers to the distinctive ways of life of such a group of people. Not all social events are culturally patterned. New types of circumstances arise for which no cultural solutions have as yet been devised.

A culture constitutes a storehouse of the pooled learning of the group. A rabbit starts life with some innate responses. He can learn from his own experience and perhaps from observing other rabbits. A human infant is born with fewer instincts and greater plasticity. His main task is to learn the answers that persons he will never see, persons long dead, have worked out. Once he has learned the formulas supplied by the culture of his group, most of his behavior becomes almost as automatic and unthinking as if it were instinctive. There is a tremendous amount of intelligence behind the making of a radio, but not much is required to learn to turn it on.

The members of all human societies face some of the same unavoidable dilemmas, posed by biology and other facts of the human situation. This is why the basic categories of all cultures are so similar. Human culture without language is unthinkable. No culture fails to provide for aesthetic expression and aesthetic delight. Every culture supplies standardized orientations toward the deeper problems, such as death. Every culture is designed to perpetuate the group and its solidarity, to meet the demands of individuals for an orderly way of life and for satisfaction of biological needs.

However, the variations on these basic themes are numberless. Some languages are built up out of twenty basic sounds, others out of forty. Nose plugs were considered beautiful by predynastic Egyptians but are not by the modern French. Puberty is a biological fact. But one culture ignores it, another prescribes informal instructions about sex but no ceremony, a third has impressive rites for girls only, a fourth for boys and girls. In this culture, the first menstruation is welcomed as a happy, natural event; in that culture the atmosphere is full of dread and supernatural threat. Each culture dissects nature according to its own system of categories ….

Every culture must deal with the sexual instinct. Some, however, seek to deny all sexual expression before marriage, whereas a Polynesian adolescent who was not promiscuous would be distinctly abnormal. Some cultures enforce lifelong monogamy; others, like our own, tolerate serial monogamy, in still other cultures, two or more women may be joined to one man or several men to a single woman. Homosexuality has been a permitted pattern in the Greco-Roman world, in parts of Islam, and in various primitive tribes. Large portions of the population of Tibet, and of Christendom at some places and periods, have practiced complete celibacy. To us marriage is first and foremost an arrangement between two individuals. In many more societies marriage is merely one facet of a complicated set of reciprocities, economic and otherwise, between two families or clans.

The essence of the cultural process is selectivity. The selection is only exceptionally conscious and rational. Cultures are like Topsy. They just grew. Once, however, a way of handling a situation becomes institutionalized, there is ordinarily great resistance to change or deviation. When we speak of "our sacred beliefs," we mean of course that they are beyond criticism and that the person who suggests modification or abandonment must be punished. No person is emotionally indifferent to his culture. Certain cultural premises may become totally out of accord with a new factual situation. Leaders may recognize this and reject the old ways in theory. Yet their emotional loyalty continues in the face of reason because of the intimate conditionings of early childhood.

A culture is learned by individuals as the result of belonging to some particular group, and it constitutes that part of learned behavior which is shared with others. It is our social legacy, as contrasted with our organic heredity. It is one of the important factors which permits us to live together in an organized society, giving us ready-made solutions to our problems, helping us to predict the behavior of others, and permitting others to know what to expect of us.

Culture regulates our lives at every turn. From the moment we are born until we die there is, whether we are conscious of it or not, constant pressure upon us to follow certain types of behavior that other men have created for us. Some paths we follow willingly, others we follow because we know no other way, still others we deviate from or go back to most unwillingly. Mothers of small children know how unnaturally most of this comes to us—how little regard we have, until we are "culturalized," for the "proper" place, time, and manner for certain acts such as eating, excreting, sleeping, getting dirty, and making loud noises. But by more or less adhering to a system of related designs for carrying out all the acts of living, a group of men and women feel themselves linked together by a powerful chain of sentiments. [American anthropologist] Ruth Benedict gave an almost complete definition of the concept when she said, "Culture is that which binds men together."

It is true any culture is a set of techniques for adjusting both to the external environment and to other men. However, cultures create problems as well as solve them. If the lore of a people states that frogs are dangerous creatures, or that it is not safe to go about at night because of witches or ghosts, threats are posed which do not arise out of the inexorable facts of the external world. Cultures produce needs as well as provide a means of fulfilling them. There exists for every group culturally defined, acquired drives that may be more powerful in ordinary daily life than the biologically inborn drives. Many Americans, for example, will work harder for "success" than they will for sexual satisfaction.

Most groups elaborate certain aspects of their culture far beyond maximum utility or survival value. In other words, not all culture promotes physical survival. At times, indeed, it does exactly the opposite. Aspects of culture which once were adaptive may persist long after they have ceased to be useful. An analysis of any culture will disclose many features which cannot possibly be construed as adaptations to the total environment in which the group now finds itself. However, it is altogether likely that these apparently useless features represent survivals, with modifications though time, of cultural forms which were adaptive in one or another previous situation.

Any cultural practice must be functional or it will disappear before long. That is, it must somehow contribute to the survival of the society or to the adjustment of the individual. However, many cultural functions are not manifest but latent. A cowboy will walk three miles to catch a horse which he then rides one mile to the store. From the point of view of manifest function this is positively irrational. But the act has the latent function of maintaining the cowboy's prestige in the terms of his own subculture. One can instance the buttons on the sleeve of a man's coat, our absurd English spelling, the use of capital letters, and a host of other apparently nonfunctional customs. They serve mainly the latent function of assisting individuals to maintain their security by preserving continuity with the past and by making certain sectors of life familiar and predictable.

Every culture is a precipitate of history. In more than one sense history is a sieve. Each culture embraces those aspects of the past which, usually in altered form and with altered meanings, live on in the present. Discoveries and inventions, both material and ideological, are constantly being made available to a group through its historical contacts with other peoples or being created by its own members. However, only those that fit the total immediate situation in meeting the group's needs for survival or in promoting the psychological adjustment of individuals will become part of the culture. The process of culture building may be regarded as an addition to man's innate biological capacities, an addition providing instruments which enlarge, or may even substitute for biological functions, and to a degree, compensating for biological limitations—as in ensuring that death does not always result in the loss of humanity of what the deceased has learned.

Culture is like a map. Just as a map isn't the territory but an abstract representation of a particular area, so also a culture is an abstract description of trends toward uniformity in the words, deeds, and artifacts of a human group. If a map is accurate and you can read it, you won't get lost; if you know a culture, you will know your way around in the life of a society....

Every group's way of life, then, is a structure—not a haphazard collection of all the different physically possible and functionally effective patterns of belief and action. A culture is an interdependent system based upon linked premises and categories whose influence is greater, rather than less, because they are seldom put in words. Some degree of internal coherence which is felt rather than rationally constructed seems to be demanded by most of the participants in any culture. As [philosopher Alfred North] Whitehead has remarked, "Human life is driven forward by its dim apprehension of notions too general for its existing language."

In sum, the distinctive way of life that is handed down as the social heritage of a people does more than supply a set of skills for making a living and a set of blueprints for human relations. Each different way of life makes its own assumptions about the ends and purposes of human existence, about what human beings have a right to expect from each other and the gods, about what constitutes a fulfillment or frustration. Some of these assumptions are made explicit in the lore of the folk; others are tacit premises which the observer must infer by finding consistent trends in word and deed.

Anthropology and the Abnormal

Ruth Benedict

As a former student of Franz Boas, Ruth Benedict must have made her mentor proud with what amounts to a position paper promoting the importance of cultural anthropology. In this 1934 article, she points out that what is considered to be "normal" or "abnormal" varies from one culture to another, that behavior perceived to be intolerable in one setting, might not only be tolerable but expected behavior in another. This viewpoint, of course, is a variation on the theme of *cultural relativity*, a long-standing principle, universally espoused, in the anthropological community.

As you read this article, please note that Ruth Benedict has brought up two issues. One has to do with whether or not some aspects of human behavior are "inevitable" (inherited) or the result of cultural factors. While some seem to be entirely social in origin, such as the extreme suspicion of others among the Dobuans, others, such as psychiatric disorders may have a hereditary component that all groups share. The other point, however, which Ruth Benedict brings home quite forcefully, is the notion that, whatever the origin of a particular form of "abnormal behavior," the degree of *social approval* it receives varies from culture to culture.

Ruth Fulton Benedict was born in New York City in 1887. She graduated Phi Beta Kappa at Vassar College with a degree in English literature in 1909. She married Stanley Benedict, a biochemist who was to become a professor at Cornell Medical School. Ruth wrote poetry and published in several literary journals under the pseudonym Anne Singleton. She enrolled at Columbia University, discovered anthropology studying with Franz Boas, and received her Ph.D. in 1923. She had also served as a teaching assistant at Barnard where she met Margaret Mead as one of her students.

Among her academic accomplishments, Ruth Benedict taught at Columbia, served as editor of Journal of American Folklore, served as president of the American Anthropological Society and the American Ethnological Association, and made many field trips among Native Americans, including the Serrano in California, the Zuni and Pima and Apache of New Mexico, and the Blackfoot of Montana.

Her most notable publications were *Patterns of Culture* (1934), *Zuni Mythology* (1935), *Race: Science and Politics* (1940), and *The Chrysanthemum and the Sword* (1946).

Ruth Benedict died in 1948.

Key Concept: "abnormal" is defined by the culture

Modern social anthropology has become more and more a study of the varieties and common elements of cultural environment and the consequences of these in human behavior. For such a study of diverse social orders, primitive peoples fortunately provide a laboratory not yet entirely vitiated by the spread of a standardized worldwide civilization. Dyaks and Hopis, Fijians and Yakuts, are significant for psychological and sociological study because only among these simpler peoples has there been sufficient isolation to give opportunity for the development of localized social forms. In the higher cultures the standardization of custom and belief over a couple of continents has given a false sense of the inevitability of the particular forms that have gained currency, and we need to turn to a wider survey in order to check the conclusions we hastily base upon this near universality of familiar customs. Most of the simpler cultures did not gain the wide currency of the one which, out of our experience, we identify with human nature, but this was for various historical reasons, and certainly not for any that gives us as its carriers a monopoly of social good or of social sanity. Modern civilization, from this point of view, becomes not a necessary pinnacle of human achievement but one entry in a long series of possible adjustments.

These adjustments, whether they are in mannerisms like the ways of showing anger or joy or grief in any society, or in major human drives like those of sex, prove to be far more variable than experience in any one culture would suggest. In certain fields, such as that of religion or of formal marriage arrangements, these wide limits of variability are well known and can be fairly described. In others it is not yet possible to give a generalized account, but that does not absolve us of the task of indicating the significance of the work that has been done and of the problems that have arisen.

One of these problems relates to the customary modern normal-abnormal categories and our conclusions regarding them. In how far are such categories culturally determined, or in how far can we with assurance regard them as absolute? In how far can we regard inability to function socially as diagnostic of abnormality, or in how far is it necessary to regard this as a function of the culture?

As a matter of fact, one of the most striking facts that emerge from a study of widely varying cultures is the ease with which our abnormals function in other cultures. It does not matter what kind of "abnormality" we choose for illustration, those which indicate extreme instability, or those which are more in the nature of character traits like sadism or delusions of grandeur or of persecution; there are well-described cultures in which these abnormals function at ease and with honor, and apparently without danger or difficulty to the society.

The most notorious of these are trance and catalepsy. Even a very mild mystic is aberrant in our culture. But most peoples have regarded even extreme psychic manifestations not only as normal and desirable, but even as characteristic of highly valued and gifted individuals. This was true even in our own cultural background in that period when Catholicism made the ecstatic experience the mark of sainthood. It is hard for us, born and brought up in a culture that makes no use of the experience, to realize how important a role it may play and how many individuals are capable of it, once it has been given an honorable place in any society....

Cataleptic and trance phenomena are, of course, only one illustration of the fact that those whom we regard as abnormals may function adequately in other cultures. Many of our culturally discarded traits are selected for elaboration in different societies. Homosexuality is an excellent example, for in this case our attention is not constantly diverted, as in the consideration of trance, to the interruption of routine activity which it implies. Homosexuality poses the problem very simply. A tendency toward this trait in our culture exposes an individual to all the conflicts to which all aberrants are always exposed, and we tend to identify the consequences of this conflict with homosexuality. But these consequences are obviously local and cultural. Homosexuals in many societies are not incompetent, but they may be such if the culture asks adjustments of them that would strain any man's vitality. Wherever homosexuality has been given an honorable place in any society, those to whom it is congenial have filled adequately the honorable roles

society assigns to them. Plato's *Republic* is, of course, the most convincing statement of such a reading of homosexuality. It is presented as one of the major means to the good life, and it was generally so regarded in Greece at that time.

The cultural attitude toward homosexuals has not always been on such a high ethical plane, but it has been very varied. Among many American Indian tribes there exists the institution of the *berdache*, as the French called them. These men-women were men who at puberty or thereafter took the dress and the occupations of women. Sometimes they married other men and lived with them. Sometimes they were men with no inversion,[1] persons of weak sexual endowment who chose this role to avoid the jeers of the women. The *berdaches* were never regarded as of first-rate supernatural power, as similar men-women were in Siberia, but rather as leaders in women's occupations, good healers in certain diseases, or, among certain tribes, as the genial organizers of social affairs. In any case, they were socially placed. They were not left exposed to the conflicts that visit the deviant who is excluded from participation in the recognized patterns of his society.

The most spectacular illustrations of the extent to which normality may be culturally defined are those cultures where an abnormality of our culture is the cornerstone of their social structure. It is not possible to do justice to these possibilities in a short discussion. A recent study of an island of northwest Melanesia by Fortune[2] describes a society built upon traits which we regard as beyond the border of paranoia. In this tribe the exogamic[3] groups look upon each other as prime manipulators of black magic, so that one marries always into an enemy group which remains for life one's deadly and unappeasable foes. They look upon a good garden crop as a confession of theft, for everyone is engaged in making magic to induce into his garden the productiveness of his neighbors; therefore no secrecy in the island is so rigidly insisted upon as the secrecy of a man's harvesting of his yams. Their polite phrase at the acceptance of a gift is, "And if you now poison me, how shall I repay you this present?" Their preoccupation with poisoning is constant; no woman ever leaves her cooking pot for a moment untended. Even the great affinal[4] economic exchanges that are characteristic of this Melanesian culture area are quite altered in Dobu since they are incompatible with this fear and distrust that pervades the culture. They go farther and people the whole world outside their own quarters with such malignant spirits that all-night feasts and ceremonials simply do not occur here. They have even rigorous religiously enforced customs that forbid the sharing of seed even in one family group. Anyone else's food is deadly poison to you, so that communality of stores is out of the question. For some months before harvest the whole society is on the verge of starvation, but if one falls to the temptation and eats up one's seed yams, one is an outcast and a beachcomber for life. There is no coming back. It involves, as a matter of course, divorce and the breaking of all social ties.

Now in this society where no one may work with another and no one may share with another, Fortune describes the individual who was regarded by all his fellows as crazy. He was not one of those who periodically ran amok and, beside himself and frothing at the mouth, fell with a knife upon anyone he could reach. Such behavior they did not regard as putting anyone outside the pale. They did not even put the individuals who were known to be liable to these attacks under any kind of control. They merely fled when they saw the attack coming on and kept out of the way. "He would be all right tomorrow." But there was one man of sunny, kindly disposition who liked work and liked to be helpful. The compulsion was too strong for him to repress it in favor of the opposite tendencies of his culture. Men and women never spoke of him without laughing; he was silly and simple and definitely crazy. Nevertheless, to the ethnologist used to a culture that has, in Christianity, made his type the model of all virtue, he seemed a pleasant fellow....

Among the Kwakiutl it did not matter whether a relative had died in bed of disease, or by the hand of an enemy; in either case death was an affront to be wiped out by the death of another person. The fact that one had been caused to mourn was proof that one had been put upon. A chief's sister and her daughter had gone up to Victoria, and either because they drank bad whiskey or because their boat capsized, they never came back.

The chief called together his warriors. "Now I ask you, tribes, who shall wail? Shall I do it or shall another?" The spokesman answered, of course, "Not you, Chief. Let some other of the tribes." Immediately they set up the war pole to announce their intention of wiping out the injury and gathered a war party. They set out and found seven men and two children asleep and killed them. "Then they felt good when they arrived at Sebaa in the evening."

The point which is of interest to us is that in our society those who on that occasion would feel good when they arrived at Sebaa that evening would be the definitely abnormal. There would be some, even in our society, but it is not a recognized and approved mood under the circumstances....

This head-hunting that takes place on the Northwest Coast after a death is no matter of blood revenge or of organized vengeance. There is no effort to tie up the subsequent killing with any responsibility on the part of the victim for the death of the person who is being mourned. A chief whose son has died goes visiting wherever his fancy dictates, and he says to his host, "My prince has died today, and you go with him." Then he kills him. In this, according to their interpretation, he acts nobly because he has not been downed. He has thrust back in return. The whole procedure is meaningless without the fundamental paranoid reading of bereavement. Death, like all the other untoward accidents of existence, confounds man's pride and can only be handled in the category of insults....

These illustrations, which it has been possible to indicate only in the briefest manner, force upon us the fact that normality is culturally defined. An adult shaped to the drives and standards of either of these cultures, if he were transported into our civilization, would fall into our categories of abnormality. He would be faced with the psychic dilemmas of the socially unavailable. In his own culture, however, he is the pillar of society, the end result of socially inculcated mores,[5] and the problem of personal instability in his case simply does not arise.

No one civilization can possibly utilize in its mores the whole potential range of human behavior. Just as there are great numbers of possible phonetic articulations, and the possibility of language depends on a selection and standardization of a few of these in order that speech communication may be possible at all, so the possibility of organized behavior of every sort, from the fashions of local dress and houses to the dicta[6] of a people's ethics and religion, depends upon a similar selection among the possible behavior traits. In the field of recognized economic obligations or sex tabus, this selection is as nonrational and subconscious a process as it is in the field of phonetics. It is a process which goes on in the group for long periods of time and is historically conditioned by innumerable accidents of isolation or of contact of peoples. In any comprehensive study of psychology, the selection that different cultures have made in the course of history within the great circumference of potential behavior is of great significance.

Every society, beginning with some slight inclination in one direction or another, carries its preference farther and farther, integrating itself more and more completely upon its chosen basis and discarding those types of behavior that are uncongenial. Most of those organizations of personality that seem to us most incontrovertibly abnormal have been used by different civilizations in the very foundations of their institutional life. Conversely, the most valued traits of our normal individuals have been looked on in differently organized cultures as aberrant. Normality, in short, within a very wide range, is culturally defined. It is primarily a term for the socially elaborated segment of human behavior in any culture; and abnormality, a term for the segment that that particular civilization does not use. The very eyes with which we see the problem are conditioned by the long traditional habits of our own society.

It is a point that has been made more often in relation to ethics than in relation to psychiatry. We do not any longer make the mistake of deriving the morality of our own locality and decade directly from the inevitable constitution of human nature. We do not elevate it to the dignity of a first principle. We recognize that morality differs in every society, and is a convenient term for socially approved habits. Mankind has always preferred to say "It is morally good" rather than "It is habitual," and the fact of this preference is matter enough for a critical science of ethics. But historically the two phrases are synonymous.

The concept of the normal is properly a variant of the concept of the good. It is that which society has approved. A normal action is one which falls well within the limits of expected behavior for a particular society. Its variability among different peoples is essentially a function of the variability of the behavior pattern that different societies have created for themselves, and can never be wholly divorced from a consideration of culturally institutionalized types of behavior.

Each culture is a more or less elaborate working-out of the potentialities of the segment [of possible human behaviors] it has chosen. Insofar as a civilization is well integrated and consistent within itself, it will tend to carry farther and farther, according to its nature, its initial impulse toward a particular type of action, and from the point of view of any other culture those elaborations will include more and more extreme and aberrant traits.

Each of these traits, in proportion as it reinforces the chosen behavior patterns of that culture, is for that culture normal. Those individuals to whom it is congenial, either congenitally or as the result of childhood sets, are accorded prestige in that culture and are not visited with the social contempt or disapproval which their traits would call down upon them in a society that was differently organized. On the other hand, those individuals whose characteristics are not congenial to the selected type of human behavior in that community are the deviants, no matter how valued their personality traits may be in a contrasted civilization....

I have spoken of individuals as having sets toward certain types of behavior, and of these sets as running sometimes counter to the types of behavior which are institutionalized in the culture to which they belong. From all that we know of contrasting cultures, it seems clear that differences of temperament occur in every society. The matter has never been made the subject of investigation, but from the available material it would appear that these temperament types are very likely of universal recurrence. That is, there is an ascertainable range of human behavior that is found wherever a sufficiently large series of individuals is observed. But the proportion in which behavior types stand to one another in different societies is not universal. The vast majority of the individuals in any group

are shaped to the fashion of that culture. In other words, most individuals are plastic to the molding force of the society into which they are born. In a society that values trance, as in India, they will have supernormal experience. In a society that institutionalizes homosexuality, they will be homosexual. In a society that sets the gathering of possessions as the chief human objective, they will amass property. The deviants, whatever the type of behavior the culture has institutionalized, will remain few in number, and there seems no more difficulty in molding the vast malleable majority to the "normality" of what we consider an aberrant trait, such as delusions of reference, than to the normality of such accepted behavior patterns as acquisitiveness. The small proportion of the number of the deviants in any culture is not a function of the sure instinct with which that society has built itself upon the fundamental sanities, but of the universal fact that, happily, the majority of mankind quite readily take any shape that is presented to them....

The problem of understanding abnormal human behavior in any absolute sense independent of cultural factors is still far in the future. The categories of borderline behavior which we derive from the study of the neuroses and psychoses of our civilization are categories of prevailing local types of instability. They give much information about the stresses and strains of Western civilization, but no final picture of inevitable human behavior. Any conclusions about such behavior must await the collection by trained observers of psychiatric data from other cultures. Since no adequate work of the kind has been done at the present time, it is impossible to say what core or definition of abnormality may be found valid from the comparative material. It is as it is in ethics: all our local conventions of moral behavior and of immoral are without absolute validity, and yet it is quite possible that a modicum of what is considered right and what wrong could be disentangled that is shared by the whole human race.

Notes

1. *inversion: male homosexuality.* [D. C. A., ed.]
2. R. F. Fortune, *Sorcerers of Dobu: The Social Anthropology of the Dobu Islanders* (New York: E. P. Dutton, 1932). [R. B.]
3. *exogamic:* marrying persons outside the group. [D. C. A.]
4. *affinal:* based on marriage. [D. C. A.]
5. *mores:* morally binding customs. [D. C. A.]
6. *dicta:* authoritative pronouncements [D. C. A.]

SELECTION 4

Godzilla Meets New Age Anthropology: Facing the Postmodernist Challenge to a Science of Culture

Robert L. Carneiro

The idea that any particular ethnographer's account of a culture should stand as the one and only word about a people has been called into question in the past few decades. There have been notable "re-studies" of particular cultural groups, such as the Robert Redfield/Oscar Lewis ethnographies of the village of Tepoztlan, Mexico, the reports of Margaret Mead/Derek Freeman in Samoa, and Napoleon Chagnon/Kenneth Good among the Yanomamo. Each of these pairs of ethnographic reports has revealed contradictions in findings that might be accounted for by such factors as the varying time periods in which the ethnographies were carried out, the kinds of "problems" they were looking to solve and/or the theoretical learnings of the anthropologists involved. Whatever the cause of the discrepancies, it is probably not coincidental that during this same time period, there has been a challenge to the very notion that anthropology should be thought of as a science at all. The challenge of *postmodernism* cuts to the core of what anthropological field investigation, *ethnography*, is all about. Does an ethnographer really collect "facts?" Do the field notes simply reflect one possible interpretation of reality versus another? Does the ethnographic account say more about the ethnographer than it does about the people being studied? Who is to say where the "truth" lies?

Anthropologist Robert Carneiro considers postmodernism to be another facet of a long-standing attack on the idea of anthropology as a science and responds accordingly. Having received his degrees in Anthropology, including a Ph.D., from the University of Michigan, Carneiro's career has been devoted to applying scientific methods to the understanding of cultures. His primary interests and research have involved cultural ecology and cultural evolution. He has done fieldwork among the Kuikuru of Brazil, the Amahuaca of Peru, and the Yanomamo of Venezuela. He is the author of *The Muse of History and the Science of Culture* (2000).

Key Concept: postmodernism

As we strive to understand nature, do we seek truth or solace?
—Stephen Jay Gould

When I began working on the first incarnation of this paper, years ago, the greatest threat to a science of culture, it seemed to me, came from those anthropologists who considered themselves humanists. Today, though, the picture has changed radically. A much greater threat now comes from that large, amorphous host who march under the banner of postmodernism. Compared to the old-fashioned humanists, the threat they pose is as the Black Plague to the chicken pox. So it is against them that my major battle will be waged. By comparison, my engagement with traditional humanists will be but a preliminary skirmish.

Nonetheless, let me begin with the humanists, for, in their distaste for a science of culture, both humanists and postmodernists have much in common. If not genetically related, the two have at least sprouted from the same seedbed.

The antagonism between humanism and science is not only deep, but old. Almost two centuries ago the poet John Keats was provoked to cry "A Confusion on Newton!". Why? Because Newton had shown the rainbow to be caused by the refraction of light through raindrops, and *that*, for Keats, destroyed the wonder of it all....

12

More recently, Joseph Wood Krutch has argued that "the experience of living is the thing which… has the greatest value, and… all the social sciences which tend to manipulate and regularize and unify human conduct result in a general lowering of the intensity of the experience … and … therefore, from my standpoint, they are bad."

Finally, E. E. Cummings expressed his contempt for science in this short verse:

> While you and I have lips and voices which,
> are for kissing and to sing with
> who cares if some oneeyed son of a bitch
> invents an instrument to measure spring with?

That scientists and humanists should be antagonists is thus nothing new or unusual. What *is* anomalous is that within something calling itself a science, there should be a large nucleus of persons who reject the ways of science and profess to practice anthropology as a humanity.

Since science vs. humanism is such a major issue, let us look at its philosophical basis. Part of this basis is the distinction between science and art, a distinction which Leslie White has expressed very nicely:

> Science is one of two basic ways of dealing with experience. The other is art.… The purpose of science and art is one: to render experience intelligible.… But although working toward the same goal, science and art approach it from opposite directions. Science deals with particulars in terms of universals: Uncle Tom disappears in the mass of Negro slaves. Art deals with universals in terms of particulars: the whole gamut of Negro slavery confronts us in the person of Uncle Tom. Art and science thus grasp a common experience, or reality, (but) by opposite poles.

White's distinction strikes me as valid. At bottom, humanists do look at the world as artists. But there is more to it than that. Humanists are not content merely to *contemplate* their subject; they also *celebrate* it. If you doubt this, just look inside the front cover of the *Anthropology and Humanism Quarterly*, a new journal published by our Association. There you will read that humanistic anthropology "celebrates" the fact that "human reality" is something that "we creative primates construct".

Now, celebration is all well and good, but it is not part of science. No physicist "celebrates" acceleration, and no chemist "celebrates" carbon tetrachloride. This is simply not a function of science. Our job, as scientists, is not to celebrate, but to *explain*, to *account for*. That's what makes us scientists. Let a poet enrapture himself over a lily, admiring the symmetry of its petals, the delicacy of its stamens, and let him sigh over the subtle fragrance of its nectar, but let him not try to pass himself off as a botanist!…

Let us not think, though, that by asserting that humanists do not do science, we are puncturing their balloon. You cannot puncture what was never inflated to begin with, and the fact is that the humanists in our ranks do not *claim* to be doing science. On the contrary, they cheerfully admit that they are *not*. But they aren't content with this. They go on to assert that *we* cannot do science, social

science, either. Indeed, many of them claim that social science *cannot* be done.

Clifford Geertz, the leading literary humanist in anthropology, finds those of us who consider ourselves social scientists "ignorant and pretentious usurpers of the mission of the humanities". So the gauntlet has been thrown down. Well, if Geertz says there can't be a social science, why not? Only two possibilities exist: either we cannot do it because it is intrinsically undoable, or, if it is theoretically possible, we cannot do it because, in practice, it is too difficult.

Let us look at each possibility in turn. To begin with, why should a science of culture be inherently impossible? The answer is, only if the things and events it studies are not subject to cause and effect. So then we must ask, is human behavior subject to strict causality? Not if there is free will.

No one has put the matter more concisely than the 19th-century British historian James Anthony Froude:

> When natural causes are liable to be set aside and neutralized by what is called volition, the word Science is out of place. If it is free to a man to choose what he will do or not do, there is no adequate science of him.…

This is not the place to attempt a formal refutation of free will. Instead, I would like to try to convince the humanists among you that determinism is not such a bad thing after all. In fact, I would argue that when you look at it deeply enough, free will turns out to be rather uncongenial to the artist. Let me present my case.

First, though, some background. Several years ago, to help us with an exhibit at the museum in which I work, we hired an artist from San Francisco. During the course of his work, I became well acquainted with him, and in one of our conversations, the subject of free will came up. As you might expect, he and I were on opposite sides of the fence on this issue. We argued about it, but neither of us made much headway in convincing the other. His work completed, the artist returned to San Francisco, but we continued to correspond. And in one of my letters, I presented an argument which I hoped might persuade him to abandon free will and embrace determinism. Here is what I wrote:

> *Dear ***,*
>
>   *It is my contention that whenever an artist creates, he is never acting outside the stream of causation. What he engenders, no matter how novel, is never fortuitous. It is neither totally unforeseen nor unaccountable. It is, in fact, the product of lots of things swirling around in his psyche, conscious and unconscious. And—here's the kicker—I would argue that, from the artist's point of view, determinism, seen in this light, is better than free will! Genuine free will implies that, whatever you produce is entirely unconstrained by anything that went before. But if that were true, your creation would be completely out of your hands, entirely at the mercy of chance.*
>
>   *And how could such a state of affairs possibly be satisfying to an artist? Isn't it much more congenial for you to think of your art as a summation and expression of everything that*

has gone into you, than for it to be unconnected and unrelated to you? Let's face it, free will—real free will—is completely depersonalizing and dehumanizing. It would work like a purely mechanical game of chance, in which you weren't even allowed to hold the dice. Surely the determinism I offer you, which puts you and your life experiences at the very heart of your artistic creation, should be much more congenial.

    Sincerely,

Now, if free will is merely an illusion, if human behavior is indeed strictly determined, there is no reason why, in principle, there cannot be a science of human behavior, a science of culture. Some humanists may grudgingly concede this, but then raise another objection: Whatever the case may be in *principle*, they say, in *practice*, human behavior is simply too complex for any genuine regularities, let alone any laws, to be teased out of it.

But is complexity of behavior solely a problem for the anthropologist? Not at all. The phenomena of physics are intricate and complex too. Of the thousands of leaves on a tree, no two fall to earth exactly the same way. Yet physics was able to see past the unique and erratic behavior of each fluttering leaf, and to formulate a general law of falling bodies. Could it be, then, that the anthropological humanist has given up finding any underlying laws in human behavior because he has not looked for them hard enough? When he triumphantly proclaims the impossibility of formulating any cultural laws, could he merely be making a virtue out of his own shortcomings? Could this, then, be nothing more than a case of the tailless fox preaching taillessness?

Having thus warded off the humanists, we come now to the main event: the challenge to the science of culture posed by postmodern anthropology. Humanism was a straightforward, innocent adversary. Postmodernism is anything *but*. Sometimes it appears quite amorphous, but at other times it has the head of a hydra and the arms of a squid. Nor is this only my opinion. C. Richard King, a not unsympathetic observer of the movement, has said that postmodernism "lacks a single, unitary definition… It appears to be, at once, everything and nothing."…

[W]hatever else postmodernism might aspire to be, it is, at bottom, one more manifestation of the old, familiar prejudice against science. Thus, in her book, *Postmodernism and the Social Sciences*, Pauline Rosenau tells us that the postmodernist "questions the validity of modern science and the notion of objective knowledge". Moreover, postmodernism's headlong retreat from science goes further than humanism's ever did. Not only does it disdain science, it declares science to be dead.

Although postmodernism has challenged anthropology on all fronts, its main attack has been leveled at ethnography. To give the devil his due, postmodernists have had a valid point to make here. Ethnographers have traditionally tended to round things off, to smooth things up. Their monographs often present a single "authoritative" statement of a particular custom or belief, as if that were all there was to it. Yet anyone who has ever done fieldwork knows that informants' versions of a custom or belief often vary all over the map. Thus, presenting only one version *masks* the actual complexity. This foreshortening of reality, though, is not done to deceive. It is done for practical reasons. Were a monograph to include 16 different versions of every custom and belief, it might be more "real," but would also become so cumbersome and wearying as to vitiate the effort. So ethnographers generally round off their accounts to the first decimal place, so to speak, and present a kind of "official" version.

But what does this "official" version of a culture really represent?, ask the critics of traditional ethnography. Is it the opinion of one's best-liked informant? Or the most reliable one? Is it the response of one informant or of several? And if several, and if their range of responses has been "averaged," then what is this "average" that gets printed in the monograph—the mean, the median, or the mode?

Postmodern critics contend that ethnography should stress the many "voices" that may be raised in a primitive society. It is certainly true that there may well be many such "voices," even in a small native village, and that most of them usually remain unheard. That, in itself, is an objective fact, and deserves to be duly noted. But to *dwell* on the myriad voices of informants—indeed, to make a *career* out of it—seems to me to attenuate and trivialize the craft of ethnography.

Yet this has become a dominant theme in postmodern anthropology. With full-throated voice, postmodernists proclaim that there is not *one* reality, but *multiple* ones. The trouble is, though, that as realities are multiplied, they are also divided; as they become more numerous, they become correspondingly smaller. And, there being more and more of them, facts now count for less and less, and so reality becomes progressively diluted and rarified. And it is but a small step from this to saying that there is *no* reality at all! And once *that* assertion has been made, the wheels come off the wagon.

*L*et us look at this dissolution of reality a little more closely. Postmodern ethnography likes to call itself "dialogical". It puts a high premium on the dialogue that takes place between ethnographer and informant. James Clifford says that in the new ethnography "monophonic authority is questioned", and in its stead "dialogism and polyphony are recognized as modes of textual production". And Stephen Tyler, another leading voice in the movement, holds that postmodern ethnography "emphasizes the cooperative and collaborative nature of the ethnographic situation in contrast to the ideology of the transcendant observer". But Tyler goes a step further, claiming that the postmodern ethnographer "rejects the ideology of 'observer-observed', there being nothing observed and no one who is observer". If this is literally true, one is left to wonder, with Richard King, whether "an anthropology which dismisses the distinctions between self and other… is possible or even imaginable?".

Setting that question aside, we come to the matter of "truth". Consider the following dilemma. If "truth" is a statement about reality, but reality has already been bargained away, where does that leave truth? "In cultural studies", says Clifford, "we can no longer know the whole truth, or even claim to approach it". But if the search for truth, the traditional objective of science, is left lying in the dust, what happens to science itself? The answer is inescapable. If, as Clifford says, "Cultures are not scientific 'objects', the science of culture loses its subject matter, and with it, its identity and even its very existence...."

With ethnographic facts now having but a tenuous reality, they are being reassigned a place in the domain of literature, namely, fiction. Clifford puts his seal of approval on this change in the following words: "Ethnographic writings can properly be called fictions in the sense of 'something made or fashioned'.... But it is important to preserve the meaning not merely of making, but also of making up, of inventing things not actually real". So there we are, in the Land of Diggledy Dan.

*A*ny serious study of literature naturally involves the use of texts. And texts have become a focus of postmodern ethnography. According to Geertz's oftquoted remark, culture itself is "an ensemble of texts, themselves ensembles, which the anthropologist strains to read over the shoulder of those to whom they properly belong". So the new ethnographer's field notes become his texts, and he proceeds to deal with them accordingly.

Yet, the more texts are scrutinized, the more they seem to proliferate, spawning *subtexts*. Now, teasing subtexts from a main text is surely slippery business, but it's also a lot of fun. It's a game *any*one can play, and *every*one can win, because there are no rules. There is no correct interpretation, no right answer. Any answer is as good as any other....

Another offshoot of literary ethnography is narrative. Its practitioners focus on *stories* rather than customs. These "stories" started out as biographies, the life histories of one's informants. But it wasn't long before biography turned into *auto*biography, and the subject of one's research became, not one's informants, but oneself. As James Clifford put it, "With the 'fieldwork account' the rhetoric of experienced objectivity yields to that of the autobiography and the ironic selfportrait. The ethnographer, a character in a fiction, is at center stage"....

Practiced with fervor, this form of postmodern ethnography becomes supremely self-centered. The ethnographer focuses, not on what he is observing, but on what he *feels* about what he is observing! He is, in effect, watching the patient, but taking his own pulse! Thus, he has become more important than his subject matter. Or rather, he has turned himself *into* his own subject matter. So, by sleight-of-hand, ethnography has become autobiography....

Needless to say, all of this is the very antithesis of science. The cornerstone of science has always been the premise that there is a real world out there, independent of our individual existences. And it is *this* world that, as scientists—as *anthropologists*—we should be studying. If anyone still doggedly prefers to contemplate his own navel, fine. But let him call his contemplation by a different name than anthropology....

I find it quite ironic that persons so concerned with "meaning" as postmodern ethnographers claim to be, should show so little regard for the process of conveying meaning, namely, communication. Yet, "meaning" is certainly what they profess to be after. Listen to Clifford Geertz:

> Believing... that man is an animal suspended in webs of significance he himself has spun, I take culture to be those webs, and the analysis of it to be therefore not an empirical science in search of law but an interpretive one in search of meaning.

Beware of those "webs of significance"! From them we have much to fear. The new ethnographer, like a spider, draws forth from his spinaret, threads of infinite subtlety, and with them, creates his own webs which, like those of the spider, are not only delicate, but sticky. And in them, he entraps his prey, holding it fast while he sucks out its meaning. Then, perhaps, he will discard the eviscerated carcass, leaving it to the old-fashioned ethnographer to find whatever vestige of structure and substance may be left in it.

Confronted with a choice between substance and meaning, it is perfectly clear that Geertz will take meaning any day. For him, nothing is what it *is*. It is what it *means*. The famous Balinese cockfight, for example, becomes, at his hands—and here I quote Geertz directly—"image", "fiction", "a model", "a metaphor". So far does he give flight to his fancies in this regard that even his fellow postmodernist, Vincent Crapanzano, feels it necessary to bring him to heel. Thus, Crapanzano says sharply, "Cockfights are surely cockfights for the Balinese—and not images, fictions, models, and metaphors". Indeed, Geertz's rendition of Balinese cockfights so disturbs Crapanzano that he characterizes it as "constructions of constructions of constructions", a simple, bloody fight between two roosters transmogrified into Cloud Cuckooland!...

*I*n the frontal attack of postmodernism on anthropology, one major casualty has been... *ethnology*. So *fixated* are postmodernists at the level of ethnography, that they have failed to fulfill ethnography's traditional obligation to ethnology. From its earliest days, ethnography has always been the handmaiden of ethnology. It quarried and dressed the stones which ethnology then used to erect its larger stuctures. For it is here, in ethnology, that broad theories are built and generalizations crafted; where the major questions of anthropology are asked and answered. *Here* it is that we debate the origin of clans, the invention of agriculture, the function of crosscousin marriage, the role of age grades, the rise of chiefdoms, and the development of states. What have postmodernists contributed to the solution of these great problems? Nothing. Has anyone even *heard* of a postmodernist theory of the origin of the state? Alas, what will happen to such questions in an age of postmodern anthropology?

The new ethnographers are not, however, unaware that they're sidestepping these issues. George Marcus, for example, notes that "because of modern ethnography's commitment to social criticism,… it has rarely been directed to answering macrosociological questions about the causes of events or the constitution of major systems and processes". The new ethnographer, then, is like a mason so enamored of the peculiarities of each brick, that he turns them over in his hands, carefully studying them, but cannot bring himself to arrange them into some larger structure. He is a mason who has neglected to apply for his architect's license. And why not? Because he doubts that major edifices can ever be built anyway.

But it gets worse. Not only does the new ethnographer refuse to start building himself, he would deny the *ethnologist* a building permit too. He is not content to say what *he* can't do, he also tells us what *we* can't do. And why can't we? Because—among other things—the tools we choose to employ are defective. They are tools of our own devising—"hegemonic concepts"—rather than the simple adzes and digging sticks of our informants. And, Stephen Tyler tells us, "postmodern ethnography… seeks… to avoid grounding itself in the theoretical and commonsense categories of… Western tradition".

Were we to follow Tyler's injunction, though, we would be severely hamstrung. Consider this example. I regard the proportion of waking time that a society spends on subsistence to be of fundamental importance in determining the general level of its culture. Accordingly, I have tried to ascertain this figure for the Kuikuru of central Brazil during the course of my field work among them. However, not being a concept the Kuikuru themselves would be likely to think of, Tyler would rule such a calculation out of court as a "hegemonic Western category". Carried to this extreme, cultural relativism surely cuts us off at the knees.…

*A*s we noted earlier, postmodernists are rather ambivalent about truth. At times, they assert there is no such thing; but at other times they tell us there are a thousand different truths. Where on earth does that leave us?

Needless to say, one can define truth any way one feels like. If one wants to define it as that which it is impossible to attain, fine. That takes care of the matter, once and for all. But what *good* does that do? It merely evades an important issue. Here's what I suggest instead. Truth

need not be regarded as some mystical, vaporous essence, a holy grail to be sought for but never found. Truth can simply be defined as an *agreement* or *correspondence* between a proposition and something in the external world. As such, it becomes quite possible to attain it. In fact, it is, and has always been, the stated goal of science.

Another notion I rebel against is that truth, if allowed to exist at all, is at best tenuous and protean, and that anyone's "truth" is just as valid as anyone else's. The implications of this view for an ethnographer working in the field are jolting, to say the least. It implies that he should be satisfied with whatever answer he gets to a question, and not try to ferret out the "truest" truth he can.…

Is this really where we want to be? Suppose, for example, that Napoleon Chagnon had accepted at face value the genealogies first given to him by the Yanomamö as being as good as any other, and let it go at that. By eschewing verification he would, according to Tyler, have been following good, postmodernist procedure. But he would also have been sorely deceived, because, as he found out months later, the Yanomamö had purposely and systematically lied to him. Now, can any postmodernist seriously hold that the spurious genealogies Chagnon first obtained were just as good, just as true, just as valid, as the ones he got later?…

I have often been struck by the fact that there is no such thing as postmodern chemistry, or postmodern geology. Why not? To begin with, no serious science would be foolish enough to define itself out of existence. Nor could it afford to spend so much of its time dabbling in hairsplitting and pettifogging. No real science would devote itself so wholeheartedly to the inconsequential. To be sure, all the sciences have their many tiny facts, but these are gathered, not for their own sake, but to serve some larger purpose. And this purpose is to formulate a series of overarching propositions that seek to explain ever larger segments of nature. And are these aims not all we really need?…

So, what is to happen? What can we expect in the future? Despite my previous lamentations, I am not altogether worried; at least not in the long run. Why? Because I'm a firm believer in the principle of natural selection, and natural selection works on ideas just as it does on organisms. In the realm of ideas, as everywhere else, it's the payoff that counts. Ultimately, any intellectual movement will be judged by its results. If it produces nothing tangible, substantial, or enlightening, it will fall by the wayside, just as so many intellectual fads have before it. Thus I am ready to predict that postmodernism, like phrenology, prohibition, and free silver, will quietly fade away, and center stage will once more be occupied by less scintillating but more productive forms of inquiry.…

Doing Fieldwork

Selection 5

E.E. EVANS-PRITCHARD, from "Fieldwork and the Empirical Tradition," *Free Press*

Selection 6

ARTURO ALVAREZ ROLDÁN, from "Malinowski and the Origins of the Ethnographic Method," *Fieldwork and Footnotes: Studies in the History of European Anthropology*

Selection 7

KATHLEEN GOUGH, from "Anthropology and Imperialism," *Monthly Review*

Fieldwork and the Empirical Tradition

E.E. Evans-Pritchard

One of the unique aspects of anthropology is *fieldwork*. This involves living with the people that one is studying—eating their food, living in their type of housing and generally "going native." This technique is called *participant observation*, and one of its primary goals is to gain an insider's perspective while maintaining the objectivity of a social scientist, all of which of course is an ideal more than a reality.

This method of research differs from that which is practiced in the other social and behavioral sciences. Anthropologists do not generally wear lab coats and experiment. They do not send out questionnaires, engage subjects in formal interviews, or perform psychological tests. It is not that they are not interested in the same things as psychologists, sociologists, and economists. It is just that they go about relating to people and trying to understand them differently.

It takes nerve to show up at someone's proverbial doorstep and expect them to be accepting. How would you feel if someone knocked on your door and said, "Hi, I am here to observe you for the next two years and, what's more, I am going to write down what I find and publish the results!?

Understandably, anthropologists have sometimes experienced a cool reception, to say the least. Author Evans-Pritchard wrote elsewhere that it took him a year to realize that the Nuer of Sudan had been lying to him, not too different from Napoleon Chagnon's experience among the Yanomamo of Venezuela, where he had to throw away most of his first year's worth of field notes.

In this essay, Evans-Pritchard gives us the historical context in which ethnography came to be the modus operandi of the anthropologist and sets forth the ground rules for what has proven to be a highly productive kind of research.

E.E. Evans-Pritchard (1902–1973) was born in Sussex, England, studied history at Exeter College, Oxford, and received his doctorate in Anthropology at the London School of Economics. He did fieldwork among the Nuer and the Azande of Sudan and is best known for his books, *Witchcraft: Oracles and Magic among the Azande* (1937) and *The Nuer* (1940).

Key Concept: ethnographic field techniques

There has always been a popular, though not unhealthy, prejudice against theory as contrasted with experience. However, an established theory is only a generalization from experience which has been again confirmed by it, and a hypothesis is merely an unconfirmed opinion that, judging by what is already known, it is reasonable to assume that further facts will be found by research to be of a certain kind. Without theories and hypotheses anthropological research could not be carried out, for one only finds things, or does not find them, if one is looking for them. Often one finds something other than what one is looking for. The whole history of scholarship, whether in the natural sciences or in the humanities, tells us that the mere collection of what are called facts unguided by theory in observation and selection is of little value.

Nevertheless, one still hears it said of anthropologists that they go to study primitive peoples with a theoretical bias and that this distorts their accounts of savage life, whereas the practical man of affairs, having no such bias, gives an impartial record of the facts as he sees them.

The difference between them is really of another kind. The student makes his observations to answer questions arising out of the generalizations of specialized opinion, and the layman makes his to answer questions arising out of the generalizations of popular opinion. Both have theories, the one systematic and the other popular.

In fact the history of social anthropology may be regarded as the substitution, by slow gradations, of informed opinion about primitive peoples for uninformed opinion, and the stage reached in this process at any time is roughly relative to the amount of organized knowledge available. In the end it is the volume, accuracy, and variety of well-authenticated fact which alone counts; and it is the function of theory to stimulate and guide observation in the collection of it. Here, however, I am not so much concerned with popular opinion as with that held by writers about social institutions.

There seems to have been a pendulum swing from extreme to extreme in speculations about primitive man. First he was a little more than an animal who lived in poverty, violence, and fear; then he was a gentle person who lived in plenty, peace, and security. First he was lawless; then he was a slave to law and custom. First he was devoid of any religious feelings or belief; then he was entirely dominated by the sacred and immersed in ritual. First he was an individualist who preyed on the weaker and held what he could; then he was a communist who held lands and goods in common. First he was sexually promiscuous; then he was a model of domestic virtue. First he was lethargic and incorrigibly lazy, then he was alert and industrious. In seeking to change a received opinion it is, I suppose, natural that in the selection and massing of evidence against it an opposite distortion is made.

The dependence of theory on available knowledge in these speculations and the shaping of each by the other may be seen throughout the development of social anthropology. The prevailing opinion about primitive man in the seventeenth and eighteenth centuries, that his life was 'solitary, poore, nasty, brutish, and short', lacked foundation in fact; but it is difficult to see what other conclusion could have been reached from the accounts of contemporary travellers, who for the most part described the primitives they saw in such terms as they have 'nothing that can entitle them to humanity but speech'—this is Sir John Chardin speaking of the Circassians whose country he traversed in 1671[1]—or that they 'differ but little from beasts'—this is Father Stanislaus Arlet speaking about the Indians of Peru in 1698.[2] These early travel accounts, whether they portrayed the savage as brutish or noble, were generally fanciful or mendacious, superficial, and full of inappropriate judgments…

Between the heyday of the moral philosophers and the earliest anthropological writings in a strict sense between, that is, the middle of the eighteenth century and the middle of the nineteenth century, knowledge of primitive peoples and of the peoples of the Far East was greatly increased. The European colonization of America had been widely expanded, British rule had been established in India, Australia, and New Zealand, and South Africa had been settled by European emigrants. The character of ethnographic description of the peoples of these regions began to change from travellers' tales to detailed studies by missionaries and administrators who not only had better opportunities to observe, but were also men of greater culture than the gentlemen of fortune of earlier times.

Much of accepted opinion about primitive peoples was seen to be wrong or one-sided in the light of this new information, and, the new information was sufficient in bulk and quality for Morgan, McLennan, Tylor, and others to build out of it a self-contained discipline devoting itself primarily to the study of primitive societies. There was at last a sufficient body of knowledge for speculations to be tested and for new hypotheses to be put forward on a solid basis of ethnographic fact.…

Many accounts written about primitive peoples by laymen were excellent, and in a few cases their descriptions have hardly been excelled by the best professional fieldworkers. They were written by men with lengthy experience of the peoples, and who spoke their languages. I refer to such books as Callaway's *The Religious System of the Amazulu* (1870), Codrington's *The Melanesians* (1891), the works of Spencer and Gillen on the Aborigines of Australia,[3] Junod's *The Life of a South African Tribe* (1912–13, French edition, 1898), and Smith and Dale's *The Ila-Speaking Peoples of Northern Rhodesia* (1920). Just as the observations of travellers continued to provide valuable information throughout this period when detailed monographs on primitive peoples were being written by missionaries and administrators, so these detailed studies by laymen continued to have great value for anthropology long after professional fieldwork had become customary.

Nevertheless it became apparent that if the study of social anthropology was to advance, anthropologists would have to make their own observations. It is indeed surprising that, with the exception of Morgan's study of the Iroquois,[4] not a single anthropologist conducted field studies till the end of the nineteenth century. It is even more remarkable that it does not seem to have occurred to them that a writer on anthropological topics might at least have a look, if only a glimpse, at one or two specimens of what he spent his life writing about. William James tells us that when he asked Sir James Frazer about natives he had known, Frazer exclaimed, 'But Heaven forbid!'[5]

Had a natural scientist been asked a similar question about the objects of his study he would have replied very differently. Maine, McLennan, Bachofen, and Morgan among the earlier anthropological writers were lawyers. Fustel de Coulanges was a classical and mediaeval historian, Spencer was a philosopher, Tylor was a foreign languages clerk, Pitt-Rivers was a soldier, Lubbock was a banker, Robertson Smith was a Presbyterian minister and a biblical scholar, and Frazer was a classical scholar. The men who now came into the subject were for the most part natural scientists. Boas was a physicist and geographer, Haddon a marine zoologist, Rivers a physiologist, Seligman a pathologist, Elliot Smith an anatomist, Balfour a zoologist, Malinowski a physicist, and Radcliffe-Brown, though he had taken the Moral Sciences Tripos at Cambridge, had also been trained in experimental psychology. These men had been taught that in science one tests hypotheses by one's own observations. One does not rely on laymen to do it for one.

Anthropological expeditions began in America with the work of Boas in Baffin Land and British Columbia, and were initiated in England shortly afterwards by Haddon of Cambridge, who led a band of scholars to conduct research in the Torres Straits region of the Pacific in 1898 and 1899. This expedition marked a turning-point in the history of social anthropology in Great Britain. From this time two important and interconnected developments began to take place: anthropology became more and more a whole-time professional study, and some field experience came to be regarded as an essential part of the training of its students.

This early professional fieldwork had many weaknesses. However well the men who carried it out might have been trained in systematic research in one or other of the natural sciences, the short time they spent among the peoples they studied, their ignorance of their languages, and the casualness and superficiality of their contacts with the natives did not permit deep investigation. It is indeed a measure of the advance of anthropology that these early studies appear today to be quite inadequate. Later studies of primitive societies became increasingly more intensive and illuminating. The most important of these was, I think, that of Professor Radcliffe-Brown, a pupil of Rivers and Haddon. His study of the Andaman Islanders from 1906 to 1908[6] was the first attempt by a social anthropologist to investigate sociological theories in a primitive society and to describe the social life of a people in such a way as to bring out clearly what was significant in it for those theories. In this respect it has perhaps greater importance in the history of social anthropology than the Torres Straits expedition, the members of which were interested in ethnological and psychological problems rather than in sociological ones.

We have noted how theoretical speculation about social institutions was at first only incidentally related to descriptive accounts of primitive peoples, and how later social anthropology may be said to have begun when in the nineteenth century these peoples became the chief field of research for some students of institutions. But the research was entirely literary and based on the observations of others. We have now reached the final, and natural, stage of development, in which observations and the evaluation of them are made by the same person and the scholar is brought into direct contact with the subject of his study. Formerly the anthropologist, like the historian, regarded documents as the raw material of his study. Now the raw material was social life itself.

Bronislaw Malinowski, a pupil of Hobhouse, Westermarck, and Seligman, carried field research a step further. If Professor Radcliffe-Brown has always had a wider knowledge of general social anthropology and has proved himself the abler thinker, Malinowski was the more thorough fieldworker. He not only spent a longer period than any anthropologist before him, and I think

after him also, in a single study of a primitive people, the Trobriand Islanders of Melanesia between 1914 and 1918, but he was also the first anthropologist to conduct his research through the native language, as he was the first to live throughout his work in the centre of native life. In these favourable circumstances Malinowski came to know the Trobriand Islanders well, and he was describing their social life in a number of bulky, and some shorter, monographs up to the time of his death.[7]

Malinowski began lecturing in London in 1924. Professor Firth, now in Malinowski's chair in London, and I were his first two anthropological pupils in that year, and between 1924 and 1930 most of the other social anthropologists who now hold chairs in Great Britain and the Dominions were taught by him. It can be fairly said that the comprehensive field studies of modern anthropology directly or indirectly derive from his teaching, for he insisted that the social life of a primitive people can only be understood if it is studied intensively, and that it is a necessary part of a social anthropologist's training to carry out at least one such intensive study of a primitive society. I shall discuss what this means when I have drawn your attention in a few words to what I think is an important feature of the earlier field studies by professional anthropologists.

These studies were carried out among very small-scale political communities—Australian hordes, Andamanese camps, and Melanesian villages—and this circumstance had the effect that certain aspects of social life, particularly kinship and ritual, were inquired into to the neglect of others, especially of political structure, which was not given the attention it deserved till African societies began to be studied. In Africa autonomous political groups often number many thousands of members, and their internal political organization as well as their interrelations forced the attention of students to specifically political problems. This is a very recent development, for professional research in Africa was not opened till the visit of Professor and Mrs. Seligman to the Anglo-Egyptian Sudan in 1909–1910, and the first intensive study in Africa by a social anthropologist was that carried out by myself among the Azande of the Anglo-Egyptian Sudan, starting in 1927. Since then, most intensive studies of primitive peoples have been made in Africa, and political institutions have received the attention they require, as, for example, in Professor Schapera's account of the Bechuana, Professor Fortes's account of the Tallensi of the Gold Coast, Professor Nadel's account of the Nupe of Nigeria, Dr. Kuper's account of the Swazi, and my own account of the Nuer of the Anglo-Egyptian Sudan.

I will now tell you, so that you may understand better what is meant by intensive fieldwork, what is today required of a person who wishes to become a professional social anthropologist. I speak particularly of our arrangements at Oxford. There a man comes to us with a degree in another subject, and he first spends a year working for the Diploma in Anthropology, a course which gives him a general knowledge of social anthropology, and also, as

I explained in my first lecture, some acquaintance with physical anthropology, ethnology, technology, and prehistoric archaeology. He spends a second year, and perhaps longer, in writing a thesis from the literature of social anthropology for the degree of B.Litt. or B.Sc. Then, if his work has been of sufficient merit and if he is lucky, he obtains a grant for field research and prepares himself for it by a careful study of the literature on the peoples of the region in which he is to conduct it, including their languages.

He then usually spends at least two years in a first field study of a primitive society, this period covering two expeditions and a break between them for collating the material collected on the first expedition. Experience has shown that a few months' break, preferably spent in a university department, is essential for sound fieldwork. It will take him at least another five years to publish the results of his research to the standards of modern scholarship, and much longer should he have other calls on his time; so that it can be reckoned that an intensive study of a single primitive society and the publication of its results take about ten years.

A study of a second society is desirable, because otherwise an anthropologist is likely to think for the rest of his life, as Malinowski did, in terms of one particular type of society. This second study usually takes a shorter time because the anthropologist has learnt from his previous experience to conduct research quickly and to write with economy, but it will certainly be several years before his researches are published. To stay this long course of training and research demands great patience....

Experience has proved that certain conditions are essential if a good investigation is to be carried out. The anthropologist must spend sufficient time on the study, he must throughout be in close contact with the people among whom he is working, he must communicate with them solely through their own language, and he must study their entire culture and social life. I will examine each of these desiderata for, obvious though they may be, they are the distinguishing marks of British anthropological research which make it, in my opinion, different from and of a higher quality than research conducted elsewhere.

The earlier professional fieldworkers were always in a great hurry. Their quick visits to native peoples sometimes lasted only a few days, and seldom more than a few weeks. Survey research of this kind can be a useful preliminary to intensive studies and elementary ethnological classifications can be derived from it, but it is of little value for an understanding of social life. The position is very different today when, as I have said, one to three years are devoted to the study of a single people. This permits observations to be made at every season of the year, the social life of the people to be recorded to the last detail, and conclusions to be tested systematically.

However, even given unlimited time for his research, the anthropologist will not produce a good account of the people he is studying unless he can put himself in a position which enables him to establish ties of intimacy with them, and to observe their daily activities from within, and not from without, their community life. He must live as far as possible in their villages and camps, where he is, again as far as possible, physically and morally part of the community. He then not only sees and hears what goes on in the normal everyday life of the people as well as less common events, such as ceremonies and legal cases, but by taking part in those activities in which he can appropriately engage, he learns through action as well as by ear and eye what goes on around him. This is very unlike the situation in which records of native life were compiled by earlier anthropological fieldworkers, and also by missionaries and administrators, who, living out of the native community in mission stations or government posts, had mostly to rely on what a few informants told them. If they visited native villages at all, their visits interrupted and changed the activities they had come to observe.

This is not merely a matter of physical proximity. There is also a psychological side to it. By living among the natives as far as he can like one of themselves the anthropologist puts himself on a level with them. Unlike the administrator and missionary he has no authority and status to maintain, and unlike them he has a neutral position. He is not there to change their way of life but as a humble learner of it; and he has no retainers and intermediaries who obtrude between him and the people, no police, interpreters, or catechists to screen him off from them.

What is perhaps even more important for his work is the fact that he is all alone, cut off from the companionship of men of his own race and culture, and is dependent on the natives around him for company, friendship, and human understanding. An anthropologist has failed unless, when he says goodbye to the natives, there is on both sides the sorrow of parting. It is evident that he can only establish this intimacy if he makes himself in some degree a member of their society and lives, thinks, and feels in their culture since only he, and not they, can make the necessary transference.

It is obvious that if the anthropologist is to carry out his work in the conditions I have described he must learn the native language, and any anthropologist worth his salt will make the learning of it his first task and will altogether, even at the beginning of his study, dispense with interpreters. Some do not pick up strange languages easily, and many primitive languages are almost unbelievably difficult to learn, but the language must be mastered as thoroughly as the capacity of the student and its complexities permit, not only because the anthropologist can then communicate freely with the natives, but for further reasons. To understand a people's thought, one has to think in their symbols. Also, in learning the language one learns the culture and the social system which are conceptualized in the language. Every kind of social relationship, every belief, every technological process —in fact everything in the social life of the natives—is expressed in words as well as in action, and when one has fully understood the meaning of all the words of their language in all their situations of reference one has finished one's study of the society. I may add that, as every experienced fieldworker knows, the most difficult task in anthropological fieldwork is to determine the meanings of a few key words, upon an understanding of which the success of the whole investigation depends; and they can only be determined by the anthropologist himself learning to use the words correctly in his converse with the natives. A further reason for learning the native language at the beginning of the investigation is that it places the anthropologist in a position of complete dependence on the natives. He comes to them as pupil, not as master.

Finally, the anthropologist must study the whole of the social life. It is impossible to understand clearly and comprehensively any part of a people's social life except in the full context of their social life as a whole. Though he may not publish every detail he has recorded, you will find in a good anthropologist's notebooks a detailed description of even the most commonplace activities, for example, how a cow is milked or how meat is cooked. Also, though he may decide to write a book on a people's law, on their religion, or on their economics, describing one aspect of their life and neglecting the rest, he does so always against the background of their entire social activities and in terms of their whole social structure....

Since in anthropological fieldwork much must depend, as I think we would all admit, on the person who conducts it, it may well be asked whether the same results would have been obtained had another person made a particular investigation. This is a very difficult question. My own answer would be, and I think that the evidence we have on the matter shows it to be a correct one, that the bare record of fact would be much the same, though there would, of course, be some individual differences even at the level of perception.

It is almost impossible for a person who knows what he is looking for, and how to look for it, to be mistaken about the facts if he spends two years among a small and culturally homogeneous people doing nothing else but studying their way of life. He gets to know so well what will be said and done in any situation—the social life becomes so familiar to him—that there ceases to be much point in his making any further observations or in asking any further questions, Also, whatever kind of person he may be, the anthropologist is working within a body of theoretical knowledge which largely determines his interests and his lines of inquiry. He is also working within the limits imposed by the culture of the people he is studying. If they are pastoral nomads, he must study pastoral nomadism. If they are obsessed by witchcraft, he must study witchcraft. He has no choice but to follow the cultural grain.

But while I think that different social anthropologists who studied the same people would record much the same facts in their notebooks, I believe that they would write different kinds of books. Within the limits imposed by their discipline and the culture under investigation anthropologists are guided in choice of themes, in selection and arrangement of facts to illustrate them, and in judgment of what is and what is not significant, by their different interests, reflecting differences of personality, of education, of social status, of political views, of religious convictions, and so forth.

One can only interpret what one sees in terms of one's own experience and of what one is, and anthropologists, while they have a body of knowledge in common, differ in other respects as widely as other people in their backgrounds of experience and in themselves. The personality of an anthropologist cannot be eliminated from his work any more than the personality of an historian can be eliminated from his. Fundamentally, in his account of a primitive people the anthropologist is not only describing their social life as accurately as he can but is expressing himself also. In this sense his account must express moral judgment, especially where it touches matters on which he feels strongly; and what comes out of a study will to this extent at least depend on what the individual brings to it. Those who know anthropologists and their writings as well as I do, would, I think, accept this conclusion. If allowances are made for the personality of the writer, and if we consider that in the entire range of anthropological studies the effects of these personal differences tend to correct each other, I do not think that we need worry unduly over this problem in so far as the reliability of anthropological findings is in question.

There is a broader aspect to the question. However much anthropologists may differ among themselves they are all children of the same culture and society. In the main they all have, apart from their common specialist knowledge and training, the same cultural categories and values which direct their attention to selected characteristics of the societies being studied. Religion, law, economics, politics, and so forth, are abstract categories of our culture into which observations on the life of primitive peoples are patterned. Certain kinds of fact are noticed, and they are seen in a certain kind of way, by people of our culture. To some extent at any rate, people who belong to different cultures would notice different facts and perceive them in a different way. In so far as this is true, the facts recorded in our notebooks are not social facts but ethnographic facts, selection and interpretation having taken place at the level of observation. I cannot now discuss, but only state, this general question of perception and evaluation.

I must say in conclusion that, as you will have noted, I have been discussing anthropological field research and the qualities and qualifications required for it in the light of the opinion I expressed in my last lecture that social anthropology is best regarded as an art and not as a natural science. Those among my colleagues who hold the opposite opinion might have discussed the questions with which I have been concerned in this lecture in a rather different way.

Notes

1. Pinkerton's *Voyages,* vol. IX, 1811, p. 143.
2. John Lockman, *Travels of the Jesuits,* vol. I, 1743, p. 93.
3. B. Spencer and F. J. Gillen, *The Native Tribes of Central Australia,* 1899; *The Northern Tribes of Central Australia,* 1904; *The Arunta,* 1927.
4. *The League of the Iroquois,* 1851.
5. Ruth Benedict, "Anthropology and the Humanities", *American Anthropologist,* 1948, p. 587.
6. A. R. Brown, *The Andaman Islanders—A Study in Social Anthropology,* 1922.
7. *Argonauts of the Western Pacific,* 1922; *The Sexual Life of Savages,* 1929; *Coral Gardens and their Magic,* 1935.

Malinowski and the Origins of the Ethnographic Method

Arturo Alvarez Roldán

At around the beginning of the 20th century, after the 19th-century evolutionary anthropologists had had their say as to how societies change over time, a strong anti-evolutionary mind-set took hold among anthropologists in both Europe and the United States. This rebellion was precipitated by what were perceived as excesses of the 19th-century theorists' claims—that all societies are destined to go through certain general stages of development (barbarism, savagery, and civilization), and that they inevitably develop along parallel lines with respect to the details of culture such as family organization and religious belief.

Once it became obvious that the 19th-century cultural evolutionists had been cherry-picking the evidence to suit pre-conceived notions, anthropologists began to call for more fieldwork and less theory. This "new" anthropology was to take two distinct forms. In the United States, under the leadership of Franz Boas, the emphasis would be upon data collection for its own sake, with the search for laws governing cultures to be put off until sufficient information could be collected in some indeterminate future. This would come to be known as *cultural anthropology*.

In Europe, led by A.R. Radcliffe-Brown and Bronislaw Malinowski (although the latter lived a good portion of his life in the United States), the perspective was more "functional," perhaps best summarized by Malinowski himself: "The functional view of culture lays down the principle that in every type of civilization, every custom, material object, idea, and belief fulfills some vital function, has some task to accomplish, represents an indispensable part within a working whole." This is what is sometimes called *social anthropology*.

In either case, anthropology was to become a study of cultures in the here and now, not the past.

Arturo Alvarez Roldán is a Lecturer in Social Anthropology at the University of Granada, Spain and has published on the history and epistemology of Darwinism and British Anthropology. He has conducted fieldwork on rituals, politics, and working-class organizations in Western Asturias in Spain.

Key Concept: functionalism

Fieldwork by participant observation is recognized within and outside anthropology as a hallmark of the discipline. It is of no interest to continue arguing about who was the inventor of this research method, or where the invention first took place. What has some significance from a historical point of view is how it was discovered. Malinowski's ethnographic experience in Melanesia is still a relevant episode in the history of European anthropology when approaching this matter. In this chapter I shall compare Malinowski's ethnography in Mailu (Samarai) with his subsequent work during his first expedition to the Trobriand Islands. I shall attempt to show how Malinowski's invention of the ethnographic method was principally a result of his praxis in the field and not a natural outcome of his previous life or theoretical ideas.

Historians of anthropology have uncovered a great deal of detail about Malinowski's life, personality, historical background and theoretical training. Yet all this information does not explain how he came to revolutionize anthropological methods.[1] Why was Malinowski's ethnographic experience in Mailu so different from his work in Kiriwina (Trobriand Islands)? What changed it in just a few months? It was certainly not Malinowski's biography or his scholarly training. What really changed was his praxis in the field. Malinowski learned to do ethnography in a modern fashion while he was in Kiriwina. My thesis is not only historical but also epistemological. It is my view that a new knowledge, including methodological knowledge, is always a consequence of a particular kind of praxis.[2] Malinowski discovered a new way of doing ethnography in Kiriwina by modifying his behaviour in the field.

There were six crucial differences in Malinowski's ethnographic practice in the Trobriand Islands in comparison with his work in Mailu. (1) In Kiriwina he lived for a long time amongst the members of the community that he studied; (2) he focused his research on a few specific subjects; (3) he studied the Trobriand people in their present existence and not their way of life in the past; (4) he learned the vernacular; (5) he increased the number of his own observations of native everyday life and institutions; and (6) he changed his style of reporting. It is my argument that these characteristics of Malinowski's Trobriand work lie at the core of the Malinowskian methodological revolution in ethnography.

'Living Right Among the Natives'

Malinowski finished his essay on 'the natives' of Mailu in Samarai at the beginning of June, 1915. From there he went to the Trobriand Islands. He expected to spend only 'one month' studying the 'material and artistic culture' of the Trobriand people, and then to continue his trip to the north-east coast (BM/CGS, 13/06/1915, in SP). Yet he stayed ten months in Kiriwina 'doing fieldwork… in the only way it is possible to do it' (BM/CGS, 30/07/1915, in SP).[3]

In the beginning he attempted to gather information from white settlers, in the same way as he had sometimes done before in Mailu. But soon he realized that 'it is quite futile to reckon on any one else but oneself' (BM/CGS, 30/07/1915, in SP). Thus, at the beginning of July, he put up his tent in a village to live among the subjects that he was going to study. It was a completely new experience for him.

Throughout his stay in Mailu, Malinowski had lived outside the local village. According to his diary, Malinowski arrived at Mailu on 16 October 1914, and he stayed there until 25 November 1914. Then he took a three-week trip to the east coast. Afterwards he came back to Mailu and stayed there from 19 December until 23 January 1915. During that time he devoted himself to collecting ethnographic information about the Magi during less than forty-two working days. He gathered the ethnographic data by setting out to find his informants and visiting the village—many times accompanied by one of the locals.

Only in Kiriwina did Malinowski begin to put into practice his Mailu *dictum* 'the nearer one lives to a village and the more one sees actually of the natives the better' (Malinowski 1988:109). Such a close contact with Kiriwinans allowed him to witness their behaviour and check the informants' accuracy. Of course, a more intense relationship with them also increased the moral and emotional tension between Malinowski and them. Malinowski reveals this sentiment very clearly in a letter he wrote to Seligman on 19 October 1915:

At times I feel damnably 'sick' (in the metaphorical sense) & I long to get away. Mind you, I am absolutely alone amongst niggers & at times they get on your nerves & add to it a bit of feverishness—any one would drink whisky under such circumstances. Now, I don't use neither whiskey nor the other 'white man's solace' [sic]—and such double abstinence makes life less merry. (BM/CGS, 19/10/1915, in SP)

When Malinowski pitched his tent in the village, he placed himself in the best circumstances to penetrate a form of life completely different from his own, but obviously he remained a member of his own culture. Malinowski's approach to the Trobrianders was cognitive, but not affective. Malinowski's virtue was not his capacity for empathy but his 'almost unbelievable capacity for work'—using Clifford Geertz's words (1967:12).

Narrowing the Focus

Unlike Mailu, the Trobriand Islands had already been studied by Seligman when Malinowski visited them. He began his work checking the information on the islands that Seligman had published in his book *The Melanesians of British New Guinea* (Seligman 1910:660–735).

I find your account of the Trobriands excellent, as far as it goes[.] (You express some misgivings in the Preface as to that part of your information; in fact, I don't think there is any essential inaccuracy in all you say about the Northern Massim). (BM/CGS, 30/07/1915, in SP)

After this quick review of Seligman's ethnographic account, Malinowski decided to continue his research on the Trobriand people, but in a different way. Instead of gathering more information on the same topics as Seligman—the table of cultural categories contained in *Notes and Queries*—Malinowski focused his investigations on a few specific topics. Later those research foci were the subjects of his principal monographs.

In Mailu, Malinowski had gathered information taking as a guide the *Notes and Queries*—the stereotyped system of cultural categories generated by the British anthropological tradition.[4] However, in the Trobriands, he left behind the traditional role of the ethnographer who went to the field to collect indiscriminately every kind of information about the ancestral customs and beliefs of 'natives' in order to provide armchair anthropologists with facts that confirmed their theories. Instead, he attempted to investigate in the field several ethnological problems that he had found formulated in books by Frazer, Durkheim, Spencer, Westermarck, Rivers, and others. Two issues had particularly attracted his attention: first, the relationship between religion, magic, and economy in primitive societies; and second, the connection between native mentality and institutions. In the field, these theoretical interests drove Malinowski to study indigenous beliefs in the spirits of the dead and reincarnation, garden magic and the Kula ring.

There are lots to be done yet—and things of extreme interest. There is their whole system of 'ceremonial gardening'—almost agricultural cult (in the Durkheimian sense); there are several beliefs and ceremonies about the spirits, BALO'M (even a belief in speedy reincarnation: a BALO'M goes to Tuma for another partial lifetime and then gets back into the first woman, it can get hold of; the annual harvest feast MILAMA'LA, connected and interwoven with the BALOM, a regular All souls day. The trading is much more peculiar and interesting, as it might appear at first sight. (BM/CGS, 30/07/1915, in SP)

Some could think that Malinowski's previous theoretical training played a definitive role in narrowing his research foci in the Trobriands. However, it should be remembered that he had carried the same theoretical ideas to Mailu, and there they did not have the same effect on his fieldwork. The reason for that change lies in the characteristics of Trobriand society and not in the theories that Malinowski had studied at home. Like a sculptor, in attempting to model his Trobriand ethnographic material, Malinowski was conditioned by the nature of the material itself. Even more, I think, Malinowski was anchored in the Trobriands by the kind of human material he found there: a matrilineal society politically organized into chieftainships, whose members were involved in a very complex system of rituals governing social life, and who, as it was phrased at the time, were ignorant of the physiological process of reproduction.

Why not Present First?

At the same time as his research focus narrowed, Malinowski lost interest in the past life of Trobriand people. While he was reading Haddon, Seligman, Rivers, and Spencer in the field, he asked himself:

why should we study the past of native institutions and not their present stage? Although Malinowski did not raise this question with his teachers in his correspondence, there is some evidence of his deep change of attitude in the notes he wrote in the margins of Rivers's book *Kinship and Social Organization*.[5]

Rivers's aim in that book was:

to show that the terminology of relationship has been rigorously determined by social conditions and that, if this position has been established and accepted, systems of relationship furnish us with a most valuable instrument in studying the history of social institutions. (Rivers 1914:1; underlined by Malinowski)

Malinowski marked this paragraph with two vertical lines and wrote next to it: 'Past[,] why not present first[?]' Until then Malinowski had been guided in his fieldwork by Seligman's directions. His work at Mailu had been 'a kind of practical training in [his mentor's] school' (BM/CGS, 20/09/1914, in SP). He had been looking for survivals of primitive society. His Mailu ethnography had been done from an evolutionist—or we might better say historicist—

point of view. In the Trobriand Islands, on the contrary, he looked at native society from a synchronic, functionalist point of view. In my opinion, this change in the way of looking at things persuaded Malinowski to learn the vernacular language and to observe natives' behaviour.

Talking Among Natives

During his stay in Kiriwina, Malinowski spent a long time learning Kiriwinian. Within three months he obtained a basic knowledge of that language. On 24 September 1915 he wrote to Seligman:

I am beginning to talk Kiriwinian quite sufficiently to work in Kiriwinian, though I have an excellent interpreter at hand. By the way I am getting up a Grammar & Vocabulary. (BM/CGS, 24/09/1915, in SP)

Some weeks later he wrote to Seligman again, telling him that he had left his interpreter and that he was already talking to the Kiriwinians in their language.

My work is going fairly smoothly, though I will have now a somewhat hard time, because I had to part with my interpreter, who was excellent in his 'professional capacity' but a bloody scoundrel in personal relations. But I have got so much Kiriwinian that for the last 3 weeks I hardly had to say a sentence or so per diem in Pidgin for the boy to interpret & having extremely intelligent natives to deal with, I am able always to get out of the difficulty. (BM/CGS, 19/10/1915, in SP)

Did Malinowski really need to learn Kiriwinian to study Trobriand people? What did he gain by learning their language? Was it just an instrument to get into touch with informants and nothing else? Could he have obtained the same information with an interpreter or by speaking a *lingua franca* such as Pidgin?

It seems that Malinowski did not consider it indispensable to learn the vernacular in order to conduct intensive ethnographic work. On 15 October 1915 he wrote to Rivers:

I am doing 'intensive work' in the Trobriands and my linguistic facilities are of some use in it, though my experience has shown me that it is possible to do almost as good work with an interpreter, though one looses [sic] much time; when one begins to understand the natives talking among themselves, the old men discussing your question, or the people gossiping in the evening, lots of things crop up automatically. (BM/WHRR, 15/10/1915, in HC: 12055)

Does this mean that his learning of the vernacular did not play a crucial role in his work in the Trobriands? I do not think so. Malinowski writes in the Introduction to *Argonauts* that he realized the importance of speaking the language, when finally he was able to understand it. He discovered that, in order to understand the meaning of a native expression, it was not enough to find a verbal equivalence in other known languages.

It was necessary to know the situation in which the expression had been pronounced. In 1923 Malinowski developed this idea in a famous paper, in which he explained his theory of meaning in primitive languages. Malinowski thought that learning a language and learning the culture in which that language is spoken are related tasks. Therefore, when he stated that he had learned the vernacular sufficiently, he did not mean to say that he had learned English or Polish verbal equivalences to native expressions. What he learned was how the native speakers used their language in their own culture. That is something he could do only by observing how the Trobrianders interact among one another, and by interacting with them himself—linguistically or not, with or without interpreter, in their language or in a different one.

What does all this have to do with the fact that Malinowski took a presentist attitude in his research? We again find the answer to this question in the critical remarks that Malinowski wrote in the margins of Rivers's *Kinship and Social Organization*.

Rivers believed that kinship terminologies were a satisfactory instrument to study the history of social institutions. He thought that 'the greatest merit' of his genealogical method was that it made it possible to obtain records of marriage and descent and other features of social organization up to 150 years old (Rivers 1910:11). Malinowski considered Rivers's concepts of 'terminology of relationship' and 'social conditions' too restricted and partially wrong. He wrote on the first pages of Rivers's book:

- Terminology of rel[ationshi]p—is [a] too fragmentary concept, when [it is] referred to reality of living language
- Terminology is a part within a determined whole—the 'indexed' language
- Terminology is accidental as far as determination goes.

Social conditions, which determine k[inship], all its symptoms & manifestations are:
The system of k[inship][,] i.e. arrangements, names, cognitive ideas & feelings which mould sentiments into definite patterns.

Malinowski accepted Rivers's idea that systems of kinship and marriage were determined by social conditions. For that reason he considered present conditions of primitive societies, and not their past, to be the cause of their kinship terminologies. From the horizon of the ethnographic present, learning the vernacular acquired new significance for Malinowski. Language was not only an instrument for collecting data from informants, but also the vehicle of native thought, and therefore a means to penetrate their mentality.[6] It was by learning the vernacular that Malinowski could gather the *corpus inscriptionum kiriwineiensium* he mentions in the famous Introduction to *Argonauts of the Western Pacific*.

Increasing the Number of Observations

Malinowski's interest in the present events of indigenous life also led him to put more emphasis on observation as a data-collection technique. In Mailu he had tried to see as many things as he could,[7] but in fact he did not witness much, and he looked at the Magi 'from his verandah' very often—an attitude that he later criticized very harshly (see, for example, Malinowski 1926:92). For his Mailu ethnography he collected most of his information through interviews with informants. In those work sessions Malinowski used an interpreter and a Motu dialect to talk to the Magi.

> If not for the miserable shade of Motuan I have got I would have to close shop, for my Motu boy is far too stupid to be used as an unchequed [unchecked] interpreter. But I picked up a certain amount of Motu before & I am rapidly perfectioning it. Thus, slowly but at a definite rate I am working out the material. (BM/CGS, 03/11/1914, in SP)

In his diary he described his Mailu stay as 'short' and 'superficial', and he wrote that he conducted his fieldwork there under 'poor circumstances' (Malinowski 1967:72). He did not live among the Mailu people and he did not observe them enough.

Malinowski achieved both aims in the Trobriands. On 24 September 1915 he wrote a letter to Seligman in which he suggested several subjects on which he could write a paper for the *Journal of the Royal Anthropological Institute*. In that letter he also gave Seligman a clear idea of the kind of materials he had collected until then:

> I am not going to be in a hurry publishing this stuff, but I shall be able to send you an article for the Journal [of the] R[oyal] A[nthropological] I[nstitute] & publish some stuff in Australia. Let me know which would you think best for the J.R.A.I.: 1) Land tenure & gardening[,] inclusive garden magic (very good informa[tio]n; [I] have seen & watched 60% as an eye witness, [I have] got magic (esoteric) from [the] biggest man in the island[.] 2) Burial, afterlife, mourning. This stuff I have got also well done: [I have] seen 3 deaths, one almost inmediately after expiration [and] 2 in wailing stage; 1 burial & any amount (over a dozen Sàgali). But this information would encroach on your stuff (that Chapter in [on] the N[orthern] Massim is the only one that needs serious amplification, as far as my present knowledge goes). I have been through 2 Milamalas, too. 3) Short article about reincarnation; ideas about conception and pregnancy. (BM/CGS, 24/09/1915, in SP)

Malinowski became an observer only when he put himself into the proper situation for observation and opened his eyes to the ethnographic present. All this happened during his first period of fieldwork in the Trobriand Islands. On 25 May 1916, while he was analysing his field material in Sydney, he wrote a letter to Haddon to tell him of the success of his enterprise:

I have spent over 8 months in one village in the Trobri-
and and this proved to me, how even a poor observer like
myself can get a certain amount of reliable information,
if he puts himself into the proper conditions for observation. (BM/ACH, 25/05/1916, in HC: 7)

A New Ethnographic Discourse

After ten months of fieldwork in the Trobriands, Malinowski
went back to Australia, where he wrote his first Trobriand
ethnography: 'Baloma' (published in 1916). In this short
monograph about Trobriand beliefs, Malinowski foreshadowed a new style of writing ethnography. It was the
first time in British anthropology that an author, in order
to anchor his discourse, included theoretical and practical
contexts of his research in an ethnographic text.

In 'Natives of Mailu' (published in 1915) Malinowski
had limited himself to presenting his facts, following too
slavishly the format of the fourth edition of *Notes and
Queries*. Contrary to his suggestion in the 'Introduction'
to this monograph, he did not introduce a new order in
his ethnographic discourse at that time. 'By adopting a
fairly systematic division' (geography, sociology, economics, magico-religious matters, etc.) of chapters and
sections, he did not deviate from 'a purely topical presentation of facts', as he claimed (Malinowski 1988:110). On
the contrary, that division just covered the topical organization of *Notes and Queries* (Young 1988:26–7). In writing
his Mailu ethnography, Malinowski remained loyal to
the style of the Cambridge school.

Malinowski left that style behind only when he began
to write 'Baloma'. This essay contains the basic lines of
the new model of ethnography that he later improved in
writing *Argonauts*. In 'Baloma', Malinowski attempted
to construct an ethnographic argument which combined
three elements: fieldwork data, information about the
research process, and theories.

Some authors have tried to analyse ethnographic texts
as if they were literary fictions (Marcus 1980, Clifford
1988, Van Maanen 1988, Atkinson 1990). In my opinion
these interpretations are one-sided, since both kinds of
texts have different aims and, what is more important,
different processes of construction. In order to write an
ethnography, it is necessary to collect data in the field
and to analyse the information afterwards. That is what
Malinowski did. Reading Malinowski's fieldnotes[8] one
realizes that the narrative structure of 'Baloma' was the
result of a qualitative analysis of his data. The division
of chapters and sections in the essay was the product of
indexing, rearranging, checking, selecting, merging, etc.
of his fieldnotes (see Alvarez Roldán 1992c). Details about
the research process (descriptions of his informants, contrasts between observations and oral reports, distinctions
between particular and general opinions of respondents,
indications of the researcher's linguistic competence, etc.)
and theoretical references (e.g. his critique of Durkheim's

concept of *conscience collective*, the classification of social
beliefs, etc.) that appear in the text should not be interpreted as mere rhetorical devices (Malinowski 1913, 1916).
The description of conditions under which Malinowski
gathered his information in the field and some of his theoretical ideas are essential elements for the assessment of
the text's ethnographic validity (Sanjek 1990). After his
Trobriand experience, Malinowski tried to ground his
monographs by building ethnographic reasoning into
them. Thus he opened a new ethnographic discourse.
With 'Baloma' ethnography took the form of a continuous constructive process, involving the tasks of doing
fieldwork and writing—two related phases of the ethnographic process. Thanks to his experience in the Trobriands Malinowski came to revolutionize ethnography not
only as a fieldwork process but also as a written product.

Notes

A preliminary version of this chapter entitled 'Malinowski's
invention of the ethnographic method revisited', was presented at the second conference of the European Association of Social Anthropologists in Prague, Czechoslovakia,
in August 1992. An early version will be published in
Russian translation in the journal *Etnograficheskoe Obozrenie*
(Moscow). I am grateful to Juan Gamella, José Luís Garcia,
Davydd Greenwood, Fermín del Pino, Marilyn Strathern, Honorio Velasco, and Han Vermeulen for their comments on the original. I am also grateful to the Syndics of
Cambridge University Library and to the British Library
of Political and Economic Science for permission to quote
from documents preserved in their manuscript collections.

1. For instance, Ernest Gellner has suggested in a thought-
    provoking paper (1985) that Malinowski's Polish back-
    ground could have influenced the way he later approached
    fieldwork, as well as his interpretations of Trobriand
    society. For a panoramic view of Malinowski's theoretical
    influences, see Stocking 1983:93-5; 1986:19-22. An example
    of partial socio-political explanation can be found in the
    recent book *The Savage Within* by Henrika Kuklick:

    > Not until after World War I, when colonial author-
    > ity seemed secure in most parts of the Empire, did it
    > become routine for anthropologists to go into the field
    > to collect their own data for analysis, and the dis-
    > cipline's altered methodology was at least a partial
    > function of political change, for anthropologists could
    > be reasonably confident that peoples accustomed to
    > defer to colonial rulers would be cooperative subjects.
    > In the prewar era, scholarly anthropological analyses
    > based on extensive field experience were written, but
    > they were produced by men who were themselves
    > colonial agents—missionaries and colonial adminis-
    > trators. (Kuklick 1993:287; my emphasis)

2. For further comments on this idea, see Alvarez Roldán
    1992a, 1992b.
3. The phrase 'living right among the natives' is taken from
    a letter that Malinowski wrote to Haddon on 15 October

1915: 'Out here one feels sometimes lonely and isolated (I am living right among the natives in a village, since beginning of July) and it is a great help in work to receive such letters as yours and the letters I am receiving from Seligman.' (BM/ACH, 15.10.1915, in HC: 7).

4. Malinowski (1988). See Young (1988:24-7).
5. The copy of Rivers's book that Malinowski took with him to the field remains in the British Library of Political and Economic Science catalogued as R (Coll). Mis. 392 (1) M 695.
6. Raymond Firth has suggested a similar idea (1981:124).
7. On 24 November 1914 he wrote to Seligman:

> I think I have got now a fairly complete all round picture of the Mailu—but it is a rough sketch in black & white. So far as the touches of colour are much more difficult to get. I am trying to *see* as many things done as I can. I hope I shall be able to see a couple of feasts in the end of December or beginning January—the great annual feast. (BM/CGS, 24.11.1914, in SP)

8. Twelve of the field notebooks that Malinowski wrote during his first period of fieldwork in the Trobriand Islands survive in the Manuscripts Room of the British Library of Political and Economic Science, London. They contain entries from the end of June 1915 until the middle of February 1916. The notes on Baloma appear in all the notebooks.

Bibliograpy

Alvarez Roldán , A. (1992a) 'La estructura de la revolución darwinista. [The structure of the Darwinian revolution]', *Asclepio*, 44, 1:243–62.

——— (1992b) 'Looking at anthropology from a biological point of view: A.C. Haddon's metaphors on anthropology', *History of the Human Sciences*, 5, 4:21–32.

——— (1992c) 'La formation del proceso etnogr·fico en la tradition británica de Tylor a Malinowski. [The formation of the ethnographical process in the British tradition from Tylor to Malinowski]', PhD dissertation, Complutense University of Madrid.

Atkinson, P. (1990) *The Ethnographic Imagination. Textual Constructions of Reality*, London: Routledge.

Clifford, J. (1988) 'On ethnographic self-fashioning: Conrad and Malinowski', in *The Predicament of Culture*, Cambridge, MA: Harvard University Press.

Firth, R. (1981) 'Bronislaw Malinowski', in Sydel Silverman (ed.) *Totems and Teachers. Perspectives on the History of Anthropology*, New York: Columbia University Press.

Geertz, C. (1967) 'Under the mosquito net', *New York Review of Books*, 9, 4 (14 September): 12–13.

Gellner, E. (1985) 'Malinowski go home. Reflections on the Malinowski Centenary Conferences', *Anthropology Today*, 1, 5:5–7.

Kuklick, H. (1993) *The Savage Within. The Social History of British Anthropology, 1885–1945*. New York: Cambridge University Press.

Malinowski, B. (1913) 'Review of *Les Formes èlémentaires de la vie réligieuse*, par E. Durkheim', *Folklore*, 24, 3, pp. 525–531.

——— (1916) 'Baloma: the spirits of the dead in the Trobriand Islands', *Journal of the Royal Anthropological Institute*, 46:353–430.

——— (1922) *Argonauts of the Western Pacific*, London: Routledge.

——— (1923) 'The problem of meaning in primitive languages', in C.L. Ogden and I.A. Richards, *The Meaning of Meaning*, London: K. Paul, Trench, Trubner.

——— (1926) *Myth in Primitive Psychology*. London: Kegan Paul.

——— (1967) *A Diary in the Strict Sense of the Term*, ed. Raymond Firth, London: Athlone Press.

——— (1988 [1915]) 'Natives of Mailu', in M. Young (ed.) *Malinowski Among the Magi*, London: Routledge.

Marcus, G.E. (1980) 'Rhetoric and the ethnographic genre in anthropological research', *Current Anthropology*, 21, 4:507–10.

Rivers, W.H.R. (1910) 'The genealogical method of anthropological inquiry', *Sociological Review*, 3:1–12.

——— (1914) *Kinship and Social Organization*, London: Constable.

Sanjek, R. (1990) 'On ethnographic validity', in R. Sanjek (ed.) *Fieldnotes. The Makings of Anthropology*, Ithaca, NY: Cornell University Press.

Seligman, C.G. (1910) *The Melanesians of British New Guinea*, Cambridge: Cambridge University Press. (Reprinted by AMS Press, New York, 1976.)

Stocking, G.W. Jr (1983) 'The ethnographer's magic. Fieldwork in British Anthropology from Tylor to Malinowski', in G.W. Stocking Jr (ed.) *Observers Observed*, Madison, WI: The University of Wisconsin Press.

——— (1986) 'Anthropology and the science of the irrational. Malinowski's encounter with Freudian Psychoanalysis', in G.W. Stocking Jr (ed.) *Malinowski, Rivers, Benedict and Others. Essays on Culture and Personality*, Madison, WI: The University of Wisconsin Press.

Van Maanen, J. (1988) *Tales of the Field. On Writing Ethnography*, Chicago: University of Chicago Press.

Young, M. (ed.) (1988) *Malinowski Among the Magi*, London: Routledge.

Manuscript Sources

HC: *Haddon Collection.* University Library, Cambridge, United Kingdom.
SP: *C.G. Seligman Papers.* British Library of Political and Economic Science, London School of Economics, London, United Kingdom.

Publication Information

Book Title: *Fieldwork and Footnotes: Studies in the History of European Anthropology.* Contributors: Arturo Alvarez Roldán—editor, Han F. Vermeulen—editor. Publisher: Routledge. Place of Publication: New York. Publication Year: 1995. Page Number: 155.

Anthropology and Imperialism

Kathleen Gough

Kathleen Gough wrote this article in 1967, after the last remaining vestiges of traditional cultures, uninfluenced by the modern Western world, had disappeared. Yet, many anthropologists continue to engage in ethnographic fieldwork as if the small-scale setting still exists as a self-contained entity. Are these anthropologists oblivious to the changes that have occurred in the larger world context of these communities, or do they stick to the tried and true as a matter of professional specialization, political expediency or economic convenience?

To say that anthropology is a child of Western imperialism, as Kathleen Gough does in this often-cited essay, is not to indict the whole profession as an accomplice in the economic exploitation of the poor and the dispossessed. Yet, it has been the imperialist side of the anthropological bread that has been buttered. In this context, it is important to distinguish between colonialism, having to do with population settlement, and imperialism, denoting political and/or economic control. Generally speaking, in the modern world, many former colonies—having achieved a semblance of political independence—are still under the political and economic influence of the more powerful nations that seek to control raw materials and world markets. It is this larger context, according to Gough, that should be taken into account in describing and explaining peoples' lives.

So to whom or to what do anthropologists owe their allegiance? To the facts? If so, which facts? Those facts that reveal a power structure that favors some over others? Or those facts that involve delving no further than the personal day-to-day experiences of individual informants?

Kathleen Gough was born in 1925 in Yorkshire, England, came to the United States in 1955, and emigrated to Canada in 1967. She received her Ph.D. at Cambridge University in Anthropology and was most recently a research associate at the University of British Columbia. She has done the bulk of her fieldwork in South Asia and has written extensively in the areas of social class, caste, and kinship organization.

Key Concept: anthropology and imperialism

Recently a number of anthropologists, and of students, have complained that cultural and social anthropology is failing to tackle significant problems of the modern world. As I have thought so for some time, I should like to make a tentative statement about where I think we stand today, and to follow it with some proposals. This being a new departure, I must ask to be excused if I am both obvious and argumentative.

Anthropology is a child of Western imperialism. It has roots in the humanist visions of the Englightenment, but as a university discipline and a modern science it came into its own in the last decades of the nineteenth and early twentieth centuries.

This was the period in which the Western nations were making their final push to bring practically the whole pre-industrial, non-Western world under their political and economic control.

Until the Second World War most of our fieldwork was carried out in societies that had been conquered by our own governments. We tended to accept the imperialist framework as given, perhaps partly because we were influenced by the dominant ideas of our time, and partly because at that time there was little anyone could do to dismantle the empires. In spite of some belief in value-free social science, anthropologists in those days seem to have commonly played roles characteristic of white liberals in other spheres of our society, sometimes of white liberal reformers. Anthropologists were of higher social status than their informants; they were usually of the dominant race, and they were protected by imperial law; yet, living closely with native peoples, they tended to take their part and to try to protect them against the worst forms of imperialist exploitation. Customary relation developed between the anthropologists and the government or the various private agencies who funded and protected them. Other types of customary relationships grew up between anthropologists and the people whose institutions they studied. Applied anthropology came into being as a kind of social work and community development effort for non-white peoples, whose future was seen in terms of gradual education, and of amelioration of conditions many of which had actually been imposed by their Western conquerors in the first place…

Whereas in the Fifties, it looked to some of us at though much of the non-Western world might gain genuine political and economic independence from the West by peaceful means, this is no longer the case. Western dominance is continuing under new guises, even expanding and hardening. At the same time, revolution now begins to appear as *the* route by which underdeveloped societies may hope to gain freedom from Western controls.

In this revolutionary and proto-revolutionary world, anthropologists are beginning to be in difficulties. We are rapidly losing our customary relationships as white liberals between the conquerors and the colonized. From the beginning, we have inhabited a triple environment involving obligations, first to the peoples we studied, second, to our colleagues and our science, and third, to the powers who employed us in universities or who funded our research. In many cases we seem now to be in danger of being torn apart by the conflicts between the first and third set of obligations, while the second set of loyalties, to our subject as an objective and humane endeavour, is being severely tested and jeopardized. On the one hand, part of the non-Western world is in revolt, especially against the American government as the strongest and most counterrevolutionary of the Western powers. The war in Vietnam has, of course, exacerhabted the non-Western sense of outrage, although the actual governments of most of these nations are so dependent on the United States, that they soften their criticisms. On the other hand, anthropologists are becoming increasingly subject to restrictions, unethical temptations, and political controls from the United States government and its subordinate agencies, as Professor Ralph Beals' report on Problems of Anthropological Research and Ethics amply shows.[1] The question tends to become: what does an anthropologist do who is dependent on a counterrevolutionary government, in an increasingly revolutionary world? To complicate matters, into the arena has stepped a fourth and most vociferous public, namely students, who once imbibed knowledge peaceably, but who are now, because of their own crises, asking awkward questions about ethics, commitments, and goals.

There is little wonder that with all these demands many anthropologists bury themselves in their specialties or, if they *must* go abroad, seek out the remotest, least unstable tribe or village they can find.

As Peter Worsley has recently pointed out, however, in a paper called "The End of Ahthropology?" we shall eventually have to choose either to remain, or become, specialists who confine themselves to the cultures of small-scale, pre-industrial societies, or else, bringing to bear all our knowledge of cultural evolution and of primitive social institutions, embark fully on the study of modern societies, including modern revolutions. If we take the former path, as our subject matter disappears, we shall become historians, and will retreat from the substantial work we have already done in contemporary societies. If we take the latter path, which is the one some of us must inevitably follow, we shall have to admit that our subject matter is increasingly the same as that of political scientists, economists, and sociologists. The only way that we can *not* admit this is by confining ourselves to studies of small segments of modern society. But as the scale of these societies widens, such studies are less and less justifiable theoretically or methodologically except within a framework of understanding of what is happening to the larger system. Anthropologists have, moreover, some right to demand of themselves that they do study the larger system as a totality, for they have fifty years of experience of analyzing the interconnectedness of political, economic, and religious institutions within smaller-scale systems. While they must necessarily depend for much of their data on the other social sciences, anthropologists do have some historical claim to play a synthesizing role.

Unfortunately we have, I think, a serious drawback in our own history which makes it very difficult for us to approach modern society as a single, interdependent, world social system; that is, although we have worked for over a hundred years in conquered societies, and although for at least fifty of them we have emphasized the interconnectedness of parts of social systems, we have virtually failed to study Western imperialism as a social system, or even adequately to explore the effects of imperialism on the societies we studied. Of late a few pioneer works have appeared which attempt this task, notably Worsley's own book, *The Third World.* Wallerstein's collection, *Social Change: the Colonial Situation,* draws together useful extracts by social scientists and nationalist leaders over the past twenty years. Wolf's study of Mexico (1959), Steward's and others' of Puerto Rico (1956), Epstein's of politics in the Zambian copper-belt (1958), and a number of others also move in this general direction. But it is remarkable how few anthropologists have studied imperialism, especially its economic system.

It is true, of course, that anthropologists have made numerous studies of modern social change in pre-industrial societies, especially in local communities. They have, however, usually handled them through very general concepts: "culture-contact," "acculturation," "social change," "modernization," "urbanization," "Westernization," or "the folk-urban continuum." Force, suffering, and exploitation tend to disappear in these accounts of structural process, and the units of study are usually so small that it is hard to see the forest for the trees. These approaches, in the main, have produced factual accounts and limited hypotheses about the impact of industrial cultures on pre-industrial ones in local communities, but have done little to aid understanding of the world distribution of power under imperialism or of its total system of economic relationships. Until recently there has also been, of course, a bias in the types of non-Western social units chosen for study, with primitive communities least touched by modern changes being preferred over the mines, cash-crop plantations, white settlements, bureaucracies, urban concentration, and nationalist movements that have played such prominent roles in colonial societies.

Why have anthropologists not studied world imperialism as a unitary phenomenon? To begin to answer this question would take another article. I will merely suggest some possible lines of enquiry, namely: (1) the very process of specialization within anthropology and between anthropology and the related dispciplines, especially political science, sociology, and economics, (2) the tradition of individual field work in small-scale societies, which at first produced a rich harvest of ethnography but later placed constraints on our methods and theories; (3) unwillingness to offend the governments that funded us, by choosing controversial subjects; and (4) the bureaucratic, counterrevolutionary setting in which anthropologists have increasingly worked in their universities, which may have contributed to a sense of impotence and to the development of machine-like models.

It may be objected that I have ignored the large volume of post-war American writing in applied anthropology and in economic and political anthropology concerned with development. This work certainly exists, and some of it is fruitful. I would argue, however, that much of it springs from erroneous or doubtful assumptions and theories that are being increasingly challenged by social scientists in the new nations themselves. Among these assumptions are: the explanation of economic backwardness in terms of values and psychological characteristics of the native population; the assumption that it is desirable to avoid rapid, disruptive changes; the refusal to take value positions that oppose official policies; the insistence on multiple causation; the assumption that the local community is a suitable unit for development programs; the belief that the main process by which development occurs is diffusion from an industrial center; and the refusal to contemplate the possibility that for some societies revolution may be the only practicable means toward economic advance.[2] In general, applied and economic anthropology stemming from North America has assumed an international capitalist economy in its framework. The harsh fact seems to be, however, that in most countries of the underdeveloped world where private enterprise predominates, the living conditions of the majority are deteriorating, and "take-off" is not occurring. If this is true it will not be surprising if the intellectuals of these countries reject the metropolitan nations' applied social science and seek remedies elsewhere.

There are of course already a large number of studies, indeed a whole literature, on Western imperialism, most although not all by writers influenced by Marx. In addition to the classic treatments by J. A. Hobson (1954), Lenin (1939) and Rosa Luxemburg (1951), Parker T. Moon (1925), Mary E. Townsend (1940), Eric Williams (1944), Fritz Steinberg (1951), the anthropologist Ramakrishna Mukherjee (1958), and Paul A. Baran (1957) have provided outstanding examples of such work. More recent studies include, of course, Baran and Sweezy's *Monopoly Capital*, Nkrumah's *Neo-Colonialism, the Last Stage of Imperialism*, René Dumont's *Lands Alive* and *False Start in Africa*, Fanon's *Wretched of the Earth* and *Studies in a Dying Colonialism*, and A. G. Frank's *Capitalism and Underdevelopment in Latin America*. Such books tend in America to be either ignored or reviewed cursorily and then dismissed. They rarely appear in standard anthropological bibliographies. I can only say that this American rejection of Marxist and other "rebel" literature, especially since the McCarthy period, strikes me as tragic. The refusal to take seriously and to defend as intellectually respectable the theories and challenges of these writers has to a considerable extent deadened controversy in our subject, as well as ruining the careers of particular individuals. It is heartening that in recent years the publications of Monthly Review Press, International Publishers, *Studies on the Left*, and other left-wing journals have become a kind of underground literature for many graduate students and younger faculty in the social sciences. But both orthodox social science and these Marxist-influenced studies suffer from the lack of open confrontation and argument between their proponents. There are of course political reasons for this state of affairs, stemming from our dependence on the powers, but it is unfortunate that we have allowed ourselves to become so subservient, to the detriment of our right of free enquiry and free speculation.

I should like to suggest that some anthropologists who are interested in these matters could begin a work of synthesis by focusing on some of the contradiction between the assertions and theories of these non-American or un-American writers and those of orthodox American social scientists, and choosing research problems that would throw light on these contradictions. Among such problems might be the following:

1. Is it true, as A. G. Frank (1967c) argues from United Nation figures, that *per capita* food production in non-Communist Asia, Africa, and Latin America has declined in many cases to below pre-war levels, since 1960, whereas it has risen, above pre-war levels in China and Cuba? Or is it generally true, as the American press asserts and many social scientists assume, that capitalist agricultural production in underdeveloped countries is poor, but socialist production is even poorer?

2. A set of research problems might be developed around comparisons of the structure and efficiency of socialist and capitalist foreign aid. One might, for example, compare the scope and results of American economic and military aid to the Dominican Republic with those of Russian aid to Cuba. Although Americans cannot go freely to Cuba, it is conceivable that a European and an American,

coordinating their research problems, might do such comparative work. In countries such as India, the UAR, or Algeria, comparable socialist and capitalist aid projects might be studied within the same locality.

3. We need comparative studies of types of modern intersocietal political and economic dominance, to define and refine such concepts as imperialism, neo-colonialism, etc. How, for example, does Russian power over one or another of the East European countries compare with that of the United States over certain Latin American or Southeast Asian countries with respect to such variables as military coercion, the disposal of the subordinate society's economic surplus, and the relations between political elites? How does Chinese control over Tibet compare, historically, structurally, and functionally, with Indian control over Kashmir, Hyderabad, or the Naga Hills, and what have been the effects of these controls on the class structures, economic productivity, and local political institutions of these regions?

4. Comparative studies of revolutionary and proto-revolutionary movements are clearly desirable if we are to keep abreast with indigenous movements for social change. In spite of obvious difficulties, it is possible to study some revolutions after they have occurred, or to study revolts in their early stages or after they have been suppressed.[3] There *are*, moreover, Westerners who live and travel with revolutionary movements; why are anthropologists seldom or never among them? We need to know, for example, whether there is a common set of circumstances under which left-wing and nationalist revolutions have occurred or have been attempted in recent years in Cuba, Algeria, Indo-China, Malaysia, the Philippines, Indonesia, Kenya, and Zanzibar. Are there any recognizable shifts in ideology or organization between these earlier revolts and the guerrilla movements now taking shape in Guaternala, Venezuela, Columbia, Angola, Mozambique, Laos, Thailand, Cameroon, Yemen, or Southern Arabia? What are the type of peasantry and urban workers most likely to be involved in these revolutions; are these typologies of leadership and organization? Why have some failed and others succeeded? How did it happen, for example, that some 1,000,000 communists and their families and supporters were killed in 1966 in Indonesia with almost no indigenous resistance, and how does this affect the self-assessment and prospects of, say, the Left Communist Party in India?

I may be accused of asking for Project Camelot, but I am not. I am asking that we should do these studies in *our* way, as we would study a cargo-cult or *kula*-ring, without the built-in biases of tainted financing, without the assumption that counterrevolution, and not revolution, is the best answer, and with the ultimate economic and spiritual welfare of our informants, and of the international community, before us rather than the shortrun military or industrial profits of the Western nations. I would also ask that these studies be attempted by individuals or self-selected teams, rather than as part of the grand artifice of some externally stimulated master-plan. Perhaps what I am asking is not possible any more in America. I am concerned that it may not be, that Americans are already too compromised, too constrained by their own imperial government. If that is so, the question really is how anthropologists can get back their freedom of enquiry and of action, and I suggest that, individually and collectively, we should place this first on the list.

Notes

1. See the *Fellow Newsletter* of the American Anthropological Association, Vol. 8, No. 1, January 1967.
2. For these and other criticisms, see Guillermo Bonfil Batalla (1966), P. Chilkwe Onwuachi, and Alvin W. Wolfe (1966), Rodolfo Stavenhagen (1966–67), and A. G. Frank (1967b).
3. For a rare example of such a study, see Donald L. Barnett and Karari Njama (1966).

References

Paul A. Baran
    1957   *The Political Economy of Growth,* Monthly Review Press.
Paul A. Baran and Paul M. Sweezy
    1966   *Monopoly Capital,* Monthly Review Press.
Donald L. Barnett and Karari Njama
    1966   *Mau-Mau from Within.* Monthly Review Press.
Guillermo Bonfill Batalla
    1966   "Conservative Though in Applied Anthropology: a Critique," *Human Organization,* Vol, 25, No. 2, Summer 1966, p. 89–92.
Wilfred Burchett
    1963   *The Furtive War,* International Publishers.
    1965   *Vietnam: Inside Story of the Guerilla War.* International Publishers.
    1966   *Vietnam North.* International Publishers.
David and Isabel Grook
    1959   *Revolution in a Chinese Village Ten Mile Inn.* Routledge and Kegan Paul.
    1966   *The First Years of Yangyi Commune.* Routledge and Kegan Paul.
Rene Dumont
    1965   *Lands Alive,* Monthly Review Press.
    1967   *False Start in Africa.* Grove Press.
A. L. Epstein
    1958   *Politics in an Urban African Community,* Manchester University Press.
Frantz Fanon
    1963   *The Wretched of the Earth.* Grove Press.
    1965   *Studies in a Dying Colonialism.* Monthly Review Press.
Andre Gunder Frank
    1966   "The Development of Underdevelopment," Monthly Review, Vol. 18, No. 4, September 1966, pp. 17–31.
    1967a *Capitalism and Underdevelopment is Latin America,* Monthly Review Press.
    1967b "Sociology of Development and Underdevelopment of Sociology," *Catalyst,* Buffalo, New York, pp. 20–73.
    1967c "Hunger," *Conadian Dimension.*
Stuart and Roma Gelder
    1964   *The Timely Rain, Travels in New Tibet.* Monthly Review Press.

Felix Greene
    1961   *China.* Doubleday.
    1964   *A Curtain of Ignorance.* Doubleday.
    1966   *Vietnam! Vietnam!* Fulton Publishers, Palo Alto, California.

William Hinton
    1966   *Fanshen.* Monthly Review Press.

J. A. Hobson
    1954   *Imperialism: A Study,* Allen and Unwin, 5th Imperssion.

Owen Lattimore
    1962   *Nomads and Commissars: Mongolia Revisited.* Oxford Universly Press.

V. I. Lenin
    1939   *Imperialism, the Highest Stage of Capitalism.* International Publishers, New York.

Rosa Luxemburg
    1951   *The Accumulation of Capital.* Yale University Press. [Reprinted by MR Press, 1964]

Parker T. Moon
    1925   *Imperialism and World Polities.* Macmillian.

Ramakrishna Mukherjee
    1958   *The Rise and Fall of the East India Company.* VEB Deutscher Vorlag der Wissenschaften, Berlin.

Gunnar Myrdal
    1956   *An International Economy.* Harper and Brothers.

Jan Myrdal
    1965   *Report from a Chinese Village.* Pantheon Books.

Kwame Nkrumah
    1966   *Neo-Colonialism, the Last Stage of Imperialism.* International Publishers, New York.

P. Chikwe Onwuachi and Alvin W. Wolfe
    1966   "The Place of Anthropology in the Furture of Africa," *Human Organization,* Vol. 25, No. 2, Summer 1966, pp. 93–95.

Joan Robinson
    1964   *Notes from China.* Oxford University Press. [Reprinted by MR. Press, 1964]

Joan Robinson and Solomon Adler
    1958   *China: An Economic Perspective.* Faban International Bureau.

Franz Schurmann
    1966   *Ideology and Organization in Communist China.* University of California Press.

Edgar Snow
    1962   *The Other Side of the River.* Random House.

Rodolfo Stavenhagen
    1966–67   "Seven Erroneous Theses about Latin America," *New University Thought,* Vol. 4, No. 4, Winter 1966–67, pp. 25–37.

Fritz Sternberg
    1951   *Capitalism and Socialism on Trial.* J. Day, New York.

Anna L. Strong
    1962   *Cash and Violence in Laos and Vietnam. Mainstream.*
    1964   *The Rise of the Chinese People's Communes—and Six Years After.* New World Press, Peking.

Julian H. Steward
    1956   *The People of Puerto Rico.* University of Illinois.

Han Suyin
    1965   *The Crippled Tree.* Jonathan Cape, London.
    1966   *A Mortal Flower,* Jonathan Cape, London.

Charles Taylor
    1966   *Reporter in Red China.* Random House.

Mary E. Townsend
    1940   *European Colonial Expansion Since 1871.* J. B. Lippincott.

Immanuel Wallenstein
    1966   *Social Change: The Colonial Situation.* John Wiley and Sons.

Eric Williams
    1944   *Capitalism and Slavery.* University of North Carolina Press.

Eric R. Wolf
    1959   *Sons of the Shaking Earth.* University of Chicago Press.

The World Almanac
    1967   Newspaper Enterprise Association, Inc.

Peter Worsley
    1964   *The Third World.* University of Chicago Press. "The End of Anthropology?" Paper prepared for the Sociology and Anthropology Working Group of the 6th World Congress of Sociology, available from Professor Peter Worsley, Department of Sociology, University of Manchester.

Theoretical Perspectives

Selection 8

ELMAN R. SERVICE, from "Evolution, Involution, and Revolution," *Cultural Evolutionism: Theory in Practice*

Selection 9

ABRAM KARDINER AND EDWARD PREBLE, from "Bronislaw Malinowski: The Man of Songs," *They Studied Man*

Selection 10

PAUL BOHANNAN, MARI WOMACK, AND KAREN SAENZ, from "Paradigms Refound: The Structure of Anthropological Revolutions," *Anthropological Theory in North America*

Selection 11

MICAELA DI LEONARDO, from "Margaret Mead vs. Tony Soprano," *The Nation*

Evolution, Involution, and Revolution

Elman R. Service

Anthropologists have always thought of themselves as objective observers, even though, as field workers, one of their goals is to understand the subjective views of others. But, just as other peoples' belief systems can only be understood in terms of their way of life, so also anthropological theories are best explained in the context of the times and conditions in which they developed. It is in this vein that Elman Service discusses the various theories as to how societies have changed over time and we get a sense, if you will, for the evolution of evolutionary ideas.

It should be expected that anthropological perspectives would change with the times, especially since, as anthropologists continue to collect information on the cultures of the world, the data base for theorizing increases. But we should not opt, argues Service, for a complete rejection of the evolutionary perspective, just because some of the older versions of it were not based upon enough sound ethnographic field work. Nor, I might add, should the work of the present-day orientation of the British and French functionalists and that of the "raw, ethnographic, 'barefoot empiricism'" of the early 20th-century American anthropologists be devalued just because of their narrow present-time orientation.

Perhaps it is time for a synthesis of the data and ideas. But, says Elman Service, "theories cannot be adjusted in conformity to their relative usefulness, if they remain—as seem to have been their destiny for so long—monolithic, schematic, and dogmatic in their use by political parties and academic schools."

Elman Service (1915–1996) received his doctorate in anthropology from Columbia University and went on to teach at Columbia, the University of Michigan, and the University of California at Santa Barbara.

Service fought for the United States in World War II and later (while still a student) joined the Abraham Lincoln Brigade in Spain where he fought fascism.

Elman Service did his fieldwork in South America and the Caribbean. His theoretical interests lay in the evolutionary change in social systems. He is perhaps best known for his books, *Primitive Social Organization* (1962) and *Profiles in Ethnology* (1963).

Key Concept: theory of cultural evolution

The development of the 18th-century evolutionary perspective must have been closely related to the actual dynamics of Europe's rapid modernization. This movement had two aspects: one was the rise of long-range commerce, urban centers, and national states with the attendant disruption of the ancient, static, feudal-monarchical order; the other combined the activities of explores, missionaries, traders, and colonizers—who opened nearly the entire world to European dominance.

The actual experience with radical social and political change suggested the fundamentals of the evolutionary view: sequential, systemic changes. This view gradually came to have great political as well as philosophical significance as it opposed the reactionary perspective of stasis: that is, of fixed, God-given, social-economic classes.

The idea that evolution involves sequences of related forms, also basically opposed it to kinds of changes is

orderly, which means that it can be analyzed scientifically in terms of cause-and-effect; and further, that characteristics of any given phenomenon cannot be fully understood, of explained, without knowing something about its ancestry—the antecedent sequence of related forms which it "unfolded."

The other stimulus to the evolutionary perspective was simply the astonishing diversity of races and cultures revealed to the Europeans as they ranged the world. How to explain this diversity? Many of the recently discovered ethnic groups seemed to have smaller and simpler societies—they seemed more "primitive" in various ways. If the idea of sequential change is added to any version of this notion about some kind of directional progress from primitive to modern societies, then we have the basis for the later, more sophisticated evolutionary schemes.

Directionality refers to the idea that societies can be arranged along a linear scale in terms of some kind of general criterion of advancement or progress. This scale was often stated explicitly in terms of "progress toward civilization," and also implicitly by the use of such descriptive epithets as "primitive" and "advanced," "simple" and "complex," "low" and "high," and in such labels as "savagery," "barbarism," and "civilization."

19th-Century Evolutionism

In the latterhalf of the 19th century, a more empirical and less ethnocentric evolutionary perspective appeared. Morgan in the U.S.A. and Tylor in England were the most influential evolutionists in anthropology; Saint-Simon, Comte, and Durkheim in France and Spencer in England were pioneers in sociology; in Germany (and later in exile) Marx and Engels were formulating an evolutionary theory of political economy. There were many others, of course, but these famous figures will serve to illustrate the major developments and disagreements within the growing evolutionary sciences.

The most significant differences among them can be reduced to three major facets of the evolutionary problem. 1. *What* is it that is evolving: stages of culture in general? separate institutions? a particular social system? 2. *How* does it evolve: by inevitable progress? improved human reason? survival of the fittest? dialectical struggle? 3. *Where* is the major evolutionary impulse: in technological developments? increased specialization of labor? political inventions? ideology? a cosmic immanence?

1. *What* Is Evolving?

E. B. Tylor is famous in anthropological history for the definition of culture with which he began his greatest work, *Primitive Culture* (1871). As the historian George Stocking (1968:Ch. 9) points out, however, Tylor's conception of culture and modern American conceptions are quite different. Tylor was concerned with general stages of advancement in culture, and also with the evolution of culture "along its many lines"—that is, sequences of improvements of weapons, forms of family, ideology, or religion. Nowhere does he evince interest in how the culture of a particular society works as a *system*. Named ethnic groups served merely as illustrations of grand cultural stages of development.

Morgan did not use the word culture, but his use of the terms "society" and "ethnical periods" were essentially similar to Tylor's "stages." A much-cited passage of Morgan's will illustrate his conception and some of the difficulties it causes (1964:6–7):

> Since mankind were one in origin, their career has been essentially one, running in different but uniform channels upon all continents, and very similarly in all the tribes and nations of mankind down to the same status of advancement. It follows that the history and experience of the

American Indian tribes, represent, more or less nearly, the history and experience of our own remote ancestors when in corresponding conditions.

This sounds "unilineal" to modern ethnologists, whose concern has been mostly with descriptive analysis of the structure and functioning of particular societies. But if Morgan's statement is read in context, it becomes apparent that he meant nothing more than that a general stage of hunting-gathering had preceded a stage of horticulture in both Europe and America and that both underlay European civilization. This seems so sensible, if commonplace, that no comment seems necessary, but in Morgan's day it was worth stating because theories of degeneration and catastrophy were still commonly opposed to evolutionism.

The sociologists, especially those under the influence of Spencer and later, Durkheim, accepted the organismic model for society. Evolution is a development of this societal whole into more parts and greater differentiation of these parts. The lack of a concept of "culture," as something distinct from "society," was an imposing intellectual handicap. Durkheim (1938) made complicated attempts to solve the problem, but he seems to have caused more confusion than clarity, even among his own students.

The Marxists were more inspired by anthropology than by sociology. Engels' *Origin of the Family, Private Property and the State*, in fact, borrowed heavily from Morgan's *Ancient Society*. As in Morgan's thought, the concept of culture was absent. It could have been appropriately used, especially because technological and economic factors were not seen by Engels as merely subserviently integrative in their function in society but as more of an initiating "prime-mover" than the sociologists believed, and this suggested functional and cause-effect kinds of relations among institutions (which are cultural) rather than among social groups alone.

2. *How* Does Culture Evolve?

The 18th-century evolutionists had thought of the improvement of the human condition as a result of the progressive evolution of thought. There was a residue of this attitude in the 19th-century as evidenced by such expressions as Morgan's "Growth of the Idea of Government" and Tylor's tendency to view progress in terms of conscious and rationalistic improvements.

How the evolutionary process worked was not otherwise described. In Tylor's view, new elements in culture sometimes tend to replace older ones if they are better, but beyond that one has the impression that evolution was taken as a "given," that immanent forces had moved mankind ever upward, however unevenly.

On the other hand, some of the most prominent of the 19th-century sociologists explicitly proposed a cause for the evolutionary process. This was the theory of "social Darwinism". Out of conflict among societies superior ones replace the inferior; within societies, competition among classes, groups, even individuals, results in "survival of the fittest." Walter Bagehot, Herbert Spencer, William Graham Sumner, and Ludwig Gumplowicz were the leading thinkers.

Although Marx and Engels were influenced by Morgan they became more consistently deterministic and materialistic than were the anthropologists and held a much more definite theory of the mechanics of evolution. To them the prime-mover in evolution was basically improvements in technology which in turn produced more goods, changed property relations, economic classes, and the state itself. (The famous "class struggle" is a precipitate out of this, not the cause of overall evolution).[1]

3. *Where* Is the Locus of the Evolutionary Impulse?

Both Morgan and Tylor saw technology, science, material culture generally, as undergoing a progressive, cumulative evolution, independent from religion and "intellectual and moral" progress. Nowhere is it plain, however, that one of these aspects is the prime-mover and the other a dependent variable. Again, it should be remembered that Morgan and Tylor were not talking about the process of systemic change in any particular society, hence the matter of functional priority of one part over another simply did not concern them.

The sociologists also seem to have taken evolution for granted. Even Herbert Spencer, the most consistently mechanistic, saw the evolutionary process as simply a grand cosmic force that generated complexity out of simplicity and heterogeneity out of homogeneity, aided only sometimes by Darwinian conflict-and-survival. Emile Durkheim (1933) posited that the division of labor in society, like the functional specialization of organs in higher biological forms, was related to population increase, greater social density, and larger, stronger societies. But these factors turn out to be indexes of evolution rather than causes. Durkheim, like functionalists today, seems to have been concerned with the relationship of one institution to another, but not with causal relations.

The Marxists, on the other hand, argued that the source of evolutionary change begins in the techno-economic sector, which subsequently affects social relations, then politics, and finally ideology, which is mere super-structure. This argument is still powerful today—although basically as dogma rather than as science....

20th-Century Evolutionism

American academic anthropologists in the early 20th century repudiated evolutionism in favor of a raw, ethnographic, "barefoot empiricism." In Britain and France, and in sociology nearly everywhere, evolutionism succumbed intellectually to a structural-functionalism that had greater utility for the practical solution of social problems, both political-administrative in colonies and ameliorative at home. Leslie A. White, Julian Steward,

and V. Gordon Childe were virtually alone in opposing the antievolutionary temper of the times. It was not until after midcentury that there was any noticeable shift of opinion toward an evolutionary outlook again, but this took place only in America, only in anthropology, and there only in small part.

Now the world is on the move again, greatly accelerated, and easily comparable in force and evolutionary significance to the earlier industrial-political revolutions of Europe. But the motive force is no longer in the European world: It resides in the rest of the world as reaction to the dominance of Western nations and the white race. It is impossible to know the precise relevance of these movements to the revival of evolutionary theories in Western social science, but it seems plain that the modern experience is at least an aid to the comprehension of the evolutionary perspective, despite the lonely academic genesis of this perspective.

The world is changing, but not in readily comprehensible ways. Certainly the simple orthogenetic evolutionary schemes and the implied "inevitability of progress" of the 18th and 19th centuries are not helpful in understanding much of what is going on in the world during the last half of the 20th century. We need some refinements in theory that can help us to understand cultural changes in all centuries, past, present, and hopefully, future.

One very simple and very general idea can be presented immediately as a key concept: Cultural changes are normally constrained by problems of adaptation. Inventions and discoveries, borrowings, unconscious "accidents," political plans, changes from whatever source, provide the cultural variations for potential evolutionary selection. But their eventual fate in the process of selection depends on the adaptive problem and context. They have to fit, to be selected for, as instruments within a complex environment (cf. Keller 1931).

Julian Steward (1955) stimulated acceptance of an important part of this perspective with his "cultural ecology." Societies are strongly influenced by their cultural adaptation to the natural environment. Walter Goldschmidt (1959:119–132) further proposed that the process of selection in adaptation has two aspects, internal and external. Cultural innovation, in other words, must either adapt to or alter preexisting traits within the culture. At the same time, they may be importantly articulated not only to the external natural environment but also to neighboring cultural systems, symbiotically, cooperatively, or competitively.

More needs to be said about this latter aspect of adaptation. As some cultures have successively become larger, more complex, more adaptable and powerful, so also have they increased their dominance over the less advanced. This dominance has taken many forms: destruction or assimilation of the weaker, occupation of its territory (as in "colonialism" in its literal sense), political rule ("imperialism"), or modern "indirect rule" with capital or commercial dominance only—and of course combinations and permutations of all these and others (cf. Kaplan 1960). In the modern world, this later indirect aspect of cultural dominance has become increasingly frequent.

We have been long committed to the notion of immanent progress that was associated with the contemporary world view of the 18th-century philosophers, and then with the later influence of the organismic analogy. It might be useful to start afresh with a look at the modern world to see what theoretical inspiration can be gained from a more recent perspective, and it may be that a useful theory of evolution thus could be inspired. If it is any good it will apply to the modern world as well as to the 18th and 19th centuries.

Evolution, Involution, and Revolution

It seems obvious that what has been missing in cultural evolutionary schemes is a way of talking in evolutionary terms plainly about what are its salient dynamics: the evolutionary dominance of modern advanced societies in the forms of colonialism and imperialism, and the reactions of some societies to this dominance in various forms of revolution. These are kinds of cultural changes that are remarkably visible today, but it seems safe to suggest that they have been going on, in one form or another, for a very long time. All it means, in effect, is that the classic evolutionary schemes failed to take into account the obvious facts of the interaction of cultures in terms of dominance, reactions to it, and the variable degrees of success on either side in the encounter. There is no inner dynamic of inevitable orthogenetic change, particularly when any change can be thwarted by another society's dominance powers.

One of the historical facts of life that has plagued all linear-orthogenetic schemes is that different societies manifest great variation in rates of evolution, from explosive rises toward "classic civilization" or industrialization, to the other extreme of stabilization or even devolution. And in many instances the same society makes a very rapid rise only to reach a long-term plateau. The theory that evolution involves adaptation, however, allows for both eventualities, taking stabilization as much for granted as progress. Stabilization, after all, is merely indicative of the success of the adaptive process: When the culture is successfully adapted, it tends to reject subsequent changes. This can render explicable what might seem paradoxical: that a culture "high" in one stage might fail to advance to further heights in the next, simply because of its earlier success. Of course, the more specialized and complicated its form of adaptation, the more deeply entrenched and committed to its extant environment it becomes.

Another historical fact of life is revolution, which often seems as much a reaction against evolution as a quest for it. Sometimes a revolution, in fact, even seeks a simplification of structure—as in Mao's China. But if we think of the cultural evolutionary process as essentially a set

of attempted solutions to environmental problems, and if the environment is to include other societies as well as nature, we need not insist that cultural changes of this sort are likely to resemble a progressive unfolding. We can then conceive of processes of adaptive change, some of which are directional in a generally progressive sense and some of which are not—although they might be very significant solutions to important local problems.

As Donald Campbell (1965:22) has noted, definitions of evolution have normally been related to theories about the presumed *course* of evolution. He advises instead that we define it in terms of the processes which produce it, and suggests a "variation-and-selective-retention" model. This is an advance, but it does not live up to the idea of definitions of process because it fails to relate the adaptive problem to the total environment in an adequate way.

To be sure, the new traits arrive, by various means, to become potentially a part of a society's culture. And, to be sure, only some are retained—often not in the original form—as they are adapted to the existing structure. But the retention of some traits over others can have vastly different consequences, in response to vastly differing environmental circumstance.

Let us retain the term evolution with as many of its originally important connotations as possible. Etymologically, it is from the Latin: *evolutis*, "unrolling." In modern ordinary usage, it is "an unfolding," "a development." Such a very general conception allows its use by many kinds of evolutionists. The central core of meaning is that of direction or progress along some kind of linear scale. Surely some cultures, institutions, and technologies have evolved strikingly in just this sense and it is useful to have an appropriate label. The argument has often been, however, about whether *every* cultural change must be of this kind—just because someone wants to call it evolutionary. The answer has to be "no," and a way out is suggested by refraining from calling all adaptive changes evolutionary.

The concept *involution* is useful in solving the labeling problem[2] This word derives from the Latin *involutum*, "rolled or wrapped up." Now, in modern usage, it means generally "an involving, a complication, or entanglement—a product of specialization." Cultural involution is a form of innovation that attempts to preserve an extant structure, solving its new problems by "fixing it up."[3] To paraphrase the famous Romer's Rule: The initial survival value of a favorable innovation is conservative in that it renders possible the maintenance of a traditional way of life in the face of changed circumstances. Thus the likelihood is that involution will be a prevalent form of cultural change.

Probably the most apt illustration of the cultural process of involution is Geertz' analysis of modern Javanese rural society. Instead of attempting modernization in order to make a long-term solution to the economic problem, the Javanese were forced to solve the problem of population pressure on food supply by continually intensifying the traditional agricultural form of production. This necessitated similar refinements and complications in other aspects of social life. "This 'late Gothic' quality of agriculture increasingly pervaded the whole economy: tenure systems grew more intricate; tenancy relationships more complicated; cooperative labor arrangements more complex—all in an effort to provide everyone with some niche, however small, in the over-all system." (Geerts 1963:82).

Wertheim (1967:59) believes that because involution frequently leads to a dead end, it ultimately may also lead to revolutionary overturns of social systems. Revolution occurs in order to free the society so that it may realize its potential for a more truly progressive evolution. But we must remember that the revolutionary impulse also typically involves some forms of adaptation to other societies. Particularly in modern times, these concern relationships of dominance and subordination.

Let us define revolution, as we have tried to define the concepts evolution and involution, as simply as possible and as close to popular usage as possible: It is derived from Latin *revolution,* "rolled, or turned, around." In ordinary usage a revolution is a radical, relatively abrupt change of the fundamental characteristics of a system. Also, the term implies that the change involves some kind of struggle *against* something or somebody. Normally, any fundamental cultural change must react against some extant form already somewhat adapted to an internal structure, and externally to nature and to other societies. We call this reaction revolutionary when it is characterized by visible disruption (cf. Brinton 1965:3–5).

This perspective on the adaptive process was stimulated by obvious characteristics of present day world-historical events. It would be particularly useful if it could also accommodate earlier events and the theories engendered by them. Let us see, by way of example, what this perspective has to say about the numerous viewpoints of the 19th century, taken in the order of their presentation in the previous section.

What is it that evolves? Is it culture in general, through grand stages, or only particular social systems? The reconciliation of these two views is easy: Both are correct. The evolution of the totality is the product of changes in the cultures of particular societies. To be sure, there is but a single adaptive process: the functional selection and adjustment of traits in particular systems. This is the way cultures become differentiated from one another; it is also the way some can become superior to others in measurable ways. Thus different theoretical perspectives are possible with respect to the varying relations of progressive change to the exigencies of adaptation. Some can be regarded as *evolutionary,* others as *involutionary,* and some, more rarely, as *revolutionary.*

How does culture evolve? Is it intentionally planned, or is it a social-Darwinistic product of competition? Surely an improvement in ideas has something to do with it and sometimes they must be by conscious and rational intention, in science and engineering most obviously, but also in the institutional realm. Many political institutions, for example, result from purposeful attempts to solve social or economic problems. Of course there are often latent and unintended consequences of even the most careful political plan.

Again it would seem that a reconciliation of the opposing views can be made by means of the adaptation-selection perspective. New culture traits or modifications can have any number of sources: discovery, invention, purposeful borrowing, accident, unconscious functional shifts, whatever. The selection or rejection of any of these also could involve conscious intentionality, even if this occurs but rarely. The selective process in cultural evolution is not often analogous to Darwinistic natural selection in biology; certainly the capacity of a person to analyze his own behavior and rearrange his affairs on that basis is a distinctively human trait ("Man is the only animal who knows he is going to die"). It is more difficult to plan and arrange things on a broad social or political basis, and the greater the demographic scope the more difficult, but it does happen. The present perspective has the great virtue of not prescribing either conscious intention or unconsciousness; it can accommodate either and still lead to comprehension of cultural change for it is concerned with outcomes rather than with motives. Furthermore, determinism in human affairs need not be equated with unawareness, nor indeterminism with awareness. Determinism is a perspective that the analyst takes, not a property of the subject matter under investigation.

Where is the locus of the evolutionary impulse? Does it lie in technology, the division of labor, "ethical and moral progress," or is it a cosmic force? A modern anthropological evolutionist should not argue this way, since the "prime-mover" in any particular instance of change is something to be discovered empirically…

The greatest virtue of the perspective on cultural change propounded in this chapter is that it should prove to have more versatile uses than the earlier evolutionary theories—even if it maintains only the single virtue of not prescribing so firmly the hypothetical answers to the "What," "How," and "Where" of the evolutionary process. If the main purpose of theories about the general processes of cultural change is to provide greater intelligibility to historical data, there ought to be some reciprocity as well, so that degrees of success and failure should result in changes and refinements in the theory itself. It is in this latter regard that the best tests of the theory are made. But they cannot be made, and theories cannot be adjusted in conformity to their relative usefulness, if they remain—as seem to have been their destiny for so long—monolithic, schematic, and dogmatic in their use by political parties and academic schools.

Notes

1. Marx said in the Author's Preface of *Capital* (1906:13): "Intrinsically, it is not a question of the higher or lower degree of development of the social antagonisms that result from the natural laws of capitalist production. It is a question of these laws themselves, of these tendencies working with iron necessity toward inevitable results."

2. I am indebted to W. F. Wertheim's ms (1967) for a description of the utility of this concept. The convenience of the idea was suggested to him by Clifford Geertz (1963), who borrowed it from Alexander Goldenweiser (1936).

3. See Harding (1960) for numerous well-taken examples of this kind of stabilization.

Bronislaw Malinowski: The Man of Songs

Abram Kardiner and Edward Preble

Some see functionalism in terms of the relationships between the institutions of a society, so that, for instance, kinship cannot be understood separately from economics and economics from politics, and so on. Malinowski's functionalism, however, not only included a broad, horizontal social framework, within which one could analyze the relationships between the parts of a society, but it was also vertical and had depth. For Malinowski, functionalism was not just a study of the relationships between the various elements of society, but it was also a way of accounting for how the various elements of a society would meet human needs. Starting with basic human nature, then, we can see how biological needs would be met by the material elements, the "derived needs" of a culture. The "derived needs" are in turn are supported by the social institutions, or "integrative needs," of a society. Even religion, as "spiritual" as it might be and as far removed from peoples' biological needs as any institution might seem, was nevertheless important for a well-functioning social order. Malinowski considered religion, therefore, as satisfying an "integrative" human need.

Abram Kardiner (1891–1981) graduated from Cornell Medical School in 1917, served a two-year internship at Mount Sinai Hospital and then went on to become a student-patient under Sigmund Freud, although he became critical of the orthodox psychiatric theory of the time. In 1930, Kardiner, along with Monroe Meyer and Bert Lewin, founded the New York Psychiatric Institute, the first training school in the United States. Kardiner later joined the department of anthropology at Columbia University, where he published *The Individual and His Society: The Psychodynamics of Primitive Social Organization* (1939) and collaborated with Ralph Linton and Cora Dubois on *The Psychological Frontiers of Society* (1945). Edward Preble taught anthropology at the New York School of Psychiatry. His fieldwork was on "street culture" in New York City.

Key Concepts: biological needs, derived needs, and integrative imperatives

The ability to understand very different kinds of people is often related to an innate lack of set values and standards. It is no accident that a great novelist like Balzac, who could penetrate and portray with impartial accuracy the character of bankers, prostitutes, and artists, was a moral relativist of psychopathic proportions. It is also no accident that the most successful field worker in the history of anthropology, Bronislaw Malinowski, was the most eccentric and controversial figure ever to enter the field of anthropology.

Malinowski recognized no boundaries. This trait infuriated professional anthropologists who wanted to establish an independent scientific discipline, but it won the confidence and trust of primitive peoples to a degree that has never been equaled. He ignored the academic partitioning of the field of human behavior into the cubicles of anthropology, sociology, and psychology, and moved freely from one medium to another according to the requirements of the problem. In the same spirit, he approached his primitive subjects free from intellectual or emotional preconception as to what constitutes the right way to live. His questions about individual behavior and cultural institutions were limited to: Does it work? How does it work? Why does it work? With these questions he founded the "functionalist" school of anthropology, and started the tradition of the "participant observer" in anthropological field work…

Malinowski was born in Cracow, Poland, April 7, 1884. His father was a nobleman of the landed gentry, but followed an academic career as professor of Slavic philology at Jagiellon University, in Cracow. Malinowski's early education was at the King Jan Sobieski Public School. From there he entered the University at Cracow, where, in 1908, he received a Ph.D. degree in physics and mathematics. His degree was awarded with the highest honors in the Austrian Empire.[1]

A promising career in the physical sciences, which began with two years of study and research in Wilhelm Ostwald's laboratory of physical chemistry at Leipzig, was canceled by Malinowski's chance reading of Frazer's

Golden Bough. Before he put down the last volume of that work, his career in the physical sciences had ended, and he had become dedicated to anthropology: "For no sooner had I begun to read this great work," wrote Malinowski, "than I became immersed in it and enslaved by it...and became bound to the service of Frazerian anthropology."

Unlike his idol and mentor, Sir James Frazer, Malinowski did not serve anthropology from the library. After four years of study, research, and writing at the London School of Economics, he set out on a field trip to Australia as secretary to a field expedition sponsored by the British Association for the Advancement of Science. He had been trained by, the greatest field worker of the day, C. G. Seligman, who thought so highly of Malinowski's potential as an anthropologist that he had offered to have his own salary cut so that Malinowski could be hired for the faculty of the London School of Economics. Besides Seligman and Frazer, he had studied with Westermarek, Rivers, and Hobhouse in London. In 1913, he published his first book, *The Family Among the Australian Aborigines.* He was well qualified to make the field trip to Australia, and no anthropologist, before or since, made so much of his training and opportunities.

It was the accident of war, however, that determined the arrangement of Malinowski's life. "Accident" and "arrangement" are contradictory terms for most people; but there are others, like Malinowski, in whom flexibility and determination are so combined that chance takes a natural place in the causal chain of events.

An Austrian subject, Malinowski had to be interned in Australia when war broke while he was on his way there. Instead of resigning himself to enforced idleness, he persuaded the Australian government to let him explore their territories during his internment. He was so convincing that the government even supplied him with funds to carry out his work.

Malinowski stayed in Australia for six years, and made three extensive field trips, one to Mailu (1915) and two to the Trobriand Islands (1915–1916 and 1917–1918). The field work in Australia was the crucial experience for Malinowski's career. He lived like a native, and with the natives experienced directly the demands and comforts of their culture. His celebrated intolerance toward a relatively academic anthropology (based on historical reconstruction, distribution studies, and other impersonal investigations), was rooted in this experience....

*T*he early background for Malinowski's work was broad and varied. His training as a chemist served as an introduction to the disciplines of physical science, and he never got over an uneasiness about the multiple assumptions and secondary inferences so common in the social sciences. His early anthropological readings (especially the works of Frazer), while they must have offended his sense of rigor, stimulated in him an enthusiasm for anthropology. At London he became acquainted with such men as Frazer, Westermarck, C. S. Seligman, W. H. R. Rivers, Haddon, Prince Kropotkin, Havelock

Ellis, Hobhouse, and Marett. Of these, he was especially influenced and stimulated by Westermarck, Seligman, Frazer, Rivers, and Haddon....

Malinowski insisted on relegating the methods of evolutionary anthropology to a minor role in the analysis of culture. Cultural processes are subject to laws, but the laws are to be found "in the function of the real elements of culture," not in the "survivals" upon which the evolutionists reconstruct the stages and processes of culture.

This departure from evolutionary theory was not new with Malinowski. Functionalism had become popular in many fields by Malinowski's time and was influencing work in science, government, philosophy, and the arts. Malinowski himself traces the functional view of culture as far back as Bastian and cites many names and "schools" as having contributed to the view. Among those he mentions are Tylor, Robertson Smith, Wundt, Frazer, Westermarck, Marett, Boas, Wissler, Kroeber, Lowie, Radin, Sapir, Benedict, and the French sociologists. With himself, however, he names only the following as having applied the functional method systematically and exclusively in ethnological field work: W. Hoernle, Radcliffe-Brown, and R. Thurnwald. Lowie names Bachofen, Fustel de Coulanges, and Boas as having made significant contributions to the study of cultures in their "intertwined state" and goes on to state that "probably everywhere scholars have followed the practice intuitively." This, however, is a little like saying that in formulating the law of gravity, Newton only made explicit what everyone knew "intuitively." Somewhat more generous is Lowie's conclusion, that, while others had preached or practiced the "faith of functionalism," Malinowski did both.

However indebted he may have been to others for his functionalism, Malinowski was certainly the one who made the integrated study of culture a popular method in anthropology. The unusual length of time he spent in the Trobriand Islands, living as a Trobriand, convinced him that a culture can be understood only by an intimate knowledge of how the individual experiences his cultural environment.

Malinowski's methodology was based on the conviction that there exist "scientific laws of culture." It is essential in a scientific theory that its assumptions be made explicit and its refutation made easy by conceivable testing and analysis. Malinowski always attempted to state his theories so that they conformed to this rule.

Although he defined anthropology as the "comparative science of cultures," Malinowski was often critical of the use made of the comparative method by the evolutionary anthropologists. He was especially critical of the concept of survival, which played such a crucial part in evolutionary reconstruction. He could not accept the implication that an institution can outlive its function and pointed out that so-called survivals disappear as we learn more about a society and the specific cultural context of a given institution. In a typical polemic Malinowski suggests how "survivals" can be misleading: "Marriage in the past did not consist merely in the eating together of fish and hard-boiled eggs, nor in the tossing of rice, nor yet in the wagging of rods or green trees. There is no reason therefore, to assume that because in some tribes the marriage act consists in a mimic capture, capture in dead earnest was the origin of marriage."

Malinowski shared Tylor's concern that anthropology not become preoccupied with "savage exoticisms" and urged that anthropology emerge from its "Herodotage" (coined from Herodotus) and "anecdotage." But, contrary to Tylor, it was the reliance on survivals that Malinowski feared would help perpetuate a distorted view of primitive societies. Society, for Malinowski, consisted of a body of institutions related to the current adaptive needs of man, and it is the study of these institutions—economic and political systems, education, law, religion, science, family organization—and the individual's relationship to them that must take precedence over historical reconstruction, whether in the hands of the evolutionists or the diffusionists.

While admitting that careful, sober, and limited evolutionary reconstructions and diffusionist hypotheses could be profitable, if secondary, enterprises, Malinowski made no such allowance for so-called "tribal-genius" studies. He criticized Boas and his students, such as Ruth Benedict, for fostering a concept of culture which was so general and vague as to defy any kind of scientific evaluation. Malinowski was uncompromising in his attack on this approach:

"I have again and again indicated that it is illegitimate to cover our inability to deal with certain facts by such mystic labels as the 'genius of culture,' or to describe this 'genius' as Appollonian, Dionysiac, megalomaniac, or hysterical." And in another place: "We might feel that it would be best to paint the warlike Masai in exaggerated colors in order to bring out the martial, boisterous, licentious 'genius' of the culture."

Malinowski's criticism of the evolutionists, diffusionists, patternists, and others, must be seen against the background of his intense crusade for an individual functionalism in anthropology. Malinowski was an "advocate"; he exaggerated the weaknesses of opposing schools and overlooked or minimized their contributions. It would be better, therefore, to turn to his own affirmative views, rather than to dwell, as some have, upon his excessive and sometimes unfair criticism of competing schools of thought.

Malinowski has defined in many places the functional method in anthropology. One of the clearest general statements is the following: "The functional view of culture lays down the principle that in every type of civilisation, every custom, material object, idea and belief fulfills some vital function, has some task to accomplish, represents an indispensable part within a working whole." The functionalist, according to Malinowski, is concerned primarily with the present workings of human culture, not with "ambitious but questionable reconstructions of the past." Cultural laws—the relations that exist between individual needs and social institutions—can be discovered only through a comparative study of cultures where the individual is seen in his day-to-day adaptations, both physical and mental. Malinowski's creed and advice was, "never to forget the living, palpitating flesh and blood organism of man which remains somewhere at the heart of every institution." The history of an institution, its form and distribution, its evolution and diffusion—all these problems are of secondary importance. The important questions are, How does an institution function *now*? How does it satisfy individual and cultural needs in the given society, and How is it related to other institutions?

Malinowski defines functionalism more specifically as "the theory of transformation of organic-that is, individual—needs into derived cultural necessities and imperatives. Society, by the collective wielding of the conditioning apparatus, molds the individual into a cultural personality."

The human individual has certain basic, physiological needs which require organized, collective responses from the members of a society. These include the need for food, shelter, safety, relaxation, movement, growth, and reproduction. The organized responses to these "basic imperatives"—the commissariat for nutrition; shelter and dress for bodily comfort; protective devices and organizations for safety; marriage and the family for reproduction-represent another, derived order of conditions which must be dealt with by the members of society. The acquisition of food, for example, requires a more or less complicated economic system where the production, processing, exchange, and distribution of food is regulated by certain social rules; proper shelter requires co-operative endeavor and communal consent regarding production, maintenance, and style; mating and parenthood must be regulated by social rules which define the rights and obligations of the persons involved to each other and to the other members of the community, and so on. Thus the great institutions of society—economic, political, legal, educational, and social—are seen by Malinowski as responses to the problems of adaptation posed by the more or less direct collective responses to the basic, physiological needs of man.

Then there is a third order of imperatives, the "integrative" or "synthetic imperatives," which result in the creation of systems of science, magic, myth, religion, and art. These, too, can be traced, although less directly, to man's organic needs. Of all living creatures man alone can accumulate experiences, reflect on them, and use them to foretell the future. These capacities make man the tragic hero that he is; they reveal new possibilities and opportunities with each generation, but they also reveal man's relative impotence and leave him striving for more than he can rationally expect to receive. Systems of knowledge, such as *science*, serve to organize and integrate human activities, so that, by the wise use of past experience, the present and the future may be made to better serve the needs of man. The gaps in man's knowledge and power create anxiety and hesitation, and here *magic* can be employed as a substitute for rational systems and give man the courage to act, even without perfect knowledge. *Myth* enhances social tradition by endowing it with awesome and glorified beginnings and thus promotes, sustains, and integrates appropriate social behavior. *Religion* promotes individual security and social cohesion by sanctifying human life and making public (by dogma and ritual) the social contracts of co-operative existence. Malinowski sees *art* as satisfying the "craving of the human organism for combinations of blended sense impressions," whether in the rhythms of bodily movement or in the blending of tones, colors, and forms.

Malinowski regarded his functionalism as differing from other social theories in its emphasis on basic bodily needs. The intellectual, emotional, and aesthetic aspects of man's behavior—the "higher side" of man's activities and the primary concern of most students—must also be seen as rooted in man's physiological needs.

Social or cultural commands, whether in the form of legal or moral codes, religious rites, economic regulation, customs, or aesthetic taste, are the reinterpretations of organic drives and impulses. They must so shape individual motives that the individual unconsciously behaves in a manner which satisfies the conditions of cultural survival and harmony. Malinowski states here (contrary to Frazer), that "Sociological aims are never present in the minds of natives, and tribal legislation on a large scale could never have occurred." It is the job of the anthropologist to discover the specific functions of the elements of a culture within the integrated scheme as outlined above. Malinowski's celebrated field work was devoted to that end. For a caricature of earlier authorities on primitive peoples Malinowski cites the response of one of them to a question about the manners and customs of certain natives: "Customs none, manners beastly." Although Malinowski's work does not in any way represent the first advance beyond the approach ridiculed here, he was the first worker to explicate and publicize the methods for investigating a primitive community in the role of a participant, with one's own cultural values left behind, in so far as that is possible. The goal of all field work, according to Malinowski, is "to grasp the native's point of view, his relation to life, to realize *his* vision of *his* world"; or, as he often put it, "to get inside the native's skin." While it is necessary to banish all preconceived ideas about how a culture must or should function, it is just as necessary that the worker have some positive theoretical framework with which to "foreshadow" the problems. For Malinowski, this was functionalism, as outlined above. Malinowski breaks scientific field work down into three areas:

1. *The organization of the tribe, and the anatomy of its culture* must be recorded in firm, clear outline. The method of *concrete, statistical documentation* is the means through which such an outline has to be given.

2. *Within this frame, the imponderabilia of actual life*, and the *type of behavior* have to be filled in. They have to be collected through minute, detailed observations, in the form of some sort of ethnographic diary, made possible by close contact with native life.

3. A collection of ethnographic statements, characteristic narratives, typical utterances, items of folklore and magical formulae has to be given as a *corpus inscriptionum*, as documents of native mentality.

These three categories correspond, in Malinowski's functional scheme, to (1) the routine prescribed by custom and tradition, (2) the manner in which it is carried out, and (3) the commentary to the routine, as contained in the native's mind. Malinowski insisted upon "statistic documentation by concrete evidence" as the method for acquiring this information about a people, but not through the procedure of the fixed interview and the native interpreter. To get an integrated picture a community worker must learn the language, live with the people, share their food and customs, and learn, as far as possible, to feel and think as they do.

This is the doctrine of the "participant observer." A field trip for Malinowski had to be a profound personal experience; from what we know of his personality, it could not have been anything else. For Malinowski there was an intense personal satisfaction in studying a foreign culture which transcended the mere satisfaction of scientific curiosity. He states: "To study the institutions, customs, and codes or to study the behavior and mentality without the subjective desire of feeling by what these people live, of realising the substance of their happiness—is, in my opinion, to miss the greatest reward which can hope to obtain from the study of man."[2]

The justification of this method does not lie in its personal satisfaction to the observer, it lies in the fact that it is the only way to central insights about a people. Malinowski claims, for example, that he discovered the function of magic when, as a frightened participant in a hurricane in Melanesia, he observed the work of a magician ordering the hurricane to stop and assuring the natives that no harm could come to the village: "I realized then and there what the real function of magic is. On the psychological side it leads to a mental integration, to that optimism and confidence in the face of danger which has won to man many a battle with nature or with his human foes. Socially, magic, by giving leadership to one man, establishes organization at a time when organized and effective action is of supreme importance."

More persuasive, however, than this personal testimonial, are Malinowski's examples of how, and how not, to get information. Do not, he urges, ask a native, "How do you treat and punish a criminal?...a real case indeed will start the natives on a wave of discussion, evoke expressions of indignation, show them taking sides—all of which will probably contain a wealth of definite views, of moral censures, as well as reveal the social mechanism set in motion by the crime committed." Malinowski gives some amusing descriptions of himself at work with this method: "... as they knew that I would thrust my nose into everything, even where a well mannered native would not dream of intruding, they finished by regarding me as part and parcel of their life, a necessary evil or nuisance, mitigated by donations of tobacco."

Although it is probably fair to describe Malinowski's method, as Kluckhohn has, as "the well-documented anecdote set firmly in a ramified context," it would be a mistake to attribute to him a lack of real scientific aims. He was convinced that cultural laws existed and that it was the primary job of the anthropologist to discover them. The job demanded more than a sensitive, intuitive participant; it demanded the patient and thorough collection and recording of vast amounts of ethnological detail, all according to a system dictated by theoretical considerations. Malinowski's reports and books, with all their maps, charts, photographs, illustrations, and case histories, still do not indicate the mass of material on which they were constructed. Much of this material has never been published.

Malinowski's serious field work was limited to the Trobriand Islands which he studied more or less intensively for six years. Although criticized as being an "ethnographic provincial" (by Lowie) and as having only a superficial knowledge of other ethnological data (by Kluckhohn), the field methods Malinowski practiced and publicized have a universal value and have been widely adopted, largely through his influence.

Before discussing Malinowski's specific ideas and theories regarding religion, magic, myth, and the family, reference should be made again to his general theory of culture.

To promote a functional analysis of society Malinowski found it necessary to define and distinguish the various elements in society. While it is true, as noted above, that other workers had, to one degree or another, employed a functional approach in their studies, Malinowski was the first anthropologist to formulate consciously and explicitly a theoretical basis for functional anthropology.

He defines *culture* as that "instrumental reality which has come into existence to satisfy the needs of man in a manner far surpassing any direct adaptation to the environment." A culture can be analyzed into *institutions*, which are defined as "a group of people united in a common task or tasks, bound to a determined portion of the environment, wielding together some technical apparatus, and obeying a body of rules." It is only by studying institutions that the worker gets a concrete picture of the social organization within a culture. Institutions are the structural units of culture. Institutions—not traits, forms, ideas, or adventitious complexes of these elements—are what diffuse and evolve, while maintaining a basic integrity. They exist to satisfy, directly or indirectly, the biological needs of man and must be studied with that central idea in mind.

Malinowski's functional approach to cultural studies marked a formal departure from the anatomical approach of many earlier anthropologists. By focusing attention on the actual behavior of the members of a community, Malinowski's institutional method resulted in a more integrated description and analysis of society. Instead, for example, of merely juxtaposing the data on dwelling construction and the data on family life, the two are considered together in the light of the functional relations which exist between them.

The key institution by which the instinctive drives of the individual are modified so as to satisfy the conditions of community survival is the family. The family, for Malinowski, is a kind of placenta through which the biological individual acquires the accumulated products of culture and is molded into a social individual. Malinowski was convinced that monogamous marriage provides the best foundation for the crucial functions of the family. It permits the most satisfactory form of sexual selection and fosters the kind of personal attachments by which the biological bonds of the family, especially between parent and child, are gradually transformed into social ties. "Love relations in the family," says Malinowski, "serve as prototypes and also as a nucleus for the loyalties of clanship, of neighborly feeling and of tribal citizenship." He cites authorities from anthropology and psychoanalysis in support of this view, including Lowie, Kroeber, Radcliffe-Brown, Freud, and Flügel. Recognition of this important function of the family was not, of course, new with these men; Darwin, in particular, had shown a very keen appreciation of the intermediary function of the family....

Although magic and religion are less directly related to biological needs than other social institutions, they are the "very foundations of culture," says Malinowski. Religion, especially, was seen by him as a basic integrative force in society.

The urgency with which the individual denies his mortality and strives to perpetuate personal attachments beyond earthly life has its origin, according to Malinowski, in the culturally determined "human sentiments." These sentiments, or emotions, are the structural elements of social cohesion, and must be fostered and maintained by social institutions. Religion, by giving supernatural and public sanction to the beliefs, attitudes, and values which comprise a social morality and make social cohesion possible, affirms and reinforces the human sentiments which morality requires.

Religion, therefore, does not arise out of illusion, speculation, or misapprehension, but as a response to the needs of cultural survival. It is an integrative institution which conditions and compensates men for the individual sacrifices required by social existence.

Malinowski contradicted his idol, Sir James Frazer, on the function of magic in society. Magic does not represent primitive science, as Frazer believed, but, on the contrary, it represents the recognition by people that human art and knowledge have definite limits. Thus, as Malinowski says, "magic and practical art are entirely independent and never fuse." It is when crucial events appear completely beyond human control and influence that magic is called upon to provide illusory gratifications. The practice of magic is a substitute activity which, in the absence of any realistic solution to vital problems, gives at least psychological support to the individual and helps to prevent submission or disintegration. Its value and validity, then, is purely subjective, but it satisfies a real biological need. As mentioned earlier, magic can also serve to organize a community in the face of a crisis by virtue of investing one or a few men with authority and leadership.

For Malinowski, magic and religion take their places alongside of rational knowledge as the foundations of culture: "Knowledge, magic and religion are the highest, the most derived imperatives of human culture.... Magic and to a much higher degree religion are the indispensable moral forces in every human culture. Grown, as they are, out of the necessity to remove internal conflict in the individual and to organize the community, they become the essential factors of spiritual and social integration. They deal with problems which affect all members of the community alike. They lead to actions on which depends the welfare of one and all. Religion and to a lesser degree magic thus became the very foundations of culture."

It is not easy to estimate Malinowski's importance in anthropology. He has been such a controversial figure as a personality that most commentators are inclined, or forced, to take a "for" or "against" position regarding his contributions. Generally speaking, his ethnological reports and his pioneer work in field methods and techniques have been acclaimed by almost all workers as belonging among the greatest contributions to cultural anthropology. But regarding his theoretical conceptions there is less agreement.

In this country Lowie and Kluckhohn have been Malinowski's chief detractors. Of these, Lowie is the more severe. He compares Malinowski with Boas on several counts and finds that Boas either anticipated Malinowski or surpassed him in insight. The only "positive achievement" that Lowie singles out is Malinowski's use of psychoanalytic concepts in his ethnographic work. Even in the area of field techniques, where few contest Malinowski's importance and priority, Lowie simply observes that his techniques "conformed to Boas' standards." Rising to a passion unmatched in the rest of his book (*History of Ethnological Theory*, 1937), Lowie writes: "In Messianic mood Malinowski is forever engaged in two favorite pastimes. Either he is battering down wide open doors or he is petulantly deriding work that does not personally attract him." And Lowie goes on: "Malinowski thumbs his nose at technology, flaunts distribution studies, sneers at reconstruction of the past... In short, Malinowski's functionalism is avowedly anti-distributional, antihistorical, and treats each culture as a closed system except insofar as its elements correspond to vital biological urges." Such an extreme condemnation by a responsible and conservative commentator must be partly attributed to Malinowski's provocative personality. Lowie himself softens his criticism by adding that "Malinowski's practice fortunately does not bear out the negative excrescences of his principle."

Kluckhohn credits Malinowski with great literary skill and the ability to dramatize field work. He also approves of Malinowski's contributions to our knowledge of the family, religion, economics, and law. Kluckhohn's chief criticism is of Malinowski's lack of "theoretical profundities." Malinowski is not subtle enough for Kluckhohn. He complains that Malinowski has "no flair for the intricate, tortuous [and precious] subtleties," and that he is only an integrator, "on a rather superficial level."

Such a general criticism is hard to evaluate. Physicists before Newton were too involved with the "subtleties" of moving objects on earth to look at the sky and bring all moving bodies under one general, unsubtle, law. One must look at Malinowski's work for himself and decide whether or not his "integrations" are superficial.

Herskovits agrees with Lowie that Malinowski's major contribution was the extension and modification of Freud's work in its application to cultural data. For his field work, Herskovits credits Malinowski with making explicit, if not inventing, field methods and procedures which facilitated a scientific treatment of anthropological data. And for his doctrine of the "participant observer," he credits Malinowski with "a real departure from the usage of many earlier students of culture...." On the theoretical side, Herskovits singles out Malinowski's understanding of the family as "a link between instinctive endowment and the acquisition of cultural inheritance," as a major insight.

Peter Murdock, whose relations with Malinowski were sometimes stormy, ranks him with Morgan, Tylor, and Boas in anthropology, and considers him to be one of the great innovators in the "behavioral sciences of man," standing with Adam Smith, Marx, Sumner, Freud, and Pavlov. He credits Malinowski with the establishment, in anthropology, of the concept of social institutions, which are the collective responses to basic human needs.

Perhaps one of the reasons that there is such a diversity of opinion among anthropologists regarding Malinowski's work is that he attempted to utilize ideas from other fields, particularly sociology and psychology. To many of the avowed specialists in the social sciences, "eclectic" is a bad word, and Malinowski respected no territorial limits in his study of man and society. If Malinowski's work is important, it is largely due to the use he made of sociological and psychological insights and techniques.

Malinowski's reputation and influence have been greater in England than in the United States. In England he stands with Radcliffe-Brown as the standard bearer of functionalism in anthropology. His empirical approach and untidy theoretical formulations have caused students to look to his work for field techniques and inspiration, but more to Radcliffe-Brown's work for a defensible theory of functionalism.

Malinowski's position in the history of anthropology has not been decided. Ultimately, it will depend on what course anthropology will take as a scientific discipline in the field of human behavior. If anthropology persists in its preoccupation with "precious subtleties" and in its suspicion of the "integrator," then Malinowski will become a forgotten hero. If, however, there should be a rebirth of the conviction that anthropology can provide the framework and perspective for an integrated study of man in his fight for survival and self-realization, then Malinowski will be listed as a great anthropologist. His passionate interest and involvement in the workaday

drama of human life kept him always in touch with the basic problems of man's cooperative endeavors to survive and to get some pleasure out of life.

Malinowski died with important work still to do, and his untimely death was a great loss to the social sciences and to society. He was intensely devoted to anthropology, and behind this devotion was a passionate sympathy for the human individual.

Notes

1. Cracow, a free city republic, was Incorporated into the Austrian Empire in 1848.
2. Malinowski was known as "The Man of Songs" to the Trobriand Islanders, a simple but convicing testimony to his successful identification with the natives.

Paradigms Refound: The Structure of Anthropological Revolutions

Paul Bohannan, Mari Womack, and Karen Saenz

In traditional cultures, most of a person's relationships are kin-based. In the modern world, even though family ties are important, especially in childhood, most of our adult relationships are determined by the routes we take in navigating through a larger and more impersonal social system. In other words, today, we position ourselves in society in relation to our educational and work experience, personal aptitudes, being in the right place at the right time, and so on, and our work relationships are not simultaneously our kinship relationships.

In the following article, the authors draw parallels between kin-based institutions found in traditional cultures and the "fictive" (made up) kin groups which characterize modern academic anthropology. If an anthropology department in a major university can be thought of as a "family," it is more like the make-shift family typical of modern America, known as the *kindred*. It exists only long enough for the individual to develop into a full-fledged anthropologist, ready to go off and establish a new family somewhere else, unlike the *lineage*, which is intergenerational and timeless. Whereas in a traditional society, it would be in one's self interest to honor one's ancestors—given the many benefits to being part of an extended family—in anthropology today, one's loyalties are much more opportunistic and so contingent, in fact, that there is even the temptation to "kill" one's ancestors and deny any lineal connection at all. This is most likely to occur, the authors contend, when an individual experiences a paradigm shift—seeing data with a new perspective or theory.

Paul Bohannan (b. 1920) is best known for his work among the Tiv of central Nigeria. He was a Rhodes Scholar at Oxford University, where he received his Ph.D. in 1951. He served there as a lecturer in social anthropology, 1951–56. He did postgraduate study at the Chicago Institute for Psychoanalysis and taught anthropology at Princeton University.

Some of Paul Bohannan's most recent publications have been *We, the Alien: An Introduction to Cultural Anthropology* (1992) *How Culture Works* (1995), and *Asking and Listening: Ethnography as Personal Adaptation* (1998).

Mari Womack received her Ph.D. in Anthropology at UCLA and has worked as a print and radio journalist, conducting what she calls *ethnography journalism*. While keeping her hand in teaching, she is also a research scholar at the UCLA Center for the Study of Women. Dr. Womack is currently working on two books: *The Artful Body, Reflections on the Human Form* and *Medical Anthropology, Models of Health and Healing*.

Key Concept: paradigm shift

*T*he Hopi, indigenous people of the U.S. Southwest, say: "This has happened before; it will come round again." The same might be said of anthropological theory. Paul Bohannan notes that a long career in anthropology allows one to witness a virtual parade of paradigms that cross and recross the anthropological stage. "As I write,… literary criticism is having considerable impact on cultural anthropology—again. My problem with that is not that I consider it wrong, but that I know it to be old hat" (1998:415). Bohannan remembers when literary critics like F. R. Leavis and William Empson had

a profound impact on social anthropology. When you remember that, it is hard to think that the same ideas, under new authorship, with more recent publication dates, championing a new set of philosophers, are an original advance.

The difference between the Hopi concept of the return of the ancestors and the parade of ancestral paradigms across the anthropological stage is significant. The Hopi believe that when loved ones die, their last breath floats upward to become a cloud, a significant contribution in a land where rain is scarce, and every drop of moisture is cherished. The ancestors are remembered when the clouds return, bringing much-needed rain for growing crops. The Hopi say: "It will come round again." Anthropologists say: "Our ancestors were blind and wrong; we now know better." That is, anthropologists kill their ancestors, then sneak the essential ideas back in, with new names.

Rediscovery of overtly discarded models, however, is common. Leslie White (1949), for example, drew on the first accepted, then rejected, models of Lewis H. Morgan and E. B. Tylor to develop his apparently radical model of cultural evolution based on the use of technology for conversion of energy. It is significant that White acknowledged his ancestral debts. White's model was rejected in turn by many of his contemporaries, although his cultural evolutionary model provides the implicit and often unacknowledged foundation for more recent economic models, including the cultural materialism of Marvin Harris or the idea (pretty generally accepted at the moment) that knowing subsistence patterns is essential to understanding other aspects of social organization.

There is a decidedly Western bias against rehabilitating previously rejected paradigms in the same field. For example, Bronislaw Malinowski's angst while in the field, recorded in his diary, is one familiar to every anthropologist who conducts fieldwork. Malinowski writes: "Feeling of absurdity less intense. Strong impression that my information about fishing is very inadequate" (1967:145). And a few days later: "Sitting in the dinghy I enjoyed being alone. Then a dominant feeling of ethnographic disappointment came back" (1967:149). Like Malinowski, we have all asked ourselves whether the ethnographic enterprise we have undertaken is really worth the effort we have put into it. Only now we call it postmodernism or the "new ethnography." Why is it so difficult for us to acknowledge that the sense of "ethnographic disappointment" we now experience was also experienced by our anthropological ancestors almost a hundred years ago? This "ethnographic disappointment" is neither new nor post-modern. It is a condition of conducting fieldwork, often alone, frustrated, and insecure.

It is not, however, the rehabilitation of previously rejected theories that strikes the eye here; it is the fact that the names of ancestral scholars are not rehabilitated along with their theories. Recognizing the contribution of others to our work does not detract from the significance of our own contribution. In fact, it makes us appear more scholarly. The process of ancestor killing is not based in logic; rather, it is embedded in the social and conceptual context of constructing new analytical models.

In his pivotal book *The Structure of Scientific Revolutions*, Thomas Kuhn deals with one conceptual basis for the killing of ancestors:

> at times of revolution, when the normal-scientific tradition changes, the scientist's perception of his environment must be reeducated—in some familiar situations he must learn to see a new gestalt. After he has done so the world of his research will seem, here and there, incommensurable with

the one he had inhabited before. That is another reason why schools guided by different paradigms are always slightly at cross-purposes (1970:112).

Kuhn's view of the adoption and rejection of scientific paradigms sounds remarkably like religious conversion, and Kuhn does not dispute this. In fact, he describes the initial period of questioning an established paradigm as a time when scientists "may begin to lose faith" but "do not renounce the paradigm that has led them into crisis" (1970:77). Kuhn notes that beginning to doubt an accepted paradigm brings angst:

> Because it demands large-scale paradigm destruction and major shifts in the problems and techniques of normal science, the emergence of new theories is generally preceded by a period of pronounced professional insecurity. As one might expect, that insecurity is generated by the persistent failure of the puzzles of normal science to come out as they should. Failure of existing rules is the prelude to a search for new ones (1970:67–68).

Kuhn frames his model of scientific revolutions primarily in intellectualist terms. However, there is also a strong political and economic basis for maintenance and rejection of paradigms. Academic communities that share a paradigm also control a great deal of political power in terms of ensuring that their shared paradigm is passed on to new generations of students. This political power is reinforced economically through control over admissions to universities, granting of Ph.D.s, hiring, granting of tenure, and awarding of research grants, as well as control over publications and literature reviews. Competing paradigms challenge a type of control that can become almost monopolistic. Discrediting competing paradigms allows a scholarly lineage to maintain control over important political and economic empires. Kuhn writes: "The very existence of science depends upon vesting the power to choose between paradigms in the members of a special kind of community" (1970:167). He adds: "A paradigm is what the members of a scientific community share, *and*, conversely, the members of a scientific community consist of men who share a paradigm" (1970:176). The "professional insecurity" described by Kuhn is reflected in the reluctance of young scholars trying to make a name for themselves to become identified with previously discredited models for fear of making themselves appear naive or unsophisticated.

At the same time, scholars can make a name for themselves by attacking dominant elders. An example in anthropology is Derek Freeman (1983), whose most significant contribution to the discipline consists of repudiating Margaret Mead's work in Samoa. The discrepancy between Freeman's and Mead's analysis of Samoan socialization and adolescent behavior is based in their differing paradigmatic stances (Shankman 1996), in that Freeman favored biological explanations for behavior whereas Mead asserted the primacy of cultural factors. However, Freeman and Mead also studied different villages and occupied different social statuses that may have given them differing aspects of data on the behavior of adolescent females (Womack 1998:128–129). Freeman was addressed by the title *manaia*, signifying his leadership within a group of untitled, unmarried men. As a young woman, Mead was a frequent companion of unmarried females. Freeman, however, framed his debate with Mead as a means of discrediting "an anthropological myth," thus reinforcing the cultural construct that biologically based paradigms are incompatible with culturally based paradigms.

Another example is Kenneth Good, whose career is based largely on attacking Napoleon Chagnon's work among the Yanomamo and on the publicity generated when Good married a Yanomamo woman. Good's book on the subject is described by the publisher as "The fascinating adventure of an American among the Yanomama— a Stone Age people of the Amazon rain forest—and one of the most remarkable love stories of our time" (1991).[1] Good's report of his "adventure" among the Yanomamo emphasizes the killing of his anthropological ancestor rather than the advancement of a new or competing paradigm.

Though it is difficult to topple reigning anthropological monarchs, doing so can provide a young anthropologist with a secure career foothold. Building a career (or "making a name") in academic anthropology in the United States is essentially a two-step process: First, the would-be careerist must ritually kill his or her intellectual ancestors; and, second, he or she must forge alliances with powerful contemporaries. Ideally, both steps must be enacted publicly in front of an audience of professional colleagues or peers. Walter Goldschmidt speaks of the first step, in Oedipal terms, as the "killing of the father" (1980, personal communication).

Is it always necessary, however, to "kill the father" in every system of kinship reckoning? Why do anthropological revolutions so often combine ancestor killing (refuting our own intellectual traditions) with borrowing from other traditions (or intellectual lineages)? Some clues may be found in the time-honored anthropological study of kinship, even though some anthropologists feel it is time to kill off this venerable branch of the family altogether.

As anthropologists have long been aware, the dynamics of kinship cannot be divorced, so to speak, from the cultural context in which they occur. Bohannan writes of his tutelage under E. E. Evans-Pritchard at Oxford in the African idiom, "He is my father and my mother" (1997: 123). In the Tiv kinship model, within which context Bohannan conducted his fieldwork, sons do not kill their fathers and mothers and, in fact, Bohannan speaks of his relationship with Evans-Pritchard in terms of filial piety (1997:123).

Malinowski (1927) rejected the idea that father-killing is a primal Oedipal urge rooted in a boy's desire to displace his father and possess his mother sexually. Instead, he said, competitive feelings toward the father are the product of patrilineal forms of inheritance, in which a man acquires his own place in society by displacing his father. Ironically, it was Malinowski who set the standard for father-killing in anthropology by turning against Sir James Frazer, the man who inspired him to become an anthropologist in the first place. Malinowski ridiculed Frazer's work, *The Golden Bough*, the very book that inspired him to enter the field of anthropology, calling its association of the succession of kings with the worship of trees "the vegetable hypothesis."

In yet another ironic twist to this primal episode in the development of anthropology, Frazer dealt in *The Golden Bough* (1890) with what he considered the widespread practice of killing kings when their powers began to fail, a ritual practice that often included sexual cohabitation with the king's wives by the successor or a mock king. Malinowski "killed" Frazer professionally by ridiculing his work, embraced Frazer's young bride Anthropology, and inherited his academic "crown" from Frazer, who gave the inaugural address when Malinowski was installed as the holder of the first chair in anthropology at the London School of Economics.

Malinowski was himself murderously assaulted by other social anthropologists, who preferred Radcliffe-Brown's "more sophisticated terminology and theoretical approach" (Lewis 1985:55) to Malinowski's "earthy, materialist view of man's motives" (Lewis 1985:53). I. M. Lewis writes: "Whereas Malinowski had invoked the aid of reductionist principles borrowed from biology, and concentrated on man's *cultural* adaptation, Radcliffe-Brown re-asserted the *social* basis of all customs and institutions" (1985: 55–56). Adam Kuper writes: "For many of Malinowski's contemporaries his theoretical naiveté was apparent from the first, and his crude utilitarianism could arouse derision" (1983:34). Kuper adds: "[Meyer] Fortes has pointed out that Malinowski was always promising a book on Trobriand kinship, and he suggests that the book was never written precisely because Malinowski could not conceive of a 'kinship system.' But so far as Malinowski was concerned, *The Sexual Life of Savages* was a book on Trobriand kinship" (1983:28).

Anthropological kinship studies are themselves currently in danger of extinction by ancestor-killing within the discipline even though, across time and across theoretical boundaries, kinship has long held a privileged place in anthropology. It has been a focus of many of our discipline's most revered ancestors, including Evans-Pritchard (1951). Contemporary scholars still rely on Lewis Henry's (1870) model of consanguinity (descent) and affinity (marriage). For example, Womack (1993) uses this model to explain the intricacies of the troubled relationship between England's Prince Charles and Princess Diana, a dynamic that can only be understood in terms of the patrilineal descent system for inheritance of the throne combined with marriage rules that prescribe endogamy for religion and social class.

The concepts of consanguinity and affinity are also useful in explaining the phenomenon of ancestor-killing in anthropology. Kuhn takes an intellectualist perspective on the tendency of scientists to vigorously reject earlier paradigms, noting that "science" is inextricably allied with "progress." It is also instructive to note that science is itself a cultural construct, developed in the Western intellectualist tradition. Scientists, too, are embedded in their genealogies. As in all kinship systems, scientists are inclined to ally themselves with relatives who can provide them with the greatest source of benefit and ignore kinship ties that might bring upon them ignominy or reduction of social status.

In particular, the American scientific community is characterized by bilateral inheritance and neolocal residence. In other words, scientists feel it is their right to borrow from whatever discipline advances their status (the rich relative syndrome associated with bilateral inheritance), while maintaining the right to cut ties of descent—which also imply obligations—in favor of establishing an entirely new area of expertise, and restricting access to resources to a small and tightly controlled reproductive unit. This shifts the emphasis from consanguineal ties to affinal ties. It also confers the advantages of bilateral inheritance and neolocal residence, which include mobility, flexibility, and the ability to expand or contract kinship bonds as advantage requires.

There are disadvantages to this system of reckoning kinship, however. One must surrender the privileges associated with unilineal or ambilineal inheritance and the extended family. Just as we are not obligated to come to the defense of anyone but our spouses and offspring, we cannot call on the resources of anyone but our spouses and offspring. We are not obligated to other lineage members, but in turn, they are not obligated to us. We claim the right to invest our resources in our offspring; our ancestors claim the right to disinherit us. We surrender the cooperative advantages of reinforcing alliances within the lineage in favor of the competitive advantages of the nuclear family.

By way of contrast, the Chinese system of ancestor reverence, with descent traced through patrilineal clans, emphasizes responsibility to the descent group. This is based on the view that an individual isolated from others cannot fulfill his or her human potential, and this philosophy is expressed formally in the "five relationships": father-son, older brother-younger brother, husband-wife, ruler-subject, and friend-friend. Of these, only the fifth relationship—friend-friend—is based on equality. In all the other cases, the position on the left side is one of responsibility, the position on the right side is one of respect and obedience. Womack writes:

Relationships within the family continue after death in a system of ritual observance that unites land ownership, the patrilineal inheritance system, and clan membership. The oldest son is responsible for "feeding" his parents even after they are dead by maintaining an ancestral altar in the family home and by ritual observances at the ancestral graveyard, which is expected to occupy the most auspicious position on the land (1998:213).

On the other hand, failure to respect and care for the ancestors brings misfortune and dishonor to the entire family. The spirits of the dead who have no one to feed them or who are neglected by their descendants must go "hungry" in the spirit world. These "hungry ghosts" retaliate by preying upon the unwary and bringing misfortune to the entire community. It is the responsibility of the community to hold a hungry ghost festival, in which people who are living provide food and paper money for the spirits of the dead who do not have family to take care of them. Womack writes: "Ancestor reverence reinforces the responsibility of the individual to the family and extends that responsibility to the community as a whole in the practice of feeding hungry ghosts" (1998:213). Rituals associated with ancestor reverence reinforce the solidarity of the lineage and bind lineage members to the land, whereas hungry ghost festivals emphasize responsibilities of individuals to the community as a whole.

The Chinese system of ancestor reverence is well-suited to an agricultural society, where land ownership is essential to survival and the labor of every family member is necessary to work the land. The scientific community, in contrast, is a product of secular segmentation, and its growth has been spurred by European colonialism and by the increasing dominance of industrialization. Industrialization is a system in which land is a resource suitable primarily for exploitation and the ideal of individual entrepreneurship is actively promoted. This is consonant with the ideology that "ancestors" are in fact "ghosts." They confer no benefits and they stick around only because they have some grievance against the living. Of course, individual entrepreneurship is a luxury for the elite and is dependent upon an abundant supply of workers who can be exploited.

In anthropology, this elitism results in a system in which an upwardly mobile individual is expected to literally abandon the family of biological origin and strike out on his or her own, exploring new territory and collecting new data. The fledgling anthropologist does not form alliances by marrying into a closely related kin group. Instead, the rite of passage that conducts the anthropologists from adolescence to maturity rests on adoption into the group being studied, in effect forming a fictive kin relationship. This amalgamation with a new lineage is not sufficient for attaining high professional status, however. The ambitious anthropologist must also adopt a paradigm advocated by powerful elders in one of the currently accepted anthropological lineages. Gaining the protection of a powerful head of an accepted lineage is sufficient for survival—getting a Ph.D., tenure, and publications—but it is not sufficient for gaining high status within the discipline. Paying homage to one's anthropological ancestors is not enough; one must also supplant the powerful lineage head, either by killing him or her or through "neolocal residence," that is, by establishing a new lineage based on a newly generated or newly defined paradigm. Bohannan notes: "We all know that history has to be rewritten every generation.

Even if the historical 'facts' do not change, the context in which they are to be read and interpreted does change" (1998:415).

In lieu of killing an ancestor in one's direct line of descent, it is also possible to make one's reputation by killing the head of another anthropological lineage. This confers the advantage of retaining the protection of one's own lineage head and, in fact, solidifying that bond by killing the head of a rival lineage. This is an ironic twist on E. B. Tylor's dictum of "marry out or die out." In this case, the individual reinforces ties within the lineage and severs ties with other lineages. Whether killed by their own descendants or by the descendants of a rival lineage, the result is the same: the loss or discrediting of essential elders in the discipline, along with the knowledge and traditions they represent.

It is doubtful whether this wholesale slaughter of ancestors is essential to the scientific enterprise or that it is beneficial to the discipline of anthropology as a whole. To draw on an evolutionary paradigm, it does not even benefit the individuals who temporarily reign supreme, though they may gain the perquisites of tenure and publications. They cannot transmit their ideas (genetic material) beyond a single generation and the name they have so carefully won is doomed to die with them.

To further delineate this kinship metaphor, it is instructive to compare American and Australian descent systems. On the surface, these two descent systems have one element in common: each has a descent rule that reckons ancestry through both male and female lines. However, the American rule of bilateral descent and the Australian rule of double unilineal descent have different effects on the production of local knowledge and "career-building" within their respective cultures. Following current convention in the anthropological study of kinship systems, here we distinguish between the descent rule, which specifies the organization of successive parent-child links, and the use of that rule as the basis for recruitment to a descent group.

The Australian system of double (or sometimes bilineal) descent, for example, recognizes that individuals simultaneously reckon ancestry patrilineally for some purposes and matrilineally for other purposes. In other words, both unilineal descent rules coexist and even intersect, but they are relevant to different circumstances. This is the case with Wardaman-speaking Aborigines, for example, who trace certain land relationships through the father and certain social relationships through the mother (Saenz 1994).

The American rule of bilateral descent, in comparison, holds that individuals reckon descent through both sides rather than both lines. This distinction may seem merely semantic when looking at the descent rule; however, when the resulting descent group is considered, the emergence of a distinction between ancestor-killing and ancestor-reverence comes into sharp relief. Specifically, the American rule of bilateral descent does not produce a descent group which is traced forward from a founding ancestor in the past, as is the case of Wardaman Aborigines who trace their corporate lineages and clans from

ancestral Dreaming beings. Rather, the American bilateral descent rule produces a descent group which is traced backward from an individual ego in the present. The Australian system produces a corporate descent group, whereas the American system produces a kindred, a set of kinship relationships specific to an individual and not shared by any group.

This distinction between kinship corporations (like lineages and clans) and kinship categories (like kindreds) cannot be overemphasized. Bilineally produced corporations, on the one hand, maintain cohesion by keeping the name of the common ancestor alive in the present. In addition to a sense of shared community, there is also a sense of shared history, or at least of continuity between the present and the past, such that descent is strongly valued in the culture. This sense of community is reinforced by the custom of naming children after ancestors. In contrast, kindred membership differs for every sibling set, since it is an ego-centered construct. Consequently, bilaterally produced kindreds reduce the community to an individual and reduce history to the present, weakening the value of ancestry (and correspondingly strengthening the value of affinity).

Similarly, the impact of this distinction between Aboriginal corporations and American kindreds on their respective cultural constructions of knowledge cannot be overemphasized. Both Wardaman culture and the American culture of academic anthropology value knowledge as a commodity; *how* the two cultures value knowledge, though, relates directly to their differing structure of descent. For Wardaman-speaking Aborigines, certain types of knowledge about "country" or land is inherited patrilineally and transmitted through the communal religious system along lines of male mentorship. Knowledge, then, both defines and is confined within the descent group. Consequently, junior members—whose "careers" are dependent upon a knowledge-wealthy descent corporation—revere senior members of their lineage, including living human mentors, former or deceased human mentors, and Dreaming-being ancestors.

American academic anthropologists, in contrast, have a vastly different cultural understanding of knowledge production and career-building. First of all, the descent system of the American culture-at-large de-emphasizes the past in favor of the present (an emphasis that is reflected in anthropology's construction of the "ethnographic present"). Secondly, the descent system of the American culture-at-large deemphasizes the descent group in favor of the individual (an emphasis that is reflected in anthropology's construction of the fieldworker-as-maverick). Finally, in the culture of academic anthropology, knowledge cannot be entirely inherited through mentorship. In the process of fieldwork, so the canon goes, one must collect one's "own" data and "make" (not inherit) one's name. In order to do this, knowledge must be produced anew (not merely reproduced), making ancestors and mentors problematic for the would-be careerist. At the very least, their existence must be denied, lest one be accused of not individuating from one's intellectual family-of-origin, thereby suffering intellectual condemnation through being labeled "derivative," a term that connotes lack of creativity and initiative. In other words, ancestors must be surpassed, when they are not killed, to achieve individuation and renown.

Ironically, we may trace both the tradition of killing our ancestors and the practice of fieldwork as a process of individuation back to our "dreamtime" ancestor, Bronislaw Malinowski. We have already noted that Malinowski established a pattern of ancestor slaughter with his attack on Sir James Frazer. In addition, he has become the very model of the intrepid anthropologist stalking the native in the field. As I. M. Lewis writes: "Although he was not the very first, [Malinowski] has come to be regarded as the pioneer, bushwhacking anthropologist, the originator of the doctrine that until you have lived cheek by jowl with an exotic tribe and spoken their language fluently you cannot claim full professional status" (1985:54).

Though bilateral inheritance and neolocal residence (combining the rich relative syndrome with the killing of ancestors) is the prevailing kinship idiom in American culture, it may not be the most beneficial idiom for the culture of anthropology. Malinowski once wrote that: "Much ink has flowed on the problem of blood" (1930:19). It may be equally true that, in anthropology, much "blood" has flowed on the problem of "ink," or publications, which may also be equated with status in the field of anthropology.

The Chinese recognize their ancestors as continuing members of one's lineage by feeding them and by acknowledging their continuing contribution to the family. It is a reciprocal relationship. Living descendants feed the ancestors to keep them from becoming "hungry ghosts" and causing trouble for the living. In return, the ancestors are expected to care for and protect their descendants. Australian Aborigines similarly recognize indebtedness to their ancestors through both matrilineal and patrilineal lines and acknowledge the continuing presence of ancestors in their lives through naming customs.

American anthropologists, on the other hand, allow their intellectual ancestors to become "hungry ghosts" and get angry when discounted theoretical models return to haunt the living. The very vehemence with which anthropologists reject what they consider outmoded theories testifies to their continuing "power" over "living" or contemporary theories. We may find that anthropologists, who have conducted such sophisticated studies and analyses of kinship, may have much to learn from the writings of their ancestors—and, indeed, from their own writings—about the importance of "blood" ties in promoting not only the

survival of the living but the eventual victories of their descendants.

Notes

Writing this chapter has been a test of the value of combining respect for one's ancestors with the advantages of neolocal residence. Paul Bohannan, Mari Womack, and Karen Saenz represent three stages of the anthropological career: respected elder, mature adult, and emerging young adult. Each has made a contribution independently of the others.

1. "Yanomamo" and "Yanomama" are alternate spellings for the same connotative term.

References

Bohannan Paul 1997 "It's Been a Good Field Trip." *Ethnos 62* (1–2):116–136. 1998 "Passing into History." In Mari Womack, *Being Human: An Introduction to Cultural Anthropology.* Upper Saddle River, NJ: Prentice-Hall.

Evans-Pritchard E. E. 1951 *Kinship and Marriage Among the Nuer.* Oxford: Clarendon Press.

Frazer James George 1890 *The Golden Bough.* London: Macmillan.

Freeman Derek 1983 *Margaret Mead and Samoa.* Cambridge, MA: Harvard University Press.

Good Kenneth (with David Chanoff) 1991 *Into the Heart: One Man's Pursuit of Love and Knowledge among the Yanomama.* New York: Simon & Schuster.

Kuhn Thomas S. 1970 *The Structure of Scientific Revolutions.* 2nd edition. Chicago, IL: University of Chicago Press.

Kuper Adam 1983 *Anthropology and Anthropologists: The Modern British School.* London: Routledge.

Lewis I. M. 1985 *Social Anthropology in Perspective.* 2nd edition. Cambridge: Cambridge University Press.

Malinowski Bronislaw 1927 *The Father in Primitive Psychology.* New York: Norton. 1930 "Kinship." *Man* 30:19–29. 1967 *A Diary in the Strict Sense of the Term*, N. Guterman, trans. Stanford, CA: Stanford University Press.

Morgan Lewis H. 1870 *Systems of Consanguinity and Affinity in the Human Family.* Washington, DC: Smithsonian Institution (Contributions to Knowledge 17).

Saenz Karen Eilene 1994 *Space, Time, and Gender: An Archaeology of Human Relations in Post-Contact Aboriginal Northern Australia*, Ph.D. dissertation, UCLA, Los Angeles.

Shankman Paul 1996 "The History of Samoan Sexual Conduct and the Mead-Freeman Controversy." *American Anthropologist* 98:555–567.

White Leslie 1949 *The Science of Culture.* New York: Grove Press.

Womack Mari. 1993 "Introduction to Love, Marriage, and Power." In Mari Womack and Judith Marti, eds., *The Other Fifty Percent.* Prospect Heights, IL: Waveland Press. 1998 *Being Human: An Introduction to Cultural Anthropology.* Upper Saddle River, NJ: Prentice-Hall.

Margaret Mead vs. Tony Soprano

Micaela di Leonardo

If anthropology is the child of imperialism, as Kathleen Gough maintained in a previous article, it is the step-child of the social and behavioral sciences. In course offerings in high schools across the United States, it is virtually invisible in comparison to history. If anthropology exists at all in the pre-collegiate curriculum, it may show up as a segment of a social studies class. And even this development has primarily taken place since World War II. Even when it is taught, the sad fact is that the overwhelming majority of high school teachers throughout this country are teaching subjects for which they have no training.

Small colleges are not likely to have an anthropology department and large colleges and universities offer few lower division anthropology classes for non-majors. Psychology is much more likely to meet the requirements for graduation.

Given the lack of knowledge most people have about anthropology and what anthropologists do, it is understandable that the images people have about the subject are going to be primarily shaped by the mass media, which is more about entertainment than it is about enlightenment. It is in this context that Micaela di Leonardo's frustration with the popular stereotypes about anthropology and anthropologists makes sense.

Micaela di Leonardo received her Ph.D. from the University of California, Berkeley in 1981. She teaches anthropology and gender studies at Northwestern University. She has been involved in ethnographic research having to do with race and gender in New Haven, CT since 1987. Her most recent book is *Exotics at Home: Anthropologies, Others, American Modernity*, and she is currently finishing *The View From Cavallaro's* having to do with one changing neighborhood in New Haven in the context of larger political and economic shifts.

Key Concept: Popular stereotypes of anthropology and anthropologists

The morning after I returned to Chicago from the recent Margaret Mead Legacy conference at Barnard College, honoring the centenary of the anthropologist's birth, a newspaper columnist rang me at dawn with the demand that I explain "from a feminist perspective" why Tony Soprano is "this millennium's first sex symbol." "Does this mean that we're all going backwards?" she asked with relish. Dumbfounded, I countered, rather crankily, with the request that she give me evidence that any women anywhere were claiming sexual attraction to a dumb, sexist and racist, unfaithful, badly out of shape, psychologically damaged organized crime capo. (Not that I don't love the show; who doesn't, even if I have to watch my own people get minstrelized to a fare-thee-well.) Nothing daunted, and with not a shred of shame that she in fact had no evidence, the columnist cleverly countered, "Well, if it were true, what would your feminist perspective be?" As Rayna Rapp of the New School had declared to the amused Barnard audience, I had that feminist anthropologist's "WWMMS moment": What Would Margaret Mead Say?

What would she say? We could easily remark about Mead what Walt Whitman, another New York-based celebrity, claimed of himself: She is large, she contains multitudes. Mead was professionally active for fully half of the last century and, by choice and her own never-ending efforts, very much a public voice for most of that time. She said a lot of different things in different decades, and she was received variously by her own professional colleagues and within a shifting American public sphere. The Barnard conferees, including the college President, Judith Shapiro, herself a feminist anthropologist, and Mead's daughter Mary Catherine Bateson, spoke on key aspects of Mead's work, on the ways in which she had inspired their own research, and on what her legacy might be in this millennium. They agreed that she and her cohort made a series of novel connections: envisioning the malleability of gender relations, seeing human corporeality, ritual and psychology as one, emphasizing the deeply enculturated nature of child-rearing and of adolescent coming of age. Elaine Charnov, director of the Margaret Mead Film Festival, and Faye Ginsburg of New

York University both spoke as well of Mead's prescience in the use of ethnographic film and her general status as technological pioneer.

"But there is no Margaret Mead now," the panelists lamented with the partisan, largely female audience crowding the auditorium, and variously attributed that fact to her heroic uniqueness, to her intellectual coming of age being the "right time and the right place" for public sphere presence, to the rise of the New Right in the West and the triumph of global neo-liberalism, to the renaissance of biological reductionism in the overwhelming American popular-cultural presence of sociobiology, to our collective retreat from public voice.

Mead became a popular icon over the course of the 1960s, and attained the status of Holy Woman in her last years, as the late Roy Rappaport commented (she died in 1978). And it is difficult to evaluate Holy Women, particularly in the long wake of a posthumous attack—by the Australian anthropologist Derek Freeman, in 1983—that quickly became a mass media firestorm. *Margaret Mead and Samoa* is a badly written and unconvincing claim that Mead, influenced in a "culturally determinist" direction by her nefarious adviser Franz Boas, falsely interpreted the Hobbesian world in which Samoan youth came of age as a gentle idyll. Freeman claimed that the true Samoa is characterized by a "primeval rank system" that dictates a "regime of physical punishment" of children and violent "rivalrous aggression" among men, "highly emotional and impulsive behavior that is animal-like in its ferocity" among chiefs, and a rape rate "among the highest to be found anywhere in the world." Scholars criticized Freeman's theoretical vacuity and empirical flaws, his ahistorical claim of an Eternal Samoa, his failure to realize that his key informants—older, high-status males—were no more a "true and accurate lens" of Samoan culture than were Mead's young female companions. Most especially, feminists noted the rank sexism of Freeman's focus on Mead's youth and size: The "liberated young American... only twenty-three years of age...[was] smaller in stature than some of the girls she was studying."

But public reception of, as opposed to in-house reaction to, Freeman's book was most importantly about the extraordinary fit between his line of attack and newly dominant New Rightist politics. Margaret Mead and Samoa provided a Heaven-sent opportunity for the press to rant against the "liberal feminist culture" and "lifestyle experiments" with which it newly identified Mead, conveniently forgetting its fervent eulogies of her of only half a decade earlier. As the late David Schneider noted at the time, Freeman's book was "a work that celebrate[d] a particular political climate by denigrating another." Freeman's vision, at one fell swoop, allowed commentators to deny female intellectual capacities across all societies; to naturalize male dominance, male sexual violence and aggression; and at the same time, to slur Samoans—and with them all so-called primitives, that is, all people of color—as violent, nasty savages. Logically self-contradictory and empirically

bankrupt though it was, Freeman's narrative was wonderfully composed to fit American Reagan-era contentions of the foolishness of the movements of the 1960s and 1970s, as you "can't change human nature," and Western, upperclass, male, heterosexual, and white dominance are natural after all.

Freeman's frisson in popular culture is now long past, victim of the increasingly rapid biodegradation of American popular consciousness. I routinely ask gender studies and anthropology classes if they have heard of Freeman or his book, and very few respond affirmatively, even when they have a niggling sense that there is some sort of blot on Mead's reputation. Only American New Rightists remember and believe in Freeman's attack on Mead: A Lexis/Nexis search for all articles referring to the two since 1990 revealed only a handful of sneering articles in rightist outlets, whereas a general search using Mead's name alone garnered thousands of "hits."

But while specific media scandals always fade, popular-cultural troping of anthropology and anthropologists is unceasing, and distorts whatever information members of the discipline may have to offer considering power and culture in human societies. The issue is more crucial than is often realized, because popular apprehensions of anthropology and anthropologists are importantly interwoven with changing American constructions of others—those deemed somehow apart from the norm by virtue of race, gender, nationality, class, religion, sexual identity. "Culture" and "biology" are the two key domains through which Americans historically have laundered politics from public sphere inspection. And anthropology, sententiously self-described as the most humanistic of the sciences, the most scientific of the humanities, has thus evolved into a cynosure of political approbation and attack, both refuge and refuse in contemporary contestations over power.

II.

I have recently identified a series of anthropological "Halloween costumes" into which, since the 1960s, American popular writing, film, television, cartoons and advertising have tended to squeeze all anthropological knowledge. Each costume—Technicians of the Sacred, Last Macho Raiders, Evil Imperialist Anthropologists, Barbarians at the Gates, and Human Nature Experts—reflects minor strands in some past or present anthropological writing. More important, each enacts a retrogressive politics with reference to culture and power on the US and global stage. The costumes, in other words, act as Procrustean beds, amputating those pesky limbs of anthropological knowledge that flop outside their predetermined grids.

Technicians of the Sacred, for example, posits anthropologists as time travelers who bring back to us visions of Noble Savages living nonviolently and cooperatively, practicing sexual equality, respecting the environment and engaging in religious worship somehow more "spiritual" than ours. Such a seemingly benign vision, however, yanks contemporaneous populations out of our shared stream of world history and prevents us from understanding the ways in which they lack political power on local and global stages. Last Macho Raiders imagines anthropologists as a guild populated by cool Harrison Ford lookalikes, virile, positive imperialists. This particular Halloween costume has long had little appeal to most members of the guild but remains widely used in popular culture. The Evil Imperialist Anthropologist, on the other hand, who is simply a Last Macho Raider seen from the viewpoint of the Raided, has roots in some Third World and Native American writing of the 1960s, became a stock postmodern character in much academic writing in the 1980s and spilled over into popular culture. Barbarians at the Gates envisions anthropologists as foolish multiculturalists, misguided salespeople hawking inferior—non-Western—cultural materials to a gullible American public. In other words, it is a rightist, racist framing of the Technicians of the Sacred trope, and has been heavily purveyed in New Rightist writing through our recent culture wars. And Human Nature Experts paints anthropologists as pure scientists—gatherers of facts alone. Of course we need to stand for empirical reality, but this particular trope functions in the public sphere today almost solely as a rationale for sociobiological arguments, as if all fact and logic were the sacred possession of that contemporary version of biological reductionism alone, and the active armies of distinguished anti-sociobiology scientists were a mere rumor in the wind.

We might say, then, that Freeman, in an act of simultaneous attack and self-aggrandizement, dressed Mead as a Barbarian at the Gates and himself as a Human Nature Expert. Ironically, though, Mead herself, over the decades, had no small hand in the fashioning of the Human Nature Expert costume. At the same time, the Halloween costumes are most definitely not unisex, and Mead, like the rest of us, never escaped her gender. Looping back to the years of Mead's intellectual coming of age and first writing helps us to trace the changing lineaments of "culture" in American politics, particularly that shifting overlap of gender and race that is so crucial to the framing of rationales for and protests against contemporary lines of stratification.

III.

In the 1920s, counter to the assertions and interpretations of more recent commentators, Mead's *Coming of Age in Samoa* was written, and was read, not as a paean to free love or women's rights or even the romantic lives of "noble savages," but rather as a scientific account of certain differing cultural features in a "more simple" society that "we," meaning middle-class white Americans, might wish to adopt in order to raise "our youth" in a less stressful manner. Mead defined herself early on, as I have written, as an objective scientist, a professional social engineer. Despite her sometimes somewhat overblown lyricism—"A group of youths may dance for the pleasure of some visiting maiden," "lovers slip home from trysts beneath the palm trees"—Mead ultimately is no Technician of the Sacred, no romantic anti-modernist. Her 1920s Samoa is a "shallow society" where "no one plays for very high stakes," of use to "us" as an object of scientific study: it is a "human experiment" under "controlled conditions."

While Mead worked almost solely with girls and women, and certainly wrote, as a contemporary reviewer put it, with the "clean, clear frankness of the scientist" about their sexual experiences, she did not draw explicitly feminist lessons from her fieldwork. Like many young women of her post-suffrage era, to whom feminism seemed both passe and potentially professionally damaging, Mead took advantage of the doors opened by the women's rights activism of her mother's and grandmother's generation (and indeed, by her own mother and grandmother) but did not herself join that ongoing movement. Nancy Lutkehaus of USC pointed out at the conference that Mead became a public intellectual in the 1920s because of her fortuitously advantageous position in time and space: based in New York, writing about the South Seas at a point when that region had caught the American public imagination, and indeed at just the point that newspapers and magazines were proliferating across the American landscape. And, I would add, because she wrote then not as a radical but as a modernist, advocating changes for the white middle classes—co-education, less authoritarian childrearing, greater frankness about the facts of birth, reproduction, and death—already in the works in the Roaring Twenties.

But scientist or not, Mead was at times portrayed in the press as many anthropologists, especially female anthropologists, have been since: with a certain condescending, inappropriately sexualizing humor, identified with her inevitably stigmatized subjects. Lutkehaus has unearthed 1920s newspaper stories claiming that Mead went to Samoa to study the "origins of the flapper." And in the 1930s, a popular magazine coyly described Mead as "a slender, comely girl who danced her way into the understanding of the Melanesian people and became an adopted daughter and a sort of princess of the Samoans. When they anointed her with palm oil and indicated that a dance was in order, she did a nice hula and they declared her in—indicating the adaptability of the modern young woman if she just has a chance to step out."

It was one of the first steps on the long road toward my Sopranos interlocutor—herself, as we shall see, merely part of a vast contemporary phenomenon.

IV.

Mead's early anthropological work reflected both developing British and American concerns: She did careful kinship and social organizational research in Samoa and

New Guinea, and studied what she construed to be varying cultural temperaments—characteristic psychological states—and their connections to sex roles and life cycles. But by 1935, when she published the widely read *Sex and Temperament in Three Primitive Societies,* her analytic twig was permanently bent in the Americanist psychological, "culture and personality" direction. *Sex and Temperament,* rather than *Coming of Age,* is the work in which Mead makes her clearest arguments concerning the plasticity of human sex role arrangements: "Many, if not all, of the personality traits that we have called masculine or feminine are as lightly linked to sex as are the clothing, the manners, and the form of head-dress that a society at a given period assigns to either sex.... We are forced to conclude that human nature is almost unbelievably malleable."

This is the modal Mead, the unpopular culture anthropologist who was rediscovered by Second Wave feminists, assigned all over the academy and read aloud in consciousness-raising groups in the 1970s. It is important to remember, though, that every generation reads selectively. Mead's "gender malleability" statements are, in fact, lodged inside a larger argument against women's equal rights as represented by the contemporary Soviet Union. Mead saw in the opening of all occupations to women there a "sacrifice in complexity" of culture: "The removal of all legal and economic barriers against women's participating in the world on an equal footing with men may be in itself a standardizing move towards the wholesale stamping-out of the diversity of attitudes that is such a dearly bought product of civilization."

Ironically, the very popular troping of anthropology for political purposes has contributed to the discipline's unpolitical reputation. Explicitly political statements in anthropological texts vanish in the course of reading, the discipline's pioneering anti-racism and near-implosion over Vietnam have succumbed to the culture of forgetting, and the long-vital left tradition in anthropology worldwide is popularly and often even professionally invisible. When I gave an early talk on Mead for a group of women's studies professors, a senior political scientist exclaimed afterward that she was surprised to learn that Mead "had any politics." All God's anthropologists got politics, most especially the very public Margaret Mead.

Those politics varied considerably over the long decades of Depression, war, de-colonization and cold war, and the 1960s and 1970s conjuncture of Vietnam, civil rights, the Second Wave of feminism and associated gay rights organizing. The one common thread across the decades, though, was Mead's adherence to Progressive social engineering, and thus her profound commitment to the notion of disinterested science and the rule of experts. In terms of gender, from the 1930s until the early 1970s, when she did take on a liberal feminist stance, Mead embraced the conservative Freudian notion of the universal "constructive receptivity of the female and the vigorous outgoing constructive activity of the male."

While Mead continued to argue against isolated, narrow nuclear families, and for careers for better-off women as long as they were "womanly" both at home and at work, it is no wonder that Betty Friedan in 1961 spent almost an entire chapter of her celebrated book attacking Mead's pernicious "super saleswomanship" of the *Feminine Mystique.* It is equally unsurprising that Second Wave feminists, in rediscovering both Friedan and Mead for their own purposes, read Friedan as selectively as they (we) did Mead.

Similarly, Mead's war work for the American government extended into both her very successful postwar advocacy of federal funding for anthropological research and her cold warrior stance against, among other actions, antinuclear and anti-Vietnam War protests. (The latter issue led to a huge fight at the 1971 American Anthropological Association meetings, during which Mead was hissed by an antiwar audience of 700.) These political actions were overwhelmed, in popular culture, by Mead's highly public approbation of "questing youth" from the mid-1960s forward, and the liberal feminist alliances of her last years. She even had her own character in the first stage version of *Hair,* who celebrated male "long hair and other flamboyant affectations," and whose song ended in the recitative, "Kids, be whatever you are, do whatever you do, just so long as you don't hurt anybody."

V.

Hair's sendup of Mead followed her thinly disguised appearance as a famous older female anthropologist in Irving Wallace's sleazy 1963 potboiler, *The Three Sirens:* "She thought of the place: the temperate trade winds, the tall, sinewy, bronze people, the oral legends, the orgiastic rites." The sexual imputations in both texts return us to consideration of my morning journalist and Tony Soprano. Like all occupational groups, anthropologists have traditions of internal self-reference, but ours have intersected in particularly damaging ways with the changing Zeitgeist. From Clyde Kluckhohn's 1940s boast that we were all "eccentrics" "interested in bizarre things," to Clifford Geertz's 1984 reference to anthropologists as "merchants of astonishment," many of us have enjoyed exoticizing ourselves, playing, as I have written, the court jesters of academe. While some of this self-exoticization has always arisen from identification with oppressed populations, the overall effect of the court jester construction is dire. Anthropologists have become the American public's "exotics at home," identified with our demonized, trivialized subjects, or rather, those who are presumed to be our sole subjects—non-Westerners around the globe, the poor, the nonwhite, and sexual minorities in every country. And, of course, in double irony, the numbers of nonwhite, non-Western and/or gay anthropologists, never insignificant, grow larger every year. By a process of infinite recursion, the stigmatized figurings of subjects and researchers repeatedly rub off on one another, denying dignity, history and human rights to domestic and foreign "exotics," and stripping anthropologists of the intellectual authority with which to contribute to progressive politics.

Ironically, the "exotics at home" complex also reifies the discipline's long historical game of peekaboo with Americanist research. Mead's own master's thesis concerned the link between exposure to English and IQ test results among Italian-American schoolchildren in New Jersey (Tony and Carmela's grandparents!), and significant numbers of anthropologists have done United States fieldwork in every decade since. All of the Barnard conference senior panelists, for example, are engaged in Americanist research. But in the grand adaptive radiation of disciplinary institutionalization as American universities grew over the twentieth century, anthropology was defined in contradistinction to sociology as the study of non-Westerners (and based on ethnographic rather than quantitative methodology), perpetrating falsehoods about actual work being done in both fields. Since at least the 1940s, anthropologists and middlebrow media have repeatedly "discovered" that anthropology is "just now coming home." In 1974 *Time* declared that

> the gimmick is that anthropologists, after decades of following Margaret Mead to Samoa and Bronislaw Malinowski to the Trobriand Islands, have staked out new territory.... U.S. anthropology, it seems, must recognize that the primary tribe to study is the Americans.

But then, fifteen years later, the *New York Times* Book Review declared:

> Pity the poor anthropologist. She has trekked the highlands, machetied the jungles, sifted the sands for new tribes to study. But the Ik have been exposed, the Tasaday tallied. What's left? Increasingly, today's would-be Meads and Benedicts are turning in their bush jackets for tweeds, for some easy poking around in their own backyards—where, lo and behold, they unearth practices as alien to Western norms as any found in the heart of New Guinea.

And so it goes. While such consistent failure to engage with empirical reality, and the condescending notion that US fieldwork must of necessity be merely "easy poking around," are extremely annoying to those of us who have done arduous research in American settings, I want to make a different point. That is, the culture of forgetting involved here enacts what I have labeled the anthropological gambit, or the pseudo-profound claim that "we" are like "primitives." The attribution of "our" characteristics to "them," and vice versa, is always good for a laugh in popular culture. "We" are only the Ik, the Tasaday, the Trobrianders. An X is only a Y.

As if to prove the point, the day before I left for the Barnard conference, the *New York Times* happily declared that "some distant day, anthropologists may discover what was surely the tribal art of 20th-century American suburbia: paint-by-number paintings."

There is nothing innately wrong with cuteness—it is after all a matter of taste. The point, though, is that the gambit, which is ubiquitous in the public sphere, is inherently political, engages in hidden rhetorical work. It certainly represents Edward Sapir's "destructive analysis of the familiar," one element of a liberatory cultural critique in use in the West at least since Michel de Montaigne's ironized cannibals. But it does so in a profoundly ahistorical, noncontextual way, and so places Others at temporal distance to ourselves and effaces the questions of history and power on both poles of the contrast.

VI.

Finally, anthropologists like Margaret Mead and Ruth Benedict pioneered an open-minded consideration of the varieties of cross-cultural human sexuality. Esther Newton, who recently published a memoir magnificently titled *Margaret Mead Made Me Gay*, spoke compellingly at the conference on the impact of her adolescent reading of Mead's "defense of cultural and temperamental difference." But that reputation for sexual frankness, combined with femaleness, the anthropological gambit and exoticism at home, has also long made women anthropologists, as I have noted for Margaret Mead, vulnerable to sexually insinuating popular-cultural costuming. In the rollicking postwar musical and film *On the Town*, recently revived on Broadway, a sex-crazed debutante "anthropology student" character throws herself at one of the sailors on leave because he "exactly resembles Pithecanthropus erectus, a man extinct since six million BC." The television series *90210* had a sluttish "feminist anthropologist" character, and Sarah Jessica Parker, in *Sex and the City*, calls herself a "sexual anthropologist." The way things seem to be going, we might want to specify another media Halloween costume for the feminist anthropologist: bustier and fishnets.

Feminist anthropologists tend to be a pretty tough bunch and certainly can take care of ourselves. (One of the conference participants pointed out to me with great glee that she was wearing fishnet hose.) The real issue is the one with which I began: the deadly intersection of the distorting Halloween costumes, the anthropological gambit and garden-variety sexism in the public sphere preventing the popular dissemination of actual knowledge on gender, culture and power. Consider my own experience. I write about gender, sexuality, race, ethnicity, and class formation in the American past and present, particularly in American cities, and I have done popular writing on racial injustice (and its connections to gender) in the present. But when does the Fourth Estate contact me? Let's just review instances from the past few years.

A *20/20* reporter called, wanting a professor to explain on-camera why "some men are sexually attracted to very obese women." (He kept trying to assure me that the show "would not be sleazy." Right.) A public radio show host invited me to do a Valentine's Day show with her on love and courtship ritual. A local television newswoman wanted my "anthropological" analysis of why women were buying Wonderbras. A *Newsweek* reporter asked for my thoughts on why, despite so many decades of feminism, American women still enlisted the aids of hair dye, makeup, plastic surgery, and diets. Didn't that prove that we were genetically encoded to try to attract men to impregnate us and protect our offspring? A young stringer for *Glamour* called, looking for "expert" analysis of why women are attracted to certain types of men. An Essence reporter wanted my thoughts on why Afro-American women, according to her, repeatedly and irrationally fell for "thugs." And last fall, a *Good Morning, America* producer begged me to appear on a show with the theme "Is Infidelity Genetic?"

So I wasn't entirely surprised by the Tony Soprano call, with its silly implications of a homogeneous feminism obsessed with mass media portrayals of sex roles. And I don't think even the Whitmanesque Margaret Mead, today, would have an easier time of it. In her memorable last years, Mead could and did play the progressive Sibyl, the wise elder using her vast cross-cultural knowledge to comment favorably, to a largely adulatory press, on the increasing social liberalization that we saw around us. But that was before Jimmy Carter, with whom Mead was closely politically allied, lost disastrously to Ronald Reagan in 1980. It was before the New Right, before the race and gender backlashes of "the underclass" and "feminazis" and the internal problematics of identity politics, before the second, more successful rise of sociobiology, before the global rightward tilt and recent neoliberal triumph, before the corporate consolidation and increasing tabloidization of the media. And, of course, it was before the "turn to language" complexified the ways in which we all envision science, culture, and knowledge.

We no longer unproblematically invoke "science," but consider it a culturally contingent, powerful process. Emily Martin of Princeton and Rayna Rapp spoke at the conference about their ongoing and highly regarded research on gender in the production and consumption of scientific knowledge. But both scholars also work actively and even teach with bench scientists. Similarly, many of us work to reposition our analyses, no matter what their regional focus, both to reduce the United States and to enlarge it, always with the goal of accurately apprehending gender, culture, history and power. That is, we no longer simply observe the world from the perspective of the West, but instead consider the long regional and global histories of contact, trade, power politics, racial and ethnic formation, and shifting political boundaries of which the United States and other Northern and Southern nations are part. At the same time, we no longer attempt to see the United States just as one among many nations—as in "an X is only a Y"—as it is still and has been the locus of global imperial power since the end of the Second World War.

These less Olympian, more nuanced understandings are a harder sell in the public sphere, but along with other progressives, we continue our Sisyphean engagement. And Mead's image, although not entirely according to her intentions, continues to inspire radical visions of American and global potentials: of international understanding, of gender, race, class and sexual equalities, of a different, more egalitarian world. Marcyliena Morgan of UCLA, for example, reported that the hip-hop-involved adolescent Afro-American girls with whom she works see Mead as "a liberating force." As Rayna Rapp ringingly concluded, "Collectively, we are surely on the case."

Language and Culture

Selection 12

JAMES P. SPRADLEY AND BRENDA J. MANN, from "How to Ask for a Drink," *The Cocktail Waitress*

Selection 13

DEBORAH TANNEN, from "Why Don't You Say What You Mean?," *The New York Times Magazine*

Selection 14

EDWARD T. HALL AND MILDRED REED HALL, from "The Sounds of Silence," *Playboy*

How to Ask for a Drink

James P. Spradley and Brenda J. Mann

People do not go to a bar just to drink. It would be less expensive to go to a liquor store and then imbibe to one's heart's content at home.

So, why do people frequent bars? As James P. Spradley and Brenda J. Mann reveal in this excerpt from their book, *Cocktail Waitress*, a bar is a place in which certain kinds of desirable social interaction are possible. Because the setting is primarily *social* and because the primary interactions are acts of communication—or *speech events*—the authors found it important to learn not only what people said to each other, but how they said it—to discern not only the "linguistic rules that generate *meaningful* utterances" but to "discover the sociolinguistic rules that generate *appropriate* utterances." In other words, the authors found it incumbent upon themselves to carry out an *ethnography of speaking*.

In the process of doing their fieldwork, Spradley and Mann found that the bar is more than a place of business. It is a ceremonial center that "reaffirms the official values of manhood." As you consider the strategies used to display such manhood, think about the authors' claim that "the masculinity rituals would not be effective without the cooperation of the waitress" and that the cultural expectations are that "she should remain dependent and passive." Would this hold true today, more than thirty years after the original publication of this article? Would today's waitress (server) be more likely to file sexual harassment charges? Would today's ethnographer find a changed "ceremonial center?" Of course, none of this negates the value of the authors' work. It is a fine ethnography done regardless of time and place.

The late Dr. James P. Spradley was best known for his ethnography *You Owe Yourself a Drunk: An Ethnography of Urban Nomads, The Cultural Experience: Ethnography in Complex Society* (with David W. McCurdy) and *Conformity and Conflict* (co-editor with David W. McCurdy. He taught at Macalester College in St. Paul, Minnesota.

Brenda J. Mann was a teaching associate at the University of Minnesota at the time this article was originally published.

Key Concept: ethnography of speaking

Brady's Bar is obviously a place to drink. Every night a crowd of college-age men and women visit the bar for this purpose. But even a casual observer could not miss the fact that Brady's is also a place to *talk*. Drinking and talking are inseparable. The lonely drinker who sits in silence is either drawn into conversation or leaves the bar. Everyone feels the anxious insecurity of such a person, seemingly alone in the crowd at Brady's. It is also believed that drinking affects the way people talk, lubricating the social interchange. If liquor flows each night in Brady's like a stream from behind the bar, talking, laughing, joking, and dozens of simultaneous conversations cascade like a torrent from every corner of the bar. Early in our research we became aware that our ethnography would have to include an investigation of this speech behavior.

The importance of drinking and talking has also been observed by anthropologists in other societies. Take, for example, the Subanun of the Philippine Islands, studied by Charles Frake.[1] Deep in the tropical rain forests of Zamboanga Peninsula on the island of Mindanao, these people live in small family groups, practicing swidden agriculture. Social ties outside the family are maintained by networks to kin and neighbors rather than through some larger formal organization. Social encounters beyond the family occur on frequent festive occasions that always include "beer" drinking. Unlike Brady's Bar with separate glasses for each person, the Subanun place fermented mash in a single, large Chinese jar and drink from this common container by using a long bamboo straw. A drinking group gathers around the jar, water is poured over the mash, and each person in turn sucks beer from the bottom of the jar. As the water passes through the mash it is transformed into a potent alcoholic beverage. There are elaborate rules for these drinking sessions that govern such activities as competitive drinking, opposite-sexed partners drinking together under the cover of a blanket, and games where drinking is done in chugalug fashion. But the drinking is secondary to the talking on these occasions, and what Frake has said about the Subanun might easily apply to Brady's Bar:

> The Subanun expression for drinking talk,… "talk from the straw," suggests an image of the drinking straw as a channel not only of the drink but also of drinking talk. The two activities, drinking and talking, are closely interrelated in that how one talks bears on how much one drinks and the converse is, quite obviously, also true… Especially for an adult male, one's role in the society at large, insofar as it is subject to manipulation, depends to a considerable extent on one's verbal performance during drinking encounters.[2]

In this chapter we will examine the verbal performances of those who participate in the social life at Brady's. We focus on a single speech event, *asking for a drink,* and the social function of this event. This chapter is intended as a partial ethnography of speaking, a description of the cultural rules at Brady's Bar for using speech.

The Ethnography of Speaking[3]

Throughout each of the preceding chapters our description has aimed at answering the fundamental ethnographic question: "What would a stranger have to act appropriately as a cocktail waitress and to interpret behavior from her perspective?" An ethnography of speaking asks this question in reference to the way people talk. It goes beyond the usual linguistic study that analyzes speech in abstraction from its usage. Instead of describing linguistic rules that generate *meaningful* utterances, we sought to discover the sociolinguistic rules that generate *appropriate* utterances. This approach is extremely important because people at Brady's are not interested in merely saying things that make sense; they seek instead to say things that reveal to others their skill in verbal performances. Indeed, this often requires that a person utter nonsense, at least so it seems to the outsider.

In order to discover the rules for using speech, we began by recording what people said to one another, noting whenever possible the gestures, tone of voice, setting, and other features of the verbal interaction. Then we examined these samples of speech usage for recurrent patterns and went back to listen for more instances. At first we sought to identify the major speech events that were typical of the bar. A speech event refers to activities that are directly governed by rules for speaking.[4] On any evening the waitress participates in many different speech events. For example, Denise enters the bar shortly after 6:30 in the evening, and almost her first act is to exchange some from of *greeting* with the bartender, the day employees who are present, and any regulars she recognizes. At the bar she *asks for a drink,* saying to John, "I'd like a gin gimlet." This particular speech event takes many forms and is one that Denise will hear repeatedly from customers throughout the evening. She will also label this speech event *taking an order.* John refuses her request, fixes a Coke instead, and replies, "You know you can't have a drink now, you start work in thirty minutes."

The evening begins slowly so Denise stands at her station talking to a regular customer. They are participating in a speech event called a *conversation.* As more customers arrive, Denise will say, "Hi, Bill," "Good to see you, George. Where have you been lately?" "Hi, how are things at the 'U' these days?" and other things to *greet* people as they walk in. She will *give orders* to the bartender, *answer the phone,* make an *announcement* about last call, and possibly get into an *argument* with one table when she tries to get them to leave on time. Like the other girls, Denise has learned the cultural rules in this bar for identifying particular speech events and participating in the verbal exchanges they involve. She has acquired the rules for greeting people, for arguing, and for giving orders, rules that define the appropriate ways to speak in such events.

It wouldn't take long for a stranger to see that *asking for a drink* is probably the most frequent speech event that occurs in the bar. But, although it is an important activity, it appears to be a rather simple act. A stranger would only have to know the name of one drink, say Pabst Beer, and any simple English utterance that expresses a desire in order to appropriately ask for a drink. The waitress approaches the table, asks, "What would you like?" and a customer can simple say, "I'll have a Pabst." And once a person knows all the names for the others' beverages, it is possible to use this sentence to ask for any drink the bartenders can provide. A stranger might even go out of the bar thinking that asking a drink is a rather trivial kind of speech behavior. That was certainly our impression during the first few weeks of fieldwork.

But as time went on we discovered that this speech event is performed in dozens of different ways. The people who come to Brady's have elaborated on a routine event, creating alternative ways for its execution. The well-socialized individual knows the rules for selecting among these alternatives and for manipulating them to his own advantage. Asking for a drink thus becomes a king of stage on which the customer can perform for the waitress and also the audience of other customers. A newcomer to the bar is frequently inept at these verbal performances, and one can observe regulars and employees smiling at one another or even laughing at some ill-timed and poorly performed effort at asking for a drink. Our goal was not to predict what people would say when they asked for a drink but to specify the alternative ways they could ask for a drink, the rules for selecting one or another alternative, and the social function of these ways of talking.[5] We especially wanted to know how the waitress would interpret the alternatives she encountered in the course of her work. At the heart of the diverse ways to ask for a drink was a large set of speech acts, and it was largely through observing the way people manipulated these different acts that we discovered how to ask for a drink in Brady's Bar.

Speech Acts

In order to describe the way people *use* speech we begin with the speech act as the minimal unit for analysis. In every society people use language to accomplish purposes: to insult, to gather information, to persuade, to greet others, to curse, to communicate, etc. An act of speaking to accomplish such purposes can be a single word, a sentence, a paragraph, or even an entire book. A speech act refers to the way any utterance, whether short or long, is used and the rules for this use.[6]

Our informants at Brady's Bar recognized many different categories of speech acts. They not only identified them for us but would frequently refer to one or another speech act during conversations in the bar. For example, at the end of a typically long evening the employees and a few real regulars are sitting around the bar talking about the events of the night. "Those guys in the upper section tonight were really obnoxious," recalls Sue. "They started off *giving me shit* about the way I took their orders and then all night long they kept *calling* my name. After last call they kept *hustling* me and when I finally came right out and said no, they really *slammed* me." The other waitress, Sandy, talks of the seven Annies who were sitting at one of her tables: "They kept *asking* me to tell them what went into drinks and they were drinking Brandy Alexanders, Singapore Slings, Brandy Manhattans, and Peapickers. Then they kept *muttering* their orders all evening so I could hardly hear and *bickering* over the prices and *bitching* about the noise—it was really awful."

Giving shit, calling, hustling, slamming, asking, muttering, bickering, and *bitching* are all ways to talk; they are speech acts used at Brady's Bar. There are at least thirty-five such named speech acts that our informants recognized and these form a folk taxonomy shown in Figure 6.1.

Components of Speech Acts[7]

The terms shown in this taxonomy refer to the *form* that messages take. But, in order to understand any speech act and the rules for its use, one must examine the various *components* of such acts. For instance, a waitress who hears a customer say, "Hey, sexy, what are you doing after work tonight?" also pays attention to the time and place of this utterance, who said it, the intention of the speaker, the tone of voice, and many other components. If said by a female customer, the waitresses would probably be shocked and offended. On the other hand, such an utterance by a *regular* male customer, especially early in the evening, might be interpreted as *teasing*. If said in a serous tone of voice by a male a few minutes before closing, the waitress would see this as *hustling*. Each of these components enters into the rules for using speech acts. Let's take a typical event to look briefly at the components that are the most important in asking for a drink.

It is Friday evening shortly before 10 P.M. In a few minutes the bouncer will assume his duties at the door. Some

WAYS TO TALK AT BRADY'S BAR	
	Slamming
	Talking
	Telling
	Giving shit
	Asking
	Begging
	Begging off
	Gossiping
	Joking
	Teasing
	Muttering
	Ordering
	Swearing
	Sweet Talking
	Pressuring
	Arguing
	Bantering
	Lying
	Bitching
	P.R.ing
	Babbling
	Harping
	Crying over a beer
	Hustling
	Introducing
	Flirting
	Daring
	Bickering
	Apologizing
	Calling
	Greeting
	Bullshitting
	Hassling
	Admitting
	Giving orders

Figure 6.1 Some Speech Acts Used in Brady's Bar.

tables are empty in both sections but the waitresses expect a rush of customers before 10:30. Two males enter and go directly to vacant stools at the bar; Sandy stands idly at her station watching them. The bartender has his back turned when they sit down, but when he turns around one of the newcomers asks quickly and firmly: "Could I please have a Schlitz?" The other one immediately adds, "Make mine Miller's." Without a word the bartender, who has never seen these two customers before, gets the beers, opens the bottles, and sets them down on the bar with two glasses. He collects their money and returns some change before turning to check other customers' needs. Sandy, her tables taken care of, has watched the brief interaction and thinks to herself, "If those *boys* had sat in my section I would have carded them both and asked them to leave—they can't be a day over 17" About five minutes later when the bartender has his attention on other matters, the two customers quietly move to one of the tables in Sandy's section and finish their beers. Later, when Sandy checks their table, one of them orders again, "Could we please have another round?" Without a word she clears their empty bottles and brings another Schlitz and Miller's. Let us look more closely at the components of these speech acts the two young customers have used to ask for drinks.

1. *Purpose.* Because asking for a drink can be done with any number of different speech acts, customers tend to select ones that will achieve certain ends. In addition to a drink they may want to tell others something about themselves, demonstrate their prowess with females generally, set the stage for later interaction with the waitress, etc. In this case, the two customers want to gain admittance to the adult world of male drinking. Even more, they want to pass as *men*, circumventing entirely the stigma of merely being *boys*. They could probably borrow I.D. cards from college friends that would legitimize their presence. But such a tactic would also announce to everyone, through the public experience of being carded, that they had not yet gained *unquestioned* right to participation in this male world. They have learned that the skillful use of language can be an world. They have learned that the skillful use of language can be an effective substitute for age and manliness.

2. *Message Content.* Schlitz and Miller's are both common drinks for young males. Had either of these customers asked for a daiquiri, a Marguerita on the rocks, or a Smith and Currants, it would have created suspicion. Not that male customers *never* drink these beverages—they do on rare occasions. But because these are female drinks it would have called attention to other characteristics of the customers. Instead of creating the impression that they were "ordinary men," such a request would have made others wonder whether they were *ordinary*, and even more important, whether they were really *men*. An order of scotch and soda, bourbon and seven, whiskey and water, or gin and tonic would not have cast doubt on their maleness but might have been a reason for others to question their age. Men often order such drinks but, in this case, asking for any one of these would obviously contrast with their youthful appearance. By ordering two

usual drinks of young men—common beers like Schlitz and Miller's—they effectively created a protective screen around their true identities.

3. *Message Form.* "Could I please have. . . " is the polite form of *asking* in Brady's Bar. The second customer also *asked* when he added, "Make mine... " But they could have *ordered* in a more direct statement. They might have *asked for information* with a question about the kinds of beers available. They could have *muttered* an order in an effort to avoid attention. Other forms were also available but asking politely helped insure an impression of knowledgeable confidence. Other speech acts could easily bring suspicion in the same way that ordering an unusual drink might have done.

4. *Channel.* People at Brady's ask for drinks by using one of several different channels. A person who regularly drinks the same beverage and does so repeatedly on a single night may receive a drink on the house. By his drinking *behavior* he can thus be asking for a free drink. When a regular enters the bar, his very presence asks for a drink, and he can merely take a place at the bar or a table and the drink appears. Various gestures are another frequently used channel as when a regular walks in and holds up his index finger or nods his head. The waitress takes his order from memory and delivers it to the waiting customer. Asking for a drink by gesture instead of the verbal channel was not possible for the two young customers because of their status as persons as persons off the street. When someone does use one of these other channels it serves as a public announcement of status in the bar.

5. *Setting.* The setting of a speech act refers to the time and place it is spoken. Even though Brady's is a small bar, the place where a person speaks can change the social significance of what it said. Individuals at the bar tend to take on some of the "sacred maleness" associated with that location. Drinking at the tables tends to convey less experience and, combined with an appearance of youth, can be sufficient reason for carding a customer. A person who enters, and walks confidently to the bar, communicates the unstated message that he is a man, a mature drinker, one whose presence at the bar is not to be questioned. By timing their entry prior to 10:00 P.M. they also circumvent the possibility of being carded by the bouncer. Once a drink is served at the bar, the same customers who would have been carded at a table, and probably excluded, can move with immunity to a table in either section. In order for a waitress to ask them for I.D.'s at that point would require that she violate the implicit rule that bartenders know better than waitresses, something few girls are eager to do in such a public manner. By timing the round ordered from a waitress to follow the drinks ordered from a bartender, the customer can ask for a drink and also accomplish other desired ends.

6. *Tone.* A customer who enters the bar is probably not always aware of the manner or tone he uses to ask for a drink. It may have been days since he asked for a drink in any his tone of voice and general manner of speech

may be conditioned by experiences earlier in the day. But, to the waitress who hears hundreds of people asking for drinks, the tone communicates a great deal. The person who asks questions about drinks or who hesitates, communicates more than the kind of drink desired. The customer who uses this occasion to hustle the waitress or tease her must carefully manipulate the tone of any utterance to avoid being seen as inept or crude. The two customers who asked for a Schlitz and Miller's exuded confidence in their manner of speaking. By eliminating any hesitancy from the speech act they effectively communicated to the bartender as well as to other customers that they were men who knew their way around in bars.

7. *Participants.* Speech acts are used between two people or between groups of people. In Brady's Bar, the participants in any communicative event can change the meaning and consequences in the same way that other components do. Asking the *bartender* instead of the *waitress* allows underage males to escape the emasculation of being carded by females. When a couple enters the bar and the girl is underage, a quick firm order for both by the male will mask the girl's discomfort and keep her from being carded. An underage *regular,* on the other hand, can order from either the bartender to waitress without worrying about being carded. As we shall see, *who* is talking to *whom* is one of the most significant variables in understanding the way people talk.[8]

But asking for a drink is not merely a communication between a customer and employee. Nearby customers and employees participate in the exchanges as an attentive audience. Many speech acts cannot be understood at Brady's unless we consider the audience before whom a speaker performs. The two young men who ordered at the bar were not only seeking to get around the barrier of carding but also to communicate their claim to adult male status, especially to those at the center of this male-oriented social world.

8. *Outcome.* The regular participants in the social life at Brady's learn to use language successfully and thereby achieve a variety of ends. Not everyone who manipulates the various features of a speech act accomplish their intentions. Some customers *hustle* a waitress when asking for a drink but to no avail. Some seek to avoid being carded, only to find themselves required to show their I.D. or leave. Others make a claim to privileged intimacy or special status, only to find their performance inept and open to derision. But there are other outcomes that often lie outside the awareness of the actors. In this case the two customers successfully escaped the degradation of carding, demonstrated their manliness and adulthood to their audience, and paved the way for an evening of uninterrupted drinking at a table served by a cocktail waitress. But equally important, their skillful performance in asking for a drink set in motion the social processes that could eventually change their status in Brady's Bar from underage persons-off-the-street to regular customers. For having escaped the carding

process once, they have established their right to drink at Brady's, and subsequent visit will reinforce this right.

Rituals of Masculinity

Probably the most important outcome of the various ways to ask for a drink at Brady's Bar is related to the way they symbolize the values of *masculinity* that lie at the heart of bar culture. During our observations of the way male customers asked for drinks it became clear that these performance had a ritual quality about them. Goffman has identified the nature of this ceremonial or ritual quality in social interaction:

> To the degree that a performance highlights the common official values of the society in which it occurs, we may look upon it, in the manner of Durkheim and Radcliffe-Brown, as a ceremony—as an expressive rejuvenation and reaffirmation of the moral values of the community.[9]

In a sense, the routine performance of asking for a drink at Brady's Bar have been transformed into rituals that express important male values. Customers and other members of this community seldom view these speech events as rituals, but nevertheless they function in this manner. These ritual performances reinforce masculine virtues and symbolize full membership in the male world of Brady's Bar.

Furthermore, these rituals take on an added meaning when we consider that the ongoing social life at Brady's often obscures the presence of a deep structural conflict. It stems from the fact that the bar functions both as a *business* and as a *men's ceremonial center* where masculine values are reaffirmed. The conflict between these two features of the bar is partially mediated by a set of speech acts that customers employ to ask for drinks. We need to examine this structural conflict briefly.

On the one hand, the bar is a business establishment that is organized to sell drinks for a profit. It has no membership dues, no initiation rituals, no rules except legal age that restrict certain classes of people from buying drinks. Any adult can open the doors, walk into the bar, and order any drink in the house. The only requirement for drinking is payment of the usual fees. As a business establishment Brady's Bar has an air of efficiency, casualness, and impersonality. There is no readily apparent organization except the division between employees and customers. Even the spatial arrangement can be seen purely in economic terms with the bar and tables arranged for the efficient distribution of drinks. It is possible for an individual to stop in for a drink without ever suspecting that the bar is much different from a restaurant, a bank, or department store except for the menu, small services rendered, or items sold. At one level, then, Brady's is primarily a place of business.

On the other hand, Brady's Bar is a *men's ceremonial center.* As we have seen in earlier chapters, there is a formal social structure that ascribes to men the places of high status. The spatial patterns in the bar reflect the values of a male-oriented culture with certain place having an almost sacred atmosphere. The language patterns also serve to reaffirm male values, providing an important symbol of membership in the informal men's association. Even the division of labor that appears to be a strict business function reflects the subordinate position of women in the bar as well as the wider society. At another level, then, Brady's Bar is primarily a place where men can come to play out exaggerated masculine roles, acting out their fantasies of sexual prowess, and reaffirming their own male identities.

The essence of the *ceremonial function is to reaffirm the official values of manhood in our culture.* But this is difficult to do when women enter almost every night to drink and talk. Some even select the same drinks as men and all have the right to sit at the bar itself. Strangers visit Brady's frequently for a quick drink, never entering into the social and ceremonial life of the bar. Students tend to be a transient group that results in a constant turnover of customers. Relationships among people in the bar are frequently impersonal and businesslike. All of this works counter to the ceremonial function that requires some common public expression of the moral values on which masculine identities are constructed. It requires some way to highlight the virtues of strength, toughness, aggressiveness, and dominance over females. Most important, it requires some corporate group of males staging the ritual performance together. It is possible that these ceremonial functions could be carried out by restricting membership to men in a formal way as done by athletic clubs or men's associations in certain New Guinea societies. Some "male only" bars still employ this device. The moral values of masculinity could be reaffirmed by aggressive physical activity from which women were excluded as is done in competitive football from Little League teams for boys to the national Football League. But Brady's managers do not even allow the escalation of the rare fights that do occur but halt them before they hardly begin. Drinks at Brady's could be restricted to men alone or special uniforms and ceremonial regalia could be created to symbolize their corporate unity and importance. But Brady's has none of these. Instead, *male values are reaffirmed by the use of elaborate patterns of language.* It is not so much *what* people say but *how* they speak that serves to mediate between the business and ceremonial functions of the bar.

Language is used to symbolize status and masculinity in public displays. Equally important, customers use speech performances to create a sense of corporate belonging, a feeling of full membership in the men's association that constitutes the hub of this society. Asking for a drink becomes not only a display of an individual's masculinity but a membership ritual announcing to those present that the speaker *belongs,* he is a man who has ties with other men, a male who is at home in a truly male world. Such rituals occur during *dominance displays, ritual reversals, reciprocal exchanges,*

drinking contests, and *asking for the wrong drink.* We shall consider each of these in turn.

Dominance Displays

One frequent way that men ask for a drink is not to ask for a drink at all. In the situation where it is appropriate to ask for a drink, they ask instead for the waitress. This may be done in the form of *teasing, hustling, hassling* or some other speech act. But, whatever the form, it serves as a ritual in which masculine values are symbolized for the people at Brady's. Consider the following example of hassling.

Sandy is working the upper section. She walks up to the corner table where there is a group of five she has never seen before: four guys and a girl who are loud and boisterous. She steps up to the table and asks, "Are you ready to order now?" One of the males grabs her by the waist and jerks her towards him. "I already know what I want, I'll take you," he says as he smiles innocently up at her. Sandy removes his hand and steps back from the table. She takes the orders from the others at the table and then turns back to the first man. He reaches over and pulls her towards him, prolonging the ritual of asking for a drink with a question, "What's good here, do you know?" Sandy patiently removes his hand for the second time, "If you haven't decided yet what you want to drink, I can come back in a few minutes," "Oh, please, don't leave me!" He grabs her by the leg this time, the only part of her he can reach and inquires, "What's your name honey? Are you new here? I don't think I've seen you before? What nights do you work?" The others at the table begin to smile and chuckle, making the situation worse; Sandy knows that several nearby customers are also watching the encounter. Finally, in desperation she heads for the bar and he calls out, "I'll have a Screwdriver."

Back at her station, she gives the bartender the order and tells Mike, a regular sitting by her station, about the *obnoxo* in the upper section. Mike listens and puts his arm protectively around her, "Look, just make them come down to the bar if they want to order. If they give you any more shit tell me and I'll take care of them." The order is ready and Sandy balances her tray as she heads back to the waiting customers, planning to stand on the opposite side of the table in hopes of avoiding a repeat performance.

This kind of performance is not exceptional. For the waitresses it is a recurrent feature of each night's work. The details vary from customer to customer but the basic features remain constant. She approaches a table where, instead of asking for a drink, a customer seizes upon the brief encounter to display his manly skills. "Where have you been all my life?" asks one. "Sit down and talk to us," says another "Have I ever told you that I love you?" "Haven't I seen you someplace before?" "Wouldn't you like to sit on my lap?" And often the verbal requests are punctuated with attempts to invade the personal space of the waitress. One customer asks for his drink in a low, muffled voice, requiring the waitress to move closer or bend down so he can hear. Another grabs her as she starts to leave. Some pinch, grab a wrist, pat, or securely retain the waitress with an arm around her waist. Except for the regular customer whom she knows well, these direct attempts at physical contact are obvious violation of the usual rules governing interaction between men and women. Indeed, their value seems to lie in this fact, as if to say there here is a real man, one who can act out his aggressive fantasies.

Thus Brady's Bar provides male customers with a stage where they can perform; it offers an audience to appreciate their displays of manliness. Furthermore, this ritual setting gives a special legitimacy to expressing one's masculinity. Asking for a drink becomes an occasion to act out fantasies that would be unthinkable in the classroom, on the street, and even perhaps when alone with a female. But here, in the protective safely of the bar, a customer can demonstrate to others that he has acquired the masculine attributes so important in our culture.

But the masculinity rituals would not be effective without the cooperation of the waitress. She had learned to respond demurely to taunts, invitations, and physical invasions of her personal space. She smiles, laughs, patiently removes hands, ignores the questions, and moves coyly out of reach. It is precisely these qualities of her response that complement the performance of male customer. When she meets a particularly aggressive and obnoxious customer she may complain to bartenders or regulars, providing these men with their opportunity to demonstrate another aspect of manliness—the protector role. But the cultural expectations are clear: *she should remain dependent and passive.* As waitresses move back and forth between the bar and their tables, they also move between these two kinds of encounters—warding off the tough, aggressive males, and leaning on the strong, protective males.

Although the girls know it is important to keep their place during these encounters, it is also clear they *could* act otherwise in dealing with aggressive customers. Like the bartenders, they might refuse to allow customers to act in offensive ways. The could become aggressive themselves, "touch broads" who brusquely reprimand customer and have them removed from the bar. On occasion the girls all have acted in this way towards a customer, something it would be *possible* to do with relative frequency. For example, one night Joyce was making her way to the table in the corner of the upper section and she had a tray load of expensive cocktails. Doug, a regular, stepped out in front of her, blocking the path. "C'mon, Doug. Don't make me spill these drinks." He was drunk. "I'll move if you give me a kiss," he replied. "Not now, Doug. I have to get these drinks to that table. Now *please* move!" Doug stood his ground, refusing to budget an inch. "If you don't move, Doug, I'm gonna kick you in the shins, and I mean it!" Doug didn't move, but instead, beer in one hand, he reached out to put the other arm around Joyce. That was all it took. Joyce gave him a good

hard kick in the shins, and then, to her surprise, Doug kicked her back! Joyce glared at him and he finally let her through to the table. She felt both angry and proud as she carried the tray of the heavy drinks to the table. Most of the frozen daiquiris were melting and the Bacardis had spilled over the tops of glasses. But for one brief moment an encounter with an aggressive male had been changed into relationship in which she felt on equal footing. But in the process she had destroyed the ritual quality of Doug's attempt to demonstrate his manliness.

Ritual Reversals

The ritual quality of asking for a drink does not always have a serious tone. Waitresses and customers often work together to create humorous scenes for the audiences around them, using speech acts like *bantering, joking,* and *teasing,* in ways that appear to be serious. These performances are particularly effective in symbolizing masculine values when they call attention to subtle possibilities that some individual is *not* acting like a woman or man. Two examples may serve to illuminate this complex use of language in asking for a drink. The first one humorously suggests that the waitress is sexually aggressive in the way reserved for men. The second implies that male customer is less than a man because of homosexual tendencies.

Recall an earlier example when Sue waited on a Cougar regular who came to Brady's with three friends. When she approached their table they were engrossed in conversation and to get their attention she placed her hand on one customer's shoulder. He turned to see who it was and then said loudly in mock anger, "Don't you touch me!" Sue jumped back, pretending to be affected by his response. "I'm sorry. Do you want another beer?" He smiled. "No, thanks, a little later." She continued on her circular path around the section. A few minutes later she was back in the area and as she passed the same table the customer reached out and grabbed her by the waist. "Watch the hands," she said. "I'll have another Pabst now," the regular said. She brought him the beer. "That was fast!" he commented as she set the bottle down. "I'm a fast girl," was her response.

"Oh, you mean with the beer?" To which she answered, as she collected the money and turned to leave, "What did you think I meant?" In this encounter, first the customer and then the waitress *jokingly* suggest that she may be a sexually aggressive female, thereby underscoring the important cultural value of actually being a passive female.

During the course of our research, a popular song included in the juke box selections at the bar had to do with a football player called Bruiser LaRue, an implied homosexual. Playing this song or making loud requests for someone to play it, provided abundant opportunities for treating homosexuality in a humorous manner. One such opportunity involved asking for a drink. Holly notices two regulars come in the door and because it is crowded they end up along the wall at the back of the lower section where she has just taken an order for another round. Because of the crowd and noise, neither bartender sees these well-known regulars or has a chance to greet them. Holly already knows their drinks so does not need to wait for their orders, but one of them says with a smile, "I'll have a Pink Lady, tell him it's for Bruiser LaRue." At the bar when Holly passes the message on, the bartender immediately scans her section to see who this "Bruiser LaRue" might be. Smiles and laughter are quickly exchanged across the noisy bar, and the ritual is complete. If either bartender or customer were to admit even the possibility of being homosexual or accuse another male of such behavior, it would be a serious violation of cultural norms. By joking about it in the presence of a waitress, they uphold the dominant masculine values, saying, in effect, "We are so manly we can even joke about being effeminate." In a similar fashion, it is not uncommon for a waitress to approach a table of male customers who have just sat down and one will say, "My friend here wants a Pink Lady," or "Bill wants a Gold Cadillac." The waitress smiles, the customers poke one another, smile, laugh, and add other comments. The incongruity of "a man like one of us" having a "female drink" has provided a brief ritual reversal of the sacred values. Because it occurs in a humors context, no one is threatened and all settle down to a night of drinking, comfortable in their sense of manhood.

Reciprocal Exchanges

There are several contexts in which customers order drinks for other people with an expectation of reciprocity. Buying in rounds is the most frequent kind of exchange and occurs with almost every group of men who stay for any length of time in the bar. A typical sequence goes something like this. Six men take their places at a table and begin with separate orders: a scotch and soda, two Buds, a Lowenbrau, a Brandy Manhattan, and a whiskey tonic. The waitress brings the drinks, arranged in order on her tray, and places each one down for the respective customer. Fred, who is sitting on the corner where the waitress stands announces, "I'll get this one," and hands her a ten dollar bill. He has assumed the temporary responsibility to ask for drinks desired by anyone at the table. Half an hour later the waitress checks the table: "How're you doin' here?" Fred shakes his head that they aren't quite ready, and the others keep right on talking. But the question has signaled the group to prepare to order soon. The next time the waitress approaches their table, Bill, sitting next to Fred, looks up and says, "Another round." The responsibility for asking has now shifted to him and he orders for everyone. In this case he might check individually or act on a knowledge of his friends' drinking habits. When the drinks arrive he pays for the second round. Soon another member of the group will take over, and before the evening ends each of the

six customers will have taken one or more turns. It is not uncommon for the composition of a table to change, adding new drinkers, losing some to other tables, expanding and contracting with the ebb and flow of people, creating ever widening circles of reciprocal exchange.

These exchanges did not seem unusual to us until we discovered that female customers almost never order or pay in rounds. Those who do are usually waitresses from other bars; they know that this practice eases the workload for the cocktail waitress, both in taking orders and making change. Why then do men almost always order in rounds, asking for drinks in this reciprocal fashion? When we observed the other ways that men typically make work difficult for waitresses it seems improbable that ordering in rounds was intended to assist the cocktail waitresses. Whatever the reason for this practice, it is a continual reminder that *males belong to groups of men in the bar*. The individual nature of asking for a drink is transformed into a shared, social experience. When men request drinks and pay for them in rounds they reaffirm their ties to one another and their common membership in a kind of men's association.

Numerous occasions occur when a single individual will buy for another person or a whole group at another table. The reciprocity in these exchanges may never occur or it can take place at a later date, but the expectation of a return drink underlies the action. In the course of an evening the waitress may have frequent orders of this nature. Two guys and a girl are drinking at a table near the lower waitress station. One of the guys signals the waitress and says, "Would you take a drink to Mark, over there? It's his birthday. Tell him it's from us." Drawing on her recollection of Mark's original order she asks the bartender for a whiskey sour and delivers it to Mark who hasn't even finished his first drink. Another friend of Mark's sitting nearby sees the extra drink arrive and when he learns it is Mark's birthday, he orders a round for everyone at the table, again in honor of the occasion.

As the bar becomes more crowded, waitresses are often kept running to take drinks to an acquaintance here who was recently engaged, a friend there who got a new job, or someone else a customer hasn't seen for a while. "Take a drink to that guy over there in the red shirt who just came in, a gin and tonic, and tell him Bob sent it," a customer tells the waitress, pointing across the bar. Fighting her way back through the crowd to the bar and then over to the man in the red shirt, the waitress says, "This is from Bob." The surprised and pleased customer looks over the crowd, locates Bob at his table and calls loudly, "Thanks, Bob, I'll talk to you later." Other people notice, look briefly in his direction, and the noisy hum of activity continues at a steady pace.

A regular at the bar motions for Stephanie: "I owe Randy one from last week. Do you know what he's drinking? Whatever it is, send him one from me." Randy is in the other waitresses section so Stephanie passes the word on to Joyce and soon Randy has an unrequested drink arrive at his table. He remembers the debt when the waitress identifies the regular; a wave and shouted words of thanks that cannot be heard above the noise complete the transaction. Later the same night customers will ask for other drinks to be delivered at other places. "I want another round for Alan—tell him congratulations on his new job." "I hear Ron got engaged, take him a drink from me."

In these and similar cases, the drink is purchased, not because someone wants a drink, but rather as a symbol of a friendship tie. On many occasions these exchanges are followed by shouting and gestures that serve not only to communicate between friends but to announce to others that the participants are inside members of the bar crowd. Even when the transaction is known only to the buyer, recipient, and waitress, the ritual performance has fulfilled its function. The customers have both demonstrated they are not alone in an impersonal, business establishment. They know people here and are known by others. The very act of establishing social ties in this manner gives these customers an additional reason for being in the bar. Their claim to membership has been announced, acknowledged, and confirmed.

Sometimes reciprocal exchanges are done in a humorous manner, emphasizing certain masculine values as well as reaffirming membership in the men's association. Recall an earlier example when one night a man at the bar called Holly over and said, "I want you to take a drink to the guy over there in the sport coat and tell him Dan said to get fucked." When the message and drink were delivered they brought a return order—a Harvey Wallbanger for Dan and a 75¢ tip for Holly. The message with its overtones of a tough man who could even use obscenity in the presence of a woman was clear. The return order of a Harvey Wallbanger, a drink with sexual connotations, brought smiles to the faces of bartenders, waitress, and customers alike. In addition, the exchange highlighted publicly the social ties between two customers.

Later on that same evening, Holly was asked to take a double vodka tonic to Gene, a regular, who was already quite intoxicated. A friend across the bar had observed Gene's steady drinking all night and increasingly boisterous behavior. Gene was finishing the last drink he would order when the "gift" arrived. "This is from Bill," said Holly with a smile, loud enough for others at the table to hear. Faced with the choice of increasing physical discomfort and a reputation that he wasn't man enough to down another drink, Gene raised the drink in a smilingly reluctant toast and finished off the double vodka tonic.

On a typical evening drinks criss-cross the bar in these ways with considerable frequency. The senders and receivers come to be recognized as full members of the bar society. Even those who do not participate in these rituals themselves gain a secure sense that there is a lot of action at Brady's. They are reassured that this is a place where male customers, in general, and themselves, in particular, truly belong.

Drinking Contests

Sometimes customers ask for drinks that involve a challenge to another man's ability to drink. In an earlier chapter we mentioned how waitresses become customer's "lucky charms" in these contests. The night is slow and two guys sitting at Joyce's station pass the time by "chugging", a kind of drinking contest. A coin was flipped and first one customer called and then the other. If a call identified the correct side of the coin, the customer who called was not required to down his drink in a single gulp. Each failure to call the coin correctly meant asking for another drink and chugging it down until one or the other contestants called a halt, thereby losing the game.

At times, such contests involve the entire bar, as customers become spectators cheering on the early demise of the participants. One evening, several of the Cougars were seated at the bar. It was late and they had been there most of the evening. The bar was noisy, but suddenly become quiet as John ceremoniously placed six empty shot glasses in front of one of the football players. "Okay, Larry, ol' boy, let's see you handle this!" Holly and Sue crowded together into the lower waitress station to get a better look as John slowly filled each shot glass with tequila. People seated at tables stood to get a better view. Someone had dared Larry to drink six straight shots of tequila and he was going to do it. John finished pouring and stepped back, bowing in deference to Larry. "It's all yours," he added. Larry picked up the first glass, toasted his audience, and downed it. Everyone applauded and cheered. He picked up the second, toasted again, and downed it too. Again, the group applauded and so it went until all six glasses were empty. Larry had met the challenge and the game was over. Someone slapped Larry on the back, he reddened and headed for the men's room. Activity returned to normal. The contest was over.

While this was one of the more dramatic contests, similar ones take place frequently at Brady's. Such drinking contests bring males together in a competitive sport, one they are allowed to play inside the bar, but in a way which symbolizes desirable masculine traits—a willingness to compete, strength, endurance, and the ability to imbibe great quantities of strong liquor. It is a contest that places emphasis on *how* one plays the game rather than who wins. Larry may have made a fast retreat to the bathroom, but he *had* played the game, and that is what counted. In addition, those who participated as spectators demonstrated their ties with Larry and others in the bar.

Asking for the Wrong Drink

One of the most curious ways that males ask for drinks involves intentional errors in ordering. This kind of asking for a drink appears to involve a combination of two speech acts: *ordering* and *telling*, or giving information. Consider the following example. Two young men enter the bar and take a table next to the wall in the lower section. The waitress approaches their table and places a napkin in front of each one. She waits in silence for their order. One of them looks up at her and says calmly:

"Two double Sloe Screws on the rocks, uhhhh, for Joe and Bill."

The waitress turns quickly, goes to the bar, and in a moment returns with two, tall, dark bottles of Hamm's beer. A stranger might think this interaction strange, and at first this kind of "asking for a drink" seemed out of place, but in time we noted other similarly strange games being played. For example, someone comes in and says. "I'll have a banana Daiquiri with Drambuie," or another person says, "Make mine a double Harvey Wallbanger." As you watch the waitress in these and other situations, you observe that frequently the drinks people ask for are not served. A scotch and soda is given instead of the banana daiquiri, a bourbon and water is served instead of the double Harvey Wallbanger, two Hamm's are delivered instead of two double Sloe Screws on the rocks.

In no case where a person asks for one drink and is given another, at least in situations like the examples noted, does the customer complain that he received the wrong drink. Two factors complicate the situation. First, sometimes people do order "Sloe Screws" or "Harvey Wallbangers" and the waitress brings these drinks. Second, occasionally the bartender mixes the wrong drink or the waitress serves the wrong drink and the customer *does* complain. If we return to our original ethnographic goal, we can now ask, "What does a stranger to Brady's Bar have to know in order to ask for a drink in this manner, or to interpret correctly when someone else asks for a drink in this manger? Furthermore, why does this kind of "asking" go on?

If the stranger were to assume the role of cocktail waitress, she would have to know at least the following:

1. That the drink requested was not actually desired.
2. That another drink was actually being requested.
3. What that other drink was.

Waitresses do acquire the rules for correctly interpreting these kinds of requests. But what are these rules and how do they operate?

Let's go back to the customer who said, "Two double sloe screws on the rocks, uhhhh, for Joe and Bill." In addition to the utterance itself, he also communicates a *metamessage*, a message about the message, that serves to identify the kind of speech act he intends it to be. The metamessage says something like, "Don't take us seriously, we really don't want two double Sloe Screws on the rocks. We aren't *ordering* but only *teasing*." But how is such a metamessage sent and how does the waitress interpret it correctly? Sometimes this information is sent by the *tone* of a speech act or by accompanying gestures or facial expressions. But when a customer uses these metamessage forms he also signals to others that he is teasing or joking. He may then be seen as a "ham," someone unsophisticated in bar culture. The ideal is to ask for a

double Sloe Screw on the rocks or a banana Daquiri with Drambuie in a perfectly serious tone of voice and manner, *sending metamessages in ways that are not obvious* to the surrounding audience. At least three alternatives are open to the sophisticated, well-enculturated customer.

First, he may choose to make a referential mistake that the waitress will recognize but other, less sophisticated customers will not. Let's take the order for two double Sloe Screws on the rocks. "On the rocks" is a feature of several drinks at Brady's. It means that liquor will be served only with ice and not the usual additional liquid. Whiskey on the rocks, for example, is whiskey without soda, water, or anything except ice. Vodka on the rocks is vodka and ice, nothing more. If a customer wants to order something "on the rocks," it usually means naming a type of liquor, not a fancy drink containing liquor and other mixtures. For example, if you order a Screwdriver on the rocks (vodka and orange juice), it would mean a screwdriver without orange juice, the same thing as vodka on the rocks. This order would be quickly recognized by waitresses as a *referential mistake*. It is a name that sounds like a drink, but no one knowledgeable in the ways of the bar would ask for this drink, but no one knowledgeable in the ways of the bar would ask for this drink, unless perhaps as a joke. A Sloe Screw is a mixture of sloe gin and orange juice. When the customer said, "Two double sloe screws on the rocks," he was talking nonsense. He asked for a drink that doesn't exist at Brady's Bar, but when he made this obvious and intentional error of reference, he also signaled to the waitress that he was *teasing*, not *ordering*. He might have asked for sloe gin on the rocks, in which case the waitress could have brought the two customers each a glass of sloe gin and ice.

A second way to unobtrusively let the waitress know that a named drink is not desired involves the connotations of certain drinks. If they are clearly female drinks such as a Pink Lady or Gold Cadillac, this can signal that the customer doesn't really want them. Both a "Sloe Screw" and a "Harvey Wallbanger" have implicit sexual connotations that are widely recognized by the people at Brady's. "A glass full of tequila" carries the connation of an impending contest and other features of the setting can make it clear that no contest is planned. If a regular wants to tease the waitress, he will not name a scotch and soda or gin and tonic for these ordinary drinks do not have the special connotations that could signal the use of a different speech act.

Finally, customers can signal the intended speech act by combining two or more speech acts. When the customer asked for two double sloe screws on the rocks, he added, "for Joe and Bill." He was *telling* the waitress something else, in addition to the apparent order. The waitress can quickly guess that the customers are teasing, but how will she know to bring them bottles of Hamm's beer? If she doesn't recognize the two customers as regulars or know their customary drinks, she can use this additional information to check with the bartenders: "What do Joe and Bill over there in the corner usually drink?"

These complicated ways of asking for drinks have many functions for both the customer and waitress. Most important, they clearly demonstrate that the customer has mastered the use of bar language. As an individual learns to use the language of this culture with skill, he also becomes recognized as a regular, one who has gained entrance to the inner circle of this little society.

Conclusion

When we began to discover the enormous range of ways that men ask for drinks and how all these patterns of talking reaffirmed masculine values as well as symbolizing full membership in the bar community, we went back to examine the way women ask for drinks. Certainly our interpretation of the significance of male speech acts would be questionable if female customers ordered drinks in the same way as males. One would expect that to women customers the bar would be seen much more as a business establishment, a place to get drinks and perhaps meet men but not a place to participate in ceremonial performance that emphasized male values. The contrast between the way men and women ordered drinks was striking. Furthermore, it shed light on why female customers seemed to unwittingly create problems for the cocktail waitresses. If we exclude the few women who came to the bar as experienced cocktail waitresses, the following significant differences are present:

1. *Female customers order separately, never in rounds.* The bar is more like a restaurant to them; they have come to purchase drinks, to get out of the dormitories for a time, perhaps to meet men, but not to become part of a ceremonial women's association.

2. *Female customers ask numerous questions about drinks.* To them, a drink is not something to use in establishing an identity as a regular customer. It is much more like an item on a restaurant menu and so it seems appropriate to inquire about the range of drinks available and their contents. After all, Brady's Bar is a place of business that sells drinks. Men hardly ever ask about drinks because such questions would reveal their ignorance and weaken the value of drinks as ceremonial markers of adulthood, masculinity, and full membership in the bar. Women, on the other hand, see drinks more as something to taste, to drink, to purchase for yourself.

3. *Female customers pay separately for their drinks.* The shared experience of ordering and paying hold little significance to women. Like a group of men who go out to lunch in a restaurant and pay separately, the women who visit Brady's are merely following the rules for purchasing things in a business establishment.

4. *Female customers are never ready to order at the same time.* Unlike the men who form small drinking *groups*, women treat the entire process of asking for a drink as an individual economic exchange between themselves and the waitress. The girls at a table who require the waitress to make six or seven trips to the bar for individual orders are not trying to create difficulties for her. They see these trips as simple acts of service for which they have paid.

5. *Female customers change their drinks frequently.* Men find it useful to stay with the same drink. They can then order in rounds. Because employees tend to recognize people by drinks, asking for the same thing on every occasion establishes one's identity as a regular, a continuing member of the bar society. Sending drinks to other people becomes easier when the waitress knows what a customer "always" drinks. But these ceremonial qualities are hardly significant to a female and so she tries new drinks, changing often for the sake of variety or in search of a drink which has little or no taste of alcohol to it.

6. *Female customers almost never tip.* We suspect that the entire cultural atmosphere of the bar communicates to women that men are receiving a special service in the form of opportunities to express their manhood. Undoubtedly competition between the female customer and the cocktail waitress also influences their reluctance to tip.

7. *Female customers never engage in reciprocal exchanges.* As we noted, they do not order in rounds. They do not send drinks across the bar to a friend who has not been seen for a time. They do not send drinks as jokes nor to a friend who gets engaged or locates a new job. The only occasion when female customers sent drinks to others, and these were rare, was on birthdays.

8. *Female customers never intentionally ask for the wrong drink.* Because the inner circle at Brady's is not open to these women, the skilled use of bar language is unimportant. Their status is relatively fixed and manipulating speech acts cannot change it.

9. *Female customers never engage in drinking contests.* Again, the symbolic meaning of such activities are only meaningful to males in the context of the bar.

It is clear that asking for a drink in Brady's Bar means one thing to men, another to women. For the female customer it is a simple economic transaction, one that takes only a few alternative speech acts. For the male customer it is an opportunity to manipulate language for a variety of ends. What Charles Frake has concluded about asking for a drink in Subanum could also apply to the men who come to Brady's Bar for drinking and talking.

> The Subanun drinking encounter thus provides a structured setting within which one's social relationships beyond his everyday associates can be extended, defined, and manipulated through the use of speech. The cultural patterning of drinking talk lays out an ordered scheme of role play through the use of terms of address, through discussion and argument, and through display of verbal art. The most skilled in "talking from the straw" are the *de facto* leaders of the society. In instructing our stranger to Subanun society how to ask for a drink, we have at the same time instructed him how to get ahead socially.[10]

Notes

1. This discussion is based on Charles O. Frake. "How to Ask for a Drink in Subanun" (1964b). This classic article provided many insights as well as the framework for the material presented in this chaptes.
2. Ibid. (1964b: 128-129).
3. One of the earliest formulations of the approach to a cultural description of speaking behavior used in this chapter is Dell H. Hymes. "The Ethnography of Speaking" (1962). Many earlier works in language and culture implicitly deal with the same issues. See Dell H. Hymes, ed., *Language, Culture and Society: A Reader in Linguistics and Anthropology* (1964) for the best of this earlier literature. Since 1962 Dell H. Hymes has published a series of articles that elaborate on his early formulation of the ethnography of speaking. This chapter and the next one draw heavily from these works. See especially his "Introduction: Toward Ethnographies of Communication" (1964); "Directions in (Ethno) Linguistic Theory" (1964); "Models of the Interaction of Language and Social Setting" (1965); "Sociolinguistics and the Ethnography of Speaking" (1971); and "Models of the Interaction of Language and Social Life" (1972). One of the earliest empirical studies based directly on Hymes' formulation of the ethnography of speaking was Charles O. Frake, "How to Ask for a Drink in Subanun" (1964b). This was published in a special issue of the *American Anthropologist*, "The Ethnography of Communication," edited by John J. Gumperz and Dell Hymes (1964), and contains other important articles in this area. For a recent collection of studies, see John J. Gumperz and Dell Hymes, eds., *The Ethnography of Communication: Directions in Sociolinguistics* (1972).
4. This definition of a speech event is based on Dell Hymes (1972:56).
5. We agree with Frake who maintaines that the goal of ethnography is not prediction but identification of culturally-appropriate alternatives. In his "Notes on Queries in Ethnography," he writes:

> The aims of ethnography, then, differ from those of stimulus-response psychology in at least two respects. First, it is not, I think, the ethnographer's task to predict behavior perse, but rather to state the rules of culturally appropriate behavior. In this respect the ethnographer is again akin to the linguist who does not attempt to predict what people will say but to state rules for constructing utterances which native speakers will judge as grammatically appropriate. The model of an ethnographic statement is not: "if a person is confronted with stimulus X, he will do Y," but: "If a person is in situation X, performance Y will be judged appropriate by native actors." The second difference is that the ethnographer seeks to discover, not prescribe, the significant stimuli in the subject's world. He attempts to describe each act in terms of the cultural situations which appropriately evoke it and each situation in terms of the acts it appropriately evokes (1964a: 133).

6. Our definition of a speech act is based on Dell Hymes (1972:56-57).
7. See Dell Hymes (1972) for an extended discussion of the components of speech acts. We have also found Joe Sherzer and Regna Darnell, "Outline Guide for the Ethnographic Study of Speech Use" (1972) especially helpful.
8. The participants in any speech event at Brady's Bar depend on their particular *identity* at the time of speaking. The range of social identities in the bar have been examined in our discussion of the social structure of Brady's Bar in Chapter 4.
9. Erving Goffman, *The Presentation of Self in Everyday Life* (1959:35). Our discussion of masculinity rituals in this section has drawn may insights from this book as well as *Interaction Ritual* (1967) and *Encounters* (1961) by Goffman.
10. Charles O. Frake, "How to Ask for a Drink in Subanum" (1964b).

Why Don't You Say What You Mean?

Directness is not necessarily logical or effective. Indirectness is not necessarily manipulative or insecure.

Deborah Tannen

In this classic article, adapted from *Talking from 9 to 5: How Women's and Men's Conversational Styles Affect Who Gets Heard, Who Gets Credit, and What Gets Done at Work,* Morrow, 1994, linguist Deborah Tannen shows us that knowledge of the fundamental elements in human communication is necessary if people are to speak to each other effectively. It is generally assumed in American culture that directness is logical and appropriate, especially when someone in authority is speaking to an underling, and that indirectness is a sign of weakness and insecurity, if not outright manipulation. Contrary to popular wisdom, however, Tannen shows that both directness and indirectness have their merits depending on their cultural context as well as the relationship between the speakers. Furthermore, indirectness is often the prerogative of those in power as they convey to subordinates what needs to be done using politeness and softened tones. A prime example of a people who place a high value on subtlety and indirectness of expression are the Japanese, whose hierarchical relationships are legendary and, yet, whose business acumen and efficiency are among the greatest in the world. Deborah Tannen (b. 1945) started out as a poet and a writer, but while teaching English in Greece became interested in interpersonal communications. Although her M.A. is in English literature from Wayne State University, she went on to study linguistics at U.C. Berkeley, where she received her M.A. in linguistics in 1976 and her Ph.D. in 1979. She has taught at several colleges, but has been a professor of linguistics at Georgetown University since 1979. Deborah Tannen is in high demand as a speaker and is the author and editor of numerous publications, including *That's Not What I Meant!: How Conversational Style Makes or Breaks Your Relations with Others* (1986), *You Just Don't Understand: Women and Men in Conversation* (1990), *The Argument Culture: Moving from Debate to Dialogue,* (1998) and *You're Wearing That? Understanding Mothers and Daughters in Conversation* (2005).

Key Concept: direct vs. indirect communication

A university president was expecting a visit from a member of the board of trustees. When her secretary buzzed to tell her that the board member had arrived, she left her office and entered the reception area to greet him. Before ushering him into her office, she handed her secretary a sheet of paper and said: "I've just finished drafting this letter. Do you think you could type it right away? I'd like to get it out before lunch. And would you please do me a favor and hold all calls while I'm meeting with Mr. Smith?"

When they sat down behind the closed door of her office, Mr. Smith began by telling her that he thought she had spoken inappropriately to her secretary. "Don't forget," he said. "*You're* the president!"

Putting aside the question of the appropriateness of his admonishing the president on her way of speaking, it is revealing—and representative of many Americans' assumptions—that the indirect way in which the university president told her secretary what to do struck him as self-deprecating. He took it as evidence that she didn't think she had the right to make demands of her secretary. He probably thought he was giving her a needed pep talk, bolstering her self-confidence.

I challenge the assumption that talking in an indirect way necessarily reveals powerlessness, lack of self-confidence or anything else about the character of the speaker. Indirectness is a fundamental element in human communication. It is also one of the elements that varies most from one culture to another, and one that can cause confusion and misunderstanding when speakers have different habits with regard to using it. I also want to dispel the assumption that American women tend to be more indirect than American men. Women and men are both indirect, but in addition to differences associated with their backgrounds—regional, ethnic and class—they tend to be indirect in different situations and in different ways.

At work, we need to get others to do things, and we all have different ways of accomplishing this. Any individual's ways will vary depending on who is being addressed—a boss, a peer or a subordinate. At one extreme are bald commands. At the other are requests so indirect that they don't sound like requests at all, but are just a statement of need or a description of a situation. People with direct styles of asking others to do things perceive indirect requests—if they perceive them as requests at all—as manipulative. But this is often just a way of blaming others for our discomfort with their styles.

The indirect style is no more manipulative than making a telephone call, asking "Is Rachel there?" and expecting whoever answers the phone to put Rachel on. Only a child is likely to answer "Yes" and continue holding the phone—not out of orneriness but because of inexperience with the conventional meaning of the questions. (A mischievous adult might do it to tease.) Those who feel that indirect orders are illogical or manipulative do not recognize the conventional nature of indirect requests.

Issuing orders indirectly can be the prerogative of those in power. Imagine, for example, a master who says "It's cold in here" and expects a servant to make a move to close a window, while a servant who says the same thing is not likely to see his employer rise to correct the situation and make him more comfortable. Indeed, a Frenchman raised in Brittany tells me that his family never gave bald commands to their servants but always communicated orders in indirect and highly polite ways. This pattern renders less surprising the finding of David Bellinger and Jean Berko Gleason that fathers' speech to their young children had a higher incidence than mothers' of both direct imperatives like "Turn the bolt with the wrench" *and* indirect orders like "The wheel is going to fall off."

The use of indirectness can hardly be understood without the cross-cultural perspective. Many Americans find it self-evident that directness is logical and aligned with power while indirectness is akin to dishonesty and reflects subservience. But for speakers raised in most of the world's cultures, varieties of indirectness are the norm in communication. This is the pattern found by a Japanese sociolinguist, Kunihiko Harada, in his analysis of a conversation he recorded between a Japanese boss and a subordinate.

The markers of superior status were clear. One speaker was a Japanese man in his late 40's who managed the local branch of a Japanese private school in the United States. His conversational partner was Japanese-American woman in her early 20's who worked at the

school. By virtue of his job, his age and his native fluency in the language being taught, the man was in the superior position. Yet when he addressed the woman, he frequently used polite language and almost always used indirectness. For example, he had tried and failed to find a photography store that would make a black-and-white print from a color negative for a brochure they were producing. He let her know that he wanted her to take over the task by stating the situation and allowed her to volunteer to do it: (This is a translation of the Japanese conversation.)

> On this matter, that, that, on the leaflet? This photo, I'm thinking of changing it to black-and-white and making it clearer.... I went to a photo shop and asked them. They said they didn't do black-and- white. I asked if they knew any place that did. They said they didn't know. They weren't very helpful, but anyway, a place must be found, the negative brought to it, the picture developed.

Harada observes, "Given the fact that there are some duties to be performed and that there are two parties present, the subordinate is supposed to assume that those are his or her obligation." It was precisely because of his higher status that the boss was free to choose whether to speak formally or informally, to assert his power or to play it down and build rapport—an option not available to the subordinate, who would have seemed cheeky if she had chosen a style that enhanced friendliness and closeness.

The same pattern was found by a Chinese sociolinguist, Yuling Pan, in a meeting of officials involved in a neighborhood youth program. All spoke in ways that reflected their place in the hierarchy. A subordinate addressing a superior always spoke in a deferential way, but a superior addressing a subordinate could either be authoritarian, demonstrating his power, or friendly, establishing rapport. The ones in power had the option of choosing which style to use. In this spirit, I have been told by people who prefer their bosses to give orders indirectly that those who issue bald commands must be pretty insecure; otherwise why would they have to bolster their egos by throwing their weight around?

I am not inclined to accept that those who give orders directly are really insecure and powerless, any more than I want to accept that judgment of those who give indirect orders. The conclusion to be drawn is that ways of talking should not be taken as obvious evidence of inner psychological states like insecurity or lack of confidence. Considering the many influences on conversational style, individuals have a wide range of ways of getting things done and expressing their emotional states. Personality characteristics like insecurity cannot be linked to ways of speaking in an automatic, self-evident way.

Those who expect orders to be given indirectly are offended when they come unadorned. One woman said that when her boss gives her instructions, she feels she should click her heels, salute, and say "Yes, Boss!" His directions strike her as so imperious as to border on the militaristic. Yet I received a letter from a man telling me that indirect orders were a fundamental part of his military training: He wrote:

> Many years ago, when I was in the Navy, I was training to be a radio technician. One class I was in was taught by a chief radioman, a regular Navy man who had been to sea, and who was then in his third hitch. The students, about 20 of us, were fresh out of boot camp, with no sea duty and little knowledge of real Navy life. One day in class the chief said it was hot in the room. The students didn't react, except to nod in agreement. The chief repeated himself: "It's hot in this room." Again there was no reaction from the students.
>
> Then the chief explained. He wasn't looking for agreement or discussion from us. When he said that the room was hot, he expected us to do something about it—like opening the window. He tried it one more time, and this time all of us left our workbenches and headed for the windows. We had learned. And we had many opportunities to apply what we had learned.

This letter especially intrigued me because "It's cold in here" is the standard sentence used by linguists to illustrate an indirect way of getting someone to do something—as I used it earlier. In this example, it is the very obviousness and rigidity of the military hierarchy that makes the statement of a problem sufficient to trigger corrective action on the part of subordinates.

A man who had worked at the Pentagon reinforced the view that the burden of interpretation is on subordinates in the military—and he noticed the difference when he moved to a position in the private sector. He was frustrated when he'd say to his new secretary, for example, "Do we have a list of invitees?" and be told, "I don't know; we probably do" rather than "I'll get it for you." Indeed, he explained, at the Pentagon, such a question would likely be heard as a reproach that the list was not already on his desk.

The suggestion that indirectness is associated with the military must come as a surprise to many. But everyone is indirect, meaning more than is put into words and deriving meaning from words that are never actually said. It's a matter of where, when and how we each tend to be indirect and look for hidden meanings. But indirectness has a built-in liability. There is a risk that the other will either miss or choose to ignore your meaning.

On Jan. 13, 1982, a freezing cold, snowy day in Washington, Air Florida Flight 90 took off from National Airport, but could not get the lift it needed to keep climbing. It crashed into a bridge linking Washington to the state of Virginia and plunged into the Potomac. Of the 79 people on board all but 5 perished, many floundering and drowning in the icy water while horror-stricken by-standers watched helplessly from the river's edge and millions more watched, aghast, on their television screens. Experts later concluded that the plane had waited too long after de-icing to take off. Fresh buildup of ice on the wings and engine brought the plane down. How could the pilot and co-pilot have made such a blunder? Didn't at least one of them realize it was dangerous to take off under these conditions?

> The co-pilot repeatedly called attention to dangerous conditions, but the captain didn't get the message.

Charlotte Linde, a linguist at the Institute for Research on Learning in Palo Alto, Calif., has studied the "black box" recordings of cockpit conversations that preceded crashes as well as tape recordings of conversations that took place among crews during flight simulations in which problems were presented. Among the black box conversations she studied was the one between the pilot and co-pilot just before the Air Florida crash. The pilot, it turned out, had little experience flying in icy weather. The co-pilot had a bit more, and it became heartbreakingly clear on analysis that he had tried to warn the pilot, but he did so indirectly.

The co-pilot repeatedly called attention to the bad weather and to ice building up on other planes:

Co-pilot: Look how the ice is just hanging on his, ah, back, back there, see that?…

Co-pilot: See all those icicles on the back there and everything?

Captain: Yeah.

He expressed concern early on about the long waiting time between de-icing:

Co-pilot: Boy, this is a, this is a losing battle here on trying to de-ice those things, it [gives] you a false feeling of security, that's all that does.

Shortly after they were given clearance to take off, he again expressed concern:

Co-pilot: Let's check these tops again since we been setting here awhile.

Captain: I think we get to go here in a minute.

When they were about to take off, the co-pilot called attention to the engine instrument readings, which were not normal:

Co-pilot: That don't seem right, does it? [three-second pause] Ah, that's not right.…

Captain: Yes, it is, there's 80.

Co-pilot: Naw, I don't think that's right. [seven-second pause] Ah, maybe it is.

Captain: Hundred and twenty.

Co-pilot: I don't know.

The takeoff proceeded, and 37 seconds later the pilot and co-pilot exchanged their last words.

The co-pilot had repeatedly called the pilot's attention to dangerous conditions but did not directly suggest they abort the takeoff. In Linde's judgment, he was expressing his concern indirectly, and the captain didn't pick up on it—with tragic results.

That the co-pilot was trying to warn the captain indirectly is supported by evidence from another airline accident—a relatively minor one—investigated by Linde that also involved the unsuccessful use of indirectness.

On July 9, 1978, Allegheny Airlines Flight 453 was landing at Monroe County Airport in Rochester, when it overran the runway by 728 feet. Everyone survived. This meant that the captain and co-pilot could be interviewed. It turned out that the plane had been flying too fast for a safe landing. The captain should have realized this and flown around a second time, decreasing his speed before trying to land. The captain said he simply had not been aware that he was going too fast. But the co-pilot told interviewers that he "tried to warn the captain in subtle ways, like mentioning the possibility of a tail wind and the slowness of flap extension." His exact words were recorded in the black box. The cross-hatches indicate words deleted by the National Transportation Safety Board and were probably expletives:

Co-pilot: *Yeah, it looks like you got a tail wind here. Yeah.*
[?]: *Yeah [it] moves awfully # slow.*
Co-pilot: *Yeah the # flaps are slower than a #.*
Captain: *We'll make it, gonna have to add power.*
Co-pilot: *I know.*

The co-pilot thought the captain would understand that if there was a tail wind, it would result in the plane going too fast, and if the flaps were slow, they would be inadequate to break the speed sufficiently for a safe landing. He thought the captain would then correct for the error by not trying to land. But the captain said he didn't interpret the co-pilot's remarks to mean they were going too fast.

Linde believes it is not a coincidence that the people being indirect in these conversations were the co-pilots. In her analyses of flight-crew conversations she found it was typical for the speech of subordinates to be more mitigated—polite, tentative or indirect. She also found that topics broached in a mitigated way were more likely to fail, and that captains were more likely to ignore hints from their crew members than the other way around. These findings are evidence that not only can indirectness and other forms of mitigation be misunderstood, but they are also easier to ignore.

In the Air Florida case, it is doubtful that the captain did not realize what the co-pilot was suggesting when he said, "Let's check these tops again since we been setting here awhile" (though it seems safe to assume he did not realize the gravity of the co-pilot's concern). But the indirectness of the co-pilot's phrasing certainly made it easier for the pilot to ignore it. In this sense, the captain's response, "I think we get to go here in a minute," was an indirect way of saying, "I'd rather not." In view of these patterns, the flight crews of some airlines are now given training to express their concerns, even to superiors, in more direct ways.

The conclusion that people should learn to express themselves more directly has a ring of truth to it—especially for Americans. But direct communication is not necessarily always preferable. If more direct expression is better communication, then the most direct-speaking crews should be the best ones. Linde was surprised to find in her research that crews that used the most mitigated speech were often judged the best crews. As part of the study of talk among cockpit crews in flight simulations, the trainers observed and rated the performances of the simulation crews. The crews they rated top in performance had a higher rate of mitigation than crews they judged to be poor.

This finding seems at odds with the role played by indirectness in the examples of crashes that we just saw. Linde concluded that since every utterance functions on two levels—the referential (what is says) and the relational (what it implies about the speaker's relationships), crews that attend to the relational level will be better crews. A similar explanation was suggested by Kunihiko Harada. He believes that the secret of successful communication lies not in teaching subordinates to be more direct, but in teaching higher-ups to be more sensitive to indirect meaning. In other words, the crashes resulted not only because the co-pilots tried to alert the captains to danger indirectly but also because the captains were not attuned to the co-pilots' hints. What made for successful performance among the best crews might have been the ability—or willingness—of listeners to pick up on hints, just as members of families or longstanding couples come to understand each other's meaning without anyone being particularly explicit.

It is not surprising that a Japanese sociolinguist came up with this explanation; what he described is the Japanese system, by which good communication is believed to take place when meaning is gleaned without being stated directly— or at all.

While Americans believe that "the squeaky wheel gets the grease" (so it's best to speak up), the Japanese say, "The nail that sticks out gets hammered back in" (so it's best to remain silent if you don't want to be hit on the head). Many Japanese scholars writing in English have tried to explain to bewildered Americans the ethics of a culture in which silence is often given greater value than speech, and ideas are believed to be best communicated without being explicitly stated. Key concepts in Japanese give a flavor of the attitudes toward language that they reveal—and set in relief the strategies that Americans encounter at work when talking to other Americans.

Takie Sugiyama Lebra, a Japanese-born anthropologist, explains that one of the most basic values in Japanese culture is *omoiyari*, which she translates as "empathy." Because of *omoiyari*, it should not be necessary to state one's meaning explicitly; people should be able to sense each other's meaning intuitively. Lebra explains that it is typical for a Japanese speaker to let sentences trail off rather than complete them because expressing ideas before knowing how they will be received seems intrusive. "Only an insensitive, uncouth person needs a direct, verbal, complete message," Lebra says.

Sasshi, the anticipation of another's message through insightful guesswork, is considered an indication of maturity.

Considering the value placed on direct communication by Americans in general, and especially by American business people, it is easy to imagine that many American readers may scoff at such conversational habits. But the success of Japanese businesses makes it impossible to continue to maintain that there is anything inherently inefficient about such conversational conventions. With indirectness, as with all aspects of conversational style, our own habitual style seems to make sense—seems polite, right and good. The light cast by the habits and assumptions of another culture can help us see our way to the flexibility and respect for other styles that is the only best way of speaking.

The Sounds of Silence

Edward T. Hall and Mildred Reed Hall

Communication between people comes in two basic types: verbal and nonverbal. Within the nonverbal, it may have to do with facial expression, body language in general or, as the Halls put it, even our "treatment of space and time and material things."

Furthermore, just as spoken language is related to other aspects of one's culture—reflecting it as well as having a determining effect upon it—so also is nonverbal language "culture specific."

The fact that nonverbal behavior can be seen as "cultural" has given rise to subfields of communication studies such as *kinesics* and *proxemics*, the subjects of this article.

Kinesics has to do with body movement as a form of communication. It was first coined in the 1950s by Ray Birdwhistell, a ballet dancer turned anthropologist who was interested in the relationship between posture and movement on the one hand and cultural meaning and communication on the other.

Proxemics, on the other hand, is a term originating with Edward T. Hall's book, *The Hidden Dimension,* and has to do with space and how people react to and use distance as a form of communication.

From 1950–1955, Edward T. Hall was the director of the Point IV Training Program at the Foreign Service Institute in Washington D.C., where he taught foreign-bound technicians and administrators how to communicate effectively across cultural boundaries.

The Halls published many articles, manuals, and books together, the most prominent being *Hidden Differences* (1987), having to do with the unstated rules for Americans doing business with the Japanese; *The Fourth Dimension in Architecture: The Impact of Building on Behavior* (1955); and *Understanding Cultural Differences: Germans, French and Americans* (1990).

Key Concept: nonverbal communication

ob leaves his apartment at 8:15 A.M. and stops at the corner drug-store for breakfast. Before he can speak, the counterman says, "The usual?" Bob nods yes. While he savors his Danish, a fat man pushes onto the adjoining stool and overflows into his space. Bob scowls and the man pulls himself in as much as he can. Bob has sent two messages without speaking a syllable.

Henry has an appointment to meet Arthur at 11 o'clock; he arrives at 11:30. Their conversation is friendly, but Arthur retains a lingering hostility. Henry has unconsciously communicated that he doesn't think the appointment is very important or that Arthur is a person who needs to be treated with respect.

George is talking to Charley's wife at a party. Their conversation is entirely trivial, yet Charley glares at them suspiciously. Their physical proximity and the movements of their eyes reveal that they are powerfully attracted to each other.

Josè Ybarra and Sir Edmund Jones are at the same party and it is important for them to establish a cordial relationship for business reasons. Each is trying to be warm and friendly, yet they will part with mutual distrust and their business transaction will probably fall through. Josè, in Latin fashion, moved closer and closer to Sir Edmund as they spoke, and this movement was miscommunicated as pushiness to Sir Edmund, who kept backing away from this intimacy, and this was miscommunicated to Josè as coldness. The silent languages of Latin and English cultures are more difficult to learn than their spoken languages.

In each of these cases, we see the subtle power of nonverbal communication. The only language used throughout most of the history of humanity (in evolutionary terms, vocal communication is relatively recent), it is the first form of communication you learn. You use this preverbal language, consciously and unconsciously, every day to tell other people how you feel about yourself and them. This language includes your posture, gestures, facial expressions, costume, the way you walk, even your treatment of time and space and material things. All people communicate on several different levels at the same time but are usually aware of only the verbal dialog and don't realize that they respond to nonverbal messages. But when a person says one thing and really believes something else, the discrepancy between the two can usually be sensed. Nonverbal-communication systems are much less subject to the conscious deception that often occurs in verbal systems. When we find ourselves thinking, "I don't know what it is about him, but he doesn't seem sincere," it's usually this lack of congruity between a person's words and his behavior that makes us anxious and uncomfortable.

Few of us realize how much we all depend on body movement in our conversation or are aware of the hidden rules that govern listening behavior. But we know instantly whether or not the person we're talking to is "tuned in" and we're very sensitive to any breach in listening etiquette. In white middle-class American culture, when someone wants to show he is listening to someone else, he looks either at the other person's face or, specifically, at his eyes, shifting his gaze from one eye to the other.

If you observe a person conversing, you'll notice that he indicates he's listening by nodding his head. He also makes little "Hmm" noises. If he agrees with what's being said, he may give a vigorous nod. To show pleasure or affirmation, he smiles; if he has some reservations, he looks skeptical by raising an eyebrow or pulling down the corners of his mouth. If a participant wants to terminate the conversation, he may start shifting his body position, stretching his legs, crossing or uncrossing them, bobbing his foot, or diverting his gaze from the speaker. The more he fidgets, the more the speaker becomes aware that he has lost his audience. As a last measure, the listener may look at his watch to indicate the imminent end of the conversation.

Talking and listening are so intricately intertwined that a person cannot do one without the other. Even when one is alone and talking to oneself, there is part of the brain that speaks while another part listens. In all conversations, the listener is positively or negatively reinforcing the speaker all the time. He may even guide the conversation without knowing it, by laughing or frowning or dismissing the argument with a wave of his hand.

The language of the eyes—another age-old way of exchanging feelings—is both subtle and complex. Not only do men and women use their eyes differently but there are class, generation, regional, ethnic, and national cultural differences. Americans often complain about the way foreigners stare at people or hold a glance too long. Most Americans look away from someone who is using his eyes in an unfamiliar way because it makes them self-conscious. If a man looks at another man's wife in a certain way, he's asking for trouble, as indicated earlier. But he might not be ill-mannered or seeking to challenge the husband. He might be a European in this country who hasn't learned our visual mores. Many American women visiting France or Italy are acutely embarrassed because, for the first time in their lives, men really look at them—their eyes, hair, nose, lips, breasts, hips, legs, thighs, knees, ankles, feet, clothes, hairdo, even their walk. These same women, once they have become used to being looked at, often return to the United States and are overcome with the feeling that "No one ever really looks at me anymore."

Analyzing the mass of data on the eyes, it is possible to sort out at least three ways in which the eyes are used to communicate: dominance vs. submission, involvement vs. detachment and positive vs. negative attitude. In addition, there are three levels of consciousness and control, which can be categorized as follows: (1) conscious use of the eye to communicate, such as the flirting blink and the intimate nose-wrinkling squint; (2) the very extensive category of unconscious but learned behavior governing where the eyes are directed and when (this unwritten set of rules dictates how and under what circumstances the sexes, as well as people of all status categories, look at each other); and (3) the response of the eye itself, which is completely outside both awareness and control—changes in that cast (the sparkle) of the eye and the papillary reflex.

The eye is unlike any other organ of the body, for it is an extension of the brain. The unconscious pupillary reflex and the cast of the eye have been known by people of Middle Eastern origin for years—although most are unaware of their knowledge. Depending on the context, Arabs and others look either directly at the eye or deeply *into* the eyes of their interlocutor. We became aware of this in the Middle East several years ago while looking at jewelry. The merchant suddenly started to push a particular bracelet at a customer and said, "You buy this one." What interested us was that the bracelet was not the one that had been consciously selected by the purchaser. But the merchant, watching the pupils of the eyes, knew what the purchaser really wanted to buy. Whether he specifically knew *how* he knew is debatable.

A psychologist at the University of Chicago, Eckhard Hess, was the first to conduct systematic studies of the pupillary reflex. His wife remarked one evening, while watching him reading in bed, that he must be very interested in the text because his pupils were dilated. Following up on this, Hess slipped some pictures of nudes into a stack of photographs that he gave to his male assistant. Not looking at the photographs but watching his assistant's pupils, Hess was able to tell precisely when the assistant came to the nudes. In further experiments, Hess retouched the eyes in a photograph of a woman. In one print, he made the pupils small, in another, large; nothing else was changed. Subjects who were given the photographs found the woman with the dilated pupils much more attractive. Any man who has had the experience of seeing a woman look at him as her pupils widen with reflex speed knows that she's flashing him a message.

The eye-sparkle phenomenon frequently turns up in our interviews of couples in love. It's apparently one of the first reliable clues in the other person that love is genuine. To date, there is no scientific date to explain eye sparkle; no investigation of the pupil, the cornea or even the white sclera of the eye shows how the sparkle originates. Yet we all know it when we see it.

One common situation for most people involves the use of the eyes in the street and in public. Although eye behavior follows a definite set of rules, the rules vary according to the place, the needs and feelings of the people, and their ethnic background. For urban whites, once they're within definite recognition distance (16-32 feet for people with average eye-sight), there is mutual avoidance of eye contact—unless they want something specific; a pickup, a handout or information of some kind. In the West and in small towns generally, however, people are much more likely to look at and greet one another, even if they're strangers.

It's permissible to look at people if they're beyond recognition distance; but once inside this sacred zone, you can only steal a glance at strangers. You *must* greet friends, however; to fail to do so is insulting. Yet, to stare too fixedly at them is considered rude and hostile. Of course, all of these rules are variable.

A great many blacks, for example, greet each other in public even if they don't know each other. To blacks, most eye behavior of whites has the effect of giving the impression that they aren't there, but this is due to white avoidance of eye contact with *anyone* in the street.

Another very basic difference between people of different ethnic backgrounds is their sense of territoriality and how they handle space. This is the silent communication, or miscommunication, that caused friction between Mr. Ybarra and Sir Edmund Jones in our earlier example. We know from research that everyone has around himself an invisible bubble of space that contracts and expands depending on several factors: his emotional state, the activity he's performing at the time and his cultural background. This bubble is a kind of mobile territory that he will defend against intrusion. If he is accustomed to close personal distance between himself and others, his bubble will be smaller than that of someone who's accustomed to greater personal distance. People of North European heritage—English, Scandinavian, Swiss, and German—tend to avoid contact. Those whose heritage is Italian, French, Spanish, Russian, Latin American, or Middle Eastern like close personal contact.

People are very sensitive to any intrusion into their spatial bubble. If someone stands too close to you, your first instinct is to back up. If that's not possible, you lean away and pull yourself in, tensing your muscles. If the intruder doesn't respond to these body signals, you may then try to body signals, you may then try to protect yourself, using a briefcase, umbrella or raincoat. Women—especially when traveling alone—often plant their pocketbook in such a way that no one get very close to them. As a last resort, you may move to another spot and position yourself behind a desk or a chair that provides screening. Everyone tries to adjust the space around himself in a way that's comfortable for him; most often, he does this unconsciously.

Emotions also have a direct effect on the size of a person's territory. When you're angry or under stress, your bubble expands and you require more space. New York psychiatrist Augustus Kinzel found a difference in what he calls Body-Buffer Zones between violent and nonviolent prison inmates. Dr. Kinzel conducted experiments in which prisoner was placed in the center of a small room and then Dr. Kinzel slowly walked toward him. Nonviolent prisoners allowed him to come quite close, while prisoners with a history of violent behavior couldn't tolerate his proximity and reacted with some vehemence.

Apparently, people under stress experience other people as looming larger and closer than they actually are. Studies of schizophrenic patients have indicated that they sometimes have a distorted perception of space, and several psychiatrists have reported patients who experience their boundaries as filling up an entire room. For these patients, anyone who comes into the room is actually inside their body, and such an intrusion may trigger a violent outburst.

Unfortunately, there is little detailed information about normal people who live in highly congested urban areas. We do know, of course, that the noise, pollution, dirt, crowding, and confusion of our cities induce feelings of stress in more of us, and stress leads to a need for greater space. The man who's packed into a subway, jostled in the street, crowded into an elevator and forced to work all day in a bull pen or in a small office without auditory or visual privacy is going to be very stressed at the end of his day. He needs places that provide relief from constant overstimulation of his nervous system. Stress from overcrowding is cumulative and people can tolerate more crowding early in the day than later; note the increased bad temper during the evening rush hour as compared with the morning melee. Certainly one factor in people's desire to commute by car is the need for privacy and relief from crowding (except, often, from other cars); it may be the only time of the day when nobody can intrude.

In crowded public places, we tense our muscles and hold ourselves stiff, and thereby communicate to others our desire, not to intrude on their space and, above all, not to touch them. We also avoid eye contact, and the total effect is that someone who has "tuned out." Walking along the street, our bubble expands slightly as we move in a stream of strangers, taking care not to bump into them. In the office, at meetings, in restaurants, our bubble keeps changing as it adjusts to the activity at hand.

Most white middle-class Americans use four main distances in their business and social relations: intimate, personal, social, and public. Each of these distances has a near and a far phase and is accompanied by changes in the volume of the voice. Intimate distance varies from direct physical contact with another person to a distance of six to eighteen inches and is used for our most private activities—caressing another person or making love. At this distance, you are overwhelmed by sensory inputs from the other person—heat from the body, tactile stimulation from the skin, the fragrance of perfume, even the sound of breathing—all of which literally envelop you. Even at the far phase, you're still within easy touching distance. In general, the use of intimate distance in public between adults is frowned on. It's also much too close for strangers, except under conditions of extreme crowding.

In the second zone—personal distance—the close phase is one and a half to two and a half feet; it's at this distance that wives usually stand from their husbands in public. If another woman moves into this zone, the wife will most likely be disturbed. The far phase—two and a half to four feet—is the distance used to "keep someone at arm's length" and is the most common spacing used by people in conversation.

The third zone—social distance—is employed during business transactions or exchanges with a clerk or repairman. People who work together tend to use close social distance—four to seven feet. This is also the distance for conversation at social gatherings. To stand up at this distance from someone who is seated has a dominating effect (e.g., teacher to pupil, boss to secretary). The far phase of the third zone—seven to twelve feet—is where people stand when someone says, "Stand back so I can look at you." This distance lends a formal tone to business or social discourse. In an executive office, the desk serves to keep people at this distance.

The fourth zone—public distance—is used by teachers in classrooms or speakers at public gatherings. At its farthest phase—25 feet and beyond—it is used for important public figures. Violations of this distance can lead to serious complications. During his 1970 U.S. visit, the president of France, Georges Pompidou, was harassed by pickets in Chicago, who were permitted to get within touching distance. Since pickets in France are kept behind barricades a block or more away, the president was outraged by his insult to his person, and President Nixon was obliged to communicate his concern as well as offer his personal apologies.

It is interesting to note how American pitchmen and panhandlers exploit the unwritten, unspoken conventions of eye and distance. Both take advantage of the fact that once explicit eye contact is established, it is rude to look away, because to do so means to brusquely dismiss the other person and his needs. Once having caught the eye of his mark, the panhandler the locks on, not letting go until he moves through the public zone, the social zone, the personal zone and, finally, into the intimate sphere, where people are most vulnerable.

Touch also is an important part of the constant stream of communication that takes place between people. A light touch, a firm touch, a blow, a caress are all communications. In an effort to break down barriers among people, there's been a recent upsurge in group-encounter activities, in which strangers are encouraged to touch one another. In special situations such as these, the rules for not touching are broken with group approval and people gradually lose some of their inhibitions.

Although most people don't realize it, space is perceived and distances are set not by vision alone but with all the senses. Auditory space is perceived with the ears, thermal space with the skin, kinesthetic space with the muscles of the body and olfactory space with the nose. And, once again, it's one's culture that determines how

his senses are programmed—which sensory information ranks highest and lowest. The important thing to remember is that culture is very persistent. In this country, we've noted the existence of culture patterns that determine distance between people in the third and fourth generations of some families, despite their prolonged contact with people of very different cultural heritages.

Whenever there is great cultural distance between two people, there are bound to be problems arising from difference in behavior and expectations. An example is the American couple who consulted a psychiatrist about their marital problems. The husband was from New England and had been brought up by reserved parents who taught him to control his emotions and to respect the need for privacy. His wife was from an Italian family and had been brought up in close contact with all the members of her large family, who were extremely warm, volatile and demonstrative.

When the husband came home after a hard day at the office, dragging his feet and longing for peace and quiet, his wife would rush to him and smother him. Clasping his hands, rubbing his brow, crooning over his weary head, she never left him alone. But when the wife was upset or anxious about her day, the husband's response was to withdraw completely and leave her alone. No comforting, no affectionate embrace, no attention—just solitude. The woman became convinced her husband didn't love her, and, in desperation, she consulted a psychiatrist. Their problem wasn't basically psychological but cultural.

Why has man developed all these different ways of communicating messages without words? One reason is that people don't like to spell out certain kinds of messages. We prefer to find other ways of showing our feelings. This is especially true in relationships as sensitive as courtship. Men don't like to be rejected and most women don't want to turn a man down bluntly. Instead, we work out subtle ways of encouraging or discouraging each other that save face and avoid confrontations.

How a person handles space in dating others in an obvious and very sensitive indicator of how he or she feels about the other person. On a first date, if a woman sits or stands so close to a man that he is acutely conscious of her physical presence—inside the intimate-distance zone—the man usually construes it to mean that she is encouraging him. However, before the man starts moving in on the woman, he should be sure what message she's really sending; otherwise, he risks bruising his ego. What is close to someone of North European background may be neutral or distant to someone of Italian heritage. Also, women sometimes use space as a way of misleading a man and there are few things that put men off more than women who communicate contradictory messages—such as women who cuddle up and then act insulted when a man takes the next step.

How does a woman communicate interest in a man? In addition to such familiar gambits as smiling at him, she may glance shyly at him, blush, and then look away. Or she may give him a real come-on look and move in very close when he approaches. She may touch his arm and ask for a light. As she leans forward to light her cigarette, she may brush him lightly, enveloping him in her perfume. She'll probably continue to smile at him and she may use what ethologists call preening gestures—touching the back of her hair, thrusting her breasts forward, tilting her hips as she stands or crossing her legs if she's seated, perhaps even exposing one thigh or putting a hand on her thigh and stroking it. She may also stroke her wrists as she converses or show the palm of her hand as a way of gaining his attention. Her skin may be unusually flushed or quite pale, her eyes brighter, the pupils larger.

If a man sees a woman whom he wants to attract, he tries to present himself by his posture and stance as someone who is self-assured. He moved briskly and confidently. When he catches the eye of the woman, he may hold her glance a little longer than normal. If he gets an encouraging smile, he'll move in close and engage her in small talk. As they converse, his glance shifts over her face and body. He, too, may make preening gestures—straightening his tie, smoothing his hair or shooting his cuffs.

How do people learn body language? The same way they learn spoken language—by observing and imitating people around them as they're growing up. Little girls imitate their mothers or an older female. Little boys imitate their fathers or a respected uncle or a character on television. In this way, they learn the gender signals appropriate for their sex. Regional, class, and ethnic patterns of body behavior are also learned in childhood and persist throughout life.

Such patterns of masculine and feminine body behavior vary widely from one culture to another. In America, for example, women stand with their thighs together. Many walk with their pelvis tipped slightly forward and their upper arms close to their body. When they sit, they cross their ankles. American men hold their arms away from their body, often swinging them as they walk. They stand with their legs apart (an extreme example is the cowboy, with legs apart and thumbs tucked into his belt). When they sit, they put their feet on the floor with legs apart and, in some parts of the country, they cross their legs by putting one ankle on the other knee.

Leg behavior indicates sex, status, and personality. It also indicates whether or not one is at ease or is showing respect or disrespect for the other person. Young Latin-American males avoid crossing their legs. In their world of *machismo*, the preferred position for young males when with one another (if there is no older dominant male present to whom they must show respect) is to sit on the base of their spine with their leg muscles relaxed and their feet wide apart. Their respect position is like our military equivalent; spine straight, heels and ankles together—almost identical to that displayed by properly brought up young women in New England in the early part of this century.

American women who sit with their legs spread apart in the presence of males are *not* normally signaling a come-on—they are simply (and often unconsciously) sitting like men. Middle-class women in the presence of other women to whom they are very close may on occasion throw themselves down on a soft chair or sofa and let themselves go. This is a signal that nothing serious will be taken up. Males, on the other hand, lean back and prop their legs up on the nearest object.

The way we walk, similarly, indicates status, respect, mood, and ethnic or cultural affiliation. The many variants of the female walk are too well known to go into here, except to say that a man would have to be blind not to be turned on by the way some women walk—a fact that made Mae West rich before scientists ever studied these matters. To white Americans, some French middleclass males walk in a way that is both humorous and suspect. There is a bounce and looseness to the French walk, as though the parts of the body were somehow unrelated. Jacques Tati, the French movie actor, walks this way; so does the great mime, Marcel Marceau.

Blacks and whites in America—with the exception of middle- and upper-middle-class professionals of both groups—move and walk very differently from each other. To the blacks, whites often seem incredibly stiff, almost mechanical in their movements. Black males, on the other hand, have a looseness and coordination that frequently makes whites a little uneasy; it's too different, too integrated, too alive, too male. Norman Mailer has said that squares walk from the shoulders, like bears, but blacks and hippies walk from the hips, like cats.

All over the world, people walk not only in their own characteristic way but have walks that communicate the nature of their involvement with whatever it is they're doing. The purposeful walk of North Europeans is an important component of proper behavior on the job. Any male who has been in the military knows how essential it is to walk properly (which makes for a continuing source of tension between blacks and whites in the Service). The quick shuffle of servants in the Far East in the old days was a show of respect. On the island of Truk, when we last visited, the inhabitants even had a name for the respectful walk that one used when in the presence of a chief or when walking past a chief's house. The term was *sufan*, which meant to be humble and respectful.

The notion the people communicate volumes by their gestures. Facial expressions, posture and walk is not new; actors, dancers, writers and psychiatrists have long been aware of it. Only in recent years, however, have scientists begun to make systematic observations of body motions. Ray L. Birdwhistell of the University of Pennsylvania is one of the pioneers in body-motion research and coined the term kinesics to describe this field. He developed an elaborate notation system to record both facial and body movements, using an approach similar to that of the linguist, who studies the basic elements of speech. Birdwhistell and other kinesicists such as Albert Sheflen,

Adam Kendon and William Condon take moves of people interacting. They run the film over and over again, often at reduced speed for frame-by analysis, so that they can observe even the slightest body movements not perceptible at normal interaction speeds. These movements are then recorded in notebooks for later analysis.

To appreciate the importance of nonverbal-communication systems, consider the unskilled inner-city black looking for a job. His handling of time and space alone is sufficiently different from the white middle-class pattern to create great misunderstandings on both sides. The black is told to appear for a job interview at a certain time. He arrives late. The white interviewer concludes from his tardy arrival that the black is irresponsible and not really interested in the job. What the interviewer doesn't know is that the black time system (often referred to by blacks as C.P.T.—colored people's time) isn't the same as that of whites. In the words of black student who had been told to make an appointment to see his professor: "Man, you *must* be putting me on. I never had an appointment in my life."

The black job applicant, having arrived late for his interview, may further antagonize the white interviewer by his posture and his eye behavior. Perhaps he slouches and avoids looking at the interviewer; to him this is playing it cool. To the interviewer, however, he may well look shifty and sound uninterested.

The interviewer has failed to notice the actual signs of interest and eagerness in the black's behavior, such as the subtle shift in the quality of the voice—a gentle and tentative excitement—an almost imperceptible change in the cast of the eyes and a relaxing of the jaw muscles.

Moreover, correct reading of black-white behavior is continually complicated by the fact that both groups are comprised of individuals—some of whom try to accommodate and some of whom make it a point of pride *not* to accommodate. At present, this means that many Americans, when thrown into contact with one another, are in the precarious position of not knowing which pattern applies. Once identified and analyzed, nonverbal-communication systems can be taught, like a foreign language. Without this training, we respond to nonverbal communications in terms of our own culture; we read everyone's behavior as if it were our own, and thus we often misunderstand it.

Several years ago in New York City, there was a program for sending children from predominantly black and Puerto Rican low-income neighborhoods to summer school in a white upper-class neighborhood on the East Side. One morning, a group of young black and Puerto Rican boys raced down the street, shouting and screaming and overturning garbage cans on their way to school. A doorman from an apartment building nearby chased them and cornered one of them inside a building. The boy drew a knife and attacked the doorman. This tragedy would not have occurred if the doorman had been familiar with the behavior of boys from low-income neighborhoods, where such antics are routine and socially acceptable and where pursuit would be expected to invite a violent response.

The language of behavior is extremely complex. Most of us are lucky to have under control one subcultural system—the one that reflects our sex, class, generation, and geographic region within the United States. Because of its complexity, efforts to isolate bits of nonverbal communication and generalize from them are in vain; you don't become an instant expert on people's behavior by watching them at cocktail parties. Body language isn't something that's independent of the person, something that can be donned and doffed like a suit of clothes.

Our research and that of our colleagues has shown that, far from being a superficial form of communication that can be consciously manipulated, nonverbal-communication systems are interwoven into the fabric of the personality and, as sociologist Erving Goffman had demonstrated, into society itself. They are the warp and woof of daily interactions with others and they influence how one expresses oneself, how one experiences oneself as a man or a woman.

Nonverbal communications signal to members of your own group what kind of person you are, how you feel about others, how you'll fit into and work in a group, whether you're assured or anxious, the degree to which you feel comfortable with the standards of your own culture, as well as deeply significant feelings about the self, including the state of your own psyche. For most of us, it's difficult to accept the reality of another's behavioral system. And, of course, none of us will ever become fully knowledgeable of the importance of every nonverbal signal. But as long as each of us realizes the power of these signals, this society's diversity can be a source of great strength rather than a further—and subtly powerful—source of division.

Social Relationships

Selection 15

MARSHALL SAHLINS, from "The Original Affluent Society," *Stone Age Economics*

Selection 16

LAURENS VAN DER POST AND JANE TAYLOR, from "Woman the Provider," *Testament to the Bushmen*

Selection 17

ERNESTINE FRIEDL, from "Society and Sex Roles," *Human Nature*

SELECTION 15

The Original Affluent Society

Marshall Sahlins

There is no better example of the need for sound anthropological fieldwork than the early, pre-ethnographic descriptions of hunter-gatherer societies. In this excerpt from his book, *Stone Age Economics*, Marshall Sahlins cites representative examples of the kind of ethnocentrism extant in Europe and the United States with regard to peoples still living a "stone age" existence.

The typical view used to be that hunter-gatherers were subsisting hand-to-mouth, had no idea where their next meal was coming from and, generally speaking, were dirt poor. Although he is not cited in this essay, Thomas Hobbes, the renowned English philosopher of the 17th century, has often been quoted as providing the definitive view of his day regarding "savage society," that life in the "state of nature" was "solitary, poor, nasty, brutish, and short." Fortunately, drawing upon decades of ethnographic fieldwork among such peoples as the Inuit (Eskimo), Mbuti (Pygmies), and the !Kung of the Kalahari, Marshall Sahlins is able to set the record straight. Centuries later, by the way, well after Sahlins published *Stone Age Economics*, Hobbes' statement is *still* taken seriously by some, especially those unfamiliar with the ethnographic evidence.

Marshall Sahlins (b. 1930) did his undergraduate work at the University of Michigan and received his Ph.D. at the University of Chicago. He taught anthropology at Columbia University from 1955 to 1957, the University of Michigan from 1957 to 1974, and has been a professor at the University of Chicago since 1974. His fieldwork has included stays in Hawaii, Fiji, New Guinea, and Turkey. His many publications have primarily dealt with Polynesian history, the evolution of culture, and social stratification.

Key Concept: hunter-gatherers as affluent societies

If economics is the dismal science, the study of hunting and gathering economies must be its most advanced branch. Almost universally committed to the proposition that life was hard in the paleolithic, our textbooks compete to convey a sense of impending doom, leaving one to wonder not only how hunters managed to live, but whether, after all, this was living? The specter of starvation stalks the stalker through these pages. His technical incompetence is said to enjoin continuous work just to survive, affording him neither respite nor surplus, hence not even the "leisure" to "build culture." Even so, for all his efforts, the hunter pulls the lowest grades in thermodynamics—less energy/capita/year than any other mode of production. And in treatises on economic development he is condemned to play the role of bad example: the so-called "subsistence economy."

The traditional wisdom is always refractory. One is forced to oppose it polemically, to phrase the necessary revisions dialectically: in fact, this was, when you come to examine it, the original affluent society. Paradoxical, that phrasing leads to another useful and unexpected conclusion. By the common understanding, an affluent society is one in which all the people's material wants are easily satisfied. To assert that the hunters are affluent is to deny then that the human condition is an ordained tragedy, with man the prisoner at hard labor of a perpetual disparity between his unlimited wants and his insufficient means.

For there are two possible courses to affluence. Wants may be "easily satisfied" either by producing much or desiring little. The familiar conception, the Galbraithean way, makes assumptions peculiarly appropriate to market economies: that man's wants are great, not to say infinite, whereas his means are limited, although improvable: thus, the gap between means and ends can be narrowed by industrial productivity, at least to the point that "urgent goods" become plentiful. But there is also a Zen road to affluence, departing from premises somewhat different from our own: that human material wants are finite and few, and technical means unchanging but on the whole adequate. Adopting the Zen strategy, a people can enjoy an unparalleled material plenty—with a low standard of living.

That, I think, describes the hunters. And it helps explain some of their more curious economic behavior:

86

their "prodigality" for example—the inclination to consume at once all stocks on hand, as if they had it made. Free from market obsessions of scarcity, hunters' economic propensities may be more consistently predicated on abundance than our own. Destutt de Tracy, "fish-blooded bourgeois doctrinaire" though he might have been, at least compelled Marx's agreement on the observation that "in poor nations the people are comfortable," whereas in rich nations "they are generally poor."

This is not to deny that a preagricultural economy operates under serious constraints, but only to insist, on the evidence from modern hunters and gatherers, that a successful accomodation is usually made....

Sources of the Misconception

"Mere subsistence economy," "limited leisure save in exceptional circumstances," "incessant quest for food," "meagre and relatively unreliable" natural resources, "absence of an economic surplus," "maximum energy from a maximum number of people"—so runs the fair average anthropological opinion of hunting and gathering.

> The aboriginal Australians are a classic example of a people whose economic resources are of the scantiest. In many places their habitat is even more severe than that of the Bushmen, although this is perhaps not quite true in the northern portion.... A tabulation of the foodstuffs which the aborigines of northwest central Queensland extract from the country they inhabit is instructive.... The variety in this list is impressive, but we must not be deceived into thinking that variety indicates plenty, for the available quantities of each element in it are so slight that only the most intense application makes survival possible (Herskovits, 1958, p 68–69).

Or again, in reference to South American hunters:

> The nomadic hunters and gatherers barely met minimum subsistence needs and often fell far short of them. Their population of 1 person to 10 or 20 square miles reflects this. Constantly on the move in search of food, they clearly lacked the leisure hours for non-subsistence activities of any significance, and they could transport little of what they might manufacture in spare moments. To them, adequacy of production meant physical survival, and they rarely had surplus of either products or time (Steward and Faron, 1959, p. 60; cf. Clark, 1953, p. 27 f; Haury, 1962, p. 113; Hoebel, 1958, p. 188; Redfield, 1953, p. 5; White, 1959).

But the traditional dismal view of the hunters' fix is also preanthropological and extra-anthropological, at once historical and referable to the larger economic context in which anthropology operates. It goes back to the time Adam Smith was writing, and probably to a time before anyone was writing.[1] Probably it was one of the first distinctly neolithic prejudices, an ideological appreciation of the hunter's capacity to exploit the earth's resources most congenial to the historic task of depriving him of the same. We must have inherited it with the seed of Jacob, which "spread abroad to the west, and to the

east, and to the north," to the disadvantage of Esau who was the elder son and cunning hunter, but in a famous scene deprived of his birthright....

The anthropological disposition to exaggerate the economic inefficiency of hunters appears notably by way of invidious comparison with neolithic economies. Hunters, as Lowie put it blankly, "must work much harder in order to live than tillers and breeders" (1946, p. 13). On this point evolutionary anthropology in particular found it congenial, even necessary theoretically, to adopt the usual tone of reproach. Ethnologists and archaeologists had become neolithic revolutionaries, and in their enthusiasm for the Revolution spared nothing denouncing the Old (Stone Age) Regime. Including some very old scandal. It was not the first time philosophers would relegate the earliest stage of humanity rather to nature than to culture. ("A man who spends his whole life following animals just to kill them to eat, or moving from one berry patch to another, is really living just like an animal himself" [Braidwood, 1957, p. 122].) The hunters thus downgraded, anthropology was free to extol the Neolithic Great Leap Forward: a main technological advance that brought about a "general availability of leisure through release from purely food-getting pursuits" (Braidwood, 1952, p. 5; cf. Boas, 1940, p. 285).

In an influential essay on "Energy and the Evolution of Culture," Leslie White explained that the neolithic generated a "great advance in cultural development...as a consequence of the great increase in the amount of energy harnessed and controlled per capita per year by means of the agricultural and pastoral arts" (1949, p. 372). White further heightened the evolutionary contrast by specifying *human effort* as the principal energy source of paleolithic culture, as opposed to the *domesticated plant and animal resources* of neolithic culture.

This determination of the energy sources at once permitted a precise low estimate of hunters' thermodynamic potential—that developed by the human body: "average power resources" of one-twentieth horsepower per capita (1949, p. 369)—even as, by eliminating human effort from the cultural enterprise of the neolithic, it appeared that people had been liberated by some labor-saving device (domesticated plants and animals). But White's problematic is obviously misconceived. The principal mechanical energy available to both paleolithic and neolithic culture is that supplied by human beings, as transformed in both cases from plant and animal sources, so that, with negligible exceptions (the occasional direct use of nonhuman power), the amount of energy harnessed per *capita* per year is the same in paleolithic and neolithic economies- and fairly constant in human history until the advent of the industrial revolution.[2]

Another specifically anthropological source of paleolithic discontent develops in the field itself, from the context of European observation of existing hunters and gatherers, such as the native Australians, the Bushmen, the Ona, or the Yahgan. This ethnographic context tends to distort our understanding of the hunting-gathering economy in two ways.

First, it provides singular opportunities for *naïvetè*. The remote and exotic environments that have become the cultural theater of modern hunters have an effect on Europeans most unfavorable to the latter's assessment of the former's plight. Marginal as the Australian or Kalahari desert is to agriculture, or to everyday European experience, it is a source of wonder to the untutored observer "how anybody could live in a place like this." The inference that the natives manage only to eke out a bare existence is apt to be reinforced by their marvelously varied diets (cf. Herskovits, 1958, quoted above). Ordinarily including objects deemed repulsive and inedible by Europeans, the local cuisine lends itself to the supposition that the people are starving to death. Such a conclusion, of course, is more likely met in earlier than in later accounts, and in the journals of explorers or missionaries than in the monographs of anthropologists; but precisely because the explorers' reports are older and closer to the aboriginal condition, one reserves for them a certain respect.

Such respect obviously has to be accorded with discretion. Greater attention should be paid a man such as Sir George Grey (1841), whose expeditions in the 1830s included some of the poorer districts of western Australia, but whose unusually close attention to the local people obliged him to debunk his colleagues' communications on just this point of economic desperation. It is a mistake very commonly made, Grey wrote, to suppose that the native Australians "have small means of subsistence, or are at times greatly pressed for want of food." Many and "almost ludicrous" are the errors travellers have fallen into in this regard: "They lament in their journals that the unfortunate Aborigines should be reduced by famine to the miserable necessity of subsisting on certain sorts of food, which they have found near their huts; whereas, in many instances, the articles thus quoted by them are those which the natives most prize, and are really neither deficient in flavour nor nutritious qualities." To render palpable "the ignorance that has prevailed with regard to the habits and customs of this people when in their wild state," Grey provides one remarkable example, a citation from his fellow explorer, Captain Sturt, who, upon encountering a group of Aboriginals engaged in gathering large quantities of mimosa gum, deduced that the "'unfortunate creatures were reduced to the last extremity, and, being unable to procure any other nourishment, had been obliged to collect this mucilaginous.'" But, Sir George observes, the gum in question is a favorite article of food in the area, and when in season it affords the opportunity for large numbers of people to assemble and camp together, which otherwise they are unable to do. He concludes:

> Generally speaking, the natives live well; in some districts there may be at particular seasons of the year a deficiency of food, but if such is the case, these tracts are, at those times, deserted. It is, however, utterly impossible for a traveller or even for a strange native to judge whether a district affords an abundance of food, or the contrary... But in his own district a native is very differently situated; he knows exactly what it produces, the proper time at which the several articles are in season, and the readiest means of procuring them. According to these circumstances he regulates his visits to different portions of his hunting ground; and I can only say that I have always found the greatest abundance in their huts (Grey, 1841, vol. 2, pp. 259-262, emphasis mine; cf. Eyre, 1845, vol. 2, p. 244f).[3]

In making this happy assessment, Sir George took special care to exclude the *lumpen-proletariat* aboriginals living in and about European towns (cf. Eyre, 1845, vol. 2, pp. 250, 254-255). The exception is instructive. It evokes a second source of ethnographic misconceptions: the anthropology of hunters is largely an anachronistic study of ex-savages—an inquest into the corpse of one society, Grey once said, presided over by members of another.

The surviving food collectors, as a class, are displaced persons. They represent the paleolithic disenfranchised, occupying marginal haunts untypical of the mode of production: sanctuaries of an era, places so beyond the range of main centers of cultural advance as to be allowed some respite from the planetary march of cultural evolution, because they were characteristically poor beyond the interest and competence of more advanced economies. Leave aside the favorably situated food collectors, such as Northwest Coast Indians, about whose (comparative) well-being there is no dispute. The remaining hunters, barred from the better parts of the earth, first by agriculture, later by industrial economies, enjoy ecological opportunities something less than the later-paleolithic average.[4] Moreover, the disruption accomplished in the past two centuries of European imperialism has been especially severe, to the extent that many of the ethnographic notices that constitute the anthropologist's stock in trade are adulterated culture goods. Even explorer and missionary accounts, apart from their ethnocentric misconstructions, may be speaking of afflicted economies (cf. *Service*, 1962). The hunters of eastern Canada of whom we read in the *Jesuit Relations* were committed to the fur trade in the early seventeenth century. The environments of others were selectively stripped by Europeans before a reliable report could be made of indigenous production: the Eskimo we know no longer hunt whales, the Bushmen have been deprived of game, the Shoshoni's piñon has been timbered and his hunting grounds grazed out by cattle.[5] If such peoples are now described as poverty-stricken, their resources "meagre and unreliable," is this an indication of the aboriginal condition—or of the colonial duress?

The enormous implications (and problems) for evolutionary interpretation raised by this global retreat have only recently begun to evoke notice (Lee and Devore, 1968). The point of present importance is this: rather than a fair test of hunters' productive capacities, their current circumstances pose something of a supreme test. All the more extraordinary, then, the following reports of their performance.

A Kind of Material Plenty

Considering the poverty in which hunters and gatherers live in theory, it comes as a surprise that Bushmen who live in the Kalahari enjoy "a kind of material plenty," at least in the realm of everyday useful things, apart from food and water:

> As the !Kung come into more contact with Europeans—and this is already happening—they will feel sharply the lack of our things and will need and want more. It makes them feel inferior to be without clothes when they stand among strangers who are clothed. But in their own life and with their own artifacts they were comparatively free from material pressures. Except for food and water (important exceptions!) of which the Nyae Nyae ! Kung have a sufficiency—but barely so, judging from the fact that all are thin though not emaciated—they all had what they needed or could make what they needed, for every man can and does make the things that men make and every woman the things that women make.... They lived in a kind of material plenty because they adapted the tools of their living to materials which lay in abundance around them and which were free for anyone to take (wood, reeds, bone for weapons and implements, fibers for cordage, grass for shelters), or to materials which were at least sufficient for the needs of the population.... The !Kung could always use more ostrich egg shells for beads to wear or trade with, but, as it is, enough are found for every woman to have a dozen or more shells for water containers—all she can carry—and a goodly number of bead ornaments. In their nomadic hunting-gathering life, travelling from one source of food to another through the seasons, always going back and forth between food and water, they carry their young children and their belongings. With plenty of most materials at hand to replace artifacts as required, the !Kung have not developed means of permanent storage and have not needed or wanted to encumber themselves with surpluses or duplicates. They do not even want to carry one of everything. They borrow what they do not own. With this ease, they have not hoarded, and the accumulation of objects has not become associated with status (Marshall, 1961, pp.243–44, emphasis mine).

Analysis of hunter-gatherer production is usefully divided into two spheres, as Mrs. Marshall has done. Food and water are certainly "important exceptions," best reserved for separate and extended treatment. For the rest, the nonsubsistence sector, what is here said of the Bushmen applies in general and in detail to hunters from the Kalahari to Labrador—or to Tièrra del Fuego, where Gusinde reports of the Yahgan that their disinclination to own more than one copy of utensils frequently needed is "an indication of self-confidence." "Our Fuegians," he writes, "procure and make their implements with little effort" (1961, p. 213).[6]

In the nonsubsistence sphere, the people's wants are generally easily satisfied. Such "material plenty" depends partly upon the ease of production, and that upon the simplicity of technology and democracy of property. Products are homespun: of stone, bone, wood, skin—materials such as "lay in abundance around them." As a rule, neither extraction of the raw material nor its working up take strenuous effort. Access to natural resources is typically direct—"free for anyone to take"—even as possession of the necessary tools is general and knowledge of the required skills common. The division of labor is likewise simple, predominantly a division of labor by sex. Add in the liberal customs of sharing, for which hunters are properly famous, and all the people can usually participate in the going prosperity, such as it is.

But, of course, "such as it is": this "prosperity" depends as well upon an objectively low standard of living. It is critical that the customary quota of consumables (as well as the number of consumers) be culturally set at a modest point. A few people are pleased to consider a few easily-made things their good fortune: some meagre pieces of clothing and rather fugitive housing in most climates;[7] plus a few ornaments, spare flints, and sundry other items such as the "pieces of quartz, which native doctors have extracted from their patients" (Grey, 1841, vol. 2, p. 266); and, finally, the skin bags in which the faithful wife carries all this, "the wealth of the Australian savage" (p. 266).

For most hunters, such affluence without abundance in the nonsubsistence sphere need not be long debated. A more interesting question is why they are content with so few possessions—for it is with them a policy, a "matter of principle" as Gusinde says (1961, p. 2), and not a misfortune.

Want not, lack not. But are hunters so undemanding of material goods because they are themselves enslaved by a food quest "demanding maximum energy from a maximum number of people," so that no time or effort remains for the provision of other comforts? Some ethnographers testify to the contrary that the food quest is so successful that half the time the people seem not to know what to do with themselves. On the other hand, *movement* is a condition of this success, more movement in some cases than others, but always enough to rapidly depreciate the satisfactions of property. Of the hunter it is truly said that his wealth is a burden. In his condition of life, goods can become "grievously oppressive," as Gusinde observes, and the more so the longer they are carried around. Certain food collectors do have canoes and a few have dog sleds, but most must carry themselves all the comforts they possess, and so only possess what they can comfortably carry themselves. Or perhaps only what the women can carry: the men are often left free to react to the sudden opportunity of the chase or the sudden necessity of defense. As Owen Lattimore wrote in a not too different context, "the pure nomad is the poor nomad." Mobility and property are in contradiction.

That wealth quickly becomes more of an encumbrance than a good thing is apparent even to the outsider. Laurens van der Post was caught in the contradiction as he prepared to make farewells to his wild Bushmen friends:

This matter of presents gave us many an anxious moment. We were humiliated by the realization of how little there was we could give to the Bushmen. Almost everything seemed likely to make life more difficult for them by adding to the litter and weight of their daily round. They themselves had practically no possessions: a loin strap, a skin blanket and a leather satchel. There was nothing that they could not assemble in one minut wrap up in their blankets and carry on their shoulders for a journey of a thousand miles. They had no sense of possession (1958, p. 276).

A necessity so obvious to the casual visitor must be second nature to the people concerned. This modesty of material requirements is institutionalized: it becomes a positive cultural fact, expressed in a variety of economic arrangements. Lloyd Warner reports of the Murngin, for example, that portability is a decisive value in the local scheme of things. Small goods are in general better than big goods. In the final analysis "the relative ease of transportation of the article" will prevail, so far as determining its disposition, over its relative scarcity or labor cost. For the "ultimate value," Warner writes, "is freedom of movement." And to this "desire to be free from the burdens and responsibilities of objects which would interfere with the society's itinerant existence," Warner attributes the Murngin's "undeveloped sense of property," and their "lack of interest in developing their technological equipment" (1964, pp. 136–137).

Here then is another economic "peculiarity"—I will not say it is general, and perhaps it is explained as well by faulty toilet training as by a trained disinterest in material accumulation: some hunters, at least, display a notable tendency to be sloppy about their possessions. They have the kind of nonchalance that would be appropriate to a people who have mastered the problems of production, even as it is maddening to a European:

They do not know how to take care of their belongings. No one dreams of putting them in order, folding them, drying or cleaning them, hanging them up, or putting them in a neat pile. If they are looking for some particular thing, they rummage carelessly through the hodgepodge of trifles in the little baskets. Larger objects that are piled up in a heap in the hut are dragged hither and yon with no regard for the damage that might be done them. The European observer has the impression that these [Yahgan] Indians place no value whatever on their utensils and that they have completely forgotten the effort it took to make them.[8] Actually, no one clings to his few goods and chattels which, as it is, are often and easily lost, but just as easily replaced.... The Indian does not even exercise care when he could conveniently do so. A European is likely to shake his head at the boundless indifference of these people who drag brandnew objects, precious clothing, fresh provisions, and valuable items through thick mud, or abandon them to their swift destruction by children and dogs.... Expensive things that are given them are treasured for a few hours, out of curiosity; after that they thoughtlessly let everything deteriorate in the mud and wet. The less they own, the more comfortable they can travel, and what is ruined they occasionally replace. Hence, they are completely indifferent to any material possessions (Gusinde, 1961, pp. 86-87).

The hunter, one is tempted to say, is "uneconomic man." At least as concerns non-subsistence goods, he is the reverse of that standard caricature immortalized in any *General Principles of Economics*, page one. His wants are scarce and his means (in relation) plentiful. Consequently he is "comparatively free of material pressures," has "no sense of possession," shows "an undeveloped sense of property," is "completely indifferent to any material pressures," manifests a "lack of interest" in developing his technological equipment....

We are inclined to think of hunters and gatherers as *poor* because they don't have anything; perhaps better to think of them for that reason as *free*. "Their extremely limited material possessions relieve them of all cares with regard to daily necessities and permit them to enjoy life" (Gusinde, 1961, p. 1)....

When Herskovits was writing his *Economic Anthropology* (1958), it was common anthropological practice to take the Bushmen or the native Australians as "a classic illustration of a people whose economic resources are of the scantiest," so precariously situated that "only the most intense application makes survival possible." Today the "classic" understanding can be fairly reversed—on evidence largely from these two groups. A good case can be made that hunters and gatherers work less than we do; and, rather than a continuous travail, the food quest is intermittent, leisure abundant, and there is a greater amount of sleep in the daytime *per capita* per year than in any other condition of society....

Reports on hunters and gatherers of the ethnological present—specifically on those in marginal environments—suggest a mean of three to five hours per adult worker per day in food production. Hunters keep bankers' hours, notably less than modern industrial workers (unionized), who would surely settle for a 21-35 hour week. An interesting comparison is also posed by recent studies of labor costs among agriculturalists of neolithic type. For example, the average adult Hanunoo, man or woman, spends 1,200 hours per year in swidden cultivation (Conklin, 1957, p. 151); which is to say, a mean of three hours twenty minutes per day. Yet this figure does not include food gathering, animal raising, cooking, and other direct subsistence efforts of these Philippine tribesmen. Comparable data are beginning to appear in reports on other primitive agriculturalists from many parts of the world. The conclusion is put conservatively when put negatively: hunters and gatherers need not work longer getting food than do primitive cultivators. Extrapolating from ethnography to prehistory, one may say as much for the neolithic as John Stuart Mill said of all labor-saving devices, that never was one invented that saved anyone a minute's labor. The neolithic saw no particular improvement over the paleolithic in the amount of time required per capita for the production of subsistence; probably, with the advent of agriculture, people had to work harder.

There is nothing either to the convention that hunters and gatherers can enjoy little leisure from tasks of sheer survival. By this, the evolutionary inadequacies of the paleolithic are customarily explained, while for the provision of leisure the neolithic is roundly congratulated. But the traditional formulas might be truer if reversed: the amount of work (per capita) increases with the evolution of culture, and the amount of leisure decreases. Hunters' subsistence labors are characteristically intermittent, a day on and a day off, and modern hunters at least tend to employ their time off in such activities as daytime sleep.... In alleging this is an affluent economy..., I do not deny that certain hunters have moments of difficulty. Some do find it "almost inconceivable" for a man to die of hunger, or even to fail to satisfy his hunger for more than a day or two (Woodburn, 1968, p. 52). But others, especially certain very peripheral hunters spread out in small groups across an environment of extremes, are exposed periodically to the kind of inclemency that interdicts travel or access to game. They suffer—although perhaps only fractionally—the shortage affecting particular immobilized families rather than the society as a whole (cf. Gusinde, 1961, pp. 306–307).

Still, granting this vulnerability, and allowing the most poorly situated modern hunters into comparison, it would be difficult to prove that privation is distinctly characteristic of the hunter-gatherers. Food shortage is not the indicative property of this mode of production as opposed to others; it does not mark off hunters and gatherers as a class or a general evolutionary stage. Lowie asks:

> But what of the herders on a simple plane whose maintenance is periodically jeopardized by plagues—who, like some Lapp bands of the nineteenth century were obliged to fall back on fishing? What of the primitive peasants who clear and till without compensation of the soil, exhaust one plot and pass on to the next, and are threatened with famine at every drought? Are they any more in control of misfortune caused by natural conditions than the hunter-gatherer? (1938, p. 286)

Above all, what about the world today? One-third to one-half of humanity are said to go to bed hungry every night. In the Old Stone Age the fraction must have been much smaller. *This* is the era of hunger unprecedented. Now, in the time of the greatest technical power, is starvation an institution. Reverse another venerable formula: the amount of hunger increases relatively and absolutely with the evolution of culture.

This paradox is my whole point. Hunters and gatherers have by force of circumstances an objectively low standard of living. But taken as their *objective*, and given their adequate means of production, all the people's material wants usually can be easily satisfied. The evolution of economy has known, then, two contradictory movements: enriching but at the same time impoverishing, appropriating in relation to nature but expropriating in relation to man. The progressive aspect is, of course, technological. It has been celebrated in many ways: as an increase in the amount of need-serving goods and services, an increase in the amount of energy harnessed to the service of culture, an increase in productivity, an increase in division of labor, and increased freedom from environmental control. Taken in a certain sense, the last is especially useful for understanding the earliest stages of technical advance. Agriculture not only raised society above the distribution of natural food resources, it allowed neolithic communities to maintain high degrees of social order where the requirements of human existence were absent from the natural order. Enough food could be harvested in some seasons to sustain the people while no food would grow at all; the consequent stability of social life was critical for its material enlargement. Culture went on then from triumph to triumph, in a kind of progressive contravention of the biological law of the minimum, until it proved it could support human life in outer space—where even gravity and oxygen were naturally lacking.

Other men were dying of hunger in the market places of Asia. It has been an evolution of structures as well as technologies, and in that respect like the mythical road where for every step the traveller advances his destination recedes by two...

The world's most primitive people have few possessions, *but they are not poor.* Poverty is not a certain small amount of goods, nor is it just a relation between means and ends; above all it is a relation between people. Poverty is a social status. As such it is the invention of civilization. It has grown with civilization, at once as an invidious distinction between classes and more importantly as a tributary relation—that can render agrarian peasants more susceptible to natural catastrophes than any winter camp of Alaskan Eskimo.

Notes

1. At least to the time Lucretius was writing (Harris, 1968, pp. 26-27). said for the mode of economic organization (cf. Polanyi, 1947, 1957, 1959; Dalton, 1961).
2. The evident fault of White's evolutionary law is the use of "per capita" measures. Neolithic societies in the main harness a *greater total amount of energy* than preagricultural communities, because of the greater number of energy-delivering humans sustained by domestication. This overall rise in the social product, however, is not necessarily effected by an increased productivity of labor—which in White's view also accompanied the neolithic revolution. Ethnological data now in hand, (see text *infra*) raise the possibility that simple agricultural regimes are not more efficient thermodynamically than hunting and gathering—that is, in energy yield per unit of human labor. In the same vein, some archaeology in recent years has tended to privilege stability of settlement over productivity of labor in explanation of the neolithic advance (cf. Braid-wood and Wiley, 1962).
3. For a similar comment, referring to missionary misinterpretation of curing by blood consumption in eastern Australia, see Hodgkinson, 1845, p. 227.
4. Conditions of primitive hunting peoples must not be judged, as Carl Sauer notes, "'from their modern survivors, now restricted to the most meagre regions of the earth, such as the interior of Australia, the American Great

Basin, and the Arctic tundra and taiga. The areas of early occupation were abounding in food' " (cited in Clark and Haswell, 1964, p. 23).

5. Through the prison of acculturation one glimpses what hunting and gathering might have been like in a decent environment from Alexander Henry's account of his bountiful sojourn as a Chippewa in northern Michigan: see Quimby, 1962.

6. Turnbull similarly notes of Congo Pygmies: "The materials for the making of shelter, clothing, and all other necessary items of material culture are all at hand at a moment's notice." And he has no reservations either about subsistence: "Throughout the year, without fail, there is an abundant supply of game and vegetable foods" (1965, p. 18).

7. Certain food collectors not lately known for their architectural achievements seem to have built more substantial dwellings before being put on the run by Europeans. See Smythe, 1871, vol. 1, pp. 125–128.

8. But recall Gusinde's comment: "Our Fuegians procure and make their implements with little effort" (1961, p. 213).

Woman the Provider

Laurens Van Der Post and Jane Taylor

If hunter-gatherer societies in general were misunderstood until recent times, the problem has been doubly so with regard to the roles that women have played in foraging cultures. Perhaps the problem can be chalked up to male bias—the fact that the earliest ethnographies were carried out primarily by men—or, perhaps it has to do with the drama and allure that is associated with the hunt. Since, in most cases, women took the responsibility of gathering fruits and vegetables, their activities were probably not deemed as exciting in print or as photogenic for ethnographic films. Then, too, at least in some cases, a male anthropologist would not have as easy access as would a female ethnographer to the more intimate aspects and meanings of, say, a young women's initiation ceremony.

In any case, the following excerpt from *Testament to the Bushmen* by Laurens Van Der Post and Jane Taylor is written from the personal experience of having accompanied women of the Kua Bushmen group on food-gathering excursions in the Kalahari Desert of southwest Africa.

As you read this essay, please note several important points made by the authors in passing, but nevertheless important in taking gathering women out of the shadows of their hunting male counterparts. First is the sheer quantity and variety of the plant life available to sustain people in this seemingly unforgiving desert. Second is the fact that, pound for pound, the food the women contribute to the sustenance of the group far outweighs and is far more predictable than the meat supplied the by men. Third is the importance of—and length of—breast-feeding of youngsters, which is not only nutritionally important, but also has a determining effect on the birth rate. Finally, there is the importance of ceremony and ritual revolving around a young woman's first menstruation, an event which in some societies is considered a time of danger whereas, among the Bushmen, it is a time of joy, a time to celebrate the ability to give life to the next generation.

Laurens Van Der Post (1906-1996) was born and raised on the South African frontier. As an outspoken critic of apartheid and co-founder of the rebellious magazine, *The Lash and the Whip*, he was to write extensively about his world travels, his service in the British Army during World War II, and his experience as a prisoner of war. His other most noted work in anthropology is *The Lost World of the Kalahari*.

Jane Taylor was born in Malaya, but lived in Sussex, England after the age of nine. After teaching history for two years, she went into publishing, journalism, and photography. She served the BBC as a researcher and interpreter on the six-part series, *The Gates of Asia*, and has since worked in film and television as well.

Key Concept: woman the gatherer

Morning began slowly in the Bushman camp. The nights were cold with the approach of winter, and figures lay huddled around the remains of fires, not stirring until the sun had risen high enough to warm them. The small children moved first, rubbing sleepy eyes as they tottered about from one inert body to another. Even /Gae≠tebe, usually a bundle of energy and merriment right through the day and half way through the night, was unrecognizably subdued.

After a while the stumblings and demands of the children roused their parents, and they too began the process of facing the day. Men prodded fires into renewed life, women put roots and knobbly gemsbok cucumbers (*Citrullus naudinianus*) onto the fires to cook and, when they were ready, handed them round to be eaten—mostly to their own immediate family, but any child who happened to be around and hungry was always given something. In late April when we arrived, there were plenty of gemsbok cucumbers (a kind of melon), brought on by the heavy rain earlier in the month, but they were nearing the end of their season as winter approached. Curiously, when Laurens van der Post was in the Kalahari Desert in the early 1950s, these same melons were referred to as eland cucumbers. It seems you can pick your antelope.

/Gae≠tebe, more awake now, came to where the melons were piled, hot and tempting, and /Ganakadi (his aunt by our reckoning, and one of his mothers by his) cut the top off one of them, mashed the flesh inside the skin with a stick, and handed it to him. He sat down and dipped into the melon with his fingers, raising the soft, steaming, yellow pulp slowly to his mouth, keeping his fingers half inside his mouth as he chewed. It was an operation of the utmost seriousness.

Gathering gemsbok cucumbers, and all other varieties of plant food is women's work among the Bushmen. A group of three or four would go out every day, usually one or more carrying a small child, and they would walk through the veld, digging with their sticks for roots, or picking melons, berries or seedpods. For much of the year there is an abundance and variety of plant food—over a hundred different species are used by the Bushmen—so there is no problem about finding sufficient to feed the whole band. So intimate and precise is their knowledge of the vegetation of the area in which they live, that the women know exactly where to go to collect each of the various plants available at that moment. Because of this there is no waste of energy. We were with them in a time of plenty, so the group of women that went out on any given day did not have to go far to gather enough food for the whole community. Each expedition that we witnessed took no longer than an hour and a half. But by the time spring has come, after several months without rain, the situation changes and more groups have to go out for considerably longer periods in order to gather enough to meet the needs of the band.

Richard Lee has estimated that among the !Kung Bushmen with whom he worked, a woman walked about 2,400 km (1,500 miles) every year. While this distance is not all covered in her search for food, quite a high proportion of it is. For most of the year this particular task is fairly undemanding and a woman may spend no more than five or six hours a week foraging; but in winter she may go out three or four days in the week, and walk for perhaps eight or nine hours at a stretch, gathering an increasing weight of vegetables as she goes. By the time she stops gathering and sets off back to camp, the load she carries can be considerable, sometimes as much as 15 kg (33 lbs).

Apart from the vegetable weight, a woman will very often have one child, and possibly two, who will need to be carried all or part of the time. On one gathering expedition that I accompanied, /Kwa-u/tee carried her young son Tshipi//xama with her all the time, slung in a kaross on her side, from which position he could reach for her breast for a feed whenever he felt like it. It was an accommodation he made full use of. He did not seem to affect her efficiency for a moment, but he was no lightweight and certainly increased the effort his mother had to put into gathering food. Small wonder that the women take every opportunity to sit and do nothing by the fire.

The women walked with a swift and easy stride in single file through the long Bushman grass which stretched away, shining in the sun, to the wide circle of the horizon. Very often the plants they were looking for revealed themselves by only the tiniest cluster of leaves above the surface, which most other people would not even notice. But they spotted everything, and the instant they saw something worth digging up they would stop and immediately set to work with rapid stabs of their digging sticks until the tuber was exposed; then they pulled it out, dusted it off, and popped it into the doubled-up kaross slung across their backs. For a small, easy plant, growing on the surface, they barely changed their gait but simply leaned down, stabbed the earth beside it, pulled it up and moved on, all in one fluid movement.

At times they would stop at a *Grewia* bush, pick the berries and suck the flesh, and then spit out the hard pip. The berries are about the size of a small grape, fibrous and not very juicy, but they have a pleasant flavour and are fairly sweet. They were rather wrinkled and past their best when we were there, so the women simply sucked them for refreshment on the way and did not bother to gather them.

One of the plants they gathered in considerable quantities was the *Bauhinia esculenta* which even I quickly learned to recognize by its long trailing creeper-like branches which ran at ground level, with pairs of flat, roundish leaves spaced at regular intervals. In late April the young tuber was at its best, and it remains good to eat for most of the winter. But by the end of August it gets hard and fibrous, and its water content, the main value of the tuber, becomes negligible. The *Bauhinia esculenta* also provides morama beans which are a much favoured food, rich in protein and oil. The whole pod is roasted in the fire, the beans taken out and either chewed as they are, or ground and mixed with other foods. A great advantage of these beans is that they can be dried and stored against a time when other foods are scarce.

The commonest root that we came across was a kind of wild turnip, *Raphionacme burkei,* known as *bi* to these Bushmen. It flourishes all the year round and is a major source of water in the dry season to those Bushmen not within easy reach of a borehole. The *bi* tuber is shredded by rapid downward movements with a sharp-edged stick, while the person doing the work holds it steady with her feet. The pulp is gathered on a piece of skin and, when there is enough, it is squeezed in one hand directly into the mouth. Children stand around with their mouths open and are usually rewarded with a squeeze of *bi* water. Then the dehydrated pulp, with what little moisture remains in it, is used to wash the face, arms and body, rather like a pulverized face cloth. In the context of a ritual, such as the washing of a girl at the end of her menarcheal rite, it is the ever-present *bi* tuber that is used. But the tuber is rather fibrous and tastes somewhat bitter, so when alternative plant water sources are available, such as the various kinds of melon, they tend to be preferred. On one occasion Aa//xama and Uyokoe/teesa overcame the problem of bitterness by mixing the *bi* pulp with the chewed-up leaves of the *Boscia albitrunca* tree.

They said that this made it sweeter, but it also required more effort on their part which would tend to put it fairly low on any list of Bushman priorities if simpler sources of sweet water were there for the taking.

Another abundant food was several species of *Scilla* which look like large spring onions. The women gathered them in quantity and, once back in their camp, roasted, peeled and ate them. Both the *Scillas* and the *bi* tuber were eaten with little discernible enthusiasm; as far as plant food was concerned, the greatest preference seemed to be for the luscious-looking green-fleshed tsama melons (*Citrullus lanatus*) that were constantly being cut open and eaten down to the skin. However, real gastronomic enthusiasm was reserved for meat alone.

Once the required root was located, it was sheer hard work to dig it out, for it was sometimes a metre (yard) or more beneath the surface. The only implement used is a digging stick, a simple straight branch of *Rhigozum brevispinosum*, a metre or more (three to four feet) in length, stripped of bark, thorns and subsidiary branches and sharpened at one end. This type of digging stick is employed throughout the Kalahari. It is fascinating, in some of the paintings of the now extinct southern Bushmen, to see that the women are carrying digging sticks of a different type, with a round knob part-way up the stick; this was a stone with a hole bored through it, which was used as a weighting device to help dig into the hard rocky ground of their terrain. The soft sand of the Kalahari demands no such refinement of design.

At Masetlheng, in the southwestern Kalahari, some of the !Xõ women showed us handfuls of what looked like large potatoes; they were truffles (*Terfezia pfeilli*), to us an expensive luxury, to them a source of vital nutrients. Truffles make a brief appearance in April to May, but they depend on rainfall and in dry years do not appear at all. At Masetlheng they were one of the very few plants available to the !Xõ for it was generally too dry for roots to survive, since the problem of water in that area is an acute one. These truffles had been brought on by a sudden downpour of rain about two weeks previously. I was astonished at the richness of their truffle harvest with no specially trained hounds (or pigs) whose help in locating these deeply hidden delicacies seems to be essential in other parts of the world. I was told it was quite simple to find them—all you have to do is to recognize a particular kind of crack in the ground, caused by the truffle growing deep down, and then dig for it. It also helps, of course, to have a Bushman's sophisticated understanding of the natural world.

The women's highly developed knowledge of plants was supplemented by their constant exchange of information as they walked along—here, perhaps, was a new cluster of plants, or there, the leaves of another plant seemed to be dying. The natural chattiness of the Bushman was channelled into a vital form of communication. In their gathering, as in everything else we saw them doing, they found an endless source of interest and amusement; with the Bushmen we found that nothing remained totally serious for very long.

It has always been the gathering of roots by the women that has provided the greatest part of the Bushman's diet. Meat may be their favourite food, and the only food to arouse real enthusiasm, but if the Bushmen had had nothing but the meat that the hunters provided, they would have disappeared without trace thousands of years ago. It is the prosaic unsung work of the women that has kept them alive. The roots, bulbs, tubers, and fruits that they eat, with the vitamins and minerals in them, provide a well-balanced diet, especially when combined with the occasional supply of protein that comes in the form of meat as well as beans and, in some areas of the northern Kalahari, nuts. It is only recently with more and more Bushmen employed on farms and being paid with food such as mealie meal, that their balanced diet has been disturbed. With free rations, and with plant food becoming scarcer as the land is increasingly heavily grazed by cattle, the women no longer go out on gathering expeditions as frequently as they used to; but mealie meal does not have the vitamins that the vegetables provided. The effects of malnutrition—distended belly and stick-like arms and legs—are not uncommon sights. They are, however, relatively new ones. Milk would help, if it were available, but Bushmen have not normally been stock-keepers, and many of them still do not regard cattle as anything more than a meal.

Another thing that has changed fairly recently, as Bushmen have increasingly settled around boreholes, is the birth rate. Nomadic Bushwomen gave birth at an average interval of between four and five years, each child continuing to breast-feed until the mother became pregnant again. Breast-feeding in itself tends to suppress ovulation, added to which it appears that fertility may be lower among Bushmen that among many other groups of people. They themselves recognize this as a good thing, a natural protection against overloading the system, especially in years of drought. There seems to be some kind of connection between drought and reduced fertility.

In extreme conditions of drought, when there is simply not enough food and water to go around, and survival is a matter of concern, the birth of another child into a nomadic band can put an impossible extra burden on the band in general, and on the mother in particular. In such a situation the mother may never allow the new baby to breathe. For people who have such a patent love for, and enjoyment of their children, the anguish this must cause is unimaginable. It is a desperate necessity, fortunately a rare one.

Even when there is no drought, the situation of the band, or the health of the mother and her other children may be so precarious that if a woman conceives too soon after the birth of her previous child, she may decide she cannot keep the new baby. Lorna Marshall questioned some of the !Kung women among whom she worked for many years and gathered that although they did not regard such infanticide as morally or socially wrong, it was deeply distressing to them. They all claimed that they had never had to do it themselves: 'When they talked about it with me, they never once spoke concretely or directly of the act itself but had much to say about the necessity of it…. They spoke of the nourishment of the children as the primary reason; they spoke in explicit detail. They want children, all the children they can possibly have, but, they explained, they cannot feed babies that are born too close together. They said Bushman children must have strong legs, and it is mother's milk that makes them strong. A mother had not enough milk to sustain completely two infants at the same time. They believe a child needs milk until it is three or four years old at least.'

Such longterm breast-feeding is certainly a good idea where there are no alternative sources of milk available for a young child. To be weaned onto rough and indigestible veld foods at the age of two or under would jeopardize the child's chances of survival, or at least its chances of a reasonably healthy life.

In our band of Kua Bushmen in the southeastern Kalahari, the spacing of the children was generally closer together than four years. Since Bushmen do not count in years, and have only a hazy notion of the time that any event occurred (even a relatively recent one), it was difficult to assess the ages of the children. Also I reckoned that they were probably older than they appeared to my western eyes, partly because of their naturally smaller stature, but also because of their somewhat slower rate of development after weaning compared with the average western child. However, the guesstimate of children's ages that I arrived at is probably more or less equally inaccurate throughout, so that the resulting number of years between each child may roughly accord with reality.

When I asked Be/tee how many children he and Khangdu had, he first of all put up four fingers and then, after due deliberation, added the thumb. In fact, as each child was named and produced, the total mounted to eight. Counting is not a common accomplishment among the parental generation. Their eldest child, Aa//xama, I reckoned to be about eighteen, a lively girl, full of wit and cheek, and with an exceptionally deep voice. She looked after her younger siblings with great affection as a kind of secondary mother. The three children next in age were at school an hour's drive away (or half a day's walk). We met them when we went to film at the school one day. Tshipikan, a boy, was about fifteen; his younger brother, Dyuogãe, about thirteen; their sister, Bia≠tebe, about eleven. The four youngest, all boys, were with their parents. Noa-adigãe was about eight; Iogãe, five; /Gae≠tebe, three, and their new baby was less than two weeks old. They said he had been born within the moon; and there had been a new moon about ten days before we arrived.

The intervals between these children range from two to three years, and this seemed to be fairly typical throughout the band. It is now several years since they were nomadic, and there is no doubt that this is a considerable factor in the more frequent births. The women no longer have to expend as much effort on gathering since almost every family has a son or daughter working on a farm, and the rations with which they are paid are shared out among the various members of the family in the traditional manner. The fact that these rations are of less nutritional value than the vegetables the women collect is not immediately obvious, and the temptation to avoid the hard labour of gathering is a powerful one, especially when they might have one or two small children to carry around with them.

To give birth to her new baby, Khangdu did as Bushman women have done for thousands of years—she went out by herself into the veld when the labour pains began, and produced her infant entirely alone, with no medical facilities of any kind. Occasionally, especially for a first birth, the woman's mother, or another close female relative, will accompany her. It is not considered necessary to go far from the camp; usually the woman goes only a few hundred yards—near enough for the baby's first cries to be heard by her family, or for them to hear if anything is going wrong.

Isaac Schapera, one of the first of the modern Bushman anthropologists, has written of a number of different practices among the various groups of Bushmen: the Heikum uprooted tufts of grass which they placed upside down on a tree as a warning to the men, who may not be present when a child is born; an Auen husband would tie his bowstring around his wife's body; a !Kung woman, when her labour pains began, had to step over her husband's legs after he had made incisions in his calves and rubbed medicine into them. These practices have largely fallen into disuse today.

The only group Schapera mentions where the women did not go out into the veld to give birth, were the Bushmen of the Namib Desert: 'When labour is far advanced the woman's husband makes a small fire outside the hut in which she is confined, and carefully keeps it going. No pot may be placed on this fire, nor may anything be cooked or roasted over it. It is believed that if this custom is neglected both the mother and new-born child will go blind. After the birth another larger fire is kindled alongside the previous one as a sign of rejoicing, irrespective of the sex of the child.'

Bushman women give birth in a squatting position which is now the favoured position among many 'advanced' people. The mother's attitude to childbirth is believed to affect the delivery; if she goes into the experience without fear then the delivery will be uncomplicated. In John Marshall's superb film, *N!ai, the Story of a !Kung Woman*, N!ai tells of her friend who resented and feared the forthcoming birth of her first child. When she dies in childbirth N!ai says it was because she had been so afraid. It is not that the Bushmen discount physical explanations, but among a deeply spiritual people the spiritual explanation has priority. For Khangdu, however, it was her eighth child, nothing had gone wrong with the previous seven births, and once again everything went as easily as she had expected. At ten days old her new son, rosy pink and with a halo of fine dark hair, was clearly doing well.

Khangdu was a quiet, unassuming woman with a ready smile and eyes that seemed to take in everything, especially anything to do with her children. When necessary she would speak in a very direct and forthright manner, and clearly expected to be listened to. If Be/tee were around she would always appear to defer to him, not expecting to assume the mantle of leadership.

There was one occasion when we inadvertently infringed one of the Bushmen's taboos concerning women. We had had a problem over filming a hunt in the area in which our three hunters lived which was severely lacking in game. After three days of fruitless searching for any kind of animal we decided, with the hunters' agreement, to move to Masetlheng, further to the west, where we had heard that game was more abundant. The Bushmen in that area were of the same language group—!Xõ—as our hunters, so that was not likely to cause undue difficulty. Our guide knew a group there to whom we could go, and he felt sure that they would understand what we wanted to do and would help us. This group did not hunt in the traditional manner any longer, so there was no question of using hunters from their own band. We arrived at Masetlheng, and all went according to plan. We filmed a successful hunt, with a gemsbok as the quarry, and the hunters brought the meat back to the camp and distributed it.

The next day our interpreter came and told us that there was much distress and anger among the men of the village because their women had received meat from strange men. By some appalling oversight we had failed to explain the full details of what we wanted to do, and the men were justly incensed at this disregard for their tradition. Our film director went with the interpreter to where the main members of the group were gathered, sat down with them, apologized from his heart and told them how distressed we were to have caused this hurt—we had thought that everything had been explained beforehand. The generosity and warmth of their response touched us deeply. They said that no white man had ever apologized to them before, but because we had done so, and had explained how the mistake had happened, and had intended no wrong, we could come again. It was a humbling moment.

As far as we knew, this was the only occasion that we made such a mistake. We were all acutely aware of the possibility of offending through ignorance or insensitivity, and also of the fact that film crews are not famous for their perception of other people's sensibilities. For this reason we avoided reference to the enlarged buttocks, or steatopygia, of the women. Bushmen are extremely modest—they do not regard breasts as sexual objects but simply as a means of feeding their children; therefore they leave them uncovered. The buttocks, however, have

considerable sexual significance and are consequently kept covered. The men are equally modest and always cover their unique portion of anatomy, the semi-erect penis. It was a feature that fascinated several early travelers who seemed to have no qualms about getting the Bushmen they met to undress and allow themselves to be inspected. I cannot see an old photograph or drawing of naked Bushmen, both men and women, without shame for the humiliation inflicted on them.

Steatopygia is caused by the accumulation of fat on the buttocks, and its existence has been the cause of some controversy. It was at one time maintained that it was a special adaptation to desert conditions. It is certainly true that this fat deposit does diminish in times of drought and food shortage, so it may indeed be an aid to survival. But paintings in the Drakensberg, and in other places that are very far from being deserts, show women with pronounced steatopygia. Also steatopygia is both more common, and of greater size, among the Hottentots (not exclusively a desert people) than among the Bushmen, so its connection with the desert must be ruled out. Phillip Tobias, Professor of Anatomy at the University of Witwatersand and an authority on early African peoples, has suggested that its evolution may be due to the occasional periods of deprivation inherent in the hunter-gatherer way of life regardless of environment.

The women's modest covering of their behinds either with western-style clothes or with their traditional clothes—a short skin hanging from the waist and a large kaross slung from the shoulders—made it difficult for us to gauge how widespread this feature was among the groups we were with. There was certainly no exaggerated steatopygia with any of them, though about half appeared to have fairly prominent behinds. There was only one occasion when the women lifted their karosses and aprons, or removed them altogether, and this was during the ritual that is performed on the occasion of a girl's first menstruation. This is very much a women's ritual, in which few men are allowed to take part, and it is a glorious celebration of a girl's passage from childhood to the beginning of womanhood.

There is a remarkable painting at Fulton's Rock in the Drakensberg mountains of Natal, which David Lewis-Williams, in his research on Bushman art, has recently identified as depicting a girl's first menstruation ritual. By piecing together references to this ritual by Bleek's southern Bushman informants in the 1870s, and present-day practice among some !Kung in the northwestern Kalahari, Lewis-Williams became increasingly convinced that some previous interpretations of this painting were missing the point. He believes that the covered figure inside the incomplete circle is in fact a girl isolated inside a hut for the duration of her first menstruation, with one or two women to keep her company; that the female figures surrounding the hut and bending forward are women performing the ritual dance, and imitating the mating behaviour of female antelopes; and that the other figures (some definitely male, others probably so) represent the few men who join in the dance, some holding sticks which represent an antelope's horns.

Among the !Kung the dance that is performed around the hut in which the girl is isolated is the eland bull dance, and it is fascinating to see in the painting executed by the southern Bushmen, that there is the shadowy figure of an eland just below the main group of figures, a symbol of the supernatural potency (*n/um*) that the girl is believed to have at this time. As we have already seen, the eland had a unique place in the imagination of the southern Bushmen; it was not only the favourite creature of Mantis, but also the source of the most powerful *n/um*. Today in the Kalahari the eland is still regard with the same kind of feeling, and it is the animal that hunters most desire to hunt.

With this painting clear in my mind, it was with a special interest that I watched the menarcheal rite that was performed by the group of !Xõ Bushmen with whom we spent some time. As one of the great rituals in the Bushmen's life, and one of the few that is still performed, we particularly wanted to film it; but the chances of our happening to be in the right place at the right time were negligible. We could hardly approach a group we did not know at all to film such a central and intimate ceremony. With the help of the school teacher at Lone Tree, Elizabeth Camm, I approached some of the women of the group we had already worked with and asked if they would perform this ritual for us to film, and I was astonished at the apparent enthusiasm with which they agreed. But first of all, they said, I must sit down and they would tell me what they were going to do.

Very often, they said, a girl would be out in the veld with her friends when she discovered that she had started to bleed. She would immediately sit down and keep very quiet, which would make the others realize what had happened. They chose a girl called !Kaekukhwe to play the main part; and what followed was exactly what the women had told me, so I could tell other people about it.

When !Kaekukhwe sat down, the game they had all been playing stopped at once and one of her friends, Zana/go, raced back to the hut where the women were sitting. With a whoop of joy, !Kaekukhwe's mother, /Kunago, leaped to her feet and ran to where her daughter was sitting, accompanied by several other women. Those who stayed back at the hut were already clapping and chanting. Zana/go ran back again to the hut to collect a kaross, and then returned like the wind to where !Kaekukhwe was surrounded by chanting and clapping women. Her mother bent down and took her daughter onto her back, while another woman covered her with the kaross so that even her face was lost to sight. Then she was carried back to the hut in which another kaross had been spread out for her to be laid on, with the original kaross covering her. Usually a special hut is quickly and roughly constructed for the girl, but on this occasion they simply used an existing one.

During the whole time of her menstruation the girl must not touch the earth, neither must the sun fall on her. She must wear no beads or clothes. Food is brought to her inside the hut where she remains alone for most of the time. For everyone else the ritual has something of a carnival atmosphere; for the girl herself is far from true as she spends long hours entirely alone with her thoughts. Only when there is dancing around the hut do one or two women come inside and sit with her. No man may see her face, for if he does it is believed that ill luck will befall him. During her first menstruation a girl is believed to have great supernatural power which can be harnessed for the good of the community if rightly treated, but if not, can turn to the detriment of an individual or the whole group.

Every day the women dance around the hut, and on some occasions two or three of the older men join in. Having only heard of the eland bull dance in connection with this ritual, I was surprised to be told that this group did the gemsbok dance. I asked why, and was told simply that this was the dance they always did. To my eyes it made little difference; and what seemed almost uncanny to me was how exact their performance was to the painting of those extinct Bushmen of the Drakensberg. Time and distance gave way to a common tradition.

As the women danced and clapped and shouted, they would tip forward with their bottoms in the air, uncovering them as they did so. This occurred especially as they danced in front of the entrance to the hut (just as in the painting), and was always accompanied by gales of bawdy laughter. The men cut forked branches which they held to their heads as they danced, in imitation of gemsbok horns, and from time to time they jerked their pelvises forward in a manner that left little to the imagination, and was a source of voluble mirth to all. At other times they would rub their horns in the bushes in the manner of rutting antelopes. The whole performance was full of earthy enjoyment, yet totally lacking the prurience that would accompany anything similar in a western 'civilized' culture.

At the end of her menstruation, the girl is washed inside the hut, with water squeezed from a *bi* tuber. Then she is scarified with a few short incisions on the back of each shoulder and in the middle of the chest above the breasts. I expressed concern for !Kaekukhwe being hurt just for our benefit, but the women regarded what I had said as a great joke. It was no problem for !Kaekukhwe, they assured me. Little girls are scarified at fairly frequent intervals from an early age in order to add to their beauty, and this would simply be another occasion for !Kaekukhwe to have her beauty enhanced. In any case, they said, she had agreed to it.

She sat there with not a flicker crossing her face as her mother made the required incisions and rubbed into them a mixture of fat and plant ash. This same mixture was then applied to her face, making a line down the center of her forehead, then from ear to ear under her chin, and large circles around her eyes—all in imitation of the facial markings of the gemsbok. Then they dressed her with a skin over her behind, and a beaded apron covering her front, put strings of beads around her neck and under her arms, crossing between her breasts, and finally a beaded band around her head. Her mother and another woman—one on either side of her—then led her out of the hut and into the dance.

Throughout the dance she was serious and unsmiling, her eyes downcast. This behaviour is also required of a girl among the !Kung, and Lewis-Williams's informant told him it was because in her enhanced state of potency she can affect the game that may be hunted in the coming days. If she keeps her eyes down, so too will the animals when they are hunted; they will not look up and see the hunter as he creeps up on them.

The dance continued into the evening, gathering momentum with the hypnotic rhythm of the clapping and chanting and the stamping of feet. Dust rose from the earth and hung in the air like an evening mist, turning to red gold as it was caught by the setting sun. By now everyone had joined in, young and old alike, and the dancing figures whirled and leaped as they circled the hut and wove their way through the bushes in a great figure of eight. The performance that had been set up for our benefit had been transformed into a celebration for the life of the whole band.

Society and Sex Roles

Ernestine Friedl

This article was written at the height of the feminist movement in the 1970's. It came as a response to the frequent claims by some that the earliest human societies were matriarchies ruled by women while others had just as vociferously charged that patriarchy, or rule by men, was the earliest order of the day. A consideration of the evidence cited in this article shows that the truth lies somewhere in between. Actually, hunting and gathering societies, taken as the earliest *kind* of human society, are egalitarian where men and women contribute equally to the food supply and tend to be more patriarchal where there is a greater emphasis upon hunting for meat. In any case, nothing should be taken for granted about which condition is "natural."

Ernestine Friedl (b. 1920 in Hungary), as a professor of anthropology at Duke University, had little interest in women's issues, not even in the anthropological study of women. Certainly, her fieldwork among the Pomo and Chippewa Indians of North America and her ethnographies in rural and urban Greece showed no such inclinations. Then, in the early 1970's, while serving on the American Anthropological Association Committee on the Status of Women, Friedl observed firsthand the discrimination against women in anthropology as well as in other academic disciplines. Since then, she has carried out cross-cultural studies on sex and gender roles and has written a book on the subject: *Women and Men: An Anthropologist's View*.

Ernestine Friedl received her Ph.D. at Columbia University in 1950. She taught at Wellesley College and Queens College of New York City before taking a professorship at Duke. She has also been a Visiting Professor at Harvard and Princeton Universities and has served as president of the American Anthropological Association and as a presidential appointee to the National Science Board (the governing body of the National Science Foundation). Friedl has also edited the *Journal of Modern Greek Studies*, with major research interests in the anthropology of modern Greece and in gender from an evolutionary perspective. Aside from this article and the book cited above, her most significant publication is *Vasilika: A Village in Modern Greece*. Today, she is professor emeritus.

Key Concept: patriarchy vs. egalitarianism

"*W*omen must respond quickly to the demands of their husbands," says anthropologist Napoleon Chagnon describing the horticultural Yanomano Indians of Venezuela. When a man returns from a hunting trip, "the woman, no matter what she is doing, hurries home and quietly but rapidly prepares a meal for her husband. Should the wife be slow in doing this, the husband is within his rights to beat her. Most reprimands... take the form of blows with the hand or with a piece of firewood.... Some of them chop their wives with the sharp edge of a machete or axe, or shoot them with a barbed arrow in some nonvital area, such as the buttocks or leg."

Among the Semai agriculturalists of central Malaya, when one person refuses the request of another, the offended party suffers *punan*, a mixture of emotional pain and frustration. "Enduring *punan* is commonest when a girl has refused the victim her sexual favors," reports Robert Dentan. "The jilted man's 'heart becomes

sad.' He loses his energy and his appetite. Much of the time he sleeps, dreaming of his lost love. In this state, he is in fact very likely to injure himself 'accidentally.' " The Semai are afraid of violence; a man would never strike a woman.

The social relationship between men and women has emerged as one of the principal disputes occupying the attention of scholars and the public in recent years. Although the discord is sharpest in the United States, the controversy has spread throughout the world. Numerous national and international conferences, including one in Mexico sponsored by the United Nations, have drawn together delegates from all walks of life to discuss such questions as the social and political rights of each sex, and even the basic nature of males and females.

Whatever their position, partisans often invoke examples from other cultures to support their ideas about the proper role of each sex. Because women are clearly subservient to men in many societies, like the Yanomamo, some experts conclude that the natural pattern is for men to dominate. But among the Semai no one has the right to command others, and in West Africa women are often chiefs. The place of women in these societies supports the argument of those who believe that sex roles are not fixed, that if there is a natural order, it allows for many different arrangements.

The argument will never be settled as long as the opposing sides toss examples from the world's cultures at each other like intellectual stones. But the effect of biological differences on male and female behavior can be clarified by looking at known examples of the earliest forms of human society and examining the relationship between technology, social organization, environment, and sex roles. The problem is to determine the conditions in which different degrees of male dominance are found, to try to discover the social and cultural arrangements that give rise to equality or inequality between the sexes, and to attempt to apply this knowledge to our understanding of the changes taking place in modern industrial society.

As Western history and the anthropological record have told us, equality between the sexes is rare; in most known societies females are subordinate. Male dominance is so widespread that it is virtually a human universal; societies in which women are consistently dominant do not exist and have never existed.

Evidence of a society in which women control all strategic resources like food and water, and in which women's activities are the most prestigious has never been found. The Iroquois of North America and the Lovedu of Africa came closest. Among the Iroquois, women raised food, controlled its distribution, and helped to choose male political leaders. Lovedu women ruled as queens, exchanged valuable cattle, led ceremonies, and controlled their own sex lives. But among both the Iroquois and the Lovedu, men owned the land and held other positions of power and prestige. Women were equal to men; they did not have ultimate authority over them. Neither culture was a true matriarchy.

Patriarchies are prevalent, and they appear to be strongest in societies in which men control significant goods that are exchanged with people outside the family. Regardless of who produces food, the person who gives it to others creates the obligations and alliances that are at the center of all political relations. The greater the male monopoly on the distribution of scarce items, the stronger their control of women seems to be. This is most obvious in relatively simple hunter-gatherer societies.

Hunter-gatherers, or foragers, subsist on wild plants, small land animals, and small river or sea creatures gathered by hand; large land animals and sea mammals hunted with spears, bows and arrows, and blow guns; and fish caught with hooks and nets. The 300,000 hunter-gatherers alive in the world today include the Eskimos, the Australian aborigines, and the Pygmies of Central Africa.

Foraging has endured for two million years and was replaced by farming and animal husbandry only 10,000 years ago; it covers more than 99 percent of human history. Our foraging ancestry is not far behind us and provides a clue to our understanding of the human condition.

Hunter-gatherers are people whose ways of life are technologically simple and socially and politically egalitarian. They live in small groups of 50 to 200 and have neither kings, nor priests, nor social classes. These conditions permit anthropologists to observe the essential bases for inequalities between the sexes without the distortions induced by the complexities of contemporary industrial society.

The source of male power among hunter-gatherers lies in their control of a scarce, hard to acquire, but necessary nutrient—animal protein. When men in a hunter-gatherer society return to camp with game, they divide the meat in some customary way. Among the !Kung San of Africa, certain parts of the animal are given to the owner of the arrow that killed the beast, to the first hunter to sight the game, to the one who threw the first spear and to all men in the hunting party. After the meat has been divided, each hunter distributes his share to his blood relatives and his in-laws, who in turn share it with others. If an animal is large enough, every member of the band will receive some meat.

Vegetable foods, in contrast, are not distributed beyond the immediate household. Women give food to their children, to their husbands, to other members of the household, and rarely, to the occasional visitor. No one outside the family regularly eats any of the wild fruit and vegetables that are gathered by the women.

The meat distributed by the men is a public gift. Its source is widely known, and the donor expects a reciprocal gift when other men return from a successful hunt. He gains honor as a supplier of a scarce item and simultaneously obligates others to him.

These obligations constitute a form of power or control over others, both men and women. The opinions of hunters play an important part in decisions to move the village; good hunters attract the most desirable women; people in other groups join camps with good hunters; and hunters, because they already participate in an internal system of exchange, control exchange with other groups for flint, salt, and steel axes. The male monopoly on hunting unites men in a system of exchange and gives them power; gathering vegetable food does not give women equal power even among foragers who live in the tropics, where the food collected by women provides more than half the hunter-gatherer diet.

If dominance arises from a monopoly on big-game hunting, why has the male monopoly remained unchallenged? Some women are strong enough to participate in the hunt and their endurance is certainly equal to that of men. Dobe San women of the Kalahari Desert in Africa walk an average of 10 miles a day carrying from 15 to 33 pounds of food plus a baby.

Women do not hunt, I believe, because of four inter-related factors: variability in the supply of game; the different skills required for hunting and gathering; the incompatibility between carrying burdens and hunting; and the small size of semi-nomadic foraging populations.

Because the meat supply is unstable, foragers must make frequent expeditions to provide the band with gathered food. Environmental factors such as seasonal and annual variation in rainfall often affect the size of the wildlife population. Hunters cannot always find game, and when they do encounter animals, they are not always successful in killing their prey. In northern latitudes, where meat is the primary food, periods of starvation are known in every generation. The irregularity of the game supply leads hunter-gatherers in areas where plant foods are available to depend on these predictable foods a good part of the time. Someone must gather the fruits, nuts, and roots and carry them back to camp to feed unsuccessful hunters, children, the elderly, and anyone who might not have gone foraging that day.

Foraging falls to the women because hunting and gathering cannot be combined on the same expedition. Although gatherers sometimes notice signs of game as they work, the skills required to track game are not the same as those required to find edible roots or plants. Hunters scan the horizon and the land for traces of large game; gatherers keep their eyes to the ground, studying the distribution of plants and the texture of the soil for hidden roots and animal holes. Even if a woman who was collecting plants came across the track of an antelope, she could not follow it; it is impossible to carry a load and hunt at the same time. Running with a heavy load is difficult, and should the animal be sighted, the hunter would be off balance and could neither shoot an arrow nor throw a spear accurately.

Pregnancy and child care would also present difficulties for a hunter. An unborn child affects a woman's body balance, as does a child in her arms, on her back, or slung at her side. Until they are two years old, many hunter-gatherer children are carried at all times, and until they are four, they are carried some of the time.

An observer might wonder why young women do not hunt until they become pregnant, or why mature women and men do not hunt and gather on alternate days, with some women staying in camp to act as wet nurses for the young. Apart from the effects hunting might have on a mother's milk production, there are two reasons. First, young girls begin to bear children as soon as they are physically mature and strong enough to hunt, and second, hunter-gatherer bands are so small that there are unlikely to be enough lactating women to serve as wet nurses. No hunter-gatherer group could afford to maintain a specialized female hunting force.

Because game is not always available, because hunting and gathering are specialized skills, because women carrying heavy loads cannot hunt, and because women in hunter-gatherer societies are usually either pregnant or caring for young children, for most of the last two million years of human history men have hunted and women have gathered.

If male dominance depends on controlling the supply of meat, then the degree of male dominance in a society should vary with the amount of meat available and the amount supplied by the men. Some regions, like the East African grasslands and the North American woodlands, abounded with species of large mammals; other zones, like tropical forests and semi-deserts, are thinly populated with prey. Many elements affect the supply of game, but theoretically, the less meat provided exclusively by the men, the more egalitarian the society.

All known hunter-gatherer societies fit into four basic types: those in which men and women work together in communal hunts and as teams gathering edible plants, as did the Washo Indians of North America; those in which men and women each collect their own plant foods although the men supply some meat to the group, as do the Hadza of Tanzania; those in which male hunters and female gatherers work apart but return to camp each evening to share their acquisitions, as do the Tiwi of North Australia; and those in which the men provide all the food by hunting large game, as do the Eskimo. In each case the extent of male dominance increases directly with the proportion of meat supplied by individual men and small hunting parties.

Among the most egalitarian of hunter-gatherer societies are the Washo Indians, who inhabited the valleys of the Sierra Nevada in what is now southern California and Nevada. In the spring they moved north to Lake Tahoe for the large fish runs of sucker and native trout. Everyone—men, women, and children—participated in the fishing. Women spent the summer gathering edible berries and seeds while the men continued to fish. In the fall some men hunted deer but the most important source of animal protein was the jack rabbit, which was captured in communal hunts. Men and women together drove the rabbits into nets tied end to end. To provide food for the winter, husbands and wives worked as teams in the late fall to collect pine nuts.

Since everyone participated in most food-gathering activities, there were no individual distributions of food and relatively little difference in male and female rights. Men and women were not segregated from each other in daily activities; both were free to take lovers after marriage; both had the right to separate whenever they chose; menstruating women were not isolated from the rest of the group; and one of the two major Washo rituals celebrated hunting while the other celebrated gathering. Men were accorded more prestige if they had killed a deer, and men directed decisions about the seasonal movement of the group. But if no male leader stepped forward, women were permitted to lead. The distinctive feature of groups such as the Washo is the relative equality of the sexes.

The sexes are also relatively equal among the Hadza of Tanzania but this near-equality arises because men and women tend to work alone to feed themselves. They exchange little food. The Hadza lead a leisurely life in the seemingly barren environment of the East African Rift Gorge that is, in fact, rich in edible berries, roots, and small game. As a result of this abundance, from the time they are 10 years old, Hadza men and women gather much of their own food. Women take their young children with them into the bush, eating as they forage, and collect only enough food for a light family meal in the evening. The men eat berries and roots as they hunt for small game, and should they bring down a rabbit or a hyrax, they eat the meat on the spot. Meat is carried back to the camp and shared with the rest of the group only on those rare occasions when a poisoned arrow brings down a large animal—an impala, a zebra, an eland, or a giraffe.

Because Hadza men distribute little meat, their status is only slightly higher than that of the women. People flock to the camp of a good hunter and the camp might take on his name because of his popularity, but he is in no sense a leader of the group. A Hadza man and a woman have an equal right to divorce and each can repudiate a marriage simply by living apart for a few weeks. Couples tend to live in the same camp as the wife's mother but they sometimes make long visits to the camp of the husband's mother. Although a man may take more than one wife, most Hadza males cannot afford to indulge in this luxury. In order to maintain a marriage, a man must supply both his wife and his mother-in-law with some meat and trade goods, such as beads and cloth, and the Hadza economy gives few men the wealth to provide for more than one wife and mother-in-law. Washo equality is based on cooperation; Hadza equality is based on independence.

In contrast to both these groups, among the Tiwi of Melville and Bathurst Islands off the northern coast of Australia, male hunters dominate female gatherers. The Tiwi are representative of the most common form of foraging society, in which the men supply large quantities of meat, although less than half the food consumed by the group. Each morning Tiwi women, most with babies on their backs, scatter in different directions in search of vegetables, grubs, worms, and small game such as bandicoots, lizards, and opossums. To track the game, they use hunting dogs. On most days women return to camp with some meat and with baskets full of *korka*, the nut of a native palm, which is soaked and mashed to make a porridge-like dish. The Tiwi men do not hunt small game and do not hunt every day, but when they do they often return with kangaroo, large lizards, fish, and game birds.

The porridge is cooked separately by each household and rarely shared outside the family, but the meat is prepared by a volunteer cook, who can be male or female. After the cook takes one of the parts of the animal traditionally reserved for him or her, the animal's "boss," the one who caught it, distributes the rest to all near kin and then to all others residing with the band. Although the small game supplied by the women is distributed in the same way as the big game supplied by the men, Tiwi men are dominant because the game they kill provides most of the meat.

The power of the Tiwi men is clearest in their betrothal practices. Among the Tiwi, a woman must always be married. To ensure this, female infants are betrothed at birth and widows are remarried at the gravesides of their late husbands. Men form alliances by exchanging daughters, sisters, and mothers in marriage and some collect as many as 25 wives. Tiwi men value the quantity and quality of the food many wives can collect and the many children they can produce.

The dominance of the men is offset somewhat by the influence of adult women in selecting their next husbands. Many women are active strategists in the political careers of their male relatives, but to the exasperation of some sons attempting to promote their own futures, widowed mothers sometimes insist on selecting their own partners. Women also influence the marriages of their daughters and granddaughters, especially when the selected husband dies before the bestowed child moves to his camp.

Among the Eskimos, representative of the rarest type of forager society, inequality between the sexes is matched by inequality in supplying the group with food. Inland Eskimo men hunt caribou throughout the year to provision the entire society, and maritime Eskimo men depend on whaling, fishing, and some hunting to feed their extended families. The women process the carcasses, cut and sew skins to make clothing, cook, and care for the young; but they collect no food of their own and depend on the men to supply all the raw materials for their work. Since men provide all the meat, they also control the trade in hides, whale oil, seal oil, and other items that move between the maritime and inland Eskimos.

Eskimo women are treated almost exclusively as objects to be used, abused, and traded by men. After puberty all Eskimo girls are fair game for any interested male. A man shows his intentions by grabbing the belt of a woman and if she protests, he cuts off her trousers and forces himself upon her. These encounters are considered unimportant by the rest of the group. Men offer their wives' sexual services to establish alliances with trading partners and members of hunting and whaling parties.

Despite the consistent pattern of some degree of male dominance among foragers, most of these societies are egalitarian compared with agricultural and industrial societies. No forager has any significant opportunity for political leadership. Foragers, as a rule, do not like to give or take orders, and assume leadership only with reluctance. Shamans (those who are thought to be possessed by spirits) may be either male or female. Public rituals conducted by women in order to celebrate the first menstruation of girls are common, and the symbolism in these rituals is similar to that in the ceremonies that follow a boy's first kill.

In any society, status goes to those who control the distribution of valued goods and services outside the family. Equality arises when both sexes work side by side in food production, as do the Washo, and the products are simply distributed among the workers. In such circumstances, no person or sex has greater access to valued items than do others. But when women make no contribution to the food supply, as in the case of the Eskimo, they are completely subordinate.

When we attempt to apply these generalizations to contemporary industrial society, we can predict that as long as women spend their discretionary income from jobs on domestic needs, they will gain little social recognition and power. To be an effective source of power, money must be exchanged in ways that require returns and create obligations. In other words, it must be invested.

Jobs that do not give women control over valued resources will do little to advance their general status. Only as managers, executives, and professionals are women in a position to trade goods and services, to do others favors, and therefore to obligate others to them. Only as controllers of valued resources can women achieve prestige, power, and equality.

Within the household, women who bring in income from jobs are able to function on a more nearly equal basis with their husbands. Women who contribute services to their husbands and children without pay, as do some middle-class Western housewives, are especially vulnerable to dominance. Like Eskimo women, as long as their services are limited to domestic distribution they have little power relative to their husbands and none with respect to the outside world.

As for the limits imposed on women by their procreative functions in hunter-gatherer societies, child-bearing and child care are organized around work as much as work is organized around reproduction. Some foraging groups space their children three to four years apart and have an average of only four to six children, far fewer than many women in other cultures. Hunter-gatherers nurse their infants for extended periods, sometimes for as long as four years. This custom suppresses ovulation and limits the size of their families. Sometimes, although rarely, they practice infanticide. By limiting reproduction, a woman who is gathering food has only one child to carry.

Different societies can and do adjust the frequency of birth and the care of children to accommodate whatever productive activities women customarily engage in. In horticultural societies, where women work long hours in gardens that may be far from home, infants get food to supplement their mothers' milk, older children take care of younger children, and pregnancies are widely spaced. Throughout the world, if a society requires a woman's labor, it finds ways to care for her children.

In the United States, as in some other industrial societies, the accelerated entry of women with preschool children into the labor force has resulted in the development of a variety of child-care arrangements. Individual women have called on friends, relatives, and neighbors. Public and private child-care centers are growing. We should realize that the declining birth rate, the increasing acceptance of childless or single-child families, and a de-emphasis on motherhood are adaptations to a sexual division of labor reminiscent of the system of production found in hunter-gatherer societies.

In many countries where women no longer devote most of their productive years to childbearing, they are beginning to demand a change in the social relationship of the sexes. As women gain access to positions that control the exchange of resources, male dominance may become archaic, and industrial societies may one day become as egalitarian as the Washo.

References

Friedl, Ernestine, *Women and Men: An Anthropologist's View*, Holt, Rinehart and Winston, 1975.

Martin, M. Kay, and Barbara Voorhies, eds., *Female of the Species*, Columbia University Press, 1977.

Murphy, Yolanda, and Robert Murphy, *Women of the Forest*, Columbia University Press, 1974.

Reiter, Rayna, ed., *Toward an Anthropology of Women*, Monthly Review Press, 1975.

Rosaldo, M. Z., and Louise Lamphere, eds., *Women, Culture, and Society*, Stanford University Press, 1974.

Schlegel, Alice, ed., *Sexual Stratification; A Cross-Cultural View*, Columbia University Press, 1977.

Strathern, Marilyn, *Women in Between: Female Roles in a Male World*, Academic Press, 1972.

Marriage and Family

Selection 18

KALMAN D. APPLBAUM, from "Marriage with the Proper Stranger: Arranged Marriage in Metropolitan Japan," *Ethnology*

Selection 19

R. JEAN CADIGAN, from "Woman-to-Woman Marriage: Practices and Benefits in Sub-Saharan Africa," *Journal of Comparative Family Studies*

Selection 20

VEENA TALWAR OLDENBURG, from "Dowry Murder: The Imperial Origins of a Cultural Crime," *Dowry Murder*

Selection 21

WILLIAM R. GARRETT, from "The Decline of the Western Family: A Review of the Evidence," *The Family in Global Transmission*

Marriage with the Proper Stranger: Arranged Marriage in Metropolitan Japan[1]

Kalman D. Applbaum

The prevailing attitude in many traditional cultures around the world has been that the decision to marry is too serious a business to be left to two young, starry-eyed, "in love" individuals. Since marriage is, generally speaking, not just a union of two people, but rather a joining together of two extended families, the relatives would understandably like to have some say in the matter.

Even in our society, although we may not officially recognize marriage as an "arrangement," it is still true that parents have considerable say-so as to who marries whom. Just consider the fact that parents decide what neighborhood their child will live in, what schools and church their child will attend, and what basic, core values their child will acquire, thereby affecting their child's future social interactions and, therefore, potential mating choices. This is not to say that children are merely pre-set, wind-up dolls, only appearing to make decisions on their own, but it does mean that, even when it comes to making that fateful choice as to with whom they will want to spend the rest of their lives, children's options are circumscribed and they, generally speaking do not fall too far from the family tree.

In contrast, consider the case of the Japanese, as described by Kalman D. Applbaum, who are experiencing the same kind of urbanization, social mobility, and weakening of extended family ties that we are. The difference seems to be that, while we have embraced the idea of "free choice" in marriage and are oblivious to the subtleties of parental influence, a good number of the Japanese have tried to maintain a semblance of tradition even while making some necessary compromises along the way. So, as you read this article, ask yourself how much real difference there is between our two societies and, in the long run, can the Japanese really maintain a modicum of tradition or are they well on their way to becoming just like us?

Kalman Applbaum teaches medical anthropology at the University of Wisconsin, Milwaukee. He is the author of *The Marketing Era: From Professional Practice to Global Provisioning* (2004). He is currently researching the effect of new anti-depressants on the practice of psychiatry and on mental health care in Japan.

Key Concept: arranged marriage

Twenty-five to 30 percent of all marriages taking place in Japan at present are arranged marriages (Kinjo 1990). Unlike "love" marriages, which are organized against the background of the relationship between two individuals, arranged marriages are premised upon the similarity of social standing of the families of the prospective couple, and the families are very much involved in the process of selecting a marriage partner. Love marriages, by contrast, are premised on the existence of affection between the two individuals entering the union and only the two principals, ideally, need be involved. Arranged marriages in Japan are typically organized by people of higher standing and age relative to the couple. In some cases this also means that the arranger is in a position of authority over the couple, such as when the introduction occurs at the workplace. Inasmuch as the couple's families are concerned with the outcome of the match, one might propose to situate arranged marriages in Japan into a classical anthropological framework of marriage rules or preferences, such as cross-cousin marriage. However, except in the very elite classes (cf. Hamabata 1990), arranged marriages in modern Japan do not structure the organization of social relations on the basis of kinship: there is no concern with alliance and descent as in connection with marriage rules elsewhere. Yet, neither can arranged marriage in Japan be thought of as merely another way of speaking about introductions for the purpose of dating because in the procedure leading up to an arranged marriage the actors are quite concerned with identifying the proper category of individuals one should marry. The question that delineates the problem of arranged marriage in metropolitan Japan therefore becomes, "How do you marry the proper stranger?"

Marrying the proper stranger means marrying someone with whom there is some basis for association either because they are known to a family member, to someone at the workplace, or to someone from one's neighborhood community. The key consideration is that the potential mate should be situated within a set of relations known through prior association to another person in that effective network (Epstein 1961). In emic terminology, one would say that arranged marriage should be with someone from the category of knowable, as compared with unknowable strangers. Typically, the potential spouse is associated to oneself through an intermediary who knows both parties and therefore is able to vouch for the appropriateness of such a union.

Appropriateness is determined by several criteria covering a range of attributes applying to both the principal and his/her family. In Japanese these attributes are referred to as iegara, which translates as birth or lineage. Iegara refers principally to family attributes and to a lesser extent personal traits. These include everything from levels of education, to income, occupation, social standing, physical appearance, lineage, reputation, and etiquette. Sometimes the term kakushiki (standing or rank) is used to denote the same thing. Iegara and kakushiki are compromised by the existence in the family of negative attributes such as divorce or mental illness. These characteristics do not strictly conform to status groups or to class. Rather the overall picture should convey a sense of a family in good standing to whom the other family could relate as equals. Too great a difference in iegara between the two families would result in embarrassment to both sides whenever they meet.

With love marriages there are no constraints against selecting individuals with whom one can trace no prior association through any of one's networks. Parents may often pressure their children to select mates coming from upbringings comparable to their own, and opportunities for meeting persons from a vastly different background in Japan may be fewer than that potential in the U.S. Consequently many love marriages end up looking something like arranged marriages. Love marriages and arranged marriages, though they invoke different value systems from the point of view of the young man and woman can be considered successive strategies for accomplishing the same goal (Edwards 1989). However, the procedural approaches to the two types of matches are considerably different and they conform to two different sets of ideologies concerning family and social network. They therefore warrant separate treatment.

"Marriage Drought"

One of the social issues in Japan today is the difficulty young people have finding desirable marriage partners

(Himeno 1989), which the term "marriage drought" (kekkon kanbatsu) describes. It is a subject of considerable political concern for a host of reasons, including a birthrate that has dropped to about 1.5 due to late marriage, among other factors. The government is concerned that there may not be enough workers in twenty years to support an aging population (Yoshida 1981). The reasons for the marriage drought are also many; some of the contributing factors are demographic, economic, and cultural. All these factors contribute to Japan's having the highest marriage age in the world; 28.6 for men, 25.9 for women.

Urban migration and greater geographical and social mobility in the society as a whole, particularly for recent college graduates, give rise to an assemblage of people with diverse backgrounds who have difficulty finding commonalities with neighbors or work mates (Ben-Ari 1991). On an individual level, this mirrors what Ahuvia and Adelman (1992:453) found to be the case in the U.S., that "many post college singles reported feeling that they had exhausted their immediate social networks as conduits to new dates."

As real estate has become increasingly dear it has become less feasible for marriageable-aged people to afford to buy their own apartment (or even rent one). Pay by seniority is still the norm. Combined with an increasing taste for privacy and independence, this means that people in their late teens and early and mid-twenties often choose to delay marriage until they can afford to live independently of their parents; this is particularly the case among the well-educated urbanites. The assignment of onerous work commitments for men during the years when they should be learning social skills and dating plays a role in protracting the period of bachelorhood.

Yet, in order to enter adulthood in Japan, one has to marry. For women this and raising children are the all-exclusive mission in life. Women who remain unmarried past the proper marriageable age (tekireiki; 22–25) are treated quite shabbily and are compared to Christmas cake (kurisumasu keeki)—fresh up until the 25th but on each succeeding day the cake becomes less appetizing and edible.

For men there is slightly more latitude (26–30) but the result is similar. A man who does not marry by about 30 or so is thought untrustworthy by colleagues and employers, who believe that such men have not been conditioned to learn the fundamental principles of co-operation and responsibility. Like unwed women, they can not be considered whole members of society (Yoshihiro 1987).

The expectations of parents and society that every person marry is not the only pressure affecting individuals as regards marriage however. In recent years the beliefs people hold regarding courtship and marriage have changed dramatically. Today's youth expect marriage to be preceded by courtship characterized by romantic love. This ideal has somewhat preceded the reality, for many young people (especially men) are ill equipped or have not had the time to pursue the romantic ideal. The fact that about

70 per cent of couples in Japan agree to marry within six months of their first encounter is said to show that dating culture is not fully developed in Japan (Mochizuki 1985).

In the 1970s it was common for sociologists in Japan to assert that marriage and romance were separate experiences and that passionate romance was not a necessary criterion for a viable relationship. Now women are regarded as more inclined to seek a romantic relationship than men (Himeno 1989). Given the differing career goals and gender enculturation of men and women, the discrepancy is not surprising. Women are by and large raised with the expectation that they may only find satisfaction within the home and are therefore perhaps more susceptible to modern brands of idealism, such as that true love will be followed by marital and domestic bliss. This, in scholarly as well as popular viewpoints in Japan, has led to expectations that are hard to fulfill. Women are in search of men who will wash the dishes and diaper the baby, who are taller than 170 cm., who are not eldest or only children (because such people will have greater responsibilities to take care of aging parents or, still worse, will require that the new spouse move in with his extended family). Women are looking for men who have secure salaries and, in many cases, who will tolerate a career ambition in their wife. This phenomenon is called the "three H syndrome" in Japan: height, high salary, high education.

New Professionalized Go-Betweens

In this context, professional go-between services modeled after (or perhaps one could say piggybacking on) the more traditional type of arranged marriage go-betweens, or nakodo, have arisen. I call these pro nakodo[2] to distinguish them from traditional regular nakodo in that they tend to be less personally involved with the individuals or families prior to the arrangement procedures; they have less to do with the couple after the marriage; and they are part of a two-person team in the arrangement of a match because a single pro nakodo will not be familiar with both sides without an introduction from another pro nakodo whose client is involved. While the same kinds of people who will engage the services of a pro nakodo might also respond to singles advertisements or go to a computer dating service, the reverse is not necessarily the case. The computer dating service's goal is to initiate romance, while pro nakodo introduce people for the purpose of marriage. The go-between introduction system permits a greater personal involvement between the customer and the agent. This creates, in their own characterization, an amae (dependency) relationship that does not exist in the more alienated dating service. The pro nakodo, whose intentions include the desire to earn a commission and a devotion to the traditional office of go-between, looks after his/her customers with a parental touch.

For the customer, the procedure begins with a modest registration fee of 10,000 yen. He or she completes a form with personal information (i.e., age, height, schooling, income, hobbies, whether one will need to live with one's parents after marriage, blood type, whether one owns land, similar information about other family members, and any special requests regarding a mate) and provides a color photograph. At the following month's go-between association (nakodokai) meeting, the photocopied application form is distributed to all the pro nakodo in the group. Each of 42 active pro nakodo in the group I studied brings in on average two or three new clients each month, so all of the nakodo review about 100 to 200 applications monthly. Each pro nakodo takes the sheets home and places them in loose-leaf notebooks, of which all the members have identical copies. The sheets are sorted into the notebooks according to age and date of registration. At the end of five years, or when they get married, whichever comes first, a person's sheet is removed from the notebook. At the time of this study, the association had registered slightly over 6,500 clients.

Nakodo, folklorists say, are people with many connections, respected, and sought after rather than self-advertised. They might also be salesmen, people of colorful personalities, raconteurs. They are trustworthy and well intentioned. Former generations of nakodo performed what today is usually divided between two or more people. And the postmarital responsibility of the nakodo to look after the couple (as reported by Dore 1958, for instance) seems to have dissipated. Much more so than in the past, the roles of introducer and wedding ceremony nakodo (tanomare nakodo) are now performed by two people. Even where a couple were introduced without a nakodo, the wedding ceremony nakodo speech should be given by an elder experienced in marriage ceremonies and preferably someone of respected status, like a director of a company or a teacher.

Additionally, the nakodo's function has become differentiated and weakened due to the shift toward informality in social relations, so the nakodo is less necessary in the introduction of the two families. Furthermore betrothal gifts (yuinokin and jisankin) have become less important in modern marriages, thus reducing the need to have an outsider negotiate the exchange. Guests are often too nervous to give the nakodo speech at a wedding and instead cede the honor to such an extent that nakodo professionals just for weddings are in considerable demand. Commercial wedding halls have retainers on hand to perform this function (Edwards 1989). Finally, many people who use pro nakodo hate to admit doing so and pro nakodo themselves are regarded as somewhat less respectable than their traditional counterparts.

The Criteria of Selection

A person registering with the pro nakodo organization is entitled to view applications and select the candidates he/she wishes to meet as often as he/she likes. The majority review the loose-leaf notebook files, alone or with a parent (usually a mother). A nakodo explained how clients proceed.

Registrants turn through the pages and examine their potential suitors:

"This one is not tall enough." A typical young woman is quoted as saying.

"This one is cute but he will have to live with his mother after getting married."

"This one indicates that she is a Christian and my family might object as they have been devout Buddhists from way back."

"She has been married once before and I was looking for someone, well, fresher."

Over 30 years ago the criteria for arranging a match were weighted towards "objective status factors such as the relative social standing of the two families, present and potential, economic earning power of the husband, appearance and refinement of the bride, all of which can be investigated by the nakodo before the miai" (Vogel 1961:115). Wealthy Japanese business families arranging strategic marriages for their children, hold similar criteria (Hamabata 1990). The matches arranged by the pro nakodo of this study also rely upon universalistic and rational criteria similar to those described by Vogel (1961), Blood (1967), Hamabata (1990), and others.

As mentioned, the objective criteria for mate selection through an arranged marriage is according to iegara, or family standing. The match must be "even" or the arrangement will not work. An interesting dilemma is raised when the qualifications of the individual are out of balance with the qualifications of his/her family. For example, if a man comes from a wealthy, high-status family but he has dropped out of school; or if the opposite case occurs where the family is of low social standing but the individual has very high qualifications. These categories of people, according to the pro nakodo, have great difficulty getting married. By the time they have reached the stage of looking for an arranged marriage the structural problems associated with their position can be all but insolvable.[3] A love marriage can be a solution to this kind of difficulty. There are also differences in criteria affecting males and females, with the emphasis on females being weighted more in the direction of social standing.

All the criteria listed on the application form are taken into consideration. Some criteria are evaluated meticulously by all the applicants. These include schooling, salary, marital history, independence from parental household, and physical attractiveness. Other characteristics, such as religion, hobbies, or having a driver's license are considered important only by a minority. Blood type is taken seriously by many of the registrants, but few people will reject a prospect entirely on the grounds that he/she is of the wrong blood type. Though emphasis on blood type does not derive from a seriously and widely held theory of personality, there does appear to be a rather deep valuation of the importance of blood in matters concerning health and Japanese identity. The term ketto, which means blood or lineage, is used frequently by nakodo and lay people when discussing marriage. It is also sometimes used to describe the ways in which Japan-born Koreans and burakumin (the outcast people of Japan) differ from "ordinary" folk. Intermarriage with these groups is considered abhorrent by many[4]. Books and magazines furnishing romantic and marital advice correlate Empedocles's four-element thesis (fire, earth, wind, water) to the four blood types and predict which of these types will mix well with other types. It seems evident, however, that even in such cases it is likely that other negative factors figure first and a candidate's being of the wrong blood type only reinforces their unacceptability.

The astrological attributes of a candidate may receive similar attention. The parents of applicants tend to take astrological factors more seriously than their children (in contrast with blood typing, where the opposite holds true). Two people, the astrological guide predicts, will or will not have a successful marriage. Also, women born on the year of the horse in the fifth cycle (hinoeuma—every sixtieth year) are bad luck. The last such year was 1966 and women born in that year are considered bad luck to marry. The belief in this is so widespread that the birthrate in Japan actually took a dip in that year (Japan Statistical Yearbook 1987). Even younger people take the hinoeuma superstition somewhat seriously, though it is rarely spoken of openly. According to my data, women born in that year often claim they were born on the following or previous year.

The overall factors included in why a candidate will be chosen or not go beyond their intrinsic qualifications. The mood of the chooser and the ability of the nakodo to be a good salesperson are both important. Though there may be hundreds of people in the correct category to choose from, the percentage ultimately sought after for a date may be very small. The two stages from there (additional dates and marriage) drop off in their respective success rates dramatically. The probable reasons for this are discussed below but, the pro nakodo concur, the number of registrants who are really serious about marriage is very small. Some people are merely satisfying the wishes of their parents when they commission the pro nakodo's services; and the parents will cover the expense. Pro nakodo pointed to the paradoxical psychology of people who craved to be married while at the same time they were incapable of making a commitment without outside help. Such a person might arbitrarily resolve to marry the "very next person they date because they cannot withstand the pressure of being single any longer." Yet, at the same time, they may be emotionally unprepared to actually go through with it.

Making the Match

I recount the procedure of getting a (omiai) date through the pro nakodo, starting at the point at which a client points at a photo and says to the pro nakodo, "I would like to meet this one." On the registration form there is a number (tanto bongo) referring to the pro nakodo who introduced the applicant. In a separate file each pro nakodo keeps the name and telephone number of the tantosha, the person handling this applicant. So when Kenji, say, selects Keiko, Kenji's pro nakodo will look up Keiko's pro nakodo through the tantosha number on the form.

Before Kenji's pro nakodo telephones Keiko's pro nakodo, however, he/she will want to get more information from Kenji about his extended family, up to the sixth degree of consanguinity. The pro nakodo probably already has personal information about his/her own clients because he/she has by and large not met the customer by impersonal means. Though there are nakodokai which encourage its members to advertise (in the phone book or even by handing out leaflets at a train station) the members of this nakodokai distinguished their organization from dating companies by virtue of not advertising. This is an attempt to legitimize their role as traditional face-to-face nakodo. Usually the client comes to the pro nakodo through a personal connection. If the pro nakodo is a teacher, for instance, then her students, or her student's children, may become clients. If the pro nakodo is an insurance salesman, a beautician, or a shopkeeper, her clientele will probably come from among her customers. Any person with a "wide forehead," that is, a broad range of contacts, may become a nakodo by virtue of their ability to introduce people to one another. Sometimes even local politicians will perform the service to expand their personal network of loyal connections.

The pro nakodo asks her client to fill out an application form and reveal information about his/her long-term family history. This knowledge may come from the keizu books, the family genealogy, recorded and kept by family members from generation to generation, often dating back into the Edo period. Though most marriage arrangements will ignore the status of one's feudal period ancestors for negative criteria, one's kakushiki is enhanced if one is descended from bushi, or samurai, which was the most honored of the four classes during the Edo period.

The other main source of information concerning an applicant comes to the nakodo through personal inquiries. If the pro nakodo does not know basic gossip about her client, she may go to the residence of her client and snoop around. (Though this practice is still common in rural areas [cf. Hendry 1981:133], in cities it is practically more difficult to manage; the pro nakodo use the antiquated term kikiawaseru, or toriawaseru, which means to ask around, to describe their activities in this matter.) She may casually strike up conversations with neighbors, asking questions about the family under consideration: Do the parents have a good relationship? Do the siblings get on well, and are they obedient to their parents? Do they take on responsibilities in the jichikai (neighborhood association)? And so on. Through such questioning the pro nakodo hopes to learn if there are an excessive number of divorces, infertility, illegitimate children, or genetic diseases in the family. Though this would seem to be a disagreeable procedure for the family under scrutiny, in fact, people do not seem to object to the practice. This is partly because it is how it has always been, to people's thinking, but also because at the same time as this nakodo is probing into their personal affairs, the nakodo of the opposite party is doing the same thing on their behalf. One cannot simply arrange a marriage with total strangers, so the investigation is justified. And the inquiries of the nakodo are only the beginning in some cases because possible marital partners are in some cases also checked out by hired, private investigators,[5] who investigate much more thoroughly into the reputation and the genetic background of the family. Should physical or mental handicaps show up nearby in the family tree, or a tendency towards certain illnesses (particularly mental illness), one's iegara is compromised considerably.

The extent to which people prepare in advance for the marriage of their children is sometimes remarkable. Especially families that bear some stigma may protect their privacy vigilantly. It takes a lifetime to build a good reputation at work, school, and neighborhood, but a single episode can besmirch one's opportunities for the best marriage and job. As Thomas Rohlen (1974:70ff.) has described of prestigious companies investigating the background of prospective employees, so too the attention paid by people to their neighborhood reputation for purposes of marriage is quite scrupulous.[6]

After an initial inquiry into the standing of the family is performed, the pro nakodo calls up the person in charge (tantosha) of the other client to decide whether the match is plausible in iegara terms. The other pro nakodo, first without consulting her client, will consult her notes on that client and decide initially whether the two people fall into the same category. If they do, the second pro nakodo will call in his client to discuss the matter. Typically the client agrees to a date solely on the basis of having been themselves selected. Many people will agree just so as not to be rude, even to a stranger.

When this is completed the go-betweens arrange for a date. On the first meeting both nakodo go to the meeting place to introduce the new couple. Sometimes the parents like to go along as well but in recent years, as omiai meetings more and more resemble regular dates, the parents wait at home for the report.[7] When the couple is introduced they are understandably shy. Because the nakodo are there with the two young people, however, the ice is broken in a hurry. The nakodo leave the couple to themselves after a short while. For their services each pro nakodo receives 20,000 yen (equivalent to U.S. $160 at the time of this research) plus expenses.[8] After the date the two parties call their respective nakodo to tell them how their date went. If the date was agreeable for both, then the pro nakodo tell their clients their date's phone number and leave it up to the couple to carry on.

Pro nakodo estimate the first meeting success rate at less than 20 per cent. Sometimes the pro nakodo encourage the one dissenting party to try a second date, saying that their partner was nervous at the initial meeting and at their worst appearance. But the more dates one makes, the stronger is the societal and circumstantial pressure to consummate the relationship in marriage. The pressure not to cause shame to another party by rejecting them, familial pressure, and a prior desideratum to marry "no matter what," sometimes tips the balance. The pro nakodo understand this dilemma, but in search of a profit (and also holding the belief of many adults that a good marriage has more to do with commitment and responsibility between evenly matched persons than with love) they may push.

If the date is successful the nakodo wait for further news. The average time taken for a couple to decide whether or not to marry is about three months. If the couple decides to get engaged, they call the pro nakodo with the news and arrange a date for the taimen (interview) with the parents. The nakodo attends this interview as well, once again, only informally participating in the "negotiations," which are said to be considerably abbreviated from the form practiced in the past. But as a smoother of social interaction between two unacquainted families that will henceforth be affinally related to each other, at least one pro nakodo's presence is requested and appreciated. For this service, the pro nakodo receives 20,000 yen. When marriage is decided, the groom's family sends a betrothal gift (yuinokin) in the form of cash to the bride's family. According to custom, the groom's family gives two-to-three times a month's income. The money is not refundable in case of a broken engagement.

These are the conditions that obtain in the event of a successfully arranged match. By and large, however, arranged marriages in this manner are not successful. Why people sign up anyway is a function of the expectations of people signing up for the service and the efforts of the pro nakodo.

The Pro Nakodo Clients

As mentioned earlier, because the two types of services are often successive strategies for some people, the pro nakodo often have clients who are unmarried because (from the go-between's point of view) they are shy, inexperienced, too picky, or are an oldest son. There is a composite of people in their late twenties and early thirties coming to terms with what they feel they have to do in order to make the next grade at work or in some other way to get out from under the constant pressure to be married. In some of these cases, the will to take an active part in the search may be lacking. The pro nakodo's job, therefore, involves a good deal of coaching, encouraging, and persuading. One pro nakodo often pressured her shy male customers to physically engage with their date by kissing or holding hands, saying, "Today it is a young woman's hope and expectation to be treated romantic-like (romanchiku) by her date. Even if there is no deep,

true love to be found in such a courtship, the illusion must be maintained." Another pro nakodo commented:

> Omiai [arranged marriage] has nothing whatsoever to do with love. Someone may look at a resume and photograph and decide yes or no, but the decision is ultimately based on whether or not they are themselves mentally prepared to get married. If they are not ready then a crooked nose or glasses may stop the proceedings.... If, however, one is mentally prepared for marriage then almost anyone will do. [In omiai] there is no "dating." There is only the getting used to the idea of marriage.

The pro nakodo recognizes that many customers, are, in addition to being shy, also inexperienced at dating. While the present generation of young people is generally more adept at the dating and romance scene than previous generations were, some people are shy, and the pro nakodo sees a high percentage of them. The pro nakodo's job, therefore, includes some coaching and encouraging (gekirei) of the customers, and the pro nakodo on both sides will exchange information in order to bring about a successful match.

From the consumers' point of view, arranged marriage is an ever-present option, although 34 of 40 unmarried individuals between the ages of 23 and 33 in the group surveyed considered arranged marriage as less desirable. People in a more general sample who were in favor of arranged marriage for themselves and others, tended at the same time to express their feelings of identification with other Japanese traditions in vogue (groupism, hometownism, human relations, extended household centeredness, etc.). On the role of marriage in modern Japan, one respondent opined, "We in Japan can not afford a sixties generation of free lovers as you have in America. In Japan, the household [ie] is a mirror image of the State.... When marriage is a matter of free will, society disintegrates, as it is doing in America."

In this oriental-occidental antilogy—arranged marriage as desirable for reasons of dignity, public legitimacy, and commendable adherence to formal goals, on the one hand, and arranged marriage as undesirable for reasons of privacy, individual freedom, and flexibility on the other—lie the visible roots of a disunity characteristic of deep cultural change. In terms existing outside of an analysis of an agglomeration of individual Japanese opinion, internalization of the value of arranged marriage implies internalization of several related cultural ideals or categories such as groupism or community-ism (kyodotai-shugi), household centeredness (ie), and social obligation (giri). In the realm of public knowledge these notions are strongly linked.

Bridging the chasm between the hopes of the clients that engaging a pro nakodo will bring the painful search for a mate to an end quickly, and the almost-uncompromisable expectation of modern youth that marriage is based upon mutual love and understanding, is a task beyond the capabilities of the pro nakodo. The problem is not located merely within the minds of those who seek the services of the pro nakodo. If that were the case then the pro nakodo could promote compromise and the illusion of satisfaction among clientele. The root of the problem lies in the unbridgeable gap between the highly charged, cultural symbols of close family ties and dependence upon a dense network of relations at work and in the neighborhood, and the actual fragmented nature of social relations in each of these domains.

Inherent in the structural (and emotional) relationship between the pro nakodo and the client is a partial antidote to the alienation of the individual from his/her social environment. Structurally, the pro nakodo locates herself at the center of a nexus of social relationships that includes the client's parents, the potential spouse's parents, and often the people in the client's surrounding neighborhood who, even if they lack a close relationship with the client, at least know the family situation well enough to be a source of information for the pro nakodo.

The "work nakodo" (usually a manager at the company) performs a mediating function similar to that of the pro nakodo. Being familiar with a certain set of context-bound characteristics of his subordinates, a work nakodo can suggest matches based upon socially relevant criteria. Moreover, because the work environment is an approved locus for demonstrating one's qualities as an adult and therefore as a potential spouse, the boss's judgment is believed to be accurate in these matters. A young person will in the main more readily accept the character evaluation of a boss (or a teacher) than that of a peer or neighbor. It is therefore considered a better option by some to avoid seeking the help of professional agencies and other noninstitutional connections and to seek, instead, the help of a relative, a boss, or a teacher, though in fact many use both sources simultaneously.

Furthermore, in the case of the work omiai, the expectations of the principals are met sooner; the uneasiness about the status and identity of one's partner is not as acute. Edwards (1989:69) notes this of two young adults, working for the same company, who have decided to marry:

> Firms like theirs check carefully on an applicant's background, so the successful applicant is certain to be of good family, well educated, and intelligent, and to come with good recommendations about his or her character. Accordingly, both felt that much of the selection process had already been completed for them, and they could hardly go wrong in choosing a co-worker as a spouse. Satoru had also wanted to marry someone who shares his interest in outdoor sports; Hiroko states that she simply wanted to get married in a hurry, before she turned thirty.

On the other hand, many respondents to our survey said they prefer to avoid the risks and costs of being responsible to their boss and to seek other means for finding marriage partners within or outside of the company context. A match made by the boss often has the burden of having to seem like a match made in heaven. Especially if the boss or some other company manager's son or daughter is involved, divorce becomes a less viable

option for settling strife in a marriage, at least for some time.[9]

The pro nakodo is an agreeable alternative because (a) one's privacy is guaranteed, (b) little or no social obligation to the go-between remains after the wedding, and (c) one's range of choice is much larger. Outside of the expectation of finding true love (though many omiai applicants do not really give up that hope), the above criteria are identical to those obtaining in the case of love marriage. In addition, it has the added advantage of, by definition, satisfying one's family because family approval is an integral part of the practice. By asking someone other than the pro nakodo to perform the ceremonial function of tanomare nakodo (lit., requested nakodo) at the wedding, some young people maintain the illusion among their peers that the match was a love marriage, while at the same time winning the ready approval of their parents because the marriage was arranged.

The Process of Arranged Marriage

If the authenticity of the pro nakodo depends on his/her being a known entity, what criteria validate this knownness? The strength of the pro nakodo system lies in its familiarity, its resemblance to traditional arranged marriage practices, and its rootedness in the popular concept of neighborhood.

Arranged marriage, by definition, means marrying someone with whom there is a basis for association either because they are (1) known to a family member, (2) respected at the workplace, or (3) are from the same hometown or neighborhood. These sources for an arranged marriage partner are identity reference groups in Japan. The identity reference group vis-a-vis arranged marriage is a cultural model held in common by the arranged marriage service providers and the consumers of that service.[10]

All three identity reference groups are somewhat compromised in today's Japan: the family through the attrition of the extended family network; work through rapidly increasing job mobility and the declining powers of paternalism; and neighborhood because of fragmenting social relations there. But love marriage is not yet capable of taking up all the slack, for reasons mentioned earlier and because some resistance to the idea of marriage grounded on romantic love as both foreign and corrosive to society persists. Arranged marriages ease the difficulties caused by social change. The challenge for the vendor of arranged marriage is how to arrange a marriage between strangers. This problem the pro nakodo solve in their own way.

Clients are buying an imagined community, or "tradition" as it is now marketed in Japanese popular culture (Robertson 1991; Tobin 1992). The candidates are also buying their place in society as well as buying off anxious parents. Though by necessity making use of a more complex and interactionist (as compared to merely symbolic) set of cultural affirmations in the pursuit of an arranged marriage service, the pro nakodo capitalize on this wave of cultural nostalgia as well as their clients' uncertainty regarding the appropriate cultural model for one of life's most important rites of passage.

That the success rate of the pro nakodo is extremely low (around .2 per cent of the total registered pool on a monthly basis) supports the view that the process is more important than the result. It is not mainly to the rational end of finding a spouse for which people register but for many other reasons—cultural expectations and group pressure figuring importantly among them—that the service endures. People buy the ideas surrounding the concept of the neighborhood go-between, not marriage itself. This is not to dismiss the ostensible logic of why people employ the service. Nor should one ignore the social maladroitness of some of the candidates, the possibly heightened expectations of the registrants (Adelman and Ahuvia 1991), or the curmudgeonliness of many of the pro nakodo as contributing factors to the low success rate of the industry. But such straightforward, pragmatic explanations of the participants' behaviors do not tell the whole story.

Pro nakodo invoke the nostalgic legitimacy of tightly knit neighborhood networks of relations in their pursuit of arranging marriages between strangers. They are in essence selling the idea of neighborhood community. The uniformity of mass culture in Japan, including a nationwide education system, makes the pro nakodo's job simpler. The familiar modus operandi of the pro nakodo enables people to transpose a pro nakodo arrangement into the meaning system of traditional, arranged marriage. Finally, the renaissance in today's Japan of traditional ideals (including the subtle reaggregation of neighborhood into one's identity reference group to which arranged marriage agglutinates) contribute to justify arranged marriage with a stranger.

Why is the marriage business so poor these days? The pro nakodo lay blame on "[t]he nuclear family, low birthrate, contrary values begotten of both imported popular culture and higher education." The pro nakodo have made it their "study" to discover the means by which they can improve their lot in a tough market. The solution many have adopted is to strengthen ties in the neighborhood, often through the neighborhood association. The strategies for the shopkeeper, the new religion promoter, the political activist, and the pro nakodo are commensurate. For by promoting neighborhood participation and co-operation all interested parties benefit.

The pro nakodo are pessimistic about the future of marriage and family in Japan. All around them, they say, are "empty households," boshi katei (mother and child households) and fushi katei (father and child households). People move often and do not care about local affairs. Old people are left to care for themselves. Social relationships lack warmth and humane (kind) feelings. The situation will not improve unless co-operative values are regained. In the view of the pro nakodo and of many Japanese politicians, the ramifications resulting from industrialization and urbanization are the breakdown of co-operation and the introduction of individualism (i.e., selfishness) into the most fundamental areas of Japanese culture. For the pro nakodo, love marriages, which represent individualism, tear away at the fabric of Japanese social relationships. Therefore the most critical means of restoring healthy societal relationships is with arranged marriage.

The pro nakodo also operate with the conviction that there is a practical coalescence of the cultural expectations and backgrounds of people living all over the central Japanese conurbations. Only if a client is predisposed to accept the notion that a person living in a different city can be as similar to oneself as someone living down the street can the pro nakodo succeed at her business. The functional and morphological similarities of Japanese metropolitan areas allow that span to be bridged. The range of the nakodokai of this study included a dozen commuter cities in north and northwestern Osaka Prefecture, including Osaka City. The boundaries of such an association obviously are based not on cultural-regional lines of demarcation but on the commuting convenience of nakodo and dates.

Conclusions

The pro nakodokai is a business, one kind of dating service. A recent innovation, the pro nakodokai is unique in the manner by which it exploits traditional symbols to fill a niche in the marriage market. Continued faith in the neighborhood as an appropriate source for an arranged marriage, and the proclivity of many to submit to parental pressure in the selection of a mate, have sustained the pro nakodo organization.

The futility of attempting to pigeonhole the pro nakodo as either a traditional or modern phenomenon bespeaks the bankruptcy of that continuum as an explanatory model of social change. Especially in Japan, where activities associated with legitimate institutions are granted instantaneous legitimacy[11] where tradition does not lie at some fixed, invariant point in the past to which people turn as a reference for legitimacy, there is little to be gained from quasi-evolutionary formulations that predict the demise of that which is old.

The coexistence of formal arranged marriage, love marriage, and pro nakodo arranged marriage in a pattern of stable diversity[12] is an indication of how Japanese culture accommodates change. Arranged marriage, by virtue of its dependence upon introduction from certain specified in-groups (at least in theory), from within the category of knowable strangers, is therefore limited by the boundaries of those in-groups, one of which is the neighborhood. As definitions of the neighborhood expand, as mobility accelerates, and as neighborhoods reproduce themselves in other locations, we may expect arranged marriage and other cultural practices characteristic of neighborhood life to change with the new circumstances.

Notes

1. This research was assisted by a grant from the Japanese Ministry of Education. The author thanks T. Bestor, X. L. Ding, I. C. Jordt, S. F. Moore, E. Ohnuki-Tierney, K. Sasaki, E. F. Vogel, N. Yalman, and S. Yoshida for their assistance.
2. The term pro nakodo will refer to both singular and plural.
3. Emiko Ohnuki-Tierney suggests that with such a dilemma individual ability will be the deciding factor. "Even the so-called economic miracle depends, from a conceptual standpoint, on the Japanese emphasis on individual's ability" (personal communication).
4. Reluctance to marry the descendants of survivors of the atom bombs (hibakusha) is also spoken of in terms of blood or genetic inheritance of disease (Lifton 1967).
5. This practice is more prevalent among wealthy people.
6. A writer on etiquette in the neighborhood says: "To prevent false critical reports by investigatory agencies, those who have daughters of marriageable age should pay a courtesy visit to the neighbors. One may even find that this countermeasure to private investigations will be good public relations for your daughter and lead to a fine marriage proposal" (Shiotsuki, in Aoki and Dardess 1981:210).
7. In traditional omiai, the first encounter is less a meeting than a viewing (kagemi). The pro nakodo do not use the term kagemi much, except sometimes in jest. The first meeting is referred to as odeito, from the English word date, but given an honorific prefix, investing the otherwise profane word date with some traditional significance. After the first meeting, odeitos are referred to as simply deitos.
8. This fee varies slightly from one organization of pro nakodo to another.
9. Discussions of workplace marriages can be found in McLendon (1983:156–82) and Rohlen (1974:235–54).
10. Cultural model here implies what Kelly (1986) and Rosaldo (1980) have called a "typification of areas of life that have gained enormous ordering power [in Japanese society]" (Kelly 1986:605). This typification is a construct that "serves less to regulate conduct than to provide the terms within which action becomes intelligible" (Rosaldo 1980:153).
11. Theodore Bestor (1985:132) eloquently states: "Japanese social institutions have a penchant for 'instant tradition'— the ability to cloak new circumstances and institutions with a mantle of traditionalism, imparting depth and resiliency to what might otherwise have shaky foundations."

Bibliography

Adelman, M., and A. C. Ahuvia. 1991. Mediated Channels for Mate Seeking: A Solution to Involuntary Singlehood? *Critical Studies in Mass Communications* 8:273–89.

Ahuvia, A. C., and M. Adelman. 1992. Formal Intermediaries in the Marriage Market: A Typology and Review. *Journal of Marriage and the Family* 54:452–63.

Aoki, M., and M. Dardess. 1981. As the Japanese See it. Honolulu.

Ben-Ari, E. 1991. Changing Japanese Suburbia. London.

Bestor, T. 1985. Tradition and Japanese Social Organization: Institutional Development in a Tokyo Neighborhood. *Ethnology* 24: 121–35.

Blood, R. O., Jr. 1967. Love Match and Arranged Marriage: A Tokyo-Detroit Comparison. New York.

Dote, R. P. 1958, City Life in Japan. Berkeley.

Edwards, W. 1989. Modern Japan Through Its Weddings. Stanford.

Epstein, A. L. 1961. The Network and Urban Social Organization. *The Rhodes-Livingstone Journal* 39:29–61.

Hamabata, M. H. 1990. Crested Kimono. Ithaca.

Hendry, J. 1981. Marriage in Changing Japan. Tokyo.

Himeno, T. 1989. Kekkon dekinai wakamonotachi [Young People Who Can't Marry]. *Aoshonen Mondai* 36:16–32.

Japan Statistical Yearbook. 1987. Bureau of Statistics, Tokyo.

Kelly, W. W. 1986. Rationalization and Nostalgia: Cultural Dynamics of New Middle-Class Japan. *American Ethnologist* 13:603–18.

Kinjo, K. 1990. Kazoku to iu kankei [The Family Relationship]. Tokyo.

Lifton, R. J. 1967. Death in Life. New York.

McLendon, J. 1983. The Office: Way Station or Blind Alley? Work and Lifecourse in Japan, ed. D. Plath, pp. 156–82. Albany.

Mochizuki, T. 1985. Hattatsu appraochi kara mita haigusha sentaku [A developmental approach to the choice of spouse]. Gendai kazoku no kiki—atarashii raifustairu sekkei, ed. H. Kimura, pp. 214–37. Tokyo.

Robertson, J. 1991. Native and Newcomer: Making and Remaking a Japanese City. Berkeley.

Rohlen, T. P. 1974. For Harmony and Strength: Japanese White Collar Organization in Anthropological Perspective. Berkeley.

Rosaldo, R. 1980. Ilongot Headhunting, 1883–1974: A Study in Society and History. Stanford.

Tobin, J. J. (ed.) 1992. Re-made in Japan. New Haven.

Vogel, E. F. 1961. The Go-Between in a Developing Society: The Case of the Japanese Marriage Arranger. *Human Organization* 20:112–20.

Yoshida, S. 1981. Koreisha Shakai [The Aging Society]. Tokyo.

Yoshihiro, K. 1987. Interviews with Unmarried Women. *Japan Quarterly* 34:305–8.

Woman-to-Woman Marriage: Practices and Benefits in Sub-Saharan Africa

R. Jean Cadigan

Anthropologists have always had a difficult time pigeon-holing marital practices. In addition, because there have been so many variations on the theme of what constitutes a marriage, it has been problematic at best to come up with a definition that would satisfy all cases and contingencies. At one "extreme," we have the Nayars of India, as reported by Kathleen Gough, who do not recognize a union between two individuals, but rather, at best, a collaborative relationship between two kinship groups, with the "husband" and "wife" identified when a child is born and according to the exigencies of the moment. At the other end of the spectrum, we have the Western ideal of the nuclear family of husband, wife, and children (which is actually in the minority).

Perhaps the least we can say is that marriage is a socially recognized union between two or more people that *may* be established for the purpose of procreation and the socialization of children. Two things about this definition should be noted. First, the idea of having children is not necessarily involved and second, the notion of *gender* is not stipulated. It is the second idea that brings us to R. Jean Cadigan's article about woman-to-woman marriage.

It is perhaps fitting that an anthropologist addresses this type of marriage system (which she claims has been largely ignored) at a time when the United States is struggling to cope with the prospect of same-sex marriage. Not that the issues are precisely the same, since woman-to-woman marriage is primarily about having children and the same-sex marriage issue in the United States is primarily about legally recognizing a relationship. Nevertheless, the differences in degree of tolerance for alternative lifestyles should be duly noted.

R. Jean Cadigan was affiliated with the Department of Anthropology, University of California, Los Angeles at the time she wrote this article for the *Journal of Comparative Family Studies.*

Key Concept: woman-to-woman marriage

Introduction

Ethnographic studies reveal that many African societies have practiced woman-to-woman marriage, and some still do (Herskovits, 1937; Krige, 1974; Obbo, 1976; O'Brien, 1977; Oboler, 1980).[1] Woman-to-woman marriage, also known as woman marriage or marriage involving a "female husband," refers to the institution whereby a woman marries another woman and assumes control over her and her offspring (Krige, 1974:11). In most cases, the wife will bear children for the female husband. All ceremonial aspects of these marriages are observed, bridewealth is paid to the girl's father, and all rules of divorce in the society apply (Herskovits, 1937:335). Despite the fact that woman-to-woman marriage has existed or exists in many societies, this institution has often been overlooked by researchers studying such topics as marriage, the family, gender relations, and the position of women in African societies. However, it is important to realize that woman-to-woman marriage has great relevance to these subjects.

The theory of male dominance and female oppression in terms of gender relations has long been discussed in the literature. Claude Meillassoux (1981) claims that senior men control the labor and produce of women through their control of the marriage (see also Potash, 1989:190). Such theories virtually ignore woman-to-woman marriage because the concept does not concur with the ideology of male dominance. However, another approach to the study of gender relations views both women and men as social actors who use various systems and their positions in society to achieve maximum personal benefits (Obbo, 1976:371; Potash, 1989:191). This article examines the relevance of woman-to-woman marriage as a strategy that women use to further their social and economic positions in society.

Cross-culturally, women take wives under three circumstances, all of which increase the status of the female husband: 1) barren women and widows take wives to obtain rights over children produced; 2) rich women accumulate wives to gain prestige and wealth in the same way men do through polygyny; and 3) in some societies where women have the right to have a daughter-in-law, women without sons can exercise their right to a daughter-in-law by marrying a woman and giving her to a non-existent son (see Huber, 1969; Krige, 1974). In each of these situations, African women are able to manipulate the existing system through woman-to-woman marriage in order to achieve higher social and economic status.

Woman-to-woman marriage can also be beneficial to persons other than the female husband. Woman-to-woman marriage involves the following persons: 1) the female husband herself; 2) if the female husband is already married, her own husband (the female husband's husband); 3) the woman who is married by the female husband—the wife; and 4) the lover(s) of the wife who may father her children. To obtain a full understanding of the topic, it is important to examine the motivations not only of the wife, but also those of the wife's lover(s) and the husband (if any) of the female husband.

This article will examine the various forms of woman-to-woman marriage in sub-Saharan Africa, discussing how each form can or could have been utilized by the female husband in order to advance her social and economic status in society. In addition, the benefits of woman-to-woman marriage to the other players involved will be examined.

Background on Woman-to-Woman Marriage

The institution of woman-to-woman marriage, which has existed at least as early as the eighteenth century (O'Brien, 1977:109), still exists in some societies today. However, as the Christian church banned polygamists (male and female) from taking communion during colonial times and Western influences have emphasized that girls have the right to choose their own husbands, woman-to-woman marriage may be dying out (Krige, 1974:17; Amadiume, 1987:132). For example, a recent study of the Western Igbo shows that women are becoming less tolerant of woman-to-woman marriage. Among women aged 15 to 24, 95 percent disapprove of the institution, as do 91 percent of women aged 25 to 44 and 89 percent of women between ages 45 to 64; only 73 percent of women above age 65 disapprove (Okonjo, 1992:350).

While some authors have argued that woman-to-woman marriage may involve lesbianism (Herskovits, 1937), most researchers vehemently oppose this idea (Krige, 1974; Obbo, 1976; O'Brien, 1977; Amadiume,

1987). For example, Amadiume (1987:7) claims that interpretations of woman-to-woman marriage as lesbianism would be "totally inapplicable, shocking and offensive to Nnobi women, since the strong bonds and support between them do not imply lesbian sexual practices." She disagrees strongly with those Western lesbians who have cited this African practice "to justify their choices of sexual alternatives which have roots and meanings in the West" (Amadiume, 1987:7).

Another topic for debate is the notion of whether the female husband is assuming a conceptual role of a male. O'Brien (1977:122) argues that the institution of woman-to-woman marriage sexually subordinates the female husband because she is forced to take on a male role. Thus, women in positions of power (usually political) must be conceptualized as male, or at least cannot be seen to hold the inferior status of wife, to justify their power and to set them apart from other women. Others argue that female husbands may or may not take on a male role (Krige, 1974; Amadiume, 1987). Among the Igbo, female husbands become heads-of-households and the Igbo word for family head is a genderless expression (Amadiume, 1987:90). The most convincing argument to date comes from Oboler's (1980) perceptions as they relate to the Nandi of Kenya. She concludes that the female husband is socially considered to assume the conceptual male role upon marriage to her wife. This is done in order to avoid the confusing situation which would arise in a patrilineal and patrilocal system whereby women have no right to land or inherited property. By conceptualizing the female husband as a man, the community recognizes that she possesses what are traditionally considered to be male rights, particularly in situations where property and inheritance are involved (Oboler, 1980). Consequently, woman-to-woman marriage may be a "pro-female" institution because it can provide women with rights that would otherwise be reserved for males (Amadiume, 1987).

Regardless of whether the female husband takes on a conceptual role of a male, it is evident that she uses the institution as a way of achieving social prestige and increased economic security. The female husband usually has the same rights over the wife and her children as a man has over his wife and children. She must financially support them and is in charge of disciplining the children (Oboler, 1980:79).

Three Reasons for the Occurrence of Woman-to-Woman Marriage

Barrenness/Increasing a Lineage

Given that in many African societies a woman's traditional social obligation is to marry and procreate, a barren woman is often considered a failure and is ostracized. Through woman-to-woman marriage, a barren woman is able to gain social prestige and her husband's favor.

Among the Kamba, a barren woman is a "social disgrace; she is a humiliation" (Kimutu, 1994). Furthermore, as long as "her husband is potent and fertile, the barren woman is obliged to accomplish her duty of providing the husband with children without interfering with their marriage" (Kimutu, 1994). A barren wife can resolve her unfortunate social position by engaging in a woman-to-woman marriage. In such cases, the wife bears children for the female husband, which brings honor and glory to the barren woman and subsequently to the husband of the barren woman. The jurisdiction of the female husband includes choosing the man with whom her wife will procreate. It may be the female husband's own husband or any of her husband's close male kin. Among the Kamba, barren women often do not succeed in finding a man to marry and thus many remain single. However, because of the social stigma attached to single women (and men), many barren women enter into a marriage with another woman while they are still single. In such cases, the wife usually chooses her own lover. The female husband in this situation also achieves prestige for taking a wife and obtaining children (Kimutu, 1999).

Among the Igbo and Kalabari communities of southern Nigeria, barren women have also been noted to enter into woman-to-woman marriages. The female husband gives her wife to her own husband or his male kin in order to procreate; an outsider would never be brought in as a lover (Herskovits, 1937:336). Often the female husband's wife is a purchased slave. Among these communities, barren women enter into woman-to-woman marriages primarily to increase their economic status. If a woman has no children, she has no claim on her husband's property upon his death and may have to leave the land on which she is likely to have lived for decades. Offspring from a woman-to-woman marriage guarantee the female husband secure economic standing by maintaining her rights to occupy property which is inherited by her children (Herskovits, 1937:336).

Huber (1969:751) claims that the occurrence of woman-to-woman marriage among the Simbiti may decrease and its importance may also decline with time. Medical advances may reduce infant mortality and barrenness. In addition, the increasing trend towards a monetary economy may alter inheritance rules. The acceptance of woman-to-woman marriage may lessen as wives of female husbands are increasingly taking advantage of their sexual freedom and behaving more like "prostitutes". The impact of Christianity and Western education may also have an effect on woman-to-woman marriage as it works to reduce the cases of polygamy (both male and female) among the Simbiti (Huber, 1969:752).

Widows entering into woman-to-woman marriages in order to increase the lineage of a deceased husband have been documented in a number of societies. Among the Kikuyu of Kenya, for example, a widow could gain social status by becoming a female husband in order to add members to her dead husband's lineage. She is able to choose between levirate or woman-to-woman marriage. Many choose to become a female husband because it gives them control over land (Mackenzie, 1990:619).

Among the Nuer, the Dinka, and the Kamba, widows often contract woman-to-woman marriages. In such cases, a widow's wife produces children in honor of the female husband's deceased husband. Nuer female husbands pay a male outsider, usually in the form of cattle, to procreate with their wives, aware that if children are produced in the name of her deceased husband, she will be revered by his family (Herskovits, 1937:336). Among Kamba widows, the first child born to the widow's wife will belong to the lineage of the widow's deceased husband. Subsequent children born to the widow's wife may be affiliated with the widow's lineage, thereby giving her the prestige associated with having an heir (Obbo, 1976:375).

As an Indication or Means of Accruing Wealth

In many societies where the institution of woman-to-woman marriage exists, wealthy women who have enough property may become female husbands. These women may be single or already married to men. The female husband may take a wife for purposes of enlarging her own family and/or for the sake of gaining public recognition and esteem. Wealthy women, just like their male counterparts, marry women to increase their social status and as a means of investing their wealth.

While this reason for woman-to-woman marriage appears to be most prevalent among West African societies where women, usually as traders, have had more opportunity to acquire wealth, it has been noted among the Kamba (Kimutu, 1994) and Simbiti (Huber, 1969) of East Africa. Kimutu (1994), a Kamba himself, notes that "when a woman marries an 'iweto' [a wife], she becomes highly esteemed, respected, influential and raised above other women because she virtually assumes the status of a [male] husband."

Traditionally among the Igbo in Nnobi, rich women were able to become female husbands in order to free themselves from domestic responsibilities (Amadiume, 1987:72). Their wives would perform all household chores while the female husband used the extra time she gained to devote her energies to other affairs, usually trading. It was the flexible gender system of the community which allowed this beneficial aspect of woman-to-woman marriage. In fact, "the ultimate indication of wealth and power, the title system, was open to men and women, as was the means of becoming rich through control over the labor of others by way of polygamy, whether man-to-woman marriage or woman-to-woman marriage" (Amadiume, 1987:42). Further, "women benefitted from the accumulation of wives in the same way as did men" (Amadiume, 1987:45).

Female textile traders in the Sokoto Caliphate in West Africa in the late nineteenth and early twentieth centuries employed woman-to-woman marriage to advance their own economic status. As females accumulated wealth through trading, they often invested it by taking wives. The institution of woman-to-woman marriage was most likely used to gain control over the labor of children and wives with the aim of producing textiles at low costs (Kriger, 1993:395). Women were engaged in weaving and spinning and were able to trade freely and to keep all profits.

In the region of the Lamai Emirate at the turn of this century, female husbands often gained profit by sending their wives on extended trading trips. Many wives, while gone, would bear children legally belonging to the female husband. As the children reached the age of five or six (usually the age when children are able to begin working), the female husband would claim them, whereupon the biological father would often pay her to transfer her paternity rights to him. It has been noted that female husbands were known to generate large profits from such encounters (Kriger, 1993:395).

Alternatively, Kriger (1993:396) speculates that the female husband might have given a man sexual access to her wife in exchange for agricultural labor. The man would have grown and harvested cotton which was cleaned and spun into yarn by the female husband's children. The yarn would then have been woven into fabrics by her wife (or wives). The entire process could have been executed at extremely low costs and managed exclusively by the female husband (Kriger, 1993:396). In colonial times, woman-to-woman marriage was condemned by missionaries and colonial officials who believed it was simply used to exploit children's labor (Kriger, 1993:395).

Marrying a "Daughter-in-Law"

Agricultural communities often recognize a woman's need for a daughter-in-law to help with domestic chores and farm work. Among the Gusii, Lovedu, and Simbiti this recognition is reflected in a form of woman-to-woman marriage whereby the female husband marries a "daughter-in-law." Closely related to the motivations caused by barrenness, women without sons would pay bridewealth for a girl and refer to the process as marrying a "daughter-in-law" for the "house." This form of woman-to-woman marriage gives a sonless female husband the opportunity to become the head of a "complete" house. Among the patrilineal Gusii and Simbiti, it also enables the female husband to expel the stigma attached to her because she failed to bear a male heir.

The matrilineal Lovedu grant every woman the right to a daughter-in-law from the home which was established through the use of her bridewealth. That is, "the brother uses his sister's bridewealth cattle to obtain a wife; the sister is then entitled to her brother's daughter" (Strobel, 1982:121). Normally, this exchange would result in the well-known form of cross-cousin marriage. However, a woman does not lose her right to a daughter-in-law if she

has no son; woman-to-woman marriage ensures her this right (Krige, 1974:15).

The Simbiti female husband, like her Lovedu counterpart, often chooses her wife from her brother's house. As her bridewealth helped to establish his home, he is often more lenient about the amount of bridewealth he demands (Huber, 1969:748). The daughter-in-law is taken on to help with various domestic chores as well as to give the female husband prestige. She essentially legitimizes the existence of the female husband's "imaginary" son, thereby increasing the female husband's status in society. While everyone realizes the female husband does not have a son, having a daughter-in-law ensures the status of obtaining grandchildren as heirs.

Unlike the Simbiti and Lovedu, the Gusii female husband does not choose a daughter-in-law to marry from her brother's home. The sonless woman does, however, use the bridewealth from one of her daughters to marry a woman on behalf of her non-existent son. The married couple refers to each other as "mother-in-law" and "daughter-in-law," and their children are considered to be the female husband's grandchildren (Hakansson, 1985:97–98). While the practice was originally rare, Hakansson reports that its occurrence has been increasing since the 1960s. Like the Lovedu and Simbiti, this form of woman-to-woman marriage among the Gusii gives the female husband the prestigious role of head-of-household and ensures male heirs in the form of grandchildren.

Motivations for those Involved to Participate in Woman-to-Woman Marriage

The Female Husband

The female husband is motivated by a number of factors to participate in woman-to-woman marriage. Cross-culturally, all women gain respect and prestige by taking wives. Barren women increase their social status by becoming "fathers" to their own heirs and increasing lineages, either their own or their husbands' (e.g., the Kamba, Nuer, and the Dinka). Female husbands benefit from the increased access to land which they achieve by "fathering" heirs (e.g., the Igbo, Kalabari, and the Kikuyu). Sonless women marry daughters-in-law in order to have domestic help and the status of having grandchildren (e.g., the Gusii, Simbiti, and the Lovedu). As a result of woman-to-woman marriage, a female husband can become powerful and wealthy through her ability to control her new family's labor.

If there are so many benefits associated with becoming a female husband, why are there not more incidences of woman-to-woman marriage? The institution appears to be dying out in many societies as a direct result of Western influences. Female husbands must be wealthy enough to pay bridewealth and, if they are married to men, they probably need to have their husband's support to enter into a marriage with a woman. Further, some women contemplating becoming female husbands have noted the difficulty associated with finding a willing and suitable wife. (Oboler, 1980:75)

While the female husband certainly has the most to gain from woman-to-woman marriage, there are certain benefits obtained by the wife, the wife's lover, and the husband of the female husband (if any).

The Wife of the Female Husband

Among the Dahomey, the wives of female husbands are not considered to be in a socially undesirable position (Herskovits, 1937:340), and indeed this may traditionally be true of wives in woman-to-woman marriages throughout Africa. Certainly among the Kamba, women gain a great deal of prestige upon marriage. In fact, a woman remains a "child" in the eyes of the community until she marries. Traditionally, a Kamba woman's main function in society is to procreate, and her duties are restricted to domestic chores and farm work (Kimutu, 1994). As a result, a woman who excels in such duties is considered to be an "ideal" woman, and therefore a good wife. Hence, if conferred with the responsibilities and duties of a wife, it is not detrimental to become a wife to another woman.

Wealth possessed by a female husband also motivates women to agree in becoming the wives of other women. Many Kamba wives of female husbands consent to woman-to-woman marriage because they may otherwise be faced with starvation or poverty (Obbo, 1976:376). Among the Nandi, women often express the opinion that it is far better to be married to a wealthy woman than to a poor man (Oboler, 1980:76). Furthermore, female husbands tend to give more bridewealth than male husbands because of the anxiety and difficulty involved in finding a willing and suitable wife (Oboler, 1980:76).

A woman may also marry a female husband because she is unable to find a man to marry. Perhaps she has a physical or mental handicap which makes her unattractive to men. Among the Nandi today, being the mother of illegitimate children is the most common reason women become wives to female husbands (Oboler, 1980:76). Woman-to-woman marriage "legitimizes" the wife's children and gives them rights of inheritance (Oboler, 1980:80).

Both the female husband and the wife gain status in society by maintaining a stable marriage. Female husbands do not usually fight as much with their wives, both verbally and physically, as male husbands (Oboler, 1980:76).

Wives of female husbands usually enjoy more freedom both socially and sexually because their role in the marriage is not as demanding as it is in man-to-woman marriage. While a wife's lover is usually chosen by the female husband, among the Nandi this arrangement must be agreed upon before marriage as wives do not like to have their freedom of choice taken from them (Oboler, 1980).

The Wife's Lover

The wife's lover, with whom she will procreate, is often chosen by the female husband. The lover rarely lives with the married couple, but instead visits the wife. His main motivation is the "free" sexual access he gets to the wife without the financial obligation to support her or their biological children. Often he may work on the farm of the female husband in exchange for the access he receives to her wife. Among the Nuer, the lover receives one cow from each of his daughters' bridewealth payments (Krige, 1974:13). Thus, the wife's lover may not only gain sexual privileges, but also certain economic advantages.

The Female Husband's Husband

While not all female husbands are already married to men, a great many are. In societies where the institution of woman-to-woman marriage exists, many male husbands urge their wives to marry a woman. If the female husband is barren, her husband virtually requires her to take a wife in order to produce children. Wealthy men are able to flaunt their wealth further by being married to women who have wives. Male and female polygamy glorifies the husbands of female husbands.

Conclusion

Women across sub-Saharan Africa have used the flexible institution of woman-to-woman marriage to achieve maximum personal benefits. In a number of different cultures, barren women have employed the system to provide themselves with the children they need in order to be considered full members of society. By marrying other women, widows have also gained status by securing children for their deceased husband's lineage. Sonless women have married daughters-in-law to provide grandchildren and domestic help. Women have been known to become female husbands in order to secure rights over land. In West Africa, female traders have manipulated the system to gain power and wealth through their marriage to women.

In most societies discussed in this article, the presence of the institution of woman-to-woman marriage is declining. As Kimutu (1994) writes about the Kamba, "the customs that prevailed within the traditional Kamba people in the pre-colonial era were eroded, altered, and to some extent obliterated by the great socioeconomic, political, and educational changes that infiltrated the traditional Kamba community from the Western world during the colonial era." In addition to the changes brought about by colonialism, the incidence of woman-to-woman marriage may have been altered in response to medical advances which reduce barrenness and infant mortality.

The study of woman-to-woman marriage provides insights into the family, marriage, gender roles, and status of women in African societies. Despite the fact that woman-to-woman marriage may also be beneficial to men, the institution is not simply given by men to women in order to appease them in the male-dominated system; rather, woman-to-woman marriage has been a way in which women could substantially advance their social status and/or increase their economic standing in their communities. The apparent decline of woman-to-woman marriage may negatively affect the position of women, particularly barren women who frequently use woman-to-woman marriage to gain the status associated with motherhood.

I am very grateful to Dominique Meekers for his encouragement, support, and valuable suggestions, and to Alice James for her comments on a version of this paper.

Note

1. O'Brien (1977:110) lists a number of societies which have practiced woman-to-woman marriage. By region they are: 1) West Africa (mainly Nigeria)—Yoruba, Ekiti, Bunu, Akoko, Yagba, Nupe, Ibo, Ijaw, and Fon (or Dahomeans); 2) South Africa (especially the Transvaal)—Venda, Lovedu, Pedi, Hurutshe, Zulu, Sotho, Phalaborwa, Narene, Koni, and Tawana; 3) East Africa—Kuria, Iregi, Kenye, Suba, Simbiti, Ngoreme, Gusii, Kipsigis, Nandi, Kikuyu, and Luo; and 4) Sudan—Nuer, Dinka, and Shilluk. In addition, others have noted the practice among the Kalabari of West Africa and the Kamba of East Africa.

References

Amadiume, I. 1987 Male Daughters, Female Husbands: Gender and Sex in an African Society. London: Zed Books.

Hakansson, N.T. 1985 "Why do Gusii women get married? A study of cultural constraints and women's strategies in a rural community in Kenya." *Folk* 27(1): 89–114.

Herskovits, M. 1937 "A note on 'woman marriage' in Dahomey." *Africa* 10(3): 335–341.

Huber, H. 1969 "'Woman marriage' in some East African societies." *Anthropos* 63–64(5–6): 745–752.

Kimutu, S.K. 1994 Letter to author discussing woman-to-woman marriage among the Kamba of Kenya, September 30.

Krige, E.J. 1974 "Woman marriage with special reference to the Lovedu—Its significance for the definition of marriage." *Africa* 44(1): 11–36.

Kriger, C. 1993 "Textile production and gender in the Sokoto Caliphate." *Journal of African History* 34(3): 361–410.

Mackenzie, F. 1990 "Gender and land rights in Murang'a District, Kenya." *The Journal of Peasant Studies* 17(4): 609–643.

Meillassoux, C. 1981 Maidens, Meal and Money: Capitalism and the Domestic Community. New York: Cambridge University Press.

Obbo, C. 1976 "Dominant male ideology and female options: Three East African case studies." *Africa* 46(4): 371–389.

Oboler, R.S. 1980 "Is the female husband a man?: Woman/woman marriage among the Nandi of Kenya." *Ethnology* 19(1): 69–88.

O'Brien, D. 1977 "Female husbands in Southern Bantu societies." Pp. 99–108 in A. Schlegel (ed.), Sexual Stratification: A Cross-Cultural View. New York: Columbia University Press.

Okonjo, K. 1992 "Aspects of continuity and change in mate selection among the Igbo West of the River Niger." *Journal of Comparative Family Studies* 23(3): 339–360.

Potash, B. 1989 "Gender relations in sub-Saharan Africa." Pp. 189–227 in S. Morgan (ed.), Gender and Anthropology: Critical Reviews for Teaching and Research. Washington, D.C.: American Anthropological Association.

Strobel, M. 1982 "African women." *Signs: Journal of Women in Culture and Society* 8(1): 109–131.

Dowry Murder: The Imperial Origins of a Cultural Crime

Veena Talwar Oldenburg

The custom of *dowry*, having to do with goods of value which accompany a bride as she moves to the groom's family home, was a long-standing tradition in pre-colonial India. As Veena Talwar indicates, its primary purposes were to serve as a mark of the social status of the bride and as a guarantee of her financial security. In addition, the transfer of wealth was also a way of ensuring that a young woman would be able to marry "properly" within her own category (caste or sub-caste) or perhaps even higher. Moreover, the very idea of a dowry transaction insured that both the bride's family and the groom's family would have some say-so as to who marries whom.

Dowry should not be confused with *bride-wealth* (or *bride-price*) which has to do with a transfer of wealth in the opposite direction, from the groom's family to the bride's family. In both cases, the residence rule is *virilocal* (or *patrilocal*), stipulating that it is the bride that is to move upon marriage, not the groom. The customs of dowry and bride-wealth serve somewhat different purposes and occur under very different social circumstances.

The problem of "bride-burning," as it has come to be associated with dowry is a fairly recent occurrence. As the author herself points out, she knew nothing about it when first asked by a television journalist in 1984. The fact that the problem is so recent and that it is *not* associated with dowry in the majority of marriages in India (nor in Europe, where dowry has also been practiced) should serve as a warning that there is something "different" going on in the places where bride-burning does occur. It is on this basis that Veena Talwar investigates the issue and finds that gender inequality, as it is expressed in both bride-burning and female infanticide, has its roots in India's colonial past.

Veena Talwar Oldenburg obtained her Ph.D. from the University of Illinois and is currently Associate Professor in the History Department at Baruch College. Her areas of scholarship are Indian History, British Colonialism, and Women's History. This article is an excerpt from her book, *Dowry Murder: The Imperial Origins of a Cultural Crime.* She is currently working on another book on the subject, *Dowry Murders: Reinvestigating A Cultural Whodunit.*

Key Concept: dowry murder

Preface

In 1984, on a quiet spring afternoon in New York, the phone rang in my study and a television journalist asked me if I knew anything about "bride burning" or "dowry murder" in my native India. I did not, but I did offer some thoughts on sati, or widow burning, along with a reading list. No, the journalist insisted, an Indian documentary on this issue was to be aired as a segment of an important national weekly news show, and the television channel was looking for informed comment. My own memories of an experience in the summer of 1966 were still surprisingly fresh, but they appeared dated and so utterly unconnected with dowry that I said nothing. That denial and the subliminal provocation instigated the book *Dowry Murder: The Imperial Origins of a Cultural Crime.*

I confess to having repressed my private suspicions about this wholly new yet chillingly remembered style of violence that appeared to have become a trend. The culprit (or culprits) used kerosene oil and a match to burn the woman to death; the motive was easily ascribed to marital conflict arising from demands for more dowry, in cash and/or as valuables, by the new husband and his family. These violent events were reported as kitchen accidents, involving the rather dangerous pressurized kerosene stoves in common use in Indian kitchens, from which other women, not just brides, and men as well frequently sustain accidental burns. Only in a very few cases of a young wife's death were the police actually summoned to the scene to file a report. Until the early 1980s, few such cases were investigated, and in even fewer was murder detected. Certainly no one had been convicted of the crime. Because violence in the home, even murder, was unofficially part of the private sphere, suspicion, innuendo, and speculation whispered in private conversations seldom became evidence in a court of law. There would be no reliable witnesses, since the mother-in-law was usually implicated as the perpetrator, often with a sister-in-law or even the husband himself as accomplice, and the crime occurred behind closed doors.

The day after the documentary was shown, colleagues and students at the small liberal arts college where I then taught besieged me with questions. They had seen the footage—a graphic depiction of a bride engulfed in flames, perhaps even the charred corpse—and they demanded answers. Appalling as the incident portrayed in the documentary might have been, it seemed clear that the U.S. media had seized an opportunity to make a spectacle of "the Orient," in this case India. I had become used to being brought to account for any Indian happening, good or bad (but chiefly bad). But never before had it been so difficult to deal with, because this time I had no satisfactory rebuttals. I tried to suggest that this could just be murder, an ordinary crime of passion or greed, as occurs against wives and girlfriends everywhere, and particularly here in the United States. No, they were quite sure that nothing they had seen could pass for a geographically or culturally neutral event. The burning death was perceived as fraught with deep Hindu religious and cultural significance. *Dahej* or dowry and its relationship to the Hindu caste system were portrayed as the key to understanding this crime. The narrator in the documentary had made it very clear that the Punjabi bride had been burned to death because she had not brought enough dowry to her husband's home, thus provoking a disappointed mother-in-law to douse her in kerosene and set her on fire.

Incidents of bargaining over dowry were not unheard of, but such behavior was customarily considered shamefully and unambiguously wrong. That matters had come to such a pass that brides were gruesomely immolated alive sounded like a postcolonial society's worst nightmare come true. This new crime against women was called "dowry death," and it was ironic that it made its appearance a quarter of a century after the passage of the Prohibition of Dowry Act in 1961. I vaguely remembered watching V. Shantaram's Hindi film *Dahej* from the late 1950s. It was a melodramatic tale, replete with singing, dancing, and pontificating, whose plot served as a vehicle to depict the evils of the dowry system. Though I was aware of the abuse of the custom, in the Indian context dowry also constituted a women's independent right to property and prestige. The burning of a bride to death for not bringing a dowry that satisfied the greed of a groom's family was a monstrous perversion of the meaning and function of the custom.

Culturally embarrassed, pedagogically nonplused, yet deeply stirred for reasons that will unfold, I knew the time had come for me to examine the alleged cultural roots of this crime. . . .

A clarification is essential at the outset: the burning of wives is neither an extension of nor culturally related to the notorious practice of sati (or "suttee," as the British called it), the voluntary self-immolation of widows on the funeral pyres of their husbands. The resonance may be confounding—the burning of women, the blurred line between suicide and murder—but the differences are significant, and they point to a serious devaluation of women in present-day India in spite of a century and a half of progressive legislation on women's rights. Sati was socially countenanced suicide because the widow perceived herself as having failed in her ritual duty to ensure the longevity of her husband by using her special power, or *shakti*. The rituals that a widow would follow to join her husband on his funeral pyre are adequately described and commented upon elsewhere; suffice it to say that it drew its cachet as a publicly witnessed act that generated social awe, status, and religious merit for the widow and made her the virtuous wife in death.

"Bride burning," on the other hand, is murder, culpable on social, cultural, and legal grounds, executed privately, and often disguised as an accident or suicide. Burning a wife is, perhaps, even more appalling than poisoning, drowning, strangling, shooting, or bludgeoning her, but it is patently chosen for the forensic advantage it has over the other methods, rather than for Hindu mythological or mystical reasons, as some reporters in the United States are fond of claiming. It is also relatively simple to execute. The crime occurs in the kitchen, where the lower- and middle-class housewife spends a lot of time each day. Kerosene stoves are in common use in such homes, and a tin of fuel is always kept in reserve. This can be quickly poured over the intended victim, and a lighted match will do the rest. It is easy to pass off the event as an accident since these stoves are, indeed, prone to explode (as confirmed by consumer reports). The now ubiquitous and inflammable nylon sari is only too wont to catch fire and engulf the wearer in flames. Signs of struggle do not show up on bodies with 90 percent or more thirddegree burns. The young widower, who has equipped himself with a cast-iron alibi, is soon in the marriage market again looking for a new bride with perhaps an even handsomer dowry. Most often it is the mother-in-law, with or without her son as a direct accomplice, who obligingly does the deed. The reason for this, I would argue, is that the son (often the breadwinner for his widowed mother) must remain innocent of all suspicion and therefore eligible for remarriage as an unfortunate widower. His income-earning activities are also not interrupted, should the event actually be investigated as a crime. This poses difficult questions: Are Indian women victims of their culture or agents of a crime they inflict upon other women? Is dowry murder a cultural crime?. . .

Seldom has there been so firm a consensus on a social issue in India as the one among scholars, journalists, feminists, politicians, legislators, and the police today that the custom of dowry has a causal relationship to prejudice and violence against women. The view that the murders of young wives are a special category of "cultural crime" linked to a high-caste Hindu cultural practice of dowry is unshakably entrenched. Women's organizations have designated the burning of wives baldly as "dowry murder." Although it is true that dowry—clothes, jewelry, household goods, cash, and property that a bride brings to a marriage—is neither new nor unique to India, just as violence against women is not an Indian cultural peculiarity, the view that dowry is a harmful, even dangerous institution has more credence in India than elsewhere. Today the dowry system is also seen as the prime, if not the sole, explanation for two other practices akin to female infanticide that are increasingly prevalent in the subcontinent: the fatal neglect of female infants, and the selective abortion of female fetuses, made possible by the abuse of recent advances in fetal diagnostic technology.

The impugning of dowry as the causal force behind gendered crimes has its roots in the collusion of the imperial state and Punjabi men who reconfigured patriarchal values and manly ideals ever more strongly in nineteenth-century Punjab. The two became meshed in an unsurprising alliance against the customary rights of women, even though the avowed purpose of social reform legislation in this period was to uplift the status of women in Indian society. We must look beyond the statute book to comprehend a central paradox of colonial policy in India that persists in post-colonial India: although the legislative record is indeed impressive, and includes the outlawing of several customs that underscored the bias against women, there was in the colonial period a profound loss of women's economic power and social worth. This was a direct consequence of the radical creation of property rights in land.

In pre-colonial India, dowry was not a "problem" but a support for women: a mark of their social status and a safety net.... dowry and associated wedding expenses neither caused the impoverishment of the Punjab peasant, which is what early colonial administrators claimed, nor were they the cause of the increase in violence against women, whether in the form of female infanticide or today's "bride burning." Rather, imperial policies created a more "masculine" economy and deepened the preference for sons that fostered the overt or hidden murder of girls. The establishment of property rights for peasants, inflexible tax demands and collection regimens, and a host of other imperial measures prepared the ground for worsening gender inequality which, in turn, increased the vulnerability of women to violence in both their natal and marital homes. The protective legislation passed for the benefit of women was aimed at protecting them from the presumed ill effects of their own cultural practices; it did little with respect to the ravages of new economic policies.

The scene of my investigation is the Punjab, in the northwestern part of the subcontinent, a varied and often partitioned space but representative of northern Indian marriage patterns and of an unabashed preference for sons. Delhi (historically part of the Punjab) became the obvious choice for the city I would concentrate on for the contemporary part of this project, for two reasons. The community most frequently implicated in these deaths consists of lower-middle-class and high-caste Punjabi Hindus and Sikhs, whose number in the capital swelled as they poured in as refugees after the partition of the Punjab in 1947. Second, the media, legal activists, and women's organizations are keenly at work there, and this affords convenient access to both historical and contemporary records. . . .

Investigating the Crime

The daily news of "bride burnings" in Delhi beckoned me urgently. I was directed to Saheli, a women's resource center, where I spent the next ten months, gleaning from files and interviews with victims the fine-grained reality of violence against women, including their narrow escapes from death. Information gathered from reading newspaper reports, going to meetings, and anti-dowry protests, and interviewing potentially endangered women and the relatives of those who had died in the corridors of hospitals did not really explain *why* dowry had become such a scourge. And I did not trust the activists' obsession with dowry. I found the thenexisting analyses of contemporary dowry murders ahistorical and counterintuitive, and the scholarly treatments of female infanticide unsatisfactory. There was enough to suggest that the custom of dowry had been corrupted, but there was little to explain why or when. The "dowry problem" had indeed a deep-but-forgotten history that had to be disinterred from the volumes of imperial records in London, Delhi, and Patiala.

The explanations from archival and contemporary sources on dowry offered glaring contradictions. The colonial finger pointed at Hindu culture, whereas present-day Indian activists and media blamed Westernization, which increased materialism, greed, and a desire for consumer goods, and commercialized human relationships. Here was the puzzle. Was this violence against women related to the ancient custom of dowry, or was it a product of acculturation to Western and modern culture? In Europe, where dowries have all but disappeared, violence against women is still rampant. Modern industrial capitalism eroded the culture of dowry in the West, but did economic distortions peculiar to the colonial setting change it for the worse in India?

In digging for the roots of the "dowry problem" to determine whether it had ever been associated with violence before 1980, I began to skim through annual compilations of administrative reports in the Punjab to see if, perhaps, a hundred years ago the custom of dowry had better press. And there it was, as a cause of the murder of females. But instead of the murder of brides, it was categorically indicted as the cause of female infanticide. The British had uncovered female infanticide in the Punjab 1851, a rampant crime that, they adduced, was directly related to the expense of wedding celebrations and dowry payments. Dowries, they reported, had impoverished Punjabi peasant families and brought them to the brink of ruin because they became heavily indebted in trying to marry off their daughters in the style demanded by upper-caste Hindu culture. It was logical, then, that the fear of future expenditure motivated peasants to kill their newborn daughters, and the imperial government, as the agent of a higher civilization, would make every effort to reform what they deemed to be culturally inbred habits engendered in a rude and ignorant people they had just conquered. Darkly, the same reports hinted at the true concern of the British: these same peasants who committed female infanticide were also defaulters on revenue payments and their lands were, therefore, up for auction by the government or foreclosure by local moneylenders. Infanticide was seen as what we might call preemptive dowry murder, with unmistakable cultural fingerprints at the site of the crime. Given these allegations, could any historical investigation of "dowry murder" be complete without looking at female infanticide, particularly in the colonial period? It became a logical necessity to include female infanticide in the ambit of this project.

But as I studied female infanticide, the popular anti-dowry explanation I had thought I would deepen and endorse began to unravel. There was, indeed, abundant colonial documentation of female infanticide among high-caste Punjabi Hindus, but statistics on sex ratios in the subcontinent pointed to a serious anomaly in the logic that underpinned the colonial verdict on the dowry system, and made the British figures suspect. A startling contradiction emerged: several families from Hindu lower castes and Sikhs who received bride-price, and Muslims who did not follow the practice of dowry, were all found guilty of committing female infanticide. This made it more than a little awkward to insist on the "Hindoo" nature of the practice, and either extravagant dowries or upper-caste "pride" (as alleged in the case of the Rajputs, the powerful landowning and ruling castes in north India) as a cultural justification for so heinous a crime. Why would colonial bureaucrats stick so adamantly to the view that the culture of Hindu caste, rather than any other rationale, explained the undeniably widespread practice of killing female infants? So I began to investigate the beginning of British rule in the Punjab, and the trail led to the transformation of rights in property, particularly land. Fortunately for the historian, officialdom was not harmoniously one on this subject. The dominant discourse against culturally induced peasant "improvidence" (in extravagant weddings and dowries) was sharply rebutted by those who more honestly saw the havoc their own policies were visiting on peasant households.

In investigating dowry-related crimes on two temporal fronts I discovered a curious symmetry in the evidence spanning the past century and a half. I needed to look at the past to flesh out the overwhelming belief (which I share) that something somewhere had gone terribly wrong with the meaning and function of dowry, to the point when activist women would urge and achieve a legal ban of the practice in 1961. For the killing of brides I needed to recover the history of this corruption that would illumine the egregious present. But the converse was true with female infanticide, where present-day sex ratios and the increasing use of new diagnostic technology to determine the sex of the fetus prior to the decision to abort illumined the age-old desire for families to have more sons in a historically war-torn region. This need for a family with many more boys than girls was greatly intensified in the colonial period. The uninterrupted use of old and new methods of reducing the number of girl children in a family are reflected in the worst female-to-male sex ratios in the world today in the space that constituted the colonial Punjab. Only such a time span enables a conjoint exploration of the past and the present, and an attempt to understand the pattern of continuities and disjunctions in colonial and postcolonial periods in turn promises to lead to a more informed perspective on one of the most troubling social issues in the history of the subcontinent. Perhaps it will also point to where future legislation must be directed.

Juxtaposing archival and activist stints in my years in Delhi in 1985–1986 and 1991–1992, and the summers of all the years in between, allowed me to treat holistically what appeared as disparate problems in disparate eras. The tragic responses shaped in the past when the colonial state and educated natives colluded in matters of social reform were being replayed as farce in modern Delhi. To suppress the murder of female infants, the colonial government passed a law in 1870, and a few years later tried to restrict the value of dowries and curb wedding expenses by assembling all the important upper-caste Hindu chiefs from the forty-odd districts of the Punjab to have them pledge an end to their "improvidence" and thriftless ways. Yet the female sex ratios in India continued to decline, which leads to the questions of whether the government campaign was successful in reducing the cost of daughters' marriages—and, if it was, if there was, in fact, no causal relationship between dowries and female infanticide.

More than a century later, Indian news media, particularly the leading feminist journal *Manushi*, waged a vigorous campaign against dowry to prevent the murder of women in their marital homes. Activists working for women's causes demanded that the Prohibition of Dowry Act of 1961 be amended "to give it teeth." This push found passionate advocates among the Delhi intelligentsia. The most committed voice for this and other deep legal reforms has been the feminist lawyer and activist Lotika Sarkar. She profiled the average victim of a dowry death: "Such a person is always a woman. . .

mostly in her twenties. She is a married woman [who has] already become a mother or is about to become a mother. . . . The woman is extremely unhappy by reason of demand for dowry. *She has no other reason or cause for unhappiness, except that resulting from, or connected with, the demand for dowry.* The demands are persistent, determined and oppressive" (Sarkar 1983: 2; emphasis added). The goal was duly accomplished in 1985, but neither dowry nor the violence blamed on it diminished, and the latter appeared steadily to rise. This raises the question of whether the unhappiness and the violence were, in fact, caused primarily by the dowry demands. In truth, the ban on dowries has had little meaning for the vast majority of the people for whom the custom has never caused serious friction, let alone provided the instigation to murder women either as infants or as brides. Yet the Delhi police proudly created a special "cell" to deal with "dowry deaths" in the late 1970s, as a model to be emulated in police departments in other major cities, and it was not until 1986 that the cell expanded its purview to deal with all violent crimes against women. . . .

Presenting the Case

The pervasive denunciation of dowry since the mid-1800s also underpins a host of corollaries that have blurred the thinking on the triangular relationship among marriage, gender, and property, which needs to be explored historically. It also pushes to the fore other, perhaps bigger, questions. Did imperial policies often create or aggravate the very problems they sought to ameliorate? For instance, were a host of new "social evils," such as accelerating chronic indebtedness and increasing drunkenness—and therefore domestic violence—in the Punjabi countryside the unwitting consequence of political economy of the new regime rather than of Hindu or Muslim cultural dictates?[6] And finally, what influence did the colonial enterprise of codifying custom into textual law and its implementation in the new courts in the Punjab have on various existing practices, particularly on the rights of women and the notions of *dahej* (dowry) and *stridhan* (women's wealth)?

The changes in the practice of dowry are uneven and ongoing, coexist in time and space, and can be best seen on a continuum rather than as sharply drawn opposites of "traditional" and "modern" dowry. Premodern dowry, I contend, was consonant with the premodern notions of rights in land. The modern notion of property that underlies the present-day pathology of dowry owes its origin to the exclusion of women from property rights in land as fashioned by the British. The social expectation that customs related to women would remain unchanged even as men's rights in property were transformed is naïve.

Dowry needs dynamic reformulation, defined neither as the timeless *stridhan* or women's wealth, as described in the third-century *Dharmashastra*, nor as the lethal custom that allegedly provokes the murders of several thousand young women annually. I therefore avoid defining dowry.

Instead, I track the course of its changing perceptions and functions over time. In tracking these changes, the Punjab and northern India in general offer a dramatic contrast to parallel-cross-cousin marriages among many communities in the south, where women remain in close proximity and touch with their natal families. Both share the custom of dowry, but the south seems to be less prone to the pathological strain of the north, where the custom of virilocal marriages (that is, the bride leaves her own home to live in the household of her husband) cuts across caste and class lines. Demands for dowry affect only a small percentage of families even in northern India, but the murder even of a minuscule fraction of the number of married women makes the problem a crucial one to investigate.

A careful rereading of historical sources and a great many interviews with women who were connected with the present-day "dowry problem" led me to conclude that dowry could be called one of the few indigenous, woman-centered institutions in an overwhelmingly patriarchal and agrarian society. I would have used the word *feminist* to describe the institution of dowry, but in India the term is resolutely rejected in some quarters as a Western idea, so I avoid its use except in reference to some individuals who would describe themselves as feminists, including myself. The word *patriarchy*, however, is widely used by activists and scholars alike. In this study I use it as shorthand, for want of a better term, for families in which a preference for sons is marked, marriage is invariably virilocal, and property is inherited by sons or agnates (among the male kin in joint households, and from fathers to sons in nuclear households). I also examine dowry in contradistinction to bride-price, which allows us to sort out the bedeviled area of high- and low-caste cultures.

Gender lines in Punjabi society, and by extension elsewhere in north India, I aver, do not create a neat binary of male and female power. The relationships of gender and power are complicated by factors such as kinship and age. For instance, a mother is more powerful than her sons and commands their obedience and loyalty; an older daughter or sister has the authority to participate in important decisions; and a wife accumulates power as she takes charge of the household and becomes a mother to the next generation. The fiercest competition for power is between the mother-in-law and her daughters-in-law, or among sisters-in-law, making gender solidarity within a multigenerational extended family difficult for women. The competition between brothers over property or other matters sunders the men in the family, too, and alliances are seldom found to run along gender lines. It is almost too facile to think that women qua women, not unlike workers of the world, can unite and eliminate the struggle for power and property.

In such a situation, dowry is an important asset for women. In the late nineteenth and early twentieth centuries, and even today, it is their economic safety net in a setting where women always marry outside their natal villages and where their rights in their natal home lapse when they leave for their marital homes. Dowry is a material resource over which a woman has had at least partial control, and her natal family has viewed it as providing her not only with goods for her use and pleasure but also with recourse in an emergency. In the absence of demands from the groom's family, a bride's dowry is reckoned as purely voluntary and comfortably within the means of her family; it serves as an index of the appreciation bestowed upon a daughter in her natal village, and the ostensible measure of her status in her conjugal village.

These parameters of the custom of dowry emerge with great clarity in the interviews conducted in Punjab villages in the 1870s to codify customary law. . . . None of the reports describes dowry as gifts demanded by the groom's family. Instead, those interviewed described it as a collection of voluntary gifts of clothes, jewelry, household goods, and cash bestowed on the bride by family and friends at the time of the wedding. In forty-nine separate volumes of customary law in an equal number of districts in the vast territory that constituted colonial Punjab—present-day Pakistan and Indian Punjab, Haryana, Jammu, Delhi, and Himachal Pradesh—this definition of dowry was reiterated. Nowhere was it treated as the prerogative of the groom and his family to demand specific consumer goods and large sums of cash for the groom's business, education, or mobility; it was voluntary and depended on the "pecuniary circumstances of the bride's parents." It also turns out that the charge of "improvidence" was not based on the expense for dowry—on what is given to the daughter—but on wedding feast and entertainment expenses for both daughters and sons. These costs were strictly itemized and evaluated in cash for three economic tiers in society and became part of the bureaucrats' handbook for enforcement. Wedding expenses did not mean only those for a daughter; many cases cited as evidence of profligacy in the handbooks refer to the weddings of sons.

Items for each daughter's dowry were, and to a lesser extent still are, accumulated gradually, not just by her immediate family but also by extended kin and friends in a village or urban neighborhood, those who share in an intricate network of reciprocal obligations.[7] Very few items were purchased; most of them were produced at home or received as part of the customary reciprocity prevalent among village families. Clothes, household furnishings, and jewelry were productive assets in terms of status (and jewelry served as collateral for loans); and cows, buffaloes, goats, and even camels, often more valuable than land, were given to daughters as income-generating assets. Cash and property began to play an increasing role in the composition of dowries as land became a marketable commodity in the colonial period and its value rose exponentially. The practical concern of families was to insure for each of their daughters a husband from a comparable family in which her life would be lived and her children would be raised; if there was unforeseen misfortune, the dowry would serve as a safety net. Why then was a strongly spun safety net twisted into a deadly noose?

Female Infanticide

A new historical understanding of the issue emerges when it is seen that as the East India Company "discovered" female infanticide they used this knowledge to further their own political ends by attributing purely traditional cultural reasons for the commission of this crime, which, in fact, had social and economic causes exacerbated by their own policies. The politics of imperial representation are far better understood today than previously, and female infanticide is a superb example to illuminate their workings.

The East India Company, originally chartered in 1600 only to trade, tasted the riches of the subcontinent by wresting the collection of revenue in the conquered province of Bengal from 1765. A century of aggressive empire building culminated in the conquest of the Punjab in 1849 and the annexation of Oudh in 1856. The company needed to make a compelling case to defend its ruthless actions to an increasingly critical Parliament and outraged public in Britain, even as it illegally assumed the substance and power of an imperial state. The development of explanations that described and blamed indigenous culture for some of its own miscalculations or the effects of misrule and greed, and justified its territorial expansion into two-thirds of the subcontinent, was perhaps the most widely deployed stratagem of the company to appease its jealous detractors at home. This stratagem is better known as Britain's "civilizing mission," with Hindu culture as its prime target. It might more aptly be called the state's alibi for its own unjust policies. For sound political reasons, imperial bureaucrats in mid-nineteenth-century Punjab reiterated the alleged causal connection between the expense of marrying a daughter and female infanticide that they had made in Bombay Presidency in the late eighteenth century. Replaying the cultural card, which had acquired a rich patina of moral superiority by the time the British conquered the Punjab in 1849, trumped most anti-imperial compunctions in Victorian England. . . .

The British used the prevalence of dowry as a litmus test for female infanticide; the corollary to this logic was that bride-price receivers must be innocent of the crime. This meant that the crime was noted and condemned only selectively. In 1851, for example, the Sikh Bedis were found guilty of female infanticide. This discovery became political capital for the British, who could retroactively justify the two unsanctioned bloody wars with the Sikhs that had led to the annexation of their rich and fertile kingdom only two years before. In their own estimation, the righteousness of their aggression was further underscored by the fact that Guru Nanak, the founder of the Sikh faith in the fifteenth century, was of the Bedi caste. In the same year, however, and in the course of the same investigation, the British judiciously overlooked the female infanticide prevalent among the Jats (a numerically preponderant agricultural caste that included Sikhs, Hindus, and Muslims), who were the favorite recruits of the British Indian Army and were in fact appreciated by the British for their strong physiques and martial qualities. Their exoneration hinged on a single, simple fact: Jats did not give dowries. On the contrary, they received bride-price for their daughters from the grooms' families. Their daughters worked in the fields, unlike Kshatriya and Brahmin daughters, and so must have been valued, and therefore they could not possibly be eliminated at birth.

The British also indicted dowry and wedding expenses as the main element of the "improvidence" that they claimed was at the root of the undeniable impoverishment of the Indian peasantry in the three decades after 1858, when the East India Company was dissolved and the Crown began its direct rule of India. As mortality from famines grew, the queries became more insistent; imperial officers generated questionnaires and reports to explain the horrifying immiseration of the victims as self-induced. It was simpler to exaggerate and condemn "wasteful" social expenditure—occasional feasts and gift giving, chiefly connected with wedding celebrations and dowry—than to acknowledge that governance by the British had created want among small landowners. . . .

Despite sumptuary regulations passed in 1853, the upward spiral in the costs of marriage in the colonial period continued. . . . Small quantitative changes added up to a big qualitative change. The British reduction or outright abolition of the customary subsidies given to village heads by Hindu, Mughal, and Sikh rulers for the maintenance of the village *chaupal* or guest house, oil lamps, the upkeep of shrines, and payment to itinerant musicians made hospitality offered during weddings more costly for individual families. The inflation that accompanied the steady rise in the price of land stood on their head the old equations of (movable) dowry for the daughters as against (immovable) property, based on virilocality, for the sons. And the increased circulation of cash and an ever-broadening range of consumer goods, chiefly British imports, generated a clamor for these items to be included in dowries.

Creating Property Titles, Erasing Entitlements

The transformation of the basic relationship between peasants and their land and the simultaneous codification of customary law caused much of the infamous indebtedness of the Punjab peasant. These two intertwined events. . . . became central in altering the texture of women's lives, their implicit rights and entitlements in their families as daughters, wives, and widows, by making men the sole proprietors. This in turn transformed the notions of women's wealth, property rights, and dowry. The new notion of peasant proprietorship produced new

perceptions of gendered rights in land, and these were recorded as "customary." Colonial investment in the Punjab in the second half of the nineteenth century, while accomplished at no cost to the British, greatly expanded arable land and agricultural production. By clearing forests and building canals, communications, and railway lines in this fertile grain-producing region, the colonial authorities linked it to a thriving international market. The British extracted wealth from the countryside in the form of heavy taxation and exports of wheat and other raw materials to Europe, but did not consider sharing their own industrial development with a people who were forcibly contributing to Britain's prosperity.

This modernizing effort remained incomplete and inept because of a greater sin of omission: the deliberate suppressing of any indigenous efforts to import modern industry. An honest-intentioned state might have created general prosperity in their empire to match their own, instead of vast pockets of landlessness and unprecedented poverty in the various subregions of the Punjab. A million and a half Punjabis perished in the famine of 1876–1877, even when Punjab did not have the severity of food shortages experienced in Madras. The conflicting interests of modern capitalism and a colonial command economy produced a half baked, deleterious version of capitalism for subsistence farmers and generated enormous social distortions that worked to the detriment of the interests of women. The new political economy with its ambivalent and hobbled capitalism created a deeper imbalance in power relations in the household. . . .

My own investigations and conclusions will make better sense if I clarify the politics of three key terms and their interrelationship on which my arguments rest: culture, imperialism (or colonialism, often used interchangeably to refer to British rule in India), and private property. The first is complicated because imperial officers used the word "culture" with deliberate political intent to create the linked pair of civilized ruler and barbaric Indian subject. In addition, there is the difficulty with what Richard Fox aptly calls "organismic conceptions of culture" (Fox 1985: 10), which render culture as static or structurally unchanging. Fox proposes that culture be viewed as a more historical and dynamic process. What is often taken as a consistent and long-lived cultural pattern, a coherent set of cultural meanings, he explains, is only the momentary and localized product of human action and contest-culture always "is," but it has always just become so. The British, for their part, had a paradoxical view of culture-they continually talked of timeless Hindu or Muslim culture, even though they believed that inferior cultures could evolve into higher ones. In their fascination with the structure of Punjabi castes and tribes, the British airbrushed historical contingency and human agency out of their voluminous descriptions of Punjabi society. Hindu culture-in contradistinction sometimes to Muslim culture but mostly to their own-was judged to be indubitably inferior. It was capricious, cruel, and barbaric, fostering criminal and amoral behavior. Thus cultural or religious motives were imputed for the crime of female infanticide. . . .

Historians of the British Raj are well aware that colonialism (or imperialism) was a continually contested and negotiated set of power relations over time and space. In other words, it would be equally misguided to think of the 250-odd years of British rule in India as an unchanging structure uniformly imposed on the colonized as to construe Hindu culture or tradition as a timeless, frozen entity. Both continually changed in the process of interaction and acculturation.

But most significantly, to understand the changing meanings of dowry and the processes that underwrote the change, it is imperative to comprehend the centerpiece of this triptych—property—also as a *dynamic* category and to understand how rights in land were differently constituted in pre-colonial and colonial times. This profound change, glossed only briefly in studies of women's right to property, is a key element in my analysis of Punjabi women's relationship to land. In the colonial period, their historical customary entitlements to the produce of the land were translated into a lack of titular rights in ownership of the land. . . . With the creation of male individual property rights in land, the British decided to create the individual peasant owner as the centerpiece of their modern revenue policy. What was to be called the *ryotwari* settlement involved giving property titles to the land directly to the peasants (*ryots*) who tilled it. The policy might well have worked as well as its predecessors had the British not clung to two of its components: fixed amounts and inelastic dates for the payment of land revenue, with little room for contingency. These fixities, along with the newly created ability of peasant proprietors, especially those with smallholdings, to alienate their land through mortgage or sale, increased their vulnerability enormously; the government's unrelenting demand for revenue even in a bad year often led to forced alienation.

These new circumstances altered the generally symbiotic relationship between borrower and lender, perhaps even bringing out an unconscionable opportunism in the latter. In pre-colonial times moneylenders had advanced small loans; the object was never to let a debt be paid off entirely, in order to keep the debtor as a permanent client. The new breed of moneylenders, with an appetite for appropriating their debtors' land—the kind of villain who chills our blood as we encounter him in numerous Indian films and fiction—emerged as a scourge of the countryside in these changed circumstances. The critical difference was that land was now a commodity that could be alienated from the original proprietor and auctioned off by the government to recover their arrears of revenue. With his land as collateral and with the value of land rising, the peasant was able to borrow far more than ever before, up to 70 percent of the value of his land; the moneylender was equally eager to lend him far more than he formerly would have, in order to foreclose on the land. The peasant was forced

to borrow in a bad year or a year when the harvest was late, chiefly to pay his taxes on time (rather than for riotous wedding parties or opulent dowries), because the dates and amounts had been clearly stipulated and there was little hope for mercy. Chronic indebtedness became the other side of the coin of prosperity for the vast majority of these small peasant proprietors.

Ironically, the price of land went up in this same period, as monetization of the economy proceeded apace with the building of canals, roads, railways, and market facilities, and as grain prices increased as exports rose. Apart from the colonial government, the grain merchant and the moneylender—not the peasant—benefited most directly from this. The merchants and moneylenders had no need to sustain the traditional symbiotic relationship with their peasant debtors; they now foreclosed on the mortgaged property as quickly as possible and hired the dispossessed proprietor as an ill-paid, wage-earning day laborer. The corollary to this was that indebtedness generated pressure to deploy women's resources—jewelry or cash—to rescue or enhance a family's holdings within the first score years of the ryotwari settlement, when approximately 40 percent of the traditional peasantry lost their lands.

Putting landed property in male hands exclusively, and holding the males responsible for payment of revenue had the effect of creating the Indian male as the dominant legal subject; this happened throughout British India and even in the independent princely states. The effects could be disastrous in the lives of women. When marital conflicts, a husband's violence, or drunkenness destroyed their marriages, the women were left landless with no legal entitlement to the land their husband or father-in-law owned. Meanwhile, their dowry might well have been spent on the husband's family's holdings. This created the very problem that has engaged feminist scholarship and activism from the late nineteenth century onward: the fight for women's rights to property.

The "masculinization" of the economy was one factor that made male children ever more desirable. In addition, the effects of recruiting the British Indian Army heavily from the ranks of Punjabi peasants, particularly the land-tilling Jats, generated a demand for strong young men who would be employed with a cash wage, awards of land, and eventually pensions. To achieve a "gender-targeted family" became vital, and in those medically primitive days it could only be done through selective female infanticide (DasGupta 1987). . . .

The Preference for Sons

The key to understanding the prejudice against women is to focus on reasons for the preference for sons. . . .

Sons were the key to survival and prosperity in the relentlessly agrarian Punjab under the British. Acquiring land during auctions or sales, finding a jobs in the lower rungs of the imperial bureaucracy or the army, or finding a niche as a retailer in the expanding market were the new plums to fight over. The newly enhanced worth of sons with such prospects came to be reflected in the confidence of some families in demanding a consideration for a marriage alliance: specific amounts of cash (sometimes to recover the cost of the education that had qualified the groom for these jobs), jewelry, or expensive consumer durables. The competition for the best-qualified and best-employed grooms within an endogamous group was fierce—for there were but a tiny number of eligible males with proper employment or economic security—and mothers of daughters knew that a good dowry was now the net to secure "the catch." The idea that a groom's family could make demands slowly infiltrated other traditional gift-giving occasions reserved by parents for their married daughters and their children. This trend, which started in the colonial period, has steadily worsened, even occasioning violence: the suicides of prospective brides to save their parents from the expense and humiliation of such alliances, and the burning to death of wives whose dowries did not meet expectations. Such perverse transactions are unfairly perceived as "dowry problems"; it would be far more accurate to think of these shameless and amoral demands as "groom price." But they came to be countenanced in a world where the relationship of power and gender had been radically reordered.

The strategic and moral imperative for peasant and warrior families in pre-colonial times was not dictated by culture or religion but by the existential needs to reproduce the ideal family to defend their lands and their rulers, to subsist, to seek opportunities for advancement, and for economic security in old age through the labor of sons. Male children were critical to the prolonged well-being of the family; sons were future soldiers and farmers of the soil to which they belonged. Daughters also worked, but their crucial role as reproducers obliged them to marry at puberty and move to the village of their husbands, where they would "plan" their own families, again engineering the survival of fewer daughters than sons. Virilocal marriages cemented communities and far-flung villages in defensive political alliances. Both sexes were needed, but the struggle was to achieve the unnatural but logical mix of several more sons than daughters. Nature played an evenhanded role by holding "normal" birth ratios at 104 males to a 100 females, but endowing female infants with greater resilience against disease. Selective female infanticide then (and to a lesser extent now) was the only available method, albeit primitive and cruel, of achieving a *deliberately planned* family—with the numbers of sons and daughters appropriate for survival in a region plagued by continual political conflict. Philip Oldenburg (1992) finds an interesting correlation between the overall murder rate and high masculine sex ratios in north India, which bolsters my own argument that the preference for sons in the Punjab was related to its being a war zone and a popular recruiting ground for soldiers. The defense of land, rather than its tilling, made the presence of a strong defenders critical to the survival of the community.

The pre-colonial logic for female infanticide was to be unwittingly strengthened by imperial revenue and land-ownership policies, even as the British outlawed the practice in 1870 and charged heavy fines and imprisonment as penalties against its perpetrators. Their remedial measures to curb infanticide focused on apprehending culprits (including the surveillance of "infanticidal tribes" at their own cost), passing sumptuary laws to restrict dowries and expenditure at weddings, and imposing penalties such as fines and imprisonment. The British never found it worthwhile to examine the social effects of their own methods of governance and development that produced the milieu in which sons became even more preferred and dowry gradually acquired the very characteristics that the British purported to reform. Despite the legislation against infanticide, colonial policies gradually worsened the already adverse sex ratios over this past century. . . .

Violence against women is universal, and perhaps timeless, but much can be done to reduce its frequency and severity by reorienting the legal universe to address economic and social inequities founded on sex and gender, and let culture adjust to the new realities. The modern secular democratic Indian state, though worlds apart from its imperial forbear, is slowly acknowledging its duty to balance the ledger where women have always been in the debit column.

The Decline of the Western Family: A Review of the Evidence

William R. Garrett

There has been considerable debate over the past few decades about the fate of the "typical" Western family of husband, wife, and children. This somewhat heated discussion began with the "counter-culture" sixties and its association with such phenomena as higher divorce rates, declining family size, and an increase in the number of women working outside the home.

The debate has had serious political repercussions as some of our nation's leaders have called for a return to "family values" and for stringent welfare reform as a way of rolling back the tide of what they perceive as an overly permissive society. All of the nation's major ills, such as crime, drug addiction, and poverty can be traced, they claim, to the weakening of the family structure.

Have our values really changed that much? Does the higher divorce rate reflect a more casual attitude toward the institution of marriage? Or does the fact that the overwhelming majority of people who get a divorce turn around and re-marry mean that they value the institution of marriage as much as ever? Does the fact that the family is shrinking in size mean that it is disappearing? Or does the smaller family today serve a different set of functions than those of an earlier day?

With the advantage of hindsight and decades of solid research, William R. Garrett answers these questions and more. Yes, the Western familial institution has been undergoing significant changes in form and function, but, to paraphrase Mark Twain, its death has been greatly exaggerated.

William R. Garrett is a Professor of Sociology at St. Michael's College in Colchester, Vermont. He received an Mdiv. at the Divinity School of Yale University and a Ph.D. in the Sociology of Religion from Drew University. He is the author of *Seasons of Marriage and Family Life* (1982), the editor of *Social Consequences of Religious Belief* (1989), and co-editor (with Roland Robertson) of *Religion and Global Order* (1991), in addition to having written many papers, book chapters, and journal articles. He has served as president of the Association for the Sociology of Religion and he is an ordained Baptist minister.

Key Concept: why people divorce

Several majors items comprise the catalogue of problem areas wherein family life is allegedly failing nowadays. Among the central issues may be enumerated the following: (1) the rising divorce rate; (2) the sexual revolution and increase in illegitimacy; (3) the decline of family size; (4) the loss of family functions; (5) the generation gap; and (6) the growth in the number of women working outside the home. We shall attend to each of these putative problem areas *seriatim*.

Divorce

Clearly no issue has troubled defenders of the family more vigorously than the rising divorce rate in Western societies, especially since the mid-1960s. The knee-jerk reaction to this phenomenon normally entails the conclusion that if the divorce rate is going up, then the quality of family life must be declining proportionately. This is one of those occasions, however, when sociologists like to point out that empirical data are not self-interpreting. One simply cannot read the health of the marital/familial institutions off of the "raw" divorce rate. Traditional, patriarchal societies typically exhibited a very low divorce rate, but this was not necessarily because a harmonious relationship prevailed between husband and wife. Rather, in traditional family contexts where marriages were arranged, a woman's family was paid a "bride-price," and divorce constituted a considerable financial loss to the groom's family. Indeed, C. K. Yang (1965: 81) reminds us that in classical China there was an old adage which advised wives that when marital life became intolerable "Good women should hang themselves, only bad women seek divorce." Surely most modern folk would agree that divorce is preferable to suicide as a means of exiting unhappy marriages. And it should be equally clear that a low divorce rate does not necessarily mean that wholesome marriages prevail in a given social order (Goode, 1993: 319–320). Accordingly, the *meaning* of the divorce rate must be extrapolated from the raw figures which only indicate what percentage of marriages are likely to end in dissolution.

There is widespread agreement among social scientific students of the family that for marriages contracted in the 1980s and thereafter in the United States the divorce rate will be approximately fifty percent (Ihinger-Tallman and Pasley, 1987:36). This figure is up from roughly twenty-five percent at the end of the decade of the 1950s (Mintz and Kellogg, 1988:178; National Center for Health Statistics, 1990:4). Although the United States continues to manifest the highest official divorce rate among the industrialized nations, other first world countries have experienced a spiraling divorce rate over the last-quarter century as well—with some evidencing a faster rate of growth than in the United States. A few modernized societies, however, have gone against the trend to retain relatively low divorce rates, notably Japan, Italy, and Israel (White, 1990:904). . . .

A number of social background factors correlate strongly with the tendency to divorce, apart from the more obvious causes such as infidelity, drug or alcohol abuse, physical/mental violence directed against either a spouse or children (Gelles and Cornell, 1985), and sexual abuse of children (Crewdson, 1988). Age at first marriage is one of the more important factors, especially for couples who marry before they enter their twenties. Teenage marriages are disproportionately likely to end in divorce because they frequently involve premarital pregnancies, immediate financial problems since schooling for a well-paying job has not been completed, and psychological immaturity (Bane, 1976: 32). (100)

The most significant factor correlated with the tendency to divorce is a difference between spouses relative to their racial and ethnic backgrounds (Tucker and Mitchell-Kernan, 1990). Black/White married couples have considerably higher rates of divorce than Asian/White or Native American/White marriages (Glick, 1990: 123–124). The high dissolution rates of interracial—and especially Black/White—couples clearly reflect the lingering effects of racial prejudice which makes marital adjustments all that much more difficult. (79)

Other factors include the presence of children—childless couples proportionately divorce more frequently than couples with children. This does not mean that children hold marriages together, but that couples typically do not begin the procreation process until they are reasonably sure that their marriage will endure. Religious affiliation also tends to reduce the tendency to divorce—no doubt because believers tend to take seriously the teachings of their religious communities pertaining to the importance

of fidelity to marital vows (Larson and Goltz, 1989). Social class standing also influences the tendency to dissolve a marriage, with lower class members exhibiting higher divorce rates than those in the higher classes (Martin and Bumpass, 1989). This is due, in large part, to the fact that lower status persons experience more social problems and have fewer social skills to deal with them effectively. (135)

And finally, marriage disruption is also correlated with the employment of wives. Women who work outside the home have higher divorce rates than those who are fulltime homemakers. The relationship between these two variables is somewhat more complex than it first appears, however, and causality is difficult to establish. Some students of the family suggest that women with their own source of income attain more independence and do not have to remain in an unhappy marriage. It may also be the case that the likelihood of divorce represents a major impetus impelling women into the labor force—since when divorce occurs the first thing a woman needs is a source of income. Also, as the income potential of women increases, the probability of divorce decreases (Greenstein , 1990), a fact which some interpret as signifying that when women contribute very significantly to the total family income, then husbands are more reluctant to engage in behaviors that would alienate the affections of their working wives. (162)

The composite of these several background factors which contribute to the likelihood of marital dissolution suggests this axiomatic conclusion, namely, that the more the backgrounds of a husband and wife diverge, then the more difficult it will be for the marriage to be sustained intact. With this insight, we are in a position to dispel at least a portion of that interpretive mystery which surrounds the whole matter of divorce. To achieve this end, we need to begin with the what has emerged in recent decades as the most highly valued feature of marriage by spouses, namely, the development of a companionate relationship in marriage (Skolnick, 1991: 146).

The importance of companionship was first demonstrated in research undertaken by Blood and Wolfe (1965) who discovered that spouses ranked companionship more important than love, sex, children, or even money as the most valued aspect of marriage. Companionship embraced such elements as emotional support, intimacy, the development of a common biography, and self-fulfillment. Marriage became after the 1960s that place where one cultivated the most important relationship one expected to experience in life. In the intimate relationship with one's spouse, a person finds a haven from the tensions and pressures of normal social interaction. The security of the companionate relationship allows a spouse the freedom to express one's feelings, dreams, fears, and hopes without fear of being penalized and in full knowledge that one's spouse will lend a sympathetic ear and be an understanding friend (Garrett, 1982: 302–303).

The nurturing of a companionate relationship takes a number of years to bring to fruition, of course, and couples are not always successful in achieving this ideal in marriage. What now appears to be occurring is that couples who do not develop a companionate relationship are more and more willing to seek a divorce, reenter the marriage market and try to find someone with whom they can develop a companionate marriage. Not only does this serve as an index of how important companionship is to contemporary marriage partners, but it also signifies a deep-rooted commitment to a high-quality marriage. If spouses cared less about marriage as an institution, therefore, they would be more willing to remain within unhappy unions. Ironically, then, the conclusion appears intractable that the relatively high divorce rate in Western societies is sustained in no small part by a commitment to a fully satisfying, companionate marriage. And another conclusion also follows indisputably, namely, that if the divorce rate could be lowered, then it would almost certainly be occasioned by a significant rise in the rate of marital dissatisfaction. One can question whether it makes good policy sense to attempt to lower the divorce rate at the cost of increasing marital unhappiness.

Corroborating evidence for the cogency of the interpretation of divorce being developed here derives in part from the remarriage rate. While the divorce rate was doubling during the period from 1960 to 1980, the remarriage rate after divorce increased at almost the same ratio. As Cherlin (1981: 28) has pointed out, almost five out of six men and three out of four women remarry after divorce. These data indicate that persons who divorce have not given up on marriage; they have simply given up on the particular partner to whom they were married. Or, as Spanier and Thompson (1987: 17) have observed: "Divorce is a response to a failing marriage, not a failing institution. The family system can remain strong while divorce rates remain high." . . .

The Sexual Revolution and the Increase in Illegitimacy

In the mid-1960s, the industrial nations of the West experienced a sexual revolution, evidenced by a sudden escalation in the rates of premarital sexual activity and a corresponding upsurge in the illegitimacy rate (Shorter, 1977). This was not the first sexual revolution in America—the first occurred during the "roaring twenties"—but through the depression, World War II, and the 1950s the rate of premarital sexual activity increased only gradually (Coontz, 1992: 193–196). Not only did premarital sexual activity dramatically increase with the emergence of the counterculture in the sixties, but other features related to sexuality also emerged with rising rates of cohabitation, gay liberation, and more explicit sexual themes openly presented in movies, novels, magazines, television, and advertising. . . .

The increase in illegitimate births has occasioned more outbursts of alarm than virtually any other by-product of the sexual revolution. Much of this discussion, especially in the op-ed pages of the newspaper, has not evidenced a very penetrating understanding of the phenomenon. The usual assumption is that the sexual revolution, along with the ready availability of the pill and other modern forms of contraception, largely produced this rise in illegitimacy. The evidence does not neatly support this interpretation. For example, Sweden has the highest rates of adolescent sexual activity in the industrialized world—while adolescents in the United States, England, France, and the Netherlands are comparable in their lower rates of sexual activity. However, the rates of teenage pregnancy are considerably higher for adolescents in the United States than in European nations (Voydanoff and Donnelly, 1990: 11–14). Moreover, most sexually active young teens are startlingly unaware of their own biological processes, sexual drives, and the means to prevent conception—a fact that should alert conservative religionists that eliminating sex education courses is almost certainly to be profoundly counterproductive (Coontz, 1992: 203). And since the growth among adolescent pregnancies has occurred among women of lower socioeconomic status with relatively poor life prospects, they are not women whose behavior has been influenced by feminist ideology. Furthermore, the rate of illegitimate births is considerably higher in the United States for Black women than Hispanics or Whites—in 1985, 60 percent of all Black births, 28 percent of Hispanic births, and 14.5 percent of White births were to unmarried mothers (Zill and Rogers, 1988: 39).

Several features stand out prominently in these data. The first is that the rise of illegitimate births has occurred disproportionately among members of the underclass, and especially the Black underclass. Moreover, while teenage out of wedlock births have stabilized since the 1980s (Voydanoff and Donnelly, 1990:15), they continue to rise in percentage terms since the overall birthrate has declined during that time. Perhaps the most serious cause for concern, however, pertains to the unraveling of the social safety net in the United States since 1980. Consequently, fewer social services—from housing to food, medical care, welfare supplements, and educational opportunities—are available to an increasing segment of the population. Other European nations continue to provide a much more viable safety net than is available in the United States (Kahn and Kamerman, 1977), and the gap between need and availability of resources will almost certainly widen in America if the proposed changes of the current Republican majority are enacted. For the tangle of pathology which poverty imposes on those trapped within it will simply foster greater impoverishment for a larger segment of the lower class population should social services be reduced even further?

The Decline in the Birth Rate

Modernization has everywhere been accompanied by a substantial decline in the fertility rate of industrializing societies. Commentators worried about the decline of the family cite this fact as evidence for the disenchantment of modern couples with family life, for if family life were still held in high esteem—so this litany runs—then spouses would also want to bring children into the union. Both survey data and actual behavior points to a quite different interpretation than that propounded by observers pessimistic about the family's prospects. . . .

While the commitment to procreation has not declined substantially over recent decades, the desired number of children has fallen quite significantly. A variety of reasons account for the declining birth rate in all Western societies. Certainly, one of the most compelling reasons is the sheer economic cost of children. Whereas during the nineteenth century, children were an economic asset—as they still are in many developing countries—by the mid-twentieth century children were becoming more economically costly and emotionally valuable (Zelizer, 1985). The financial burden of raising a child from birth through four years of public higher education now runs around $175,000—and this only includes direct and indirect maintenance costs; it does not include lost income if one parent leaves the labor force to provide in-home childcare. In light of these figures, it is not surprising that fertility rates have fallen to or below zero population growth (which is 2.2 children per husband-wife unit) in most Western societies (Goode, 1993: 34).

The accelerating cost of having children is only one explanation for why the fertility rate is dropping so sharply in industrialized societies, however, and it is apparently not even the most significant reason. Numerous studies have also revealed that parents more and more regard children as emotionally valuable and that, as a consequence, they are willing to invest considerably more time and psychological energy in nurturing their offspring (Zelizer, 1985). With large families of five, six, or more children, it would simply be impossible to allocate both emotional and time resources on a scale parents now regard as appropriate. Thus, we are currently witnessing the continuation of what Blood and Wolfe (1965: 121) described some time ago as a shift "... from quantity to quality with respect to children."

In sum, then, the decline of family size reflects neither a disenchantment with family life nor a preference for childless marriages, but a practical adjustment to the inevitable limits of time, money, and emotional resources insofar as childrearing is concerned. (Curiously, world population pressures do not seem to have played a very significant role in fertility decisions among members of Western nations, since they are already near or below zero population growth.) Moreover, just as Western societies manifested the trend toward smaller family size, there emerged a countervailing trend toward valuing children as emotionally "priceless," Unfortunately, the heightened valuation of children in private families has not carried over into the collective realm to counteract indifference to children's needs and more effective child welfare policies, especially in the United States (Sidel, 1992).

The Loss of Family Functions

There once was a time when the family was, in the words of John Demos (1971), "a little commonwealth," by which he meant that the family performed a whole variety of functions of an economic, governmental, welfare, educational, social control, and religious character. Prior to the modern age, the family was, in effect, a miniature society. Nowadays many of these functions have been transferred to other social institutions. For example, industrialization occasioned the separation of the domicile from the workplace; monetary loans more often come now from banks or other lending institutions rather than family members; the care of the elderly has shifted to a very great extent to governmental agencies; most education—even in practical skills such as driving a car, home economics skills, and manual skills in home maintenance and repair, and even the transmission of knowledge relative to sexual matters—now takes place outside the home, and frequently in the schools; social control over the behavior of offspring is now a largely shared function with school officials and local police forces; and religious institutions have assumed major responsibility for training young persons in the basic tenets of the faith.

The wholesale transfer of functions from the family to other institutions has prompted some commentators to conclude that the family has, perforce, become less important as a consequence of its reduced social responsibilities. Talcott Parsons (1955:9–10) cogently argued some time ago, however, that the loss of family functions does not represent a decline of the family in a general sense, but rather it has facilitated the emergence of a new family form wherein this institution has now become, at once, more specialized and more proficient.

Specialization has taken place in two discrete but crucial areas, namely, the socialization of children and the stabilization of adult personalities through the cultivation of a companionate relationship between spouses. While socialization has long been a function of the family, there is a mounting body of data suggesting that parents are intensifying their efforts and consciously honing their skills in this area (Johnson, 1988: 261–265). Indeed, one notable sphere of change has surrounded the role of fatherhood. Male parenting has taken on renewed significance of late, perhaps in response to feminist critiques of the manner in which fathers typically were performing. Most fathers regarded their breadwinning function as their most important contribution to their children, but today for more and more fathers the emphasis is shifting toward nurturing as an equally important function (Griswold, 1993: 249–250).

A renewal of commitment to the companionate ideal has also figured prominently in the expectations of spouses in recent years (Skolnick, 1991: 191–196). Some students of family life have, in fact, posed the question of whether expectations have been ratcheted so high that few men, in particular, are now able to meet them, given the historic difficulty of men to engage in expressive behaviors. Nevertheless, it is clear that the companionate ideal has enlarged its sphere of influence by spreading from the white collar into the working class in recent decades. The experience of many working class women is expressed in this statement given to Lillian Rubin (1976: 93) when one informant declared relative to her husband, "I guess I can't complain. He's a steady worker; he doesn't drink; he doesn't hit me." But subsequent interviews revealed that this woman was not satisfied with having met these minimal conditions in marriage based on expectations from her former lower-class background; she wanted in addition what many middle-class women typically experienced, namely, a relationship of sharing, companionship, and emotional intimacy. . . .

The Generation Gap

When Christopher Lasch (1979b: xx) observed that "...the family has been slowly coming apart for more than a hundred years. The divorce crisis, feminism, and the revolt of youth originated in the nineteenth century, and they have been the subject of controversy ever since," it is interesting to note that conflict between the generations figured prominently in what he perceived as one of the crucial ills of modern family life. The generation gap, as such, however, was not usually singled out for special attention until after the counterculture revolution in the mid-1960s. Unfortunately, the precise nomenclature, generation gap, was popularized by journalists before it was empirically tested by social scientists. The concept pointed to a putative widening gap between parents and their children on such matters as basic values, political attitudes, sexual norms, and aesthetic tastes. When the data were finally in, what they revealed was that a gap existed, but it was less often between generations than between social classes and liberal/conservative constituencies. . . .

On issues pertaining to equality for racial, ethnic, class, and gender groups; the search for self-fulfillment; and the expansion of the scope of discretionary individual behaviors, the counterculture challenged the staid conservative culture of the 1950s, while it also ushered in a more liberal perspective which many parents and societal authorities in Western nations could heartily embrace. Thus, the youth peer culture has enjoyed a variegated relationship with members of the adult world—with some aspects of the peer culture eliciting adult approval and other features triggering harsh condemnation (Yinger, 1982: 285–288).

Clearly, not all the issues bound up in the larger counterculture revolution have yet been resolved. For example, Christopher Lasch (1979a) soundly condemned the search for self-fulfillment promoted by counterculture participants as an exercise in banal narcissism, self-indulgence, materialism, and intellectual erosion, while, several years later, Robert Wuthnow (1991) gathered data which showed that members of the "me generation" in pursuit of self-fulfillment actually found it through vigorous and widespread participation in altruistic activities, volunteer and charity work. The discovery that the search for self-fulfillment had in fact manifested itself in altruistic behavior to the extent that some 45 percent of adult Americans contributed over twenty billion hours of service to their communities per year suggests at the very least that some values carried by the counterculture have managed to produce profoundly constructive consequences. To be sure, this high rate of altruism cannot be wholly attributed to countercultural influences, but a significant portion of compassionate Americans were products of counterculture social movements and deeply influenced by its value perspectives.

Women in the Labor Force

Since at least the 1950s, scholars have expressed concern over women's labor force participation, fearing that women employed outside the home would (1) leave the family nest unattended and (2) encounter more opportunities for entering into romantic relationships that could jeopardize marriage (Parsons, 1955; Shorter, 1977). Moreover, we have known for some time that trends in the rates of marital disruption and women's labor force participation have generally moved upward in unison during the post-World War II era (South and Lloyd, 1995: 33). What has not been clear, however, is how these two variables are interrelated. An attempt to weave together a coherent interpretation of the interaction of the two variables will be undertaken after baseline data on female employment is reviewed.

By 1985, 61 percent of all married women with a husband present in the household worked outside the home. Women with children under age six were slightly less likely to be employed (53.7 percent) than women with children between the ages of 6 to 17 (68.1 percent) (Voydanoff, 1987: 24). These rates are somewhat higher than those for other European nations, with the exception of Sweden. For example, from 1966 to 1986, the percentage of women aged 15 to 64 who were employed increased by 20 percent in the United States, compared to roughly 11 percent in Britain, only 2 percent in West Germany, and 3 percent in Austria (from 1970 to 1986) (Davis and Robinson, 1991: 82–83). In Sweden, the number of women in the labor force is only 4 percent less than that of men—giving Sweden by far the highest rate of female labor force participation of any Western society (Casper, McLanahan, and Garfinkel, 1994:600).

Assessing the meaning of these data in relation to the rising divorce rate since the 1960s is considerably more complex a task than simply reporting them. Patricia Voydanoff (1987: 46) flatly declares that "(t)here is no consistent body of evidence indicating that wife employment is associated with divorce." This, she continues, is due to the operation of two counteracting processes, variously labeled the "independence effect" and the "income effect."

The "independence effect" entails the following argument: for members of a dual-earner family, divorce is less difficult. Historically, many men have been held in their marriages by the responsibility to provide for their wives' financial dependence. When a wife works, this responsibility is no longer felt as keenly and men in unhappy marriages are much more likely to seek divorce. Similarly, women who are financially independent are more likely to terminate an unhappy union. Thus, we have a situation in which "...people are dissatisfied with their particular marriage partners, unafraid of leaving them, and willing to try again (Matthaei, 1982: 311).

Andrew Cherlin (1981: 53–54) describes an alternative scenario that has come to be known as the "income effect." In this instance, the earnings a wife brings home could ease the financial tension experienced by a family unit and thereby reduce the likelihood of marital dissolution. Moreover, a wife's earnings may well make her more desirable as a marriage partner and a husband less willing to consider divorce, since this action would result in a substantial decline in the family's income (Voydanoff, 1987: 46). Employed wives with high levels of education who are working out of choice and who receive both support and approval from their husbands have notably higher levels of marital satisfaction than women who are homemakers (Voydanoff, 1987: 47). And higher marital satisfaction translates into a lower likelihood of marriage dissolution.

A more disconcerting argument has recently been developed which suggests another interpretation to the conundrum of the relationship between working women and the probability of divorce. The first stage of this alternative account was developed by Norval Glenn (1991), who proposed that something new may have entered into the outlook of couples nowadays, namely, that the commitment to marital permanence has declined rather substantially. The upshot is that, while partners are still marrying, they are not leaving the marriage market. Accordingly, if they find a more attractive marriage prospect, then they are less hesitant nowadays to divorce their present spouse and remarry the more desirable person.

Evidence partially in support of this interpretation has recently been provided by South and Lloyd (1995) who found a positive association between an area's unmarried female labor force participation rate and martial dissolution. Specifically, they discovered that when there was a large pool of young women in the labor force in a particular region, then there was an increased probability that men will find a more attractive alternative to their current wife. Moreover, this is especially the case where the marriage market is set within a social climate that is increasingly tolerant of divorce, where skepticism abounds about the permanence of marriage, when even married persons tentatively remain within the marriage market, and when there is the opportunity afforded at work for men and women to encounter a more attractive mate than their present spouse (South and Lloyd, 1995: 33).

The ambiguity of these various research findings makes it impossible to render a definitive account of the relationship between working women and the divorce rate. The best that can be said, perhaps, is that working women may well increase the probability of subsequent marital instability, but there are also other benefits to family living derived from women's increasing participation in the labor force which may outweigh the putative risks. This appears to be the case, primarily, in those instances where women work by choice, enjoy interesting jobs, are well-paid, and have the support of their husbands. On this issue, however, considerably more research will have to be undertaken before we can rise above the level of conjecture and hypothesis and propound a more definitive account of the relationship between working women and family stability.

Conclusion: The Status of the Western Family

Several observations are warranted in light of this relatively swift review of the evidence in support of the decline-of-the-Western-family thesis. Perhaps the most obvious is that the marriage and family systems in the West have experienced considerable social change and transformation over the last four decades or so. Family forms are much more pluralistic today than ever before in Western history. Change does not automatically mean the decline of the family system, however, since what we may be witnessing is what Talcott Parsons (1955:4) long ago termed the "disorganization of transition." Indeed, one subplot to this survey has been to demonstrate that assessing the meaning of trends relative to family matters is a complicated process which entails teasing out the implications of various forms of data rather than simply jumping to hasty conclusions.

What, then, shall we say about the status of the contemporary Western family? At the risk of appearing naively optimistic, the sociological data facilitate the interpretation that the Western family is remarkably stable, given the sorts of changes with which it has had to cope over the last forty years or so. This judgment is based on the fact that none of the alleged problems confronting the family appear to have undermined its essential stability and proficiency. The rising divorce rate is not *ipso facto* an indication of familial decline. Indeed, as we suggested above, to a large extent, the high divorce rate is a function of the Western commitment to high quality marriages. Similarly, the sexual revolution, with its associated rise in the illegitimacy rate, the declining birth rate, the loss of family functions, and the generation gap are all symptoms of change, but not necessarily of decline or decay. Many of these changes have, in fact, made the family stronger and more specialized in the performance of its central functions. The increase in the number of working women poses a somewhat more complex interpretative problem. The data with respect to this issue are somewhat more mixed in comparison to other analytical areas. My own hunch is that subsequent data will reveal that working women enhance the quality of the marital experience—in part through their own increased levels of personal fulfillment and in part through the added resources which they are able to bring to family life. The collective import of the trends surveyed in this analysis, then, tends to suggest that the Western familial institution is not in danger of social disintegration anytime soon. If this is the case, then how do we account for the numerous expressions of concern over the health and stability attending marriage and family life in the West? The answer to this question is a kind of Catch-22. That is to say, so long as societal members worry over the decline of the family, we may be fairly well assured that the family is in reasonably good shape. And conversely, when members of Western societies stop feeling concerned about the quality of their family life, then decline will probably already have begun in earnest.

References

Arendell Terry, 1986. *Mothers and Divorce*. Berkeley, CA: University of California Press.

Bane Mary Jo, 1976. *Here to Stay: American Families in the Twentieth Century*. New York: Basic Books.

Berger Brigitte and Peter L. Berger, 1984. *The War Over the Family*. Garden City, NY.: Anchor Books.

Birnbaum Jeffrey H., 1995. "The Gospel According to Ralph." *Time*. 145:20:28-35.

Blood Robert O., Jr., and Donald M. Wolfe, 1965. *Husbands Wives: The Dynamics of Married Living*. New York: Free Press.

Casper Lynne M., Sara S. McLanahan, and Irwin Garfinkel, 1994. "The Gender-Poverty Gap: What We Can Learn From Other Countries." *American Sociological Review*. 59:4:594–605.

Cherlin Andrew J., 1981. *Marriage, Divorce, Remarriage*. Cambridge, MA: Harvard University Press.

Coontz Stephanie, 1992. *The Way We Never Were: American Families and the Nostalgia Trap*. New York: Basic Books.

Crewdson John, 1988. *By Silence Betrayed*. New York: Harper & Row, Publishers.

Houseknecht Sharon K., 1987. *Voluntary Childlessness*. In Marvin B. Sussman and Suzanne K. Steinmetz, eds., *Handbook of Marriage and the Family*. New York: Plenum Press.

Hunt Morton, 1974. *Sexual Behavior in the Seventies*. Chicago: Playboy Press.

Hunter James Davidson, 1991. *Culture Wars*. New York: Basic Books.

Johnson Miriam M., 1988. *Strong Mothers. Weak Wives*. Berkeley, CA: University of California Press.

King Karl, Jack O. Balswick, and Ira E. Robinson, 1977. "The Continuing Premarital Sexual Revolution Among College Females." *Journal of Marriage and the Family*. 39:455–459.

Ihinger-Tallman Marilyn, and Kay Pasley, 1987. *Remarriage*. Newbury Park, CA: Sage Publications.

Kahn Alfred J., and Sheilia B. Kamerman, 1977. *Not for the Poor Alone: European Social Services*. New York: Harper.

Larson Lyle E., and Walter Goltz, 1989. "Religious Participation and Marital Commitment." *Review of Religious Research*. 30:4: 387–400.

LaRossa Ralph, 1986. *Becoming a Parent*. Newbury Park, CA: Sage Publications.

Lasch Christopher, 1979a. *The Culture of Narcissism*. New York: Warner Books.

Lasch Christopher, 1979b. *Haven in a Heartless World: The Family Besieged*. New York: Basic Books.

Martin Teresa Castro, and Larry Bumpass, 1989. "Recent Trends in Marital Disruption." *Demography*. 26:37–51.

Matthaei Julie A., 1982. *An Economic History of Women in America*. New York: Schocken Books.

Mintz Steven, and Susan Kellogg, 1988. *Domestic Revolutions: A Social History of American Family Life*. New York: Free Press.

Murray Charles, 1993. "The Coming White Underclass." *The Wall Street Journal*. October 29.

Murstein Bernard I., 1986. *Paths to Marriage*. Newbury Park, CA: Sage Publications.

National Center for Health Statistics, 1990. "Births, Marriages, Divorces, and Deaths for June 1990." *Monthly Vital Statistics Report*. Hyattsville, MD: Public Health Service.

Parsons Talcott, 1955. *Family, Socialization and Interaction Process*. New York: Free Press.

Popenoe David, 1987. "Beyond the Nuclear Family: A Statistical Portrait of the Changing Family in Sweden." *Journal of Marriage and the Family*. 49:1:173–183.

Riley Glenda, 1991. *Divorce: An American Tradition*. New York: Oxford University Press.

Shorter Edward, 1977. *The Making of the Modern Family*. New York: Basic Books.

Sidel Ruth, 1992. *Women and Children Last: The Plight of Poor Women in Affluent America*. New York: Penguin Books.

Skolnick Arlene, 1991. *Embattled Paradise: The American Family in Age of Uncertainty*. New York: Basic Books.

South Scott J., and Kim M. Lloyd, 1995. "Spousal Alternatives and Marital Dissolution." *American Sociological Review*. 60:1:21–35.

Spanier Graham B., and Linda Thompson, 1987. *Parting: The Aftermath of Separation and Divorce*. Updated Edition. Newbury Park, CA: Sage Publications.

Tucker M. Belinda, and Claudia Mitchell-Kernan, 1990. "New Trends in Black American Interracial Marriages: The Social Structural Context." *Journal of Marriage and the Family*. 52:1: 209–218.

Voydanoff Patricia, 1987. *Work and Family Life*. Newbury Park, CA: Sage Publications.

Voydanoff Patricia, and Brenda W. Donnellly, 1990. *Adolescent Sexuality and Pregnancy*. Newbury Park, CA: Sage Publications.

Weitzman Lenore J., 1985. *The Divorce Revolution*. New York: Free Press.

White Lynn K., 1990. "Determinants of Divorce: A Review of Research in the Eighties." *Journal of Marriage and the Family*. 52:4:904–912.

Wright Gerald C., and Dorothy M. Stetson, 1978. "The Impact of No-Fault Divorce Law Reform on Divorce in American States." *Journal of Marriage and the Family*. 40:575–580.

Wuthnow Robert, 1991. *Acts of Compassion: Caring for Others and Helping Ourselves*. Princeton, NJ.: Princeton University Press.

Yankelovich Daniel, 1974. *The New Morality: A Profile of American Youth in the 70s*. New York: McGraw-Hill.

Yinger J. Milton, 1982. *Countercultures*. New York: Free Press.

Zelizer Viviana A., 1985. *Pricing the Priceless Child*. New York: Basic Books.

Zill Nicholas, and Carolyn C. Rogers, 1988. *Recent Trends in the Well-Being of Children in the United States and Their Implications for Public Policy*. pp. 31–115 in Andrew J. Cherlin, ed., *The Changing American Family and Public Policy*. Washington, DC.: The Urban Institute Press.

Magic, Religion, and Witchcraft

Selection 22

ABRAM KARDINER AND EDWARD PREBLE, from "Edward Tylor: Mr. Tylor's Science," *They Studied Man*

Selection 23

BRONISLAW MALINOWSKI, from "Essay I," *Magic, Science and Religion: And Other Essays*

Selection 24

E.E. EVANS-PRITCHARD, from "Witchcraft Explains Unfortunate Events," *Reader in Comparative Religion*

Edward Tylor: Mr. Tylor's Science

Abram Kardiner and Edward Preble

Although he never received a formal education in anthropology, Edward Tylor (1832–1917) spent a year of his youth in Mexico doing archeological fieldwork and making cultural observations under the guidance of Henry Christy, a noted businessman-turned-archeologist/ethnologist. Tylor's early publications, including *Anahuac* (1861), an account of the Mexican expedition and *Researches in the Early History of Mankind* (1865), immediately established him as a leading figure in anthropology. He was eventually to take a teaching position at Oxford University from where he would send many fieldworkers out to various parts of the world to collect ethnographic information. In his most widely read book, *Primitive Culture: Researches into the Development of Mythology*, *Philosophy, Religion, Art, and Custom* (1871), Tylor takes a position against racism and stresses the humanity of all people even though they may differ culturally.

This article is excerpted from *They Studied Man* by Abram Kardiner and Edward Preble. (Please refer to selection 9 for background information on them.) Edward Tylor is best known for his writings on religion. The authors make several key points about Tylor. First, he was a product of nineteenth-century evolutionary thinking, not just in the Darwinian biological sense, but also in the Spencerian social evolutionary sense. Second, Tylor's concept of *survival* is important to his evolutionary reconstruction of religious development. Just as one may find a stone arrow point embedded in the soil and deduce that it represents a time when stone age people hunted in the vicinity, so also Tylor claimed that religious beliefs systems should be seen as "relics" or carry-overs from the past. Third, Tylor believed in the psychic unity (equality) of humankind and opposed the concept of degeneration, the notion that contemporary "primitive" peoples represent a backsliding down from civilization rather than precursors to it. In other words, in his free-thinking Quaker essence, he truly believed that the variety of human societies in the world represented various stages of developmental progress toward civilization. Finally, just as so many social institutions can be seen to have changed, developed, and improved over time, so also have peoples' beliefs in the supernatural.

Key Concept: the psychic unity of man

A butcher is handed a Tasmanian skin-scraper and asked to test it on a side of beef; a children's street game is interrupted for the benefit of a bystander who wants the rules explained; gamblers, busy at their trade, are the uneasy objects of quiet, intensive scrutiny. In studying such cases of everyday work and play, Edward Burnett Tylor, the founder of modern anthropology, had been at work patiently reconstructing the past from observations of the present.

As modern highways are often laid upon remains of ancient tracks of barbaric roads, so, thought Tylor, was modern thought and behavior following the courses of primitive existence. To a university man, steeped in the traditions of academic learning, the commonplaces and trivia of daily life might seem a strange place to look for the origins and development of cultural history. To Tylor, who was denied a university career, it seemed natural to study the living for knowledge of the dead.

Tylor was born at Camberwell, England, October 2, 1832, the third son of Joseph Tylor and Harriet Skipper. The father ran a prosperous brass foundry, which belonged to the family. Both parents were Quakers, and Tylor was to make the most of his inheritance of freedom from religious formality. This independence cost him a classical education, however, because he could not pass the tests of religious orthodoxy which were then required for admission to the universities. He received, instead, a brief and informal education at a school maintained by the Society of Friends.

He entered the family business at the age of sixteen and worked there for seven years. In 1855, at the age of twenty-three, his health showed signs of breaking down, and he was advised to quit work and indulge his health by leisurely travel.

He spent almost a year traveling in the United States, and in the spring of 1856 was in Cuba. Here his Quaker affiliations provided the chance opportunity that so often gives direction to a man's life. While on a Havana bus he overheard a passenger use the pronoun "thou," which at that time identified the speaker as a Quaker. Tylor approached the stranger and introduced himself as a fellow Quaker. The man happened to be Henry Christy, a prosperous businessman, who had become an archaeologist and ethnologist of considerable reputation. He was one of the archaeologists who later made the important confirmation of the validity of Boucher de Perthes' discoveries concerning the antiquity of man. The two men took an immediate liking to each other, and Christy persuaded Tylor to accompany him on an archaeological expedition to Mexico. Tylor turned out to be one of Christy's greatest "finds" for anthropology.

Under Christy's expert and mature guidance (he was twenty years Tylor's senior), Tylor's curiosity and natural capacity for careful observation and balanced judgment were turned to good account in the reconstruction of the pre-history of Mexico. He was especially interested in the problem of the development of society, which was suggested by the material remains of culture discovered by the two travelers, as well as by the antiquities of popular rites, customs, beliefs, and legends which were to be observed among the contemporary peoples of Mexico. He observed that many extant customs were similar or identical to the customs of ancient peoples. He noticed, for example, the practice of Mexican penitents scourging themselves at church under the fierce exhortations of a monk, and was reminded of the identical rite at the Egyptian festival of Isis. This early interest in the survival of ancient customs in civilized societies was the starting point of one of Tylor's most important achievements in anthropology: the formulation of the "doctrine of survivals."

Another problem that interested Tylor on the Mexican expedition was that of the independent origin or diffusion of cultural institutions. This question was to become a crucial one in anthropology, with important implications for social, political, and religious thought. After considering a specific problem in this area, Tylor employed a caution which characterized much of his subsequent works: "Set the difficulties on one side of the question against those on the other, and they will nearly balance. We must wait for further evidence."

Although it was of much shorter duration (six months), Tylor's expedition in Mexico played the same role in his career that the *Beagle* voyage played for Darwin: it shaped once and for all the course of his life's work. His life was henceforth to be devoted to the founding of a science of culture.

Tylor is everywhere described as a commanding, benevolent figure. He was tall, well-built, and extremely handsome. His simplicity, patience, and quiet humor made him popular as a teacher and organizer, and contributed to an easy, persuasive style which won a wide audience for his writings. His writings were always free of jargon or pretension of any kind, a consequence, perhaps,

of the fact that he was taken from school at sixteen and never again became a "student" in the academic sense.

His life, as much as his work, exemplified what Lowie has called Tylor's "sense of fitness." His relationship to Anna Fox, whom he married in 1858, was regarded as a model of marital life. They lived together quietly and happily for fifty-nine years, until Tylor's death in 1917. It is said that Lady Tylor always attended a certain series of her husband's lectures, and that on one occasion, before a large audience, Tylor turned toward his wife after a lengthy exposition and said absent-mindedly, "And so my dear Anna, we observe. . . . "

In 1861 Tylor published *Anahuac*, an account of the Mexican expedition with Christy. His *Researches in the Early History of Mankind* was published in 1865, and it immediately established him as a leading figure in anthropology. His professional maturity came at a time when several lines of inquiry and speculation were converging toward a point which would radically alter man's conception of himself and his place in nature.

In geology Charles Lyell, building on the work of James Hutton, had successfully challenged the cataclysmic theories required by Biblical cosmology, and had shown the earth to have evolved over many millions of years instead of the few thousand required by scriptural authority. With the doctrine of "uniform causes," which assumed that the processes of geological change in the past were similar to those observable in the present, it was possible to block out an approximate chronological series for earthly formations.

In archaeology the confirmation in 1858 of Boucher de Perthes' discoveries of fashioned implements of great antiquity climaxed almost three centuries of fragmentary discoveries and speculations about man's ancient past; the existence of paleolithic man was definitely established.

In biology Darwin's work established the evolutionary view of nature as a key to the general problem of origin and development.

These developments in the mid-nineteenth century constituted a challenge of survival to religious orthodoxy. One of the many heresies the ecclesiastics had to combat was the idea that man had gradually evolved, not only from the lower animals, but, what was perhaps even worse, from a primitive state of humanity comparable to existing savages. The savage with his naked body, many wives, and pagan gods was regarded as a poor representative of Christian morality and hardly worthy of God's initial human creation.

To combat this particular heresy, the "degeneration (or degradation) theory" was advanced as an alternative to the evolutionary theory. According to this doctrine, man was created in a highly civilized, moral condition, but had, in some cases, degenerated to a savage state—become "outcasts of the human race," as the Duke of Argyll put it.

The degeneration theory became a popular alternative to the developmental (evolutionary) theory and was defended by such influential men as Richard Whately,

Archbishop of Dublin, and the Duke of Argyll, among others. But while this theory established the glory of man's beginning, it suggested a dim view of his future. To those who had inherited the optimism of the eighteenth century regarding man's capacity for self-improvement, the degeneration theory was intolerable and had to be smothered. Sir John Lubbock (Lord Avebury) complained that "if the past history of man has been one of deterioration, we have but groundless expectation of future improvement." Lubbock, along with Lyell and others, carried on a spirited debate over the question with the clerics and their supporters. The following is a typical exchange: The Duke of Argyll was explaining why the highland Eskimos do not have any weapons or any idea of war: "No wonder, poor people! They have been driven into regions where no stronger race could desire to follow them. But that the fathers had once known what war and violence meant there is no more conclusive proof than the dwelling place of their children." Lubbock responds: "It is perhaps natural that the leader of a great highland clan [Argyll] should regard with pity a people who, having 'once known what war and violence meant,' have no longer any neighbors to pillage or to fight, but a Lowlander can hardly be expected seriously to regard such a change as one calculated to excite pity, or as any evidence of degradation."

Tylor, a freethinking Quaker and firm believer in man's rationality and capacity for improvement, plunged into the very middle of this controversy. There is little doubt that he considered the implications of the degeneration theory to be a serious threat to man's confidence in himself and his future. The developmental theory of civilization had to be established beyond all doubt if the faith in progress was to be sustained.

Two general premises were necessary for the establishment of a progressive theory of cultural development: (1) the basic similarity of human minds and, (2) the priority of Primitive Man in the chronological series. Tylor's second book, *Researches Into the Early History of Mankind* (1865), dealt largely with the first question (among other things), and his third book, *Primitive Culture* (1871), completed the argument by establishing the second.

That Tylor's aims had a missionary quality to them is suggested by these stanzas which he contributed anonymously to Andrew Lang "Double Ballade Of A Primitive Man":

From a status like that of the Cres,
Our society's fabric arose,—
Develop'd, evolved, if you please,
But deluded chronologists chose,
In a fancied accordance with Moses,
4000 B.C. for the span
When he rushed on the world and its woes,—

But the mild anthropologist,—he's
Not recent inclined to suppose
Flints Palaeolithic like these,

Quaternary bones such as those,
In Rhinoceros, Mammouth and CO.s,
First Epoch, the Human Began,
Theologians all to expose,—
'Tis the mission of Primitive Man.

Tylor was the first serious student of culture to embrace the entire field of man and his environment. For him, the scope of anthropology should include man's body, his physical and cultural environment, and his soul.

Tylor was not a field worker, but, as Lowie has insisted, he was far from being an "armchair anthropologist." He studied culture wherever he happened to be—in a junk store of a big city; at a school for the deaf and dumb (where he worked out important features of his work on gesture-language); at a knitting mill; a butcher shop; and at festivals and religious ceremonies. The greater part of his time was spent with the literature which dealt in any way with the history of civilizations and institutions, artifacts, beliefs, and customs of primitive peoples. He became, as has been said, a "circumnavigator of books," and his knowledge of the literature was both wide and profound.

Not being a field worker, Tylor had to rely largely on material gathered from the accounts and publications of travelers, missionaries, adventurers, colonists, sailors, and the like. These reports were largely fragmentary, uncritical, biased, and generally unreliable. The facile use of this kind of material by other workers had resulted in confusion and contradictions. Practically any assertion about primitive cultures could be supported by citations from the literature.

Tylor was very much aware of this problem and set about constructing canons of "internal evidence" which could be applied to the sifting out of reliable data from the mass of testimony. His main tool here was the "test of recurrence," or "undesigned coincidence," by which statements were evaluated according to their frequency in other accounts, the most unique statements being assigned the highest probability. Lowie has said that "The student of Tylor in 1890 could profit from a vast mass of thoroughly sifted and authenticated material, interpreted from a unifying evolutionary point of view, tempered with sanity."

After he had established anthropology as a discipline at Oxford, Tylor was able to send students all over the world, as "the field naturalists of human nature." They went into the field with precise instructions and techniques for gathering data and for organizing the material so that it would yield useful relationships and generalizations.

Most impressive of all was the actual bulk of material that Tylor collected and employed. A reviewer of the French translation of *Primitive Culture* commented: "What one notes above all is the abundance of documents. One finds them by piles, by heaps, by mountains, and when these are cleared there are still others."

Tylor is famous for the caution and tentativeness with which he advanced his theories and ideas. Many references are made to his "infinite respect for facts," his "great patience in eliciting the universal from a multitude of particulars," and his patience in allowing the facts themselves to "crystallize into generalizations." Tylor's obituary in the *London Times* praised this aspect of his work: "he [Tylor] held that the enumeration of facts must form the staple of the argument, and that the limit of needful detail was reached only when each group of facts so displayed its general law that fresh ones came to range themselves in their proper riches as new instances of an already established rule."

It should be noted, however, that it was the fashion in the early development of the social sciences to emulate the attitudes and techniques that had been so successful in the rapid advance of the physical science in the seventeenth and eighteenth centuries. The Baconian ideal of perfect induction in science was considered the only reliable method for arriving at scientific generalizations, and even a verbal adherence to this ideal was impressive. It has been seen how Herbert Spencer, one of the most "deductive" minds in the social sciences, claimed and believed that his was a completely inductive work. Tylor was undoubtedly more careful and thorough than Spencer, but it would be a mistake to picture him as a man without definite preconceptions and vested interests in the work he was doing. His early work, especially, is boldly speculative and, in fact, owes much of its greatness to a zealous, partisan point of view.

Tylor approached his main subject—primitive man—with a sense of cultural relativity unusual for his time. "Measuring other people's corn by one's own bushel," was a cardinal mistake, according to Tylor, and had to be guarded against at all times. And although he is not completely free from censure on this point, he succeeded better than most of his contemporaries.

Above all, Tylor believed that the "inner springs of human behavior," the beliefs and attitudes that underlie institutions, comprise the most reliable evidence of man's history and development. Myth, folklore, religion, and custom were the sources for such information and must be studied along with written materials and artifacts if a reliable reconstruction is to be made. Tylor erred in certain of his emphases, but he exposed a whole new dimension for the study of culture.

Tylor was a thoroughgoing Darwinian in his biological views, but he specifically denied any direct influence from Darwin's work. He states in the preface to the second edition of *Primitive Culture:* "It may have struck some readers as an omission, that in a work on civilization insisting so strenuously on a theory of development on evolution, mention should scarcely have been made of Mr. Darwin and Mr. Spencer, whose influence on the whole course of modern thought on such subjects should not be left without formal recognition. This absence of particular reference is accounted for by the present work, arranged on its own lines, coming scarcely into contact or detail with the previous works of these eminent philosophers." Many of

today's anthropologists, such as Lowie, Herskovits, and Kroeber, have expressed the same judgment regarding the influence of Darwin on Tylor and on the development of anthropology in general. It is a question which can be argued with authority from either side. Tylor, though not a strict unilinear evolutionist (one who believed that every society must pass through the same definite stages), employed many concepts which paralleled the methods and ideas employed in the Darwinian reconstruction of organic evolution.

One of Tylor's problems was to establish the essential similarity of human minds; the "psychic unity of mankind," as it was called. Similarities of artifacts, customs, and beliefs between past and present cultures had been pointed out by many workers already, but Tylor saw that where there was a chance of cultural contact and the transmission of culture traits (which he always admitted according to the evidence), similarities did not require an independent development. What had to be shown was that under like conditions men's minds would work in like ways. The argument here would have to rest more on psychological than on historical data, because the history of a given culture trait could seldom rule out the possibility of cultural borrowing. It would be essential that the traits selected for study be those which have not, as Tylor says "travelled far from their causes." A great variety of cultural traits had resulted from generations of cumulative training and no longer reflected initial mental and environmental conditions. In certain areas, however, there had been little change, such as in picture-writing and gesture-language; games, proverbs, and riddles; myth, legend, folklore, and religion. Such traits represent more directly the untrained mental processes and provide for a safer reconstruction of the human mind, as such. Accordingly, in the *Researches* (1865), Tylor chose to offer a history of civilization based primarily on an examination of language, myths, rites, customs, and beliefs.

The similarities of gesture-language in societies separated in time and place were convincing evidence to Tylor "that the mind of uncultured men works in much the same way at all times and everywhere." The history of magic everywhere pointed to one underlying phenomenon: the outward projection on to material reality of the inner processeses of individual thought. In the lengthy, detailed treatment of mythology, Tylor identifies eight mythological themes which commonly occur in North and South America, and in Asia: World-Tortoise, Man Swallowed by Fish, Sun Catcher, Accent of Heaven by the Tree, Bridge of Dead, Fountain of Youth, Tail-Fisher, Diable Boiteux. Here again was telling evidence for the fundamental similarity of the human mind.

With the assumption of psychic unity established, Tylor was in a position to accept the evidence of either diffusion or independent development. They both appeared to be due to the similarity of the human mind: in the first case, the transfer of traits seemed to be made possible by the similarity of the inventing and the borrowing mind; and in the second, a parallel development seemed to be due to the action of like minds working under like conditions.

The *Researches*, then, proved a landmark in anthropology on two counts: it advanced the developmental theory by its treatment of the problem of similarities, and it made theoretical use of an important and neglected body of cultural material.

Having established the psychic unity of man, the next step for Tylor was to establish a cultural reconstruction which would show a progressive development from primitive to civilized man. He accomplished this in the publication of *Primitive Culture* (1871), an anthropological classic which marks the beginning of the scientific study of culture. Two major contributions to cultural anthropology emerged from this work: The "doctrine of survivals" and the theory of "animism."

Tylor considered two methods of evolutionary reconstruction which suggested the method of survivals to him. One was the reconstruction of material culture by the archaeologists and geologists on the basis of the discoveries of material relics (artifacts) in the geological strata. The archaeologist, working with the geologist, could establish from a few surviving artifacts (such as fragments of weapons, implements, pottery) a general picture of the material culture of an ancient society, and its approximate place in a chronological series. The three well-known stages (stone, bronze, iron) of material culture had been established in this way. The other suggestion for a method may have come from the use the biologists made of rudimentary (vestigial) organs in the reconstruction of organic evolution, where nonfunctional parts of the body were considered as survivals from ancestral forms in which they had a functional role.

In brief, Tylor's doctrine of survivals considered the quaint and nonfunctional customs and beliefs of civilized peoples as ancient "artifacts," or "vestigial remains." As stated previously, Tylor was interested as early as 1856 in the existence of quaint and unrealistic customs and beliefs in modern civilization. What are these, asked Tylor, but the relics of a cultural past, which have been preserved in the "strata" of human behavior.

With the assumption of man's essential rationality within a given environmental context, these "survivals" become trustworthy clues to man's cultural past: "When in the process of time there has come general change in the condition of a people, it is usual, notwithstanding, to find much that manifestly has not its origin in the new state of things, but has simply lasted on into it. On the strength of these survivals, it becomes possible to declare that the civilization of the people they are observed among must have been derived from an earlier state in which the proper home and meaning of these things are to be found; and thus collections of such facts are to be worked as mines of historical knowledge." They exist in our midst, Tylor continues, as the "primeval monuments of barbaric thought and life."

The doctrine of survivals added utility and prestige to the "comparative method" as the key to ethnological research; Tylor, in fact, is often referred to as the founder of "comparative ethnology." The comparative method had rested on the almost gratuitous assumption that contemporary savage peoples represented earlier stages of cultural development which had been traversed by civilized peoples. By the study of survivals (material and nonmaterial) in modern societies, it was now possible, according to Tylor, to find the actual traces of these stages in modern society: "Look at the modern European peasant," says Tylor, "using his hatchet and his hoe, see his food boiling or roasting over the log-fire, observe the exact place which beer holds in his calculation of happiness, hear his tale of the ghost in the nearest haunted house, and of the farmer's niece who was bewitched with knots in her inside till she fell into fits and died. If we choose out in this way things which have altered little in a long course of centuries we may draw a picture where there shall be scarce a hand's breadth difference between an English ploughman and a Negro of Central Africa. . . . We have continued reason to be thankful for fools. . . . It is quite wonderful . . . to see how large a share stupidity and impractical conservatism and dogged superstition have had in preserving for us traces of the history of our race, which practical utilitarianism would have remorselessly swept away."

Tylor's doctrine of survivals became the most valuable tool of the evolutionary anthropologists and resulted in a growing body of valuable ethnological material, which can be summed up under the general heading of "folklore."

Before taking up Tylor's influential theory of animism it may be useful to consider his approach to myth in general, because it paves the way for his exposition of animism.

Tylor believed that myth originated in the human intellect when it was in a childlike state. Myths represented for Tylor the crude but essentially rational attempts of childlike peoples to make sense out of their environment and experiences. "Legend," he states, ". . . is only telling the perennial story of the world's daily life." He believed that in myth and legend one had access to the primitive philosophy of nature and life. The following Polynesian nature-myth is an example of the kind of evidence on which Tylor founded his "primitive philosopher" idea:

Sky (father) and Earth (mother) created all things in nature. But at first there was no light because Sky and Earth still cleaved to each other. The children counseled with one another on whether to slay the parents or rend them apart so as to admit the light. The "father of the forests" advised that the parents be separated, the sky to become a "stranger" and the earth a nursing mother. Several of the children tried and failed to separate Sky and Earth and finally the father of the forests tried. He placed his head against the earth, his feet against the sky, and sundered them as they cried, groaned, and shrieked aloud. The father of wind and storms had not consented to the plan of his brothers, and followed his father into the heavens. He then waged war on his brothers by sending wind and storms to stir up the sea, break down the forests, and destroy the plant and animal life. In the course of the battle the reptiles fled from the sea to seek safety in the woods. The Earth caught up the gods of the plants and animals and hid them from the storm god. Finally the storm god attacked the "father of fierce men," the one who had planned the destruction of the parents; but the storm god could not shake him, and man remained erect and unshaken upon the bosom of mother Earth. Man was furious at having been deserted by his brethren in the battle and has exploited them for his benefit ever since. He conquered all but the storm god who still attacks him periodically with tempest and hurricane. And until this time Sky and Earth have remained separated, but their love continues. The warm sighs of the Earth's bosom (the mists) are directed to the parted spouse, and the Sky drops frequent tears (dew-drops) on his beloved Earth.

Tylor says of this myth that there is "scarcely a thought that is not still transparent, scarcely even a word that has lost its meaning to us." He means, of course, that it is a realistic, if childlike, interpretation of natural phenomena. This is characteristic of Tylor's rationalistic approach to all folklore, and it underlies his entire theory of animism.

Tylor called the belief in spiritual beings animism and considered it to be the minimum definition of religion. Tylor's animism in fact is a comprehensive theory of the origin and development of religious systems everywhere, and it served to illustrate the kind of reconstruction that can be made with a developmental theory. Animism rests on one very simple idea: that where men dream by night, have phantasms by day, and die, the belief in spiritual beings will arise. He divided the animism of primitive peoples into two principal ideas: the concept of the *soul* and the derivative belief in *other spirits*.

The idea of the soul Tylor thought to be a crude but reasonable inference on the part of primitive man. The savage, like every man, is confronted daily with the dual nature of existence. At death certain phenomena disappear-breath, pulse, consciousness, and the capacity for voluntary movement. The body remains, but that complex of phenomena known as "life" has disappeared, "passed away," as we say today. Life, or soul, has left the body.

Dreams and phantasms suggest a related duality. Here, human shapes appear which are images of individuals who may be some distance away, or even dead. The savage reasonably concludes that man's body has a phantom copy which may leave the body and have independent experiences.

According to Tylor, the primitive mentality makes a natural connection between these two separable attributes of the body—the phantom copy and the soul—and brings them together in an apparitional-soul, or ghost-soul. It is the ghost-soul which accounts for death as well as dreams, visions, sleep, swoons, illness, coma, and the like; conditions, that is, where life processes are impaired, distorted, or destroyed. It is the key to the entire psycho-biology of primitive man: "It is a thin unsubstantial human image, in its nature a sort of vapour, film, or shadow; the cause of life and thought in the individual it animates; independently possessing the personal consciousness and volition of its corporeal owner, past or present; capable of leaving the body far behind, to flash swiftly from place to place; mostly impalpable and invisible, yet also manifesting physical power, and especially appearing to men waking or asleep as a phantasm separate from the body of which it bears the likeness; continuing to exist and appear to men after death of that body; able to enter into, possess, and act in the bodies of other men, of animals, and even things."

The next stage in the development of animism is the natural extension of souls and phantom-copies to animals, there being only a small distinction in the primitive mind between man and the other animals. Animals appear in dreams, and they die; hence the ghost-soul can account for animal as well as human existence. To support this theory, Tylor cites many examples of animal sacrifice which are made at human burials—the idea being that the ghostsoul of the sacrificed animal will accompany the ghost-soul of the individual and serve him in the next world as it did in this. Dogs, for example, are buried with children in some primitive cultures, to lead them to the land of souls. Horses are led to a warrior's grave, killed and thrown in the grave with their master. Tylor found a case of this kind occurring as late as 1781 in Europe and stated that it was still practiced in Asia.

The next extension of the ghost-soul is to non-living objects. Things also appear in dreams and must have phantom-copies. Unlike animals, they do not "die," but this requirement is probably overlooked on the ground that where one (the phantom) is evident, the other (the soul) can be assumed. Evidence for this idea is found in the common practice of sending objects, such as weapons, implements, pottery, and so on, along with the dead man in his grave, for his use in the next life.

Three general beliefs concerning the existence of ghost-souls after death are derived from these early stages of animism: (1) the conviction that the ghost-souls hover around the earth and take an interest in the living—sometimes visiting their former homes, (2) the belief in metempsychosis—the transmigration of souls into other human beings, or even into animals, plants, and things, (3) the idea of a special residence in another world, such as the Western Islands, the Underworld, the Mountains, and Heaven. This last kind of belief falls into one of two categories, which Tylor calls the "continuance theory" and the "retribution theory." In the first, a life similar to earthly life is carried on, and in the second, the ghost-souls are rewarded or punished according to the deeds of their earthly life. The second theory would, of course, have a special effect on the social behavior of the people who adopted the belief.

The general idea of the primitive ghost-soul animating men, animals, plants, and things naturally leads to the belief in another order of spiritual beings which are on a higher level. These are called "manes," which are souls in origin but which acquire a special quality raising them to the level of demons or deities. This development resulted in one of the great branches of religion: Manes-Worship.

Manes are souls of individuals who, in real life, were in a position of authority with respect to the worshiper. This will often be a parent, hence ancestor-worship becomes a common form of Manes-Worship. But it might also be the soul of a tribal-chief, a tribal-hero, or any other powerful person. He can have been a power for good or evil, and thus become either a deity or a demon.

Regarding Manes-Worship, Tylor says: "Its principles are not difficult to understand, for they plainly keep up the social relations of the living world. The dead ancestor, now passed into a deity, simply goes on protecting his own family and receiving suit and service from them as of old; the dead chief still watches over his own tribe, still holds his authority by helping friends and harming enemies, still rewards the right and sharply punishes the wrong."

Manes-Worship was especially instructive for Tylor in the reconstruction of animism, because he saw it as intermediate in the hierarchy of the spiritual world, standing between ordinary souls and superhuman demons and deities. It was clear evidence for Tylor of the modeling of superior spirits on the human soul. He cites the worship of saints in modern religion as a clear case of Manes-Worship, being as it is the worship of dead men and women who form a class of inferior deities.

Another important feature in the development of primitive religion is the general idea of the *embodiment* of spirits. As the soul may be in or out of the body, so are spirits free to run in and out of objects—living and non-living. This idea serves two important purposes in lower animism: As a theory of "demoniacal possession," it explains all forms of human disease and derangement. Tylor gives a particularly vivid account of this phenomenon:

> As in normal conditions, the man's soul, inhabiting his body, is held to give it life, to think, speak, and act through it, so an adaptation of the self-same principle explains abnormal conditions of body or mind, by considering the new symptoms as due to the operation of a second soul-like being, a strange spirit. The possessed man, tossed and shaken in fever, pained and wrenched as though some live creature were tearing or twisting him within, pining as though it were devouring his vitals day by day, rationally finds a personal spiritual cause for his sufferings. In hideous dreams he may even sometimes see the very ghost or nightmare-fiend that plagues him. Especially when the mysterious unseen power throws him helpless to the ground, jerks and writhes him in convulsions, makes him leap upon the bystanders with a giant's strength and a wild beast's ferocity, impels him, with distorted face and frantic gesture, and voice not his own nor seemingly human, to pour forth with incoherent raving, or with thought and eloquence beyond his sober faculties to command, to counsel, to foretell—such a one seems to those who watch him, and even to himself, to have become the mere instrument of a spirit which has seized him or entered into him, a possessing demon in

whose personality the patient believes so implicitly that he often imagines a personal name for it, which it can declare when it speaks in its own voice and character through his organs of speech; at last, quitting the medium's spent and jaded body, the intruding spirit departs as it came.

The practice of exorcism emerges as the therapeutic device for dealing with the invading demon spirits. The exorcist removes the spirit by cajolery, bribes, threats, or by persuading or driving it to another abode.

Related to the "possession theory" (above), is the next important application of the Embodiment idea, known as fetishism. As the savage may "lay" a demon spirit in a foreign body, so may he manipulate a useful spirit to his advantage. It may be carried around in an object to fend off enemies and disease, or it may be set up as a deity in a material object, for propitiation and worship.[1]

Fetishism merges into idolatry when a fetish object is altered in some material way by the worshiper so as to indicate its special function as the abode for a spirit. A few scratches on a dab of paint may serve to construct an idol, or a more elaborate job may be done in the construction of a definite image, as in a statue or picture. The important thing is that the idol takes on a "personality," or soul, which is absent in the pure fetish. An idol, for Tylor, must thus combine the characteristics of portrait (no matter how crude) and fetish. The connection between souls and other spirits—the crucial factor in Tylor's theory—is further reinforced by this view of Idolatry: soul and spirit are both embodied in the idol, just as they are both embodied in human bodies, at least on occasions.

The next stage in animism occurs when the primitive mind draws the analogy between human behavior and the behavior of nature at large. As the human body functions by virtue of its inhabiting ghost-soul, so does nature in general appear to be animated by analogous agents. Thus animism, beginning as a philosophy of human life, becomes a comprehensive philosophy of all nature. The "causes" of all natural phenomena are nature-spirits. They cause the wind to blow, the sky to rain, the rivers to move, the volcanoes to erupt.

Beginning, most likely, from very particular spirits for particular events, the idea of nature-spirits becomes generalized, and there arise the species-deities: the gods of Forest, Heaven, Earth, Water, Sun, and Moon. Next, invisible species-deities emerge: the gods of Agriculture, War, Peace, Good, and Evil. This is the great stage of polytheism.

And finally, the concept of one Supreme Deity arrives. Above the souls, manes, nature-spirits, and species-deities of class and element—one deity is elevated to divine supremacy. Monotheism, the great belief of civilized peoples, has evolved from the primitive past. A developmental theory can adequately account for monotheism and the entire history of religion; there is no need of Divine Revelation. Tylor has answered the clerics who would defend the degeneration theory—and on their own ground.

Lowie has said of Tylor's method of "adhesions" that "nothing that Tylor ever did serves so decisively to lift him above the throng of his fellow-workers." Briefly, the method involved the application of statistical methods of probability to ethnological data. The method aimed at discovering the causal relationships, if any, between culture traits; whether, for example, the customs of residence are related to, or are independent of, customs of avoidance. If relationships, or adhesions, can be discovered, then, thought Tylor, inferences of cultural causality can be made over the whole range of mankind; "social arithmetic" could be employed to disclose the course of social history. His attempt, according to Lowie, was to "substitute the mathematical concept of function for the metaphysical concept of cause."

Tylor employed the method in the following way: He was interested, for example, in the cultural laws of marriage and descent and had data on these customs from over 300 peoples, from "savage hordes" to "cultured nations." All customs related to the subject were tabulated and classified. By consulting the tables, the investigator could easily determine what customs accompanied other customs, such as teknonymy (the term invented by Tylor for the custom of naming parents after children) and matrilocal residence. If the recurrence of the given coincidence in the tables exceeded significantly the number that could be expected on a chance distribution, then a causal relationship could be assumed. In the above example—teknonymy and residence—the "reckoning of the adhesions" showed a connection between teknonymy and matrilocal. residence in twenty-two cases, where accidental distribution would yield eleven. Teknonymy was even more closely related to avoidance, fourteen cases occurring, with a chance expectation of four. Taking the three customs together—teknonymy, matrilocal residence, and avoidance—they would appear by chance only once or twice among all the peoples studied; they actually appear together eleven times, giving odds of about six to one for a causal relationship.

Tylor realized that many refinements must be made before this method could be applied with complete confidence, but his experience so far with it made it clear to him "that the rules of human conduct are amenable to classification in compact masses, so as to show by strict numerical treatment their relations to one another."

Except for a few detractors, such as G. Elliot Smith and other extreme diffusionists, and those who incorrectly place Tylor among the uncritical unilinear evolutionists, Tylor is rated among the very greatest in anthropology. He is considered the founder of cultural anthropology and has had enormous influence. Sir James Frazer, to name one individual, was greatly indebted to Tylor for his work. Max Müller referred consistently to ethnology as "Mr. Tylor's Science"; Andrew Lang stated, in 1907, that Tylor, along with Lubbock, "towered above all British Anthropologists, like Saul above his people"; Lowie states that "the lapse of time has merely confirmed the earlier judgment of his greatness."

The most common and obvious criticism of Tylor's work centers around his extreme rationalistic interpretations of ethnological data. His "sense of probability," as Lowie called it, was carried to the extreme in conceiving of all human beings as relatively sophisticated philosophers. Tylor recognizes this one-sidedness in some places, as where, after the exposition of animism, he states that "the intellectual rather than the emotional side of religion has been kept in view." And then he goes on: "Even in the life of the rudest savages, religious belief is associated with intense emotion, with awful reverence, with agonizing terror, with rapt ecstasy when sense and thought utterly transcend the common level of daily life." But he justifies the exclusion of a treatment of these emotional factors on the ground that they represent divergencies from his main purpose of showing the transmission of certain main features of cultural history, in this case animism.

Probably part of Tylor's rationalistic emphasis can be attributed to his conscious polemic against the clerics, who would create an impassable gulf between civilized man and his primitive ancestors. Tylor had to show that the "rude savage" was potentially an English gentleman, with the capacities for rational inference within his limited historical sphere. There is no mistaking the delight with which Tylor directs the attention of theologians to the beginnings and transmission of their noble doctrines and beliefs. "Theologians all to expose," was "the *mission* of primitive man," as Tylor could say in poetry.

Probably most important, as far as his influence is concerned, was Tylor's justification of the evolutionary method as a technique of investigation and interpretation in the social sciences. It may be said that many of the followers of this method lacked Tylor's relatively critical and sophisticated use of it, and finally brought it into general discredit; but in one form or another it has continued to exert great influence to the present day.

Finally, the general influence of Tylor's personality may be mentioned again. With Tylor, as with Darwin, a quiet but shrewd geniality helped pave the way for the early acceptance of ideas and methods which were loaded with explosive implications for contemporary thought and society.

Note

1. It may be noted here that for Comte, to whom Tylor was consciously indebted for many ideas, fetishism was used to designate primitive religion in general. Tylor used the term to indicate a subordinate department of animism, and restricted its use for spirits embodied in, or related to material objects, living or non-living.

Magic, Science and Religion: And Other Essays

Bronislaw Malinowski

In this essay, excerpted from *Magic, Science and Religion: And Other Essays*, the pioneering social anthropologist Bronislaw Malinowski provides us with a clear-cut delineation between the realm of the *sacred*, or supernatural, and the world of the *profane*, the latter having to do with cause-and-effect relationships and knowledge based upon experience and reason.

Most importantly, Malinowski draws from his own extensive fieldwork experiences in the Trobriand Islands to show that these distinctions are not simply the product of a modern-day perspective or even an anthropological dichotomy, but are an integral part of the way "primitive" people think as well.

People everywhere, argues Malinowski, operate on the basis of their objective understanding of the world around them. But, it is also true that people everywhere are subjected to circumstances beyond their comprehension and control and, when this happens, they resort to supernatural means to achieve their goals. So, whether embarking on a fishing expedition on the dangerous open sea or facing death as the result of advancing old age, people will, in a practical manner of speaking, do what they can to ward off the impending danger, but additionally, knowing full well that their fate is not entirely in their hands, will look to the sacred for guidance and understanding.

Bronislaw Malinowski was born in 1884 in Krakow, Poland and received a doctorate in mathematics and physics from the University of Krakow. Inspired by a chance reading of Sir James George Frazer's book, *Golden Bough*, Malinowski decided to do fieldwork in anthropology and went on to study at the London School of Economics. It was from there that he embarked upon a field trip to Australia, which in turn led to his doing fieldwork in the Trobriand Islands. He taught at the University of London, Cornell, Harvard, and then Yale. He died in New Haven, Connecticut in 1942.

Malinowski is noted for having been one of the first anthropologists to do extensive ethnographic fieldwork, for being a founder of the "functional school" of anthropology, and for his many publications, especially those on the Trobriand Islands, including *The Family among the Australian Aborigines: A Sociological Study*, *Argonauts of the Western Pacific*, *Sex and Repression in Savage Society*, *Coral Gardens and their Magic: A Study of the Methods of Tilling the Soil and of Agricultural Rites in the Trobriand Islands*, and, the volume from which the following excerpt is taken.

Key Concepts: magic, science and religion

Primitive Man and His Religion

There are no peoples however primitive without religion and magic. Nor are there, it must be added at once, any savage races lacking either in the scientific attitude or in science, though this lack has been frequently attributed to them. In every primitive community, studied by trustworthy and competent observers, there have been found two clearly distinguishable domains, the Sacred and the Profane; in other words, the domain of Magic and Religion and that of Science.

On the one hand there are the traditional acts and observances, regarded by the natives as sacred, carried out with reverence and awe, hedged around with prohibitions and special rules of behavior. Such acts and observances are always associated with beliefs in supernatural forces, especially those of magic, or with ideas about beings, spirits, ghosts, dead ancestors, or gods. On the other hand, a moment's reflection is sufficient to show that no art or craft however primitive could have been invented or maintained, no organized form of hunting, fishing, tilling, or search for food could be carried out without the careful observation of natural process and a firm belief in its regularity, without the power of reasoning and without confidence in the power of reason; that is, without the rudiments of science.

The credit of having laid the foundations of an anthropological study of religion belongs to Edward B. Tylor. In his well-known theory he maintains that the essence of primitive religion is animism, the belief in spiritual beings, and he shows how this belief has originated in a mistaken but consistent interpretation of dreams, visions, hallucinations, cataleptic states, and similar phenomena. Reflecting on these, the savage philosopher or theologian was led to distinguish the human soul from the body. Now the soul obviously continues to lead an existence after death, for it appears in dreams, haunts the survivors in memories and in visions and apparently influences human destinies. Thus originated the belief in ghosts and the spirits of the dead, in immortality and in a nether world. But man in general, and primitive man in particular, has a tendency to imagine the outer world in his own image. And since animals, plants, and objects move, act, behave, help man or hinder him, they must also be endowed with souls or spirits. Thus animism, the philosophy and the religion of primitive man, has been built up from observations and by inferences, mistaken but comprehensible in a crude and untutored mind.

Tylor's view of primitive religion, important as it was, was based on too narrow a range of facts, and it made early man too contemplative and rational. Recent field work, done by specialists, shows us the savage interested rather in his fishing and gardens, in tribal events and festivities than brooding over dreams and visions, or explaining "doubles" and cataleptic fits, and it reveals also a great many aspects of early religion which cannot be possibly placed in Tylor's scheme of animism.

The extended and deepened outlook of modern anthropology finds its most adequate expression in the learned and inspiring writings of Sir James Frazer. In these he has set forth the three main problems of primitive religion with which present-day anthropology is busy: magic and its relation to religion and science; totemism and the sociological aspect of early faith; the cults of fertility and vegetation. It will be best to discuss these subjects in turn.

Frazer's *Golden Bough*, the great codex of primitive magic, shows clearly that animism is not the only, nor even the dominating belief in primitive culture. Early man seeks above all to control the course of nature for practical ends, and he does it directly, by rite and spell, compelling wind and weather, animals and crops to obey his will. Only much later, finding the limitations of his magical might, does he in fear or hope, in supplication or defiance, appeal to higher beings; that is, to demons, ancestor-spirits or gods. It is in this distinction between direct control on the one hand and propitiation of superior powers on the other that Sir James Frazer sees the difference between religion and magic. Magic, based on man's confidence that he can dominate nature directly, if only he knows the laws which govern it magically, is in this akin to science. Religion, the confession of human impotence in certain matters, lifts man above the magical level, and later on maintains its independence side by side with science, to which magic has to succumb.

This theory of magic and religion has been the starting point of most modern studies of the twin subjects. Professor Preuss in Germany, Dr. Marett in England,

and MM. Hubert and Mauss in France have independently set forth certain views, partly in criticism of Frazer, partly following up the lines of his inquiry. These writers point out that similar as they appear, science and magic differ yet radically. Science is born of experience, magic made by tradition. Science is guided by reason and corrected by observation, magic, impervious to both, lives in an atmosphere of mysticism. Science is open to all, a common good of the whole community, magic is occult, taught through mysterious initiations, handed on in a hereditary or at least in very exclusive filiation. While science is based on the conception of natural forces, magic springs from the idea of a certain mystic, impersonal power, which is believed in by most primitive peoples. This power, called *mana* by some Melanesians, *arungquiltha* by certain Australian tribes, *wakan*, *orenda*, *manitu* by various American Indians, and nameless elsewhere, is stated to be a well-nigh universal idea found wherever magic flourishes. According to the writers just mentioned, we can find among the most primitive peoples and throughout the lower savagery a belief in a supernatural, impersonal force, moving all those agencies which are relevant to the savage and causing all the really important events in the domain of the sacred. Thus *mana*, not animism, is the essence of "pre-animistic religion," and it is also the essence of magic, which is thus radically different from science.

There remains the question, however, what is *mana*, this impersonal force of magic supposed to dominate all forms of early belief? Is it a fundamental idea, an innate category of the primitive mind, or can it be explained by still simpler and more fundamental elements of human psychology or of the reality in which primitive man lives? The most original and important contribution to these problems is given by the late Professor Durkheim, and it touches the other subject, opened up by Sir James Frazer: that of totemism and of the sociological aspect of religion.

Totemism, to quote Frazer's classical definition, "is an intimate relation which is supposed to exist between a group of kindred people on the one side and a species of natural or artificial objects on the other side, which objects are called the totems of the human group." Totemism thus has two sides: it is a mode of social grouping and a religious system of beliefs and practices. As religion, it expresses primitive man's interest in his surroundings, the desire to claim an affinity and to control the most important objects: above all, animal or vegetable species, more rarely useful inanimate objects, very seldom man-made things. As a rule species of animals and plants used for staple food or at any rate edible or useful or ornamental animals are held in a special form of "totemic reverence" and are tabooed to the members of the clan which is associated with the species and which sometimes performs rites and ceremonies for its multiplication. The social aspect of totemism consists in the subdivision of the tribe into minor units, called in anthropology *clans*, *gentes*, sibs, or *phratries*.

In totemism we see therefore not the result of early man's speculations about mysterious phenomena, but a blend of a utilitarian anxiety about the most necessary objects of his surroundings, with some preoccupation in those which strike his imagination and attract his attention, such as beautiful birds, reptiles, and dangerous animals. With our knowledge of what could be called the totemic attitude of mind, primitive religion is seen to be nearer to reality and to the immediate practical life interests of the savage, than it appeared in its "animistic" aspect emphasized by Tylor and the earlier anthropologists.

By its apparently strange association with a problematic form of social division, I mean the clan system; totemism has taught anthropology yet another lesson: it has revealed the importance of the sociological aspect in all the early forms of cult. The savage depends upon the group with whom he is in direct contact both for practical cooperation and mental solidarity to a far larger extent than does civilized man. Since—as can be seen in totemism, magic, and many other practices—early cult and ritual are closely associated with practical concerns as well as with mental needs, there must exist an intimate connection between social organization and religious belief. This was understood already by that pioneer of religious anthropology, Robertson Smith, whose principle that primitive religion "was essentially an affair of the community rather than of individuals" has become a *Leitmotiv* of modern research. According to Professor Durkheim, who has put these views most forcibly, "the religious" is identical with "the social." For "in a general way . . . a society has all that is necessary to arouse the sensation of the Divine in minds, merely by the power that it has over them; for to its members it is what a God is to its worshippers."[1] Professor Durkheim arrives at this conclusion by the study of totemism, which he believes to be the most primitive form of religion. In this the "totemic principle" which is identical with *mana* and with "the God of the clan . . . can be nothing else than the clan itself."[2] . . .

The third great subject introduced into the *Science of Religion* by Sir James Frazer is that of the cults of vegetation and fertility. In *The Golden Bough*, starting from the awful and mysterious ritual of the wood divinities at Nemi, we are led through an amazing variety of magical and religious cults, devised by man to stimulate and control the fertilizing work of skies and earth and of sun and rain, and we are left with the impression that early religion is teeming with the forces of savage life, with its young beauty and crudity, with its exuberance and strength so violent that it leads now and again to suicidal acts of self-immolation. The study of *The Golden Bough* shows us that for primitive man death has meaning mainly as a step to resurrection, decay as a stage of rebirth, the plenty of autumn and the decline of winter as preludes to the revival of spring. Inspired by these passages of *The Golden Bough* a number of writers have developed, often with greater precision and with a fuller analysis than by Frazer himself, what could be called the *vitalistic* view of religion. Thus Mr. Crawley in his *Tree of Life*, M. van

Gennep in his *Rites de Passage*, and Miss Jane Harrison in several works, have given evidence that faith and cult spring from the crises of human existence, "the great events of life, birth, adolescence, marriage, death . . . it is about these events that religion largely focuses."[3] The tension of instinctive need, strong emotional experiences, lead in some way or other to cult and belief. "Art and Religion alike spring from unsatisfied desire."[4] How much truth there is in this somewhat vague statement and how much exaggeration we shall be able to assess later on.

There are two important contributions to the theory of primitive religion which I mention here only, for they have somehow remained outside the main current of anthropological interest. They treat of the primitive idea of one God and of the place of morals in primitive religion respectively. It is remarkable that they have been and still are neglected, for are not these two questions first and foremost in the mind of anyone who studies religion, however crude and rudimentary it may be? Perhaps the explanation is in the preconceived idea that "origins" must be very crude and simple and different from the "developed forms," or else in the notion that the "savage" or "primitive" is really savage and primitive!

The late Andrew Lang indicated the existence among some Australian natives of the belief in a tribal All-Father, and the Rev. Pater Wilhelm Schmidt has adduced much evidence proving that this belief is universal among all the peoples of the simplest cultures and that it cannot be discarded as an irrelevant fragment of mythology, still less as an echo of missionary teaching. It looks, according to Pater Schmidt, very much like an indication of a simple and pure form of early monotheism.

The problem of morals as an early religious function was also left on one side, until it received an exhaustive treatment, not only in the writings of Pater Schmidt but also and notably in two works of outstanding importance: the *Origin and Development of Moral Ideas* of Professor E. Westermarck, and *Morals in Evolution* of Professor L. T. Hobhouse.

It is not easy to summarize concisely the trend of anthropological studies in our subject. On the whole it has been towards an increasingly elastic and comprehensive view of religion. Tylor had still to refute the fallacy that there are primitive peoples without religion. Today we are somewhat perplexed by the discovery that to a savage all is religion, that he perpetually lives in a world of mysticism and ritualism. If religion is co-extensive with "life" and with "death" into the bargain, if it arises from all "collective" acts and from all "crises in the individual's existence," if it comprises all savage "theory" and covers all his "practical concerns"—we are led to ask, not without dismay: What remains outside it, what is the world of the "profane" in primitive life? Here is a first problem into which modern anthropology, by the number of contradictory views, has thrown some confusion, as can be seen even from the above short sketch. We shall be able to contribute towards its solution in the next section.

Primitive religion, as fashioned by modern anthropology, has been made to harbor all sorts of heterogeneous things. At first reserved in animism for the solemn figures of ancestral spirits, ghosts and souls, besides a few fetishes, it had gradually to admit the thin, fluid, ubiquitous *mana*; then, like Noah's Ark, it was with the introduction of totemism loaded with beasts, not in pairs but in shoals and species, joined by plants, objects, and even manufactured articles; then came human activities and concerns and the gigantic ghost of the Collective Soul, Society Divinized. Can there be any order or system put into this medley of apparently unrelated objects and principles? This question will occupy us in the third section.

One achievement of modern anthropology we shall not question: the recognition that magic and religion are not merely a doctrine or a philosophy, not merely an intellectual body of opinion, but a special mode of behavior, a pragmatic attitude built up of reason, feeling, and will alike. It is a mode of action as well as a system of belief, and a sociological phenomenon as well as a personal experience. But with all this, the exact relation between the social and the individual contributions to religion is not clear, as we have seen from the exaggerations committed on either side. Nor is it clear what are the respective shares of emotion and reason. All these questions will have to be dealt with by future anthropology, and it will be possible only to suggest solutions and indicate lines of argument in this short essay.

Rational Mastery by Man of His Surroundings

The problem of primitive knowledge has been singularly neglected by anthropology. Studies on savage psychology were exclusively confined to early religion, magic and mythology. Only recently the work of several English, German, and French writers, notably the daring and brilliant speculations of Professor Lévy-Bruhl, gave an impetus to the student's interest in what the savage does in his more sober moods. The results were startling indeed: Professor Lévy-Bruhl tells us, to put it in a nutshell, that primitive man has no sober moods at all, that he is hopelessly and completely immersed in a mystical frame of mind. Incapable of dispassionate and consistent observation, devoid of the power of abstraction, hampered by "a decided aversion towards reasoning," he is unable to draw any benefit from experience, to construct or comprehend even the most elementary laws of nature. "For minds thus orientated there is no fact purely physical." Nor can there exist for them any clear idea of substance and attribute, cause and effect, identity and contradiction. Their outlook is that of confused superstition, "prelogical," made of mystic "participations" and "exclusions." I have here summarized a body of opinion, of which the brilliant French sociologist is the most decided and competent spokesman,

but which numbers besides, many anthropologists and philosophers of renown.

But there are also dissenting voices. When a scholar and anthropologist of the measure of Professor J. L. Myres entitles an article in *Notes and Queries* "Natural Science," and when we read there that the savage's "knowledge based on observation is distinct and accurate," we must surely pause before accepting primitive man's irrationality as a dogma. Another highly competent writer, Dr. A. A. Goldenweiser, speaking about primitive "discoveries, inventions and improvements"—which could hardly be attributed to any pre-empirical or prelogical mind—affirms that "it would be unwise to ascribe to the primitive mechanic merely a passive part in the origination of inventions. Many a happy thought must have crossed his mind, nor was he wholly unfamiliar with the thrill that comes from an idea effective in action." Here we see the savage endowed with an attitude of mind wholly akin to that of a modern man of science!

To bridge over the wide gap between the two extreme opinions current on the subject of primitive man's reason, it will be best to resolve the problem into two questions. First, has the savage any rational outlook, any rational mastery of his surroundings, or is he, as M. Lévy-Bruhl and his school maintain, entirely "mystical"? The answer will be that every primitive community is in possession of a considerable store of knowledge, based on experience and fashioned by reason.

The second question then opens: Can this primitive knowledge be regarded as a rudimentary form of science or is it, on the contrary, radically different, a crude empiry, a body of practical and technical abilities, rules of thumb, and rules of art having no theoretical value? This second question, epistemological rather than belonging to the study of man, will be barely touched upon at the end of this section and a tentative answer only will be given.

In dealing with the first question, we shall have to examine the "profane" side of life, the arts, crafts and economic pursuits, and we shall attempt to disentangle in it a type of behavior, clearly marked off from magic and religion, based on empirical knowledge and on the confidence in logic. We shall try to find whether the lines of such behavior are defined by traditional rules, known, perhaps even discussed sometimes, and tested. We shall have to inquire whether the sociological setting of the rational and empirical behavior differs from that of ritual and cult. Above all we shall ask, do the natives distinguish the two domains and keep them apart, or is the field of knowledge constantly swamped by superstition, ritualism, magic or religion?

Since in the matter under discussion there is an appalling lack of relevant and reliable observations, I shall have largely to draw upon my own material, mostly unpublished, collected during a few years' field work among the Melanesian and Papuo-Melanesian tribes of Eastern New Guinea and the surrounding archipelagoes. As the Melanesians are reputed, however, to be specially magic-ridden, they will furnish an acid test of the existence of empirical and rational knowledge among savages living in the age of polished stone.

These natives, and I am speaking mainly of the Melanesians who inhabit the coral atolls to the N.E. of the main island, the Trobriand Archipelago and the adjoining groups, are expert fishermen, industrious manufacturers and traders, but they rely mainly on gardening for their subsistence. With the most rudimentary implements, a pointed diggingstick and a small axe, they are able to raise crops sufficient to maintain a dense population and even yielding a surplus, which in olden days was allowed to rot unconsumed, and which at present is exported to feed plantation hands. The success in their agriculture depends—besides the excellent natural conditions with which they are favored-upon their extensive knowledge of the classes of the soil, of the various cultivated plants, of the mutual adaptation of these two factors, and, last not least, upon their knowledge of the importance of accurate and hard work. They have to select the soil and the seedlings, they have appropriately to fix the times for clearing and burning the scrub, for planting and weeding, for training the vines of the yam plants. In all this they are guided by a clear knowledge of weather and seasons, plants and pests, soil and tubers, and by a conviction that this knowledge is true and reliable, that it can be counted upon and must be scrupulously obeyed.

Yet mixed with all their activities there is to be found magic, a series of rites performed every year over the gardens in rigorous sequence and order. Since the leadership in garden work is in the hands of the magician, and since ritual and practical work are intimately associated, a superficial observer might be led to assume that the mystic and the rational behavior are mixed up, that their effects are not distinguished by the natives and not distinguishable in scientific analysis. Is this so really?

Magic is undoubtedly regarded by the natives as absolutely indispensable to the welfare of the gardens. What would happen without it no one can exactly tell, for no native garden has ever been made without its ritual, in spite of some thirty years of European rule and missionary influence and well over a century's contact with white traders. But certainly various kinds of disaster, blight, unseasonable droughts rains, bush-pigs, and locusts, would destroy the unhallowed garden made without magic.

Does this mean, however, that the natives attribute all the good results to magic? Certainly not. If you were to suggest to a native that he should make his garden mainly by magic and scamp his work, he would simply smile on your simplicity. He knows as well as you do that there are natural conditions and causes, and by his observations he knows also that he is able to control these natural forces by mental and physical effort. His knowledge is limited, no doubt, but as far as it goes it is sound and proof against mysticism. If the fences are broken down, if the seed is destroyed or has been dried or washed away, he will have recourse not to magic, but to work, guided by knowledge and reason. His experience has taught him also, on the other hand, that in spite of all his forethought and beyond all his efforts there are agencies and forces which one year bestow unwonted and unearned benefits of fertility, making everything run smooth and well, rain and sun appear at the right moment, noxious insects remain in abeyance, the harvest yields a superabundant crop; and another year again the same agencies bring ill luck and bad chance, pursue him from beginning till end and thwart all his most strenuous efforts and his best-founded knowledge. To control these influences and these only he employs magic.

Thus there is a clear-cut division: there is first the well-known set of conditions, the natural course of growth, as well as the ordinary pests and dangers to be warded off by fencing and weeding. On the other hand there is the domain of the unaccountable and adverse influences, as well as the great unearned increment of fortunate coincidence. The first conditions are coped with by knowledge and work, the second by magic.

This line of division can also be traced in the social setting of work and ritual respectively. Though the garden magician is, as a rule, also the leader in practical activities, these two functions are kept strictly apart. Every magical ceremony has its distinctive name, its appropriate time and its place in the scheme of work, and it stands out of the ordinary course of activities completely. Some of them are ceremonial and have to be attended by the whole community, all are public in that it is known when they are going to happen and anyone can attend them. They are performed on selected plots within the gardens and on a special corner of this plot. Work is always tabooed on such occasions, sometimes only while the ceremony lasts, sometimes for a day or two. In his lay character the leader and magician directs the work, fixes the dates for starting, harangues and exhorts slack or careless gardeners. But the two roles never overlap or interfere: they are always clear, and any native will inform you without hesitation whether the man acts as magician or as leader in garden work.

What has been said about gardens can be paralleled from any one of the many other activities in which work and magic run side by side without ever mixing. Thus in canoe building empirical knowledge of material, of technology, and of certain principles of stability and hydrodynamics, function in company and close association with magic, each yet uncontaminated by the other.

For example, they understand perfectly well that the wider the span of the outrigger the greater the stability yet the smaller the resistance against strain. They can clearly explain why they have to give this span a certain traditional width, measured in fractions of the length of the dugout. They can also explain, in rudimentary but clearly mechanical terms, how they have to behave in a sudden gale, why the outrigger must be always on the weather side, why the one type of canoe can and the other cannot beat. They have, in fact, a whole system of principles of sailing, embodied in a complex and rich terminology, traditionally handed on and obeyed as rationally and consistently as is modern science by modern sailors. How could they sail otherwise under eminently dangerous conditions in their frail primitive craft?

But even with all their systematic knowledge, methodically applied, they are still at the mercy of powerful and incalculable tides, sudden gales during the monsoon season, and unknown reefs. And here comes in their magic, performed over the canoe during its construction, carried out at the beginning and in the course of expeditions and resorted to in moments of real danger. If the modern seaman, entrenched in science and reason, provided with all sorts of safety appliances, sailing on steel-built steamers, if even he has a singular tendency to superstition—which does not rob him of his knowledge or reason, nor make him altogether prelogical—can we wonder that his savage colleague, under much more precarious conditions, holds fast to the safety and comfort of magic?

An interesting and crucial test is provided by fishing in the Trobriand Islands and its magic. While in the villages on the inner lagoon, fishing is done in an easy and absolutely reliable manner by the method of poisoning, yielding abundant results without danger and uncertainty, there are on the shores of the open sea dangerous modes of fishing and also certain types in which the yield greatly varies according to whether shoals of fish appear beforehand or not. It is most significant that in the lagoon fishing, where man can rely completely upon his knowledge and skill, magic does not exist, while in the open-sea fishing, full of danger and uncertainty, there is extensive magical ritual to secure safety and good results.

Again, in warfare the natives know that strength, courage, and agility play a decisive part. Yet here also they practice magic to master the elements of chance and luck.

Nowhere is the duality of natural and supernatural causes divided by a line so thin and intricate, yet, if carefully followed up, so well marked, decisive, and instructive, as in the two most fateful forces of human destiny: health and death. Health to the Melanesians is a natural state of affairs and, unless tampered with, the human body will remain in perfect order. But the natives know perfectly well that there are natural means which can affect health and even destroy the body. Poisons, wounds, burns, falls, are known to cause disablement or death in a natural way. And this is not a matter of private opinion of this or that individual, but it is laid down in traditional lore and even in belief, for there are considered to be different ways to the nether world for those who died by sorcery and those who met "natural" death. Again, it is recognized that cold, heat, overstrain, too much sun, overeating, can all cause minor ailments, which are treated by natural remedies such as massage, steaming, warming at a fire and certain potions. Old age is known to lead to bodily decay and the explanation is given by the natives that very old people grow weak, their oesophagus closes up, and therefore they must die.

But besides these natural causes there is the enormous domain of sorcery and by far the most cases of illness and death are ascribed to this. The line of distinction between sorcery and the other causes is clear in theory and in most cases of practice, but it must be realized that it is subject to what could be called the personal perspective. That is, the more closely a case has to do with the person who considers it, the less will it be "natural," the more "magical." Thus a very old man, whose pending death will be considered natural by the other members of the community, will be afraid only of sorcery and never think of his natural fate. A fairly sick person will diagnose sorcery in his own case, while all the others might speak of too much betel nut or overeating or some other indulgence.

But who of us really believes that his own bodily infirmities and the approaching death is a purely natural occurrence, just an insignificant event in the infinite chain of causes? To the most rational of civilized men health, disease, the threat of death, float in a hazy emotional mist, which seems to become denser and more impenetrable as the fateful forms approach. It is indeed astonishing that "savages" can achieve such a sober, dispassionate outlook in these matters as they actually do.

Thus in his relation to nature and destiny, whether he tries to exploit the first or to dodge the second, primitive man recognizes both the natural and the supernatural forces and agencies, and he tries to use them both for his benefit. Whenever he has been taught by experience that effort guided by knowledge is of some avail, he never spares the one or ignores the other. He knows that a plant cannot grow by magic alone, or a canoe sail or float without being properly constructed and managed, or a fight be won without skill and daring. He never relies on magic alone, while, on the contrary, he sometimes dispenses with it completely, as in fire-making and in a number of crafts and pursuits. But he clings to it, whenever he has to recognize the impotence of his knowledge and of his rational technique. . . .

This brings us to the second question: Can we regard primitive knowledge, which, as we found, is both empirical and rational, as a rudimentary stage of science, or is it not at all related to it? If by science be understood a body of rules and conceptions, based on experience and derived from it by logical inference, embodied in material achievements and in a fixed form of tradition and carried on by some sort of social organization—then there is no doubt that even the lowest savage communities have the beginnings of science, however rudimentary.

Most epistemologists would not, however, be satisfied with such a "minimum definition" of science, for it might apply to the rules of an art or craft as well. They would maintain that the rules of science must be laid down explicitly, open to control by experiment and critique by reason. They must not only be rules of practical behavior, but theoretical laws of knowledge. Even accepting this stricture, however, there is hardly any doubt that many of the principles of savage knowledge are scientific in this sense. The native shipwright knows not only practically of buoyancy, leverage, equilibrium, he has to obey these laws not only on water, but while making the canoe he must have the principles in his mind. He instructs his helpers in them. He gives them the traditional rules, and in a crude and simple manner, using his hands, pieces of wood, and a limited technical vocabulary, he explains some general laws of hydrodynamics and equilibrium. Science is not detached from the craft, that is certainly true, it is only a means to an end, it is crude, rudimentary, and inchoate, but with all that it is the matrix from which the higher developments must have sprung.

Notes

1.   *The Elementary Forms of the Religious Life,* p. 206.
2.   *Ibid.*
3.   J. Harrison, *Themis,* p. 42.
4.   J. Harrison, op. cit. p. 44

Witchcraft Explains Unfortunate Events

E. E. Evans-Pritchard

In this classic analysis of witchcraft beliefs, Evans-Pritchard shows the Azande of Africa to be just as rational as we are when it comes to explaining unfortunate events.

If a potter breaks a pot or if a farmer watches helplessly as his crops fail, the Azande will acknowledge the same cause-and-effect relationships that we do. Of course, an inexperienced potter is going to break more pots than would an accomplished artisan. Of course, blight may cause one farmer's crop to fail. But, the Azande reason, why does even an *experienced* potter have a pot break if he has successfully used the same materials in the same way time after time? Why did one farmer's crop fail, but the crops of his neighbors did not, even though the same soil and weather conditions seemed to prevail? Tough luck? That is what we would say. Witchcraft? The Azande are convinced of it.

But, what do we mean by "tough luck?" and how is it any better of an explanation than the notion that someone is out to harm you?

Consider a more contemporary example. A motorist is driving through an intersection with the green light in his favor. Another motorist runs the red and hits him. Now, the victim certainly knows the immediate cause of the accident—the other motorist. Yet, there remains that nagging element of uncertainty in his mind as he thinks to himself: "I have driven through many intersections without getting hit and there are many motorists who run red lights without hitting anyone. Why did *I* happen to be driving through *this* intersection *precisely when* that guy ran a red light?" Chance? Law of averages? At least, to the Azande, a witch is more tangible practical target, i.e. an actual person that one can confront if one chooses to do so.

The fact that E.E. Evans-Pritchard (1902–1973) studied at the London School of Economics under Bronislaw Malinowski probably has something to do his emphasis on the role of religion in satisfying peoples' social needs and in resolving human conflicts.

Evans-Pritchard did his fieldwork among the Nuer of Sudan and taught at the London School of Economics, the Egyptian University in Cairo, and at Cambridge University during the 1930s. From 1946 until his retirement in 1970, he held the chair of social anthropology at Oxford University.

Key Concept: witchcraft

In few societies of the world does witchcraft assume a more focal interest than among the Azande, a large and complex group situated both north and south of the Sudan-Belgian Congo border. The Azande recognize witchcraft to be a psychic act, and they clearly differentiate it from sorcery, which concerns itself with spells and medicines. They believe that a person is a witch because of an inherited organ or substance called *mangu*. Mangu is oval, is located somewhere between the breastbone and the intestines, and is variously described as reddish, blackish, or hairy. A male can inherit mangu only from a male, a female only from a female. An autopsy may be performed to determine the presence or absence of mangu. Since an accusation of witchcraft may result in a stigma or a fine, or both, autopsies are sometimes carried out to clear a family name.

Witchcraft explains unfortunate events, but only if these events are unusual and inexplicable. An event which is clearly due to carelessness, sorcery, or a taboo violation would not be explained as being due to witchcraft. It is the uncommon event, the event which cannot be understood through normal causal interpretation, which is "obviously" due to witchcraft. The logic used in positing witchcraft as the cause of such strange events is impeccable. It is the basic premise, not be logic, which is at fault.

There are many plausible functions of Zande witchcraft. A man who is too successful, for example, one who finds three honeycombs in one day, is accused of witchcraft. Such accusations militate against any strong striving for success. The economic efficiency of the *kpolo* (extended family) is maintained by directing all conflicts outside the kpolo through accusations of witchcraft. A member of one's own extended family cannot be accused of witchcraft. The fact that the Azande have not engaged in feuds or raids may indicate the ability of accusations and angers against witches to absorb latent hostilities.

Most important, however, is the usefulness of witchcraft in explaining why an event occurred. Science cannot tell us what happened, beyond mentioning the laws of probability. The Azande find both comfort and an opportunity to retaliate in their explanation of why an unfortunate and unusual event took place.

It is an inevitable conclusion from Zande descriptions of witchcraft that it is not an objective reality. The physiological condition which is said to be the seat of witchcraft, and which I believe to be nothing more than food passing through the small intestine, is an objective condition, but the qualities they attribute to it and the rest of their beliefs about it are mystical. Witches, as Azande conceive them, cannot exist.

The concept of witchcraft nevertheless provides them with a natural philosophy by which the relations between men and unfortunate events are explained and with a ready and stereotyped means of reacting to such events. Witchcraft beliefs also embrace a system of values which regulate human conduct.

Witchcraft is ubiquitous. It plays its part in every activity of Zande life; in agricultural, fishing, and hunting pursuits; in domestic life of homesteads as well as in communal life of district and court; it is an important theme of mental life in which it forms the background of a vast panorama of oracles and magic; its influence is plainly stamped on law and morals, etiquette and religion; it is prominent in technology and language; there is no niche or corner of Zande culture into which it does not twist itself. If blight seizes the groundnut crop it is witchcraft; it the bush is vainly scoured for game it is witchcraft; if women laboriously bail water out of a pool and are rewarded by but a few small fish it is witchcraft; if termites do not rise when their swarming is due and a cold useless night is spent in waiting for their flight, it is witchcraft; if a wife is sulky and unresponsive to her husband it is witchcraft; if a prince is cold and distant with his subject it is witchcraft; if a magical rite fails to achieve its purpose it is witchcraft; if, in fact, any failure or misfortune falls upon any one at any time and in relation to any of the manifold activities of his life it may be due to witchcraft. Those acquainted either at firsthand or through reading with the life of an African people will realize that there is no end to possible misfortunes, in routine tasks and leisure hours alike, arising not only from miscalculation, incompetence, and laziness, but also from causes over which the African, with his meager scientific knowledge, has no control. The Zande attributes all these misfortunes to witchcraft unless there is strong evidence, and subsequent oracular confirmation, that sorcery or one of those evil agents which I mentioned in the preceding section has been at work, or unless they are clearly to be attributed to incompetence, breach of a taboo, or failure to observe a moral rule.

When a Zande speaks of witchcraft he does not speak of it as we speak of the weird witchcraft of our own history. Witchcraft is to him a commonplace happening and he seldom passes a day without mentioning it. Where we talk about the crops, hunting, and our neighbors' ailments the Zande introduces into these topics of conversation the subject of witchcraft. To say that witchcraft has blighted the groundnut crop, that witchcraft has scared away game, and that witchcraft had made so-and-so ill is equivalent to saying in terms of our own culture that the groundnut crop has failed owing to blight, that game is scarce this season, and that so-and-so has caught influenza. Witchcraft participates in all misfortunes and is the idiom in which Azande speak about them and in which they explain them. Witchcraft is a classification of misfortunes which while differing from each other in other respects have this single common character, their harmfulness to man.

Unless the reader appreciates that witchcraft is quite a normal factor in the life of Azande, one to which almost any and every happening may be referred, he will entirely misunderstand their behavior towards it. To us witchcraft is something which haunted and disgusted our credulous forefathers. But the Zande expects to come across witchcraft at any time of the day or night. He would be just as surprised if he were not brought into daily contact with it as we would be if confronted by its appearance. To him there is nothing miraculous about it. It is expected that a man's hunting will be injured by witches, and he has at his disposal means of dealing with them. When misfortunes occur he does not became awe-struck at the play of supernatural forces. He is not terrified at the presence of an occult enemy. He is, on the other hand, extremely annoyed. Some one, out of spite, has ruined his groundnuts or spoiled his hunting or given his wife a chill, and surely this is cause for anger! He has done no one harm, so what right has anyone to interfere in his affairs? It is an impertinence, an insult, a dirty, offensive trick! It is the aggressiveness and not the eeriness of these actions which Azande emphasize when speaking of them, and it is anger and not awe which we observe in their response to them.

Witchcraft is not less anticipated than adultery. It is so intertwined with everyday happenings that it is part of a Zande's ordinary world. There is nothing remarkable about a witch—you may be one yourself, and certainly many of your closest neighbors are witches. Nor is there anything awe-inspiring about witchcraft. We do not become psychologically transformed when we hear that someone is ill—we expect people to be ill—and it is the same with Azande. They expect people to be ill, i.e., to be bewitched, and it is not a matter for surprise or wonderment.

But is not Zande belief in witchcraft a belief in mystical causation of phenomena and events to the complete exclusion of all natural causes? The relations of mystical to commonsense thought are very complicated and raise problems that confront us on every page of this book. Here I wish to state the problem in a preliminary manner and in terms of actual situations.

I found it strange at first to live among Azande and listen to naïve explanations of misfortunes which, to our minds, have apparent causes, but after a while I learned the idiom of their thought and applied notions of witchcraft as spontaneously as themselves in situations where the concept was relevant. A boy knocked his foot against a small stump of wood in the center of a bush path, a frequent happening in Africa, and suffered pain and inconvenience in consequence. Owing to its position on his toe it was impossible to keep the cut free from dirt and it began to fester. He declared that witchcraft had made him knock his foot against the stump. I always argued with Azande and criticized their statements, and I did so on this occasion. I told the boy that he had knocked his foot against the stump of wood because he had been careless, and that witchcraft had not placed it in the path, for it had grown there naturally. He agreed that witchcraft had nothing to do with the stump of wood being in his path but added that he had kept his eyes open for stumps, as indeed every Zande does most carefully, and that if he had not been bewitched he would have seen the stump. As a conclusive argument for his view he remarked that all cuts do not take days to heal but, on the contrary, close quickly, for that is the nature of cuts. Why, then, had his sore festered and remained open if there were no witchcraft behind it? This, as I discovered before long, was to be regarded as the Zande explanation of sickness. Thus, to give a further example, I had been feeling unfit for several days, and I consulted Zande friends whether my consumption of bananas could have had anything to do with my indisposition and I was at once informed that bananas do not cause sickness, however many are eaten, unless one is bewitched. I have described at length Zande notions of disease in Part IV, so I shall record here a few examples of witchcraft being offered as an explanation for happenings other than illness.

Shortly after my arrival in Zandeland we were passing through a government settlement and noticed that a hut had been burnt to the ground on the previous night. Its owner was overcome with grief as it had contained the beer he was preparing for mortuary feast. He told us that he had gone the previous night to examine his beer. He had lit a handful of straw and raised it above his head so that light would be cast on the pots, and in so doing he had ignited the thatch. He, and my companions also, were convinced that the disaster was caused by witchcraft.

One of my chief informants, Kisanga, was a skilled wood carver, one of the finest carvers in the whole kingdom of Gbudwe. Occasionally the bowls and stools which he carved split during the work as one may well imagine in such a climate. Though the hardest woods be selected they sometimes split in process of carving or on completion of the utensil even if the craftsman is careful and well acquainted with the technical rules of his craft. When this happened to the bowls and stools of this particular craftsman he attributed the misfortune to witchcraft and used to harangue me about the spite and jealousy of his neighbors. When I used to reply that I thought he was mistaken and that people were well disposed towards him he used to hold the split bowl or stool toward me as concrete evidence of his assertions. If people were not bewitching his work, how would I account for that? Likewise a potter will attribute the cracking of his pots during firing to witchcraft. An experience potter need have no fear that his pots will crack as a result of error. He selects the proper clay, kneads it thoroughly till he has extracted all grit and pebbles, and builds it up slowly and carefully. On the night before digging out his clay he abstains from sexual intercourse. So he should have nothing to fear. Yet pots sometimes break, even when they are the handiwork of expert potters, and this can only be accounted for by witchcraft. "It is broken—there is witchcraft," says the potter simply. Many similar situations in which witchcraft is cited as an agent are instanced throughout this and following chapters.

In speaking to Azande about witchcraft and in observing their reactions to situations of misfortune it was obvious that they did not attempt to account for the existence of phenomena, or even the action of phenomena, by mystical causation alone. What they explained by witchcraft were the particular conditions in a chain of causation which related an individual to natural happenings in such a way that he sustained injury. The boy who knocked his foot against a stump of wood did not account for the stump by reference to witchcraft, nor did he suggest that whenever anybody knocks his foot against a stump it is necessarily due to witchcraft, not yet again did he account for the cut by saying that it was caused by witchcraft, for he knew quite well that it was caused by the stump of wood. What he attributed to witchcraft was that on this particular occasion, when exercising his usual care, he struck his foot against a stump of wood, whereas on a hundred other occasions he did not do so, and that on this particular occasion the cut, which he expected to result from the knock, festered whereas he had had dozens of cuts which had not festered. Surely these peculiar conditions demand an explanation. Again, if one eats a number of bananas this does not in itself cause sickness. Why should it do so? Plenty of people eat bananas but are not sick in consequence, and I myself had often done so in the past. Therefore my indisposition could not possibly be attributed to bananas alone. If bananas alone had caused my sickness, then it was necessary to account for the fact that they had caused me sickness on this single occasion and not on dozens of previous occasions, and that they had made only me ill and not other people who were eating them. Again, every year hundreds of Azande go and inspect their beer by night and they always take with them a handful of straw in order to illuminate the hut in which it is fermenting. Why then should this particular man on this single occasion have ignited the thatch of his hut? I present the Zande's explicit line of reasoning—not my own. Again my friend the wood carver had made scores of bowls and stools without mishap and he knew all there was to know about the selection of wood, use of tools, and conditions of carving. His bowls and stools did not split like the products of craftsmen who were unskilled in their work, so why on rare occasions should his bowls and stools split when they did not split usually and when he had exercised all his usual knowledge and care? He knew the answer well enough and so, in his opinion, did his envious, backbiting neighbors. In the same way, a potter wants to know why his pots should break on an occasion when he uses the same material and techniques as on other occasions; or rather he already knows, for the reason is known in advance, as it were. If the pots break it is due to witchcraft.

We must understand, therefore, that we shall give a false account of Zande philosophy if we say that they believe witchcraft to be the sole cause of phenomena. This proposition is not contained in Zande patterns of thought, which only assert that witchcraft brings a man into relation with events in such a way that he sustains injury.

My old friend Ongosi was many years ago injured by an elephant while out hunting, and his prince, Basongoda, consulted the oracles to discover who had bewitched him. We must distinguish here between the elephant and its prowess, on the one hand, and the fact that a particular elephant injured a particular man, on the other hand. The Supreme Being, not witchcraft, created elephants and gave them tusks and a trunk and huge legs so that they are able to pierce men and filing them sky high and reduce them to pulp by kneeling on them. But whenever men and elephants come across one another in the bush these dreadful things do not happen. They are rare events. Why, then, should this particular man on this one occasion in a life crowded with similar situations in which he and his friends emerged scatheless have been gored by this particular beast? Why he and not someone else? Why on this occasion and not on other occasions? Why by this elephant and not by other elephants? It is the particular and variable conditions of an event and not the general and universal conditions that witchcraft explains. Fire is hot, but it is not hot owing to witchcraft, for that is its nature. It is universal quality of fire to burn, but is not a universal quality of fire to burn *you*. This may

never happen; or once in a lifetime, and then only if you have been bewitched.

In Zandeland sometimes an old granary collapses. There is nothing remarkable in this. Every Zande knows that termites eat the supports in course of time and that even the hardest woods decay after years of service. Now a granary is the summerhouse of a Zande homestead and people sit beneath it in the heat of the day and chat or play the African hole game or work at some craft. Consequently it may happen that there are people sitting beneath the granary when it collapses and they are injured, for it is a heavy structure made of beams and clay and may be stored with eleusine as well. Now why should these particular people have been sitting under this particular granary at the particular moment when it collapsed? That it should collapse is easily intelligible, but why should it have collapsed at the particular moment when these particular people were sitting beneath it? Through years it might have collapsed, so why should it fall just when certain people sought its kindly shelter? We say that the granary collapsed because its supports were eaten away by termites. That is the cause that explains the collapse of the granary. We also say that people were sitting under it at the time because it was in the heat of the day and they thought that it would be a comfortable place to talk and work. This is the cause of people being under the granary at the time it collapsed. To our minds the only relationship between these two independently caused facts is their coincidence in time and space. We have no explanation of why the two chains of causation intersected at a certain time and in a certain place, for there is no interdependence between them.

Zande philosophy can supply the missing link. The Zande knows that the supports were undermined by termites and that people were witting beneath the granary in order to escape the heat and glare of the sun. But he knows besides why these two events occurred at a precisely similar moment in time and space. It was due to the action of witchcraft. If there had been no witchcraft people would have been sitting under the granary and it would not have fallen on them, or it would have collapsed but the people would not have been sheltering under it at the time. Witchcraft explains the coincidence of these two happenings.

Cults and Ritual

Selection 25
PETER M. WORSLEY, from "Cargo Cults," *Scientific American*

Selection 26
RALPH LINTON, from "Totemism and the A. E. F.," *American Anthropologist*

Selection 27
CLIFFORD GEERTZ, from "Deep Play: Notes on the Balinese Cockfight," *Daedalus*

Selection 28
MARVIN HARRIS, from "Mother Cow," *Cows, Pigs, Wars, and Witches: The Riddles of Culture*

Cargo Cults

Peter M. Worsley

We tend to think of the last few centuries of Western expansion in terms of what it meant to people of European extraction—the finding of new worlds of people and resources initially strange to them. We often forget, however, that the indigenous peoples of the world have had their own thoughts about the colonial encounter. Among the first impressions of native peoples is the fact of the vast discrepancies in terms of material wealth between what they had and what the Europeans brought with them. Moreover, amazingly to them, white people seemed to make no effort in acquiring trade goods—"cargo" in the Pidgin English of New Guinea. The belief soon spread that the cargo was actually made by the dead ancestors and intended for the hardworking and deserving natives, but that the Europeans, holding the "secret" of the cargo, were intercepting the goods. (The fact that cargo planes dropped goods by parachute in World War II reinforced this belief.) Furthermore, the world as it was known would soon come to an end, the whites would leave, and the native peoples would get what they justly deserved.

Peter Worsley (b. 1924) acquired a B.A. in anthropology and an M.A. in archeology from Cambridge University in 1947. He was then appointed a readership at Manchester University, where he got his M.A. He eventually moved to Australia, where he did research on Melanesian cultures and then obtained a Ph.D. at the Australian National University. In 1955, he returned to England and taught sociology at the University of Hull until 1964 when he was appointed to the sociology chair at Manchester University. His best known book is *The Trumpet Shall Sound: A Study of Cargo Cults in Melanesia* (2nd rev. edition, 1957, New York: Schocken)

Key Concept: Cargo Cults

Patrols of the Australian Government venturing into the "uncontrolled" central highlands of New Guinea in 1946 found the primitive people there swept up in a wave of religious excitement. Prophecy was being fulfilled: The arrival of the Whites was the sign that the end of the world was at hand. The natives proceeded to butcher all of their pigs—animals that were not only a principal source of subsistence but also symbols of social status and ritual pre-eminence in their culture. They killed these valued animals in expression of the belief that after three days of darkness "Great Pigs" would appear from the sky. Food, firewood, and other necessities had to be stock-piled to see the people through to the arrival of the Great Pigs. Mock wireless antennae of bamboo and rope had been erected to receive in advance the news of the millennium. Many believed that with the great event they would exchange their black skins for white ones.

This bizarre episode is by no means the single event of its kind in the murky history of the collision of European civilization with the indigenous cultures of the southwest Pacific. For more than 100 years traders and missionaries have been reporting similar disturbances among the peoples of Melanesia, the group of Negro-inhabited islands (including New Guinea, Fiji, the Solomons, and the New Hebrides) lying between Australia and the open Pacific Ocean. Though their technologies were based largely upon stone and wood, these peoples had highly developed cultures, as measured by the standards of maritime and agricultural ingenuity, the complexity of their varied social organizations and the elaboration of religious belief and ritual. They were nonetheless ill prepared for the shock of the encounter with the Whites, a people so radically different from themselves and so infinitely more powerful. The sudden transition from the society of the ceremonial stone ax to the society of sailing ships and now of airplanes has not been easy to make.

After four centuries of Western expansion, the densely populated central highlands of New Guinea remain one of the few regions where the people still carry on their primitive existence in complete independence of the world outside. Yet as the agents of the Australian Government penetrate into ever more remote mountain valleys, they find these backwaters of antiquity already deeply disturbed by contact with the ideas and artifacts of European civilization. For "cargo"—Pidgin English for trade goods—has long flowed along the indigenous channels of communication from the seacoast into the wilderness. With it has traveled the frightening knowledge of the white man's magical power. No small element in the white man's magic is the hopeful message sent abroad by his missionaries: the news that a Messiah will come and that the present order of Creation will end.

The people of the central highlands of New Guinea are only the latest to be gripped in the recurrent religious frenzy of the "cargo cults." However variously embellished with details from native myth and Christian belief, these cults all advance the same central theme: the world is about to end in a terrible cataclysm. Thereafter God, the ancestors or some local culture hero will appear and inaugurate a blissful paradise on earth. Death, old age, illness, and evil will be unknown. The riches of the white man will accrue to the Melanesians.

Although the news of such a movement in one area has doubtless often inspired similar movements in other areas, the evidence indicates that these cults have arisen independently in many places as parallel responses to the same enormous social stress and strain. Among the movements best known to students of Melanesia are the "Taro Cult" of New Guinea, the "Vailala Madness" of Papua, the "Naked Cult" of Espiritu Santo, the "John Frum Movement" of the New Hebrides, and the "Tuka Cult" of the Fiji Islands.

At times the cults have been so well organized and fanatically persistent that they have brought the work of government to a standstill. The outbreaks have often taken the authorities completely by surprise and have confronted them with mass opposition of an alarming kind. In the 1930s, for example, villagers in the vicinity of Wewak, New Guinea, were stirred by a succession of "Black King" movements. The prophets announced that the Europeans would soon leave the island, abandoning their property to the natives, and urged their followers to cease paying taxes, since the government station was about to disappear into the sea in a great earthquake. To the tiny community of Whites in charge of the region, such talk was dangerous. The authorities jailed four of the prophets and exiled three others. In yet another movement, that sprang up in declared opposition to the local Christian mission, the cult leader took Satan as his god.

Troops on both sides in World War II found their arrival in Melanesia heralded as a sign of the Apocalypse. The G.I.'s who landed in the New Hebrides, moving up for the bloody fighting on Guadalcanal, found the natives furiously at work preparing airfields, roads and docks for the magic ships and planes that they believed were coming from "Rusefel" (Roosevelt), the friendly king of America.

The Japanese also encountered millenarian visionaries during their southward march to Guadalcanal. Indeed, one of the strangest minor military actions of World War II occurred in Dutch New Guinea, when Japanese forces had to be turned against the local Papuan inhabitants of the Geelvink Bay region. The Japanese had at first been received with great joy, not because their "Greater East Asia Co-Prosperity Sphere" propaganda had made any great impact upon the Papuans, but because the natives regarded them as harbingers of the new world that was dawning, the flight of the Dutch having already given the first sign. Mansren, creator of the islands and their peoples, would now return, bringing with him the ancestral dead. All this had been known, the cult leaders declared, to the crafty Dutch, who had torn out the first page of the Bible where these truths were inscribed. When Mansren returned, the existing world order would be entirely overturned. White men would turn black like Papuans, Papuans would become Whites; root crops would grow in trees, and coconuts and fruits would grow like tubers. Some of the islanders now began to draw together into large "towns"; others took Biblical names such as "Jericho" and "Galilee" for their villages. Soon they adopted military uniforms and began drilling. The Japanese, by now highly unpopular, tried to disarm and disperse the Papuans; resistance inevitably developed. The climax of this tragedy came when several canoe-loads of fanatics sailed out to attack Japanese warships, believing themselves to be invulnerable by virtue of the holy water with which they had sprinkled themselves. But the bullets of the Japanese did not turn to water, and the attackers were moved down by machine-gun fire.

Behind this incident lay a long history. As long ago as 1857 missionaries in the Geelvink Bay region had made note of the story of Mansren. It is typical of many Melanesian myths that became confounded with Christian doctrine to form the ideological basis of the movements. The legend tells how long ago there lived an old man named Manamakeri ("he who itches"), whose body was covered with sores. Manamakeri was extremely fond of palm wine, and used to climb a huge tree every day to tap the liquid from the flowers. He soon found that someone was getting there before him and removing the liquid. Eventually he trapped the thief, who turned out to be none other than the Morning Star. In return for his freedom, the Star gave the old man a wand that would produce as much fish as he liked, a magic tree and a magic staff. If he drew in the sand and stamped his foot, the drawing would become real. Manamakeri, aged as he was, now magically impregnated a young maiden; the child of this union was a miracle-child who spoke as soon as he was born. But the maiden's parents were horrified, and banished her, the child, and the old man. The trio sailed off in a canoe created by Mansren ("The Lord"), as the old man now became known. On this journey Mansren rejuvenated himself by stepping into a fire and flaking off his scaly skin, which changed into valuables. He then sailed around Geelvink Bay, creating islands where he stopped, and peopling them with the ancestors of the present-day Papuans.

The Mansren myth is plainly a creation myth full of symbolic ideas relating to fertility and rebirth. Comparative evidence—especially the shedding of his scaly skin—confirms the suspicion that the old man is, in fact, the Snake in another guise. Psychoanalytic writers argue that the snake occupies such a prominent part in mythology the world over because it stands for the penis, another fertility symbol. This may be so, but its symbolic significance is surely more complex than this. It is the "rebirth" of the hero, whether Mansren of the snake, that exercises such universal fascination over men's minds.

The 19th-century missionaries thought that the Mansren story would make the introduction of Christianity easier, since the concept of "resurrection," not to mention that of the "virgin birth" and the "second coming," was already there. By 1867, however, the first cult organized around the Mansren legend was reported.

Though such myths were widespread in Melanesia, and may have sparked occasional movements even in the pre-White era, they took on a new significance in the late 19th century, once the European powers had finished parceling out the Melanesian region among themselves. In many coastal areas the long history of "blackbirding"—the seizure of islanders for work on the plantations of Australia and Fiji—had built up a reservoir of hostility to Europeans. In other areas, however, the arrival of the Whites was accepted, even welcomed, for it meant access to bully beef and cigarettes, shirts and paraffin lamps, whisky, and bicycles. It also meant access to the knowledge behind these material goods, for the Europeans brought missions and schools as well as cargo.

*P*ractically the only teaching the natives received about European life came from the missions, which emphasized the central significance of religion in European society. The Melanesians already believed that man's activities—whether gardening, sailing canoes or bearing children—needed magical assistance. Ritual without human effort was not enough. But neither was human effort on its own. This outlook was reinforced by mission teaching.

The initial enthusiasm for European rule, however, was speedily dispelled. The rapid growth of the plantation economy removed the bulk of the able-bodied men from the villages, leaving women, children and old men to carry on as best they could. The splendid vision of the equality of all Christians began to seem a pious deception in face of the realities of the color bar, the multiplicity of rival Christian missions and the open irreligion of many Whites.

For a long time the natives accepted the European mission as the means by which the "cargo" would eventually be made available to them. But they found that acceptance of Christianity did not bring the cargo any nearer. They grew disillusioned. The story now began to be put about that it was not the Whites who made the cargo,

but the dead ancestors. To people completely ignorant of factory production, this made good sense. White men did not work; they merely wrote secret signs on scraps of paper, for which they were given shiploads of goods. On the other hand, the Melanesians labored week after week for pitiful wages. Plainly the goods must be made for Melanesians somewhere, perhaps in the Land of the Dead. The Whites, who possessed the secret of the cargo, were intercepting it and keeping it from the hands of the islanders, to whom it was really consigned. In the Madang district of New Guinea, after some 40 years' experience of the missions, the natives went in a body one day with a petition demanding that the cargo secret should now be revealed to them, for they had been very patient.

So strong is this belief in the existence of a "secret" that the cargo cults generally contain some ritual in imitation of the mysterious European customs which are held to be the clue to the white man's extraordinary power over goods and men. The believers sit around tables with bottles of flowers in front of them, dressed in European clothes, waiting for the cargo ship or airplane to materialize; other cultists feature magic pieces of paper and cabalistic writing. Many of them deliberately turn their backs on the past by destroying secret ritual objects, or exposing them to the gaze of uninitiated youths and women, for whom formerly even a glimpse of the sacred objects would have meant the severest penalties, even death. The belief that they were the chosen people is further reinforced by their reading of the Bible, for the lives and customs of the people in the Old Testament resemble their own lives rather than those of the Europeans. In the New Testament they find the Apocalypse, with its prophecies of destruction and resurrection, particularly attractive.

Missions that stress the imminence of the Second Coming, like those of the Seventh Day Adventists, are often accused of stimulating millenarian cults among the islanders. In reality, however, the Melanesians themselves rework doctrines the missionaries teach them, selecting from the Bible what they themselves find particularly congenial in it. Such movements have occurred in areas where missions of quite different types have been dominant, from Roman Catholic to Seventh Day Adventist. The reasons for the emergence of these cults, of course, lie far deeper in the life-experience of the people.

*T*he economy of most of the islands is very backward. Native agriculture produces little for the world market, and even the European plantations and mines export only a few primary products and raw materials: copra, rubber, gold. Melanesians are quite unable to understand why copra, for example, fetches 30 pounds sterling per ton one month and but 5 pounds a few months later. With no notion of the workings of world-commodity markets, the natives see only the sudden closing of plantations, reduced wages and unemployment, and are inclined to attribute their insecurity to the whim or evil in the nature of individual planters.

Such shocks have not been confined to the economic order. Governments, too, have come and gone, especially during the two world wars: German, Dutch, British and French administrations melted overnight. Then came the Japanese, only to be ousted in turn largely by the previously unknown Americans. And among these Americans the Melanesians saw Negroes like themselves, living lives of luxury on equal terms with white G.I.'s. The sight of these Negroes seemed like a fulfillment of the old prophecies to many cargo cult leaders. Nor must we forget the sheer scale of this invasion. Around a million U. S. troops passed through the Admiralty Islands, completely swamping the inhabitants. It was a world of meaningless and chaotic changes, in which anything was possible. New ideas were imported and given local twists. Thus in the Loyalty Islands people expected the French Communist Party to bring the millennium. There is no real evidence, however, of any Communist influence in these movements, despite the rather hysterical belief among Solomon Island planters that the name of the local "Masinga Rule" movement was derived from the word "Marxian"! In reality the name comes from a Solomon Island tongue, and means "brotherhood."

Europeans who have witnessed outbreaks inspired by the cargo cults are usually at a loss to understand what they behold. The islanders throw away their money, break their most sacred taboos, abandon their gardens and destroy their precious livestock; they indulge in sexual license or, alternatively, rigidly separate men from women in huge communal establishments. Sometimes they spend days sitting gazing at the horizon for a glimpse of the long-awaited ship or airplane; sometimes they dance, pray and sing in mass congregations, becoming possessed and "speaking with tongues."

Observes have not hesitated to use such words as "madness," "mania," and "irrationality" to characterize the cults. But the cults reflect quite logical and rational attempts to make sense out of a social order that appears senseless and chaotic. Given the ignorance of the Melanesians about the wider European society, its economic organization and its highly developed technology, their reactions form a consistent and understandable pattern. They wrap up all their yearning and hope in an amalgam that combines the best counsel they can find in Christianity and their native belief. If the world is soon to end, gardening or fishing is unnecessary; everything will be provided.

If the Melanesians are to be part of a much wider order, the taboos that prescribe their social conduct must now be lifted or broken in a newly prescribed way.

Of course the cargo never comes. The cults nonetheless live on. If the millennium does not arrive on schedule, then perhaps there is some failure in the magic, some error in the ritual. New breakaway groups organize around "purer" faith and ritual. The cult rarely disappears, so long as the social situation which brings it into being persists.

At this point it should be observed that cults of this general kind are not peculiar to Melanesia. Men who feel themselves oppressed and deceived have always been ready to pour their hopes and fears, their aspirations and frustrations, into dreams of a millennium to come or of a golden age to return. All parts of the world have had their counterparts of the cargo cults, from the American Indian ghost dance to the communist-millenarist "reign of the saints" in Münster during of Reformation, from medieval European apocalyptic cults of African "witch-finding" movements and Chinese Buddhist heresies. In some situations men have been content to wait and pray; in others they have sought to hasten the day by using their strong right arms to do the Lord's work. And always the cults serve to bring together scattered groups, notably the peasants and urban plebeians of agrarian societies and the peoples of "stateless" societies where the cult unites separate (and often hostile) villages, clans, and tribes into a wider religiopolitical unity.

Once the people begin to develop secular political organizations, however, the sects tend to lose their importance as vehicles of protest. They begin to relegate the Second Coming to the distant future or to the next world. In Melanesia ordinary political bodies, trade unions, and native councils are becoming the normal media through which the islanders express their aspirations. In recent years continued economic prosperity and political stability have taken some of the edge of their despair. It now seems unlikely that any major movement along cargo-cult lines will recur in areas where the transition to secular politics has been made, even if the insecurity of prewar times returned. I would predict that the embryonic nationalism represented by cargo cults is likely in future to take forms familiar in the history of other countries that have moved from subsistence agriculture to participation in the world economy.

Totemism and the A. E. F.

Ralph Linton

Much has been written about the concept of the *totem* over the past 150 years and, after all is said and done, there is very little that can be set forth in the way of generalization that would not be contradicted in some way, somewhere. Perhaps the safest things that can be said about totems is that they are generally symbolic, typically represent groups rather than individuals, and their insignia can be borrowed from just about any plant, animal, object or idea from the physical or social environment. As such, we can see the totemic notion being used in all kinds of societies, ranging from the very simplest to the most technologically modern.

Because anthropologists have focused primarily upon kinship as a key element of social organization, their primary interest in totemism has had to do with kinship group identification and marriage regulation. In many non-western cultures, for instance, a totem may be symbolic of clan membership and would usually mean that if two people, male and female, were strangers to each other and, yet, were to discover that they belonged to the same clan—identified by its totemic symbol—they would not be able to marry no matter how distantly they might be related.

But totems serve functions other than marriage regulation and, as Ralph Linton shows in the following article, the 42nd Army Division of the American Expeditionary Force of World War I found that being identified as the Rainbow division fostered group solidarity. Since the same can be said of the totems for modern-day sports team such as the Chicago Bears as well as "brotherhood" organizations such as the Elks Club, a focus on the general thought processes and social functions involved in totemic systems leads us to see them everywhere.

Ralph Linton (1893–1953) was born into the Hicksite faction of Quakers that emphasized hard work, high intellect, and no fun. His rebellious nature eventually led him away from his father and into anthropology. In fact, his service in the Forty-second (Rainbow) Division during World War I led to his being read out of the Friends Meeting for his willingness to bear arms. Although he attended graduate school at Columbia University, where he seemed to clash with Franz Boas (a pacifist and pro-German), Linton was to eventually get his Ph.D. from Harvard University. Linton began his career as an archeologist, but gravitated toward cultural anthropology and did fieldwork in Madagascar. Ralph Linton is best known for his book, *The Study of Man*, an introduction to cultural anthropology. He was then hired to replace Franz Boas at Columbia, where he was to become chair of the anthropology department.

Key Concept: totemism

$\mathcal{M}$any modern anthropologists discount the supposed differences in the mental processes of civilized and uncivilized peoples and hold that the psychological factors which have controlled the growth of the so-called primitive cultures are still at work in modern society. It is difficult to obtain evidence on this point, and a record of the development in the American army of a series of beliefs and practises which show a considerable resemblance to the totemic complexes existing among some primitive peoples may, therefore, be of interest. The growth of one of these pseudo-totemic complexes can be fully traced in the case of the 42nd or Rainbow Division. The name was arbitrarily chosen by the higher officials and is said to have been selected because the organization was made up of units from many states whose regimental colors were of every hue in the rainbow. Little importance was attached to the name while the division was in America and it was rarely used by enlisted men. After the organization arrived in France, its use became increasingly common, and the growth of a feeling of divisional solidarity finally resulted in its regular employment as a personal appellation. Outsiders usually addressed division members as "Rainbow," and to the question "What are you?" nine out of ten enlisted men would reply "I'm a Rainbow." This personal use of the name became general before any attitude toward the actual rainbow was developed. A feeling of connection between the organization and its namesake was first noted in February, 1918, five to six months after the assignment of the name. At this time it was first suggested and then believed that the appearance of a rainbow was a good omen for the division. Three months later it had become an article of faith in the organization that there was always a rainbow in the sky when the division went into action. A rainbow over the enemy's lines was considered especially auspicious, and after a victory men would often insist that they had seen one in this position even when the weather conditions or direction of advance made it impossible. This belief was held by most of the officers and enlisted men, and anyone who expressed doubts was considered a heretic and overwhelmed with arguments.

The personal use of the divisional name and the attitude toward the rainbow had both become thoroughly established before it began to be used as an emblem. In the author's regiment this phase first appeared in May, when the organization came in contact with the 77th Division which had its namesake, the Goddess of Liberty, painted on its carts and other divisional property. The idea was taken up at once, and many of the men decorated the carts and limbers in their charge with rainbows without waiting for official permission. As no two of the painted rainbows were alike, the effect was grotesque and the practice was soon forbidden. Nevertheless it continued, more or less surreptitiously, until after the armistice, when it was finally permitted with a standardized rainbow.

The use of rainbows as personal insignia appeared still later, in August or September. The history of the development of shoulder insignia in the American army is well known and need not be given here. The idea apparently originated with the Canadian forces, but the A. E. F. received it indirectly through one of the later American organizations which had adopted it before their arrival in France. The use of such insignia became general in the rear areas before it reached the divisions at the front. The first shoulder insignia seen by the author's regiment were worn by a salvage corps and by one of the newer divisions. This division was rumored to have been routed in its first battle, and it was believed that its members were forced to wear the insignia as punishment. The idea thus reached the 42nd Division under unfavorable auspices, but it was immediately taken up and passed through nearly the same phases as the use of painted insignia on divisional property. The wearing of shoulder insignia was at first forbidden by some of the regimental commanders, but even while it was proscribed many of the men carried insignia with them and pinned them on whenever they were out of reach of their officers. They were worn by practically all members of the division when in the rear areas, and their use by outsiders, or even by the men sent to the division as replacements, was resented and punished. In the case of replacements, the stricture was relaxed as they became recognized members of the group.

All the other army organizations which were in existence long enough to develop a feeling of group solidarity seem to have built up similar complexes centering about their group names. The nature of some of these names precluded the development of the ideas of the namesake's guardianship or omen giving, but in such cases the beliefs which were associated with the rainbow by the 42nd Division were usually developed in connection with something other than the group namesake. In some organizations the behavior of an animal mascot, or even of an abnormal person, was considered ominous. In one instance a subnormal hysteric acquired a reputation as a soothsayer and was relieved of regular duty by the other enlisted men on condition that he foretell the outcome of an expected attack. The successive stages in the development of these complexes were not always the same as in the case of the 42nd Division. Many of the later organizations seems to have taken over such complexes with little change except the substitution of their namesake for that of the group from which they borrowed.

By the end of the war, A. E. F. had become organized into a series of well-defined, and often mutually jealous, groups each of which had its individual complex of ideas and observances. These complexes all conformed to the same general pattern but differed in content. The individual complexes bound the members of each group together and enabled them to present a united front against other groups. In the same way the uniformity of pattern gave a basis for mutual understanding and tolerance and united all the groups against persons or organizations outside the system.

The conditions in the American army after these group complexes had become fully developed may be summarized as follows:

1. A division of the personnel into a number of groups conscious of their individuality;
2. the possession by each of these groups of a distinctive name derived from some animal, object or natural phenomenon;
3. the use of this name as a personal appellation in conversation with outsiders;
4. the use of representations of the group namesake for the decoration of group property and for personal adornment, with a taboo against its use by members of other groups;
5. a reverential attitude toward the group namesake and its representations;
6. in many cases, an unformulated belief that the group namesake was also a group guardian capable of giving omens.

Almost any investigator who found such a condition existing among an uncivilized people would class these associated beliefs and practices as a totemic complex. It shows a poverty of content when contrasted with the highly developed totemism of the Australians or Melanesians, but is fully as rich as the totemic complexes of some of the North American Indian tribes. The main points in which it differs from true totemism are the absence of marriage regulations, of beliefs in descent from, or of blood relationship with, the totem, and of special rites or observances to propitiate the totem. Each of these features is lacking in one or another of the primitive complexes which are usually classed as totemic and one of the most important marriage regulation is clearly a function of the clan or gentile system of organization and occurs in primitive groups for which totemism can not be proved.

It seems probable that both the A. E. F. complexes and primitive totemism are results of the same social and supernaturalistic tendencies. The differences in the working out of these tendencies can readily be accounted for by the differences in the framework to which they have attached themselves and in the cultural patterns which have shaped their expression. In the army, the military unit offered a crystallization point for these tendencies, and this precluded the development of marriage regulations or of a belief in the common of the group. The American culture pattern stimulated the development of the eponymous and decorative features, but offered no formulae for the rationalization of the relation felt to exist between the group and its namesake, or for the development of observances for the namesake's propitiation. In primitive groups, on the other hand, the same tendencies usually crystallized about a clan or gentile system, and the marriage regulation features of this system became incorporated into the complex. Membership in the clan or gens was based on common descent, and in a group which drew no clear line between mankind and the rest of nature, the idea of blood relationship provided a convenient formula for the explanation of the group-namesake relation. Animistic or polytheistic concepts, and the existence of observances for the propitiation of a number of supernatural beings, afforded a pattern for the development of religious attitudes and special observances in connection with the namesake.

Even if we are willing to admit the essential unity of the tendencies which produced the army complexes on one hand and the totemic complexes on the other, it does not follow that the observed development of the army complexes will throw much light on the history of primitive totemism. Even in the army no universal rule of evolution was evident, for although the starting-points were always the group and name, the other features appeared in different order in the various units. The ease and rapidity with which the army complexes were developed suggests that the tendencies underlying them were deepseated and only awaited a chance for expression. The importance of diffusion in the growth of these complexes is suggestive, and the army conditions may afford a clue to the true significance of some totemic phenomena. The often quoted example of the Australian who declared he was a kangaroo is a case in point. The author repeatedly heard soldiers declare that they were sunsets, wild cats, etc. and it would have required a good deal of questioning to obtain any coherent explanation of the relation which they felt existed between themselves and their namesakes. Such a cross-examination would have been impossible with the limited vocabulary of a trade, jargon and very difficult with an ordinary interpreter. Although the army attitudes and practices were definite enough, their background was emotional rather than rational and the average soldier never attempted to formulate the ideas underlying them. Explanations elicited by questioning would be made up on the spur of the moment and would represent only his individual opinion. It seems probable that in primitive groups also a whole series of attitudes and practices could be developed without the individual feeling any need for their rationalization until he was confronted by some anthropological investigator.

Deep Play:
Notes on the Balinese Cockfight

Clifford Geertz

In this classic article, originally published in 1973, Clifford Geertz discusses the cockfight as a metaphor for just about everything else that happens in Bali, whether it is a war, a political contest, or a street fight. For each and every man involved, the cockfight symbolizes the struggle for status, dignity, self-esteem, and respect. And yet, the results of a cockfight rarely change anything. While it is true that bets are made, in the long run and for the overwhelming majority of people, the amounts are insignificant. And just as American sports fans metaphorically live and die each weekend, depending on the box scores, wins and losses and the chances that their team will make it to the playoffs, when all is said and done, their lives remain the same. While others run with the bulls in Pamplona, climb Mount Everest, or compete in the Iditarod, the Balinese attend cockfights, assemble along lines of allegiance, and scream their bets as if it truly made a difference. And who is to say that it does not lend excitement and meaning to their lives? In Geertz's ethnographic experience, it certainly does. This article also serves as a good example of Geertz's take on anthropology: it is "not an empirical science in search of law but an interpretive one in search of meaning." (see 1.4 "Godzilla Meets New Age Anthropology") Thus, Geertz is the leader of a movement referred to as "symbolic" or "interpretive" anthropology, which holds that culture imposes meaning and that the best an anthropologist can do is faithfully interpret the guiding symbols of that culture. It is safe to say that he is not into functional or causal interpretations of society or the notion that there can even be such a thing as a "science of culture."

Clifford Geertz was born in 1926. After serving in the Navy in World War II, he received a B.A. from Antioch in 1950 and a Ph.D. from Harvard University in 1956. He has taught and held fellowships too numerous to cite here, but his primary tenures have been at the University of Chicago (1960–70) and at the Institute for Advanced Study in Princeton from 1970–2000, where he is now emeritus. His primary fieldwork and writing has had to do with Bali, Java, and Morocco. Some of his most cited works are *The Development of the Javanese Economy: A Socio-Cultural Approach* (1956), *Modjokuto: Religion in Java, Agricultural Involution: The Process of Ecological Change in Indonesia* (1964), and *Works and Lives* (1988).

Key Concept: anthropology as a search for *meaning*

ali, mainly because it is Bali, is a well-studied place. Its mythology, art, ritual, social organization, patterns of child rearing, forms of law, even styles of trance, have all been microscopically examined for traces of that elusive substance Jane Belo called "The Balinese Temper."[1] But, aside from a few passing remarks, the cockfight has barely been noticed, although as a popular obsession of consuming power it is at least as important a revelation of what being a Balinese "is really like" as these more celebrated phenomena.[2] As much of America surfaces in a ballpark, on a golf links, at a race track, or around a poker table, much of Bali surfaces in a cock ring. For it is only apparently cocks that are fighting there. Actually, it is men.

To anyone who has been in Bali any length of time, the deep psychological identification of Balinese men with their cocks is unmistakable. The double entendre here is deliberate. It works in exactly the same way in Balinese as it does in English, even to producing the same tired jokes, strained puns, and uninventive obscenities. Bateson and Mead have even suggested that, in line with the Balinese conception of the body as a set of separately animated parts, cocks are viewed as detachable, self-operating penises, ambulant genitals with a life of their own.[3] And while I do not have the kind of unconscious material either to confirm or disconfirm this intriguing notion, the fact that they are masculine symbols par excellence is about as indubitable, and to the Balinese about as evident, as the fact that water runs down-hill.

The language of everyday moralism is shot through, on the male side of it, with roosterish imagery. Sabung, the word for cock (and one which appears in inscriptions as early as A.D. 922), is used metaphorically to mean "hero," "warrior," "champion," "man of parts," "political candidate," "bachelor," "dandy," "ladykiller," or "tough guy." A pompous man whose behavior presumes above his station is compared to a tailless cock who struts about as though he had a large, spectacular one. A desperate man who makes a last, irrational effort to extricate himself from an impossible situation is likened to a dying cock who makes one final lunge at his tormentor to drag him along to a common destruction. A stingy man, who promises much, gives little, and begrudges that is compared to a cock which, held by the tail, leaps at another without in fact engaging him. A marriageable young man still shy with the opposite sex or someone in a new job anxious to make a good impression is called "a fighting cock caged for the first time."[4] Court trials, wars, political contests, inheritance disputes, and street arguments are all compared to cockfights.[5] Even the very island itself is perceived from its shape as a small, proud cock, poised, neck extended, back taut, tail raised, in eternal challenge to large, feckless, shapeless Java.[6]

But the intimacy of men with their cocks is more than metaphorical. Balinese men, or anyway a large majority of Balinese men, spend an enormous amount of time with their favorites, grooming them, feeding them, discussing them, trying them out against one another, or just gazing at them with a mixture of rapt admiration and dreamy self-absorption. Whenever you see a group of Balinese men squatting idly in the council shed or along the road in their hips down, shoulders forward, knees up fashion, half or more of them will have a rooster in his hands, holding it between his thighs, bouncing it gently up and down to strengthen its legs, ruffling its feathers with abstract sensuality, pushing it out against a neighbor's rooster to rouse its spirit, withdrawing it toward his loins to calm it again. Now and then, to get a feel for another bird, a man will fiddle this way with someone else's cock for a while, but usually by moving around to squat in place behind it, rather than just having it passed across to him as though it were merely an animal.

In the houseyard, the high-walled enclosures where the people live, fighting cocks are kept in wicker cages, moved frequently about so as to maintain the optimum balance of sun and shade. They are fed a special diet, which varies somewhat according to individual theories but which is mostly maize, sifted for impurities with far more care than it is when mere humans are going to eat it and offered to the animal kernel by kernel. Red pepper is stuffed down their beaks and up their anuses to give them spirit. They are bathed in the same ceremonial preparation of tepid water, medicinal herbs, flowers, and onions in which infants are bathed, and for a

prize cock just about as often. Their combs are cropped, their plumage dressed, their spurs trimmed, their legs massaged, and they are inspected for flaws with the squinted concentration of a diamond merchant. A man who has a passion for cocks, an enthusiast in the literal sense of the term, can spend most of his life with them, and even those, the overwhelming majority, whose passion though intense has not entirely run away with them, can and do spend what seems not only to an outsider, but also to themselves, an inordinate amount of time with them. "I am cock crazy," my landlord, a quite ordinary afficianado by Balinese standards, used to moan as he went to move another cage, give another bath, or conduct another feeding. "We're all cock crazy."

The madness has some less visible dimensions, however, because although it is true that cocks are symbolic expressions or magnifications of their owner's self, the narcissistic male ego writ out in Aesopian terms, they are also expressions—and rather more immediate ones—of what the Balinese regard as the direct inversion, aesthetically, morally, and metaphysically, of human status: animality.

The Balinese revulsion against any behavior regarded as animal-like can hardly be overstressed. Babies are not allowed to crawl for that reason. Incest, though hardly approved, is a much less horrifying crime than bestiality. (The appropriate punishment for the second is death by drowning, for the first being forced to live like an animal.[7]) Most demons are represented—in sculpture, dance, ritual, myth—in some real or fantastic animal form. The main puberty rite consists in filing the child's teeth so they will not look like animal fangs. Not only defecation but eating is regarded as a disgusting, almost obscene activity, to be conducted hurriedly and privately, because of its association with animality. Even falling down or any form of clumsiness is considered to be bad for these reasons. Aside from cocks and a few domestic animals—oxen, ducks—of no emotional significance, the Balinese are aversive to animals and treat their large number of dogs not merely callously but with a phobic cruelty. In identifying with his cock, the Balinese man is identifying not just with his ideal self, or even his penis, but also, and at the same time, with what he most fears, hates, and ambivalence being what it is, is fascinated by—The Powers of Darkness.

The connection of cocks and cockfighting with such Powers, with the animalistic demons that threaten constantly to invade the small, cleared-off space in which the Balinese have so carefully built their lives and devour its inhabitants is quite explicit. A cockfight, any cockfight, is in the first instance a blood sacrifice offered, with the appropriate chants and oblations, to the demons in order to pacify their ravenous, cannibal hunger. No temple festival should be conducted until one is made. (If it is omitted someone will inevitably fall into a trance and command with the voice of an angered spirit that the oversight be immediately corrected.) Collective responses to natural evils—illness, crop failure, volcanic eruptions—almost always involve them. And that famous holiday in Bali,

The Day of Silence (Njepi), when everyone sits silent and immobile all day long in order to avoid contact with a sudden influx of demons chased momentarily out of hell, is preceded the previous day by large-scale cockfights (in this case legal) in almost every village on the island.

In the cockfight, man and beast, good and evil, ego and id, the creative power of aroused masculinity and the destructive power of loosened animality fuse in a bloody drama of hatred, cruelty, violence, and death. It is little wonder that when, as is the invariable rule, the owner of the winning cock takes the carcass of the loser—often torn limb from limb by its enraged owner—home to eat, he does so with a mixture of social embarrassment, moral satisfaction, aesthetic disgust, and cannibal joy. Or that a man who has lost an important fight is sometimes driven to wreck his family shrines and curse the gods, an act of metaphysical (and social) suicide. Or that in seeking earthly analogues for heaven and hell the Balinese compare the former to the mood of a man whose cock has just won, the latter to that of a man whose cock has just lost.

Cockfights (tetadjen; sabungan) are held in a ring about fifty feet square. Usually they begin toward late afternoon and run three or four hours until sunset. About nine or ten separate matches (sehet) comprise a program. Each match is precisely like the others in general pattern: there is no main match, no connection between individual matches, no variation in their format, and each is arranged on a completely ad hoc basis. After a fight has ended and the emotional debris is cleaned away—the bets paid, the curses cursed, the carcasses possessed—seven, eight, perhaps even a dozen men slip negligently into the ring with a cock and seek to find there a logical opponent for it. This process, which rarely takes less than ten minutes, and often a good deal longer, is conducted in a very subdued, oblique, even dissembling manner. Those not immediately involved give it at best but disguised, sidelong attention; those who, embarrassedly, are, attempt to pretend somehow that the whole thing is not really happening.

A match made, the other hopefuls retire with the same deliberate indifference, and the selected cocks have their spurs (tadji) affixed—razor sharp, pointed steel swords, four or five inches long. This is a delicate job which only a small proportion of men, a half-dozen or so in most villages, know how to do properly. The man who attaches the spurs also provides them, and if the rooster he assists wins its owner awards him the spur-leg of the victim. The spurs are affixed by winding a long length of string around the foot of the spur and the leg of the cock. For reasons I shall come to presently, it is done somewhat differently from case to case, and is an obsessively deliberate affair. The lore about spurs is extensive—they are sharpened only at eclipses and the dark of the moon, should be kept out of the sight of women, and so forth. And they are handled, both in use and out, with the same curious combination of fussiness and sensuality the Balinese direct toward ritual objects generally.

The spurs affixed, the two cocks are placed by their handlers (who may or may not be their owners) facing one another in the center of the ring.[8] A coconut pierced with a small hole is placed in a pail of water, in which it takes about twenty-one seconds to sink, a period known as a tjeng and marked at beginning and end by the beating of a slit gong. During these twenty-one seconds the handlers (pengangkeb) are not permitted to touch their roosters. If, as sometimes happens, the animals have not fought during this time, they are picked up, fluffed, pulled, prodded, and otherwise insulted, and put back in the center of the ring and the process begins again. Sometimes they refuse to fight at all, or one keeps running away, in which case they are imprisoned together under a wicker cage, which usually gets them engaged.

Most of the time, in any case, the cocks fly almost immediately at one another in a wing-beating, head-thrusting, leg-kicking explosion of animal fury so pure, so absolute, and in its own way so beautiful, as to be almost abstract, a Platonic concept of hate. Within moments one or the other drives home a solid blow with his spur. The handler whose cock has delivered the blow immediately picks it up so that it will not get a return blow, for if he does not the match is likely to end in a mutually mortal tie as the two birds wildly hack each other to pieces. This is particularly true if, as often happens, the spur sticks in its victim's body, for then the aggressor is at the mercy of his wounded foe.

With the birds again in the hands of their handlers, the coconut is now sunk three times after which the cock which has landed the blow must be set down to show that he is firm, a fact he demonstrates by wandering idly around the rink for a coconut sink. The coconut is then sunk twice more and the fight must recommence.

During this interval, slightly over two minutes, the handler of the wounded cock has been working frantically over it, like a trainer patching a mauled boxer between rounds, to get it in shape for a last, desperate try for victory. He blows in its mouth, putting the whole chicken head in his own mouth and sucking and blowing, fluffs it, stuffs its wounds with various sorts of medicines, and generally tries anything he can think of to arouse the last ounce of spirit which may be hidden somewhere within it. By the time he is forced to put it back down he is usually drenched in chicken blood, but, as in prizefighting, a good handler is worth his weight in gold. Some of them can virtually make the dead walk, at least long enough for the second and final round.

In the climactic battle (if there is one; sometimes the wounded cock simply expires in the handler's hands or immediately as it is placed down again), the cock who landed the first blow usually proceeds to finish off his weakened opponent. But this is far from an inevitable outcome, for if a cock can walk he can fight, and if he can fight, he can kill, and what counts is which cock expires first. If the wounded one can get a stab in and stagger on until the other drops, he is the official winner, even if he himself topples over an instant later.

Surrounding all this melodrama—which the crowd packed tight around the ring follows in near silence, moving their bodies in kinesthetic sympathy with the movement of the animals, cheering their champions on with wordless hand motions, shiftings of the shoulders, turnings of the head, falling back en masse as the cock with the murderous spurs careens toward one side of the ring (it is said that spectators sometimes lose eyes and fingers from being too attentive), surging forward again as they glance off toward another—is a vast body of extraordinarily elaborate and precisely detailed rules.

These rules, together with the developed lore of cocks and cockfighting which accompanies them, are written down in palm-leaf manuscripts (lontar; rontal) passed on from generation to generation as part of the general legal and cultural tradition of the villages. At a fight, the umpire (saja komong; djuru kembar)—the man who manages the coconut—is in charge of their application and his authority is absolute. I have never seen an umpire's judgment questioned on any subject, even by the more despondent losers, nor have I ever heard, even in private, a charge of unfairness directed against one, or, for that matter, complaints about umpires in general. Only exceptionally well-trusted, solid, and, given the complexity of the code, knowledgeable citizens perform this job, and in fact men will bring their cocks only to fights presided over by such men. It is also the umpire to whom accusations of cheating, which, though rare in the extreme, occasionally arise, are referred; and it is he who in the not infrequent cases where the cocks expire virtually together decides which (if either, for, though the Balinese do not care for such an outcome, there can be ties) went first. Likened to a judge, a king, a priest, and a policeman, he is all of these, and under his assured direction the animal passion of the fight proceeds within the civic certainty of the law. In the dozens of cockfights I saw in Bali, I never once saw an altercation about rules. Indeed, I never saw an open altercation, other than those between cocks, at all.

This crosswise doubleness of an event which, taken as a fact of nature, is rage untrammeled and, taken as a fact of culture, is form perfected, defines the cockfight as a sociological entity. A cockfight is what, searching for a name for something not vertebrate enough to be called a group and not structureless enough to be called a crowd, Erving Goffman has called a "focused gathering"—a set of persons engrossed in a common flow of activity and relating to one another in terms of that flow.[9] Such gatherings meet and disperse; the participants in them fluctuate; the activity that focuses them is discreet—a particulate process that reoccurs rather than a continuous one that endures. They take their form from the situation that evokes them, the floor on which they are placed, as Goffman puts it; but it is a form, and an articulate one, nonetheless. For the situation, the floor is itself created, in jury deliberations, surgical operations, block meetings, sit-ins, cockfights, by the cultural preoccupations—here, as we shall see, the celebration of status rivalry—which

not only specify the focus but, assembling actors and arranging scenery, bring it actually into being.

In classical times (that is to say, prior to the Dutch invasion of 1908), when there were no bureaucrats around to improve popular morality, the staging of a cockfight was an explicitly societal matter. Bringing a cock to an important fight was, for an adult male, a compulsory duty of citizenship; taxation of fights, which were usually held on market day, was a major source of public revenue; patronage of the art was a stated responsibility of princes; and the cock ring, or wantilan, stood in the center of the village near those other monuments of Balinese civility—the council house, the origin temple, the marketplace, the signal tower, and the banyan tree. Today, a few special occasions aside, the newer rectitude makes so open a statement of the connection between the excitements of collective life and those of blood sport impossible, but, less directly expressed, the connection itself remains intimate and intact. To expose it, however, it is necessary to turn to the aspect of cockfighting around which all the others pivot, and through which they exercise their force, an aspect I have thus far studiously ignored. I mean, of course, the gambling.

The Balinese never do anything in a simple way that they can contrive to do in a complicated one, and to this generalization cockfight wagering is no exception.

In the first place, there are two sorts of bets, or toh.[10] There is the single axial bet in the center between the principals (toh ketengah), and there is the cloud of peripheral ones around the ring between members of the audience (toh kesasi). The first is typically large; the second typically small. The first is collective, involving coalitions of bettors clustering around the owner; the second is individual, man to man. The first is a matter of deliberate, very quiet, almost furtive arrangement by the coalition members and the umpire huddled like conspirators in the center of the ring; the second is a matter of impulsive shouting, public offers, and public acceptances by the excited throng around its edges. And most curiously, and as we shall see most revealingly, where the first is always, without exception, even money, the second, equally without exception, is never such. What is a fair coin in the center is a biased one on the side.

The center bet is the official one, hedged in again with a webwork of rules, and is made between the two cock owners, with the umpire as overseer and public witness.[11] This bet, which, as I say, is always relatively and sometimes very large, is never raised simply by the owner in whose name it is made, but by him together with four or five, sometimes seven or eight, allies—kin, village mates, neighbors, close friends. He may, if he is not especially well-to-do, not even be the major contributor, though, if only to show that he is not involved in any chicanery, he must be a significant one.

Of the 57 matches for which I have exact and reliable data on the center bet, the range is from 15 ringgits to 500, with a mean at 85 and with the distribution being rather noticeably trimodal: small fights (15 ringgits either side of 35) accounting for about 45 percent of the total number; medium ones (20 ringgits either side of 70) for about 25 percent; and large (75 ringgits either side of 175) for about 20 percent, with a few very small and very large ones out at the extremes. In a society where the normal daily wage of a manual laborer—a brickmaker, an ordinary farmworker, a market porter—was about 3 ringgits a day, and considering the fact that fights were held on the average about every 2.5 days in the immediate area I studied, this is clearly serious gambling, even if the bets are pooled rather than individual efforts.

The side bets are, however, something else altogether. Rather than the solemn, legalistic pact-making of the center, wagering takes place rather in the fashion in which the stock exchange used to work when it was out on the curb. There is a fixed and known odds paradigm which runs in a continuous series from 10-9 at the short end to 2-1 at the long: 10-9, 9-8, 8-7, 7-6, 6-5, 5-4, 4-3, 3-2, 2-1. The man who wishes to back the underdog cock (leaving aside how favorites, kebut, and underdogs, ngai, are established for the moment) shouts the short-side number indicating the odds he wants to be given. That is, if he shouts gasal, "five," he wants the underdog at 5-4 (or, for him, 4-5); if he shouts "four," he wants it at 4-3 (again, he putting up the "three"), if "nine," at 9-8, and so on. A man backing the favorite, and thus considering giving odds if he can get them short enough, indicates the fact by crying out the color type of that cock—"brown," "speckled," or whatever.[12]

As odds-takers (backers of the underdog) and odds-givers (backers of the favorite) sweep the crowd with their shouts, they begin to focus in on one another as potential betting pairs, often from far across the ring. The taker tries to shout the giver into longer odds, the giver to shout the taker into shorter ones.[13] The taker, who is the wooer in this situation, will signal how large a bet he wishes to make at the odds he is shouting by holding a number of fingers up in front of his face and vigorously waving them. If the giver, the wooed, replies in kind, the bet is made; if he does not, they unlock gazes and the search goes on.

The side betting, which takes place after the center bet has been made and its size announced, consists then in a rising crescendo of shouts as backers of the underdog offer their propositions to anyone who will accept them, while those who are backing the favorite but do not like the price being offered, shout equally frenetically the color of the cock to show they too are desperate to bet but want shorter odds. . . .

As the moment for the release of the cocks by the handlers approaches, the screaming, at least in a match where the center bet is large, reaches almost frenzied proportions as the remaining unfulfilled bettors try desperately to find a last-minute partner at a price they can live with. (Where the center bet is small, the opposite tends to occur: betting dies off, trailing into silence, as odds lengthen and people lose interest.) In a large bet, well-made match—the kind

of match the Balinese regard as "real cockfighting"—the mob scene quality, the sense that sheer chaos is about to break loose, with all those waving, shouting, pushing, clambering men is quite strong, an effect which is only heightened by the intense stillness that falls with instant suddenness, rather as if someone had turned off the current, when the slit gong sounds, the cocks are put down, and the battle begins.

When it ends, anywhere from fifteen seconds to five minutes later, all bets are immediately paid. There are absolutely no IOUs, at least to a betting opponent. One may, of course, borrow from a friend before offering or accepting a wager, but to offer or accept it you must have the money already in hand and, if you lose, you must pay it on the spot, before the next match begins. This is an iron rule, and as I have never heard of a disputed umpire's decision (though doubtless there must sometimes be some), I have also never heard of a welshed bet, perhaps because in a worked-up cockfight crowd the consequences might be, as they are reported to be sometimes for cheaters, drastic and immediate.

It is, in any case, this formal asymmetry between balanced center bets and unbalanced side ones that poses the critical analytical problem for a theory which sees cockfight wagering as the link connecting the fight to the wider world of Balinese culture. It also suggests the way to go about solving it and demonstrating the link.

The first point that needs to be made in this connection is that the higher the center bet, the more likely the match will in actual fact be an even one. Simple considerations of rationality suggest that. If you are betting 15 ringgits on a cock, you might be willing to go along with even money even if you feel your animal somewhat the less promising. But if you are betting 500 you are very, very likely to be loathe to do so. Thus, in large-bet fights, which of course involve the better animals, tremendous care is taken to see that the cocks are about as evenly matched as to size, general condition, pugnacity, and so on as is humanly possible. The different ways of adjusting the spurs of the animals are often employed to secure this. If one cock seems stronger, an agreement will be made to position his spur at a slightly less advantageous angle—a kind of handicapping, at which spur affixers are, so it is said, extremely skilled. More care will be taken, too, to employ skillful handlers and to match them exactly as to abilities.

In short, in a large-bet fight the pressure to make the match a genuinely fifty-fifty proposition is enormous, and is consciously felt as such. For medium fights the pressure is somewhat less, and for small ones less yet, though there is always an effort to make things at least approximately equal, for even at 15 ringgits (5 days' work) no one wants to make an even-money bet in a clearly unfavorable situation. And, again, what statistics I have tend to bear this out. In my 57 matches, the favorite won 33 times overall, the underdog 24, a 1.4 to 1 ratio. But if one splits the figures at 60 ringgits center bets, the ratios turn out to be 1.1 to 1 (12 favorites, 11 underdogs) for those above this line, and 1.6 to 1 (21 and 13) for those below it. Or, if you take the extremes, for very large fights, those with center bets over 100 ringgits the ratio is 1 to 1 (7 and 7); for very small fights, those under 40 ringgits, it is 1.9 to 1 (19 and 10).[14]

Now, from this proposition—that the higher the center bet the more exactly a fifty-fifty proposition the cockfight is—two things more or less immediately follow: (1) the higher the center bet, the greater is the pull on the side betting toward the short-odds end of the wagering spectrum and vice versa; (2) the higher the center bet, the greater the volume of side betting and vice versa.

The logic is similar in both cases. The closer the fight is in fact to even money, the less attractive the long end of the odds will appear and, therefore, the shorter it must be if there are to be takers. That this is the case is apparent from mere inspection, from the Balinese's own analysis of the matter, and from what more systematic observations I was able to collect. Given the difficulty of making precise and complete recordings of side betting, this argument is hard to cast in numerical form, but in all my cases the odds-giver, odds-taker consensual point, a quite pronounced minimax saddle where the bulk (at a guess, two-thirds to three-quarters in most cases) of the bets are actually made, was three or four points further along the scale toward the shorter end for the large-center-bet fights than for the small ones, with medium ones generally in between. In detail, the fit is not, of course, exact, but the general pattern is quite consistent: the power of the center bet to pull the side bets toward its own even-money pattern is directly proportional to its size, because its size is directly proportional to the degree to which the cocks are in fact evenly matched. As for the volume question, total wagering is greater in large-center-bet fights because such fights are considered more "interesting," not only in the sense that they are less predictable, but, more crucially, that more is at stake in them—in terms of money, in terms of the quality of the cocks, and consequently, as we shall see, in terms of social prestige.[15]

The paradox of fair coin in the middle, biased coin on the outside is thus a merely apparent one. The two betting systems, though formally incongruent, are not really contradictory to one another, but part of a single larger system in which the center bet is, so to speak, the "center of gravity," drawing, the larger it is the more so, the outside bets toward the short-odds end of the scale. The center bet thus "makes the game," or perhaps better, defines it, signals what, following a notion of Jeremy Bentham's, I am going to call its "depth."

The Balinese attempt to create an interesting, if you will, "deep," match by making the center bet as large as possible so that the cocks matched will be as equal and as fine as possible, and the outcome, thus, as unpredictable as possible. They do not always succeed. Nearly half the matches are relatively trivial, relatively uninteresting—in my borrowed terminology, "shallow"—affairs.

But that fact no more argues against my interpretation than the fact that most painters, poets, and playwrights are mediocre argues against the view that artistic effort is directed toward profundity and, with a certain frequency, approximates it. The image of artistic technique is indeed exact: the center bet is a means, a device, for creating "interesting," "deep" matches, not the reason, or at least not the main reason, why they are interesting, the source of their fascination, the substance of their depth. The question why such matches are interesting—indeed, for the Balinese, exquisitely absorbing—takes us out of the realm of formal concerns into more broadly sociological and social-psychological ones, and to a less purely economic idea of what "depth" in gaming amounts to.[16]

Bentham's concept of "deep play" is found in his *The Theory of Legislation*.[17] By it he means play in which the stakes are so high that it is, from his utilitarian standpoint, irrational for men to engage in it at all. If a man whose fortune is a thousand pounds (or ringgits) wages five hundred of it on an even bet, the marginal utility of the pound he stands to win is clearly less than the marginal disutility of the one he stands to lose.

In genuine deep play, this is the case for both parties. They are both in over their heads. Having come together in search of pleasure they have entered into a relationship which will bring the participants, considered collectively, net pain rather than net pleasure. Bentham's conclusion was, therefore, that deep play was immoral from first principles and, a typical step for him, should be prevented legally.

But more interesting than the ethical problem, at least for our concerns here, is that despite the logical force of Bentham's analysis men do engage in such play, both passionately and often, and even in the face of law's revenge. For Bentham and those who think as he does (nowadays mainly lawyers, economists, and a few psychiatrists), the explanation is, as I have said, that such men are irrational—addicts, fetishists, children, fools, savages, who need only to be protected against themselves. But for the Balinese, though naturally they do not formulate it in so many words, the explanation lies in the fact that in such play money is less a measure of utility, had or expected, than it is a symbol of moral import, perceived or imposed.

It is, in fact, in shallow games, ones in which smaller amounts of money are involved, that increments and decrements of cash are more nearly synonyms for utility and disutility, in the ordinary, unexpanded sense—for pleasure and pain, happiness and unhappiness. In deep ones, where the amounts of money are great, much more is at stake than material gain: namely, esteem, honor, dignity, respect—in a word, though in Bali a profoundly freighted word, status.[18] It is at stake symbolically, for (a few cases of ruined addict gamblers aside) no one's status is actually altered by the outcome of a cockfight; it is only, and that momentarily, affirmed or insulted. But for the Balinese, for whom nothing is more pleasurable than an affront obliquely delivered or more painful than one obliquely received—particularly when mutual acquaintances, undeceived by surfaces, are watching—such appraisive drama is deep indeed.

This, I must stress immediately, is not to say that the money does not matter, or that the Balinese is no more concerned about losing 500 ringgits than 15. Such a conclusion would be absurd. It is because money does, in this hardly unmaterialistic society, matter and matter very much that the more of it one risks the more of a lot of other things, such as one's pride, one's poise, one's dispassion, one's masculinity, one also risks, again only momentarily but again very publicly as well. In deep cockfights an owner and his collaborators, and, as we shall see, to a lesser but still quite real extent also their backers on the outside, put their money where their status is.

It is in large part because the marginal disutility of loss is so great at the higher levels of betting that to engage in such betting is to lay one's public self, allusively and metaphorically, through the medium of one's cock, on the line. And though to a Benthamite this might seem merely to increase the irrationality of the enterprise that much further, to the Balinese what it mainly increases is the meaningfulness of it all. And as (to follow Weber rather than Bentham) the imposition of meaning on life is the major end and primary condition of human existence, that access of significance more than compensates for the economic costs involved.[19] Actually, given the even-money quality of the larger matches, important changes in material fortune among those who regularly participate in them seem virtually nonexistent, because matters more or less even out over the long run. It is, actually, in the smaller, shallow fights, where one finds the handful of more pure, addict-type gamblers involved—those who are in it mainly for the money—that "real" changes in social position, largely downward, are affected. Men of this sort, plungers, are highly dispraised by "true cockfighters" as fools who do not understand what the sport is all about, vulgarians who simply miss the point of it all. They are, these addicts, regarded as fair game for the genuine enthusiasts, those who do understand, to take a little money away from, something that is easy enough to do by luring them, through the force of their greed, into irrational bets on mismatched cocks. Most of them do indeed manage to ruin themselves in a remarkably short time, but there always seems to be one or two of them around, pawning their land and selling their clothes in order to bet, at any particular time.[20]

This graduated correlation of "status gambling" with deeper fights and, inversely, "money gambling" with shallower ones is in fact quite general. Bettors themselves form a sociomoral hierarchy in these terms. As noted earlier, at most cockfights there are, around the very edges of the cockfight area, a large number of mindless, sheer-chance type gambling games (roulette, dice throw, coin-spin, pea-under-the-shell) operated by concessionaires. Only women, children, adolescents, and various other sorts of people who do not (or not yet) fight cocks—the extremely poor, the socially despised, the personally idiosyncratic—play at these games, at, of course, penny ante levels. Cockfighting men would be ashamed to go anywhere near them. Slightly above these people in standing are those who, though they do not themselves fight cocks, bet on the smaller matches around the edges. Next, there are those who fight cocks in small, or occasionally medium matches, but have not the status to join in the large ones, though they may bet from time to time on the side in those. And finally, there are those, the really substantial members of the community, the solid citizenry around whom local life revolves, who fight in the larger fights and bet on them around the side. The focusing element in these focused gatherings, these men generally dominate and define the sport as they dominate and define the society. When a Balinese male talks, in that almost venerative way, about "the true cockfighter," the bebatoh ("bettor") or djuru kurung ("cage keeper"), it is this sort of person, not those who bring the mentality of the pea-and-shell game into the quite different, inappropriate context of the cockfight, the driven gambler (potet, a word which has the secondary meaning of thief or reprobate), and the wistful hanger-on, that they mean. For such a man, what is really going on in a match is something rather closer to an affaire d'honneur (though, with the Balinese talent for practical fantasy, the blood that is spilled is only figuratively human) than to the stupid, mechanical crank of a slot machine.

What makes Balinese cockfighting deep is thus not money in itself, but what, the more of it that is involved the more so, money causes to happen: the migration of the Balinese status hierarchy into the body of the cockfight. Psychologically an Aesopian representation of the ideal/demonic, rather narcissistic, male self, sociologically it is an equally Aesopian representation of the complex fields of tension set up by the controlled, muted, ceremonial, but for all that deeply felt, interaction of those selves in the context of everyday life. The cocks may be surrogates for their owners' personalities, animal mirrors of psychic form, but the cockfight is—or more exactly, deliberately is made to be—a simulation of the social matrix, the involved system of crosscutting, overlapping, highly corporate groups—villages, kingroups, irrigation societies, temple congregations, "castes"—in which its devotees live.[21] And as prestige, the necessity to affirm it, defend it, celebrate it, justify it, and just plain bask in it (but not, given the strongly ascriptive character of Balinese stratification, to seek it), is perhaps the central driving force in the society, so also—ambulant penises, blood sacrifices, and monetary exchanges aside—is it of the cockfight. This apparent amusement and seeming sport is, to take another phrase from Erving Goffman, "a status bloodbath."[22]

The easiest way to make this clear, and at least to some degree to demonstrate it, is to invoke the village whose cockfighting activities I observed the closest. . .

As all Balinese villages, this one—Tihingan, in the Klungkung region of southeast Bali—is intricately organized, a labyrinth of alliances and oppositions. But, unlike many, two sorts of corporate groups, which are also status groups, particularly stand out, and we may concentrate on them, in a part-for-whole way, without undue distortion.

First, the village is dominated by four large, patrilineal, partly endogamous descent groups which are constantly vying with one another and form the major factions in the village. Sometimes they group two and two, or rather the two larger ones versus the two smaller ones plus all the unaffiliated people; sometimes they operate independently. There are also subfactions within them, subfactions within the subfactions, and so on to rather fine levels of distinction. And second, there is the village itself, almost entirely endogamous, which is opposed to all the other villages round about in its cockfight circuit (which, as explained, is the market region), but which also forms alliances with certain of these neighbors against certain others in various supravillage political and social contexts. The exact situation is thus, as everywhere in Bali, quite distinctive; but the general pattern of a tiered hierarchy of status rivalries between highly corporate but various based groupings (and, thus, between the members of them) is entirely general.

Consider, then, as support of the general thesis that the cockfight, and especially the deep cockfight, is fundamentally a dramatization of status concerns, the following facts, which to avoid extended ethnographic description I will simply pronounce to be facts—though the concrete evidence-examples, statements, and numbers that could be brought to bear in support of them is both extensive and unmistakable:

1. A man virtually never bets against a cock owned by a member of his own kingroup. Usually he will feel obliged to bet for it, the more so the closer the kin tie and the deeper the fight. If he is certain in his mind that it will not win, he may just not bet at all, particularly if it is only a second cousin's bird or if the fight is a shallow one. But as a rule he will feel he must support it and, in deep games, nearly always does. Thus the great majority of the people calling "five" or "speckled" so demonstratively are expressing their allegiance to their kinsman, not their evaluation of his bird, their understanding of probability theory, or even their hopes of unearned income.

2. This principle is extended logically. If your kingroup is not involved you will support an allied kingroup against an unallied one in the same way, and so on through the very involved networks of alliances which, as I say, make up this, as any other, Balinese village.

3. So, too, for the village as a whole. If an outsider cock is fighting any cock from your village you will tend to support the local one. If, what is a rarer circumstance but occurs every now and then, a cock from outside your cockfight circuit is fighting one inside it you will also tend to support the "home bird."

4. Cocks which come from any distance are almost always favorites, for the theory is the man would not have dared to bring it if it was not a good cock, the more so the further he has come. His followers are, of course, obliged to support him, and when the more grand-scale legal cockfights are held (on holidays, and so on) the people of the village take what they regard to be the best cocks in the village, regardless of ownership, and go off to support them, although they will almost certainly have to give odds on them and to make large bets to show that they are not a cheapskate village. Actually, such "away games," though infrequent, tend to mend the ruptures between village members that the constantly occurring "home games," where village factions are opposed rather than united, exacerbate.

5. Almost all matches are sociologically relevant. You seldom get two outsider cocks fighting, or two cocks with no particular group backing, or with group backing which is mutually unrelated in any clear way. When you do get them, the game is very shallow, betting very slow, and the whole thing very dull, with no one save the immediate principals and an addict gambler or two at all interested.

6. By the same token, you rarely get two cocks from the same group, even more rarely from the same subfaction, and virtually never from the same sub-subfaction (which would be in most cases one extended family) fighting. Similarly, in outside village fights two members of the village will rarely fight against one another, even though, as bitter rivals, they would do so with enthusiasm on their home grounds.

7. On the individual level, people involved in an institutionalized hostility relationship, called puik, in which they do not speak or otherwise have anything to do with each other (the causes of this formal breaking of relations are many: wife-capture, inheritance arguments, political differences) will bet very heavily, sometimes almost maniacally, against one another in what is a frank and direct attack on the very masculinity, the ultimate ground of his status, of the opponent.

8. The center bet coalition is, in all but the shallowest games, always made up by structural allies—no "outside money" is involved. What is "outside" depends upon the context, of course, but given it, no outside money is mixed in with the main bet; if the principals cannot raise it, it is not made. The center bet, again especially in deeper games, is thus the most direct and open

expression of social opposition, which is one of the reasons why both it and match making are surrounded by such an air of unease, furtiveness, embarrassment, and so on.

9. The rule about borrowing money—that you may borrow for a bet but not in one—stems (and the Balinese are quite conscious of this) from similar considerations: you are never at the economic mercy of your enemy that way. Gambling debts, which can get quite large on a rather short-term basis, are always to friends, never to enemies, structurally speaking.

10. When two cocks are structurally irrelevant or neutral so far as you are concerned (though, as mentioned, they almost never are to each other) you do not even ask a relative or a friend whom he is betting on, because if you know how he is betting and he knows you know, and you go the other way, it will lead to strain. This rule is explicit and rigid; fairly elaborate, even rather artificial precautions are taken to avoid breaking it. At the very least you must pretend not to notice what he is doing, and he what you are doing.

11. There is a special word for betting against the grain, which is also the word for "pardon me" (mpura). It is considered a bad thing to do, though if the center bet is small it is sometimes all right as long as you do not do it too often. But the larger the bet and the more frequently you do it, the more the "pardon me" tack will lead to social disruption.

12. In fact, the institutionalized hostility relation, puik, is often formally initiated (though its causes always lie elsewhere) by such a "pardon me" bet in a deep fight, putting the symbolic fat in the fire. Similarly, the end of such a relationship and resumption of normal social intercourse is often signalized (but, again, not actually brought about) by one or the other of the enemies supporting the other's bird.

13. In sticky, cross-loyalty situations, of which in this extraordinarily complex social system there are of course many, where a man is caught between two more or less equally balanced loyalties, he tends to wander off for a cup of coffee or something to avoid having to bet, a form of behavior reminiscent of that of American voters in similar situations.[23]

14. The people involved in the center bet are, especially in deep fights, virtually always leading members of their group-kinship, village, or whatever. Further, those who bet on the side (including these people) are, as I have already remarked, the more established members of the village—the solid citizens. Cockfighting is for those who are involved in the everyday politics of prestige as well, not for youth, women, subordinates, and so forth.

15. So far as money is concerned, the explicitly expressed attitude toward it is that it is a secondary matter. It is not, as I have said, of no importance; Balinese are no happier to lose several weeks' income than anyone else. But they mainly look on the monetary aspects of the cockfight as self-balancing, a matter of just moving money around, circulating it among a fairly well-defined group of serious cockfighters. The really important wins and losses are seen mostly in other terms, and the general attitude toward wagering is not any hope of cleaning up, of making a killing (addict gamblers again excepted), but that of the horseplayer's prayer: "Oh, God, please let me break even." In prestige terms, however, you do not want to break even, but, in a momentary, punctuate sort of way, win utterly. The talk (which goes on all the time) is about fights against such-and-such a cock of So-and-So which your cock demolished, not on how much you won, a fact people, even for large bets, rarely remember for any length of time, though they will remember the day they did in Pan Loh's finest cock for years.

16. You must bet on cocks of your own group aside from mere loyalty considerations, for if you do not people generally will say, "What! Is he too proud for the likes of us? Does he have to go to Java or Den Pasar [the capital town] to bet, he is such an important man?" Thus there is a general pressure to bet not only to show that you are important locally, but that you are not so important that you look down on everyone else as unfit even to be rivals. Similarly, home team people must bet against outside cocks or the outsiders will accuse it—a serious charge—of just collecting entry fees and not really being interested in cockfighting, as well as again being arrogant and insulting.

17. Finally, the Balinese peasants themselves are quite aware of all this and can and, at least to an ethnographer, do state most of it in approximately the same terms as I have. Fighting cocks, almost every Balinese I have ever discussed the subject with has said, is like playing with fire only not getting burned. You activate village and kingroup rivalries and hostilities, but in "play" form, coming dangerously and entrancingly close to the expression of open and direct interpersonal and intergroup aggression (something which, again, almost never happens in the normal course of ordinary life), but not quite, because, after all, it is "only a cockfight." . . .

"Poetry makes nothing happen," Auden says in his elegy of Yeats, "it survives in the valley of its saying . . . a way of happening, a mouth." The cockfight too, in this colloquial sense, makes nothing happen. Men go on allegorically humiliating one another and being allegorically humiliated by one another, day after day, glorying quietly in the experience if they have triumphed, crushed only slightly more openly by it if they have not. But no one's status really changes. You cannot ascend the status ladder by winning cockfights; you cannot, as an individual, really ascend it at all. Nor can you descend it that way.[24] All you can do is enjoy and savor, or suffer and withstand, the concocted sensation of drastic and momentary movement along an aesthetic semblance of that ladder, a kind of behind-the-mirror status jump which has the look of mobility without its actuality.

As any art form—for that, finally, is what we are dealing with—the cockfight renders ordinary, everyday experience comprehensible by presenting it in terms of acts and objects which have had their practical consequences removed and been reduced (or, if you prefer, raised) to the level of sheer appearances, where their meaning can be more powerfully articulated and more exactly perceived. The cockfight is "really real" only to the cocks—it does not kill anyone, castrate anyone, reduce anyone to animal status, alter the hierarchical relations among people, nor refashion the hierarchy; it does not even redistribute income in any significant way. What it does is what, for other peoples with other temperaments and other conventions, *Lear* and *Crime and Punishment* do; it catches up these themes—death, masculinity, rage, pride, loss, beneficence, chance—and, ordering them into an encompassing structure, presents them in such a way as to throw into relief a particular view of their essential nature. It puts a construction on them, makes them, to those historically positioned to appreciate the construction, meaningful—visible, tangible, graspable—"real," in an ideational sense. An image, fiction, a model, a metaphor, the cockfight is a means of expression; its function is neither to assuage social passions nor to heighten them (though, in its play-with-fire way, it does a bit of both), but, in a medium of feathers, blood, crowds, and money, to display them. . . .

As a dramatic shape, the fight displays a characteristic that does not seem so remarkable until one realizes that it does not have to be there: a radically atomistical structure.[25] Each match is a world unto itself, a particulate burst of form. There is the match making, there is the betting, there is the fight, there is the result—utter triumph and utter defeat—and there is the hurried, embarrassed passing of money. The loser is not consoled. People drift away from him, look through him, leave him to assimilate his momentary descent into nonbeing, reset his face, and return, scarless and intact, to the fray. Nor are winners congratulated, or events rehashed; once a match is ended the crowd's attention turns totally to the next, with no looking back. A shadow of the experience no doubt remains with the principals, perhaps even with some of the witnesses, of a deep fight, as it remains with us when we leave the theater after seeing a powerful play well-performed; but it quite soon fades to become at most a schematic memory—a diffuse glow or an abstract shudder—and usually not even that. Any expressive form lives only in its own present—the one it itself creates. But, here, that present is severed into a string of flashes, some more bright than others, but all of them disconnected, aesthetic quanta. Whatever the cockfight says, it says in spurts. . . .

Every people, the proverb has it, loves its own form of violence. The cockfight is the Balinese reflection on theirs: on its look, its uses, its force, its fascination. Drawing on almost every level of Balinese experience, it brings together themes—animal savagery, male narcissism, opponent gambling, status rivalry, mass excitement, blood sacrifice—whose main connection is their involvement with rage and the fear of rage, and, binding them into a set of rules which at once contains them and allows them play, builds a symbolic structure in which, over and over again, the reality of their inner affiliation can be intelligibly felt. If, to quote Northrop Frye again, we go to see *Macbeth* to learn what a man feels like after he has gained a kingdom and lost his soul, Balinese go to cockfights to find out what a man, usually composed, aloof, almost obsessively self-absorbed, a kind of moral autocosm, feels like when, attacked, tormented, challenged, insulted, and driven in result to the extremes of fury, he has totally triumphed or been brought totally low. The whole passage, as it takes us back to Aristotle (though to the *Poetics* rather than the *Hermeneutics*), is worth quotation:

> But the poet [as opposed to the historian], Aristotle says, never makes any real statements at all, certainly no particular or specific ones. The poet's job is not to tell you what happened, but what happens: not what did take place, but the kind of thing that always does take place. He gives you the typical, recurring, or what Aristotle calls universal event. You wouldn't go to *Macbeth* to learn about the history of Scotland—you go to it to learn what a man feels like after he's gained a kingdom and lost his soul. When you meet such a character as Micawber in Dickens, you don't feel that there must have been a man Dickens knew who was exactly like this: you feel that there's a bit of Micawber in almost everybody you know, including yourself. Our impressions of human life are picked up one by one, and remain for most of us loose and disorganized. But we constantly find things in literature that suddenly co-ordinate and bring into focus a great many such impressions, and this is part of what Aristotle means by the typical or universal human event.[26]

It is this kind of bringing of assorted experiences of everyday life to focus that the cockfight, set aside from that life as "only a game" and reconnected to it as "more than a game," accomplishes, and so creates what, better than typical or universal, could be called a paradigmatic human event—that is, one that tells us less what happens than the kind of thing that would happen if, as is not the case, life were art and could be as freely shaped by styles of feeling as *Macbeth* and *David Copperfield* are. Enacted and reenacted, so far without end, the cockfight enables the Balinese, as, read and reread, *Macbeth* enables us, to see a dimension of his own subjectivity. As he watches fight after fight with the active watching of an owner and a bettor (for cockfighting has no more interest as a pure spectator sport than croquet or dog racing do), he grows familiar with it and what it has to say to him, much as the attentive listener to string quartets or the absorbed viewer of still lifes grows slowly more familiar with them in a way which opens his subjectivity to himself.[27]

Yet, because—in another of those paradoxes, along with painted feelings and unconsequenced acts, which haunt aesthetics—that subjectivity does not properly exist until it is thus organized, art forms generate and regenerate the very subjectivity they pretend only to display. Quartets, still lifes, and cockfights are not merely reflections of a preexisting sensibility analogically represented; they are positive agents in the creation and maintenance of such a sensibility. If we see ourselves as a pack of Micawbers it is from reading too much Dickens (if we see ourselves as unillusioned realists, it is from reading too little); and similarly for Balinese, cocks, and cockfights. It is in such a way, coloring experience with the light they cast it in, rather than through whatever material effects they may have, that the arts play their role, as arts, in social life[28]. . . .

Notes

1. Jane Belo, "The Balinese Temper," in Jane Belo, ed., *Traditional Balinese Culture* (New York: Columbia University Press, 1970; originally published in 1935). 85–110.

2. The best discussion of cockfighting is again Bateson and Mead's (*Balinese Character*, 24–25, 140), but it, too, is general and abbreviated.

3. Ibid., 25–26. The cockfight is unusual within Balinese culture in being a single sex public activity from which the other sex is totally and expressly excluded. Sexual differentiation is culturally extremely played down in Bali and most activities, formal and informal, involve the participation of men and women on equal ground, commonly as linked couples. From religion, to politics, to economics, to kinship, to dress, Bali is a rather "unisex" society, a fact both its customs and its symbolism clearly express. Even in contexts where women do not in fact play much of a role—music, painting, certain agricultural activities—their absence, which is only relative in any case, is more a mere matter of fact than socially enforced. To this general pattern, the cockfight, entirely of, by, and for men (women—at least Balinese women—do not even watch), is the most striking exception.

4. Christiaan Hooykaas. *The Lay of the Jaya Prana* (London: Luzac, 1958), 39. The lay has a stanza (no. 17) with the reluctant bridegroom use. Jaya Prana, the subject of a Balinese Uriah myth, responds to the lord who has offered him the loveliest of six hundred servant girls: "Godly King, my Lord and Master / I beg you, give me leave to go / such things are not yet in my mind; / like a fighting cock encaged / indeed I am on my mettle / I am alone / as yet the flame has not been fanned."

5. For these, see V. E. Korn, *Het Adatrecht van Bali,* 2d ed. (s'Gravenhage: G. Naeff, 1932), index under toh.

6. There is indeed a legend to the effect that the separation of Java and Bali is due to the action of a powerful Javanese religious figure who wished to protect himself against a Balinese culture hero (the ancestor of two Ksatria castes) who was a passionate cockfighting gambler. See Christiaan Hooykaas, *Agama Tirtha* (Amsterdam: Noord-Hollandsche, 1964), 184.

7. An incestuous couple is forced to wear pig yokes over their necks and crawl to a pig trough and eat with their mouths there. On this, see Jane Belo, "Customs Pertaining to Twins in Bali," in Belo, ed., *Traditional Balinese Culture*, 49; on the abhorrence of animality generally, Bateson and Mead, *Balinese Character*, 22.

8. Except for unimportant, small-bet fights (on the question of fight "importance," see below) spur affixing is usually done by someone other than the owner. Whether the owner handles his own cock or not more or less depends on how skilled he is at it, a consideration whose importance is again relative to the importance of the fight. When spur affixers and cock handlers are someone other than the owner, they are almost always a quite close relative—a brother or cousin—or a very intimate friend of his. They are thus almost extensions of his personality, as the fact that all three will refer to the cock as "mine," say "I" fought So-and-So, and so on, demonstrates. Also, owner-handler-affixer triads tend to be fairly fixed, though individuals may participate in several and often exchange roles within a given one.

9. Erving Goffman, *Encounters: Two Studies in the Sociology of Interaction* (Indianapolis: Bobbs-Merrill, 1961), 9-10.

10. This word, which literally means an indelible stain or mark, as in a birthmark or a vein in a stone, is used as well for a deposit in a court case, for a pawn, for security offered in a loan, for a stand-in for someone else in a legal or ceremonial context, for an earnest advanced in a business deal, for a sign placed in a field to indicate its ownership is in dispute, and for the status of an unfaithful wife from whose lover her husband must gain satisfaction or surrender her to him. See Korn, *Het Adatrecht van Bali;* Theodoor Pigeaud, *Javaans-Nederlands Handwoordenboek* (Groningen: Wolters, 1938); H. H. Juynboll, *Oudjavaansche-Nederlandsche Woordenlijst* (Leiden: Brill, 1923).

11. The center bet must be advanced in cash by both parties prior to the actual fight. The umpire holds the stakes until the decision is rendered and then awards them to the winner, avoiding, among other things, the intense embarrassment both winner and loser would feel if the latter had to pay off personally following his defeat. About 10 percent of the winner's receipts are subtracted for the umpire's share and that of the fight sponsors.

12. Actually, the typing of cocks, which is extremely elaborate (I have collected more than twenty classes, certainly not a complete list), is not based on color alone, but on a series of independent, interacting, dimensions, which include, beside color, size, bone thickness, plumage, and temperament. (But not pedigree. The Balinese do not breed cocks to any significant extent, nor, so far as I have been able to discover, have they ever done so. The asil, or jungle cock, which is the basic fighting strain everywhere the sport is found, is native to southern Asia, and one can buy a good example in the chicken section of almost any Balinese market for anywhere from 4 or 5 ringgits up to 50 or more.) The color element is merely the one normally used as the type name, except when the two cocks of different types—as on principle they must be—have the same color, in

which case a secondary indication from one of the other dimensions ("large speckled" v. "small speckled," etc.) is added. The types are coordinated with various cosmological ideas which help shape the making of matches, so that, for example, you fight a small, headstrong, speckled brown-on-white cock with flat-lying feathers and thin legs from the east side of the ring on a certain day of the complex Balinese calendar, and a large, cautious, all-black cock with tufted feathers and stubby legs from the north side on another day, and so on. All this is again recorded in palm-leaf manuscripts and endlessly discussed by the Balinese (who do not all have identical systems), and full-scale componential-cum-symbolic analysis of cock classifications would be extremely valuable both as an adjunct to the description of the cockfight and in itself. But my data on the subject, though extensive and varied, do not seem to be complete and systematic enough to attempt such an analysis here. For Balinese cosmological ideas more generally see Belo, ed., *Traditional Balinese Culture*, and J. L. Swellengrebel, ed., *Bali: Studies in Life, Thought, and Ritual* (The Hague: W. van Hoeve, 1960); for calendrical ones, Clifford Geertz, *Person, Time, and Conduct in Bali: An Essay in Cultural Analysis* (New Haven, Conn.: Southeast Asia Studies, Yale University, 1966), 45–53.

13. For purposes of ethnographic completeness, it should be noted that it is possible for the man backing the favorite—the odds-giver—to make a bet in which he wins if his cock wins or there is a tie, a slight shortening of the odds (I do not have enough cases to be exact, but ties seem to occur about once every fifteen or twenty matches). He indicates his wish to do this by shouting sapih ("tie".) rather than the cock-type, but such bets are in fact infrequent.

14. Assuming only binomial variability, the departure from a fifty-fifty expectation in the 60 ringgits and below case is 1.38 standard deviations, or (in a one-direction test) an 8 in 100 possibility by chance alone; for the below 40 ringgits case it is 1.65 standard deviations, or about 5 in 100. The fact that these departures though real are not extreme merely indicates, again, that even in the smaller fights the tendency to match cocks at least reasonably evenly persists. It is a matter of relative relaxation of the pressures toward equalization, not their elimination. The tendency for high-bet contests to be coin-flip propositions is, of course, even more striking, and suggests the Balinese know quite well what they are about.

15. The reduction in wagering in smaller fights (which, of course, feeds on itself; one of the reasons people find small fights uninteresting is that there is less wagering in them, and contrariwise for large ones) takes place in three mutually reinforcing ways. First, there is a simple withdrawal of interest as people wander off to have a cup of coffee or chat with a friend. Second, the Balinese do not mathematically reduce odds, but bet directly in terms of stated odds as such. Thus, for a 9-8 bet, one man wagers 9 ringgits, the other 8; for 5-4, one wagers 5, the other 4. For any given currency unit, like the ringgit, therefore, 6.3 times as much money is involved in a 10-9 bet as in a 2-1 bet, for example, and, as noted, in small fights betting settles toward the longer end. Finally, the bets which are made tend to be one- rather than two-, three-, or in some of the very largest fights, four- or five-finger ones. (The fingers indicate the multiples of the stated bet odds at issue, not absolute figures. Two fingers in a 6–5 situation

means a man wants to wager to ringgits on the underdog against 12, three in an 8-7 situation, 21 against 24, and so on.)

16. Besides wagering there are other economic aspects of the cockfight, especially its very close connection with the local market system which, though secondary both to its motivation and to its function, are not without importance. Cockfights are open events to which anyone who wishes may come, sometimes from quite distant areas, but well over 90 percent, probably over 95, are very local affairs, and the locality concerned is defined not by the village, nor even by the administrative district, but by the rural market system. Bali has a three-day market week with the familiar "solar-system" type rotation. Though the markets themselves have never been very highly developed, small morning affairs in a village square, it is the microregion such rotation rather generally marks out—ten or twenty square miles, seven or eight neighboring villages (which in contemporary Bali is usually going to mean anywhere from five to ten or eleven thousand people) from which the core of any cockfight audience, indeed virtually all of it, will come. Most of the fights are in fact organized and sponsored by small combines of petty rural merchants under the general premise, very strongly held by them and indeed by all Balinese, that cockfights are good for trade because "they get money out of the house, they make it circulate." Stalls selling various sorts of things as well as assorted sheer-chance gambling games (see below) are set up around the edge of the area so that this even takes on the quality of a small fair. This connection of cockfighting with markets and market sellers is very old, as, among other things, their conjunction in inscriptions (Roelof Goris, *Prasasti Bali*, 2 vols. [Bandung: N. V. Masa Baru, 1954]) indicates. Trade has followed the cock for centuries in rural Bali and the sport has been one of the main agencies of the island's monetization.

17. The phrase is found in the Hildreth translation, *International Library of Psychology*, 1931, note to 106; see L. L. Fuller, *The Morality of Law* (New Haven, Conn.: Yale University Press, 1964), 6ff.

18. Of course, even in Bentham, utility is not normally confined as a concept to monetary losses and gains, and my argument here might be more carefully put in terms of a denial that for the Balinese, as for any people, utility (pleasure, happiness. . .) is merely identifiable with wealth. But such terminological problems are in any case secondary to the essential point: the cockfight is not roulette.

19. Max Weber, *The Sociology of Religion* (Boston: Beacon Press, 1963). There is nothing specifically Balinese, of course, about deepening significance with money, as Whyte's description of corner boys in a working-class district of Boston demonstrates: "Gambling plays an important role in the lives of Cornerville people. Whatever game the corner boys play, they nearly always bet on the outcome. When there is nothing at stake, the game is not considered a real contest. This does not mean that the financial element is all-important. I have frequently heard men say that the honor of winning was much more important than the money at stake. The corner boys consider playing for money the real test of skill and, unless a man performs well when money is at stake, he is not considered a good competitor." W. F. Whyte, *Street Corner Society*, 2d ed. (Chicago: University of Chicago Press, 1955), 140.

20. The extremes to which this madness is conceived on occasion to go—and the fact that it is considered madness—is demonstrated by the Balinese folktale I Tuhung Kuning. A gambler becomes so deranged by his passion that, leaving on a trip, he orders his pregnant wife to take care of the prospective newborn if it is a boy but to feed it as meat to his fighting cocks if it is a girl. The mother gives birth to a girl, but rather than giving the child to the cocks she gives them a large rat and conceals the girl with her own mother. When the husband returns the cocks, crowing a jingle, inform him of the deception and, furious, he sets out to kill the child. A goddess descends from heaven and takes the girl up to the skies with her. The cocks die from the food given them, the owner's sanity is restored, the goddess brings the girl back to the father who reunites him with his wife. The story is given as "Geel Komkommertje" in Jacoba Hooykaas-van Leeuwen Boomkamp, *Sprookjes en Verhalen van Bali* (s'Gravenhage: Van Hoeve, 1956), 19–25.

21. For a fuller description of Balinese rural social structure, see Clifford Geertz, "Form and Variation in Balinese Village Structure," *American Anthropologist* 61 (1959): 94-108; "Tihingan, A Balinese Village," in R. M. Koentjaraningrat, *Villages in Indonesia* (Ithaca, N.Y.: Cornell University Press, 1967), 210–243; and, though it is a bit off the norm as Balinese villages go, V. E. Korn, *De Dorpsrepubliek tnganan Pagringsingan* (Santpoort [Netherlands]: C. A. Mees, 1933).

22. Goffman, Encounters, 78.

23. B. R. Berelson, P. F. Lazersfeld, and W. N. McPhee, *Voting: A Study of Opinion Formation in a Presidential Campaign* (Chicago: University of Chicago Press, 1954).

24. Addict gamblers are really less declassed (for their status is, as everyone else's, inherited) than merely impoverished and personally disgraced. The most prominent addict gambler in my cockfight circuit was actually a very high caste satria who sold off most of his considerable lands to support his habit. Though everyone privately regarded him as a fool and worse (some, more charitable, regarded him as sick), he was publicly treated with the elaborate deference and politeness due his rank. On the independence of personal reputation and public status in Bali, see Geertz, *Person, Time, and Conduct,* 28–35.

25. British cockfights (the sport was banned there in 1840) indeed seem to have lacked it, and to have generated, therefore, a quite different family of shapes. Most British fights were "mains," in which a preagreed number of cocks were aligned into two teams and fought serially. Score was kept and wagering took place both on the individual matches and on the main as a whole. There were also "battle Royales," both in England and on the Continent, in which a large number of cocks were let loose at once with the one left standing at the end the victor. And in Wales, the so-called "Welsh main" followed an elimination pattern, along the lines of a present-day tennis tournament, winners proceeding to the next round. As a genre, the cockfight has perhaps less compositional flexibility than, say, Latin comedy, but it is not entirely without any. On cockfighting more generally, see Arch Ruport, *The Art of Cockfighting* (New York: Devin-Adair, 1949); G. R. Scott, *History of Cockfighting* (London: Charles Skilton, 1957); and Lawrence Fitz-Barnard, *Fighting Sports* (London: Odhams Press, 1921).

26. Frye, The Educated Imagination, 63–64.

27. The use of the, to Europeans, "natural" visual idiom for perception—"see," "watches," and so forth—is more than usually misleading here, for the fact that, as mentioned earlier, Balinese follow the progress of the fight as much (perhaps, as fighting cocks are actually rather hard to see except as blurs of motion, more) with their bodies as with their eyes, moving their limbs, heads, and trunks in gestural mimicry of the cocks' maneuvers, means that much of the individual's experience of the fight is kinesthetic rather than visual. If ever there was an example of Kenneth Burke's definition of a symbolic act as "the dancing of an attitude" (*The Philosophy of Literary Form*, rev. ed. [New York: vintage Books, 1957], 9) the cockfight is it. On the enormous role of kinesthetic perception in Balinese life, Bateson and Mead, *Balinese Character*, 84–88; on the active nature of aesthetic perception in general, Goodman, *Language of Art*, 241–244.

28. All this coupling of the occidental great with the oriental lowly will doubtless disturb certain sorts of aestheticians as the earlier efforts of anthropologists to speak of Christianity and totemism in the same breath disturbed certain sorts of theologians. But as ontological questions are (or should be) bracketed in the sociology of religion, judgmental ones are (or should be) bracketed in the sociology of art. In any case, the attempt to deprovincialize the concept of art is but part of the general anthropological conspiracy to deprovincialize all important social concepts—marriage, religion, law, rationality—and though this is a threat to aesthetic theories which regard certain works of art as beyond the reach of sociological analysis, it is no threat to the conviction, for which Robert Graves claims to have been reprimanded at his Cambridge tripos, that some poems are better than others.

SELECTION 28

Mother Cow

Marvin Harris

Marvin Harris always loved a challenge, especially when others would chalk off religious beliefs to the inscrutable, irrational motives of mankind. It did not matter whether the issue had to do with why people fight or why Jews and Moslems do not eat pork. The greater the riddle, the more exhaustively he would research the matter until he came up with a rational, down-to-earth explanation.

"Cow love" in India is a good example. The Hindu taboo on eating beef, in a country in which so many people seem to be dirt poor and starving, appeared to be the height of irrationality—until Marvin Harris looked into it. In this essay, taken from his book, *Cows, Pigs, Wars and Witches* (1974), Harris claims that most of the people in India are better off not consuming the sacred cow than they would be if they did indulge.

Marvin Harris' approach in this essay, in fact in his entire book, is what he termed the *cultural materialist perspective*, meaning that one needs to know the actual circumstances of people's lives before one can understand their beliefs and behavior. Moreover, one should never rely solely on a people's conscious awareness of themselves as a guide to understanding their beliefs. The personal perspective is as much a product of their circumstances as is the behavior to be explained. In other words, we get nowhere by explaining aspects of culture as culturally determined.

Marvin Harris (1927–2001) received his Ph.D. from Columbia University in 1953. He began his teaching career at Columbia in 1952, until he became a graduate research professor at the University of Florida. He retired in 2000. He also served as a technical adviser to the Ministry of Education in Brazil (where he had done fieldwork) in 1953, was executive secretary of the Columbia-Cornell-Harvard-Illinois Summer Field Studies Program from 1960-66, and lectured at the Foreign Service Institute, beginning in 1966.

Among his most significant publications were *The Rise of Anthropological Theory: A History of Theories of Culture* (1968), *Culture, Man and Nature: An Introduction to General Anthropology* (1971), *Cannibals and Kings: The Origin of Cultures* (1974), *Cultural Materialism: The Struggle for a Science of Culture* (1979), *Why Nothing Works: The Anthropology of Daily Life* (1987), and *Good to Eat: Riddles of Food and Culture* (1986)

Key Concept: Cow love in India

---

*W*henever I get into discussions about the influence of practical and mundane factors on lifestyles, someone is sure to say, "But what about all those cows the hungry peasants in India refuse to eat?" The picture of a ragged farmer starving to death alongside a big fat cow conveys a reassuring sense of mystery to Western observes. In countless learned and popular allusions, it confirms our deepest conviction about how people with inscrutable Oriental minds ought to act. It is comforting to know—somewhat like "there will always be an England"—that in India spiritual values are more precious than life itself. And at the same time it makes us feel sad. How can we ever hope to understand people so different from ourselves? Westerners find the idea that there might be a practical explanation for Hindu love of cow more upsetting than Hindus

do. The sacred cow—how else can I say it?—is one of our favorite sacred cows.

Hindus venerate cows because cows are the symbol of everything that is alive. As Mary is to Christians the mother of God, the cow of Hindus is the mother of life. So there is no greater sacrilege for a Hindu than killing a cow. Even the taking of human life lacks the symbolic meaning, the unutterable defilement, that is evoked by cow slaughter.

According to many experts, cow worship is the number one cause of India's hunger and poverty. Some Western-trained agronomists say that the taboo against cow slaughter is keeping one hundred million "useless" animals alive. They claim that cow worship lowers the efficiency of agriculture because the useless animals contribute neither milk nor meat while competing for croplands and foodstuff with useful animals and hungry human beings. A study sponsored by the Ford Foundation in 1959 concluded that possibly half of India's cattle could be regarded as surplus in relation to feed supply. And an economist from the University of Pennsylvania stated in 1971 that India has thirty million unproductive cows.

It does seem that there are enormous numbers of surplus, useless, and uneconomic animals, and that this situation is a direct result of irrational Hindu doctrines. Tourists on their way through Delhi, Calcutta, Madras, Bombay, and other Indian cities are astonished at the liberties enjoyed by stray cattle. The animals wander through the streets, browse off the stalls in the market place, break into private gardens, defecate all over the sidewalks, and snarl traffic by pausing to chew their cuds in the middle of busy intersections. In the countryside, the cattle congregate on the shoulders of every highway and spend much of their time taking leisurely walks down the railroad tracks.

Love of cow affects life in many ways. Government agencies maintain old age homes for cows at which owners may board their dry and decrepit animals free of charge. In Madras, the police round up stray cattle that have fallen ill and nurse them back to health by letting them graze on small fields adjacent to the station house. Farmers regard their cows as member of the family, adorn them with garlands and tassels, pray for them when they get sick, and call in their neighbors and a priest to celebrate the birth of a new calf. Throughout India, Hindus hang on their walls calendars that portray beautiful, bejeweled young women who have the bodies of big fat white cows. Milk is shown jetting out of each teat of these half-woman, half-zebu goddesses.

Aside from the beautiful human face, cow pinups bear little resemblance to the typical cow one sees in the flesh. For most of the year their bones are their most prominent feature. Far from having milk gushing from every teat, the gaunt beasts barely manage to nurse a single calf to maturity. The average yield of whole milk from the typical humpbacked breed of zebu cow in India amounts to less than 500 pounds a year. Ordinary American dairy cattle produce over 5,000 pounds, while for champion milkers, 20,000 pounds is not unusual. But this comparison doesn't tell the whole story. In any given year about half of India's zebu cows give no milk at all—not a drop.

To make matters worse, love of cow does not stimulate love of man. Since Moslems spurn pork but eat beef, many Hindus consider them to be cow killers. Before the partition of the Indian subcontinent into India and Pakistan, bloody communal riots aimed at preventing the Moslems from killing cows became annual occurrences. Memories of old cow riots—as, for example, the one in Bihar in 1917 when thirty people died and 170 Moslem villages were looted down to the last doorpost—continue to embitter relations between India and Pakistan.

Although he deplored the rioting, Mohandas K. Gandhi was an ardent advocate of cow love and wanted a total ban on cow slaughter. When the Indian constitution was drawn up, it included a bill of rights for cows which stopped just short of outlawing every form of cow killing. Some states have since banned cow slaughter altogether, but others still permit exceptions. The cow question remains a major cause of rioting and disorders, not only between Hindus and the remnants of the Moslem community, but between the ruling Congress Party and extremist Hindu factions of cow lovers. On November 7, 1966, a mob of 120,000 people, led by a band of chanting, naked holy men draped with garlands of marigolds and smeared with white cow-dung ash, demonstrated against cow slaughter in front of the Indian House of Parliament. Eight persons were killed and forty-eight injured during the ensuing riot. This was followed by a nationwide wave of fasts among holy men, led by Muni Shustril Kumar, president of the All-Party Cow Protection Campaign Committee.

To Western observers familiar with modern industrial techniques of agriculture and stock raising, cow love seems senseless, even suicidal. The efficiency expert yearns to get his hands on all those useless animals and ship them off to a proper fate. And yet one finds certain inconsistencies in the condemnation of cow love. When I began to wonder if there might be a practical explanation for the sacred cow, I came across an intriguing government report. It said that India had too many cows but too few oxen. With so many cows around, how could there be a shortage of oxen? Oxen and male water buffalo are the principal source of traction for plowing India's fields. For each farm of ten acres or less, one pair of oxen or water buffalo is considered adequate. A little arithmetic shows that as far as plowing is concerned, there is indeed a shortage rather than a surplus of animals. India has 60 million farms, but only 80 million traction animals. If each farm had its quota of two oxen or two water buffalo, there ought to be 120 million traction animals—that is, 40 million more than are actually available.

The shortage may not be quite so bad since some farmers rent or borrow oxen from their neighbors. But the sharing of plow animals often proves impractical. Plowing must be coordinated with the monsoon rains, and by the time one farm has been plowed, the optimum moment for plowing another may already have passed. Also, after plowing is over, a farmer still needs his own pair of oxen to pull his oxcart, the mainstay of bulk transport throughout rural India. Quite possibly private ownership of farms, livestock, plows, and oxcarts lowers the efficiency of Indian agriculture, but this, I soon realized, was not caused by cow love.

The shortage of draft animals is a terrible threat that hangs over most of India's peasant families. When an ox falls sick a poor farmer is in danger of losing his farm. If he has no replacement for it, he will have to borrow money at usurious rates. Millions of rural households have in fact lost all or part of their holdings and have gone into sharecropping or day labor as a result of such debts. Every year hundreds of thousands of destitute farmers end up migrating to the cities, which already teem with unemployed and homeless persons.

The Indian farmers who can't replace his sick or deceased ox is in much the same situation as an American farmer who can neither replace nor repair his broken tractor. But there is an important difference: tractors are made by factories, but oxen are made by cows. A farmer who owns a cow owns a factory for making oxen. With or without cow love, this is a good reason for him not to be too anxious to sell his cow to the slaughterhouse. One also begins to see why Indian farmers might be willing to tolerate cows that give only 500 pounds of milk per year. If the main economic function of the zebu cow is to breed male traction animals, then there's no point in comparing her with specialized American dairy animals, whose main function is to produce milk. Still, the milk produced by zebu cows plays an important role in meeting the nutritional needs of many poor families. Even small amounts of milk products can improve the health of people who are forced to subsist on the edge of starvation.

When Indian farmers want an animal primarily for milking purposes they turn to the female water buffalo, which has longer lactation periods and higher butterfat yields than zebu cattle. Male water buffalo are also superior animals for plowing in flooded rice paddies. But oxen are more versatile and are preferred for dry-field farming and road transport. Above all, zebu breeds are remarkably rugged, and can survive the long droughts that periodically afflict different parts of India.

Agriculture is part of a vast system of human and natural relationships. To judge isolated portions of this "ecosystem" in terms that are relevant to the conduct of American agribusiness leads to some very strange impressions. Cattle figure in the Indian ecosystem in ways that are easily overlooked or demeaned by observers from industrialized, high energy societies. In the United States, chemicals have almost completely replaced animal manure as the principal source of farm fertilizer. American farmers stopped using manure when they began to plow with tractors rather than mules or horses. Since tractors excrete poisons rather than fertilizers, a commitment to large-scale machine farming is almost of necessity a commitment to the use of chemical fertilizers. And around the world today there has in fact grown up a vast integrated petrochemical-tractor-truck industrial complex that produces farm machinery, motorized transport, oil and gasoline, and chemical fertilizers and pesticides upon which new high-yield production techniques depend.

For better or worse, most of India's farmers cannot participate in this complex, not because they worship their cows, but because they can't afford to buy tractors. Like other underdeveloped nations, India can't build factories that are competitive with the facilities of the industrialized nations nor pay for large quantities of imported industrial products. To convert from animals and manure to tractors and petrochemicals would require the investment of incredible amount of capital. Moreover, the inevitable effect of substituting costly machines for cheap animals is to reduce the number of people who can earn their living from agriculture and to force a corresponding increase in the size of the average farm. We know that the development of large-scale agribusiness in the United States has meant the virtual destruction of the small family farm. Less than 5 percent of U.S. families now live on farms, as compared with 60 percent about a hundred years ago. If agribusiness were to develop along similar lines of India, jobs and housing would soon have to be found for a quarter of a billion displaced peasants.

Since the suffering caused by unemployment and homelessness in India's cities is already intolerable, an additional massive build-up of the urban population can only lead to unprecedented upheavals and catastrophes.

With this alternative in view, it becomes easier to understand low-energy, small-scale, animal-based systems. As I have already pointed out, cows and oxen provide low energy substitutes for tractors and tractor factories. They also should be credited with carrying out the functions of a petrochemical industry. India's cattle annually excrete about 700 million tons of recoverable manure. Approximately half of this total is used as fertilizer, while most of the remainder is burned to provide heat for cooking. The annual quantity of heat liberated by this dung, the Indian housewife's main cooking fuel, is the thermal equivalent of 27 million tons of kerosene, 35 million tons of coal, or 68 million tons of wood. Since India has only small reserves of oil and coal and is already the victim of extensive deforestation, none of these fuels can be considered practical substitutes for cow dung. The thought of dung in the kitchen may not appeal to the average American, but Indian women regard it as a superior cooking fuel because it is finely adjusted to their domestic routines. Most Indian dishes are prepared with clarified butter known as *ghee*, for which cow dung is the preferred source of heat since it burns with a clean, slow, long-lasting flame that doesn't scorch the food. This enables the Indian housewife to start cooking her meals and to leave them unattended for several hours while she takes care of the children, helps out in the fields, or performs other chores. American housewives achieve a similar effect through a complex set of electronic controls that come as expensive options on late-model stoves.

Cow dung has at least one other major function. Mixed with water and made into a paste, it is used as a household flooring material. Smeared over a dirt floor and left to harden into a smooth surface, it keeps the dust down and can be swept clean with a broom.

Because cattle droppings have so many useful properties, every bit of dung is carefully collected. Village small fry are given the task of following the family cow around and of bringing home its daily petrochemical output. In the cities, sweeper castes enjoy a monopoly on the dung deposited by strays and earn their living by selling it to housewives.

From an agribusiness point of view, a dry and barren cow is an economic abomination. But from the viewpoint of the peasant farmer, the same dry and barren cow may be a last desperate defense against the moneylenders. There is always the chance that a favorable monsoon may restore the vigor of even the most decrepit specimen and that she will fatten up, calve, and start giving milk again. This is what the farmer prays for; sometimes his prayers are answered. In the meantime, dung-making goes on. And so one gradually begins to understand why a skinny old hag of a cow still looks beautiful in the eyes of her owner.

Zebu cattle have small bodies, energy-storing humps on their back, and great powers of recuperation. These features are adapted to the specific conditions of Indian agriculture. The native breeds are capable of surviving for long periods with little food or water and are highly resistant to diseases that afflict other breeds in tropical climates. Zebu oxen are worked as long as they continue to breathe. Stuart Odend'hal, a veterinarian formerly associated with Johns Hopkins University, performed field autopsies on Indian cattle which had been working normally a few hours before their deaths but whose vital organs were damaged by massive lesions. Given their enormous recuperative powers, these beasts are never easily written off as completely "use-less" while they are still alive.

But sooner or later there must come a time when all hope of an animal's recovery is lost and even dung-making ceases. And still the Hindu farmer refuses to kill if for food or sell it to the slaughterhouse. Isn't this incontrovertible evidence of a harmful economic practice that has no explanation apart from the religious taboos on cow slaughter and beef consumption?

No one can deny that cow love mobilizes people to resist cow slaughter and beef eating. But I don't agree that the anti-slaughter and beef-eating taboos necessarily have an adverse effect on human survival and well-being. By slaughtering or selling his aged and decrepit animals, a farmer might earn a few more rupees or temporarily improve his family's diet. But in the long run, his refusal to sell to the slaughterhouse or kill for his own table may have beneficial consequences. An established principle of ecological analysis states that communities of organisms are adapted not to average but to extreme conditions. The relevant situation in India is the recurrent failure of the monsoon rains.

To evaluate the economic significance of the anti-slaughter and anti-beef-eating taboos, we have to consider what these taboos mean in the context of periodic droughts and famine.

The taboo on slaughter and beef eating may be as much a product of natural selection as the small bodies and fantastic recuperative powers of the zebu breeds. During droughts and famines, farmers are severely temped to kill or sell their livestock. Those who succumb to this temptation seal their doom, even if they survive the drought, for when the rains come, they will be unable to plow their fields. I want to be even more emphatic: Massive slaughter of cattle under the duress of famine constitutes a much greater threat to aggregate welfare than any likely miscalculation by particular farmers concerning the usefulness of their animals during normal times. It seems probable that the sense of unutterable profanity elicited by cow slaughter has its roots in the excruciating contradiction between immediate needs and long-run conditions of survival. Cow love with its sacred symbols and holy doctrines protects the farmer against calculations that are "rational" only in the short term. To Western experts it looks as if "the Indian farmer would rather starve to death then eat his cow." The same kinds of experts like to talk about the "inscrutable Oriental mind" and think that "life is not so dear to the Asian masses." They don't realize that the farmer would rather eat his cow than starve, but that he will starve if he does eat it.

Even with the assistance of the holy laws and cow love, the temptation to eat beef under the duress of famine sometimes proves irresistible. During World War II, there was a great famine in Bengal caused by droughts and the Japanese occupation of Burma. Slaughter of cows and draft animals reached such alarming levels in the summer of 1944 that the British had to use troops to enforce the cow-protection laws. In 1967 *The New York Times* reported;

> Hindus facing starvation in the drought-stricken area of Bihar are Slaughtering cows and eating the meat even though the animals are sacred to the Hindu religion.

Observers noted that "the misery of the people was beyond imagination."

The survival into old age of a certain number of absolutely useless animals during good times is part of the price that must be paid for protecting useful animals against slaughter during bad times. But I wonder how much is actually lost because of the prohibition on slaughter and the taboo on beef. From a Western agribusiness viewpoint, it seems irrational for India not to have a meat-packing industry. But the actual potential for such an industry in a country like India is very limited. A substantial rise in beef production would strain the entire ecosystem, not because of cow love but because of the laws of thermodynamics. In any food chain the interposition of additional animal links results in sharp decrease in the efficiency of food production. The caloric value of what an animal has eaten is always much greater than the caloric value of its body. This means that more calories are available per capita when plant food is eaten directly by a human population than when it is used to feed domesticated animals.

Because of the high level of beef consumption in the United States, three-quarters of all our croplands are used for feeding cattle rather than people. Since the per capita calorie intake in India is already below minimum daily requirements, switching croplands to meat production could only result in higher food prices and a further deterioration in the living standards for poor families I doubt it more than 10 percent of the Indian people will ever be able to make beef an important part of their diet, regardless of whether they believe in cow love or not.

I also doubt that sending more aged and decrepit animals to existing slaughterhouses would result in nutritional gains for the people who need it most. Most of these animals get eaten anyway, even if they aren't sent to the slaughterhouse, because throughout India there are low-ranking castes whose members have the right to dispose of the bodies of dead cattle. In one way of another, twenty million cattle die every year, and a large portion of their meat is eaten by these carrion-eating "untouchables."

My friend Dr. Joan Mencher, an anthropologist who has worked in India for many years, points out that the existing slaughterhouse cater to urban middle-class non-Hindus. She notes that "the untouchables get their food in other ways. It is good for the untouchable if a cow dies of starvation in a village, but not if it gets sent to Muslims of Christians." Dr. Mencher's informants at first denied that "upper-caste" Americans liked steak, they readily confessed their taste for beef curry.

Like everything else I have been discussing, meat eating by untouchables is finely adjusted to practical conditions. The meat-eating castes also tend to be the leather-working castes, since they have the right to dispose of the skin of the fallen cattle. So despite cow love, India manages to have a huge leathercraft industry. Even in death, apparently useless animals continue to be exploited for human purposes.

I could be right about cattle being useful for traction, fuel, fertilizer, milk, floor covering, meat, and leather, and still misjudge the ecological and economic significance of the whole complex. Everything depends on how much all of this costs in natural resources and human labor relative to altenative modes of satisfying the needs of India's huge population. These costs are detemined largely by what the cattle eat. Many experts assume that man and cow are locked in a deadly competition for land and food crops. This might be true if Indian farmers followed the American agribusiness model and fed their animals on food crops. But the shameless truth about the sacred cow is that she is an indefatigable scavenger. Only an insignificant portion of the food consumed by the average cow comes from pastures and food corps set aside for their use.

This ought to have been obvious from all those persistent reports about cows wandering about and snarling traffic, What are those animals doing in the markets, on the lawns, along the highways and railroad tracks, and up on the barren hillsides? What are they doing if not eating every morsel of grass, stubble, and garbage that cannot be directly consumed by human beings and converting it into milk and other useful products! In his study of cattle in West Bengal, Dr. Odend'hal discovered that the major constituent in the cattle's diet is inedible by-products of human food crops, principally rice straw, wheat bran, and rice husks. When the Ford Foundation estimated that half of the cattle were surplus in relation to feed supply, they meant to say that half of the cattle manage to

survive even without access to fodder crops. But this is understatement. Probably less than 20 percent of what the cattle eat consists of humanly edible substances; most of this is fed to working oxen and water buffalo rather than to dry and barren cows. Odend'hal found that in his study area there was no competition between cattle and humans for land of the food supply: "Basically, the cattle convert items of little direct human value into products of immediate utility."

One reason why cow love is so often misunderstood is that it has different implications for the rich and the poor. Poor farmers use it as a license to scavenge while the wealthy farmers resist it as a rip-off. To the poor farmer, the cow is a holy beggar; to the rich farmer, it's a thief, Occasionally the cows invade someone's pastures or planted fields. The landlords complain, but the poor peasants plead ignorance and depend on cow love to get their animals back. If there is competition, it is between man and man or caste and caste, not between man and beast.

City cows also have owners who let them scrounge by day and call them back at night to be milked. Dr. Mencher recounts that while she lived for a while in a middle-class neighborhood in Madras her neighbors were constantly complaining about "stray" cows breaking into the family compounds. The strays were actually owned by people who lived in a room above a shop and who sold milk door in the neighborhood. As for the old age homes and police cowpounds, they serve very nicely to reduce the risk of maintaining cows in a city environment. If a cow stops producing milk, the owner may decide to let it wander around until the police pick it up and bring it to the precinct house. When the cow has recovered, the owner pays a small fine and returns it to its usual haunts. The old age homes operate on a similar principle, providing cheap government-subsidized pasture that would otherwise not be available to city cows.

Incidentally, the preferred form of purchasing milk in the cities is to have the cow brought to the house and milked on the spot. This is often the only way that the householder can be sure that he is buying pure milk rather than milk mixed with water or urine.

What seems most incredible about these arrangements is that they have been interpreted as evidence of wasteful, anti-economic Hindu practices, while in fact they reflect a degree of economizing that goes far beyond Western, "Protestant" standards of savings and husbandry. Cow love is perfectly compatible with a merciless determination to get the literal last drop of milk out of the cow. The man who takes the cow door to door brings along a dummy calf made out of stuffed calfskin which he sets down beside the cow to trick it into performing. When this doesn't work, the owner may resort to *phooka*, blowing air into the cow's uterus through a hollow pipe, or *doom dev*, stuffing its tail into the vaginal orifice. Gandhi believed that cows were treated more cruelly in India than anywhere else in the world. "How we bleed her to take the last drop of milk from her," he lamented. "How we starve her to emaciation, how we ill-treat the calves, how we deprive them of their portion of milk, how cruelly we treat the oxen, how we castrate them, how we beat them, how we overload them."

No one understood better than Gandhi that cow love had different implications for rich and poor. For him the cow was a central focus of the struggle to rouse India to authentic nationhood. Cow love went along with small-scale farming, making cotton thread on a hand spinning wheel, sitting cross-legged on the floor, dressing in a loincloth, vegetarianism, reverence for life, and strict non-violence. To these themes Gandhi owed his vast popular following among the peasant masses, urban poor, and untouchables. It was his way of protecting them against the ravages of industrialization.

The asymmetrical implications of *ahimsa* for rich and poor are ignored by economists who want to make Indian agriculture more efficient by slaughtering "surplus" animals. Professor Alan Heston, for example, accepts the fact that the cattle perform vital functions for which substitutes are not readily available. But he proposes that the same functions could be carried out more efficiently if there were 30 million fewer cows. This figure is based on the assumption that with adequate care only 40 cows per 100 male animals would be needed to replace the present number of oxen. Since there are 72 million adult male cattle, by this formula, 24 million breeding females ought to be sufficient. Actually, there are 54 million cows. Subtracting 24 million from 54 million, Heston arrives at the estimate of 30 million "useless" animals to be slaughtered. The fodder and feed that these "useless" animals have been consuming are to be distributed among the remaining animals, who will become healthier and therefore will be able to keep total milk and dung production at or above previous levels. But whose cows are to be sacrificed? About 43 percent of the total cattle population is found on the poorest 62 percent of the farms. These farms, consisting of give acres or less, have only 5 percent of the pasture and gazing land. In other words, most of the animals that are temporarily dry, barren, and feeble are owned by the people who live on the smallest and poorest farms. So that when the economists talk about getting rid of 30 million cows, they are really talking about getting rid of 30 million cows that belong to poor families, not rich ones. But most poor families own only one cow, so what this economizing boils down to is not so much getting rid of 30 million cows as getting rid of 150 million people—forcing them off the land and into the cities.

Cow-slaughter enthusiasts base their recommendation on an understandable error. They reason that since the farmers refuse to kill their animals, and since there is a religious taboo against doing so, therefore it is the taboo that is mainly responsible for the high ratio of cows to oxen. Their error is hidden in the observed ratio itself: 70 cows to 100 oxen. If cow love prevents farmers from killing cows that are economically useless, how is it there are 30 percent fewer cows than oxen? Since approximately as many female as male animals are born, something must be causing the death of more females than males. The solution to this puzzle is that while no Hindu farmer deliberately slaughters a female calf or decrepit cow with a club or a knife, he can and does get rid of them when they become truly useless from his point of view. Various methods short of direct slaughter are employed. To "kill" unwanted calves, for example, a triangular wooden yoke is placed about their necks so that when they try to nurse they jab the cow's udder and get kicked to death. Older animals are simply tethered on short ropes and allowed to starve—a process that does not take too long if the animal is already weak and diseased. Finally, unknown numbers of decrepit cows are surreptitiously sold through a chain a Moslem and Christian middlemen and end up in the urban slaughterhouses.

If we want to account for the observed proportions of cows to oxen, we must study rain, wind, water, and land-tenure patterns, not cow love. The proof of this is that the proportion of cows to oxen varies with the relative importance of different components of the agricultural system in different regions of India. The most important variable is the amount or irrigation water available for the cultivation of rice. Wherever there are extensive wet rice paddies, the water buffalo tends to be the preferred traction animal, and the female water buffalo is then substituted for the zebu cow as a source of milk. That is why in the vast plains of northern India, where the melting Himalayan snows and monsoons create the Holy River Ganges, the proportion of cows to oxen drops down to 47 to 100. As the distinguished Indian economist K. N. Raj has pointed out, districts in the Ganges Valley where continuous year-round rice-paddy cultivation is practiced, have cow-to-oxen ratios that approach the theoretical optimum. This is all the more remarkable since the region in question—the Gangetic plain—is the heartland of the Hindu religion and contains its most holy shrines.

The theory that religion is primarily responsible for the high proportion of cows to oxen is also refuted by a comparison between Hindu India and Moslem West Pakistan. Despite the rejection of cow love and the beef-slaughter and beef-eating taboos, West Pakistan as a whole has 60 cows for every 100 male animals, which is considerably higher than the average for the intensely Hindu Indian state of Uttar Pradesh. When districts in Uttar Pradesh are selected for the importance of water buffalo and canal irrigation and compared with ecologically similar districts in West Pakistan, ratios of female to male cattle turn out to be virtually the same.

Do I mean to say that cow love has no effect whatsoever on the cattle sex ratio or on other aspects of the agricultural system? No. What I am saying is that cow love is an active element in a complex, finely articulated material and cultural order. Cow love mobilizes the latent capacity of human beings to persevere in a low-energy ecosystem in which there is little room for waste or indolence. Cow love contributes to the adaptive resilience of the human population by preserving temporarily dry or barren but still useful animals; by discouraging the growth of an energy-expensive beef industry; by protecting cattle that fatten in the public domain or at landlord's expense; and by preserving the recovery potential of the cattle population during droughts and famines. As in any natural or artificial system, there is some slippage, friction, or waste associated with these complex interactions. Half a billion people, animals, land, labor, political economy, soil, and climate are all involved. The slaughter enthusiasts claim that the practice of letting cows breed indiscriminately and then thinning their numbers through neglect and starvation is wasteful and inefficient. I do not doubt that this is correct, but only in a narrow and relatively insignificant sense. The savings that an agricultural engineer might achieve by getting rid of an unknown number of absolutely useless animals must be balanced against catastrophic losses for the marginal peasants, especially during droughts and famines, if cow love ceases to be a holy duty.

Since the effective mobilization of all human action depends upon the acceptance of psychologically compelling creeds and doctrines, we have to expect that economic systems will always oscillate under and over their points of optimum efficiency. But the assumption that the whole system can be made to work better simply by attacking its consciousness is native and dangerous. Major improvements in the present system can be achieved by stabilizing India's human population, and by making more land, water, oxen, and water buffalo available to more people on a more equitable basis. The alternative is to destroy the present system and replace it with a completely new set of demographic, technological, politico-economic, and ideological relationships—a whole new ecosystem. Hinduism is undoubtedly a conservative force, one that makes it more difficult for the "development" experts and "modernizing" agents to destroy the old system and to replace it with a high-energy industrial and agribusiness complex. But if you think that a high-energy industrial and agribusiness complex will necessarily be more "rational" or "efficient" than the system that now exists, forget it.

Contrary to expectations, studies of energy costs and energy yields show that India makes more efficient use of its cattle than the United States does. In Singer district in West Bengal, Dr. Odend'hal discovered that the cattle's gross energetic efficiency, defined as the total of useful calories produced per year divided by the total calories consumed during the same period, was 17 percent. This compares with a gross energetic efficiency of less than 4 percent for American beef cattle raised on Western range land. As Odend'hal says, the relatively high efficiency of the Indian cattle complex comes about not because the animals are particularly productive, but because of scrupulous product utilization by humans: "The villagers are extremely utilitarian and nothing is wasted."

Wastefulness is more a characteristic of modern agribusiness than of traditional peasant economies. Under the new system of automated feed-lot beef production in the United States, for example, cattle manure not only goes unused, but it is allowed to contaminate ground water over wide areas and contributes to the pollution of nearby lakes and streams.

The higher standard of living enjoyed by the industrial nations is not the result of greater productive efficiency, but of an enormously expanded increase in the amount of energy available per person. In 1970 the United States used up the energy equivalent of twelve tons of coal per inhabitant, while the corresponding figure for India was one-fifth ton per inhabitant. The way this energy was expended involved far more energy being wasted per person in the United States than in India. Automobiles and airplanes are faster than oxcarts, but they do not use energy more efficiently. In fact, more calories go up in useless heat and smoke during a single day of traffic jams in the United States than is wasted by all the cows of India during an entire year. The comparison is even less favorable when we consider the fact that the stalled vehicles are burning up irreplaceable reserves of petroleum that it took the earth tens of millions of years to accumulate. If you want to see a real sacred cow, go out and look at the family car.

Social Change

Selection 29

LAURISTON SHARP, from "Steel Axes for Stone-Age Australians," *Steel Axes for Stone-Age Australians*

Selection 30

E. RICHARD SORENSON, from "Growing Up as a Fore Is to Be 'In Touch' and Free," *Smithsonian*

Steel Axes for Stone-Age Australians

Lauriston Sharp

Although most ethnographic accounts are like snapshots, giving us a view of cultures at given moments in time with the impression that they are unchanging, the truth of the matter is that social change has been almost constant over the past few centuries, particularly because of colonization by Europeans and their descendants.

Australian natives (in this 1952 article, referred to as "aboriginals") are no exception. Note, however, that the changes taking place as a result of introducing steel axes to the Yir Yoront were as gradual, piecemeal, and, in a sense, unintentional as they were inevitable.

At first, it seems amazing that a simple device such as a steel axe, which did not function too differently from the stone axe that it replaced, could be the stimulus for such major changes. But when one considers that the steel axe came from a different source and, in this way, disrupted the previous trading, owning, and lending relationships that had prevailed in relation to the stone ax, one begins to understand how native peoples become engulfed by European culture.

Lauriston Sharp (1907–1993) was born and raised in Madison, Wisconsin. Although he did attend the University of Wisconsin briefly, he received a Certificate in Anthropology from the University of Vienna in 1931 and received an M.A. in anthropology from Harvard University, partially based on his fieldwork on the Fox Indian project in Iowa. He went on to teach at Cornell University, where he became Chairman, Department of Sociology and Anthropology. In 1945–46, he served as the assistant chief of the division of Southeast Asian Affairs in the State Department. He also did fieldwork in Thailand and created the Cornell-Thailand Project. He wrote many books, including *Tribes and Totemism in Northeast Australia* (1939) and *Ethnographic Notes from Northern Thailand* (1965).

The fieldwork upon which this study was based was supported by the Australian National Research Council through the award of a Fellowship to the author in 1933–35.

Key Concept: social change

I.

Like other Australian aboriginals, the Yir Yoront group which lives at the mouth of the Coleman River on the west coast of Cape York Peninsula originally had no knowledge of metals. Technologically their culture was of the old stone age or Paleolithic type. They supported themselves by hunting and fishing, and obtained vegetables and other materials from the bush by simple gathering techniques. Their only domesticated animal was the dog; they had no cultivated plants of any kind. Unlike some other aboriginal groups, however, the Yir Yoront did have polished stone axes hafted in short handles which were most important in their economy.

Towards the end of the 19th century metal tools and other European artifacts began to filter into the Yir Yoront territory. The flow increased with the gradual expansion of the white frontier outward from southern and eastern Queensland. Of all the items of western technology thus made available, the hatchet, or short handled steel axe, was the most acceptable to and the most highly valued by all aboriginals.

In the mid 1930's an American anthropologist lived alone in the bush among the Yir Yoront for 13 months without seeing another white man. The Yir Yoront were thus still relatively isolated and continued to live an essentially independent economic existence, supporting themselves entirely by means of their old stone age techniques. Yet their polished stone axes were disappearing fast and being replaced by steel axes which came to them in considerable numbers, directly or indirectly, from various European sources to the south.

What changes in the life of the Yir Yoront still living under aboriginal conditions in the Australian bush could be expected as a result of their increasing possession and use of the steel axe?

II. The Course of Events

Events leading up to the introduction of the steel axe among the Yir Yoront begin with the advent of the second known group of Europeans to reach the shores of the Australian continent. In 1623 a Dutch expedition landed on the coast where the Yir Yoront now live.[1] In 1935 the Yir Yoront were still using the few cultural items recorded in the Dutch log for the aboriginals they encountered. To this cultural inventory the Dutch added beads and pieces of iron which they offered in an effort to attract the frightened "Indians." Among these natives metal and beads have disappeared, together with any memory of this first encounter with whites.

The next recorded contact in this area was in 1864. Here there is more positive assurance that the natives concerned were the immediate ancestors of the Yir Yoront community. These aboriginals had the temerity to attack a party of cattle men who were driving a small herd from southern Queensland through the length of the then unknown Cape York Peninsula to a newly established government station at the northern tip.[2] Known as the "Battle of the Mitchell River," this was one of the rare instances in which Australian aboriginals stood up to European gunfire for any length of time. A diary kept by the cattle men records that: ". . . 10 carbines poured volley after volley into them from all directions, killing and wounding with every shot with very little return, nearly all their spears having already been expended. . . . About 30 being killed, the leader thought it prudent to hold his hand, and let the rest escape. Many more must have been wounded and probably drowned, for 59 rounds were counted as discharged." The European party was in the Yir Yoront area for three days; they then disappeared over the horizon to the north and never returned. In the almost three-year long anthropological investigation conducted some 70 years later—in all the material of hundreds of free association interviews, in texts of hundreds of dreams and myths, in genealogies, and eventually in hundreds of answers to direct and indirect questioning on just this particular matter—there was nothing that could be interpreted as a reference to this shocking contact with Europeans.

The aboriginal accounts of their first remembered contact with whites begin in about 1900 with references to persons known to have had sporadic but lethal encounters with them. From that time on whites continued to remain on the southern periphery of Yir Yoront territory. With the establishment of cattle stations (ranches) to the south, cattle men made occasional excursions among the "wild black-fellows" in order to inspect the country and abduct natives to be trained as cattle boys and "house girls." At least one such expedition reached the Coleman River where a number of Yir Yoront men and women were shot for no apparent reason.

About this time the government was persuaded to sponsor the establishment of three mission stations along the 700-mile western coast of the Peninsula in an attempt to help regulate the treatment of natives. To further this purpose a strip of coastal territory was set aside as an aboriginal reserve and closed to further white settlement.

In 1915, an Anglican mission station was established near the mouth of the Mitchell River, about a three-day march from the heart of the Yir Yoront country. Some Yir Yoront refused to have anything to do with the mission, others visited it occasionally while only a few eventually settled more or less permanently in one of the three "villages" established at the mission.

Thus the majority of the Yir Yoront continued to live their old self-supporting life in the bush, protected until 1942 by the government reserve and the intervening mission from the cruder realities of the encroaching new order from the south. To the east was poor, uninhabited country. To the north were other bush tribes extending on along the coast to the distant Archer River Presbyterian mission with which the Yir Yoront had no contact. Westward was the shallow Gulf of Carpentaria on which the natives saw only a mission lugger making its infrequent dry season trips to the Mitchell River. In this protected environment for over a generation the Yir Yoront were able to recuperate from shocks received at the hands of civilized society. During the 1930's their raiding and fighting, their trading and stealing of women, their evisceration and two- or three-year care of their dead, and their totemic ceremonies continued, apparently uninhibited by western influence. In 1931 they killed a European who wandered into their territory from the east, but the investigating police never approached the group whose members were responsible for the act.

As a direct result of the work of the Mitchell River mission, all Yir Yoront received a great many more western artifacts of all kinds than ever before. As part of their plan for raising native living standards, the missionaries made it possible for aboriginals living at the mission to earn some western goods, many of which were then given or traded to natives still living under bush conditions; they also handed out certain useful articles gratis to both mission and bush aboriginals. They prevented guns, liquor, and damaging narcotics, as well as decimating diseases, from reaching the tribes of this area, while encouraging the introduction of goods they considered "improving." As has been noted, no item of western technology available, with the possible exception of trade tobacco, was in greater demand among all groups of aboriginals than the short handled steel axe. The mission always kept a good supply of these axes in stock; at Christmas parties or other mission festivals they were given away to mission or visiting aboriginals indiscriminately and in considerable numbers. In addition, some steel axes as well as other European goods were still traded in to the Yir Yoront by natives in contact with cattle stations in the south. Indeed, steel axes had probably come to the Yir Yoront through established lines of aboriginal trade long before any regular contact with whites had occurred.

III. Relevant Factors

If we concentrate our attention on Yir Yoront behavior centering about the original stone axe (rather than on the axe—the object—itself) as a cultural trait or item of cultural equipment, we should get some conception of the role this implement played in aboriginal culture. This, in turn, should enable us to foresee with considerable accuracy some of the results stemming from the displacement of the stone age by the steel axe.

The production of a stone axe required a number of simple technological skills. With the various details of the axe well in mind, adult men could set about producing it (a task not considered appropriate for women or children). First of all a man had to know the location and properties of several natural resources found in his immediate environment: pliable wood for a handle, which could be doubled or bent over the axe head and bound tightly; bark, which could be rolled into cord for the binding; and gum, to fix the stone head in the haft. These materials had to be correctly gathered, stored, prepared, cut to size, and applied or manipulated. They were in plentiful supply, and could be taken from anyone's property without special permission. Postponing consideration of the stone head, the axe could be made by any normal man who had a simple knowledge of nature and of the technological skills involved, together with fire (for heating the gum), and a few simple cutting tools—perhaps the sharp shells of plentiful bivalves.

The use of the stone axe as a piece of capital equipment used in producing other goods indicates its very great important to the subsistence economy of the aboriginal. Anyone—man, woman, or child—could use the axe; indeed, it was used primarily by women, for theirs was the task of obtaining sufficient wood to keep the family campfire burning all day, for cooking or other purposes, and all night against mosquitoes and cold (for in July, winter temperature might drop below 40 degrees). In a normal lifetime a woman would use the axe to cut or knock down literally tons of firewood. The axe was also used to make other tools or weapons, and a variety of material equipment required by the aboriginal in his daily life. The stone axe was essential in the construction of the wet season domed huts which keep out some rain and some insects; of platforms which provide dry storage; of shelters which give shade in the dry summer when days are bright and hot. In hunting and fishing and in gathering vegetable or animal food the axe was also a necessary tool, and in this tropical culture, where preservatives or other means of storage are lacking, the natives spend more time obtaining food than in any other occupation—except sleeping. In only two instances was the use of the stone axe strictly limited to adult men: for gathering wild honey, the most prized food known to the Yir Yoront; and for making the secret paraphernalia for ceremonies. From this brief listing of some of the activities involving the use of the axe, it is easy to understand why there was at least one stone axe in every camp, in every hunting or fighting party, and in every group out on a "walk-about" in the bush.

The stone axe was also prominent in interpersonal relations. Yir Yoront men dependent upon interpersonal relations for their stone axe heads, since the flat, geologically recent, alluvial country over which they range provides no suitable stone for this purpose. The stone they used came from quarries 400 miles to the south, reaching the Yir Yoront through long lines of male trading partners. Some of these chains terminated with the Yir Yoront men, others extended on farther north to other groups, using Yir Yoront men as links. Almost every older adult man had one or more regular trading partners, some to the north and some to the south. He provided his partner or partners in the south with surplus spears, particularly fighting spears tipped with the barbed spines of sting ray which snap into vicious fragments when they penetrate human flesh. For a dozen such spears, some of which he may have obtained from a partner to the north, he would receive one stone axe head. Studies have shown that the sting ray barb spears increased in value as they move south and farther from the sea. One hundred and fifty miles south of Yir Yoront one such spear may be exchanged for one stone axe head. Although actual investigations could not be made, it was presumed that farther south, nearer the quarries, one sting ray barb spear would bring several stone axe heads. Apparently people who acted as links in the middle of the chain and who made neither spears nor axe heads would receive a certain number of each as a middleman's profit.

Thus trading relations, which may extend the individual's personal relationships beyond that of his own group, were associated with spears and axes, two of the most important items in a man's equipment. Finally, most of the exchanges took place during the dry season, at the time of the great aboriginal celebrations centering about initiation rites or other totemic ceremonials which attracted hundreds and were the occasion for much exciting activity in addition to trading.

Returning to the Yir Yoront, we find that adult men kept their axes in camp with their other equipment, or carried them when travelling. Thus a woman or child who wanted to use an axe—as might frequently happen during the day—had to get one from a man, use it promptly, and return it in good condition. While a man might speak of "my axe," a woman or child could not.

This necessary and constant borrowing of axes from older men by women and children was in accordance with regular patterns of kinship behavior. A woman would expect to use her husband's axe unless he himself was using it; if unmarried, or if her husband was absent, a woman would go first to her older brother or to her father. Only in extraordinary circumstances would she seek a stone axe from other male kin. A girl, a boy, or a young man would look to a father or an older brother to provide an axe for their use. Older men, too, would follow similar rules if they had to borrow an axe.

It will be noted that all of these social relationships in which the stone axe had a place are pair relationships and that the use of the axe helped to define and maintain their character and the roles of the two individual participants. Every active relationship among the Yir Yoront involved a definite and accepted status of superordination or subordination. A person could have no dealings with another on exactly equal terms. The nearest approach to equality was between brothers, although the older was always superordinate to the younger. Since the exchange of goods in a trading relationship involved a mutual reciprocity, trading partners usually stood in a brotherly type of relationship, although one was always classified as older than the other and would have some advantage in case of dispute. It can be seen that repeated and widespread conduct centering around the use of the axe helped to generalize and standardize these sex, age, and kinship roles both in their normal benevolent and exceptional malevolent aspects.

The status of any individual Yir Yoront was determined not only by sex, age, and extended kin relationships, but also by membership in one of two dozen patrilineal totemic clans into which the entire community was divided.[3] Each clan had literally hundreds of totems, from one or two of which the clan derived its name, and the clan members their personal names. These totems included natural species or phenomena such as the sun, stars, and daybreak, as well as cultural "species": imagined ghosts, rainbow serpents, heroic ancestors; such eternal cultural verities as fires, spears, huts; and such human activities, conditions, or attributes as eating, vomiting, swimming, fighting, babies and corpses, milk and blood, lips and loins. While individual members of such totemic classes or species might disappear or be destroyed, the class itself was obviously ever-present and indestructible. The totems, therefore, lent permanence and stability to the clans, to the groupings of human individuals who generation after generation were each associated with a set of totems which distinguished one clan from another.

The stone axe was one of the most important of the many totems of the Sunlit Cloud Iguana clan. The names of many members of this clan referred to the axe itself, to activities in which the axe played a vital part, or to the clan's mythical ancestors with whom the axe was prominently associated. When it was necessary to represent the stone axe in totemic ceremonies, only men of this clan exhibited it or pantomimed its use. In secular life, the axe could be made by any man and used by all; but in the sacred realm of the totems it belonged exclusively to the Sunlit Cloud Iguana people.

Supporting those aspects of cultural behavior which we have called technology and conduct, is a third area of culture which includes ideas, sentiments, and vales. These are most difficult to deal with, for they are latent and covert, and even unconscious, and must be deduced from overt actions and language or other communicating behavior. In this aspect of the culture lies the significance of the stone axe to the Yir Yoront and to their cultural way of life.

The stone axe was an important symbol of masculinity among the Yir Yoront (just as pants or pipes are to us). By a complicated set of ideas the axe was defined as "belonging" to males, and everyone in the society (except untrained infants) accepted these ideas. Similarly spears, spear throwers, and fire-making sticks were owned only by men and were also symbols of masculinity. But the masculine values represented by the stone axe were constantly being impressed on all members of society by the fact that females borrowed axes but not other masculine artifacts. Thus the axe stood for an important theme of Yir Yoront culture: the superiority and rightful dominance of the male, and the greater value of his concerns and of all things associated with him. As the axe also had to be borrowed by the younger people it represented the prestige of age, another important theme running through Yir Yoront behavior.

To understand the Yir Yoront culture it is necessary to be aware of a system of ideas which may be called their totemic ideology. A fundamental belief of the aboriginal divided time into two great epochs: (1) a distant and sacred period at the beginning of the world when the earth was peopled by mildly marvelous ancestral beings or culture heroes who are in a special sense the forebears of the clans; and (2) a period when the old was succeeded by a new order which includes the present. Originally there was no anticipation of another era supplanting the present. The future would simply be an eternal continuation and reproduction of the present which itself had remained unchanged since the epochal revolution of ancestral times.

The important thing to note is that the aboriginal believed that the present world, as a natural and cultural environment, was and should be simply a detailed reproduction of the world of the ancestors. He believed that the entire universe "is now as it was in the beginning" when it was established and left by the ancestors. The ordinary cultural life of the ancestors became the daily life of the Yir Yoront camps, and the extraordinary life of the ancestors remained extant in the recurring symbolic pantomimes and paraphernalia found only in the most sacred atmosphere of the totemic rites.

Such beliefs, accordingly, opened the way for ideas of what *should be* (because it supposedly *was*) to influence or help determine what actually *is*. A man called Dog-chases-iguana-up-a-tree-and-barks-at-him-all-night had that and other names because he because he believed his ancestral alter ego had also had them; he was a member of the Sunlit Cloud Iguana clan because his ancestor was; he was associated with particular countries and totems of this same ancestor; during an initiation he played the role of a dog and symbolically attacked and killed certain members of other clans because his ancestor (conveniently either anthropomorphic or kynomorphic) really did the same to the ancestral alter egos of these men; and he would avoid his mother-in-law, joke with a mother's distant brother, and make spears in a certain way because his and other people's ancestors did these things. His behavior in these specific ways was outlined, and to that extent determined for him, by a set of ideas concerning the past and the relation of the present to the past.

But when we are informed that Dog-chases-etc. had two wives from the Spear Black Duck clan and one from the Native Companion clan, one of them being blind, that he had four children with such and such names, that he had a broken wrist and was left handed, all because his ancestor had exactly these same attributes, then we know (though he apparently didn't) that the present has influenced the past, that the mythical world has been somewhat adjusted to meet the exigencies and accidents of the inescapably real present.

There was thus in Yir Yoront ideology a nice balance in which the mythical was adjusted in part to the real world, the real world in part to the ideal pre-existing mythical world, the adjustments occurring to maintain a fundamental tenet of native faith that the present must be a mirror of the past. Thus the stone axe in all its aspects, uses, and associations was integrated into the context of Yir Yoront technology and conduct because a myth, a set of ideas, had put it there.

IV. The Outcome

The introduction of the steel axe indiscriminately and in large numbers into the Yir Yoront technology occurred simultaneously with many other changes. It is therefore impossible to separate all the results of this single innovation. Nevertheless, a number of specific effects of the change from stone to steel axes may be noted, and the steel axe may be used as an epitome of the increasing quantity of European goods and implements received by the aboriginals and of their general influence on the native culture. The use of the steel axe to illustrate such influences would seem to be justified. It was one of the first European artifacts to be adopted for regular use by the Yir Yoront, and whether made of stone or steel, the axe was clearly one of the most important items of cultural equipment they possessed.

The shift from stone to steel axes provided no major technological difficulties. While the aboriginals themselves could not manufacture steel axe heads, a steady supply from outside continued; broken wooden handles could easily be replaced from bush timbers with aboriginal tools. Among the Yir Yoront the new axe was never used to the extent it was on mission or cattle stations (for carpentry work, pounding tent pegs, as a hammer, and so on); indeed, it had so few more uses than the stone axe that its practical effect on the native standard of living was negligible. It did some jobs better, and could be used longer without breakage. These factors were sufficient to make it of value to the native. The white man believed that a shift from steel to stone axe on his part would be a definite regression. He was convinced that his axe was much more efficient, that its use would save time, and that it therefore represented technical "progress" towards goals which he had set up for the native. But this assumption was hardly borne out in aboriginal practice. Any leisure time the Yir Yoront might gain by using steel axes or other western tools was not invested in "improving the conditions of life," nor, certainly, in developing aesthetic activities, but in sleep—an art they had mastered thoroughly.

Previously, a man in need of an axe would acquire a stone axe head through regular trading partners from whom he knew what to expect, and was then dependent solely upon a known and adequate natural environment, and his own skills or easily acquired techniques. A man wanting a steel axe, however, was in no such self-reliant position. If he attended a mission festival when steel axes were handed out as gifts, he might receive one either by chance or by happening to impress upon the mission staff that he was one of the "better" bush aboriginals (the missionaries' definition of "better" being quite different from that of his bush fellows). Or, again almost by pure chance, he might get some brief job in connection with the mission which would enable him to earn a steel axe. In either case, for older men a preference for the steel axe helped change the situation from one of self-reliance to one of dependence, and a shift in behavior from well-structured or defined situations in technology or conduct to ill-defined situations in conduct alone. Among the men, the older ones whose earlier experience or knowledge of the white man's harshness made them suspicious were particularly careful to avoid having relations with the mission, and thus excluded themselves from acquiring steel axes from that source.

In other aspects of conduct or social relations, the steel axe was even more significantly at the root of psychological stress among the Yir Yoront. This was the result of new factors which the missionary considered beneficial: the simple numerical increase in axes per capita as a result of mission distribution, and distribution directly to younger men, women, and even children. By winning the favor of the mission staff, a woman might be given a steel axe which was clearly intended to be hers, thus creating a situation quite different from the previous custom which necessitated her borrowing an axe from a male relative. As a result a woman would refer to the axe as "mine," a possessive form she was never able to use of the stone axe. In the same fashion, young men or even boys also obtained steel axes directly from the mission, with the result that older men no longer had a complete monopoly of all the axes in the bush community. All this led to a revolutionary confusion of sex, age, and kinship roles, with a major gain in independence and loss of subordination on the part of those who now owned steel axes when they had previously been unable to possess stone axes.

The trading partner relationship was also affected by the new situation. A Yir Yoront might have a trading partner in a tribe to the south whom he defined as a younger brother and over whom he would therefore have some authority. But if the partner were in contact with the mission or had other access to steel axes, his subordination obviously decreased. Among other things, this took some of the excitement away from the dry season fiesta-like tribal gatherings centering around initiations. These had traditionally been the climactic annual occasions for exchanges between trading partners, when a man might seek to acquire a whole year's supply of stone axe heads. Now he might find himself prostituting his wife to almost total strangers in return for steel axes or other white man's goods. With trading partnerships weakened, there was less reason to attend the ceremonies, and less fun for those who did.

Not only did an increase in steel axes and their distribution to women change the character of the relations between individuals (the paired relationships that have been noted), but a previously rare type of relationship was created in the Yir Yoront's conduct towards whites. In the aboriginal society there were few occasions outside of the immediate family when an individual would initiate action to several other people at once. In any average group, in accordance with the kinship system, while a person might be superordinate to several people to whom he could suggest or command action, he was also subordinate to several others with whom such behavior would be tabu. There was thus no overall chieftainship or authoritarian leadership of any kind. Such complicated operations as grass-burning animal drives or totemic ceremonies could be carried out smoothly because each person was aware of his role.

On both mission and cattle stations, however, the whites imposed their conception of leadership roles upon the aboriginals, consisting of one person in a controlling relationship with a subordinate group. Aboriginals called together to receive gifts, including axes, at a mission Christmas party found themselves facing one or two whites who sought to control their behavior for the occasion, who disregarded the age, sex, and kinship variables of which the aboriginals were so conscious, and who considered them all at one subordinate level. The white also sought to impose similar patterns on work parties. (However, if he placed an aboriginal in charge of a mixed group of post-hole diggers, for example, half of the group, those subordinate to the "boss," would work while the other half, who were superordinate to him, would sleep.) For the aboriginal, the steel axe and other European goods came to symbolize this new and uncomfortable form of social organization, the leader-group relationship.

The most disturbing effects of the steel axe, operating in conjunction with other elements also being introduced from the white man's several sub-cultures, developed in the realm of traditional ideas, sentiments, and values. These were undermined at a rapidly mounting rate, with no new conceptions being defined to replace them.

The result was the erection of a mental and moral void which foreshadowed the collapse and destruction of all Yir Yoront culture, if not, indeed, the extinction of the biological group itself.

From what has been said it should be clear how changes in overt behavior, in technology and conduct, weakened the values inherent in a reliance on nature, in the prestige of masculinity and of age, and in the various kinship relations. A scene was set in which a wife, or a young son whose initiation may not yet have been completed, need no longer defer to the husband or father who, in turn, became confused and insecure as he was forced to borrow a steel axe from them. For the woman and boy the steel axe helped establish a new degree of freedom which they accepted readily as an escape from the unconscious stress of the old patterns—but they, too, were left confused and insecure. Ownership became less well defined with the result that stealing and trespassing were introduced into technology and conduct. Some of the excitement surrounding the great ceremonies evaporated and they lost their previous gaiety and interest. Indeed, life itself became less interesting, although this did not lead the Yir Yoront to discover suicide, a concept foreign to them.

The whole process may be most specifically illustrated in terms of totemic system, which also illustrates the significant role played by a system of ideas, in this case a totemic ideology, in the breakdown of a culture.

In the first place, under pre-European aboriginal conditions where the native culture has become adjusted to a relatively stable environment, few, if any, unheard of or catastrophic crises can occur. It is clear, therefore, that the totemic system serves very effectively in inhibiting radical cultural changes. The closed system of totemic ideas, explaining and categorizing a well-known universe as it was fixed at the beginning of time, presents a considerable obstacle to the adoption of new or the dropping of old culture traits. The obstacle is not insurmountable and the system allows for the minor variations which occur in the norms of daily life. But the inception of major changes cannot easily take place.

Among the bush Yir Yoront the only means of water transport is a light wood log to which they cling in their constant swimming of rivers, salt creeks, and tidal inlets. These natives know that tribes 45 miles further north have a bark canoe. They know these northern tribes can thus fish from midstream or out at sea, instead of clinging to the river banks and beaches, that they can cross coastal waters infested with crocodiles, sharks, sting rays, and Portuguese men-of-war without danger. They know the materials of which the canoe is made exist in their own environment. But they also know, as they say, that they do not have canoes because their own mythical ancestors did not have them. They assume that the canoe was part of the ancestral universe of the northern tribes. For them, then, the adoption of the canoe would not be simply a matter of learning a number of new behavioral skills for its manufacture and use. The adoption would require a much more difficult procedure; the acceptance by the entire society of a myth, either locally developed or borrowed, to explain the presence of the canoe, to associate it with some one or more of the several hundred mythical ancestors (and how decide which?), and thus establish it as an accepted totem of one of the clans ready to be used by the whole community. The Yir Yoront have not made this adjustment, and in this case we can only say that for the time being at least, ideas have won out over very real pressures for technological change. In the elaborateness and explicitness of the totemic ideologies we seem to have one explanation for the notorious stability of Australian cultures under aboriginal conditions, an explanation which gives due weight to the importance of ideas in determining human behavior.

At a later stage of the contact situation, as has been indicated, phenomena unaccounted for by the totemic ideological system begin to appear with regularity and frequency and remain within the range of native experience. Accordingly, they cannot be ignored (as the "Battle of the Mitchell" was apparently ignored), and there is an attempt to assimilate them and account for them along the lines of principles inherent in the ideology. The bush Yir Yoront of the mid-thirties represent this stage of the acculturation process. Still trying to maintain their aboriginal definition of the situation, they accept European artifacts and behavior patterns, but fit them into their totemic system, assigning them to various clans on a par with original totems. There is an attempt to have the myth-making process keep up with these cultural changes so that the idea system can continue to support the rest of the culture. But analysis of overt behavior, of dreams, and of some of the new myths indicates that this arrangement is not entirely satisfactory, that the native clings to his totemic system with intellectual loyalty (lacking any substitute ideology), but that associated sentiments and values are weakened. His attitude towards his own and towards European culture are found to be highly ambivalent.

All ghosts are totems of the Head-to-the-East Corpse clan, are thought of as white, and are of course closely associated with death. The white man, too, is closely associated with death, and he and all things pertaining to him are naturally assigned to the Corpse clan as totems. The steel axe, as a totem, was thus associated with the Corpse clan. But as an "axe," clearly linked with the stone axe, it is a totem of the Sunlit Cloud Iguana clan. Moreover, the steel axe, like most European goods, has no distinctive origin myth, nor are mythical ancestors associated with it. Can anyone, sitting in the shade of a *ti* tree one afternoon, create a myth to resolve this confusion? No one has, and the horrid suspicion arises as to the authenticity of the origin myths, which failed to take into account this vast new universe of the white man. The steel axe, shifting hopelessly between one clan and the other, is not only replacing the stone axe physically, but is hacking at the supports of the entire cultural system.

The aboriginals to the south of the Yir Yoront have clearly passed beyond this stage. They are engulfed by European culture, either by the mission or cattle station sub-cultures or, for some natives, by a baffling, paradoxical combination of both incongruent varieties. The totemic ideology can no longer support the inrushing mass of foreign culture traits, and the myth-making process in its native form breaks down completely. Both intellectually and emotionally a saturation point is reached so that the myriad new traits which can neither be ignored nor any longer assimilated simply force the aboriginal to abandon his totemic system. With the collapse of this system of ideas, which is so closely related to so many other aspects of the native culture, there follows an appallingly sudden and complete cultural disintegration, and a demoralization of the individual such as has seldom been recorded elsewhere. Without the support of a system of ideas well devised to provide cultural stability in a stable environment, but admittedly too rigid for the new realities pressing in from outside, native behavior and native sentiments and values are simply dead. Apathy reigns. The aboriginal has passed beyond the realm of any outsider who might wish to do him well or ill.

Returning from the broken natives huddled on cattle stations or on the fringes of frontier towns to the ambivalent but still lively aboriginals settled on the Mitchell River mission, we note one further devious result of the introduction of European artifacts. During a wet season stay at the mission, the anthropologist discovered that his supply of tooth paste was being depleted at an alarming rate. Investigation showed that it was being taken by old men for use in a new tooth paste cult. Old materials of magic directed towards the mission staff and some of the younger aboriginal men. Old males, largely ignored by the missionaries, were seeking to regain some of their lost power and prestige. This mild aggression proved hardly effective, but perhaps only because caonfidence in any kind of magic on the mission was by this time at a low ebb.

For the Yir Yoront still in the bush, a time could be predicted when personal deprivation and frustration in a confused culture would produce an overload of anxiety. The mythical past of the totemic ancestors would disappear as a guarantee of a present of which the future was supposed to be a stable continuation. Without the past, the present could be meaningless and the future unstructured and uncertain. Insecurities would be inevitable. Reaction to this stress might be some form of symbolic aggression, or withdrawal and apathy, or some more realistic approach. In such a situation the missionary with understanding of the processes going on about him would find his opportunity to introduce his forms of religion and to help create a new cultural universe.

Notes

1. An account of this expedition from Amboina is given in R. Logan Jack, *Northmost Australia* (2 vols.), London, 1921, Vol. 1, pp. 18–57.
2. R. Logan Jack, *op. cit.,* pp. 298–335.
3. The best, although highly concentrated, summaries of totemism among the Yir Yoront and the other tribes of north Queensland will be found in R. Lauriston Sharp, "Tribes and Totemism in Northeast Australia," *Oceania,* Vol. 8, 1939, pp. 254–275 and 439–461 (especially pp. 268–275); also "Notes on Northeast Australian Totemism," in *Papers of the Peabody Museum of American Archaeology and Ethnology,* Vol. 20, *Studies in the Anthropology of Oceania and Asia,* Cambridge, 1943, pp. 66–71.

Growing Up as a Fore Is to Be 'In Touch' and Free

E. Richard Sorenson

It took a long time for Europeans to happen upon the interior of highland New Guinea. The Portuguese reached the islands in the early 1600s and named them *Ilhas dos Papuas*, or "Land of the Fuzzy-Haired People." In the mid-1800s, European missionaries began to settle in the coastal areas, but it was not until the 1930s that the outsiders explored the highland region (using air craft) and found that there were over one million people living there. Neither the New Guineans nor the Europeans knew about each other's existence. From the standpoint of the traditional cultures that existed there for millennia, it was all downhill after that.

As anthropologist E. Richard Sorenson tells us in this very personal account, one group of New Guinea highlanders, the Fore, were just beginning to change as result of outside intrusion into their economy and way of life. We are fortunate to have this ethnographic description, in both Sorenson's words and on film because no such record would have been possible much earlier than when Sorenson got there in the early 1960s nor much later, since their way of life was already beginning to change.

As Sorenson describes it, there was an "Achilles heel" in the traditional Fore culture, which apparently hastened their demise. This "weakness" consisted of an openness and willingness to try anything new. While such traits might be considered admirable and functional in the context of their traditional way of life, they made for vulnerability in the face of the emerging market culture.

E. Richard Sorenson (b. 1929) was the director of the Smithsonian Institute's National Film Center. His book, *The Edge of the Forest* (1976) recounts his experiences with the Fore. Sorenson is now retired and lives on an island, Phuket, in southern Thailand, which he uses as his base for anthropological studies. Although Phuket was one of the hardest places hit by the tsunami of December 26, 2004, and Sorenson was temporarily listed as missing, his home was on high ground and he escaped injury. Distraught by the loss of so many friends, he was soon flying off to interview some tribal people in Laos.

Key Concept: adaptation to social change

*U*ntouched by the outside world, they had lived for thousands of years in isolated mountains and valleys deep in the interior of Papua New Guinea. They had no cloth, no metal, no money, no idea that their homeland was an island or that what surrounded it was salt water. Yet the Fore (for'ay) people had developed remarkable and sophisticated approaches to human relations, and their child-rearing practices gave their young unusual freedom to explore. Successful as hunter-gatherers and as subsistence gardeners, they also had great adaptability, which brought rapid accommodation with the outside world after their lands were opened up.

It was alone that I first visited the Fore in 1963—a day's walk from a recently built airstrip. I stayed six months. Perplexed and fascinated, I returned six times in the next ten years, eventually spending a year and a half living with them in their hamlets.

Theirs was a way of life different from anything I had seen or heard about before. There were no chiefs, patriarchs, priests, medicine men or the like. A striking personal freedom was enjoyed even by the very young, who could move about at will and be where or with whom they liked. Infants rarely cried, and they played confidently with knives, axes, and fire. Conflict between old and young did not arise; there was "no generation gap."

Older children enjoyed deferring to the interests and desires of the younger, and sibling rivalry was virtually undetectable. A responsive sixth sense seemed to attune the Fore hamlet mates to each other's interests and needs. They did not have to directly ask, inveigle, bargain or speak out for what they needed or wanted. Subtle, even fleeting expressions of interest, desire, and discomfort were quickly read and helpfully acted on by one's associates. This spontaneous urge to share food, affection, work, trust, tools, and pleasure was the social cement that held the Fore hamlets together. It was a pleasant way of life, for one could always be with those with whom one got along well.

Ranging and planting, sharing and living, the Fore diverged and expanded through high virgin lands in a pioneer region. They hunted out their gardens, tilled them while they lasted, then hunted again. Moving ever away from lands peopled and used they had a self-contained life with its own special ways.

The underlying ecological conditions were like those that must have encompassed the world before agriculture set its imprint so broadly. Abutting the Fore was virtually unlimited virgin land, and they had food plants they could introduce into it. Like hunter-gatherers they sought their sources of sustenance first in one locale and then another, across an extended range, following opportunities provided by a providential nature. But like agriculturalists they concentrated their effort and attention more narrowly on selected sites of production, on their gardens. They were both seekers and producers. A pioneer people in a pioneer land, they ranged freely into a vast territory, but they planted to live.

Cooperative groups formed hamlets and gardened together. When the fertility of a garden declined, they abandoned it. Grass sprung up to cover these abandoned sites of earlier cultivation, and, as the Fore moved on to other parts of the forest, they left uninhabited grasslands to mark their passage.

The traditional hamlets were small, with a rather fluid system of social relations. A single large men's house provided shelter for 10 to 20 men and boys and their visiting friends. The several smaller women's houses each normally sheltered two married women, their unmarried daughters and their sons up to about six years of age. Formal kinship bonds were less important than friendship was. Fraternal "gangs" of youths formed the hamlets; their "clubhouses" were the men's houses.

During the day the gardens became the center of life. Hamlets were virtually deserted as friends, relatives and children went to one or more garden plots to mingle their social, economic and erotic pursuits in a pleasant and emotionally filled Gestalt of garden life. The boys and unmarried youths preferred to explore and hunt in the outlying lands, but they also passed through and tarried in the gardens.

Daily activities were not scheduled. No one made demands, and the land was bountiful. Not surprisingly the line between work and play was never clear. The transmission of the Fore behavioral pattern to the young began in early infancy during a period of unceasing human physical contact. The effect of being constantly "in touch" with hamlet mates and their daily life seemed to start a process which proceeded by degrees: close rapport, involvement in regular activity, ability to handle seemingly dangerous implements safely, and responsible freedom to pursue individual interests at will without danger.

While very young, infants remained in almost continuous bodily contact with their mother, her house mates or her gardening associates. At first, mothers' laps were the center of activity, and infants occupied themselves there by nursing, sleeping, and playing with their own bodies or those of their caretakers. They were not put aside for the sake of other activities, as when food was being prepared or heavy loads were being carried. Remaining in close, uninterrupted physical contact with those around them, their basic needs such as rest, nourishment, stimulation, and security were continuously satisfied without obstacle.

By being physically in touch from their earliest days, Fore youngsters learned to communicate needs, desires and feelings through a body language of touch and response that developed before speech. This opened the door to a much closer rapport with those around them than otherwise would have been possible, and led ultimately to the Fore brand of social cement and the sixth sense that bound groups together through spontaneous, responsive sharing.

As the infant's awareness increased, his interests broadened to the things his mother and other caretakers did and to the objects and materials they used. Then these youngsters began crawling out to explore things that attracted their attention. By the time they were toddling, their interests continually took them on short sorties to nearby objects and persons. As soon as they could walk well, the excursions extended to the entire hamlet and its gardens, and then beyond with other children. Developing without interference or supervision, this personal exploratory learning quest freely touched on whatever was around, even axes, knives, machetes, fire, and the like. When I first went to the Fore, I was aghast.

Eventually I discovered that this capability emerged naturally from Fore infant-handling practices in their milieu of close human physical proximity and tactile interaction. Because touch and bodily contact lend themselves naturally to satisfying the basic needs of young children, an early kind of communicative experience fostered cooperative interaction between infants and their caretakers, also kinesthetic contact with the activities at hand. This made it easy for them to learn the appropriate handling of the tools of life.

The early pattern of exploratory activity included frequent return to one of the "mothers." Serving as home base, the bastion of security, a woman might occasionally give the youngster a nod of encouragement, if he glanced in her direction with uncertainty. Yet rarely did the women attempt to control or direct, nor did they participate in the child's quests or jaunts.

As a result Fore children did not have to adjust to rule and schedule in order to find their place in life. They could pursue their interests and whims wherever they might lead and still be part of a richly responsive world of human touch which constantly provided sustenance, comfort, diversion, and security.

Learning proceeded during the course of pursuing interests and exploring. Constantly in touch with people who were busy with daily activities, the Fore young quickly learned the skills of life from example. Muscle tone, movement, and mood were components of this learning process; formal lessons and commands were not. Kinesthetic skills developed so quickly that infants were able to casually handle knives and similar objects before they could walk.

Even after several visits I continued to be surprised that the unsupervised Fore toddlers did not recklessly thrust themselves into unappreciated dangers, the way our own children tend to do. But then, why should they? From their earliest days, they enjoyed a benevolent sanctuary from which the world could be confidently viewed, tested and appreciated. This sanctuary remained ever available, but did not demand, restrain or impose. One could go and come at will.

In close harmony with their source of life, the Fore young were able confidently, not furtively, to extend their inquiry. They could widen their understanding as they chose. There was no need to play tricks or deceive in order to pursue life.

Emerging from this early childhood was a freely ranging young child rather in tune with his older and younger hamlet mates, disinclined to act out impulsively, and with a capable appreciation of the properties of potentially dangerous objects. Such children could be permitted to move out on their own, unsupervised and unrestricted. They were safe.

Such a pattern could persist indefinitely, re-creating itself in each new generation. However, hidden within the receptive character it produced was an Achilles heel; it also permitted adoption of new practices, including child-handling practices, which did not act to perpetuate the pattern. In only one generation after Western contact, the cycle of Fore life was broken.

Attuned as they were to individual pursuit of economic and social good, it did not take the Fore long to recognize the value of the new materials, practices and ideas that began to flow in. Indeed, change began almost immediately with efforts to obtain steel axes, salt, medicine, and cloth. The Fore were quick to shed indigenous practices in favor of Western example. They rapidly altered their ways to adapt to Western law, government, religion, materials and trade.

Sometimes change was so rapid that many people seemed to be afflicted by a kind of cultural shock. An anomie, even cultural amnesia, seemed to pervade some hamlets for a time. There were individuals who appeared temporarily to have lost memory of recent past events. Some Fore even forgot what type and style of traditional garments they had worn only a few years earlier, or that they had used stone axes and had eaten their dead close relatives.

Remarkably open-minded, the Fore so readily accepted reformulation of identity and practice that suggestion or example by the new government officers, missionaries and scientists could alter tribal affiliation, place names, conduct and hamlet style. When the first Australian patrol officer began to map the region in 1957, an error in communication led him to refer to these people as the "Fore." Actually they had had no name for themselves and the word, Fore, was their name for a quite different group, the Awa, who spoke another language and lived in another valley. They did not correct the patrol officer but adopted his usage. They all now refer to themselves as the Fore. Regional and even personal names changed just as readily.

More than anything else, it was the completion of a steep, rough, always muddy Jeep road into the Fore lands that undermined the traditional life. Almost overnight their isolated region was opened. Hamlets began to move down from their ridgetop sites in order to be nearer the road, consolidating with others.

The power of the road is hard to overestimate. It was a great artery where only restricted capillaries had existed before. And down this artery came a flood of new goods, new ideas and new people. This new road, often impassable even with four-wheel-drive vehicles, was perhaps the single most dramatic stroke wrought by the government. It was to the Fore an opening to a new world. As they began to use the road, they started to shed traditions evolved in the protective insularity of their mountain fastness, to adopt in their stead an emerging market culture.

The Coming of the Coffee Economy

"Walkabout," nonexistent as an institution before contact, quickly became an accepted way of life. Fore boys began to roam hundreds of miles from their homeland in the quest for new experience, trade goods, jobs, and money. Like the classic practice of the Australian aborigine, this "walkabout" took one away from his home for periods of varying length. But unlike the Australian practice, it usually took the boys to jobs and schools rather than a solitary life in traditional lands. Obviously it sprang from the earlier pattern of individual freedom to pursue personal interests and opportunity wherever it might lead. It was a new expression of the old Fore exploratory pattern.

Some boys did not roam far, whereas others found ways to go to distant cities. The roaming boys often sought places where they might be welcomed as visitors, workers or students for a while. Mission stations and schools, plantation work camps, and the servants' quarters of the European population became way-stations in the lives of the modernizing Fore boys.

Some took jobs on coffee plantations. Impressed by the care and attention lavished on coffee by European planters and by the money they saw paid to coffee growers, these young Fore workers returned home with coffee beans to plant.

Coffee grew well on the Fore hillsides, and in the mid-1960s, when the first sizable crop matured, Fore who previously had felt lucky to earn a few dollars found themselves able to earn a few hundred dollars. A rush to coffee ensued, and when the new gardens became productive a few years later, the Fore income from coffee jumped to a quarter of a million dollars a year. The coffee revolution was established.

At first the coffee was carried on the backs of its growers (sometimes for several days) over steep, rough mountain trails to a place where it could be sold to a buyer with a jeep. However, as more and more coffee was produced, the villagers began to turn with efforts to planning and constructing roads in association with neighboring villages. The newly built roads, in turn, stimulated further economic development and the opening of new trade stores throughout the region.

Following European example, the segregated collective men's and women's houses were abandoned. Family houses were adopted. This changed the social and territorial arena for all the young children, who hitherto had been accustomed to living equally with many members of their hamlet. It gave them a narrower place to belong, and it made them more distinctly someone's children. Uncomfortable in the family houses, boys who had grown up in a freer territory began to gather in "boys' houses," away from the adult men who were now beginning to live in family houses with their wives. Mothers began to wear blouses, altering the early freer access to the breast. Episodes of infant and child frustration, not seen in traditional Fore hamlets, began to take place along with repeated incidents of anger, withdrawal, aggressiveness and stinginess.

So Western technology worked its magic on the Fore, its powerful materials and practices quickly shattering their isolated autonomy and life-style. It took only a few years from the time Western intruders built their first grass-thatched patrol station before the Fore way of life they found was gone.

Fortunately, enough of the Fore traditional ways were systematically documented on film to reveal how unique a flower of human creation they were. Like nothing else, film made it possible to see the behavioral patterns of this way of life. The visual record, once made, captured data which was unnoticed and unanticipated at the time of filming and which was simply impossible to study without such records. Difficult-to-spot subtle patterns and fleeting nuances of manner, mood and human relations emerged by use of repeated reexamination of related incidents, sometimes by slow motion and stopped frame. Eventually the characteristic behavioral patterns of Fore life became clear, and an important aspect of human adaptive creation was revealed.

The Fore way of life was only one of the many natural experiments in living that have come into being through thousands of years of independent development in the world. The Fore way is now gone; those which remain are threatened. Under the impact of modern technology and commerce, the entire world is now rapidly becoming one system. By the year 2000 all the independent natural experiments that have come into being during the world's history will be merging into a single world system.

One of the great tragedies of our modern time may be that most of these independent experiments in living are disappearing before we can discover the implication of their special expressions of human possibility. Ironically, the same technology responsible for the worldwide cultural convergence has also provided the means by which we may capture detailed visual records of the yet remaining independent cultures. The question is whether we will be able to seize this never-to-be repeated opportunity. Soon it will be too late. Yet, obviously, increasing our understanding of the behavioral repertoire of humankind would strengthen our ability to improve life in the world.

Medical Anthropology

Selection 31
ANN McELROY AND PATRICIA K. TOWNSEND, from "The Ecology of Health and Disease," *Medical Anthropology in Ecological Perspective*

Selection 32
THOMAS ADEOYE LAMBO, from "Psychotherapy in Africa," *Human Nature*

Selection 33
EDWARD T. HALL, from "Proxemics: The Study of Man's Spatial Relations," *Culture, Curers, and Contagion: Readings for Medical Social Science*

The Ecology of Health and Disease

Ann McElroy and Patricia K. Townsend

Medical Anthropology is a sub-discipline of the general field of anthropology. Its emphasis is upon the health aspects of human biological and cultural adaptations to environmental circumstances. As the authors point out, this focus upon both the biological and the social is what makes medical anthropology a truly integrative and holistic field.

As you read the following essay, excerpted from *Medical Anthropology in Ecological Perspective* by Ann McElroy and Patricia K. Townsend, just consider the great range of knowledge brought to bear upon the questions of Eskimo adaptations and health and you will understand how the "holistic" claim can be made. An understanding of Inuit adaptive patterns requires knowledge from such fields as geography, climatology, biology, botany, physiology, nutrition, epidemiology, cultural ecology, cultural anthropology, demography, and architecture—just to name the more obvious ones!

Ann McElroy received her Ph.D. in 1973 at the University of North Carolina at Chapel Hill and is an associate professor of anthropology at State University of New York at Buffalo. She is also the director of a two-year training program for students preparing for careers in research, medicine or public health.

Patricia K. Townsend is a research associate professor at State University of New York at Buffalo and serves on the advisory board of the *Journal of Ecological Anthropology*.

Key Concept: medical anthropology

Anthropological Subdisciplines and Medical Anthropology

Anthropology has four subdisciplines: physical anthropology, archaeology, cultural anthropology, and linguistics. Ideally, each anthropologist receives training in all four areas. To be truly holistic in studying human behavior, one needs to know something about human biology, prehistory, cultural systems, and language, and needs to be able to integrate this knowledge. But as the subdisciplines drifted apart into increasing specialization, most anthropologists received research training in only one or two subfields. Medical anthropology, with its emphasis on viewing humans as both biological and cultural creatures, is one of the few topical fields that bridges the subdisciplines. An unexpected dividend of recent work in medical anthropology has been the possibility of reintegrating the subdisciplines. . . .

As medical anthropology grew into a distinct discipline, it developed its own methodological and topical specialties. Although some medical anthropologists work comfortably in several subfields, combining and integrating diverse approaches, the field has become so complex and large that many researchers confine their activities to one specialty. Biomedical study of adaptation to disease is one specialty. The term "biomedical" refers to the dominant medical system in Europe and North America, with research fields such as genetics, epidemiology, nutrition, and public health. Biomedical and ecological models can be used in studies of any population by imposing western diagnostic categories and environmental models on the cultures being studied.

Ethnomedical studies of health and healing are a second major emphasis in medical anthropology. Researchers studying ethnomedicine often attempt to discover the insiders' viewpoints in describing and analyzing health and systems of healing. Among the topics studied in this subfield are ethnoscience, shamanism, ethnopharmacology, altered states of consciousness, alternative therapies, midwifery, and medical pluralism.

Third, many anthropologists focus their work on social problems and carry out interventions through applied medical anthropology. Among the areas of this subfield are studies of addictions, disabilities, and mental health issues; public health and family planning; clinical anthropology and health care delivery in pluralistic settings.

Examples of applied research and ethnomedicine will be found throughout this text within the framework of the biomedical and ecological perspective introduced in this chapter.

A Focus on Adaptation

Whatever their subdisciplinary orientation, whether biomedical, ethnomedical, or applied, many medical anthropologists agree that the concept of adaptation is a core theoretical construct. We define adaptation as changes, modifications, and variation enabling a person or group to survive in a given environment. Like any other animal, humans adapt through a variety of biological mechanisms and behavioral strategies, but they depend on cultural adaptation more than other species. They use cultural mechanisms in banding together and coordinating their efforts to get food, in protecting themselves from the weather, and in training their young. However harsh or dangerous the environment, humans usually have the flexibility to survive, although it is only in groups that they go beyond sheer survival to achieve well-being. So pervasive is the human dependence on learning rather than on innate or instinctive strategies that it makes sense to consider culture as an adaptive mechanism specific to human evolution.

As humans hunt animals and cultivate crops, find protection against extreme heat or cold through clothing and dwellings, teach young about the environment, form alliances, and exchange goods with neighbors, they create survival-promoting relationships within an environmental system. These are relationships within the group, with neighboring groups, and with the plants and animals of the habitat. A central premise of medical anthropology is that the group's level of health reflects the nature and quality of these relationships. . . .

The following section demonstrates the ecology of health model by describing traditional arctic peoples known as Eskimos or, the preferred term, *Inuit* ("human beings" or "people"). The profile describes adaptations that hunting peoples of the North maintained for centuries. Today, in the twenty-first-century, few Inuit live in the manner we describe here, but some remember a childhood when people lived totally "on the land," as they say. Because hunting and foraging peoples evolved successful methods for surviving, anthropologists study these strategies, attempting through archaeology, ethnohistory, and ethnography to reconstruct a way of life that existed only a few hundred years ago.

Profile: Arctic Adaptations

Inuit tell a story of a woman who raised a polar bear cub as her son, naming him *Kunikdjuaq*. She nursed him, gave him a soft warm bed next to hers, and talked to the cub as if to a child. When the bear grew up, he brought seals and salmon home to his adoptive mother.

Because of his skill in hunting, the people in the camp became envious and decided to kill him. The old woman offered her own life in place of the bear's, but the people refused. In tears she told him to go away and save his life. The bear gently placed his huge paw on her head and hugged her, saying "Good mother, *Kunikdjuaq* will always be on the lookout for you and serve you as best he can" (Boas 1964:230–231).

Of all animals, the polar bear is the most admired by Inuit. They point out how the bear's hunting techniques resemble their own: slowly stalking seals who lie sunning themselves on ice floes or waiting quietly at the seals' breathing-holes in the ice. Because they admire and envy the bear and compete with it for food, Inuit feel a sense of ambivalent kinship with the bear, and sometimes they even name a child *nanuq*, or "bear."

The symbolic closeness of the two species, bear and human, reflects their ecological relationship. They face similar problems: to get enough to eat in an ecosystem that supports few species of animals and almost no edible plants, and to conserve body heat in a harsh climate. Both bears and humans are large animals with high caloric needs. Because food resources are dispersed and only seasonally available, both bears and humans must also remain dispersed in small mobile units. Neither was seriously subjected to predation until humans acquired rifles about seventy years ago. Avoiding predators was far less a problem than finding food, keeping warm, and keeping population size within the limits of available food.

Bears have evolved solutions to these problems such as thick fur, semi-hibernation in winter, and small social units; male bears are usually solitary while cubs stay with the mother the first eighteen months of their lives. Human solutions to the same problems are quite different. Humans lack fur but know—not instinctively but rather through observation and training—how to turn animal fur into clothing for protection against cold. They do not remain in dens in the winter but continue a vigorous life of travel in bands of twenty or thirty people, all ages and both males and females. Unable to swim in icy arctic waters, as bears do, Inuit build boats. Rather than eating only a few species of large marine mammals, as bears do, humans use most species from both land and sea habitats in some manner, if not for food, then for clothing, fuel, or tools.

Humans and bears live in the same habitat, but their adaptations differ because of the cultural component in human behavior. This health profile will describe traditional human adaptive patterns in the central and eastern Arctic and discuss how these patterns affected health. The description is mostly in the present tense to show a way of life that persisted for thousands of years and only gradually changed after the arrival of explorers, traders, and whalers. The information comes partly from publications by anthropologists and medical scientists and partly from ethnohistorical research by Ann McElroy in eastern Canada.

Accessing Energy: Selectivity in Exploitation

The Arctic is depicted in movies and novels as a barren, frozen land where famine constantly threatens and people must eat everything available just to stay alive. It is true that arctic regions are limited by high winds and severe wind chill, low precipitation, and poor, thin soil, but boreal habitats provide more resources than is generally known. The tundra is a simple ecosystem compared to tropical rain forests, but twenty-nine species of game are available to Inuit for food. They exploit heavily only four categories: fish, seals, whales, and caribou. Some animals are not eaten at all except during severe shortages. Before contact with traders, Inuit manufactured all artifacts from natural resources, mostly from animal products because wood and usable stone were scarce. Bone, ivory, sinew, antler, skin, fur, feathers, blubber—every part of the animal was used for something, from sewing needles to harpoons, water buckets to boats, snow shovels, lamp fuel, and boots.

The growing season is short, usually no more than ten weeks, but the long hours of daylight allow plants to complete their life cycles before they become dormant for another winter. Some plants are collected for immediate consumption, like the berries so abundant in August. Others are dried as medicinal herbs and teas. Everyone is taught from childhood to recognize and harvest edible and useful plants, but it is traditional midwives who most regularly depend on plants. Arctic cotton grass, for example, is mixed with charcoal and placed on babies' navels to hasten the drying and healing of the umbilical stump. If a woman continues to bleed after giving birth, the midwife puts shredded grass into the vagina and gives the new mother tea made from sorrel or from Labrador tea leaves (Traditional Medicine Project 1983).

Inuit traditionally exploit both coastal and inland food resources, often following the seasonal patterns of the migratory species. They pursue game animals that provide maximal yield for minimal energy output or relatively low risk. They prefer species such as seals and whales that provide a good return of meat and by-products such as skin, bones, and oil. Arctic char, similar to salmon, is an important seasonal resource. The return is high for the energy the men, women, and children invest in netting and spearing as the fish swim upstream to spawn. The surplus can be cut into strips and dried in the sun, providing an important protein source in late autumn. Migratory caribou herds also return a good yield, each animal contributing several hundred pounds of meat as well as skins for clothing and tents.

Not all animals in the ecosystem are used for food. Musk ox herds, in past centuries reliable sources of food and by-products, no longer figure in arctic ecosystems. The few remaining herds are protected by law from being hunted. Polar bear hunting is also regulated by government quotas, but bears were never an important source of food, for several reasons. Hunting them was risky because a wounded bear might maul humans and dogs. Also, cooking polar bear meat, which is necessary to prevent trichinosis, is wasteful of fuel (most foods could safely be eaten raw). Finally, bear liver, so rich in vitamin A, can be toxic.

Some species such as the tiny and unpalatable lemmings are rarely eaten by humans, although the lemming skin makes an effective bandage for treatment of wounds and boils (Traditional Medicine Project 1983). Lemmings have "high handling costs" (that is, they take too much time to catch and prepare relative to their yield in nutrients) and others like sea gulls simply don't taste good (Smith 1991:209–210).

Only rarely were Inuit so short of food that they resorted to cannibalism. During shortages the small hunting band, usually fifteen to fifty people, would disperse into smaller units of one or two families. They would eat their dogs long before they would consider killing a person for food, an abhorrent idea to Inuit. Thus dogs provide not only transportation but also a reserve food supply. However, dogs, foxes, and wolves carry a tapeworm that can be transmitted to humans and cause severe effects if lodged in the brain, bone marrow, or kidneys (Oswalt 1967:79). We have no evidence that Inuit were aware of the risk of tapeworm, but they ate these animals only in times of great need.

Human relationships with dogs are as ambivalent as they are with polar bears. This is reflected in tales of dogs who married women. Their offspring became the ancestors of Indians, the traditional enemy of Inuit. Inuit have no love for their dogs, which can viciously maim a child, but they do depend on them for travel, and they must feed them. Much energy goes into providing food for dogs. A Banks Island trapper brought in an average of 6,226 pounds of meat annually; 4,627 pounds fed his nine dogs, while only 1,599 pounds were consumed by his family (Usher 1971:85).

Food-sharing partnerships among hunters are an important feature of Inuit cultural ecology (Balikci 1970). These alliances not only create political stability but also ensure cooperation rather than competition in exploitation of the environment. Food is rarely hoarded. When there is surplus, people feast, and the little that is left over may be stored under rocks. Travelers without food can help themselves to these caches.

Consuming Energy: Dietary Patterns

Life in the Arctic requires high energy levels. Traveling by dogsled means much running, pushing, and pulling; rarely is there a chance to ride. When the family is traveling, each evening a new snowhouse or tent must be erected, and in summer, water is hauled from inland pools and willow and heather are gathered for bedding and insulation. Men construct fish weirs by carrying hundreds of boulders, and women scrape animal skins for hours to soften them for sewing. Babies are nursed and carried on their mothers' backs up to three years. Breast milk production requires extra calories, and it takes energy to carry a growing child five to ten hours a day. To keep warm, Inuit enjoy strenuous wrestling, acrobatics, and races.

Some subsistence activities have higher energy costs than others. For example, people fishing in summer (jumping from rock to rock and spearing fish) have almost twice the oxygen costs as men sealing in winter on the floe edge. The average energy expenditure for Inuit hunters is about twice that of more sedentary arctic groups (Shephard and Rode 1996:22). However, arctic hunters do not maintain such high levels of activity every day. About 160 days a year are spent hunting, fishing, trapping, and traveling; the rest of the time is spent relaxing, repairing equipment, visiting, trading, and feasting.

Inuit look stocky because of their bulky clothing and relatively short limbs, but they are actually lean and muscular and have little body fat to burn during food shortages. The body fat measured in one eastern Arctic community averaged only 13 percent (Shephard and Rode 1996:29). Adult men expend about 2,700 calories per day (and at peak activity periods, 3,600 calories) and require between 2,800 and 3,100 calories to maintain a weight of about 140 pounds (63 kg) at an average height of 5 feet 3 inches (160 cm) (Rodahl 1963:103). Women's caloric needs are somewhat less because they do not hunt but stay in camp preparing skins and tending children. But when they are nursing a child, digging clams, chasing ptarmigan, or traveling, they need almost as many calories as the men do.

Inuit consume an average of 200 grams of protein per day, about 32 percent of their total caloric intake (Draper 1977:311). Some Greenlandic Inuit consume protein as 44 percent of their diet. In contrast, only 15 percent of Americans' caloric intake is protein, with an average of 77 grams a day (Nutrition Today 1995). In most low-income countries, protein constitutes only about 2 percent of the diet. Inuit carbohydrate consumption is very low, 10 grams daily and between two and eight percent of total intake, compared to U.S. levels (50 percent) and to less developed countries (60 to 75 percent). Because of the cold and the long months of little daylight, it is not possible to raise food plants or to gather sufficient quantities of wild plants. Small portions of berries, sourgrass and sorrel, and sea kelp gathered in summer add variety but not enough vitamins to meet nutritional needs. Nearly all available food comes from seal, caribou, whale, walrus, fish, and birds—all high in protein and fat. Fat consumption averages 66 percent of the diet and 185 grams daily, while the average North American's consumption of fat in the 1990s represented about 34 percent of caloric intake.

With this diet of high protein, high fat, and low carbohydrates, we might expect health problems. And yet Inuit are well nourished, without deficiency diseases such as scurvy and rickets or heart disease from cholesterol build-up. How do they manage to thrive on this diet?

In large quantities, meat can provide adequate amounts of all vitamins except ascorbic acid (vitamin C). Seal oil and fish are especially rich in vitamins A and D, and the B vitamins are adequate in the traditional foods. Inuit prepare and eat meat in ways that maximize its nutritional value. For example, by eating meat raw, they preserve small quantities of vitamin C that would be lost in cooking. This was shown by the anthropologist-explorer Stefansson, who ate meat raw, frozen, or only lightly cooked just as the Inuit do in order to avoid developing scurvy. The plankton in the stomachs of raw fish provides vitamin C, as do the stomach contents of walrus and caribou. Whale skin, a popular delicacy, is high in vitamin C.

The all-meat diet is high in phosphorus and low in calcium. By eating the soft parts of animal bones, as well as dried fish and bird bones, Inuit compensate for the lack of other sources of calcium. Adult's molars are so hard, and their jaw muscles so strong, that they can crunch through bones easily. Nevertheless, some suffer from mild calcium deficiency, especially in winter when the lack of vitamin D from sunlight inhibits calcium absorption. This puts a particular strain on nursing women. Probably because they are nursed for long periods, children rarely have rickets. Among adults, however, there is elevated risk of loss of bone minerals due to low calcium and vitamin D intake and to high phosphorus intake. The elderly are especially prone to osteoporosis, a decrease in bone mass that increases the risk of fractures (Mazess and Mather, 1978:138). From age 40 on, Inuit men and women loss bone mass at a more rapid rate than the general U.S. population (Draper 1980).

The low proportion of carbohydrates seems to pose a risk of impaired glucose homeostasis. Glucose is needed for quick energy and for brain function. An all-meat diet provides 10 grams of glucose a day; the brain consumes ten times this much. Additional glucose may be synthesized from the amino acids released from digested protein (Draper 1977). Laboratory tests and medical records show that Inuit populations have very efficient glucose metabolism and rarely show signs of diabetes. In fact, may show intolerance to glucose, sucrose, and lactose.

Inuit diets are high in fat, yet the Inuit have low cholesterol levels in the blood, low blood pressure, and low rates of heart disease, perhaps because the meat they eat is significantly lower in saturated fats than beef. For instance, caribou meat has much higher proportion of polyunsaturated fatty acid contents, 21 percent as compared to only 3 percent in beef (Draper 1977). Diets rich in the omega-3 polyunsaturated fatty acids found in fish, seal, whale, and polar bear lipids are associated with a low rate of atherosclerosis and cardiovascular problems (Innis and Kuhnlein 1987).

Some of the animals of the Arctic, for example, caribou and rabbit, provide very lean meat. Although this would seem desirable, a diet of lean meat is not an adequate source of energy and essential fatty acids. The blubbery animals of the Arctic, especially the seal, provide these, and arctic groups that subsist too heavily on caribou may face nutritional deficiencies (Speth and Spielmann 1983).

A number of cultural anthropologists, including Franz Boas as early as 1888, have attempted to show adaptive aspects of the ideologies of arctic peoples. Food customs and beliefs, especially seasonal hunting taboos, do not invariably demonstrate pragmatic benefits, but rules prohibiting people from consuming caribou and seal in the same season show intuitive understanding that food differ nutritionally. Borré's work (1991) on Baffin Island demonstrates Inuit beliefs about the importance of "country food," particularly marine mammals, to maintain identity as an Inuk and to reinforce involvement of people in the community in procuring and sharing highly nourishing food. Inuit say that seal meat is a "rejuvenator of human blood" and "Seal blood gives us our blood. Seal is life-giving" (Borré 1991:54). Because of these beliefs, seal meat is invariably given to sick people as a remedy.

Conserving Energy: Staying Warm

How can humans cope with the severe temperatures of the Arctic, which remain usually well below freezing eight to nine months of the year? How can they work, travel, even play out of doors in –30°F (–34°C)? Do Inuit have an extra layer of body fat? Or perhaps an unusually high metabolism?

The extra fat idea has been disproved by skinfold measurements. Inuit are no fatter then racially similar people such as Chinese and Japanese living in temperate climates (Laughlin 1964). They do, however, respond to cold with an increase in cellular metabolism through nonshivering thermogenesis. This response, associated with a special kind of fat called brown adipose tissue, is found in all human infants and is maintained in adult arctic natives (Little and Hochner 1973:6–7).

Inuit basal metabolism is between 13 and 33 percent higher than among people in temperate climates, increasing core body temperature and reducing the risk of hypothermia. Diet contributes to higher metabolic rates. When some Alaskan Eskimos were placed on a white man's diet, lower in protein and higher in carbohydrates, their basal metabolism fell. Eskimo hunters had a metabolism rate 25 percent higher than a group of Eskimos living in a city (Hammel 1969:335–336).

Because of this higher metabolism Inuit have excellent blood circulation and resistance to cold in the hands and feet (Laughlin 1969:414). (See Fig. 31.1.) Frostbite is very infrequent. When Inuit are exposed to cold, the blood flow to their hands and feet rapidly increases. The response is cyclical, alternating between vasoconstriction and vasodilation. This ability to respond quickly to cold, called high core to shell conductance, is up to 60 percent faster among Inuit than among whites (Moran 2000:125). This is more related to diet than to genetic inheritance. It is an important physiological adaptation because the hands are the only part of the body frequently exposed to

wet cold. There is a relatively thick layer of subcutaneous fat in the hands and feet, allowing tasks like untangling dog harnesses, spearing fish, or butchering seals to be done efficiently without mittens.

Under normal circumstances, only the hands and face are exposed to extremely low temperatures. Scientists once believed that the facial flatness and eyefolds of Inuit were a genetic adaptation to cold, but these characteristics have been shown not to offer significant protection (Steegmann 1970). Out of doors, Inuit are clothed in double-layered caribou furs; which provide three or more inches of excellent insulation, and waterproof sealskin boots lined with caribou fur. Caribou hairs are hollow and very dense, providing good insulation, light weight, and softness. Traditional Inuit clothing "provides thermal equilibrium for a resting subject at –40° C" (–40° F) (Shephard and Rode 1996:31). This creates a microclimate as warm as a person could desire, sometimes even too warm during strenuous activity, but the "chimney effect" of venting at the hood, sleeves, and other openings in the parka helps prevent excessive sweating and hyperthermia. (See Fig. 1.5.) In addition, arctic peoples tend to sweat less from the trunk area and more from the face.

Inuit take advantage of body heat to keep their infants warm on the mother's back in the spacious pouch of the mother's parka, or *amaut*. (See Fig. 1.6.) The waistband of the *amaut* can be loosened to allow the infant to be shifted around to the front to nurse without being exposed to the air. Indoors on the elevated sleeping platform, Inuit sleep in close body contact, sharing the warmth of thick caribou furs insulated with a layer of heather branches.

Heated only by melted seal blubber and small flames from a length of moss wick in a stone lamp, plus the heat of human bodies, snowhouses, or igluit, become remarkably warm, often 30 to 60°F (17 to 33°C) higher than outside temperatures. Snow houses are excellent insulators because the ice contains small air cells. The heat of the seal oil lamp slightly melts the inside snow surfaces. They refreeze at night to a smooth reflecting surface that conserves radiant heat. Attaching entrance tunnels with openings at right angles helps to prevent drafts and heat loss (Moran 2000:121).

From May to November, Inuit live not in snowhouses, but in tents lined with animal skin and in some regions, small huts called a *qarmaq* made with whale bone or timber frame and layers of skins and sod. Moss and heather, gathered in late summer and early autumn and stuffed between the walls of these dwellings, provide effective insulation.

Conserving Energy: Limiting Population Growth

Food resources are a critical factor limiting population size and density in the Arctic. Availability of fish or caribou is always unpredictable. It is hard to accumulate surplus against hard times because of the mobile lifestyle and the

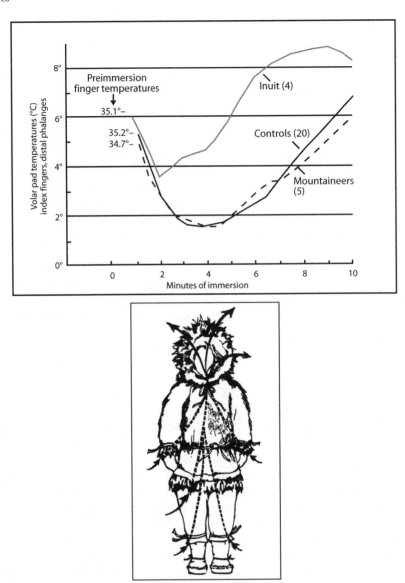

Figure 31.1 (Top) Physiological adaptation in vascular responses to cold. Inuit retain warmer fingers after ice water immersion than other subjects. (Bottom) The chimney effect in fur clothing, a cultural adaptation. Vents are opened by release of drawstrings during exhertion to prevent accumulation of sweat. Figures from Emilio Moran, *Human Adaptability,* Second edition. Westview Press, 2000. Pp. 125 (top) and 121 (top). Source of top figure: C. J. Eagan. 1963. Introduction and Terminology: Habituation and Peripheral Tissue Adaptations. Fed. Proc. 22:930–1933.

need to travel lightly. Food supply is rarely dependable enough to allow people to settle in one place for long. Thus population density was traditionally very low: approximately .03 persons per square kilometer (.08 per square mile) in Canada and .04 (.1 per square mile) in Alaska. Total population in mid-twentieth century was estimated at 25,000 in Alaska and approximately 35,000 in Greenland and Canada combined (Black 1980:39; Oswalt 1967:113–114; Guemple 1972:95).

If population size in any given region exceeds the area's resources, starvation threatens. Inuit avoid this by keeping well under the upper limits, usually fewer than a hundred persons per camp, with a social structure that allows easy fissioning of groups and a seasonal cycle

in which the size of the camp varies depending on the resources being exploited (Smith 1991). Several factors can maintain stability in population size: predation, starvation, disease, accidents, and social mortality. Humans are rarely preyed on in the Arctic, although polar bears stalk people occasionally. Starvation has not been a frequent cause of death, but it is certain that mortality increased among old people and small children during serious food shortages as recently as the 1960s.

Disease is also rare, for two reasons. One is that a simple ecosystem like the tundra has few parasitic and infectious organisms and few species of animals or insects that transmit diseases to humans (Dunn 1968:226). The second reason is that communities were too small to sustain epidemic diseases before the days of European whaling and trading stations. Thus, before contact with Europeans, Inuit did not experience contagious diseases such as measles, smallpox, rubella, and flu.

The health problems of Inuit, before moving into settlements, are primarily chronic conditions such as arthritis, eye damage, deficiency in enamel formation on the teeth, loss of incisors, and osteoporosis. A hysterical syndrome called *pibloktoq* affects people in winter. There is a risk of contracting tapeworm and trichinosis. Eating aged meat, considered a delicacy, poses a risk of fatal botulism. Many problems of modern societies, such as high blood pressure, heart disease, and diabetes, are absent. Cancer is rare, but there are cases of tumors of the nasopharynx, the salivary glands, and the esophagus (Shephard and Rode 1996:41). By far the most common health problems involve intestinal parasites, including protozoa, flukes from fish, and pinworms, and hydatid disease can be contracted from dogs. Tapeworms contracted from eating raw fish are most prevalent, in some communities reaching 83 percent infection rate, but they do not cause serious illness. The risk is seasonal, as freezing the fish will kill the tapeworm. Rabies among dogs and other animals posed a problem for humans in Alaska but was not introduced to northern Canada until 1945 (Shephard and Rode 1996:235, 236).

By far the major cause of injury and natural death is accidents, especially drowning or freezing to death after capsizing, but including house fires and attacks by sled dogs. Hunting accidents among men account for 15 percent of the deaths of a southern Baffin Island group (Kemp 1971). Young adult males have a high frequency of an unusual skeletal defect in the lower back called spondylolysis. This is due to stress fracturing during adolescence, probably incurred during kayak paddling, harpooning, wrestling, and lifting heavy objects (Merbs 1996).

Another important regulator of population is what Dunn (1968) calls "social mortality," such as feuds and murders. Warfare did not occur in the eastern Arctic. Suicide was frequent, especially by old people who could not keep up with the group and wished not to be a burden, and in younger people because of blindness or other crippling disability, guilt, or despair. Among the Netsilik Eskimos of Canada, in fifty years there were thirty-five successful and four unsuccessful suicides in a group of about 300 people (Balikci 1970:163).

A final important form of social mortality before acceptance of Christianity was infanticide. Rates of newborn female infanticide averaged 21 percent and ranged from 0 percent to 40 percent (Smith and Smith 1994:595). One group, the Netsilik, showed highly disproportionate gender ratios among children, with 66 girls and 138 boys in 1902, giving a ratio of 209 boys for every 100 girls. Since the normal ratio of males to females born in humans is 105 to 100, this gender discrepancy reveals the high infanticide rate as well as possible neglect of female offspring. Not all Inuit groups had high infanticide rates.

Nineteenth-century data on nine Baffin Island groups showed a ratio of 76 men to 100 women (Smith and Smith 1994:597).

Infanticide keeps population down in several ways: It is a direct check on the effective birth rate and reduces the number of potential reproducers in the next generation. In populations with high death rates among adult males from hunting accidents and homicides, female infanticide served to balance the gender ratio over the long run, increasing the proportion of food-producing males to non-food-producing females. However, we have no evidence that Inuit rationally calculated these long-range effects.

There may have been more immediate reasons to allow a newborn to die. The breast milk that comes in after childbirth could be used to continue nursing a two- or three-year-old toddler. During times of scarcity or frequent travel when a newborn was a burden, or if the mother were in poor health, infanticide might be chosen. Given the limits of the traditional curative system and the skills of traditional midwives, infanticide was safer than abortion.

In addition to these health reasons, hunters greatly preferred sons. A man had to feed a daughter at least fourteen or fifteen years, knowing that she would marry and usually leave her family. A son, however, provides food to the family at an early age and might very well stay with his father's group after marriage, providing labor and sharing food. Sons contribute more to the survival and reproductive success of the parents and other close relatives than do daughters after marriage (Smith and Smith 1994:610–612). It was most often the father, not the mother, who decided that a newborn baby must die. This was done, usually by exposure to the cold, immediately after the birth. The infant might be spared if the name of a deceased person were spoken, allowing the soul of the person to enter the child. Betrothal before birth, or an arrangement to let another family adopt her, also ensured a female infant's chance to live (Balikci 1970).

Resources for Survival

The adaptive traits that distinguish Inuit from other mammals of the Arctic include the ability to make tools, to use speech, to coordinate and plan hunting activities, and to teach their young necessary skills. An important aspect of the training of the young was to pass on knowledge and awareness about the sea ice, the snow, the weather, animal behavior, geography, and navigation (Nelson 1969). Children, learning not from books but from observation and from trial and error participation, became highly sensitive to subtle environmental cues such as shifts in the wind, changing humidity, the color of ice, the restlessness of a caribou herd. This sensitivity was extremely important for survival.

Inuit fully exploited the resources of the ecosystem, yet they remained a part of the system without changing it enough to threaten its equilibrium. Their health was a reflection of this equilibrium. Inuit lived in northern Canada, Greenland, and Alaska for 5,000 years or more in a relatively stable way of life, as a part of nature rather than separate from it. They could feel a kinship with *nanuq*, the bear, yet because of their tools, language, and creativity, they also felt a sense of competition and separation from the bear.

An old Inuk once showed Ann McElroy an ivory chess set he was carving. He had chosen *nanuq* to be king of all the animals and *inuk* (the man) to be king of a whimsical ensemble of dogs, children, sleds, and snow-houses. The set was skillfully carved and would bring a fine price in Toronto, but it was more than just tourist art. It seemed symbolic of the human niche in the arctic biome: bear and human as equals and opponents in the carver's conception of the game.

A Working Model of Ecology and Health

The working model shown in Figure 31.2 will help the reader to organize the variables presented in this chapter. A model like this is a visual aid that shows that the environment that impinges on people can be broken down into three parts: the physical, or abiotic, environment; the biotic environment; and the cultural environment. The parts are interdependent and continually in interaction;

a change in one variable frequently leads to a change in another (this is what a system means). Although we usually focus on the separate parts and think of them as causes and effects of change processes, it is also possible to imagine all these individual spheres and variables functioning as a single unit. If you look at the whole this way, you have a model of an ecosystem, a set of relationships among organisms and their environments.

In analyzing the impact of people on their environment and the impact of environment on people, we can shift focus from individual to population, and back, depending on our purpose. For example, a hunter puts on his snow goggles to protect his eyes from the glare of sun on snow and ice. The goggles are a material artifact, a part of the cultural environment that impinges on the hunter. They modify the impact of the physical environment on his vision and preventing snow blindness, a temporary but debilitating condition. The goggles themselves are made from bone, a material coming from the biotic environment. As we look at this simple act of putting on snow goggles, we can focus on the effect on the whole population, considering the role of this artifact in the group's long-term adaptation to an environment with long winters. We can shift the focus to the individual and consider his day-to-day success in finding food. We can even ask about the effect of the snow goggles on the hunter's eyes, lowering the focus to the organ, tissue, or even molecular level.

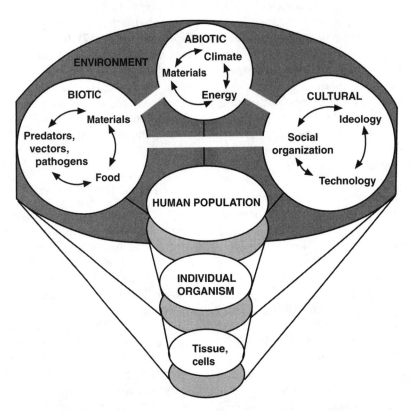

Figure 31.2 The environment that affects human health is made up of physical, biological, and cultural components forming a total ecosystem.

Where do health and disease fit into this model? A change in any one of the variables in the model in Figure 1.7 can lead to certain imbalances, contributing to disease or stress. For instance, change in climate may lead to a sharp decrease in human food supplies. Erosion of soil may undermine agricultural productivity. Politically and economically powerful groups may impose changes that further disadvantage vulnerable groups. This was the case in the Aral Sea region of the Soviet Union. From the late 1950s until 1991, Moscow sent out directives, passed on through layers of corrupt bureaucracy, to increase production of cotton in this region. Poorly designed irrigation and the overuse of fertilizer and pesticides led to air and water pollution. The Aral sea lost two-thirds of its volume and became salty, and infant mortality spiked during the crisis over the water supply (Brookfield 1999).

Our model builds on certain premises about the ecology of health and disease. First, there is no single cause of disease. The immediate, clinically detectable stimulus for disease may be a virus, vitamin deficiency, or an intestinal parasite, but disease itself is ultimately due to a chain of factors related to ecosystem imbalances. Second, health and disease develop within a set of physical, biological, and cultural subsystems that continually affect one another. Third, environment is not merely the physical habitat, the soil, air, water, and terrain in which we live and work, but also the culturally constructed environments—streets and buildings, farms and gardens, slums and suburbs. Further, people also create and live within social and psychological environments, and their perception of the physical habitat and of their proper role is influenced by social values and worldview. Thus our model linking environment and health fully acknowledges the impact of human behavior on environment.

The holistic approach in medical ecology attempts to account for as many environmental variables as possible. But the analysis of so many variables is difficult conceptually and not always possible, as research is always limited by time and money. The model allows us to look at only part of the overall system; for example, we can consider how technological change (say, increase in low-level radiation) and change in health indices (rates of cancer) are related. While remaining aware that many ecosystem variables are involved in this change, we can choose to study only a few variables in systematic comparisons of populations or communities. A system approach precludes easy explanations, but it does allow you to think about health and disease in ways that are both realistic and challenging. With this open model, you can analyze many of the specific cases discussed in this text, assessing the relative impact of one or another variable on health and comparing the adaptive strategies of various populations in terms of health benefits and disease risks.

The model presented here provides a framework for the study of health in environmental context. It does not specify what factors maintain health other than to suggest that change in ecological relations may adversely affect

health, but not invariably, for adaptation to disease often involves ecological changes. Ecology in a narrow sense does not fully explain why people are sick, hungry, displaced from their homeland, or deprived of basic rights. Politics and economics always play a large role in a community's health and must be considered in any model of ecology and health. Humans live in behavioral environments in which sources of threat and stress often come from other humans who impose oppressive conditions and introduce life-threatening hazards and pathogens (McElroy 1990). Poor outcomes of these encounters are not to be construed as failures in adaptation but rather as disastrous transformations of environments in which benefits to one group often put others at risk.

To be useful, an ecological model must be expanded to fit those cases, with permeable boundaries that account for external influences as well as internal dynamics. Modifications of the ecological approach to include political and economic factors are leading to productive collaboration among biological and cultural anthropologists. It is through collaborative development of theory and methodology, the focus of the next chapter, that medical anthropology continues to contribute to the study of health and environment.

Resources

Readings

Balikci, Asen. 1970. *The Netsilik Eskimo.* Garden City, NY: Natural History Press.

Coimbra, Carlos, et al. 2002. *The Xavante in Transition: Health, Ecology and Bioanthropology in Central Brazil.* Ann Arbor: University of Michigan Press.

Panter-Brick, Catherine. 2002. Street Children, Human Rights, and Public Health: A Critique and Future Directions. *Annual Review of Anthropology* 31: 147–171.

Panter-Brick, Catherine, and Malcolm T. Smith, Eds. 2000. *Abandoned Children.* Cambridge, UK: Cambridge University Press.

Schull, William J., and Francisco Rothhammer. 1990. *The Aymará: Strategies in Human Adaptation to a Rigorous Environment.* Dordrecht: Academic Publishers.

Smith, Eric A. 1991. *Inujjuamiut Foraging Strategies: Evolutionary Ecology of an Arctic Hunting Economy.* Hawthorne, NY: Aldine de Gruyter.

Journals

Medical Anthropology Quarterly—International Journal for the Cultural and Social Analysis of Health. The official journal of the Society for Medical Anthropology is published by the American Anthropological Association.

Medical Anthropology, Cross-Cultural Studies in Health and Illness. Published as a quarterly by Taylor & Francis, Ltd.

Social Science and Medicine. An international journal that includes articles by anthropologists, sociologists, geographers, economists, and other social scientists. Published by Pergamon and Elsevier Science Ltd.

Anthropology and Medicine (formerly the British Medical Anthropology Review). Published by Taylor & Francis, Ltd.

Films

"A Fistful of Rice." Bullfrog Productions, U.S. distributor. http://www.bullfrogfilms.com/
In UK, contact: Television Trust for the Environment, http://www.tve.org/
This video deals with poverty and homelessness in Kathmandu, Nepal.

Netsilik Eskimo Series. 1967–1971. Available in video format from Documentary Educational Resources, Cambridge, MA, and in 16 mm films from Pennsylvania State University. The films include: At the Autumn River Camp; At the Caribou Crossing Place; At the Spring Sea-Ice Camp; At the Winter Sea—Ice Camp; Jigging for Lake Trout; Stalking Seal on the Spring Ice; Group Hunting on the Spring Ice; Building a Kayak; and Fishing at the Stone Weir.

Psychotherapy in Africa

Thomas Adeoye Lambo

The kind of treatment people seek for their ailments will depend not only on what kind of medical facilities are available, but also on their perceptions of the causes of illness and the types of therapeutic procedures called for. This is particularly true of mental and emotional disorders in which both the causes and the treatment options are not always obvious.

In this classic article having to do with African concepts of health and illness, Thomas Adeoye Lambo shows how modern medicinal practices can incorporate traditional methods of healing for a viable treatment program. Based on the premise that clinical problems such as stress, depression, and emotional incapacity are rooted in an individual's social environment and, therefore, the treatment as well should be social, Dr. Lambo and his colleagues initiated what has come to be known as the "Aro experiment." Aro is an area of four villages in western Nigeria. The experiment consisted of building a day hospital and using a village care system to treat the patients.

The program became so successful that Dr. Thomas Adeoye Lambo was considered to be the father of African psychiatry and the UN produced a film about the hospital, which has served as a model for other African mental health systems.

Dr. Lambo was born in Abeokuta, Nigeria in 1923. After studying medicine at the University of Birmingham, England, he trained in psychiatry at Maudsley Hospital (1952–54). Returning to Nigeria, he set up the Neuropsychiatric Hospital Aro, where he worked until 1963, when he was appointed Professor of Psychiatry at Unversity College Hospital Ibadan. He later became Dean of Medicine (1966–68) and Vice Chancellor of the University of Ibadan (1968–1971).

Lambo joined the World Health Organization in 1971 as Assistant Director General, with special responsibility for the Divisions of Mental Health, Non-communicable diseases, Therapeutics & Prophylactic Substances and Health Manpower Development. He later became Deputy Director of the World Health Organization in 1973, and worked in that capacity until 1988. He was honored by many institutions during his life, including appointment to the Pontifical Academy of Sciences (1974), Haile Selassie Africa Research Award (1970), and honorary doctorates from University of Benin, University of Birmingham, Kent State University, Université d'Aix-Marseille, Long Island University, and Catholic University of Louvan. He was awarded Nigeria's highest honour, the National Merit Award.

Dr. Thomas Adeoye Lambo was active until his death in 2004, but his legacy, including the Neuropsychiatric Hospital Aro and the Department of Psychiatry at the University of Ibadan, lives on.

Key Concept: The power of the group in healing

Some years ago, a Nigerian patient came to see me in a state of extreme anxiety. He had been educated at Cambridge University and was, to all intents and purposes, thoroughly "Westernized." He had recently been promoted to a top-level position in the administrative service, bypassing many of his able peers. A few weeks after his promotion, however, he had had an unusual accident from which he barely escaped with his life. He suddenly became terrified that his colleagues had formed a conspiracy and were trying to kill him.

His paranoia resisted the usual methods of Western psychiatry, and he had to be sedated to relieve his anxiety. But one day he came to see me, obviously feeling much better. A few nights before, he said, his grandfather had appeared to him in a dream and had assured him of a long and healthy life. He had been promised relief from fear and anxiety if he would sacrifice a goat. My patient bought a goat the following day, carried out all the detailed instructions of his grandfather, and quickly recovered. The young man does not like to discuss this experience because he feels it conflicts with his educational background, but occasionally, in confidence, he says: "There is something in these native things, you know."

To the Western eye, such lingering beliefs in ritual and magic seem antiquated and possibly harmful—obstacles in the path of modern medicine. But the fact is that African cultures have developed indigenous forms of psychotherapy that are highly effective because they are woven into the social fabric. Although Western therapeutic methods are being adopted by many African therapists, few Africans are simply substituting new methods for traditional modes of treatment. Instead, they have attempted to combine the two for maximum effectiveness.

The character and effectiveness of medicine for the mind and the body always and everywhere depend on the culture in which the medicine is practiced. In the West, healing is often considered to be a private matter between patient and therapist. In Africa, healing is an integral part of society and religion, a matter in which the whole community is involved. To understand African psychotherapy one must understand African thought and its social roots.

It seems impossible to speak of a single African viewpoint because the continent contains a broad range of cultures. The Ga, the Masai, and the Kikuyu, for example, are as different in their specific ceremonies and customs as are the Bantus and the Belgians. Yet in sub-Saharan black Africa the different cultures do share a consciousness of the world. They have in common a characteristic perception of life and death that makes it possible to describe their overriding philosophy. (In the United States, Southern Baptists and Episcopalians are far apart in many of their rituals and beliefs, yet one could legitimately say that both share a Christian concept of life.)

The basis of most African value systems is the concept of the unity of life and time. Phenomena that are regarded as opposites in the West exist on a single continuum in Africa. African thought draws no sharp distinction between animate and inanimate, natural and supernatural, material and mental, conscious and unconscious. All things exist in dynamic correspondence, whether they are visible or not. Past, present, and future blend in harmony; the world does not change between one's dreams and the daylight.

Essential to this view of the world is the belief that there is continuous communion between the dead and the living. Most African cultures share the idea that the strength and influence of every clan is anchored by the spirits of its deceased heroes. These heroes are omnipotent and indestructible, and their importance is comparable to that of the Catholic saints. But to Africans, spirits and deities are ever present in human affairs; they are the guardians of the established social order.

The common element in rituals through out the continent—ancestor cults, deity cults, funeral rites, agricultural rites—is the unity of the people with the world of spirits, the mystical and emotional bond between the natural and supernatural worlds.

Because of the African belief in deities and ancestral spirits, many Westerners think that African thought is more concerned with the supernatural causes of events than with their natural causes. On one level this is true. Africans attribute nearly all forms of illness and disease, as well as personal and communal catastrophes, accidents, and deaths to the magical machinations of their enemies and to the intervention of gods and ghosts. As a result there is a deep faith in the power of symbols to produce the effects that are desired. If a man finds a hair, or a piece of material, or a bit of a fingernail belonging to his enemy, he believes he has only to use the object ritualistically in order to bring about the enemy's injury or death.

As my educated Nigerian patient revealed by sacrificing a goat, the belief in the power of the supernatural is not confined to uneducated Africans. In a survey of African students in British universities conducted some years ago, I found that the majority of them firmly believed that their emotional problems had their origin in, or could at least be influenced by, charms and diabolical activities of other African students or of people who were still in Africa. I recently interviewed the student officers at the Nigeria House in London and found no change in attitude.

The belief in the power of symbols and magic is inculcated at an early age. I surveyed 1,300 elementary-school children over a four-year period and found that 85 percent used native medicine of some sort—incantations, charms, magic—to help them pass exams, to be liked by teachers, or to ward off the evil effects of other student "medicines." More than half of these children came from Westernized homes, yet they held firmly to the power of magic ritual.

Although most Africans believe in supernatural forces and seem to deny natural causality, their belief system is internally consistent. In the Western world, reality rests on the human ability to master things, to conquer objects, to subordinate the outer world to human will. In the African world, reality is found in the soul, in a religious acquiescence to life, not in its mastery. Reality rests on the relations between one human being and another, and between all people and spirits.

The practice of medicine in Africa is consistent with African philosophy. Across the African continent, sick people go to acknowledged diviners and healers—they are often called witch doctors in the West—in order to discover the nature of their illness. In almost every instance, the explanation involves a deity or an ancestral spirit. But this is only one aspect of the diagnosis, because the explanation given by the diviner is also grounded in natural phenomena. As anthropologist Robin Horton observes: "The diviner who diagnoses the intervention of a spiritual agency is also expected to give some acceptable account of what moved the agency in question to intervene. And this account very commonly involves reference to some event in the world of visible, tangible happenings. Thus if a diviner diagnoses the action of witchcraft influence or lethal medicine spirits, it is usual for him to add something about the human hatreds, jealousies, and misdeeds that have brought such agencies into play. Or, if he diagnoses the wrath of an ancestor, it is usual for him to point to the human breach of kinship morality which has called down this wrath."

The causes of illness are not simply attributed to the unknown or dropped into the laps of the gods. Causes are always linked to the patient's immediate world of social events. As Victor Turner's study of the Ndembu people of central Africa revealed, diviners believe a patient "will not get better until all the tensions and aggressions in the group's interrelations have been brought to light and exposed to ritual treatment." In my work with the Yoruba culture, I too found that supernatural forces are regarded as the agents and consequences of human will. Sickness is the natural effect of some social mistake—breaching a taboo or breaking a kinship rule.

African concepts of health and illness, like those of life and death, are intertwined. Health is not regarded as an isolated phenomenon but reflects the integration of the community. It is not the mere absence of disease but a sign that a person is living in peace and harmony with his neighbors, that he is keeping the laws of the gods and the tribe. The practice of medicine is more than the administration of drugs and potions. It encompasses all activities—personal and communal—that are directed toward the promotion of human well-being. As S. R. Burstein wrote, to be healthy requires averting the wrath of gods or spirits, making rain, purifying streams or habitations, improving sex potency or fecundity or the fertility of fields and crops—in short, it is bound up with the whole interpretation of life.

Native healers are called upon to treat a wide range of psychiatric disorders, from schizophrenia to neurotic syndromes. Their labels may not be the same, but they recognize the difference between an incapacitating psychosis and a temporary neurosis, and between a problem that can be cured (anxiety) and one that cannot (congenital retardation or idiocy). In many tribes a person is defined as mad when he talks nonsense, acts foolishly and irresponsibly, and is unable to look after himself.

It is often assumed that tribal societies are a psychological paradise and that mental illness is the offspring of modern civilization and its myriad stresses. The African scenes in Alex Haley's *Roots* tend to portray a Garden of Eden, full of healthy tribesmen. But all gardens have snakes. Small societies have their own peculiar and powerful sources of mental stress. Robin Horton notes that tribal societies have a limited number of roles to be filled, and that there are limited choices for individuals. As a result each tribe usually has a substantial number of social misfits. Traditional communities also have a built-in set of conflicting values: aggressive ambition versus a reluctance to rise above one's neighbor; ruthless individualism versus acceptance of one's place in the lineage system. Inconsistencies such as these, Horton believes, "are often as sharp as those so well known in modern industrial societies. . . . One may even suspect that some of the young Africans currently rushing from the country to the towns are in fact escaping from a more oppressive to a less oppressive psychological environment."

Under typical tribal conditions, traditional methods are perfectly effective in the diagnosis and treatment of mental illness. The patient goes to the tribal diviner, who follows a complex procedure. First the diviner (who may be a man or a woman) determines the "immediate" cause of the illness—that is, whether it comes from physical devitalization or from spiritual possession. Next he or she diagnoses the "remote" cause of the ailment: Had the patient offended one of his ancestor spirits or gods? Had a taboo been violated? Was some human agent in the village using magic or invoking the help of evil spirits to take revenge for an offense?

The African diviner makes a diagnosis much as a Western psychoanalyst does: through the analysis of dreams, projective techniques, trances and hypnotic states (undergone by patient and healer alike), and the potent power of words. With these methods, the diviner defines the psychodynamics of the patient and gains insight into the complete life situation of the sick person.

One projective technique of diagnosis—which has much in common with the Rorschach test—occurs in *Ifa* divination, a procedure used by Yoruba healers. There are 256 *Odus* (incantations) that are poetically structured; each is a dramatic series of words that evoke the patient's emotions. Sometimes the power of the *Odus* lies in the way the words are used, the order in which they are arranged, or the starkness with which they express a deep feeling. The incantations are used to gain insight into the patient's problem. Their main therapeutic value, as in the case with the Rorschach ink blots, is to interpret omens, bring up unconscious motives, and make unknown desires and fears explicit.

Once the immediate and remote causes are established, the diagnosis is complete and the healer decides on the course of therapy. Usually this involves an expiatory sacrifice meant to restore the unity between man and deity. Everyone takes part in the treatment; the ritual involves the healer, the patient, his family, and the community at large. The group rituals—singing and dancing, confessions, trances, storytelling, and the like—that follow are powerful therapeutic measures for the patient. They release tensions and pressures and promote positive mental health by tying all individuals to the larger group. Group rituals are effective because they are the basis of African social life, an essential part of the lives of "healthy" Africans.

Some cultures, such as the N'jayei society of the Mende in Sierra Leone and the Yassi society of the Sherbro, have always had formal group therapy for their mentally ill. When one person falls ill, the whole tribe attends to his physical and spiritual needs.

Presiding over all forms of treatment is the healer, or *nganga*. My colleagues and I have studied and worked with these men and women for many years, and we are consistently impressed by their abilities. Many of those we observed are extraordinary individuals of great common sense, eloquence, boldness, and charisma. They are highly respected within their communities as people who through self-denial, dedication, and prolonged meditation and training have discovered the secrets of the healing art and its magic (a description of Western healers as well, one might say).

The traditional *nganga* has supreme self-confidence, which he or she transmitsto the patient. By professing an ability to commune with supernatural beings—and therefore to control or influence them—the healer holds boundless power over members of the tribe. Africans regard the *nganga's* mystical qualities and eccentricities fondly, and with awe. So strongly do people believe in the *nganga's* ability to find out which ancestral spirit is responsible for the psychological distress of the patient, that pure suggestion alone can be very effective.

For centuries the tribal practice of communal psychotherapy served African society well. Little social stigma was attached to mental illness; even chronic psychotics were tolerated in their communities and were able to function at a minimal level. (Such tolerance is true of many rural cultures.) But as the British, Germans, French, Belgians, and Portuguese colonized many African countries, they brought a European concept of mental illness along with their religious, economic, and educational systems.

They built prisons with special sections set aside for "lunatics" usually vagrant psychotics and criminals with demonstrable mental disorders—who were restricted with handcuffs and ankle shackles. The African healers had always drawn a distinction between mental illness and criminality, but the European colonizers did not.

In many African cultures today, the traditional beliefs in magic and religion are dying. Their remaining influence serves only to create anxiety and ambivalence among Africans who are living through a period of rapid social and economic change. With the disruption and disorganization of family units, we have begun to see clinical problems that once were rare: severe depression, obsessional neurosis, and emotional incapacity. Western medicine has come a long way from the shackle solution, but it is not the best kind of therapy for people under such stress. In spite of its high technological and material advancement, modern science does not satisfy the basic metaphysical and social needs of many people, no matter how sophisticated they are.

In 1954 my colleagues and I established a therapeutic program designed to wed the best practices of traditional and contemporary psychology. Our guiding premise was to make use of the therapeutic practices that already existed in the indigenous culture, and to recognize the power of the group in healing.

We began our experiment at Aro, a rural suburb of the ancient town of Abeokuta, in western Nigeria. Aro consists of four villages that lie in close proximity in the beautiful rolling countryside. The villages are home to Yoruba tribesmen and their relatives, most of whom are peasant farmers, fishermen, and craftsmen.

Near these four villages we built a day hospital that could accommodate up to 300 patients, and then we set up a village care system for their treatment. Our plan was to preserve the fundamental structure of African culture: closely knit groups, well-defined kin networks, an interlocking system of mutual obligations and traditional roles.

Patients came to the hospital every morning for treatment and spent their afternoons in occupational therapy, but they were not confined to the hospital. Patients lived in homes in the four villages or, if necessary, with hospital staff members who lived on hospital grounds—ambulance drivers, clerks, dispensary attendants, and gardeners. (This boarding-out procedure resembles a system that has been practiced for several hundred years in Gheel, a town in Belgium, where the mentally ill live in local households surrounding a central institution.)

We required the patients, who came from all over Nigeria, to arrive at the village hospital with at least one relative—a mother, sister, brother, or aunt—who would be able to cook for them, wash their clothes, take them to the hospital in the morning, and pick them up in the afternoon.

These relatives, along with the patients, took part in all the social activities of the villages: parties, plays, dances, storytelling. Family participation was successful from the beginning. We were able to learn about the family influences and stresses on the patient, and the family members learned how to adjust to the sick relative and deal with his or her emotional needs.

The hospital staff was drawn from the four villages, which meant that the hospital employees were the landlords of most of the patients, in constant contact with them at home and at work. After a while, the distinction between the two therapeutic arenas blurred and the villages became extensions of the hospital wards.

Doctors, nurses, and superintendents visited the villages every day and set up therapy groups—often for dancing, storytelling, and other rituals—as well as occupational programs that taught patients traditional African crafts.

It is not enough to treat patients on a boarding-out or outpatient basis. If services are not offered to them outside of the hospital, an undue burden is placed on their families and neighbors. This increases the tension to which patients are exposed. As essential feature of our plan was to regard the villages as an extension of the hospital, subject to equally close supervision and control.

But we neither imposed the system on the local people nor asked them to give their time and involvement without giving them something in return. We were determined to inflict no hardships. The hospital staff took full responsibility for the administration of the villages and for the health of the local people. They held regular monthly meetings with the village elders and their councils to give the villagers a say in the system. The hospital also arranged loans to the villagers to expand, repair, or build new houses to take care of the patients; it paid for the installation of water pipes and latrines; it paid for a mosquito eradication squad; it offered jobs to many local people and paid the landlords a small stipend.

Although these economic benefits aided the community, no attempt was ever made to structure the villages in any way, or to tell the villagers what to do with the patients or how to treat them. As a result of economic benefits, hospital guidance, and a voice in their own management, village members supported the experiment.

In a study made after the program began, we learned that patients who were boarded out under this system adapted more quickly and responded more readily to treatment than patients who lived in the hospital. Although the facilities available in the hospital were extensive—drug medication, group therapy sessions, modified insulin therapy, electro-convulsive shock treatments we found that the most important therapeutic factor was the patient's social contacts, especially with people who were healthier than the patient. The village groups, unlike the hospital group, were unrehearsed, unexpected, and voluntary. Patients could choose their friends and activities; they were not thrown together arbitrarily and asked to "work things out." We believe that the boarded-out patients improved so quickly because of their daily contact with settled, tolerant, healthy people. They learned to function in society again without overwhelming anxiety.

One of the more effective and controversial methods we used was to colaborate with native healers. Just as New Yorkers have faith in their psychoanalysts, and pilgrims have faith in their priests, the Yoruba have faith in the *nganga;* and faith, as we are learning, is half the battle toward cure.

Our unorthodox alliance proved to be highly successful. The local diviners and religious leaders helped many of the patients recover, sometimes through a simple ceremony at a village shrine, sometimes in elaborate forms of ritual sacrifice, sometimes by interpreting the spiritual or magical causes of their dreams and illnesses.

At the beginning of the program patients were carefully selected for admission, but now patients of every sort are accepted: violent persons, catatonics, schizophrenics, and others whose symptoms make them socially unacceptable or emotionally withdrawn. The system is particularly effective with emotionally disturbed and psychotic children, who always come to the hospital with a great number of concerned relatives. Children who have minor neurotic disorders are kept out of the hospital entirely and treated exclusively and successfully in village homes.

The village care system was designed primarily for the acutely ill and for those whose illness was manageable, and the average stay for patients at Aro was, and is, about six months. But patients who were chronically ill and could not recover in a relatively short time posed a problem. For one thing, their relatives could not stay with them in the villages because of family and financial obligations in their home communities. We are working out solutions for such people on a trial-and-error basis. Some of the incapacitated psychotic patients now live on special farms; others live in Aro villages near the hospital and earn their keep while receiving regular supervision. The traditional healers keep watch over these individuals and maintain follow-up treatment.

We have found many economic, medical, and social advantages to our program. The cost has been low because we have concentrated on using human resources in the most effective and strategic manner. Medically and therapeutically, the program provides a positive environment for the treatment of character disorders, sociopathy, alcoholism, neuroses, and anxiety. Follow-up studies show that the program fosters a relatively quick recovery for these problems and that the recidivism rate and the need for aftercare are significantly reduced. The length of stay at Aro, and speed of recovery, is roughly one third of the average stay in other hospitals, especially for all forms of schizophrenia. Patients with neurotic disorders respond most rapidly. Because of its effectiveness, the Aro system has been extended to four states in Nigeria and to five countries in Africa, including Kenya, Ghana, and Zambia. At each new hospital the program is modified to fit local conditions.

Some observers of the Aro system argue that it can operate only in nonindustrial agrarian communities, like those in Africa and Asia, where families and villages are tightly knit. They say that countries marked by high alienation and individualism could not import such a program. Part of this argument is correct. The Aro approach to mental health rests on particularly African traditions, such as the *nganga,* and on the belief in the continuum of life and death, sickness and health, the natural and the supernatural.

But some lessons of the Aro plan have already found their way into Western psychotherapy. Many therapists recognize the need to place the sick person in a social context; a therapist cannot heal the patient without attending to his beliefs, family, work, and environment. Various forms of group therapy are being developed in an attempt to counteract the Western emphasis on curing the individual in isolation. Lately, family therapy has been expanded into a new procedure called network therapy in which the patient's entire network of relatives, coworkers, and friends become involved in the treatment.

Another lesson of Aro is less obvious than the benefits of group support. It is the understanding that treatment begins with a people's indigenous beliefs and their world view, which underlie psychological functioning and provide the basis for healing. Religious values that give meaning and coherence to life can be the healthiest route for many people. As Jung observed years ago, religious factors are inherent in the path toward healing, and the native therapies of Africa support his view.

A supernatural belief system, Western or Eastern, is not a sphere of arbitrary dreams but a sphere of laws that dictate the rules of kinship, the order of the universe, the route of happiness. The Westerner sees only part of the African belief system, such as the witch doctor, and wonders how wild fictions can take root in a reasonable mind. (His own fictions seem perfectly reasonable, of course.) But to the African, the religious-magical system is a great poem, allegorical of human experience, wise in its portrayal of the world and its creatures. There is more method, more reason, in such madness than in the insanity of most people today.

References

Burstein, S. R. "Public Health and Prevention of Disease in Primitive Communities." *The Advancement of Science,* Vol. 9, 1952, pp. 75–81.

Horton, Robin. "African Traditional Thought and Western Science." *Africa*, Vol. 37, 1967, pp. 50–71.

Horton, Robin. *The Traditional Background of Medical Practice in Nigeria.* Institute of Africa Studies, 1966.

Lambo, T. A. "A World View of Mental Health: Recent Developments and Future Trends." *American Journal of Orthopsychiatry,* Vol. 43, 1973, pp. 706–716.

Lambo, T. A. "Psychotherapy in Africa." *Psychotherapy and Psychosomatics,* Vol. 24, 1974, pp. 311–326.

Proxemics: The Study of Man's Spatial Relations

Edward T. Hall

The placement of an article on spatial relationships in a section dealing with medical anthropology may seem peculiar, but remember that medical anthropology deals with many different factors having to do with human health, and *proxemics*, the study of the human use of spatial relationships, is one of those factors. As Edward T. Hall points out, the medical profession needs to know when to put people close to each other and when—and how far—to keep them apart.

As a young man in the 1930s, Hall was employed by the Bureau of Indian Affairs as a camp manager on a New Deal Project building roads and dams in Arizona. It was in this capacity that he came to know the Navajo and the Hopi, some of whom were workers on the project, and he developed an interest in the "language of behavior" and, by extension, the notion of proxemics, a concept that he himself developed.

Edward T. Hall was born in 1914 and received his Ph.D. from Columbia University in 1942. He served in WWII as a white officer in a black regiment. In the 1950s, for the U.S. State Department, he taught inter-cultural communication skills to Foreign Service personnel. He also taught on several different campuses, including the Harvard Business School, the Illinois Institute of Technology, and Northwestern University.

His most significant books have been *The Silent Language* (1959), *The Hidden Dimension* (1966), and *An Anthropology of Everyday Life: An Autobiography* (1992).

Key Concept: proxemics is the study of human spatial relationships

Several years ago, I encountered an examination question concerning what could be done about a situation where there were too few health facilities to serve a large population. In the facetious part of my response I suggested that one solution would be to design and provide mediocre services—fewer people would seek help and the problem of shortages would disappear. Authors such as Kunnes (1971) and the Ehrenreichs (1970) argue in a very political way that such mediocre services have, in fact, been consistently provided on a grand scale (though not with the above mentioned results). In the following article, using the health setting as a focus, Hall presents insights of a non-political nature concerning an often neglected realm of culture. We are given an opportunity to examine proxemic factors that can affect a person's well-being. People accustomed to modern medical procedures in one culture may be made to feel uncomfortable in an equally modern but different setting in another. Some clues are provided, then, about why many people might be reluctant to adopt "scientific" medicine. Proxemic considerations provide, to be sure, only part of the answer concerning acceptance and rejection of services. However, a cross-cultural examination of proxemics in medical settings might provide us with some interesting insights into the provision of services in a heterogeneous society.

There are many differences in the spatial layout of the hospital, the clinic, and the office of the private practitioner. Man's responses to these differences are not haphazard. Vincent Kling [1959] remarks that there are "happy spaces and gloomy ones." It's the anthropologist's job—using the tools of his trade—to isolate the significant variables at work, and to discover what spatial cues cause people to differentiate between "happy" and "gloomy" spaces, and how space molds behavior in various contexts.

Fixed Feature Space

Winston Churchill once observed: "We shape our buildings and later they shape us" [Kling, 1959]. Much can be discovered by observing how man uses fixed space in an organizational setting. Given a knowledge of the culture, it is possible to form a reasonably firm picture of the structure and function of an organization from its layout. Centrally located functions take precedence over those on the periphery; places at a maximum distance from the center are used for unimportant or low status activities, or for isolation of danger—such commonplace observations are often ignored because they seem to be so obvious.

Searles [1960] thinks that patients occupying rooms at the ends of corridors tend to do less well than patients who are more centrally located. In the same wards, he also noted that patients would put up with a disagreeable roommate, rather than be moved away from the nurses' station, which is the center of gravity of the ward. The pioneering statement on this proposition by Baker, Davies, and Sivadon describes the influence of fixed feature space on the recovery of psychiatric patients [1959].

Space and the Mental Hospital. There is a slowly accumulating body of evidence pointing to the need for a complete re-evaluation and restudy of hospital layout, taking into account cultural, as well as strictly functional factors.

In a series of penetrating papers on the relationship of architecture to the treatment of psychosis, Osmond [1957, 1959] and Izumi [1957] take vigorous exception to the conventional design of modern mental hospitals. They maintain that most are actually antitherapeutic, and tend to aggravate patients' conditions rather than to improve them. They suggest a design that will allow the patient a small place to be away—to shut himself off—from the suffering of others, a place where he can "pull himself together" from time to time. In their conception, these very small spaces radiate in a circle off slightly larger rooms, in which two to four people can interact. These, in turn, are placed around a community day room, in which larger groups can meet. The nursing staff and administrative functions form the core of this radial system.

Paralleling Osmond's thinking is Sivadon's [n.d.] highly unique approach, originated at Neuilly-sur-Marne, and currently being incorporated in a new addition being built for the Château de la Verrière at Le Mesnil-St.-Denis (Seine-et-Oise), France. This new hospital is being built according to World Health Organization plans [Baker, Davies, and Sivadon, 1959]. The entire plant uses space as a therapeutic agent. There are three "villages," arranged in a hierarchy from simple to complex. Ninety patients are housed in each village, 30 to a ward. Open spaces are used to contain the patients, rather than fences and walls. Internal space is designed so that room size can be altered by opening and closing sliding sections of the walls. This feature has much in common with the Japanese practice of opening and closing sections of the house for different occasions and moods, and for different times of the day.

An added consideration in such hospital plans is the distorted space perception of schizophrenic patients. For schizophrenics, distances are exaggerated, so that long halls make them feel small and insignificant. Weckowitz [1957], commenting on the perceptual world of the schizophrenic, describes how size-constancy becomes distorted, and the schizophrenic underestimates the size of objects seen at a distance. He therefore over-estimates distance, which puts a strain on his cybernetic mechanisms. Sivadon treats this condition by re-educating his patients in their use of space. It would be interesting to discover how normal, as well as psychotic, people in different cultures vary in their spatial perceptions.

Room Size. Hospital rooms, as currently designed, take into account virtually everything except the psychological influence of size, proportions, and outside view on the patient.[1]

For example, in a new hospital in the Washington area the rooms are so small that they barely can hold the furniture. How crowding of this type influences the patient's recovery is unknown. In another hospital (also in Washington), a private room in the surgery ward is so small that people constantly deteriorate in this room, and have to be moved. There is undoubtedly a point at which spatial economies begin to bring diminishing returns. We need to know the ideal room size for treating different conditions. We need to know the limits above and below which room size should not go.[2]

Man's tolerance of confining space and crowding is, in general, a function of time and situation [United States Navy . . . , 1959]. In this sense the consequences of bad design and crowded conditions may ultimately be less serious in hospitals than in dwellings and offices, where most people spend significant portions of their lives.

In a study I am currently conducting on space as an inducer and reliever of stress in man, office space has been examined using a variety of techniques.[3] Preliminary results indicate that office size is of crucial importance to man's comfort, productivity, and general well-being. Culture is, of course, a very significant variable that has to be taken into account, since cultures vary in the space required for the person. That is, "personal distance" as well as social distance varies from culture to culture [Calhoun, 1961].

Consequences of Crowding. The social consequences of crowding in dwelling rooms has only very recently been isolated from other factors and studies in a systematic way. The usual practice was to collect data on the number of persons or families per room or dwelling unit. It was not until Chombart de Lauwe [1959a, 1959b] calculated the number of square meters available to each individual in different situations that additional significant information became available.

His studies indicate that there are critical limits below which and above which French working-class families show the consequences of either crowding, or its opposite, which is something akin to neglect. When there is less than 8 to 10 square meters per person, social and physical disorders double. Between 8 square meters and 14 square meters per person, pathology is at a minimum. Above 14 meters, there is an increase again. Chombart de Lauwe's explanation of the latter finding is that these statistics came from upwardly mobile homes, where the parents were more interested in status symbols and getting ahead than in the family. Hence, they isolated their children in separate rooms, and did not pay enough attention to them.

It is important also to stress that 8 square meters, as a minimum, is not a constant that remains fixed. It changes in time and space, with culture and with the situation. My own observations indicate that individual distance with middle class and working class French people is much less than that for the same groups in the United States. In France, therefore, it is possible to fit more people into a given space, without their personal distances overlapping too much, than it is in the United States.

The Hospital in a Transcultural Setting. In the transfer of the fixed features of hospital designs across cultural boundaries, there is a constant danger that there will be an automatic reproduction of the familiar patterns of the donor. Failure to recognize intangibles of the other's culture is not surprising when it is considered that, even within the context of our own culture, anatomy and convention are largely responsible for space allocation and layout. It is possible to measure a man, a bed, and a chair and calculate the cost of building and maintaining a square foot of floor, but not the cost of crowding. The data are meager on the behavioral side, and the temptation to act on the basis of simple tangibles is strong in both the transcultural and intracultural situation.

Sollenberger [1951–1955] provides the classic example, that of the transmittal of a four-story hospital plant plan, *unaltered*, from the United States to the center of China. He describes a four-story mission hospital built on the northwest plains of China, for which literally everything had to be packed in by animal back, including a boiler to run the heating plant. From the very beginning, the Chinese patients disliked the hospital and there was difficulty getting them to enter it. Because of its very great distance from urban centers, and the difficulty of maintaining equipment, it soon became apparent that the second-story wards were a luxury that even the Western medical missionaries could ill afford. The hospital limped along as a little-used, rather unpopular affair until the Chinese Communists arrived. Then, it was torn down, brick by brick, and reassembled according to the Chinese pattern. Instead of wards, there were small huts, separated in space, and clustered around a clinical and administrative center. The small huts in which the patients were housed were designed in that way so that the families would stay with the patients and care for them.

The "family care" plan, as a matter of fact, is popular in many parts of the world. A new hospital in El Salvador attracted considerable attention a number of years ago because it incorporated this feature in the design of the wards. The Salvadorians thought that the Americans (who designed the hospital) were at last beginning to acknowledge that the culture of El Salvador was different from their own—and not necessarily inferior.

Cultural Determinants in Crowding and Health. Western medicine stresses the isolation of the sick and the minimization of their contact with the healthy. Yet, there are a number of instances, in other cultures, where leaving the patient alone or with only a very few people around him would signify approaching death. This pattern used to characterize the Navaho, and undoubtedly is still extant in many of the more remote regions of the Navaho reservation.

Traditionally, cure of the Navaho requires the presence and active cooperation of many people. There are special ceremonial houses (fixed-feature hogans) for curing ceremonies. Illness also provides virtually the only occasion for everyone in these widely scattered communities to get together. If the patient dies, however, the ground and the building immediately become contaminated. According to Navaho belief, evil spirits will infect anyone who steps on this ground, for untold years to come. For this reason, the white hospitals used to be avoided by the Navahos, because people died in them.

Paul [1953] reports how he and his wife, visiting a patient in a local dwelling in Guatemala, attempted to reduce the crowding in the room in order to make things more comfortable for the person they were visiting—not realizing that, as in the case of the Navaho, a lack of crowding would have been taken by the patient as a sign that death was near. Paul's example is a good one because it illustrates the fact that one never knows the significance of an action in a foreign culture in advance, even if one is a trained anthropologist, as he is.

Semi-fixed Spatial Features

The study of furniture arrangement, screens, movable partitions and the like as factors in human interactions constitutes the core of the studies that have been done on semi-fixed spatial features.

Osmond [1959] coined the terms *sociopetal* and *sociofugal* as a way of characterizing two contrasting spatial arrangements. Sociofugal space discourages human interaction and tends to keep people apart. Railroad stations, libraries, and many hospitals have their furniture set in a sociofugal mold. Sociopetal space has just the opposite effect. The small face-to-face conversational groups in the living rooms of many American houses, booths in the old-style drug store, restaurant tables and the sidewalk cafés in France and Italy are all sociopetal.

Robert Sommer [1959, 1961, 1958, 1961], in a pioneering study on the effect of space on human interaction, rearranged the furniture in a "model" ward, in which the patients had been observed to be apathetic, in spite of "bright and cheerful surroundings." As a result of these rearrangements, the number of conversations doubled, and intake of information through reading tripled. Sommer also demonstrated that apathetic patients in a large mental hospital tended to be observed in halls and corridors, where the space is sociofugal, five times more frequently than non-apathetic patients, who were constructively occupied in day rooms and shops.

The custodial nature of such hospitals, and the mechanics of house-keeping in many, tend to encourage sociofugal, isolating arrangements of furniture. Nurses do not normally arrange the chairs so that they will encourage conversation, but rather so that they will look neat and orderly. In another study, Sommer reports on the influence of seating arrangement on table conversation. Fifty observation sessions were conducted at controlled intervals of people sitting at 36x72-inch tables in a cafeteria. Side-by-side conversations were three times as frequent as face-to-face conversations (across the table). Corner-to-corner conversations were twice as frequent as the side-by-side conversations, and therefore six times as frequent as the face-to-face ones. That is, face-to-face placing at a 36-inch distance is more sociofugal than corner-to-corner placing.

There is a chance that one may feel that I imply that sociofugal arrangements are bad and sociopetal ones are good. This is not the case. There are times when each is appropriate and desirable.

It should also be noted here that *what is sociofugal for one culture may be sociopetal in another.* Americans have great difficulty carrying on conversations across a room; a few remarks, perhaps, but if the conversation is to continue they generally have to move closer together. In the mountain villages of Lebanon and Syria this is the accepted way for men to converse in the evening. They will sit on opposite sides of the room and talk across the room at each other, something that it would be virtually impossible for Americans to do. Similarly, a Chinese subject whom I interviewed a few years ago was positively tongue-tied when speaking face-to-face or at an angle, but became quite talkative when I discovered he was accustomed to a side-by-side arrangement of the furniture, and placed myself appropriately.

Dynamic Use of Space as Space in Human Transactions

In addition to the fixed and semi-fixed aspects of space, of the types described above, there is *dynamic* space, in which man actively uses the fixed and semi-fixed features given to him. People can be put at ease, shut up, or frozen, depending on where they place themselves in relationship to each other. A big desk is often employed to impress others, to emphasize status, or as a hiding place. The desk has other communicative functions, depending whether the

man who occupies it stays fixed behind it or departs from it. Technical, consultative, or "strictly business" transactions among intimates are very often conducted across a desk or around a table. Leaving the desk and sitting away from it can be a way of staying away from business, or it can signal friendship or a personal relationship.

The Doctor and the Patient. Sullivan [1947, 1954], one of the first to emphasize the relationship of anthropology to psychiatry, used to sit at 90 degrees to the patient because he felt that schizophrenics were embarrassed by being stared at.

Park's distinction between the "foot-of-the-bed" doctor and the "beside-the-bed" doctor is also relevant in this context.[4] The foot-of-the-bed position is a little more than six feet from the patient's head. Six feet is in the "impersonal" conversational zone. This is a strictly consultative public distance. Use of this distance by the physician communicates less interest in the patient than in his condition. Patients recognize this, but are hard put to say on what cues they base their appraisal of the doctor's attitude.

The beside-the-bed position is personal, and communicates to the patient a sense of the doctor's interest in him as a person. It is a position at which personal subjects, or those about which there is some anxiety, can be discussed. Standing versus sitting, however, is a matter of dominance. If the doctor sits, he puts himself on a more or less equal level with the patient. If he wants to elicit information about which the patient feels anxious, he may find it easier to do so seated. His bending down will also sometimes achieve the same result.

A cautionary note must be injected at this point: consistency is always desirable in communication. Tone of voice, stance, and attitude of the body communicate [Birdwhistell, 1952]. A physician who is more interested in the condition under treatment than the patient is well advised not to feign, by moving from one place to another, an interest in the patient that he does not feel.

Winick and Holt [1961], reporting on the space dynamics of group therapy, noted that many patients seemed to prefer not to sit on a sofa because they did not want to be touched by other patients. The preference for individual chairs indicated that a human being experiences his own body border, as well as a need for a "life space," in the literal sense. It appeared, however, that the strength of preference for a specific, individual space was a function of the degree of neurosis.[5]

Attempts by Winick and Holt to arrange a new therapy group in a circle led to anxiety, particularly in those members whose problems included fear of closeness to other people. They also observed that when a group wished to express anxiety, whether or not the patients or therapists were aware of their anxiety, the members would often spontaneously move their chairs into a circle. As the group addressed itself with increasing anxiety to the situation, the members drew even closer together. The circle became smaller and smaller. As anxiety diminished, the circle expanded, and the seating arrangement became more rectangular again.

As one might anticipate, the groups became freer in their use of space as their ability to cope with their hostility toward their parents and others increased. Also, the members were less insistent that "their" chairs not be used by anyone else.

Territoriality in the Mentally Ill. For the institutionalized psychotic, laying claim to a territory is more basic than speech (in some instances). At least, it is still manifest in mute patients. Woodbury [1958] reports that space was the "currency" of one of the large, seldom-visited wards in Washington, D.C.'s St. Elizabeth's Hospital. The dominant patient in the ward hierarchy had complete run of the ward; he could go anywhere. Lesser lights could move freely, but they had smaller divisions of space. No one invaded the territory of someone higher than himself in the social structure of the ward. At the bottom, there was one patient who was restricted to the bench under which he slept. This patient could not even spit in the drain hole in the middle of the ward, nor was he allowed to use the toilet. His incontinence was more a symptom of his social status in the ward than of his psychosis.

Woodbury also reports that 50 percent of the incontinent patients ceased to be incontinent when they were moved; that is, with a definite alteration in the structuring of territory, behavioral changes ensued.

Some St. Elizabeth's patients took violent exception to being touched. There was what Woodbury terms the *crise de contact* through which these patients had to pass. After this crisis, the violent fights between these patients ceased. (Lewin [1958] reported that enuresis may respond to a change in environment.)

Searles [1960], reporting on patients' spatial distortions, states that some of the patients confuse their own physical boundaries with those of the room. Davie and Freeman [1961] also comment on the "disturbed perception of the body boundaries." In an interview, Searles mentioned that he had patients who objected violently to being approached too closely during therapy.[6] One female patient would place her chair in a niche under a gable, at the maximum possible distance from the therapist (about 20 feet). As treatment progressed, she became more able to tolerate closeness: a signal of her recovery was her ability to tolerate normal interaction distances.

Anxiety and the Perception of Space. Anxiety is a significant factor in perception, and is therefore an element to be considered in space studies. In some instances, the space itself apparently induces anxiety, which in turn distorts the perceptions, thus creating a vicious circle from which it is hard to escape. Data on spatial distortions are available for both normal and psychiatric populations.

In a study of normal subjects' responses to crowding in a bomb shelter, the walls at first appeared to "close in upon them." As they became more accustomed to the space, and anxiety diminished, the walls receded [United States Navy . . . , 1959]. Wittreich, Grace, and Radcliffe [1961] have demonstrated that man distorts his perceptions under conditions of anxiety. The greater the anxiety, the greater the distortions.

Interviews with psychiatrists in private practice failed to reveal one who did not use space consciously in treatment; that is, their placement of both themselves and their patients was far from haphazard. Some had a greater repertoire at their command than others. Several used space as a means of reassuring dependent patients. Another sat in his chair in such a way that his outstretched hand would be inside the patient's personal space. He noticed that as treatment progressed he was gradually able to withdraw his hand. Still another doctor put his foot against the patient's chair during treatment as a means of maintaining contact.

Summary

It is hoped that this review of proxemics will serve as an introduction to its study. My purpose has been simply to indicate who has been working in this field, and what results have been achieved. The physician, architect, biologist, psychologist, sociologist, and anthropologist all have contributions to make, each in his own specialty; I have emphasized those contributions that are of relevance to the physician and the anthropologist.

The subject is so vast in scope that I cannot help but feel frustrated concerning all that I have had to leave unsaid. However, for my anthropological colleagues, I want to summarize some of my own reasons for pursuing research in this field.

Technically, the anthropologist is drawn to the study of space for the following reasons: *(a)* it is a bio-basic, culturally modified system of behavior; *(b)* it is measurable; *(c)* as cultural systems go, it is reasonably simple; *(d)* it provides a means for comparing behavior across cultural lines in concrete terms; *(e)* it is an activity which man shares with other vertebrates, and there is a growing wealth of comparative material on related life forms; *(f)* all cultural activities occur in a spatial frame; *(g)* a great many spatial acts are so highly patterned and so automatic that they function almost totally out-of-awareness, and therefore are not subject to the kind of control and distortion that conscious words are; and *(h)* time and space are also admirably suited to multidisciplinary studies [Moholy-Nagy, 1949].

Notes

1. One of the few exceptions is the previously mentioned Château de la Verrière. Here, actively disturbed schizophrenic patients are given large rooms and terraces with a view, instead of restraints. The more disturbed the patient, the more space he is given. Tubular halls are avoided.
2. A recent report of the American Institute of Architects' Committee on Hospitals and Health (*AIA Journal*, Sept., 1960) states that *the average size of single rooms in American*

hospitals of recent date is 117 to 172 square feet of floor space. Double rooms average 157 to 210 square feet.

3. "Social Space as Bio-communication," under a grant from the United States Public Health Service.

4. John Parks, Dean of the Medical School of George Washington University, used these distinctions in lectures to interns and resident physicians.

5. Lawrence K. Frank's [1958] insightful and provocative treatment of life space and tactile communication is also relevant in this regard.

6. Data collected in one of a series of interviews with physicians on proxemics in relation to psychiatric disorders.

Applied Anthropology

Selection 34
MARIANNE ELISABETH LIEN, from "Fame and the Ordinary: 'Authentic' Constructions of Convenience Foods," *Advertising Cultures*

Selection 35
MONTGOMERY McFATE, from "Anthropology and Counterinsurgency: The Strange Story of their Curious Relationship," *Military Review*

Selection 36
LEE CRONK, from "Chapter 7: Gardening Tips," *That Complex Whole: Culture and the Evolution of Human Behavior*

Fame and the Ordinary: 'Authentic' Constructions of Convenience Foods

Marianne Elisabeth Lien

When most of us think of convenience food, we think of something simple to prepare and eat. Little thought, if any, is given to the process which resulted in our purchase of the item.

In the following account, we get an anthropological, "insider" ethnographic description of the decision-making process that goes into the manufacture and promotion of so-called convenience foods. As an anthropologist, Marianne Elisabeth Lien provides us with the larger context—a highly competitive, but limited market—in which the only way to enhance profit is not to expect any increase in consumption, but to capture a larger market share and to add value to the product in order to justify a price increase. All of this is done, of course, while keeping the product cost-effective as well as attractive and convenient to the consumer.

As much as textbooks on advertising may try to capture the process on paper, the actual workings of the marketing maneuvers involve many cultural contingencies with respect to the "target group," the shared understandings between producer and consumer, and the desire to have the product appear exotic, yet familiar. Such a complicated matter can only be carried off by someone who combines the skills of a product manager with those of the marketing profession. And its true significance—in all of its intricate detail—can only be understood and described by a skilled ethnographer!

Marianne Elisabeth Lien was once a researcher for the National Institute for Consumer Research in Norway, concentrating upon nutritional policies, advertising, and mediations between consumers and suppliers in the marketplace and food production. She is currently an Associate Professor of Social Anthropology at the University of Oslo Norway, where she conducts research related to globalization of the marketplace. In addition to contributing to several anthologies having to do with markets, consumption and culture, she has published *Marketing and Modernity* (Berg, 1997).

Key Concept: marketing exotic food

Convenience Foods in Norway: Fertile Ground for Growth

In the early 1990s, food manufacturers in Norway observed a paradox. On the one hand, research on demography, family structure, and eating habits indicated a significant demand for convenience foods among Norwegian consumers. On the other hand, the actual consumption of convenience foods was very low, compared with countries in the EU and with the US. For Viking Foods,[1] this was good news. For some time, they had searched for ways to increase the so-called 'added value' of their product range. Convenience foods appeared as a promising area in which they might achieve this aim.

The term 'convenience food' (*ferdigmat* in Norwegian) usually refers to an industrial product, which combines elements that have previously been put together in the home. For instance, a package of dry spaghetti is usually not referred to as a convenience food, as the possibility of making spaghetti from raw materials is generally not considered. Once the pasta is purchased in a mixture with a pre-prepared sauce, however, the product is more likely to be referred to as convenience food, as the preparation of pasta sauce in the home is fairly common. Convenience food may thus be conceived of as a relative rather than an absolute term. Its meaning derives not only from industrial processing, but also from the absence of culinary elaboration in the household. An increase in the consumption of convenience foods thus indicates a transfer of certain household activities from the private sphere to the industrial domain.

The case that is about to unfold took place in the early 1990s in the marketing department of Viking Foods, one of the largest private food manufacturers in Norway, and the market leader in the field of frozen convenience foods. . . .

The Bon Appetit Project

'Bon Appetit' is the name of a range of frozen dinner products, launched by Viking Foods in March 1991. I first entered the project half a year later, in October 1991, when I joined Henrik, a product manager in charge of Bon Appetit on his visit to *ANUGA,* a biannual international food fair in Cologne. Henrik was in his early thirties. With a degree in marketing, and several years of experience in Viking Foods' marketing department, he clearly represented the marketing profession. The main purpose of his visit to ANUGA was to see other products, which might give him some ideas to take home, and to get a general update of what was going on in the international market. As we stopped at a stand with German convenience foods, Henrik spent a long time looking at the varieties of ethnic convenience foods offered, many of which I had never encountered in Norwegian food stores. I noticed that while some dishes caught his interest, others were immediately discarded. It seemed to me that these judgments were made intuitively, and when I asked him about what he was actually doing, he replied:

Henrik: I just pick up some ideas. A lot of these are not relevant for the Norwegian market. It is simply too strange. Like for instance *Deutsche Knodeln*.[2] This is food for the Germans. But then there are other things that are interesting.
Marianne: Like what?
Henrik: Lots of things. Italian dishes, obviously. And spring rolls as well. I think spring rolls have now reached a point which is suitable in terms of a launch.
Marianne: How do you know?
Henrik: I guess it relates to an overall knowledge of the Norwegian market.

At this time, Bon Appetit had been on the market for about six months, and the product range included lasagne, tagliatelle, spaghetti bolognese, tortellini, chop suey, oriental stew and a popular Norwegian dish called *'lapskaus.'* However, as the Bon Appetit product range was a flexible concept, with single products being added or eliminated over time, product development remained an issue that Henrik constantly had to consider.

According to the Brand Strategy, the Bon Appetit product range consisted of 'complete meals' characterized by 'high quality and good taste at a reasonable price' that could 'be heated in the package either in an oven, a microwave oven or in hot water.' The primary target group was defined as 'modern, busy urban people with a high income, eating conveniently during weekdays' and 'not particularly gourmet oriented. This group had been labeled 'live for the present' by consumer segmentation surveys, and was described in the Brand Strategy as being

'engaged and active' and 'with an individual, unstructured meal pattern.' The secondary target group was referred to as the gourmet segment. However, as it turned out, this target group was difficult to please. In relation to this segment, convenience food was described as having 'a credibility problem in appearing as natural products precisely because (they are) pre-prepared at the factory.'[3] Thus the ability to come up with new products that were palatable and appealing to critical consumers was a key challenge.

Getting Things Right; Technology and Taste

To a great degree it was Henrik who defined the further choice of direction, specifying to the product development experts what to do, and in what order of priority. These negotiations involved a level of detail, which was quite far removed from the abstract product concept defined in the Brand Strategy. Decisions about the right amounts of cheese and carrots, and the correct viscosity of a particular sauce could hardly be made by referring, for example, to the degree of modernity of the target group. Henrik's task may thus be perceived as the work of translation between the abstract level of general consumer characteristics, and the very concrete level of material composition (and vice versa). Clearly, the Brand Strategy provided no manual of how to go about this. And the target group analysis, which explored in detail the characteristics of the most relevant consumers, hardly provided any clues with regard to the taste and flavor of the actual product. How then, did Henrik manage these translations? How did he know that the pasta sauce was too thick, and on what basis did he select the combination of cheese and carrots?

Faced with such questions, Henrik used the expertise that was most readily available: himself, his family and a few colleagues in the marketing department. In the middle of the marketing department office area, there was a tiny kitchen, which allowed for certain experiments. Sometimes the smell of hot food spread into the office area, whereupon Henrik, mostly without any advance warning, gathered whoever was present to try something out. Other times, during discussions, he jokingly referred to recent test results from *'Edvard Griegs vei* 54,' his home address, and to informal trials that he had undertaken together with his wife. Thus, while the written documents mostly reflected professional market research, informal, ad hoc testing was part of decision-making as well, although it was not always referred to as such.

Frank Cochoy (1998) has described marketing as a distinct body of knowledge located halfway between supply and demand, but also between science and practice. Henrik's pragmatic combination of formal and informal marketing strategies illustrates this. He consulted consumer surveys and applied market research when it was available or appeared to be a practical solution. But formal market research can never provide answers to every single issue that needs to be solved on a day-to-day basis, particularly when the issues relate to product development. Consequently, Henrik did what was expected with regard to formal market research, but beyond that he relied on his own 'gut feeling' and common sense. . . .

Why Pasta?
The Foreign and the Familiar. . .

The strong emphasis on dishes of foreign origin, and particularly on Italian pasta dishes, reflected a general tendency during the 1990s associating convenience foods with foods of foreign origin.[4] But how can this connection be explained? And why did Italian cuisine gain such a strong position? During a period when Henrik planned to launch another two pasta dishes in the product range, I had the chance to discuss this with him. He explained that a recent consumer survey on Norwegian eating habits had indicated that among all ethnic foods, Italian food was rated number one.[5] He continued: 'In addition, pasta is the kind of dish which tastes good even when there is not a lot of meat in it. In other words, we avoid some of the problems related to high costs of production.'

At the same time, Henrik also tried to establish more typically Norwegian products. . . . One of the most promising products was *finnebiff*, a common and fairly popular Norwegian dish based on thinly sliced reindeer meat. For Henrik, this was part of a deliberate strategy, and when I asked about the rationale behind it he replied:

Henrik: Part of our product strategy goes kind of like this: in order to protect ourselves against foreign competitors, our only possibility is to develop typically Norwegian dishes out of Norwegian raw materials. Here we have a competitive advantage compared to the foreign competitors, while with international dishes, we are more equal. I don't mean to push Norwegian food down people's throats. But the idea is that we can develop such Norwegian dishes, which sell fairly well, then that's a good thing. In addition, there are signals from the sales corps. They often ask why there aren't any more Norwegian products in the product range. Especially from peripheral areas of Norway, we tend to get such signals.

Marianne: I would assume that it is precisely in peripheral areas that you find consumers who'd rather cook such traditional dishes themselves, and are less ready to accept convenience foods?

Henrik: We've thought about that. That's why we deliberately do not launch *farikal* (a meat and cabbage stew) and *kjfittkaker* (meatballs). Instead, we try to make other things, like for instance *finnebiff*. I believe in that. And *rensdyrkaker* (reindeer meatballs). I don't know if that will work, whether people will want it. But if it works, it is something we might compete on. Norwegian casserole is another attempt: something which is Norwegian, but which is not prepared exactly like this in the households.

As Henrik strived to achieve a balance between foreign and domestic culinary traditions, several voices of interest could be identified. First of all there were the consumers, whose attitudes and interests were voiced directly through aggregate purchase behavior, through the success of competitors or indirectly through market research interpretations. When Henrik decided to introduce two new pasta varieties, he referred explicitly to consumers' preferences for Italian foods, as reflected in external market research surveys. In addition, his decision was in accordance with current sales figures.

Further, the popularity of Italian dishes could be explained in terms of the material advantages involved. Norwegian consumers generally perceived convenience foods to be expensive. In the marketing department, controlling the cost of production was therefore of key importance, and dishes made with inexpensive raw materials were at a definite advantage. Pasta, which is filling and inexpensive compared with meat, fulfills this requirement. As an additional quality, pasta is a culinary concept which may be varied endlessly, thus giving rise to a wide variety of different products (tortellini, spaghetti, lasagne, and so on). These features may partly explain the dominant emphasis of 'Italianness' in the Bon Appetit product range, and in convenience foods in general. This exemplifies how certain material characteristics of product components contribute to shaping the symbolic connotations of a product range.

Imagined Cuisines

But the popularity of pasta and other foreign food items may also be related to the way they mediate between the realms of culinary knowledge, food experience and imagination. In creating a new product, a product manager seeks to achieve a certain coherence between the material product (in terms of taste, texture, etc.) and the anticipations evoked by the product through name, appearance and visual design. Put more simply, there is an expectation among the consumers that the product should be what it claims to be. Such judgments of coherence are based upon knowledge and previous experience on the part of the consumer, and imply a shared cultural repertoire between producer and consumer. Almost intuitively, Henrik knew that *farikdl* was not going to work: *farikdl* is a dish which most Norwegian consumers are accustomed to preparing at home, and for which judgments of coherence are likely to be very precise. Norwegians 'know' what *fadrikal* should taste like. Hence, any deviation from the homemade variety (due to requirements of industrial production) is likely to be detected immediately and judged negatively. When it comes to foreign culinary concepts, however, knowledge among consumers is generally far more limited, their expectations are less precise, and they themselves are much less likely to be critical. Consequently, when creating new products based on foreign culinary concepts such as Chinese chop suey, the producer is, to a far greater extent, free to define the product in a way that suits the specific requirements and conditions of industrial mass production.

Many authors have argued that food provides a particularly suitable medium for representing 'the other,' making ethnic cuisine an excellent paradigm, or metaphor, for ethnicity itself.[6] However, such representations of the other are also locally constructed, as they tend to be influenced not so much by the 'others' they claim to represent as by cultural configurations of 'otherness' among the consumers they address. This is particularly salient in industrial food manufacturing and marketing.[7] Foreign ethnic cuisines, as they are expressed in modern manufacture, are therefore largely based upon local imagery of the other, and may be conceived as *imagined cuisines*.[8]

As we have seen, certain culinary formats such as pasta are particularly suitable for the requirements of low-cost mass production. In addition, a foreign cuisine which few consumers have first-hand knowledge of will easily lend itself to the technical requirements of mass manufacture. I suggest, therefore, that it is precisely the 'imagined-ness' of foreign cuisines which makes them suitable for industrial production. This applies especially to convenience foods, for which scepticism with regard to product quality is perhaps most enhanced.

Each time a locally defined image of the exotic is disseminated through a commercial food product on the Norwegian market, it will also contribute to a process of routinization. Through processes of routinization, elements that were previously exotic will eventually become familiar to consumers. This, in turn, may force product managers to search for other, still unspoiled, imagined cuisines in order to present their products as exotic, thus contributing to a constant acceleration of new culinary concepts offered to Norwegian consumers. These mechanisms, I contend, may account for the constant attempts in food marketing and manufacture at appropriating and launching foreign novelties, and contribute to what we may refer to as a *routinization of the exotic*.

Appropriation of exotic elements must, however, be balanced with some level *of familiarity* and of *significance*. Even though the appropriation of food from, for instance, New Guinea would imply an extreme degree of freedom on the part of the manufacturer to define the cuisine in a suitable—and potentially profitable—manner, this strategy was rarely pursued. The reason for this, I suggest, is that a place like New Guinea still fails to constitute the careful balance between foreign-ness and familiarity that is required for marketing purposes. Most importantly, New Guinea cannot be said to represent a significant 'other' for Norwegian consumers, in the way that, for instance, 'America' or 'Italy' does. Although all nations are 'foreign' in the strict sense of the term, only the latter two nations are familiar enough to be elaborated in the construction of imagined cuisines.

The extent to which a manufacturer's definition of a certain product influences consumers' concepts of an exotic cuisine depends, however, on whether or not the manufacturer is able to present the product as authentic. This ability, in turn, depends on the extent to which the product manager succeeds in choosing culinary elements that still retain a promise of something exotic or unique—that is, elements whose meanings are not yet eroded by the mechanisms of routinization.

The struggle to get the dishes right is, though, only half of a story, of which advertising constitutes the other half. While product development staff were busy with trials for new Bon Appetit products, an advertising agency at the other end of town worked hard to develop ideas for a TV commercial. As product manager, Henrik was in charge of both processes, and, as both responsibilities demanded a strong engagement on his part, his working days involved abrupt shifts of perspective, and required the ability to attend closely to different projects simultaneously. Most of the time, these processes went on independently of each other, but, as we shall see, there were also times when the problems on the product development side had direct relevance for the marketing activities.

Constructing a Testimonial: Fame and the Ordinary

About six months after the product launch, plans began for the first Bon Appetit TV commercial. Henrik had limited experience with TV commercials, and, as in the case of product development, he had to rely on the advice of experts, in this case advertising agencies and professional film producers. At the same time, as in the case of product development, he was the one who had the final word on any decision, and who would ultimately be held responsible for failure or success.

In the Brand Strategy, benefits of Bon Appetit were defined as a set of 'promises' that would be communicated to the consumer. 'Functional promises' included a wide selection of dishes and portion sizes, time saving, convenience and simplicity in the sense that the dishes would not require any skills to prepare. 'Emotional promises' were defined as an experience of a tasty meal, a healthy convenient food, and a meal that would provide more time for other activities. In addition, the product range would be slightly less expensive than main competitors.

In October 1991, shortly after our visit to ANUGA, Henrik received a storyboard for a Bon Appetit commercial from Viking Foods' long-term advertising partner, an agency called Publicity. A storyboard is an illustrated summary and a key preparatory tool in film production, which indicates the basic chronology of a film by means of shorts pieces of text and a series of visual images. Two films were planned at this stage, one with a male and the other with a female spokesperson. . .

It became clear that the main criterion for selecting a character was his or her appeal to the target group, a feature that was partly grounded on his or her assumed ability to evoke feelings of identification within the target group. . . . Furthermore, the person should not be too controversial. This was why a famous comedian, whose performances were often quite satirical, was discarded. In addition, the concept of ordinariness must not imply a publicly low profile: a musician, who had played with a very successful band, but still remained in the shadow of the front-figure of that band, was described as a person whom, in spite of his talents, 'nobody really knows,' and was dropped as a result. In other words, a certain level of fame was required. At the same time, there was a consistent tradeoff between fame and financial cost. Obviously, there were many celebrities who were more famous than the ones mentioned during the meeting whose charges would exceed the Viking Foods marketing budget.

One name after another had been brought up and then quickly dropped when someone mentioned a national broadcast program director called Kjell Gregers. For the first time, as the following summary of comments indicates, an appropriate candidate was in sight: 'He's known. He's ordinary. Not controversial. He's in *Se & Hør* [a celebrity magazine] almost every week. He gets a lot of attention. And he goes to all first night performance parties. It seems like he's on the way up. And besides, he just bought a new car. I read in an article that he was crazy about cars.' At this moment, the film director, Martin—a man in his mid-thirties—arrived, together with a younger female secretary. Instantly, Martin became the center of attention. Without any further introduction, he suggested a celebrity whom he considered to be the right male character for a Bon Appetit testimonial: his choice was Vidar Sande, a well-known racing driver from rural Norway, who was known both for his speed driving talent, and for his rough and outspoken behavior. It seemed as if the film director had made up his mind before entering the meeting, and he spent most of his presentation defending this choice. As he explained:

A lot of people like him. He may be a 'bully' and a reckless driver, but he's a good guy. And one can easily understand that he has little time for cooking. Things must happen fast. And he has a charming dialect. He is likely to appeal to the segment we are talking about. There's a lot to play upon, film-wise.

According to the film director, Sande had already agreed to participate. He had asked a price that was considered quite reasonable, and gradually, as Martin presented his arguments, a consensus was reached to contract Vidar Sande. Shortly afterwards, Anne left the room in order to call him and make an appointment. She returned a few minutes later, saying that he would be home in an hour.

The film director spent the rest of the time elaborating his concept. He wanted pictures of Sande returning to his home in the evening, flashbacks from his busy day, the sound of car tires against gravel, and Sande's voice all along. Now and then, he intended to interrupt this sequence by delicious pictures of raw food material.

Henrik expressed some worry that the film might introduce too many different sequences, but the director assured him that it would not. Towards the end of the film, the voice and image would be synchronized, and we would see Sande speaking right into the camera. Then there would be so-called pack shots, and a voice-over saying something about Viking Foods.

A week later, Henrik commented on the meeting this way:

Now, after a while, I'm starting to feel comfortable about these plans for using Vidar Sande. I was more sceptical at first about whether he had a kind of. . . nice and attractive appeal. But then, on the other hand, he might just appeal to the target group of slightly 'rough men' that we are thinking of, so then it's OK.

Henrik's last comment indicates the extent to which he differentiated between his own subjective likes and dislikes, and the assumed preferences of his target group. Clearly, his immediate personal reaction was replaced by a more objective judgment. But what did he look for in a spokesperson? Which characteristics of the potential candidates turned out to be decisive? The discussion prior to the arrival of the film director had given some clues. The spokesperson should be famous, and yet ordinary. Obviously, finding such as person was not an easy task, as fame tends to be based on some personal trait or activity that makes the person stand apart as different, unordinary. . . . Television is important in this respect. Due to frequent appearances on television, Gregers, a fairly 'ordinary' person had become publicly known. His fame was *not* based on any particular trait that made him stand apart, but was rather a function of frequent exposure. In this way, nationwide broadcasting provides possibilities for fame for persons who are *not* talented or outstanding in any particular way, and, in a sense, constructs a celebrity out of the person next door. Television thus helps produce celebrities in which the criteria of fame and 'ordinariness' are reconciled.[9]

While television provides an answer to the question of *how* fame and ordinariness may be reconciled, the question *why* still remains. More precisely, we may ask: why did the spokesperson have to be so ordinary?. . . Sande was famous for being a successful racing driver, although his popularity seemed to be related to his ordinary appeal. The fame of the spokeswoman, Maria Mortensen, was definitely based on her abilities as a singer; yet she left the impression of a person who was straightforward, 'natural' and unpretentious, thus contributing to a cultural image of an 'ordinary' Norwegian woman. In other words, the process of selecting a celebrity demonstrates the importance of ordinariness as the common denominator that is required.

This search for ordinariness may be analyzed in light of what Marianne Gullestad refers to as the typically Norwegian notion of equality as sameness. She writes: 'Because sameness (being alike) is a central value, it is problematic to demand prestige and recognition. Norwegians are no less interested in recognition than others, but for them an initiative to attain recognition must be inscribed in the ideal of sameness. Modesty is a virtue, and self-assertion is seen as bragging'.[10] Searching for a character who is famous, yet ordinary, may thus be interpreted as a way of ensuring recognition while at the same time under-communicating social difference. As mentioned above, one way of handling this delicate balance between public fame and ordinariness is through the use of a TV celebrity. But what about the situations in which fame stems from the demonstration of talent? When fame must be inscribed in the ideal of sameness, rendering any explicit claims for extraordinary talent somewhat illegitimate, how then is public popularity achieved?

Looking more closely at the racing driver and the female singer, we find that they share one important characteristic; namely, a direct way of expressing themselves which is readily conceptualized in Norwegian as natural (*naturlig*) or honest (*cerlig*). For the male character this is expressed through a rough and unpolished way of speaking (which also includes a rural dialect). For the female character, it is expressed more subtly through a nice and unpretentious image, which makes her similar to any girl next door. Hence, when Maria Mortensen comes off as ordinary and natural, what we see may be a certain avoidance of artificiality in social encounters that serves to substantiate an implicit claim of being herself; that is to say, of being authentic. Expressing naturalness and authenticity through their behavior, both these celebrities present their talents within a context of ordinariness. It seems reasonable to suggest that it was precisely this ability that made them both stand out as more popular than others who were equally talented, and thus also as preferred candidates for a testimonial. This interpretation is in accordance with Gullestad's assertion that the notion of being natural is a central cultural symbol in Norway: 'Artfulness and style are often experienced as unnatural and artificial and therefore as negative oppositions to the natural.'[11]. . .

Authenticity and the Consumers' Gaze

. . . as consumers, we may conceive products as more or less authentic representations of whatever they claim to portray, be it 'nature,' 'Italy' or typically 'Norwegian cuisine.' Particularly with regard to claims of foreign origin, we may observe that a wide range of products are, in fact, 'Italian'; yet at the same time we may decide that some of them are more 'Italian' than others. Thus, the competition in the market place is partly structured in terms of another contest in which different products are ranked according to their ability to represent authentically what they claim to represent.

Another significant dimension of Western modernity may be referred to as reflexive disengagement.[12] According to Taylor, the Cartesian notion of a disengaged subject

articulates one of the most important developments of the modern era, and has brought about: 'The growing ideal of a human agent who is able to remake himself by methodical and disciplined action. What this calls for is the ability to take an instrumental stance to one's given properties, desires, inclinations, tendencies, habits of thought, and feeling so that they can be *worked* on ... until one meets the desired specifications.'[13] Although Taylor refers to a reflexive disengagement in relation to the self, reflexive disengagement is also an apt description of the product manager's approach to products in the making. Contrary to what many consumers are led to believe, modern food products rarely exist prior to the production of their Brand Strategy. Although advertising may involve narratives that situate products historically and create an image of continuity through the use of traditional recipes or preparation methods, most products are constructed with a future consumer in mind. In other words, the material process of food manufacture is essentially open-ended, and guided by definitions of potential target groups. Thus, when food products appear in the grocery store, their symbolic and social meaning is literally baked into them.[14] Product managers are, of course, fully aware of this. They know that any successful brand product is the result of the effort to successfully create an image that appears as authentic: that is, a brand is thoroughly constructed and 'authentic' at the same time. The swiftness by which this apparent contradiction is handled by product managers may be interpreted as an expression of reflexive disengagement—of ways of being in the world that are firmly located within the condition described by Taylor as Western modernity.

However, the anticipation of consumers' gaze provides some restrictions. As we have seen, exotic food from New Guinea, or 'strange' food from more familiar places, such as *Deutsche Knodeln*, were *not* appropriated in the routinization of the exotic, in spite of their authentic and exotic potential. I suggest that this is because product managers knew that the 'authentic' is only valuable in so far as it is made comparable within a common format, and this common format is defined by the gaze of Norwegian consumers. Thus, when Henrik constructed the Bon Appetit product range, he acted in accordance with an immediate and general knowledge of Norwegian consumers. At the same time, he demonstrated that the quest for authenticity had its limits. It was precisely this awareness, and the disengaged instrumentality with which he selected certain properties, and discarded others, that enabled him to construct and market products that 'met the desired specifications.'

Being There; Between Models and Reality

The production of advertising is rarely a smooth process. While textbooks on marketing and advertising offer a range of rational models on how to proceed, the experience of marketing on a day-to-day basis leaves an impression of a process that is much more pragmatic and contingent upon a variety of exogenous factors. . . . I found it interesting, and slightly peculiar, when, during one of our very first meetings, a marketing director told me that I would probably find the process of decision-making in Viking Foods far more contingent than I had originally thought. Similar points were frequently made by product managers, often apologetically, as if they knew they were not always doing things 'right,' and expected me to discover this. Entering the field with little knowledge of marketing, I was clearly much less predisposed to judge their activities critically than my informants assumed. At the same, I learned that marketing is structured through a dialectic between practice and knowledge, or between the need to act pragmatically in relation to day-to-day decisions, and the need to justify such decisions in relation to a body of marketing knowledge which includes models and guidelines for action.

My interest as an anthropologist in this field is not the fact that ideal models do not correspond to everyday realities. Discontinuities between 'maps' and 'territories' are commonplace in ethnographic research and a trivial dimension of social life. However, the exact configurations of such discontinuities, and the ways in which people reflect upon them, differ markedly from one field to another. Thus, the anxiety expressed by my informants, and their frequent comparisons with an idealized model for action (usually drawn from marketing textbooks or seminar material) revealed a field of social practice that is highly self-conscious, reflexive, and struggling to come to terms with a state of professional uncertainty.[15] This finding could be a characteristic expression of a marketing department in a part of the world which, in relation to marketing and advertising, is after all in a marginal location. But it could also be a more general trait of the marketing and advertising professions. Anyhow, it is a finding that sharply contrasts with the image of marketing and advertising which is usually portrayed of—and by—the professions themselves in relation to the general public.

Ethnographic research is particularly well equipped to grasp such cultural idiosyncrasies. The fact of being there, and of meticulously tailing informants in and out of meetings, elevators, boardrooms and trade exhibitions, allows us to trace the shifting contexts in which people operate. Through the peculiar combination of the gaze of a distant observer and the emphatic mode of a partner or companion, the anthropologist acquires a sensitivity to the significance of such cultural discontinuities. In this way, the ethnographic approach to marketing and advertising enables us to compare these practices with other practices elsewhere, providing for the profession what is often the most valuable contribution: a view from the outside.

Notes

1. Viking Foods is a fictitious name, as are all other names of persons and products in this chapter.
2. *Deutsche Knodeln* are a kind of dumpling, typical of central European cuisine.
3. Target group analysis, May 1990.
4. A content analysis of Norwegian food adverts during the same period revealed that out of all product attributes referred to in the adverts, the correlation between terms referring to foreign origin and the term convenient was the strongest of all bivariate correlations (Lien 1995).
5. Spisevaneunders0kelsen' (The food habits survey), the Market and Media Institute (MMI) 1991/1992.
6. See, for instance, Van den Berghe (1984), Levenstein (1985), and Appadurai (1988).
7. For a more thorough discussion elaborating the case of frozen pizza, see Lien (2000).
8. The term 'imagined cuisines' is inspired by Benedict Anderson's (1983) concept of nations as 'imagined communities.'
9. These events took place about eight years before so-called 'reality' TV was introduced in Norway. With the emergence of 'reality' TV the production of celebrities out of ordinary persons is even more pronounced.
10. Gullestad (1992: 192).
11. Gullestad (1992: 206).
12. See, for instance, Taylor (1992) or Giddens (1991).
13. Taylor (1992: 99).
14. According to Hennion and Meadel (1989: 208) the production of advertising implies that: 'When the object appears at the end of the process, it already contains its market just as it has its technical components. It is just as aware of its own future consumer as of its manufacture.'
15. For a more thorough analysis, see Lien (1997).

Anthropology and Counterinsurgency: The Strange Story of their Curious Relationship

Montgomery McFate

Throughout this book, it has been taken for granted that we, as students of anthropology, would want to know about others and would want to better understand ourselves. This kind of enlightenment, we presume, would build bridges of understanding between diverse peoples and, in general, enrich the lives of all of us.

But, then, an article like this one comes along to remind us that anthropology was once the "handmaiden of imperialism," that some anthropologists have contributed to "the war effort" and have participated in counterinsurgency programs and that, used in the "right way," anthropology has something to contribute to a governmental power's struggle to "win the hearts and minds of the people."

If nothing else, it is an informative and provocative essay, making us think about such issues as "selling out," "compromising the science," and adhering to a code of ethics. Although the author makes a good case for incorporating anthropology into military culture, it is not so certain that anthropologists would want to go along.

Dr. Montgomery McFate received her Ph.D. in cultural anthropology from Yale University and a J.D. from Harvard Law School. Her Ph.D. dissertation focused on British counterinsurgency policy in Northern Ireland. She held an Everett Fellowship in Human Rights Watch Arms Project and a clinical internship on the United States Attorney's Office Organized Crime and Drug Enforcement Task Squad. Dr. McFate was also a litigation associate at the law firm of Baker & McKenzie in San Francisco, CA. She is currently an AAAS Defense Policy Fellow at the Office of Naval Research, where she is promoting the use of social science research in the national security area.

Dr. McFate is a member of the Council for Emerging National Security Affairs and has published in such journals as *Journal of Conflict Studies, Harvard Journal of International Law,* and *Peace and Conflict Studies.*

Key Concept: anthropology and foreign policy

Something mysterious is going on inside the U.S. Department of Defense (DOD). Over the past 2 years, senior leaders have been calling for something unusual and unexpected—cultural knowledge of the adversary. In July 2004, retired Major General Robert H. Scales, Jr., wrote an article for the Naval War College's Proceedings magazine that opposed the commonly held view within the U.S. military that success in war is best achieved by overwhelming technological advantage. Scales argues that the type of conflict we are now witnessing in Iraq requires "an exceptional ability to understand people, their culture, and their motivation."[1] In October 2004, Arthur Cebrowski, Director of the Office of Force Transformation, concluded that "knowledge of one's enemy and his culture and society may be more important than knowledge of his order of battle."[2] In November 2004, the Office of Naval Research and the Defense Advanced Research Projects Agency (DARPA) sponsored the Adversary Cultural Knowledge and National Security Conference, the first major DOD conference on the social sciences since 1962.

Why has cultural knowledge suddenly become such an imperative? Primarily because traditional methods of warfighting have proven inadequate in Iraq and Afghanistan. U.S. technology, training, and doctrine designed to counter the Soviet threat are not designed for low-intensity counterinsurgency operations where civilians mingle freely with combatants in complex urban terrain.

The major combat operations that toppled Saddam Hussein's regime were relatively simple because they required the U.S. military to do what it does best—conduct maneuver warfare in flat terrain using overwhelming firepower with air support. However, since the end of the "hot" phase of the war, coalition forces have been fighting a complex war against an enemy they do not understand. The insurgents' organizational structure is not military, but tribal. Their tactics are not conventional, but asymmetrical. Their weapons are not tanks and fighter planes, but improvised explosive devices (IEDs). They do not abide by the Geneva Conventions, nor do they appear to have any informal rules of engagement.

Countering the insurgency in Iraq requires cultural and social knowledge of the adversary. Yet, none of the elements of U.S. national power—diplomatic, military, intelligence, or economic—explicitly take adversary culture into account in the formation or execution of policy. This cultural knowledge gap has a simple cause—the almost total absence of anthropology within the national-security establishment.

Once called "the handmaiden of colonialism," anthropology has had a long, fruitful relationship with various elements of national power, which ended suddenly following the Vietnam War. The strange story of anthropology's birth as a warfighting discipline, and its sudden plunge into the abyss of postmodernism, is intertwined with the U.S. failure in Vietnam. The curious and conspicuous lack of anthropology in the national-security arena since the Vietnam War has had grave consequences for countering the insurgency in Iraq, particularly because political policy and military operations based on partial and incomplete cultural knowledge are often worse than none at all.

A Lack of Cultural Awareness

In a conflict between symmetric adversaries, where both are evenly matched and using similar technology, understanding the adversary's culture is largely irrelevant. The Cold War, for all its complexity, pitted two powers of European heritage against each other. In a counterinsurgency operation against a non-Western adversary, however, culture matters. U.S. Department of the Army Field Manual (FM) (interim) 3-07.22, Counterinsurgency Operations, defines insurgency as an "organized movement aimed at the overthrow of a constituted government through use of subversion and armed conflict. It is a protracted politico-military struggle designed to weaken government control and legitimacy while increasing insurgent control. Political power is the central issue in an insurgency [emphasis added]." Political considerations must therefore circumscribe military action as a fundamental matter of strategy. As British Field Marshall Gerald Templar explained in 1953, "The answer lies not in pouring more troops into the jungle, but rests in the hearts and minds of the ... people." Winning hearts and minds requires understanding the local culture.[3]

Aside from Special Forces, most U.S. soldiers are not trained to understand or operate in foreign cultures and societies. One U.S. Army captain in Iraq said, "I was never given classes on how to sit down with a sheik. . . . He is giving me the traditional dishdasha and the entire outfit of a sheik because he claims that I am a new sheik in town so I must be dressed as one. I don't know if he is trying to gain favor with me because he wants something [or if it is] something good or something bad." In fact, as soon as coalition forces toppled Saddam Hussein, they became de facto players in the Iraqi social system. The young captain had indeed become the new sheik in town and was being properly honored by his Iraqi host.[4]

As this example indicates, U.S. forces frequently do not know who their friends are, and just as often they do not know who their enemies are. A returning commander from the 3d Infantry Division observed: "I had perfect situational awareness. What I lacked was cultural awareness. I knew where every enemy tank was dug in on the outskirts of Tallil. Only problem was, my soldiers had to fight fanatics charging on foot or in pickups and firing AK-47s and RPGs [rocket-propelled grenades]. Great technical intelligence. Wrong enemy."[5]

While the consequences of a lack of cultural knowledge might be most apparent (or perhaps most deadly) in a counterinsurgency, a failure to understand foreign cultures has been a major contributing factor in multiple national-security and intelligence failures. In her 1962 study, Pearl Harbor. Warning and Decision, Roberta Wohlstetter demonstrated that although the U.S. Government picked up Japanese signals (including conversations, decoded cables, and ship movements), it failed to distinguish signals from noise—to understand which signals were meaningful—because it was unimaginable that the Japanese might do something as "irrational" as attacking the headquarters of the U.S. Pacific fleet.[6]

Such ethnocentrism (the inability to put aside one's own cultural attitudes and imagine the world from the perspective of a different group) is especially dangerous in a national-security context because it can distort strategic thinking and result in assumptions that the adversary will behave exactly as one might behave. India's nuclear tests on 11 and 13 May 1998 came as a complete surprise because of this type of "mirror-imaging" among CIA analysts. According to the internal investigation conducted by former Vice Chairman of the Joint Chiefs of Staff David Jeremiah, the real problem was an assumption by intelligence analysts and policymakers that the Indians would not test their nuclear weapons because Americans would not test nuclear weapons in similar circumstances. According to Jeremiah, "The intelligence and the policy communities had an underlying mind-set going into these tests that the B.J.R [Bharatiya Janata Party] would behave as we [would] behave."[7]

The United States suffers from a lack of cultural knowledge in its national-security establishment for two primary, interrelated reasons. First, anthropology is largely and conspicuously absent as a discipline within our national-security enterprise, especially within the intelligence community and DOD. Anthropology is a social science discipline whose primary object of study has traditionally been non-Western, tribal societies. The methodologies of anthropology include participant observation, fieldwork, and historical research. One of the central epistemological tenets of anthropology is cultural relativism—understanding other societies from within their own framework.

The primary task of anthropology has historically been translating knowledge gained in the "field" back to the West. While it might seem self-evident that such a perspective would be beneficial to the national-security establishment, only one of the national defense universities (which provide master's degree-level education to military personnel) currently has an anthropologist on its faculty. At West Point, which traditionally places a heavy emphasis on engineering, anthropology is disparagingly referred to by cadets as "nuts and huts." And, although political science is well represented as a discipline in senior policymaking circles, there has never been an anthropologist on the National Security Council.

The second and related reason for the current lack of cultural knowledge is the failure of the U.S. military to achieve anything resembling victory in Vietnam. Following the Vietnam War, the Joint Chiefs of Staff collectively put their heads in the sand and determined they would never fight an unconventional war again. From a purely military perspective, it was easier for them to focus on the threat of Soviet tanks rolling through the Fulda Gap, prompting a major European land war—a war they could easily fight using existing doctrine and technology and that would have a clear, unequivocal winner.[8]

The preference for the use of overwhelming force and clear campaign objectives was formalized in what has become known as the Weinberger doctrine. In a 1984 speech, Secretary of Defense Caspar Weinberger articulated six principles designed to ensure the Nation would never become involved in another Vietnam. By the mid-1980s, there was cause for concern: deployment of troops to El Salvador seemed likely and the involvement in Lebanon had proved disastrous following the bombing of the U.S. Marine barracks in Beirut. Responding to these events, Weinberger believed troops should be committed only if U.S. national interests were at stake; only in support of clearly defined political and military objectives; and only "with the clear intention of winning."[9]

In 1994, Chairman of the Joint Chiefs of Staff Colin Powell (formerly a military assistant to Weinberger) rearticulated the Weinberger doctrine's fundamental elements, placing a strong emphasis on the idea that force, when used, should be overwhelming and disproportionate to the force used by the enemy. The Powell-Weinberger doctrine institutionalized a preference for "major combat operations"—big wars—as a matter of national preference. Although the Powell-Weinberger doctrine was eroded during the Clinton years; during operations other than war in Haiti, Somali, and Bosnia; and during

the second Bush Administration's pre-emptive strikes in Afghanistan and Iraq, no alternative doctrine has emerged to take its place.[10]

We have no doctrine for "nationbuilding," which the military eschews as a responsibility because it is not covered by Title 10 of the U.S. Code, which outlines the responsibilities of the military as an element of national power. Field Manual 3-07, Stability Operations and Support Operations, was not finalized until February 2003, despite the fact the U.S. military was already deeply engaged in such operations in Iraq. Field Manual 3-07.22—meant to be a temporary document—is still primarily geared toward fighting an enemy engaged in Maoist revolutionary warfare, a type of insurgency that has little application to the situation in Iraq where multiple organizations are competing for multiple, confusing objectives.[11]

Since 1923, the core tenet of U.S. warfighting strategy has been that overwhelming force deployed against an equally powerful state will result in military victory. Yet in a counterinsurgency situation such as the one the United States currently faces in Iraq, "winning" through overwhelming force is often inapplicable as a concept, if not problematic as a goal. While negotiating in Hanoi a few days before Saigon fell, U.S. Army Colonel Harry Summers, Jr., said to a North Vietnamese colonel, "You know, you never defeated us on the battlefield." The Vietnamese colonel replied, "That may be so, but it is also irrelevant."[12] The same could be said of the conflict in Iraq.

Winning on the battlefield is irrelevant against an insurgent adversary because the struggle for power and legitimacy among competing factions has no purely military solution. Often, the application of overwhelming force has the negative, unintended effect of strengthening the insurgency by creating martyrs, increasing recruitment, and demonstrating the "brutality" of state forces.

The alternative approach to fighting insurgency, such as the British eventually adopted through trial and error in Northern Ireland, involves the following: A comprehensive plan to alleviate the political conditions behind the insurgency; civil-military cooperation; the application of minimum force; deep intelligence; and an acceptance of the protracted nature of the conflict. Deep cultural knowledge of the adversary is inherent to the British approach.[13]

Although cultural knowledge of the adversary matters in counterinsurgency, it has little importance in major combat operations. Because the Powell-Weinberger doctrine meant conventional, large-scale war was the only acceptable type of conflict, no discernable present or future need existed to develop doctrine and expertise in unconventional war, including counterinsurgency. Thus, there was no need to incorporate cultural knowledge into doctrine, training, or warfighting. Until now, that is.

On 21 October 2003, the House Armed Services Committee held a hearing to examine lessons learned from Operation Iraqi Freedom. Scales' testimony at the hearing prompted U.S. Representative "Ike" Skelton to write a letter to Secretary of Defense Donald Rumsfeld in which he said: "In simple terms, if we had better under-stood the Iraqi culture and mindset, our war plans would have been even better than they were, the plan for the postwar period and all of its challenges would have been far better, and we [would have been] better prepared for the 'long slog' ... to win the peace in Iraq."[14]

Even such DOD luminaries as Andrew Marshall, the mysterious director of the Pentagon's Office of Net Assessment, are now calling for "anthropology-level knowledge of a wide range of cultures" because such knowledge will prove essential to conducting future operations. Although senior U.S. Government officials such as Skelton are calling for "personnel in our civilian ranks who have cultural knowledge and understanding to inform the policy process," there are few anthropologists either available or willing to play in the same sandbox with the military.[15]

The Current State of the Discipline

Although anthropology is the only academic discipline that explicitly seeks to understand foreign cultures and societies, it is a marginal contributor to U.S. national-security policy at best and a punch line at worst. Over the past 30 years, as a result of anthropologists' individual career choices and the tendency toward reflexive self-crit-icism contained within the discipline itself, the discipline has become hermetically sealed within its Ivory Tower.

Unlike political science or economics, anthropology is primarily an academic discipline. The majority of newly minted anthropologists brutally compete for a limited number of underpaid university faculty appointments, and although there is an increasing demand from industry for applied anthropologists to advise on product design, marketing, and organizational culture, anthropologists still prefer to study the "exotic and useless," in the words of A.L. Kroeber.[16]

The retreat to the Ivory Tower is also a product of the deep isolationist tendencies within the discipline. Following the Vietnam War, it was fashionable among anthropologists to reject the discipline's historic ties to colonialism. Anthropologists began to reinvent their dis-cipline, as demonstrated by Kathleen Gough's 1968 arti-cle, "Anthropology. Child of Imperialism," followed by Dell Hymes' 1972 anthology, *Reinventing Anthropology,* and culminating in editor Talal Asad's *Anthropology and the Colonial Encounter.*[17]

Rejecting anthropology's status as the handmaiden of colonialism, anthropologists refused to "collaborate" with the powerful, instead vying to represent the interests of indigenous peoples engaged in neocolonial struggles. In the words of Gayatri Chakravorti Spivak, anthropologists would now speak for the "subaltern." Thus began a sys-tematic interrogation of the contemporary state of the dis-cipline as well as of the colonial circumstances from which it emerged. Armed with critical hermeneutics, frequently backed up by self-reflexive neo-Marxism, anthropology

began a brutal process of self-flagellation, to a degree almost unimaginable to anyone outside the discipline.[18]

The turn toward postmodernism within anthropology exacerbated the tendency toward self-flagellation, with the central goal being "the deconstruction of the central-ized, logocentric master narratives of European culture." This movement away from descriptive ethnography has produced some of the worst writing imaginable. For example, *Cultural Anthropology,* one of the most respected anthropology journals in the United States, commonly publishes such incomprehensible articles as "Recover-ing True Selves in the Electro-Spiritual Field of Universal Love" and "Material Consumers, Fabricating Subjects: Perplexity, Global Connectivity Discourses, and Transna-tional Feminist Research."[19]

Anthropologist Stephen Tyler recently took fourth place in the Bad Writing Contest with this selection from *Writing Culture,* a remarkable passage describ-ing postmodern ethnography: "It thus relativizes dis-course not just to form—that familiar perversion of the modernist; nor to authorial intention—that conceit of the romantics; nor to a foundational world beyond discourse—that desperate grasping for a separate real-ity of the mystic and scientist alike; nor even to history and ideology—those refuges of the hermeneuticist; nor even less to language—that hypostasized abstraction of the linguist; nor, ultimately, even to discourse—that Nietzschean playground of world-lost signifiers of the structuralist and grammatologist, but to all or none of these, for it is anarchic, though not for the sake of anar-chy, but because it refuses to become a fetishized object among objects—to be dismantled, compared, classified, and neutered in that parody of scientific scrutiny known as criticism."[20]

The Colonial Era

From the foregoing discussion, it might be tempting to conclude that anthropology is absent from the policy arena because it really is "exotic and useless." However, this was not always the case. Anthropology actually evolved as an intellectual tool to consolidate imperial power at the mar-gins of empire.

In Britain the development and growth of anthropol-ogy was deeply connected to colonial administration. As early as 1908, anthropologists began training admin-istrators of the Sudanese civil service. This relationship was quickly institutionalized: in 1921, the International Institute of African Languages and Cultures was estab-lished with financing from various colonial govern-ments, and Lord Lugard, the former governor of Nigeria, became head of its executive council. The organization's mission was based on Bronislaw Malinowski's article, "Practical Anthropology," which argued that anthropo-logical knowledge should be applied to solve the problems faced by colonial administrators, including those posed by "'savage law, economics, customs, and institutions."[21]

Anthropological knowledge was frequently useful, especially in understanding the power dynamics in traditional societies. In 1937, for example, the Royal Anthropological Institute's Standing Committee on Applied Anthropology noted that anthropological research would "indicate the persons who hold key positions in the community and whose influence it would be important to enlist on the side of projected reforms." In the words of Lord Hailey, anthropologists were indeed "of great assistance in providing Government with knowledge which must be the basis of administrative policy."[22]

Anthropology as a tool of empire was, however, not without its detractors. In 1951, Sir Philip E. Mitchell wrote: "Anthropologists busied themselves [with] all the minutiae of obscure trial and personal practices, especially if they were agreeably associated with sex or flavoured with obscenity. There resulted a large number of painstaking and often accurate records of interesting habits and practices, of such length that no one had time to read them and [which were] often, in any case, irrelevant. . . ."[23]

The World War I Era

After the classic age of empire came to a close, anthropologists and archeologists became key players in the new game in town—espionage. Their habits of wandering in remote areas and skill at observation proved to be quite useful to the government. Although a number of anthropologists worked as spies during World War I (including Arthur Carpenter, Thomas Gann, John Held, Samuel Lothrop, and Herbert Spinden), the most famous was Harvard-trained archaeologist Sylvanus Morley, who had discovered the ancient city of Naachtun and had directed the reconstruction of Chichen Itza while serving as head of the Carnegie Archaeological Program from 1914 to 1929. Morley, who was one of the most respected archeologists of the early 20th century, was also the "best secret agent the United States produced during World War I."[24]

In 1916, when German agents were allegedly attempting to establish a Central American base for submarine warfare, the Office of Naval Intelligence recruited Morley, who used archeological fieldwork as cover to traverse 2,000 miles of remote Central American coastline, enduring "ticks, mosquitoes, fleas, sand flies, saddle-sores, seasickness, bar running, indifferent grub, and sometimes no grub at all, rock-hard beds, infamous hostelries, and even earthquakes." While Morley and company found no German submarine bases, he did produce nearly 10,000 pages of intelligence reports documenting everything from navigable shoreline features to the economic impact of sisal production.[25]

Morley's activities were not well regarded by many anthropologists. On 20 December 1919, Franz Boas, the most well-known anthropologist in America, published a letter in *The Nation*, to the effect that Morley and others (although they were not named directly) "have prostituted science by using it as a cover for their activities as spies. A soldier whose business is murder as a fine art ... accept[s] the code of morality to which modern society still conforms. Not so the scientist. The very essence of his life is the service of truth."[26]

A German Jew by birth, Boas was an adamant pacifist and an outspoken critic of the war, writing multiple editorials and newspaper articles expressing his opinion that World War I was a war of imperialist aggression. (Ironically, many of Boas' students, including Margaret Mead and Ruth Benedict went on to work for the military in roles Boas would have, no doubt, questioned.)

For his public allegations against the unnamed anthropologists, the American Anthropological Association censured Boas in 1919. The criticism of Morley by his peers for his espionage activities and the resulting scuffle within the American Anthropological Association (AAA) foreshadowed the reemergence of the issue of covert anthropological support to the U.S. Government during the 1960s.

The World War II Era

During World War II, the role of anthropologists within the national-security arena was greatly expanded. Many anthropologists served in the Office of Strategic Services (OSS), the institutional predecessor to both the CIA and Special Forces. Anthropologists served in a research capacity and as operatives. Carleton Coon, a professor of anthropology at Harvard, trained Moroccan resistance groups in sabotage, fought in the battle of Kasserine Pass, and smuggled arms to French resistance groups in German-occupied Morocco. His book about life in the OSS, *A North Africa Story: The Anthropologist as OSS Agent*, contains a highly amusing account of developing an IED in the shape of a donkey dropping.[27]

Other anthropologists also saw direct action: British ethnologist Tom Harrisson parachuted into Borneo to train indigenous guerrillas to fight the Japanese. Cora Du Bois, who served as Chief of the Indonesia section in the OSS Research and Analysis Branch, became the head of the Southeast Asia Command in Ceylon, where she ran resistance movements in Southeast Asian countries under Japanese occupation. Du Bois received the Exceptional Civilian Service Award in 1945 for her work with the Free Thai underground movement.[28]

Perhaps the most famous anthropologist who served in the OSS was Gregory Bateson. Bateson, a British citizen, spent many years conducting ethnographic research in New Guinea, the results of which were published in 1936 as *Naven*. At the beginning of World War II, having failed to find a position with the British War Office, Bateson returned to the United States and was recruited by the OSS, where he served as a civilian member of a forward intelligence unit in the Arakan Mountains of Burma.[29]

In addition to intelligence analysis, Bateson designed and produced "black propaganda" radio broadcasts intended to undermine Japanese propaganda in the Pacific Theater. He found the work distasteful, however, because he believed that truth, especially the unpleasant truth, was healthy. Despite his misgivings about deceitful propaganda, Bateson was a willing and competent operative. In 1945, he volunteered to penetrate deep into enemy territory to attempt the rescue of three OSS agents who had escaped from their Japanese captors. For this service, Bateson was awarded the Pacific Campaign Service Ribbon.[30]

Bateson had remarkable strategic foresight concerning the effect of new technology on warfare. While in the Pacific Theater, he wrote to the legendary director of the OSS, "Wild Bill" Donovan, that the existence of the nuclear bomb would change the nature of conflict, forcing nations to engage in indirect methods of warfare. Bateson recommended to Donovan that the United States not rely on conventional forces for defense but to establish a third agency to employ clandestine operations, economic controls, and psychological pressures in the new warfare.[31] This organization is, of course, now known as the Central Intelligence Agency.

Later in his career, Bateson was allegedly involved with a number of experimental psychological warfare initiatives, including the CIA's Operation MK Ultra, which conducted mind-control research. It is generally accepted that Bateson "turned on" the Beat poet Allen Ginsberg to LSD at the Mental Research Institute, where Bateson was working on the causes of schizophrenia.[32]

Among anthropologists, Bateson is generally remembered not for his activities in the OSS, but as Mead's husband. In 1932, he met Mead in the remote Sepik River area of New Guinea. After conducting fieldwork together in New Guinea, Bateson and Mead coproduced ethnographic films and photodocumentation of Balinese kinesics.[33]

Like her husband, Mead was also involved in the war effort. In addition to producing pamphlets for the Office of War Information, she produced a study for the National Research Council on the cultural food habits of people from different national backgrounds in the United States. She also investigated food distribution as a method of maintaining morale during wartime in the United States. Along with Bateson and Geoffrey Gorer, Mead helped the OSS establish a psychological warfare training unit for the Far East.[34]

Like Bateson, Mead had reservations about the use of deceitful propaganda, believing that such methods have "terrible possibilities of backfiring." Mead's larger concern, however, was the "tremendous amount of resentment" against using anthropological insights during the war. In particular, she noted that using anthropologists to advise advisers is ineffective; to be useful, anthropologists must work directly with policymakers.[35]

In 1942, Mead published *And Keep Your Powder Dry*, a book on U.S. military culture. According to Mead, Americans see aggression as a response rather than a primary behavior; believe in the use of violence for altruistic, never for selfish purposes; and view organized conflict as a finite task to be completed. Once finished, Americans walk away and move on to the next task. William O. Beeman points

out that Mead's observations of U.S. national strategic character seem to be borne out by the current administration's characterization of the conflict in Iraq as a defensive war, prompted by the imminent threat of weapons of mass destruction ready for imminent use and undertaken for altruistic reasons, such as "bringing Democracy to Iraq," that would be short and limited in scope.[36]

In 1943, Benedict, Mead's long-time friend and collaborator, became the head (and initially the sole member) of the Basic Analysis Section of the Bureau of Overseas Intelligence of the Office of War Information (OWI), a position Benedict sought to use "to get policy makers to take into account different habits and customs of other parts of the world." While at OWI, Benedict coauthored The Races of Mankind, a government pamphlet which refuted the Nazi pseudo-theories of Aryan racial superiority. Conservative congressmen attacked the pamphlet as communist propaganda, and the publicity surrounding it led to the sale of 750,000 copies, its translation into seven languages, and the production of a musical version in New York City.[37]

Benedict also undertook research on Japanese personality and culture, the effect of which cannot be overstated. Near the end of the war, senior military leaders and U.S. President Franklin Delano Roosevelt were convinced the Japanese were "culturally incapable of surrender" and would fight to the last man. Benedict and other OWI anthropologists were asked to study the view of the emperor in Japanese society. The ensuing OWI position papers convinced Roosevelt to leave the emperor out of the conditions of surrender (rather than demanding unconditional surrender as he did of dictators Adolph Hitler and Benito Mussolini). Much of Benedict's research for OWI was published in 1946 as *The Chrysanthemum and the Sword*, considered by many as a classic ethnography of Japanese military culture, despite Benedict never having visited the country.[38]

Since fieldwork in the traditional sense was impossible during wartime, culture had to be studied remotely. The theoretical contribution of World War II anthropologists to the discipline is commonly known as "culture at a distance." Following the war, from 1947 to 1952, Mead, Benedict, and others established a research program at Columbia University. Working under contract to the U.S. Office of Naval Research, anthropologists developed techniques for evaluating cultural artifacts, such as immigrant and refugee testimonies, art, and travelers' accounts, to build up a picture of a particular culture.[39]

Most of the culture-at-a-distance studies were rooted in the premises of developmental psychology, such as that the so-called national character of any group of people could be traced to commonalities in psychological-development processes. While some of their conclusions now seem ridiculous (for example, Gorer's "swaddling hypothesis" to explain the bipolar swings in Russian culture from emotional repression to aggressive drinking), other research results were not only accurate but useful in a military context.[40]...

The Vietnam War

Anthropologists such as Gerald Hickey, who went to Vietnam as a University of Chicago graduate student and remained throughout the war as a researcher for the RAND Corporation, found that their deep knowledge of Vietnam (valuable for counterinsurgency) was frequently ignored by U.S. military leaders who increasingly adopted a conventional-war approach as the conflict progressed. Hickey's career raises a number of issues that even now plague anthropological research in a military context, such as the politics of research inside the beltway, the inability to change counterproductive policies, and backbiting by other anthropologists hostile to the military enterprise.

Hickey, who wrote *Village in Vietnam*, a classic ethnography of a southern Vietnamese lowland village, was recruited by RAND in 1961 to produce a study funded by DARPA. The study followed the newly established Strategic Hamlet Program that sought to consolidate governmental authority in pacified areas through a defense system and administrative reorganization at the village level. Central to the study was the question of how highland tribes could be encouraged to support the South Vietnamese Government.

Hickey's research indicated that the strategic hamlets might be successful if farmers saw evidence their communal labor and contribution of time, land, and building materials actually resulted in physical and economic security. Although Hickey's observations were probably correct, his views were often dismissed as too pacifistic.[41] When Hickey debriefed Marine General Victor Krulak, the general pounded his fist on his desk and said, "We are going to make the peasants do what's necessary for strategic hamlets to succeed!"[42] As Hickey noted, peasants have many methods of passive and active resistance, and force is often counterproductive as a motivator. Disliking the results of the study, the Pentagon pressured RAND to change the findings and, in the interest of impartial research, RAND refused. In the end, none of Hickey's findings were implemented, and the Strategic Hamlet Program was a failure.

In 1964, a major uprising of Montagnard highland tribal groups occurred under the banner of FULRO (The United Front for the Struggle of Oppressed Races). Although the Montagnards sided with the United States against the communist north and were supplied by (and fought alongside) U.S. troops, they violently opposed the South Vietnamese Government's efforts to control their region and assimilate the population.

Dealing with the revolt was a major imperative for the military and the South Vietnamese Government because the central highlands were of strategic importance and included the Ho Chi Minh Trail, which was the main North Vietnamese infiltration and supply route. Hickey, who had worked closely with the Montagnards for years, advised the senior commander of U.S. forces in Vietnam, General William Westmoreland, on the reasons for the rise of ethno-nationalism among the tribes and how to cope with the revolt. Hickey also successfully acted as an intermediary between highland leaders and the U.S. and South Vietnamese governments.[43]

As the war dragged on, Hickey became increasingly frustrated with the military-strategy viewpoint held by officers such as U.S. Army General William E. Depuy, who believed a war of attrition would defeat the communists. Hickey's view was that the war in Vietnam was a political struggle that could only be resolved in political terms, not through pure military force. As an anthropologist, he recognized that elements of Vietnam's own culture could be used to promote peace between the existing nationalist political parties, religious groups, and minorities—none of whom welcomed communist rule.

In a remarkable paper titled "Accommodation in South Vietnam: the Key to Sociopolitical Solidarity," Hickey explored the indigenous Vietnamese cultural concept of accommodation. While Taoist roots of the Vietnamese value system stressed individualism, in the Vietnamese worldview, accommodation was also necessary to restore harmony with the universe. In Washington, D.C., Hickey's views on accommodation were treated as heresy. In 1967, at the conclusion of Hickey's brief to a Pentagon audience, Richard Holbrooke said, "What you're saying, Gerry, is that we're not going to win a military victory in Vietnam." Because it did not conform to the prevailing view of the conflict, Hickey's message was promptly dismissed. Regardless of the improbability of a military victory, to U.S. leaders, "accommodation" meant "giving in," and that was not an acceptable alternative. In the end, the American solution to the conflict was the use of overwhelming force in the form of strategic bombing and the Accelerated Pacification Campaign, neither of which resulted in victory.[44]

For his "ethnographic studies," "contributions to the enhancement of U.S. Advisor/Vietnamese Counterpart relationship," and "presence and counsel during periods of attack by Viet Cong Forces and Montagnard uprisings," Hickey was awarded the medal for Distinguished Public Service by Secretary of Defense Robert McNamara. Despite his medal (or perhaps because of it), Hickey was not able to get an academic job when he returned to the United States. He was refused a position at the University of Chicago by fellow anthropologists who objected to his association with RAND. Ironically, Hickey was also forced out of RAND because it was no longer interested in counterinsurgency. Following the lead of the Joint Chiefs of Staff, RAND was no longer going to undertake research on unconventional warfare, but turn its attention to "longer-range problems of tactical, limited war and deterrence under the Nixon Doctrine."[45]

Project Camelot

Testifying before the U.S. Congress in 1965, R.L. Sproul, director of DARPA said: "It is [our] primary thesis that remote area warfare is controlled in a major way by the environment in which the warfare occurs, by the sociological and anthropological characteristics of the people involved in the war, and by the nature of the conflict itself."[46]

The recognition within DOD that research and development efforts to support counterinsurgency operations must be oriented toward the local human terrain led to the establishment of the Special Operations Research Office (SORO) at the American University in Washington, D.C. With anthropologists and other social scientists on staff, SORO functioned as a research center into the human dimension of counterinsurgency. Many SORO reports took a unique approach. In 1964, the Army commissioned an unusual paper titled "Witchcraft, Sorcery, Magic, and Other Psychological Phenomena, and Their Implications on Military and Paramilitary Operations in the Congo." Authored by James R. Price and Paul Jureidini, the report is a treatise on paranormal combat, discussing "counter-magic" tactics to suppress rebels who are backed by witch doctors, charms, and magic potions.[47]

In 1964, SORO also designed the infamous Project Camelot. According to a letter from the Office of the Director of the Special Operations Research Office, Project Camelot was "a study whose objective [was] to determine the feasibility of developing a general social systems model which would make it possible to predict and influence politically significant aspects of social change in the developing nations of the world." The project's objectives were "to devise procedures for assessing the potential for internal war within national societies; to identify with increased degrees of confidence those actions which a government might take to relieve conditions which are assessed as giving rise to a potential for internal war; [and] to assess the feasibility of prescribing the characteristics of a system for obtaining and using the essential information needed for doing the above two things."[48]

Project Camelot, which was initiated during a time when the military took counterinsurgency seriously as an area of competency, recognized the need for social science insights. According to the director's letter: "Within the Army there is especially ready acceptance of the need to improve the general understanding of the processes of social change if the Army is to discharge its responsibilities in the overall counterinsurgency program of the U.S. Government."[49]

Chile was to be the first case study for Project Camelot. Norwegian sociologist Johan Galtung was invited to design a seminar for Project Camelot. Although he refused, he shared information about the project with colleagues. Meanwhile, Hugo Nuttini, who taught anthropology at the University of Pittsburgh, accepted an assignment for Project Camelot in Chile. While there, he concealed Camelot's military origin, but word leaked out. Protests arose from Chile's newspapers and legislature and the Chilean Government lodged a diplomatic protest with the U.S. Ambassador. In Washington, D.C., following congressional hearings on the subject, McNamara canceled Project Camelot in 1965.

The Thai Scandal

Shortly after the Project Camelot scandal, the issue of clandestine research surfaced again in Thailand. In March 1970, documents that appeared to implicate social scientists in U.S. counterinsurgency programs in Thailand were stolen from a university professor's file cabinet. The documents were given to the Student Mobilization Committee to End the War in Vietnam and were subsequently published in The Student Mobilizer. A number of anthropologists and other social scientists were allegedly gathering data for DOD and the Royal Thai Government to support a counterinsurgency program that would use development aid to encourage tribal villages to remain loyal to the Thai Government rather than joining the insurgents. Although anthropologists claimed to have been using their expertise to prevent Thai villages from being harmed, heated debates took place within the AAA's Committee on Ethics.[50]

As a result of Project Camelot and the Thai scandal, government funding and use of social science research became suspect. Anthropologists feared that, were such research to continue, the indigenous people they studied would assume they were all spies, closing off future field opportunities abroad. Many anthropologists also believed the information would be used to control, enslave, and even annihilate many of the communities studied. The result of these debates is the determination that for anthropologists to give secret briefings is ethically unacceptable. The AAA's current "Statement of Professional Responsibility" says: "Anthropologists should undertake no secret research or any research whose results cannot be freely derived and publicly reported.... No secret research, no secret reports or debriefings of any kind should be agreed to or given." These guidelines reflect a widespread view among anthropologists that any research undertaken for the military is de facto evil and ethically unacceptable.[51]

The Perils of Incomplete Knowledge

DOD yearns for cultural knowledge, but anthropologists en masse, bound by their own ethical code and sunk in a mire of postmodernism, are unlikely to contribute much of value to reshaping national security policy or practice. Yet, if anthropologists remain disengaged, who will provide the relevant subject matter expertise? As Anna Simons, an anthropologist who teaches at the Naval Postgraduate School, points out: "If anthropologists want to put their heads in the sand and not assist, then who will the military, the CIA, and other agencies turn to for information? They'll turn to people who will give them the kind of information that should make anthropologists want to rip their hair out because the information won't be nearly as directly connected to what's going on on the local landscape."[52]

Regardless of whether anthropologists decide to enter the national-security arena, cultural information will inevitably be used as the basis of military operations and public policy. And, if anthropologists refuse to contribute, how reliable will that information be? The result of using incomplete "bad" anthropology is, invariably, failed operations and failed policy. In a May 2004 *New Yorker* article, "The Gray Zone: How a Secret Pentagon Program Came to Abu Ghraib," Seymour Hersh notes that Raphael Patai's 1973 study of Arab culture and psychology, *The Arab Mind*, was the basis of the military's understanding of the psychological vulnerabilities of Arabs, particularly to sexual shame and humiliation.[53]

Patai says: "The segregation of the sexes, the veiling of the women ..., and all the other minute rules that govern and restrict contact between men and women, have the effect of making sex a prime mental preoccupation in the Arab world." Apparently, the goal of photographing the sexual humiliation was to blackmail Iraqi victims into becoming informants against the insurgency. To prevent the dissemination of photos to family and friends, it was believed Iraqi men would do almost anything.[54]

As Bernard Brodie said of the French Army in 1914, "This was neither the first nor the last time that bad anthropology contributed to bad strategy." Using sexual humiliation to blackmail Iraqi men into becoming informants could never have worked as a strategy since it only destroys honor, and for Iraqis, lost honor requires its restoration through the appeasement of blood. This concept is well developed in Iraqi culture, and there is even a specific Arabic word for it: *al-sharaf,* upholding one's manly honor. The alleged use of Patai's book as the basis of the psychological torment at Abu Ghraib, devoid of any understanding of the broader context of Iraqi culture, demonstrates the folly of using decontextualized culture as the basis of policy.[55]

Successful counterinsurgency depends on attaining a holistic, total understanding of local culture. This cultural understanding must be thorough and deep if it is to have any practical benefit at all. This fact is not lost on the Army. In the language of interim FM 3-07.22: "The center of gravity in counterinsurgency operations is the population. Therefore, understanding the local society and gaining its support is critical to success. For U.S. forces to operate effectively among a local population and gain and maintain their support, it is important to develop a thorough understanding of the society and its culture, including its history, tribal/family/social structure, values, religions, customs, and needs."[56]

To defeat the insurgency in Iraq, U.S. and coalition forces must recognize and exploit the underlying tribal structure of the country; the power wielded by traditional authority figures; the use of Islam as a political ideology; the competing interests of the Shia, the Sunni, and the Kurds; the psychological effects of totalitarianism; and the divide between urban and rural, among other things. Interim FM 3-07.22 continues: "Understanding and working within the social fabric of a local area is initially

the most influential factor in the conduct of counterinsurgency operations. Unfortunately, this is often the factor most neglected by U.S. forces."[57]

And, unfortunately, anthropologists, whose assistance is urgently needed in time of war, entirely neglect U.S. forces. Despite the fact that military applications of cultural knowledge might be distasteful to ethically inclined anthropologists, their assistance is necessary.

Notes

1. MG Robert H. Scales, Jr., "Culture-Centric Warfare," *Proceedings* (October 2004).
2. Megan Scully, "'Social Intel' New Tool For U.S. Military," *Defense News*, 26 April 2004, 21.
3. U.S. Department of the Army Field Manual (FM) (Interim) 3-07.22, Counterinsurgency Operations (Washington, DC: U.S. Government Printing Office [GPO], 1 October 2004), sec. 1-1; David Charters, "From Palestine to Northern Ireland: British Adaptation to Low-Intensity Operations," in *Armies in Low-Intensity Conflict: A Comparative Analysis*, eds., D. Charters and M. Tugwell (London: Brassey's Defence Publishers, 1989), 195.
4. Leonard Wong, "Developing Adaptive Leaders: The Crucible Experience of Operation Iraqi Freedom," Strategic Studies Institute, U.S. Army War College, Carlisle Barracks, Pennsylvania, July 2004, 14.
5. Scales, "Army Transformation: Implications for the Future," testimony before the House Armed Services Committee, Washington, D.C., 15 July 2004.
6. Roberta Wohlstetter, *Pearl Harbor: Warning and Decision* (California: Stanford University Press, 1962).
7. Jeffrey Goldberg, "The Unknown: The C.I.A. and the Pentagon take another look at Al Qaeda and Iraq," *The New Yorker,* 10 February 2003.
8. See Max Boot, *The Savage Wars of Peace: Small Wars and the Rise of American Power* (New York: Basic Books, 2003).
9. Casper W. Weinberger, "The Uses of Military Power," speech at the National Press Club, Washington, D.C., 28 November 1984.
10. Jeffrey Record, "Weinberger-Powell Doctrine Doesn't Cut It," *Proceedings* (October 2000) The Powell doctrine also "translates into a powerful reluctance to engage in decisive combat, or to even risk combat, and an inordinate emphasis at every level of command on force protection." Stan Goff, "Full-Spectrum Entropy: Special Operations in a Special Period," Freedom Road Magazine, on-line at <www.freedom.road.org/fr/03/english/07_entropy.html>, accessed 18 February 2005.
11. U.S. Code, Title 10, "Armed Forces," on-line at <www.access.gpo.gov/uscode/title10/title10.html>, accessed 18 February 2005; FM 3-07, Stability Operations and Support Operations (Washington, DC: GPO, February, 2003); FM 3-07.22, Interim.
12. The 1923 Field Service Regulations postulate that the ultimate objective of all military operations is the destruction of the enemy's armed forces and that decisive results are obtained only by the offensive. The Regulations state that the Army must prepare to tight against an "opponent organized for war on modern principles and equipped with all the means of modern warfare. . . ." The preference for

use of offensive force is found continuously in U.S. military thought, most recently in FM 3-0, Operations (Washington, DC: GPO, 2001), which says: "The doctrine holds warfighting as the Army's primary focus and recognizes that the ability of Army forces to dominate land warfare also provide the ability to dominate any situation in military operations other than war"; Richard Darilek and David Johnson, "Occupation of Hostile Territory: History, Theory, Doctrine; Past and Future Practice, "conference presentation, Future Warfare Seminar V. Carlisle, Pennsylvania, 18 January 2005; Peter Grier, "Should US Fight War in Bosnia? Question Opens an Old Debate," *Christian Science Monitor,* 14 September 1992, 9.

13. For a full discussion of British principles of counterinsurgency, see Thomas Mockaitis, *British Counterinsurgency, 1919–1960* (New York: St. Martin's Press, 1990); Ian Beckett and John Pimlott, eds., *Armed Forces and Modern Counter-Insurgency* (London: Croom Helm, 1985).

14. Office of Congressman Ike Skelton, "Skelton Urges Rumsfeld To Improve Cultural Awareness Training," press release, 23 October 2003, on-line at <www.house.gov/skelton/pr031023.html>, accessed 18 February 2005.

15. Jeremy Feller, "Marshall. U.S. Needs To Sustain Long-Distance Power Projection," *Inside The Pentagon,* 4 March 2004, 15.

16. A.L. Kroeber, "The History of the Personality of Anthropology," *American Anthropologist* 61 (1959).

17. Kathleen Gough, "Anthropology: Child of Imperialism," *Monthly Review* 19, 11 (April 1968); Dell Hymes, ed., *Reinventing Anthropology* (New York: Random House, 1972); Talal Asad, ed., *Anthropology and the Colonial Encounter* (London: Ithaca Press, 1973).

18. Gayatri Chakravorty Spivak, "Can the Subaltem Speak?" in *Marxism and the Interpretation of Culture,* eds., Cary Nelson and Larry Grossberg (Chicago: University of Illinois Press, 1988).

19. Bill Ashcroft, Gareth Griffiths, and Helen Tiffin, eds., *The Post-Colonial Studies Reader* (London: Routledge, 1995), 117; Pazderic Nickola, "Recovering True Selves in the Electro-Spiritual of Universal Love," *Cultural Anthropology* 19, 2 (2003); Priti Ramamurthy, "Material Consumers, Fabricating Subjects: Perplexity, Global Connectivity Discourses, and Transnational Feminist Research." *Cultural Anthropology* 18, 4 (2003).

20. Stephen A Tyler "Post-modern Ethnography: From Document of the Occult to Occult Document," in *Writing Culture: The Poetics and Politics of Ethnography,* eds., James Clifford and George E. Marcus (Berkeley: University of California Press, 1986), 122-40. Sadly, the Bad Writing Contest, sponsored by *The Journal of Philosophy and Literature,* is defunct.

21. Stephan Feuchtwang, "The Discipline and its Sponsors," in Asad, *Anthropology and the Colonial Encounter,* 82; Bronislaw Malinowski, "Practical Anthropology," *Africa,* 2 (1929), 22–23.

22. Feuchtwang, "The Discipline and its Sponsors," 84, 85.

23. Philip E Mitchell, "Review of Native Administration in the British Territories in Africa," *Journal of African Administration* 3 (1951): 56–57.

24. Sylvanus G. Morley wrote a number of classic archeological texts including *The Ancient Maya* (California: Stanford University Press, 1946) and *An Introduction to the Study of Maya Hieroglyphs* (Washington, DC: The Smithsonian, 1915);

25. Charles H. Harris and Louis R. Sadler, *The Archaeologist was a Spy.* Sylvanus G. Morley and the Office of Naval Intelligence (Albuquerque: University of New Mexico Press, 2003).

25. Harris and Sadler.

26. Franz Boas, "Scientists as Spies," *The Nation* 109 (20 December 1919): 797.

27. Carleton Coon, *A North Africa Story.* The Anthropologist as OSS Agent 1941–1943 (Ipswich, MA: Gambit, 1980).

28. Chris Bunting, "I Spy with My Science Eye," *Times Higher Education Supplement,* 12 April 2002; Cora Du Bois Obituary, *Chicago Tribune,* 14 April 1991; E. Bruce Reynolds, *Thailand's Secret War: The Free Thai, OSS, and SOE during World War II* (United Kingdom: Cambridge University Press, 2005).

29. Gregory Bateson, *Naven* (California: Stanford University Press, 1936).

30. Carleton Mabee, "Margaret Mead and Behavioral Scientists in World War II: Problems in Responsibility, Truth, and Effectiveness," *Journal of the History of Behavioral Sciences* 23, 1 (23 January 1987): 7; David H Price, "Gregory Bateson and the OSS: World War II and Bateson's Assessment of Applied Anthropology" *Human Organization* 57, 4 (Winter 1998): 3794–84.

31. Arthur 8. Darling, The Birth of Central Intelligence, Sherman Kent Center for the Study of Intelligence, on-line at <www.cia.gov/csi/kent_csi/docs/v10i2a01p_0001.htm>, accessed 18 February 2005.

32. Conspiracy theories abound concerning Bateson's involvement with MK-Ultra. See, for example, Colin A Ross, *Bluebird. Deliberate Creation of Multiple Personality by Psychiatrists* (Richardson, TX: Manitou Communications, 2000). See also on-line at <www.phinnweb.com/livingroom/rosemary/>, accessed 18 February 2005; John Marks, *The Search for the Manchurian Candidate* (New York: New York Times Books, 1979). Bateson invented the "Double Blind" theory of schizophrenia See Bateson, "Cultural problems posed by a study of schizophrenic process," in *Schizophrenia, an Integrated Approach,* ed, A. Auerbach (New York: Ronald Press, 1959).

33. See Margaret Mead and Gregory Bateson, *Balinese Character: A Photographic Analysis* (New York: New York Academy of Sciences Press, 1942).

34. Mead, "Anthropological Contribution to National Policies during and Immediately after World War II," in *The Uses of Anthropology,* ed., Walter Goldschmidt (Washington, DC: American Anthropological Association, 1979), 145–57; Mabee, 8.

35. Mabee, 8, 5.

36. Mead, *And Keep Your Powder Dry. An Anthropologist Looks at America* (New York: Morrow, 1942); William O. Beeman, "Postscript to September 11—What Would Margaret Mead Say?" The Institute for Intercultural Studies, on-line at <www.mead 2001.org/beeman.html>, accessed 18 February 2005.

37. Linda Rapp, "Benedict, Ruth (1887-1948)," *GLBTQ: An Encyclopedia of Gay, Lesbian, Bisexual Transgender, and Queer Culture* (Chicago: glbtq, Inc., 2004); Cora Sol Goldstein, "Ideological Constraints and the American Response to Soviet Propaganda in Europe: The Case of Race," paper presented at the Conference of Europeanists, Chicago, Illinois, March 2004.

38. David H. Price, "Lessons From Second World War Anthropology: Peripheral, Persuasive and Ignored Contributions" *Anthropology Today* 18, 3 (June 2002): 181 Ruth Benedict, *The*

Chrysanthemum and the Sword: Patterns of Japanese Culture (New York: Houghton Mifflin, 1946).

39. Beeman, "Introduction: Margaret Mead, Cultural Studies, and International Understanding," in *The Study of Culture at a Distance*, eds., Margaret Mead and Rhoda Métraux (New York: Berghahn Books, 2000).

40. Geoffrey Gofer and John Rickman, *The People of Great Russia* (London: Groset, 1949); Roberta LeVine, "Culture and Personality Studies, 1918-1960: Myth and History," *Journal of Personality* 69, 6 (December 2001).

41. Gerald Hickey, *Village in Vietnam* (New Haven: Yale University Press, 1964).

42. Hickey, *Window on a War: An Anthropologist in the Vietnam Conflict* (Lubbock: Texas Tech University Press, 2002), 99–101.

43. Ibid., Window, 149–82.

44. Hickey, "Accommodation in South Vietnam: The Key to Sociopolitical Solidarity," RAND Corporation, 1967; Hickey, Window, 199–201.

45. Ibid., Window, 313.

46. Eric Wakin, *Anthropology Goes to War: Professional Ethics and Counterinsurgency in Thailand* (Madison: University of Wisconsin Press, 1992), 85.

47. In general, see Ron Robin, *The Making of the Cold War Enemy. Culture and Politics in the Military-Intellectual Complex* (New Jersey: Princeton University Press, 2001); James R. Price and Paul Jureidini, "Witchcraft, Sorcery, Magic, and Other Psychological Phenomena, and Their Implications on Military and Paramilitary Operations in the Congo," Special Operations Research Office, SORO/CINFAC/6-64, 8 August 1964, online at <www.ksinc.net/~devilsad/psyops5.htm>, accessed 18 February 2005.

48. Irving Louis Horowitz, ed, *The Rise and Fall of Project Camelot: Studies in the Relationship Between Social Science and Practical Politics* (Cambridge, MA: MIT Press, 1967), 47–49.

49. Ibid.

50. Eric R. Wolf and Joseph G. Jorgensen, "Anthropology on the Warpath in Thailand," *New York Review of Books*, 19 November 1970, 26-35.

51. Council of the American Anthropological Association (AAA), "Statement on Ethics: Principles of Professional Responsibility," adopted by the AAA, May 1971 (as amended through November 1986), on-line at <www.aaanet.org/stmts/ethstmnt.htm>, accessed 18 February 2005.

52. Renee Montagne, "Interview: Anna Simons and Catherine Lutz on the involvement of anthropologists in war," National Public Radio's Morning Edition, 14 August 2002.

53. Raphael Patai in Seymour M. Hersh, "The Gray Zone How a secret Pentagon program came to Abu Ghraib," *The New Yorker*, 24 May 2004; Patai, *The Arab Mind* (Now York: Scribner's 1973).

54. Patai.

55. Bernard Brodie, *Strategy in the Missile Age* (New Jersey: Princeton University Press, 1959), 52.

56. Amatzia Baram, "Victory in Iraq, One Tribe at a Time," *New York Times,* 28 October 2003; FM (Interim) 3-07.22, sec 4–11.

57. FM (Interim) 3-07.22, sec. 4–11.

Gardening Tips

Lee Cronk

In this essay, excerpted from the last chapter of Lee Cronk's book, *That Complex Whole: Culture and the Evolution of Human Behavior*, the author deals with the uses and misuses of a very important anthropological concept: *cultural relativity*. This is the notion that the best way to understand people's behavior is to consider it from the perspective of the people being studied rather than from the point of view of one's own culture.

As Lee Cronk points out, however, holding to the principle of cultural relativity does not necessarily lead to an "anything goes" approval of what happens in another society, just because it is part of someone's way of life. After all, the mission of anthropology is to *explain* behavior, not to justify it—to describe what "is," not to specify what "ought" to be.

Human beings—anthropologists included—should not sit idly by while atrocities are committed elsewhere in the world, any more than they should tolerate such actions in their own society. It is possible, says, Cronk, to deplore a particular action without indicting the whole culture. If so, what is the source of such a moral code? If it is derived from one's own culture, one would be guilty of *ethnocentrism*, blindly condemning other people's behavior because it does not conform to one's own standards.

Lee Cronk draws the line at human suffering or—to put it more positively—human well-being which, for him, becomes the standard for a universal moral code. This is a position that we might hold, not as reasoning anthropologists, but as caring human beings.

Lee Cronk received his Ph.D. in anthropology at Northwestern University in 1989. He has done ethnographic fieldwork among the Mukogodo of Kenya and taught at Texas A&M Univesity from 1995-1999. He is now a professor of anthropology at Rutgers University, where he is the Graduate Program Director. His primary interests are in human evolutionary ecology, human behavioral ecology, and generally bridging the gap between cultural anthropology and evolutionary anthropology.

Key Concept: cultural relativity and ethnocentrism

The final chapter is where, by tradition, the author attempts to demonstrate how all that went before can solve social problems, improve morality, make one a more effective competitor, or in some other manner contribute to making life better for us all. Now that we have a framework for understanding the evolution of the human mind and of culture, are we better off? Do we have the basis for a science of social engineering?

—Jerome Barkow[1]

"Social engineering" is an ugly and frightening phrase to many people, but, like so many of the ideas discussed in this book, it is only a metaphor. "Social gardening" would be every bit as apt a way to describe the efforts of people to alter, in big and little ways, their behavior, the behavior of others, and the institutional frameworks in which they all live. Even those of us who prefer the decentralized, naturalistic, bottoms-up approach of an English-style social garden to the rigid lines and neatly trimmed hedges of the French style are still advocating a type of gardening, at a minimum, a set of policies favoring some sorts of behaviors and social arrangements over others. Although as a scientist I am a strong advocate of knowledge for its own sake, I also recognize that for many people this is not enough. For them, science must justify itself not just in terms of the intellectual satisfaction it provides scientists, but by the practical benefits it provides everyone else.

Tolerating the Intolerable

Let's begin by looking at the practical benefits provided by one alternative: cultural determinism. What practical good has the average person received from the doctrine that culture is the only significant influence on human behavior? It can be argued, with some justification, that when the culturalist approach was new it was a key element in the argument against racism in particular and against the broader idea that biology is destiny. In the intellectual milieu of the early twentieth century, it was a major step forward. Nativist and racist doctrines of the inherent superiority of Whites in general, and of northern Europeans in particular, were rampant and were fueled in the United States by alarm over growing rates of immigration mainly from Eastern and Southern Europe. In response to arguments that such immigrants were watering down America's good Anglo-Saxon stock, Franz Boas, the founder of academic anthropology in the United States, conducted a key piece of research, showing that although immigrants' physical forms, particularly the shapes of their heads, may have varied from the American average on arrival, their children's bodies and head shapes showed a definite shift toward the American pattern.[2] Not only was biology not destiny as far as behavior was concerned, in this case it was not even destiny for the development of the human body!

Research such as this, along with ethnographies that revealed the wisdom and logic behind the customs of culturally different peoples, set the stage for the tremendous advances in race relations, such as the desegregation of schools and armed forces, that followed World War II, as well as for the widespread interest in cultural diversity that has bloomed in the late twentieth century. As an anthropologist and as a citizen of the world, I consider these accomplishments to be enormous and, I hope, pivotal in human history. Before the development of the culture concept, only two explanations were given for the behavior of people different from oneself: ignorance or stupidity. The first left open the possibility that these others could be taught the "correct" way to behave; the second did not. It is a privilege to be part of the discipline that made such explanations unacceptable.

Perhaps because the doctrine of cultural relativism has had such an admirable history in terms of its influence on our social lives, there has been a tendency in recent years to take it a bit too far, to allow an idea that began simply as the scientist's disinterested detachment from his subject to slide into moral relativism. College students in particular tend to be relativistic and tolerant to a fault. When I have raised the issue of cultural relativism in my own classes, some students—students with otherwise mainstream political and moral opinions—have earnestly used the idea of "culture" to exonerate the efforts of the Nazis to exterminate European Jewry. "It's *their* culture, so who are *we* to judge it?" is the reasoning offered, implicitly putting the Holocaust on the same moral level as eating bratwurst.

The same sort of radical relativism has stymied. . . African women who have sought asylum in the United States because of the threat and promise of female circumcision in their homelands. Although the practice of female circumcision is becoming more widely known in the West, most people in our society are not clear on what it entails. The name is really a euphemism. To call it "circumcision" is to call what Lorena Bobbit did to her husband John

"circumcision."[3] While the male operation involves only the removal of the foreskin, the female operation is usually much more drastic. While in some societies it involves only a ceremonial knick of the hood covering the clitoris, in most cases it involves anything ranging from removal of the clitoris to removal of the clitoris and some or all of the labia minora, to removal of the clitoris and labia minora and sewing up the opening, leaving only a small passage for menstrual blood and urine. In some societies it is performed on babies and young girls, while others, including the Mukogodo and other Maasai-speakers, wait until a girl has had her first menses. It is a common practice in some parts of Africa and the Middle East, though even in the West removal of the clitoris was used by a few physicians in the nineteenth century to control women thought to have an excessive interest in sex.[4] My wife, Beth Leech, is one of the few Westerners to have seen a female circumcision. Here are her field notes, reproduced here with only minor editing to preserve the privacy of those mentioned, from the first of two circumcisions she witnessed in 1986, one that involved a girl from an ethnic group neighboring the Mukogodo who was preparing to marry a man from yet another neighboring group:

Arrived at the settlement just before 6:00 A.M. Still dark out. Stood at gate and a girl saw me, greeted me, and asked me why I was there. I told her for the circumcision, so she said, "Let's go" and led me through the settlement to her mother's house. Outside the house, dressed in a white cloak, was Natito, her head freshly shaved. With her was a girl about her age dressed in a school uniform. Natito asked if I had brought a knife. I didn't understand except literally, so said quizzically, "You want a knife? No, I don't have one." Later I heard her ask others the same question and figured out that it was rhetorical and meant to show that she wasn't afraid. By about 6:10 several girls had gathered and Natito's aunt came up and told us, "Sing now." So the girls, including Natito and I, stood up by the side of the house and began to sing. Natito's older sister and Natito were among the song leaders. After we'd sung for a while, the leaders stopped. During a several-minute silence, tears filled the eyes of Natito's older sister, and Natito and several others seemed to be trying to force tears to their eyes. Some young brides and young mothers came up and we began to sing again, sometimes with one of them leading. Mostly just the girls sang, although a young married woman would occasionally lead a verse.

About 6:30 Natito's aunt said, "Now." The girls and young women joined the old women a few steps away outside the door of the house. A hide was brought out of the house and arranged in the doorway. The men now all were outside the settlement. Another lady brought a pot of water. The pot looked like it hadn't been washed—like there was cooked-on porridge around the edges. The lady took a spearhead out of the water and put it on top of the house. Natito was led onto the hide. She removed her white cape and stood naked on the hide, her body shielded from the view of men outside by a semicircle of women and girls. Cold water from the pot was poured over Natito's head. She shivered. More water was splashed on her body, and the pot was set down on the edge of the hide. Natito kicked it angrily (part of the ceremony) all over me (not part of the ceremony). Natito then sat on the hide, facing me, arms akimbo, legs bent and spread. Her aunt holds one of her shoulders; three other women hold the other shoulder and her two legs. The circumcision lady unwrapped her razorblade and the operation began. All I can see is the woman's butt and the squinched-up face of Natito. She does not cry or cry out, just squinches her face tighter and tighter. Her aunt kept saying the equivalent of "Come on, that's right, chin up, you're almost done, brave girl, you can do it, come on." The lady's butt moved aside and I could see her fingering the bloody area, moving the lips aside. It was as if the clitoris was a plant: she had cut the stem and now must dig out the root. The women and girls crowded closer, watching every movement. Within two minutes it was over. The mother brought a gourd of milk from the house. A woman poured milk in the lid, allowing the milk to splatter onto the ground and onto what was left of Natito's genitals. Sheep fat was then smeared, globbed over the wound. Natito was then picked up under the arms and by the legs and carried into the house. On the hide I could see about a pint of Natito's blood, mixed with milk. She still had not cried out, but as they carried her in, her eyes were wet and her breath came in high wheezes. As Natito was carried in, another woman carried in the hide, folding it in half and lifting up the ends to keep in the blood and milk. An old woman picked up a broom of branches and swept the doorway clean.

Natito was married the next day.

A strict application of the logic of cultural relativism would lead us to tolerate and even support this practice, despite how reluctant we might be to have it performed on ourselves, our daughters, our sisters, or our wives. This is the position taken by John E Gossart, Jr., an immigration judge in Baltimore. In refusing the asylum claim of a woman from Sierra Leone in 1995, Judge Gossart described female circumcision as "an important ritual" that "binds the tribe," noting that "while some cultures view FGM [female genital mutilation] as abhorrent and/or even barbaric, others do not." The woman from Sierra Leone, he said, "cannot change that she is a female, but she can change her mind with regards to her position toward the FGM practices. It is not beyond [her] control to acquiesce to the tribal position on FGM."[5] Not all immigration judges take similar positions. Judge Paul Nejelsky of Arlington, Virginia, ruled in favor of the asylum claim of another woman from Sierra Leone, arguing that "forced female genital mutilation clearly merits being recognized as a form of persecution."[6]

Absolutist Alternatives

Explaining behavior and justifying behavior are two very different things. Although one of the central arguments of this book is that culture is overused as an explanation for behavior, it is still a perfectly good and legitimate explanation in many, many cases. Yet, to move from using culture as an explanation of behavior to using it as a moral

justification for behavior in the style of radical relativists like Judge Gossart is to slide from an "is" statement to an "ought" statement, a violation of a principle laid down convincingly by the Scottish philosopher David Hume more than two centuries ago.[7] Ironically, many of those who are quick to justify and defend others' behaviors on cultural grounds also denounce biological approaches to behavior because they imagine that biological explanations might be used to justify unsavory, antisocial behaviors. To do so is to commit what is often called the "naturalistic fallacy," the idea that if something is "natural" it must therefore be "good."[8] This sort of logic may work for granola, but it does not work for behavior. There may be biological reasons for jealousy, rape, xenophobia, and murder, but no biological explanation of those behaviors can be used to justify them in a moral sense. To use the culture concept to give a moral defense of any behavior is to commit the naturalistic fallacy in a new guise—call it the "culturatistic fallacy." No explanation of a behavior, whether it is based on biology, culture, or the phases of the moon, can ever be used to justify a behavior in moral terms.

If culture cannot be used to justify behavior, then perhaps we should get rid of cultural relativism entirely and replace it with something else, some approach to human affairs based on an absolute and universalistic moral code. For example, perhaps rather than just marveling at human diversity we should be social activists engaged in a moralistic quest to identify oppressors and oppressed, exploiters and exploited. This is what is advocated by, for example, Nancy Scheper-Hughes, an anthropologist at the University of California at Berkeley. Scheper—Hughes has shown how the poor of northeastern Brazil are kept poor and their children are kept sick and undernourished by a system involving physicians and the folk medical notion of a condition called "nervos." People who suffer from nervos may show a variety of symptoms including weakness, sleeplessness, headaches, and fainting. Scheper-Hughes argues that it is far from coincidental that these symptoms are the same one would expect from anyone who is chronically hungry. The solution offered by the Brazilian medical establishment is not food but tranquilizers, which make it doubly difficult for the people to do anything about their condition.[9] Other cultural practices around the world as troubling as the notion of nervos are not difficult to find. One that sometimes shocks Americans even more than female circumcision is the practice of hacking off little girls' fingers among the Dani of Irian Jaya, the western part of the island of New Guinea. The practice is part of a particular Dani mourning ritual, and as a result of it some adult Dani women end up with only the thumb and two adjacent fingers of one hand remaining.[10] People all over the political spectrum are bothered by the doctrine of cultural relativism in light of human rights abuses around the world.

Recently Donald Hodel, a former Reagan administration official and now president of the Christian Coalition, a conservative, religious lobbying organization, argued in favor of a bill in Congress that would tie American foreign policy to religious freedom overseas. At a press conference where he lent the bill his group's support, Hodel argued that "this is an atrocity that's going on out there, and for people to suggest for a moment that well maybe we shouldn't be too concerned about somebody being hung upside down and beaten nearly to death and boiling oil poured over his feet . . . because maybe that's a cultural problem, I think is an abdication of our responsibility as free citizens of what ought to be a religiously safe world."[11] Scheper-Hughes gets the moral code she applies to other societies from leftist political doctrines; Hodel gets his from the Judeo-Christian tradition and ideas about human rights developed during the Enlightenment. Still others propose a biological route around the problem of cultural relativism and toward a universal ethical system. Edward O. Wilson, for example, has recently argued that the naturalistic fallacy is no fallacy at all, and that, rather than rejecting evolutionary biology as a source of moral and ethical insights, we should be using it as the basis of a new and potentially universal ethical code. Ethical precepts, he writes, are not "ethereal messages outside humanity awaiting revelation" but rather "physical products of the brain and culture." Wilson argues that individuals are "predisposed biologically to make certain choices" about what is right and what is wrong that are then elevated through a process of cultural evolution to general principles. For example, here is the development he sees behind rules against adultery:

1. "Let's not go further; it doesn't feel right, it would lead to trouble."
2. "Adultery not only causes feelings of guilt, it is generally disapproved of by society, so these are other reasons to avoid it."
3. "Adultery isn't just disapproved of, it's against the law."
4. "God commands that we avoid this mortal sin."[12]

Does Wilson's "empirical" approach to ethics really let us escape from the problem of cultural relativism? What if someone with a somewhat different cultural background (say, a Mukogodo man) were faced with a similar concern with adultery? His ethical code might develop in quite a different way, such as this:

1. "Adultery is a problem. It destroys families and causes conflict in our society."
2. "One of the main reasons for adultery is women in pursuit of sexual pleasure."
3. "The clitoris is the main organ of sexual pleasure for most women."
4. "Therefore we should remove the clitorises of our women."
5. "Failure to remove the clitoris is shameful and dirty. No man should marry such an unclean woman."
6. "God wants us to perform clitoridectomies on all our women."

Although I certainly agree with Wilson that biology has much to teach us about the choices people make in life and also that evolutionary biology has an important role to play in the empirical study of moral sentiments and systems, it is not clear that it is a sound basis on which to develop a system of ethics or that it truly offers us any way around the problem of cultural relativism.

Finding a Middle Ground

The very fact that, despite their common Western, Euro-American, Judeo-Christian cultural backgrounds, Scheper-Hughes, Hodel, and Wilson all come up with different sorts of absolutist moral codes suggests that there may be some life left in the old doctrine of cultural relativism after all. In defense of relativism, it is helpful to remember that our own behaviors are often just as disturbing to people with other cultural backgrounds as, say, female genital mutilation and the removal of little girls' fingers among the Dani are to us. This was brought home to me white I was among the Mukogodo. A teenage boy had heard from someone else that white people do not circumcise their girls and asked me whether it was true. When I told him that it was and then confirmed his logical conclusion that my own wife must not be circumcised, he came close to vomiting. To him, an uncircumcised woman is unclean, and certainly not to be married. Capital punishment is another custom that disturbs many people from other societies. Although it is popular among the American voting public, it is opposed as a human rights abuse by international human rights organizations and the governments of many other Western democracies. Clearly, some approach must be found that allows us to reap the benefits of cultural relativism while avoiding its pitfalls—to make moral judgments without assuming that ours is always the only "right" way of doing things.

I can offer three simple suggestions for how to reconcile our species' cultural diversity with our desire for a common, universal moral code. First, we need to stop thinking of cultures as coherent, integrated, bounded wholes and replace this with the idea that they are amorphous, unbounded bundles of ideas, knowledge, and beliefs that are continually being contested and renegotiated. . . . This allows us to better understand the diversity that exists within cultures as well as between them; it also allows us to be less hesitant in judging the effects of culture traits. I can, for example, feel free to deplore the practice of female circumcision as a specific Mukogodo culture trait while simultaneously having deep respect for the rest of Mukogodo culture. I can love and respect my own American culture while opposing the death penalty. And so on.

Second, we need to keep in mind that culture traits are not and cannot be rights-bearing entities. The only things capable of having rights are people. . . . Students who defend the Holocaust and the judges who deny asylum to women avoiding circumcision on the grounds that such things are simply someone else's culture are, in effect, elevating the rights of culture traits above those of real, living people. The realization that culture is often a tool used by some people to manipulate others also helps us to see through the cloak that extreme relativism draws around it. If some cultural idea amounts to an attempt by some people to manipulate others, whether it is the concept of *nervos*, the doctrine of the divine right of kings, or the idea that those people who are different from us are somehow our enemies, then it is easy to see how protecting such a notion under the protective banner of cultural relativism can serve to perpetuate oppression and exploitation.

There is another, more defensible and legitimate argument for the preservation of cultural traits, but acting on it does not require violating anyone's rights. We may wish to preserve the many cultural traits that are rapidly disappearing from the world's societies for their potential usefulness in the future. Just as genetic diversity may be worth preserving because it may help the world deal with future biological crises, so we might be wise to keep a storehouse of the world's cultural knowledge in case it, too, can help us through hard times ahead. We are already beginning to recognize, for example, that we can learn a thing or two from traditional medical practices around the world, and it is likely that we would benefit from preserving and learning to appreciate many other sorts of folk knowledge and skills. Indeed, helping to preserve the world's cultural diversity, just as it is so rapidly disappearing, is one of the main ways in which anthropology can make itself useful. Fortunately for all concerned, doing so does not involve the violation of anyone's rights or forcing anyone to conform to traditional cultural traits that they no longer wish to follow.

Third, we need to foster the development of connections between the social sciences and the rest of the sciences. To reject all attempts to separate facts from values puts anthropologists and all other social scientists who deal with cultural difference on no firmer ground than religious missionaries, zealots with a passion not for understanding but for righting the wrongs of the world as they see them. As Roy D'Andrade of the University of California at San Diego has pointed out, we are more likely to have positive effects on the world if we first attempt to understand other societies before attempting to change them.[13] Understanding behavior across cultural gaps requires a sort of limited relativism that is no different from the usual detachment scientists show toward their subjects. Medical science is a good example of the power of this sort of attitude. Physicians, whose job it is to apply biological knowledge, have clear ideas about good and bad. Things that make people suffer, like viruses, are bad. Relieving people of problems caused by viruses and other pathogens is good. To achieve their goals, physicians must make use of knowledge gained by scientists about things like viruses. But it does not do any good for virologists to think of viruses as "bad" in some moralistic sense. They are simply fascinating and worthy of study in their own right. Similarly, it does the social scientist no good to make value judgments about the people, cultures, and societies he studies if his goal is simply to understand them. Such judgments may simply cloud his mind and make his primary tasks of explanation and understanding all the more difficult. Connecting the study of human affairs with the rest of the scientific project will help to foster an appropriate attitude of scientific detachment. . . .

Notes

1. Barkow 1989, 373.
2. Boas 1940, 60–75.
3. On June 23, 1993 in Prince William County, Virginia, Lorena Bobbitt sliced off her husband John's penis while he slept. Unlike the clitorides of women who experience clitoridectomies, John Bobbitt's penis was recovered and surgically reattached.
4. The nineteenth-century British physician Isaac Baker Brown was a prominent advocate of clitoridectomies to treat such symptoms of "uterine madness" and nymphomania as masturbation, though he was eventually expelled from the Obstetrical Society of London for coercing patients into accepting the treatment (Moscucci 1990, 105; see also Dedman 1991).
5. Judgment made on April 28, 1995 in the case of an asylum applicant referred to as "D.J."
6. Judgment made August 9, 1995 in the case of an asylum applicant from Sierra Leone.
7. Hume 1739/40.
8. Moore 1903, 10.
9. Scheper-Hughes 1992, 1995.
10. Heider 1991.
11. Quoted in a story reported by Lynn Neary on the National Public Radio program "All Things Considered" aired August 26, 1997.
12. Wilson 1998, 250.
13. D'Andrade 1995.

Acknowledgments

Chapter 1

SELECTION 1 From *Race, Language and Culture* by Franz Boas, (1940, Macmillan) pp. 626–629, 635–37, 638. Copyright © 1940 by Franz Boas. Reprinted by permission of The Free Press, a division of Simon & Schuster Adult Publishing Group.

SELECTION 2 Section 2.1 from *Mirror for Man: The Relation of Anthropology to Modern Life,* McGraw-Hill, 1949. Copyright © 1949 by the estate of Clyde Kluckhohn.

SELECTION 3 From *Journal of General Psychology,* 10(2), January 1934, pp. 59+.

SELECTION 4 From *EUROPÆA,* 1995, I-1. Copyright © 1995 by EUROPÆA. Reprinted by permission.

Chapter 2

SELECTION 5 From Essay IV. of *Social Anthropology and Other Essays,* Free Press, 1966, pp. 64–85 excerpts.

SELECTION 6 From chapter 8 of *Fieldwork and Footnotes: Studies in the History of European Anthropology,* Roldan & Vermeulen, eds., Routledge 1995, pp. 143–155. Copyright © 1995 by Routledge. Reprinted by permission of Taylor & Francis Books and Arturo Álvarez Roldán

SELECTION 7 From *Monthly Review,* Vol. 19, no. 11, 1968, pp. 12–13, 17–27. Copyright © 1968 by MR Press. Reprinted by permission of Monthly Review Foundation.

Chapter 3

SELECTION 8 From chapter 1 of *Cultural Evolutionism: Theory in Practice,* 1st ed., by Elman R. Service, 1971 (Holt), pp. 5–14. Copyright © 1971 Wadsworth. Reprinted by permission of Wadsworth, a division of Thomson Learning: www.thomsonrights.com. Fax 800 730–2215.

SELECTION 9 From chapter 7 of *They Studied Man,* by Abram Kardiner and Edward Preble, pp. 140–141, 151, 162–186. First published by World Publishing Co. in 1961.

SELECTION 10 From *Anthropological Theory in North America,* E. L. Cerroni-Long, editor, Greenwood/Bergin 1999, pp. 19–32. Copyright © 1999 by Greenwood Publishing Group, Inc., Westport, CT. Reprinted by permission.

SELECTION 11 Reprinted by permission from the May 21, 2001, issue of *The Nation,* Vol. 272, Iss. 20, pp. 29–35. Copyright © 2001 by The Nation. For subscription information, call 1-800-333-8536. Portions of each week's Nation magazine can be accessed at www.thenation.com.

Chapter 4

SELECTION 12 From chapter 7 of *The Cocktail Waitress* (John Wiley & Sons, Inc., 1975), pp. 120–143. Copyright © 1975 by James P. Spradley and Brenda J. Mann. Reprinted by permission of Random House, Inc.

SELECTION 13 As seen in *New York Times Magazine,* August 28, 1994, pp. 46–49, adapted from chapter 3 of *Talking from 9 to 5: Women and Men at Work,* by Deborah Tannen, PhD (William Morrow, 1994), pp. 78–106. Copyright © 1994 by Deborah Tannen, PhD. Reprinted by permission of HarperCollins Publishers.

SELECTION 14 From *Playboy,* 1971, pp. 139–140, 204, 206. Copyright © 1971 by Edward T. Hall. Reprinted by permission of the author.

Chapter 5

Chapter 6

Chapter 7

Chapter 8

Chapter 9

Index

A

abnormal behavior, 8–11
aboriginals, of Australia, 43; economic
    resources of, 87, 88, 89; introduction
    of steel axes to, 186–192
adaptation: concept of, 200; constraint of, 38
advertising, product development of
    convenience foods and, 225, 226, 227
affluent societies, hunter-gatherers as, 86–91
Africa: autonomous political groups in, 20;
    group healing power in, 209–214; woman-
    to-woman marriage in, 115–120
agriculture: in India, 179–183; Melanesian,
    150–151
aid projects, 33
Air Florida Flight 90, 76, 77
airplane, indirect communication on, 76–77
Allegheny Airline Flight 453, 76–77
America: evolutionism in, 38; expeditions in,
    20; foreign economic aid of, 32; military
    aid and, 32
American Anthropological Association,
    on anthropologists and warfare, 233, 236
American Expeditionary Force, totemism
    and, 162–164
American Indian tribes, homosexuals in, 9
ancestor killing, 49, 50, 51–52
ancestor reverence in, 52
Andamanese, 2, 20
animism, 142, 143, 146–147, 149
anthropologists, counterinsurgency programs
    and, 229–237
anxiety, space perception and, 219
Applbaum, on arranged marriage in Japan,
    106–114
Arabs, eye contact of, 80
Argonauts of the Western Pacific (Malinowski),
    26
Army, U.S., totemism in, 162–164
Aro experiment, 212–213
arranged marriage, in Japan, 106–114
art: functionalism and, 45; science and, 13
Artic, Inuit life in, 201
Azande, of Africa, witchcraft among, 153–156

B

Bali, cockfight as metaphor in, 165–177
Baloma (Malinowski), 28
Balzac, 42
bar, speech behaviors in, 62–73
"barefoot empiricism," 38
barrenness, woman-to-woman marriage and,
    116–117

basal metabolism, of Inuit, 203
bears, Inuit and, 200, 201
Bechuana, 20
behavior, human: abnormal, 8–11; causality,
    13; justifying, 242; mores and, 10; normal,
    10–11; physiological needs of, 45; science
    of, 14; social anthropology and, 8;
belief, standardization and, 8
Benedict, Ruth, 8, 44, 59, 234; on abnormal
    behavior, 8–11
berdache, 9
bereavement, 10
betting, Balinese cockfight and, 168–173
birth rates: of Bushwoman, 95; decline in
    family and, 132–133; illegitimate, 132
black magic, 9
"blackbirding," 160
black(s), eye behavior of, 81; -white behavior,
    84
Boas, Franz, on ethnocentrism and fieldwork,
    1–3
body language, 83
Bohannan, Paul, on paradigm shift, 49–54
Brady's Bar, 62–73
brand strategy, 225
breast feeding, among Bushwomen, 95
bride burning, in India, 121–129
Britain: anthropology expeditions and, 20;
    female infanticide and, 126, 127; foreign
    policy in, 232–233; in India, 125, 126,
    127–128, 129
Bushmen, 1, 2, 93–99

C

Cadigan, R. Jean, on woman-to-woman
    marriage, 115–120
Campbell, Donald, definitions of evolution
    and, 39
cargo cults, in New Guinea, 158–161
Carneiro, Robert L., on postmodernism,
    12–16
cataleptic phenomena, 9
Cecrops, family in, 2
celibacy, 6
"ceremonial gardening," 26
Chagnon, Napoleon, 16
Childe, V. Gordon, 38
children, 55, 102, 104, 131, 194–197, 205
Christianity, Mansren legend and, 159–160
Christy, Henry, 139
Circassians, 19
"class struggle," 38
Clifford, James, 14, 15
cockfights, Balinese, 15, 165–177

coffee economy, and Fore people, 196–197
colonialism, 30–34, 39
communication, 74–78, 195, 218
companionship, marriage and, 131–132, 133
comparative ethnology, 142
conflict-and-survival, 38
continuance theory, 143
convenience foods, marketing of, 222–228
counterinsurgency programs, anthropologists
    and, 229–237
cow worship, in India, 178–184
Crapanzano, Vincent, 15
Cronk, Lee, on cultural relativity, 240–244
crowding, social consequences of, 216, 217
cults, cargo, 158–161
cultural ecology, 38
cultural evolution, theory of, 36–41
cultural knowledge, of adversary, 229–237
cultural relativity, 240–244
Cummings, E. E., on science, 13
custom, standardization of, 8

D

Dahomey people, 119
data collection, 1–3, 27
daughter-in-law, woman-to-woman marriage
    and, 118
de Lauwe, Chombart, 216–217
death, 10, 25, 49–50, 143, 147
deep play, 170, 171, 172
degeneration theory, 139–140
determinism, 13
developmental theory, 141, 142
di Leonardo, Micaela, on stereotypes of
    anthropologists, 55–60
diet, of Inuit, 202–203
dieties, species-, 144
direct communication, 74–78
directionality, of societies, 37
disease, adaptation to, 199
distance, personal, 81–82. See also space
diviners, 210, 213
divorce, 130–136
DobeSan, women, 101
dogs, Inuit and, 201
dowry murder, in India, 121–129
dreams, 143
drinking talk, rituals of, 62–73
Durkheim, Emile, 38
dynamic space, 218

E

East India Company, 126
ecology, and health, 206–207

economy, of hunter-gatherers, 88
egalitarianism vs. patriarch, 100–104
eland bull dance ritual, 98–99
employer-employee communication, 75–76
Energy and the Evolution of Culture (White), 87
environment, selective use of, 5
equality, between sexes, 100–104
Eskimos. *See* Inuits
espionage, 233
ethnic backgrounds, divorce rates and, 131
ethnocentrism, Boas and, 1–3
ethnography, postmodernism and, 12–16
ethnology, 15
Evans-Pritchard, E. E.: on ethnographic field techniques, 18–23; on witchcraft, 153–156
evolutionism, 36, 37–38, 39, 141
exorcism, practice of, 144
eyes, language of, 80–81, 82

F

fact, authenticated, 19
family, 2, 46, 130–136. *See also* kinship
Family among the Australian Aborigines (Malinowski), 43
Fazer, James, primitive religions and, 147, 148
female genital mutilation, 241–242, 243
female husband, 115, 116, 117, 118–119
female infanticide, 126, 127, 205
feminist, 58, 59
fetishism, 144
fieldwork, 14, 15; in Australia, 43–48; Boas and, 1–3; ethnographic techniques of, 18–23; imperialism and, 30–34; Malinowski and, 50, 51, 54; participant observation and, 24–29; in United States, 59
fishing, 151, 202
focused gathering, 168
food production, 32, 39–40, 90
Fore people, adaptation to social change and, 194–197
forgers. *See* gatherers
free will, 13, 14
Freeman, Derek: on behavior, 50; on Martha Mead, 56
Friedl, Ernestine, on sex roles and society, 100–104
Froude, James Anthony, on free will, 13
functionalism, 24–29, 42–48

G

gambling, Balinese cockfight, 165–177
garden magic, 25, 27
Garrett, William R., on decline of Western family structure, 130–136
gatherers: Bushwomens' role as, 93–99; women as, 101, 102, 103, 104
Geertz, Clifford, 13, 15, 39–40; on Balinese cockfight as metaphor, 165–177
generation gap, 134
gesture-language, similarities of, 141
ghost(s), belief in, 147, 149
ghost-soul, 143
go-between, in Japan. *See* pro nakodo
Golden Bough, The (Frazer), 51, 147, 148
goods, portability of, 88, 89
Gough, Kathleen, on anthropology and imperialism, 30–34

government, anthropologists and, 31
Grey, Sir George, 88
group(s): healing power of, 209–214; human survival and, 200; solidarity of, 163, 164

H

Hadza of Tanzania, 102
Hall, Edward T.: on human spatial relationships, 215–220; on nonverbal communication, 79–84
Hall, Mildred Reed Hall, on nonverbal communication, 79–84
Harris, Marvin, on cow worship in India, 178–184
healers, tribal, 211, 212, 213
health: cultural adaptations to, 199, 205, 206–207; spatial relationships and, 215–220
Hess, Eckhard, 80
Hickey, Gerald, 235
Hindu: dowry practice and, 122, 123, 124; sacred cows and, 178, 179, 183
Hodel, Donald, 242
homosexuality, 6, 9, 11, 68, 69
Hopi, ancestral paradigms and, 49–50
Horton, Robert, 211
hospitals, space and health in, 216, 217
human rights, 242, 243
humanism, vs. science, 12–13
"hungry ghosts," 52, 54
hunter-gatherers: as affluent societies, 86–91; Fore people as, 194–197; male power among, 101, 102; productive capabilities of, 88, 89, 90; standard of living of, 91
hustling, speech acts and, 64

I

idoltry, 144
Igbo, woman-to-woman marriage and, 116, 117
Ila-Speaking Peoples of Northern Rhodesia (Smith and Dale), 19
illegitimate births, 132
immigrants, 241
imperialism: anthropology and, 30–34; European, environments and, 88; evolutionary dominance and, 39
India: cow worship in, 178–184; dowry murder in, 121–129; farming in, 179–180
indirect communication, 74–78
industrialization, 39
infanticide: among Bushwomen, 95; female, 123, 124, 126–127, 129; hunter-gatherers and, 104; Inuit and, 205; among !Kung, 95–96; patrilineal system, 51, 52
insignia, shoulder, development of, 163
institutions, of society, functionalism and, 42–48
Inuit, 3; adaptive patterns of, 199–208; inequality between the sexes and, 103
involution, cultural, concept of, 39
Israel, lost tribes of, 3

J

Japan: arranged marriage in, 106–114; birth rate, 107; communication in, 75, 77

K

Kalabari, woman-to-woman marriage and, 117
Kamba, woman-to-woman marriage and, 117
Kardiner, Abram: on Bronislaw Malinowski, 42–48; on Edward Tylor, 138–145
Keats, John, on Newton, 12
Kikuyu of Kenya, female husband and, 117
King, C. Richard, 14
kinship: steel axes and, 188–189, 191; study of, 51, 53; terminology, 27
Kiriwina. *See* Trobriand Islands
Kluckhohn, Clyde: on meaning of culture, 4–7; on Malinowski, 47
knowledge: cultural, of adversary, 229; theory on, 24
Krutch, Joseph Wood, 13
Kuhn, Thomas, ancestor killing and, 50, 52
Kula ring, 25
!Kung: infanticide among, 95–96; menstruation ritual of, 98, 99
Kwakiutl, death in, 10

L

labor force: division of, 38, 39; women in, 134–135
Lambo, Thomas Adeoye, on group healing power, 209–214
language: fieldwork and, 45; human culture and, 6; -gesture, similarities of, 141; learning native, 21–22; Trobriand fieldwork and, 26, 27; use of, 62–73
Lien, Marianne Elisabeth, on marketing convenience foods, 222–228
Life of a South African Tribe (Junod), 19
Linton, Ralph, on totemism, 162–164
listening behavior, 80
literature: ethnography, 15; underground, 32
Lycians, family in, 2

M

magic: function of, 44, 45, 46, 47; power of, 210; primitive man and, 146–149
Mailu, fieldwork in, 24, 25, 26, 27, 28
male dominance, over women, 100–104
Malinowski, Bronislaw: fieldwork of, 20, 24–29, 50, 51, 54; on functionalism, 42–48; on magic, science, and religion, 146–152
Man of Songs, The, 42–48. *See also* Bronislaw Malinowski
mana, 147, 149
"manes," 143–144
mangu, witchcraft and, 153
Mann, Brenda J., on ethnography of speaking, 62–73
Mansren legend, 159–160
Marco Polo, 2
Marcus, George, 16
marketing, of convenience foods, 222–228
marriage, 6; arranged, in Japan, 106–114; communal, 2; dowry murder in India and, 121–129; decline of family structure and, 130–136; love, in Japan, 107;

Malinowski on, 44; plural wives and, 5; variability limits of, 9; woman-to-woman, in Africa, 115–120

Marxism, 32, 37, 38

masculinity: axe as symbol of, 189, 191; Balinese cockfight and, 165–177; language and, 65, 66, 67, 68, 69; leg behavior and, 83

matrilineal society, in Trobriand Islands, 26

McElroy, Ann, on ecology of health and disease, 199–208

McFate, Montgomery, on anthropology and foreign policy, 229–239

Mead, Margaret, 50, 55–60, 234

meaning, search for, and Balinese cockfight metaphor, 165–177

media: marketing of convenience foods and, 226, 227, 228; stereotypes of anthropologists and, 59–60

medical anthropology, 199–208

Melanesians, 20, 24, 149–150, 151, 159–160, 161

Melanesians of British New Guinea, The (Seligman), 25

Melanesians, The (Codrington), 19

men, arranged marriage and, 106–114

menarcheal ritual, 97–99

mental illness: native healers and, 211; space as therapy for, 216–219

metamessages, in bar situations, 70–71

military: anthropology and, 229–237; burden of interpretation in, 76; totemism in, 162–164

Mitchell River Mission, in Australia, 187

monotheism, 144

morals, early religion and, 148

Morley, Sylvanus, espionage and, 233

Moslems, Indian cow worship and, 179

Mukogodo, 241–242, 243

mystics, 9

myths, 45, 141, 142, 143

N

Nandi, wives of female husbands, 119

national-security, anthropology and, 230, 232–237

Natives of Mailu (Malinowski), 28

naturalistic fallacy, 242

needs, basic, 44

Negro tribes, in Africa, 3

Neolithic Great Leap Forward, 87

New Guinea, Western expansion to, 158–161

Nigeria, Aro experiment in, 212–213

nonverbal communication, 77, 79–84

normality, culturally defined, 10–11

Norway, marketing convenience foods in, 222–228

Nuer, 20

Nupe, 20

O

objectivity, of social scientist, 18–23

observation, as data-collection technique, 27

Oldenburg, Veena Talwar on dowry murder, 121–129

organismic model, for society, 37

outcasts, customs and, 9–10

oxen, in India, 179, 183

P

paradigm shift, 49–54

parents: arranged marriage and, 107–114; decline of family structure and, 130–136

participant observation, 18–23, 45

patriarchies, 100–104, 189

perception, influence of culture on, 22

Peruvian Indians, 19

Phaëthon tale, 3

phantasms, 143

philosopher, primitive, 142

plants, Bushwomens' knowledge of, 95

political groups, autonomous, in Africa, 20

population control, of Inuit, 203–204

postmodernism, 12–16

Postmodernism and the Social Sciences (Rosenau), 14

Powell-Weinberger doctrine, 231

power, distribution of, under imperialism, 32

Preble, Edward: on Bronislaw Malinowski, 42–48; on Edward Tylor, 138–145

primative peoples: customs of, 2, religion and, 146–149; speculations about, 19; studies of, 19, 20; Tylor's study of, 138–145

private enterprise, underdeveloped world and, 32

pro nakodo, Japanese arranged marriage and, 108–114

product development, 222–228

Prohibition of Dowry Act, 122, 124

Project Camelot, 235–236

propaganda, 234

proxemics, 215–220

psychic manifestations, 9

psychic unity, of mankind, 141–145

psychological warfare, 234

psychotherapy, in Africa, 209–214

puberty: cultures and, 6; and menarcheal ritual, 97–99

public distance, 82

R

race(s), 36, 38, 131

Radcliffe-Brown, and Andaman Islanders, 20

Rainbow Division, of 42nd Army Division, 162–164

reality: dissolution of, 14; truth and, 15

reasoning power: of Bushmen, 1; primitive man's, 149

reciprocal exchanges, in bar situations, 69–70

reflexive disengagement, 227

reincarnation, 25, 26

relationships: companionate, 131–132, 133; terminology of, 27

religion, 2; developmental theory and, 144; Malinowski on, 45, 46, 47; primitive man and, 146–149; variability limits of, 9

Religious System of the Amazula, The (Callaway), 19

retribution theory, 143

revolution(s): anthropological, 49–54; as reaction against evolution, 39, 40

rituals: ancestral spirits and, 210; group, 211

roads, effect on economic development and, 196, 197

Roldán, Arturo Alvarez, on Malinowski and ethnographic method of fieldwork, 24–29

routinization, process of, 225

S

Saenz, Karen, on paradigm shift, 49–54

Sahlins, Marshall, on hunter-gatherers as affluent society, 86–92

Samarai. *See* Mailu

Samoa: Margaret Mead in, 56, 57, 58; socialization in, 50

Scheper-Hughes, Nancy, 242–243

science: laws of culture and, 43; primitive man and, 146–149; vs. humanism, 12–13

scientific laws of culture, 43

Seligman, C. G., 25, 43

Semai, women and men relationships in, 100, 101

Service, Elman R., on cultural evolution theory, 36–41

sex roles, society and, 100–104

sexual revolution, illegitimacy and, 132

shallow games, 170–171

Shamans, 103

sharing, customs of, 89

Sharp, Lauriston, on effect of steel axes on Australian aboriginals, 186–193

silence, as nonverbal communication, 77, 79–84

Simbiti, woman-to-woman marriage and, 117

social anthropology, 18–19, 20, 22

social change: adaptation to, by Fore people, 194–197; introduction of steel axe and, 186–192

"social Darwinism," 37

social distance, in business, 82

social life study, 22

social science, 13

societies: group interaction in, 5; imperialism and, 31; primitive, 19, 20

sociofugal space, 217–218

sociopetal space, 217

Sorenson, E. Richard, on adaptation to social change, 194–197

space, perception of, 81–82, 215–220

spatial relationships, human health and, 215–220

speaking, ethnography of, 62–73

speech behavior, in bars, 62–73

Spencer, Herbert, 38

spirits, embodiment of, 144

spiritualism, modern, 3

Spradley, James P., on ethnography of speaking, 62–73

steatopygia, of Bushwomen, 97

steel axe, introduction of, to Australians, 186–192

stereotypes, of anthropologists, 55–60

Steward, Julian, and cultural ecology, 38

Sunlit Cloud Iguana clan, 189, 192

supernatural, beliefs in, 146–149, 210, 213–214

survival, culture and, 6, 7, 37–38, 43, 142, 200

Swazi, 20

T

taboos, concerning Bushwomen, 97

Tallensi, 20

Tannen, Deborah, on direct and indirect communication, 74–78

target groups, marketing and, 223, 225–226

Taylor, Jane, on role of Bushwomen, 93–99

teasing, speech acts in bars and, 64

territoriality, in mental illness, 219

Thai Scandal, 236

thought, progressive evolution of, 37

Tiwi of North Australia, 102, 103

totemism, 147–148; American Expeditionary Force and, 162–164; of clans, 189

touch, as part of communication, 82

Townsend, Patricia K., on ecology of health and disease, 199–208

trade: in New Guinea, 159–161; steel axe and, 186–192

trance phenomena, 9, 11

"tribal-genius" studies, 44

Trobriand Islanders of Melanesia (Malinowski), 20

Trobriand Islands, 24, 25, 26, 27, 28; magic and fishing in, 151; Malinowski fieldwork in, 43

truth, reality and, 15, 16

Tyler, Stephen, 14, 16

Tylor, Edward Burnett, 37, 38, 138–145, 146–147

U

universities, anthropological studies in, 20–21

V

van der Post, Laurens, 89–90; on role of Bushwomen, 93–99

verbal performances, in bars, 62–73

Viking Foods, marketing, 222–228

village care system, in Africa, 212–213

W

warfare, magic and, 151

war-fighting strategies, cultural knowledge of adversary and, 229–237

Washo Indians of North America, 102

water buffalo, in India, 179, 180

way of life, culture and, 5

Wertheim, on cultural involution, 39

Western expansion, 30, 32; and Fore life, 196–197; to New Guinea, 158–161; steel axes to aboriginals and, 186–192

White, Leslie A., 13, 38

whites: -black behavior, 84; eye behavior of, 81

widows, self-immolation and, 122

Wilson, Edward O., 243

witch doctors, 210

witchcraft, among Azande, 153–156

Womack, Mari, 51, 52; on paradigm shift, 49–54

women: anthropologists, 55–60; arranged marriage and, 106–114; body behavior of, 80, 82, 83; among Bushmen, 93–99; axe use by, 188, 190; dowry death in India and, 121–129; indirect communication and, 75; in labor force, 134–135; property rights of Indian, 125, 127, 128; social relationships between men and, 100–104; woman-to-woman marriage of, 115–120

woman-to-woman marriage, in Africa, 115–120

World War I, espionage and, 233

World War II era, role of anthropologists during, 233–234

world, end of, cargo cults and, 159

Worsley, Peter M., on Cargo Cults, 158–161

Y

Yanomamö, 16

Yir Yoront, introduction of steel axes to, 186–192